LATE HELLENISTIC GREEK LITERATURE IN DIALOGUE

Late Hellenistic Greek literature, both prose and poetry, stands out for its richness and diversity. Recent work has tended to take an author-by-author approach that underestimates the interconnectedness of the literary culture of the period. The chapters assembled here set out to change that by offering new readings of a wide range of late Hellenistic texts and genres, including historiography, geography, rhetoric and philosophy, together with many verse texts and inscriptions. In the process, they offer new insights into the various ways in which late Hellenistic literature engaged with its social, cultural and political contexts, while interrogating and revising some of the standard narratives of the relationship between late Hellenistic and imperial Greek literary culture, which are too often studied in isolation from each other. As a whole the book prompts us to rethink the place of late Hellenistic literature within the wider landscape of Greek and Roman literary history.

JASON KÖNIG is Professor of Classics at the University of St Andrews. He has published widely on the Greek literature and culture of the Roman Empire. His books include *Athletics and Literature in the Roman Empire* (Cambridge, 2005) and *Saints and Symposiasts: The Literature of Food and the Symposium in Greco-Roman and Early Christian Culture* (Cambridge, 2012).

NICOLAS WIATER is Senior Lecturer in Classics at the University of St Andrews. He specialises in Hellenistic and early imperial Greek literature. His publications include *The Ideology of Classicism: Language, History, and Identity in Dionysius of Halicarnassus* (Berlin, 2011) and, with T. A. Schmitz, *The Struggle for Identity. Greeks and their Past in the First Century* BCE (Stuttgart, 2011).

GREEK CULTURE IN THE ROMAN WORLD

Series Editors
JAŚ ELSNER, University of Oxford
SIMON GOLDHILL, University of Cambridge
CONSTANZE GÜTHENKE, University of Oxford
MICHAEL SQUIRE, King's College London

Founding Editors
SUSAN E. ALCOCK
JAŚ ELSNER
SIMON GOLDHILL

The Greek culture of the Roman Empire offers a rich field of study. Extraordinary insights can be gained into processes of multicultural contact and exchange, political and ideological conflict, and the creativity of a changing, polyglot empire. During this period, many fundamental elements of Western society were being set in place: from the rise of Christianity, to an influential system of education, to long-lived artistic canons. This series is the first to focus on the response of Greek culture to its Roman imperial setting as a significant phenomenon in its own right. To this end, it will publish original and innovative research in the art, archaeology, epigraphy, history, philosophy, religion, and literature of the empire, with an emphasis on Greek material.

Recent titles in the series:

Late Hellenistic Greek Literature in Dialogue Edited by Jason König and Nicolas Wiater

The Death of Myth on Roman Sarcophagi: Allegory and Visual Narrative in the Late Empire Mont Allen

The Invention of Christian Time: Temporality and the Literature of Late Antiquity Simon Goldhill

The Moon in the Greek and Roman Imagination: Myth, Literature, Science and Philosophy Karen ní Mheallaigh

The Resurrection of Homer in Imperial Greek Epic: Quintus Smyrnaeus' Posthomerica and the Poetics of Impersonation Emma Greensmith

Oppian's Halieutica: Charting a Didactic Epic Emily Kneebone

Preposterous Poetics: The Politics and Aesthetics of Form in Late Antiquity Simon Goldhill

The Aesthetics of Hope in Late Greek Imperial Literature: Methodius of Olympus' Symposium and the Crisis of the Third Century Dawn LaValle Norman

LATE HELLENISTIC GREEK LITERATURE IN DIALOGUE

EDITED BY

JASON KÖNIG

University of St Andrews, Scotland

NICOLAS WIATER

University of St Andrews, Scotland

Shaftesbury Road, Cambridge CB2 8EA, United Kingdom

One Liberty Plaza, 20th Floor, New York, NY 10006, USA

477 Williamstown Road, Port Melbourne, VIC 3207, Australia

314–321, 3rd Floor, Plot 3, Splendor Forum, Jasola District Centre, New Delhi – 110025, India

103 Penang Road, #05–06/07, Visioncrest Commercial, Singapore 238467

Cambridge University Press is part of Cambridge University Press & Assessment, a department of the University of Cambridge.

We share the University's mission to contribute to society through the pursuit of education, learning and research at the highest international levels of excellence.

www.cambridge.org
Information on this title: www.cambridge.org/9781009015950

DOI: 10.1017/9781009030878

© Cambridge University Press & Assessment 2022

This publication is in copyright. Subject to statutory exception and to the provisions of relevant collective licensing agreements, no reproduction of any part may take place without the written permission of Cambridge University Press & Assessment.

First published 2022
First paperback edition 2023

A catalogue record for this publication is available from the British Library

Library of Congress Cataloging-in-Publication data
NAMES: König, Jason, editor. | Wiater, Nicolas, editor.
TITLE: Late Hellenistic Greek literature in dialogue / edited by Jason König, Nicolas Wiater.
OTHER TITLES: Greek culture in the Roman world.
DESCRIPTION: Cambridge, United Kingdom : Cambridge University Press, 2022. | SERIES: Greek culture in the Roman world | Most of the papers in this volume derive from a confrence entitled Rethinking late Hellenistic literature and the Second Sophistic, held at the School of Classics, University of St. Andrews. | Includes bibliographical references and index.
IDENTIFIERS: LCCN 2021054143 (print) | LCCN 2021054144 (ebook) | ISBN 9781316516683 (hardback) | ISBN 9781009015950 (paperback) | ISBN 9781009030878 (epub)
SUBJECTS: LCSH: Greek literature, Hellenistic–History and criticism–Congresses. | LCGFT: Conference papers and proceedings.
CLASSIFICATION: LCC PA3081 .L38 2022 (print) | LCC PA3081 (ebook) | DDC 880.9/001–dc23/eng/20220106
LC record available at https://lccn.loc.gov/2021054143
LC ebook record available at https://lccn.loc.gov/2021054144

ISBN 978-1-316-51668-3 Hardback
ISBN 978-1-009-01595-0 Paperback

Cambridge University Press & Assessment has no responsibility for the persistence or accuracy of URLs for external or third-party internet websites referred to in this publication and does not guarantee that any content on such websites is, or will remain, accurate or appropriate.

Contents

List of Figures | page vii
List of Contributors | viii
Preface | xiii
List of Abbreviations | xiv

Introduction | 1
Jason König and Nicolas Wiater

1 The Empire Becomes a Body: Power, Space and Movement in Polybius' *Histories*
   Nicolas Wiater | 36

2 Pyrenaean Mountains and Deep-Valleyed Alps: Geography and Empire in the *Garland of Philip*
   Thomas A. Schmitz | 69

3 Sailing the Sea, Sailing an Image: *Periplus* and Mediality in Diodorus' *Bibliotheke* and Philostratus' *Imagines*
   Mario Baumann | 94

4 Ecocritical Readings in Late Hellenistic Literature: Landscape Alteration and *Hybris* in Strabo and Diodorus
   Jason König | 119

5 Civic and Counter-Civic Cosmopolitanism: Diodorus, Strabo and the Later Hellenistic *Polis*
   Benjamin Gray | 149

6 The Wrath of the Sibyl: Homeric Reception and Contested Identities in the Sibylline Oracles 3
   Emma Greensmith | 178

7 Imagining Belonging: The Use of Athens in Hellenistic Rome
   Joy Connolly   211

8 Philosophical Self-Definition in Strabo's *Geography*
   Myrto Hatzimichali   231

9 Narrating 'the Swarm of Possibilities': Plutarch, Polybius
   and the Idea of Contingency in History
   Felix K. Maier   251

10 'Asianist' Style in Hellenistic Oratory and Philostratus'
   Lives of the Sophists   272
   Lawrence Kim

11 Greek Reading Lists from Dionysius to Dio: Rhetorical
   Imitation in the Augustan Age and the Second Sophistic
   Casper C. de Jonge   319

12 Envoi: To Live in Hellenistic Times
   Simon Goldhill   351

References   366
Index Locorum   403
General Index   409

Figure

6.1 Marble relief showing the *apotheosis* of Homer, Archelaos of Priene; *c.* 200 BCE; from Bovillae; height 1.15 m. London, British Museum. © The Trustees of the British Museum. *page* 182

Contributors

MARIO BAUMANN is Juniorprofessor für Kulturen der Antike/Griechische Literatur at Technische Universität Dresden. He is the author of *Bilder schreiben: Virtuose Ekphrasis in Philostrats Eikones* (De Gruyter, 2011) and *Welt erzählen: Narration und das Vergnügen des Lesers in der ersten Pentade von Diodors Bibliotheke* (Vandenhoeck & Ruprecht, 2020). His current major research project, funded by the Deutsche Forschungsgemeinschaft (DFG), is a commentary on Herodian's *History of the Empire from the Death of Marcus*.

JOY CONNOLLY is President of the American Council of Learned Societies, after service as provost and interim president of the CUNY Graduate Center and as dean for humanities at NYU. She is the author of two books, including *The Life of Roman Republicanism* (Princeton University Press, 2014), and over seventy scholarly articles and essays and reviews in the popular press. She is currently preparing a series of lectures on classical studies in the contemporary world for the University of Pennsylvania, which will be published by Princeton University Press.

CASPER C. DE JONGE is Professor of Greek Language and Literature at Leiden University. His research concentrates on Greek literature in the Roman world, ancient migrant literature, ancient literary criticism, classical rhetoric, the sublime, and the reception of antiquity in classical music. He has received Veni and Vidi grants from the Netherlands Organization of Scientific Research (NWO).

SIMON GOLDHILL is Professor of Greek at the University of Cambridge, and Foreign Secretary of the British Academy. He has written broadly on Greek literature and culture: his works have been translated into ten languages and won three international prizes. He has lectured all over the world and has broadcast regularly on radio and television in the UK, USA, Canada, and Australia. His most recent book is *Preposterous*

Poetics: The Politics and Aesthetics of Form in Late Antiquity (Cambridge University Press, 2020).

BENJAMIN GRAY is Senior Lecturer in Ancient History at Birkbeck, University of London. He is the author of *Stasis and Stability: Exile, the Polis, and Political Thought, c. 404–146 BC* (Oxford University Press, 2015) and co-editor of *The Hellenistic Reception of Classical Athenian Democracy and Political Thought* (Oxford University Press, 2018, with M. Canevaro). He is currently working on a project, from which his chapter in this volume derives, on the interaction between political thought and civic rhetoric in the later Hellenistic world.

EMMA GREENSMITH is Associate Professor of Classical Languages and Literature at the University of Oxford and a Fellow of St John's College. She specialises in imperial Greek literature, particularly epic, poetics and religious culture. Her recent book, *The Resurrection of Homer in Imperial Greek Epic: Quintus Smyrnaeus' Posthomerica and the Poetics of Impersonation* (Cambridge University Press, 2020), offers a new reading of the role of epic and the reception of Homer in Greco-Roman poetic culture. She has also written recent articles on Nonnus, Triphiodorus and Colluthus, and is editing a new *Cambridge Companion to Greek Epic*.

MYRTO HATZIMICHALI is University Senior Lecturer in Classics (Philosophy) at the University of Cambridge. She is author of *Potamo of Alexandria and the Emergence of Eclecticism in Late Hellenistic Philosophy* (Cambridge University Press, 2011). Her research interests include Greco-Roman philosophy in the first century BCE (where she has published on the fate of the Aristotelian corpus, the doxography of Arius Didymus, Antiochus of Ascalon and Philodemus). They also range over Greek intellectual life more broadly, with publications on the Library of Alexandria and the scholars associated with it, including the Jewish author of the *Letter of Aristeas*. She is currently working on a series of papers on Aristotle's biological works.

LAWRENCE KIM is Professor of Classical Studies at Trinity University in San Antonio, Texas. He is the author of *Homer between History and Fiction in Imperial Greek Literature* (Cambridge University Press, 2010) as well as numerous articles on the ancient novel, ancient literary criticism, Atticism and imperial Greek prose literature. His current project treats the idea of the 'archaic' in Greek and Latin literary-historical thinking.

List of Contributors

JASON KÖNIG is Professor of Greek at the University of St Andrews. He has published widely on the Greek literature and culture of the Roman Empire. His publications include *Athletics and Literature in the Roman Empire* (Cambridge University Press, 2005), *Saints and Symposiasts: The Literature of Food and the Symposium in Greco-Roman and Early Christian Culture* (Cambridge University Press, 2012), and a series of volumes on knowledge-ordering and encyclopaedic writing in the imperial period. He is currently working on representations of landscape, environment, and especially mountains in ancient Mediterranean culture. His latest book, *The Folds of Olympus: Mountains in Ancient Greek and Roman Culture*, is forthcoming with Princeton University Press.

FELIX K. MAIER is Heisenberg Professor at the University of Würzburg (Germany). His research centres on ancient Greek historiography, imperial representation in Late Antiquity, conflict escalation models and Digital Classics. He is the author of the monographs *Überall mit dem Unerwarteten rechnen: Die Kontingenz historischer Prozesse bei Polybios* (C. H. Beck, 2012) and *Palastrevolution: Der Weg zum hauptstädtischen Kaisertum im Römischen Reich des vierten Jahrhunderts* (Brill, 2019). He is also the chief editor of *Die Fragmente der Griechischen Historiker* Part v. Currently he is working on identity and power in the early imperial era.

THOMAS A. SCHMITZ studied classics and comparative literature in Bonn, Paris and Harvard. He teaches Greek Literature at Bonn University and has held positions at Kiel, Heidelberg, Frankfurt, Stanford and Paris. His main research interests are imperial Greek culture, the connections between modern literary theories and classical texts, and classical receptions. He has published on imperial Greek literature, Hellenistic poetry, and literary theory. His most recent book is a commented edition of Sophocles' *Electra* (De Gruyter, 2016). He is currently preparing a book on the classical tradition in European literature.

NICOLAS WIATER is Senior Lecturer in Classics at the University of St Andrews. He specialises in Hellenistic and early imperial Greek literature, especially Greek authors engaging with Rome. His major publications include *The Ideology of Classicism: Language, History, and Identity in Dionysius of Halicarnassus* (De Gruyter, 2011), a multi-volume German translation, with introduction and commentary, of Dionysius' *Early Roman History* (so far, 2 vols, Hiersemann, 2014,

2018), and *The Struggle for Identity: Greeks and Their Past in the First Century BCE*, co-edited with Thomas A. Schmitz (Franz Steiner Verlag, 2011). His current projects include a commentary on Polybius, *Histories* III for Oxford University Press and a monograph on the debate about Hannibal's march from Polybius to the twenty-first century (funded by The Leverhulme Trust).

Preface

Many of the chapters in this volume were delivered in preliminary form at a conference entitled 'Rethinking Late Hellenistic Literature and the Second Sophistic', at the School of Classics, University of St Andrews. We are grateful to the British Academy and the Leverhulme Trust for their generous funding of that event, via the BA/Leverhulme Small Research Grants scheme. Thanks also to Michael Sharp, the series editors, and the anonymous readers for Cambridge University Press; to Jenny Messenger at Atomic Typo for indexing; and to Peter Bing, Matthew Fox, Regina Höschele, Katarzyna Jazdzewska, Emily Kneebone and Karen ní Mheallaigh for important contributions at various stages in the project.

Abbreviations

Journal abbreviations are from *Année philologique*. All other abbreviations are from the *Oxford Classical Dictionary*, fourth edition; or in the case of abbreviations not included there, from Liddell-Scott-Jones, *A Greek–English Lexicon* or from the *Oxford Latin Dictionary*. Abbreviations not included in those works are listed below.

Billerbeck = Billerbeck, M. (ed.) 2006. *Stephani Byzantii Ethnica Volumen I: Α-Γ*. Berlin.
Boissonade = Boissonade, J. F. (ed.) 1851. *Tzetzae Allegoriae Iliadis*. Paris.
Edelstein-Kidd = Edelstein, L. and Kidd, I. (eds) 1989. *Posidonius. Volume 1, The Fragments* (second edition; first published in 1972). Cambridge.
K (Galen) = Kühn, K. G. (ed.) 1821–33. *Opera omnia Claudii Galeni* (22 volumes). Leipzig.
Or. Sib. = Sibylline Oracles
R^3 = Ribbeck, O. (ed.) 1897–8. *Scaenicae Romanorum poesis fragmenta* (third edition). Leipzig.
Tzetz. *Alleg.* = John Tzetzes, *Allegories of the Iliad*.

Introduction

Jason König and Nicolas Wiater

Late Hellenistic Literature: Creativity and Diversity

The last few decades have seen an explosion of interest in the Greek literature of the Roman Empire, from the works of Plutarch and Dio Chrysostom in the late first century through to Philostratus in the early third. One starting point has been closer examination of the phenomenon described by Philostratus as the 'Second Sophistic', the flourishing of performance oratory that is such a distinctive feature of that period.[1] The Greek novels have been a major focus of interest for many decades now.[2] More recently that development has been further expanded to cover a wide range of texts and genres, with attention also to links between Greek and Latin prose, and to the wider social and historical context of imperial Greek literature.[3] Much of that work has focused on the way in which imperial Greek literature reflects and performs a complex range of identities and cultural affiliations.

By contrast, interest in late Hellenistic and Augustan Greek literature, and prose literature in particular, has developed much more slowly.[4] The reasons for that are various. One factor is the state of our surviving sources. Many key works do not survive for the second and first centuries BCE. A lot of scholarly energy in the past has understandably gone into reconstructing what is missing, rather than attempting to take a broader view of the literary culture of this period. The situation improves a little in the late

---

[1] E.g., see Bowersock 1969, Gleason 1995, Schmitz 1997, Korenjak 2000, Whitmarsh 2005; and for good recent overviews, Schmitz 2017 and Pernot 2017, both with further bibliography.
[2] See Whitmarsh 2008 for starting points.
[3] See Swain 1996, Goldhill 2001, Whitmarsh 2001a, König 2009 and more recently Johnson and Richter 2017, which includes discussion of Greek and Latin prose literature side by side.
[4] However, see Schmitz and Wiater 2011a for one exception, esp. Schmitz and Wiater 2011b: 15–16 and 44–5 for some starting points on the relationship between conceptions of Greek identity in the late Hellenistic and imperial periods; Hunter and de Jonge 2019b: 6–17 for discussion along similar lines; and further bibliography on individual authors below; also Meeus 2018c.

first century BCE and early first century CE under Augustus, but there is then an even more striking absence of surviving texts from the second and especially the third quarter of the first century CE, which has encouraged the perception of a significant break between late Hellenistic and imperial Greek literature – although of course there would have been no rigid dividing line between these two 'periods' of literary production for the inhabitants of the Roman empire (we will have more to say on problems of periodisation below). The connotations of decline and weakness that used to be associated with Greek culture under Roman rule have also been slower to shift for the late Hellenistic world than they have for the later imperial period. The idea, proclaimed even in recent reference works on Hellenistic literature, that 'real' rhetoric ceased to exist with the end of the classical period is a case in point: it stems directly from the (equally mistaken) assumption that 'real' political and cultural life became impossible after the end of the fourth century.[5] That stereotype has been challenged for the wealthy cities of the Greek east in the second century CE, as we shall see further below, but much less so for the first and second centuries BCE.[6]

Late Hellenistic literature has also suffered from competition with the Alexandrian poetry of the third century BCE.[7] The brilliant works of the poet-scholars of Alexandria between them form an unusually coherent body of work, focused around a well-defined set of recurring themes and aesthetic and methodological principles. They were produced over a relatively short period of time within a well-documented historical and cultural context. Hellenistic Alexandria has thus produced nothing short of an intellectual goldmine comparable only to the literary culture of classical Athens in its geographical and intellectual consistency. Add to this the enormous influence these poets have exerted on the literature of subsequent generations, and it is understandable that Alexandrian poetry has attracted the attention and energy of such a large proportion of scholars with an interest in post-classical Greek literature. Compared to the concentrated 'unity' of third-century Alexandrian poetry, other, later Hellenistic poetry has been seen as much less inviting. As we shall see in

---

[5] E.g., Kühnert and Vogt 2005: 912–13.
[6] There are some signs, though, that the tide is slowly turning: e.g., see Grieb 2008; Canevaro and Gray 2018; cf. Cuypers 2010: 323–4 and Wiater 2014a: 860–1, both with further references; Alcock 1993 for a related attempt to challenge stereotypes of economic decline in mainland Greece in the late Hellenistic and early imperial periods.
[7] Rengakos 2017: 74–5 traces the origins of the tendency to privilege Alexandrian poetry in studies of Hellenistic literature to Wilamowitz and Pfeiffer.

Greensmith's chapter, late Hellenistic verse texts are constantly at risk of being ignored – viewed as culturally and aesthetically marginal, by comparison with their Alexandrian equivalents, and harder to categorise and confine within a set of common concerns and approaches (to some extent the same goes for the Greek poetry of the imperial period, although that long-standing misconception is increasingly being dismantled by important works on imperial and late antique Greek epic in particular).[8]

Hellenistic prose has also had a bad deal within the scholarship of the last century, with the exception of a few key ancient authors. Chapter 3 ('Authors and Genres') of Kathryn Gutzwiller's excellent *Guide to Hellenistic Literature* devotes only two out of nine sections, or 23 out of 117 pages, to prose authors, with one section on Polybius and another on 'technical prose writing' (also a few pages on philosophical prose writing in a section on 'parodic and philosophical literature' that is primarily concerned with verse).[9] The rest of the chapter deals exclusively with Hellenistic poets. Hellenistic prose appears to be 'all over the place', with a huge diversity of different, often highly specialised works,[10] including a staggering range of different types of historical narratives covering events in an enormous range of periods and geographical locations;[11] technical

---

[8] For surveys of the main landmarks of imperial Greek verse, see Bowie 1989b and 1990, and Baumbach 2017; and for recent developments in the scholarship see Greensmith's chapter below, esp. p. 185, n. 25.

[9] Gutzwiller 2007: 50–167. Three years later, Martine Cuypers stated that 'Hellenistic prose typically fills little space in surveys of Greek literature' (2010: 317). This has changed somewhat thanks to the publication, in the meantime, of Zimmermann and Rengakos 2014, but Cuypers' statement does still ring true today. On the state of the history of Hellenistic literature see also Rengakos 2017; and cf. Meeus 2018b: esp. 1–4 (with a particular emphasis on historiography).

[10] As Cuypers 2010: 317 points out, not all of these different kinds of texts are treated equally: philosophical authors and Polybius, for example, tend to receive more scholarly attention than technical and scientific writers.

[11] To name only a few, Polybius' 'universal' history, covering the rise of Rome from the First Roman–Carthaginian War (264–241 BCE) to the fall of Carthage and Corinth in 146 BCE in forty books; the history of the Diadochs, covering the time from the death of Pyrrhus (272) to the death of Cleomenes (220–219), in twenty-eight books by Phylarchus; the histories focusing on the deeds of Antiochus III and Eumenes II by the same author; the large number of historians describing the deeds of Alexander the Great; the various local historians, including the Atthidographers such as Philochorus of Athens (340–262), the most important representative of the genre; the Σαμίων ὧροι, a history centred on Samos but including extended characterisations of important historical characters (and, hence, overlapping with biography) by Duris (from 350–340 to 280–270), and the *Sicilian Histories* of Timaeus (350–260) in thirty-eight books; related, but with a more ethnographic focus, are the *Babylonian History* by Berossus of Babylon (early third century), the *Aegyptiaka* by Manetho and the *Asiatika* (ten books on the history of the Diadochs), *Europiaka* (forty-nine books) and the treatise *On the Red Sea* (five books) by Agatharchides of Cnidus (200–120); and the increasing number of historians focusing on various aspects of Roman history, such as Polybius (mentioned above), whose work was continued in the first century by the Stoic philosopher, historian and scientist Posidonius of Apameia (covering the years from 145 to

treatises on medicine, music, biology, astronomy, mechanics and strategy as well as grammar;[12] writings on rhetoric and literary criticism;[13] and the works of the influential philosophical schools, the Peripatetics, Stoics, Epicureans and Sceptics.[14] The later Hellenistic period also sees many inscriptions with a strongly 'literary' character, especially long honorary decrees which draw on biographical, rhetorical and philosophical motifs: they need to be counted as part of the late Hellenistic literary landscape, rather than as a background to 'literature' proper.[15]

This plurality is one of the defining features of Hellenistic prose. 'Hellenistic prose' is best imagined as a dynamic, constantly shifting field, with authors re-working, adopting and adapting the works of their predecessors in the light of their own social, cultural and political circumstances, and in many cases pushing the boundaries of literary and generic conventions. Many of these authors are just as polymathic as their poetic counterparts in Alexandria. Think of Posidonius, for example, who wrote on history, philosophy and the sciences; of Strabo, who wrote geography and history; Polybius, who is the author of a biography and a technical military treatise as well as his famous historical work and a treatise on the habitability of the equatorial zones; Dionysius of Halicarnassus, who taught 'classical' style and aesthetics as well as being the author of the *Early Roman History*; and Agatharchides, whose works crossed the boundaries between history and ethnography, to name only a few.[16]

The plethora of different approaches to historical writing in Hellenistic literature illustrates this well. Theopompus, for example, initially followed well-established models of historical narrative in his *Hellenika* (designed to continue Thucydides' work and, as such, a direct competitor of Xenophon's work with the same title) but then abandoned this design

---

86/5 in fifty-two books), and the *Early Roman History* by Dionysius of Halicarnassus, which treated the history of Rome from the ethnic origins of the Romans and the foundation of the city to the beginning of the First Roman–Carthaginian War originally in twenty books; the 'universal' history of Diodorus of Sicily, which narrated the history of the entire *oikoumene* from mythical times down to the Britannic expedition of Julius Caesar originally in forty books; the 'Hannibal historians' Silenus and Sosylus (on the Second Roman–Carthaginian War); the 'world history' by Nicolaus of Damascus (born c. 64 BCE) in 144 books from the earliest times to the death of Herodes (4 BCE); and the 'universal history' (*Hypomnemata Historika*) by Strabo of Amaseia (64 BCE–23/27 CE) originally in forty-three books. This list is far from exhaustive and meant merely to give an impression of the incredible variety of Hellenistic prose literature even just within the field of historiography; for a helpful overview see Zimmermann and Rengakos 2014: 617–77.

[12] Zimmermann and Rengakos 2014: 453–616.   [13] Zimmermann and Rengakos 2014: 860–6.
[14] Zimmermann and Rengakos 2014: 392–452.
[15] See Benjamin Gray's chapter below, with Robert 1960: 213. Angelos Chaniotis has done much pioneering work in this field, e.g., Chaniotis 1987, 2013a, 2013b.
[16] Cf. also Cuypers 2010: 332 with further examples.

'midway through' to centre his historical narrative on the person of Philip of Macedon, thus producing his *Philippika*. The fragmentary nature of what little remains of Theopompus' works makes it impossible for us to assess the effect of this change precisely, but the inventive and controversial nature of Theopompus' move is still perceptible in Polybius' harsh criticism, that Theopompus should have kept history and biography neatly separate (8.11.3–6 = BNJ 115 T19). As Polybius' objection makes clear, Theopompus' change could be seen as a radical (and, in Polybius' view, failed and morally questionable) experiment that challenged conventional narrative modes and conventional views on the relationship between genres, specifically the relationship between history and biography, which Polybius believes ought to be kept strictly separate.[17] At the same time, it is possible to recapture a more positive impression of Theopompus' creativeness: for example the preserved fragments of the *Philippika* show that Theopompus supplemented his bio-historiographical approach with long topographical, geographical and ethnographical digressions, anecdotes, and *thaumasia*, while covering the deeds of Greeks as well as non-Greeks, thus aligning his narrative more with a Herodotean type of historical writing and combining a personalised, biographical focus with a more universalising one.[18]

It is too simplistic to view Polybius' extensive engagement with Theopompus and other historical predecessors (most prominently Timaeus, but Ephorus, Phylarchus, Fabius Pictor and many others also feature heavily in Polybius' methodological passages)[19] simply as an expression of his peculiar penchant for belligerent criticism. Polybius' critical passages testify to the power of multiple approaches and the drive for constant innovation in prose narrative in this period. Moreover, Polybius himself shares some aspects of Theopompus' inventiveness by, for example, seeking to establish the idea of the *symploke*, the 'weaving together' of the entire Mediterranean under Roman power, as the 'key' to understanding past and present,[20] but also by engaging with a wide range of different kinds of writing such as inscriptions in order to inscribe his work into larger political contexts of Greek arbitration and Roman political discussion.[21]

---

[17] Cf. Polybius 10.21.8, where he refers to his biography of Philopoemen as an *enkomion*.
[18] Cf. Zimmermann and Rengakos 2014: 634, with further bibliography.
[19] Meister 1975 is still the most comprehensive treatment; cf., more recently, Scardino 2018 on Polybius' engagement with his historical predecessors; Parmeggiani 2018 on fourth-century historiography in particular.
[20] Cf. Wiater 2017 and in this volume. [21] See Wiater 2018b.

We argue, then, that generic inventiveness and multiplicity are hallmarks of literary production, in prose as well as poetry, for the Hellenistic period as a whole. Conventional accounts of Hellenistic literature, focused on third-century Alexandrian verse, have tended to foreground the first of those features, but to underestimate the second.[22] In the same way in which we now prefer to speak of 'cultures' and 'identities', we ought to think of Hellenistic 'literatures' in the plural, rather than the singular. In that sense Hellenistic literature defies any attempt at a unifying, 'Great Story' type of approach. This has important implications for scholarly works like this one which set out to take a broad view of the literature of these centuries. What 'Hellenistic literature' is lies in the eye of the beholder to an even greater extent than for the literature of the archaic and classical periods.

Because of the extraordinary diversity of Hellenistic literary production, a selective and hence to some degree arbitrary approach is unavoidable. No discussion of Hellenistic literature can ever lay a claim to being comprehensive or uncovering some sort of 'essence' of Hellenistic literary production. Although we cover many of the key genres and authors of late Hellenistic Greek literature – the most obvious exception is scientific or technical writing –[23] the approach adopted in this volume is, therefore, deliberately selective. The chapters collected here are intended as samples and stimuli; they do not add up to a fully comprehensive discussion of Hellenistic literature; instead they showcase and explore the viability and profitability of many different approaches. Maier in this volume discusses the technique of 'sideshadowing' in Polybius and Plutarch, which allows them to draw attention to possible pathways not taken in the unfolding historical events they describe. This volume too invites a kind of sideshadowing. It is possible to imagine versions of this project or even this introduction that give their main attention to a very different selection of texts, for example moving Polybius or Strabo or Dionysius of Halicarnassus more into the background, and giving more weight in turn to late Hellenistic philosophical writing, to some of the other late Hellenistic historiographical texts that are covered only in passing in this volume, or to the late Hellenistic Jewish literature whose importance is sketched briefly at a later stage in this introduction, and then in the chapters by Greensmith and Goldhill. We hope that others will take up

---

[22] Cf. Rengakos 2017.
[23] For a helpful, concise overview of this aspect of Hellenistic literary production, with further literature, see Cuypers 2010: 330–4.

the opportunity to explore quite different combinations of texts in future, and in doing so to open up fresh perspectives on the landscape of late Hellenistic literature.

Re-bounding the Late Hellenistic

We argued in the preceding section that any unifying approach to the themes and genres of 'late Hellenistic literature' is likely to be inadequate, given the diversity and multiplicity of that material. The same holds true for any attempt to define 'late Hellenistic' texts by clear-cut and rigid temporal boundaries. In this section we offer a more extensive discussion of issues of periodisation, in order to explore what is at stake in the term 'late Hellenistic' as we use it in this volume, before moving on to examine the way in which our view of the multiplicity of Hellenistic literature and the difficulty of demarcating it within well-defined temporal boundaries informs our approach to individual texts and authors.

What constitutes the 'Hellenistic' period of Greek literature has always been a matter of contention.[24] The concept of a 'Hellenistic' period of Greek literature itself does not, as Rudolf Kassel has shown, originate with Droysen, who offered preciously little concrete discussion of literature and literary history.[25] It is found already in Friedrich August Wolf's lectures on the history of Greek literature at the end of the eighteenth century. Wolf distinguished six periods of Greek literature, the fourth of which begins in 323/2 BCE with the deaths of Alexander and Aristotle – the end of the period of *Attica elegantia litterarum et artium* – and ends with Augustus' victory at Actium in 31 BCE and the arrival of Dionysius of Halicarnassus in Rome a year later.[26] Wolf calls it the *aetas studiorum Alexandrinorum seu polymathiae Alexandrinae*, with 'Alexandrian' being synonymous with 'Hellenistic' (i.e., covering all forms of literary production of that period), as it remained until Wilamowitz.[27] It was Wilamowitz who first

---

[24] Our remarks here are influenced by the crucial contribution of Kassel 1987.
[25] See Kassel 1987: esp. 10 on Droysen and literary history; also Bichler 1983 on the concept of 'Hellenismus', which was well-established, in a plethora of different meanings, before Droysen published the first volume of his *Geschichte des Hellenismus* in 1836, and which was immediately criticised after the publication of Droysen's work and has remained controversial ever since. Cf. Bonnet 2015: 19–23, with further literature.
[26] It is worth pointing out that Wolf is here adopting Dionysius' own periodisation; see *Orat. vett.* 1.1.2 with Wiater 2011: 60–5 (with further literature); cf. also Kim's chapter in this volume.
[27] Kassel 198: 10–11. Susemihl's two-volume *Geschichte der griechischen Litteratur in der Alexandrinerzeit* (1891–2), which remains the best overview of the staggering variety and sheer mass of Hellenistic literature, is a case in point.

systematically and programmatically associated the 'Hellenistic' period of Greek literature with Droysen's concept of 'Hellenismus' because he shared with Droysen – in stark contrast to most of his scholarly precursors – a positive view of this period and an enthusiasm for what we would call today the 'globalisation' of Greek culture.[28]

Wolf's definition of the start and end points of his 'Alexandrian' (as we would call it, 'Hellenistic') period, 323/2–30 BCE, happen to be identical with the ones commonly accepted today but were, in fact, never uncontroversial. In his *Grundriß der griechischen Litteratur* (vol. 1: 1836, vol. 2: 1845) Wolf's disciple Bernhardy took the beginning of Alexander's reign, rather than his death as the starting point for the period. Theodor Bergk, by contrast, argued in his treatise 'When Did the Alexandrian Period of Greek Literature Begin' (1872) for 300 BCE, because only the time of peace after the battle of Ipsus could have provided the environment essential for the thriving academic culture that Bergk, like many others, regarded as the defining characteristic of 'Alexandrian' literature. A more radical approach was proposed in 1925 by Richard Laqueur, who argued for 400 BCE, while Kenneth Dover suggested in the introduction to his commented selection of Theocritus' poems (1971) that 'Hellenistic' poetry began as early as the deaths of Sophocles and Euripides.[29]

A similar picture emerges from an examination of the proposed end dates of the period. In Bergk's *Griechische Literaturgeschichte*, published some twenty years after the treatise mentioned above, it stretches down to 146 BCE (incidentally also the end point of the final edition of Polybius' *Histories*), followed by an 'unproductive' period down to 44 BCE (the death of Caesar); both these periods, however, are part of a larger, bipartite division of Greek literature into a 'classical period in the sense proper', from the beginnings to 300 BCE, and the 'afterlife', a period generally devoid of originality, from 300 BCE to 527 CE![30] Along similar lines, Bernhardy had treated 'Alexandrian poetry' and Greek literature of the imperial period together. Wilamowitz, by contrast, distinguished a 'Hellenistic' period, lasting from 320 to 30 BCE, from the preceding 'Attic' and the following 'Roman' ones. Within that 'Hellenistic period', however, he identified, with reference to poetry in particular, a 'productive' and an 'unproductive' phase, with the latter beginning in 200, in later editions even in 250 BCE.[31]

---

[28] See Kassel 1987: 11 on Wilamowitz and Droysen, and 1–11 on scholarly views (usually negative) of Hellenistic literature and culture; Bichler 1983: 55–109 on Droysen.
[29] Kassel 1987: 5–16.   [30] Kassel 1987: 7.   [31] Kassel 1987: 8–9.

To finish this survey with the two most recent standard treatments of Greek literary history, von Christ, Schmid and Stählin distinguish 'the creative period of post-classical literature', which they additionally define as 'Hellenistic literature', from 320 to 146 BCE, from the 'period of the transition to neo-classicism', from 146 BCE to 100 CE.[32] Zimmermann and Rengakos, by contrast, treat the literature of the archaic, classical and Hellenistic periods in two volumes. The first one, entitled *The Literature of Archaic and Classical Times*, ends at around 400 BCE – a time, the editors claim, that was perceived by contemporaries, for example, Aristophanes in the *Frogs* (405 BCE), as an 'epochal break' ('Epocheneinschnitt').[33] The second volume, entitled *The Literature of Classical and Hellenistic Times* covers literature from 400 BCE to the Augustan and even Tiberian periods (both Strabo and Dionysius of Halicarnassus, for example, are included among the historians), but begins with a characterisation of the Hellenistic period and 'Hellenistic poetry', thus leaving the fourth century, despite the volume's title, strangely undefined: is it part of the 'classical' or the 'Hellenistic' period, or does it, in some ways, belong to both?

This brief survey confirms – if any such confirmation was necessary – that periodisations are artificial constructs that respond to their creators' needs and reflect their prejudices rather than being based on any kind of 'objective' criteria. Our time has settled on 323 to 30 BCE, not least, one suspects, because those dates mark symbolically charged, significant political events.[34] They appeal because they are convenient, but many others could be and have, indeed, been chosen, and usually with good reason. The best approach thus seems to be the one adopted by Zimmermann and Rengakos (even though they never make this explicit) of operating with fluid concepts of period 'boundaries'.[35] Ways of writing and thinking did not suddenly and radically change in 323/2 BCE or, for that matter, 30 BCE. Recent studies on Dionysius of Halicarnassus, for example, have shown that both his historical and his critical works are firmly rooted in Hellenistic and, indeed, classical Greek (but also Roman Republican) traditions of thinking and writing, while also reflecting crucial aspects of his Augustan present.[36] Polybius, on the other hand, foreshadows in

---

[32] von Christ, Schmid and Stählin 1920: I, Table of Contents.
[33] Zimmermann and Rengakos 2011: vii.   [34] Cf. Kassel 1987: 15–16.
[35] Cf. also Prag and Quinn 2013b: 3–10; Whitmarsh 2017 for a challenge to the perception of a clear dividing line between the Hellenistic and imperial periods; and A. König and Whitton 2018b: 3–9 and 14–16 for parallel reflections on periodisation in relation to 'Nervan, Trajanic and Hadrianic literary culture' (4).
[36] See, e.g., de Jonge 2008 and the contributions in Hunter and de Jonge 2019a; Wiater 2018c, 2019.

significant ways views of space and empire that are often associated with the imperial period.[37]

Looking at literature other than Greek problematises the boundary between Hellenistic and imperial still further. From the perspective of Jewish authors, for example, there is no clear dividing line between 'Hellenistic' and 'imperial'.[38] The word 'Hellenistic' is often used by researchers who work on Jewish and even early Christian literature to cover what most classicists would see as a combination of 'Hellenistic' and 'early imperial' material, without reference to the conventional classicist's end date of the late 30s BCE. That is partly because many works are not securely dateable. Scholars of this literature are used to looking at them together partly because they have no choice, and that necessity has given them the freedom to understand connections and common features.[39] Jewish literature also does not see the gap in literary production in the second and third quarters of the first century CE that in non-Jewish literature contributes to the impression (itself, as we have seen, not uncontroversial) of a clean break between 'Hellenistic' and 'imperial' literature. Philo and Josephus are among the most important writers in Greek from those decades: they bridge us smoothly from Augustus to the Flavians.[40]

With that background in mind it is clear that any attempt to define a late Hellenistic 'period' rigidly would be counter-productive. That is not to say that we should reject periodisation entirely. Individual authors and their works will always need to be discussed in terms of the literary and intellectual traditions on which they draw as well as the ways in which they respond to specific cultural, social, political and literary developments of their own time. All of the chapters that follow draw among others on texts that were written in the second and/or first centuries BCE, and we use 'late Hellenistic' as a convenient shorthand for that time-span. It is not meant, however, to carry any 'essentialist' meaning of the kind ascribed to it by Droysen.[41] Neither in terms of dates, nor in terms of 'contents', as we

---

[37] See Wiater in this volume. [38] Cf. Gruen 1998a: xvii; Siegert 2016.
[39] For example, see further p. 18 below on the work of Erich Gruen.
[40] See Niehoff 2018: esp. 18–22 on the way in which Philo's work anticipates many of the features of later imperial Greek literature.
[41] Jameson 1981: 27 writes about the 'fatally reductive' quality of periodisation, and the way in which it gives 'an impression of facile totalization, a seamless web of phenomena each of which, in its own way, "expresses" some inner truth – a world view or a period style or a set of structural categories which marks the whole length and breadth of the "period" in question'; at the same time even Jameson himself acknowledges the necessity and the potential rewards of periodisation; see also

argued in the previous section, does the idea of 'Hellenistic' or 'late Hellenistic' literature lend itself to unifying, 'one-size-fits-all' approaches.

The prominence of Polybius as a starting point for thinking about late Hellenistic literary production is a case in point. There are pragmatic reasons for seeing Polybius' *Histories* as an important landmark, and it is taken as such in several of the chapters that follow. Within the fragmented landscape of post-classical Greek prose literature, Polybius' *Histories* is a work of which we have a significant amount of text, a considerable part of which, namely the first five books, constitutes an integral, coherent narrative sequence. In part, then, it is the coincidence of textual survival that endows Polybius with a prominent position. But Polybius is also, as far as we can tell, the first author to make Rome the main focus and organising principle of his narrative. His choice of subject represents a watershed in the orientation of Greek historical thinking and testifies to the perception of Rome as the upcoming new centre of power of the Mediterranean among Greeks. He therefore seems particularly suited as a boundary marker for the present exploration of Hellenistic and imperial Greek literature in which Greek interaction with Roman texts and culture invariably plays a role.

Moreover, it so happens that the state of preservation of Hellenistic literature improves a little after Polybius. While Polybius' *Histories* stands out even in its fragmentary state as extraordinarily well preserved within the scarce remains of third- and second-century BCE Greek prose literature,[42] substantial parts of large-scale literary works have been preserved from the first centuries BCE and CE, such as the *Roman Antiquities* and critical essays of Dionysius of Halicarnassus, Strabo's *Geography*, and the *Life of Augustus* and historical narrative of Nicolaus of Damascus. Hellenistic literature, visible only in its broad contours in the third and second centuries BCE, takes on a more concrete form from the first century BCE onwards. In all of these ways Polybius is an important landmark. We have therefore opted, in the end, for Polybius as the starting point for the present volume, and the main focus of the chapters that follow is, consequently, a span of a little under 200 years, from Polybius to Strabo, who wrote under Augustus and perhaps Tiberius.[43] It is, however, important to

---

Besserman 1996: 3, who quotes this passage from Jameson at the start of his wide-ranging discussion of the problems and opportunities in period-based approaches.

[42] An important exception to this rule, as Cuypers 2010: 317 remarks, is the category of scientific texts.

[43] See Pothecary 2005: 1–2 for debate over the date of Strabo, with further bibliography.

stress that Polybius' work is only one of many possible starting points for mapping out the Greek literature of these centuries.[44]

Dealing with Diversity: Dialogue and Interplay

What are the consequences of those reflections on the plurality and diversity of late Hellenistic literature for the contributions to this volume? While there is some merit, of course, in discussing Hellenistic texts by genre, or in focusing on individual texts on their own, such an approach is, we believe, less likely to produce exciting new results. We have seen that Hellenistic authors of poetry as well as prose programmatically engaged with a plethora of texts, literary as well as non-literary. Our contributors have therefore been encouraged to adopt a 'dialogic approach' and explore different texts, and kinds of texts, alongside each other, just as Hellenistic works themselves entered – consciously or unconsciously – into dialogue with many different kinds of writing. One of our main aims in the volume, in other words, is to open up some new insights into the interconnectedness of the Greek literature of those centuries. This is the first of the two kinds of dialogue in which we are interested in the volume. Traditionally there has been a reluctance to accept that most of these late Hellenistic authors deserve the same sophisticated analysis as their great 'classical' predecessors,[45] but there is now a promising number of important studies that explore individual authors such as Polybius,[46] Diodorus,[47] Dionysius,[48] Parthenius,[49] and Strabo,[50] among others. In verse, some areas of late Hellenistic epigram are now well studied.[51] What is missing, however, is work that attempts a more wide-ranging analysis of late Hellenistic Greek texts and their interrelations with each other.[52]

---

[44] Cf. Cuypers 2010: 318 on the way in which scholars dealing with Hellenistic literature often look to Polybius as a sort of 'safe haven', and 319 for qualms about this 'primacy' of Polybius in survey accounts of Hellenistic literature.
[45] Cf. Weißenberger 2012, reviewing Wiater 2011.
[46] E.g., Eckstein 1995, Champion 2004, Maier 2012b, Miltsios 2013, Wiater 2017.
[47] E.g., Sacks 1990, Sulimani 2011, Muntz 2017.
[48] E.g., Gabba 1991, Fox 1993, Wiater 2014b and 2018a, among others, on Dionysius' *Early Roman History*; de Jonge 2008 and Wiater 2011 on his critical works; most recently, Hunter and de Jonge 2019a for a volume giving attention to both.
[49] E.g., Lightfoot 1999. [50] E.g., Dueck 2000, Dueck, Lindsay and Pothecary 2005.
[51] For a recent example, see Ypsilanti 2018 on Crinagoras.
[52] In that sense this book is intended as a follow-up to Schmitz and Wiater 2011a: many of the chapters in that volume too focus on individual authors, but several others, especially the introduction, offer assessments of the period as a whole, juxtaposing a wide range of different texts. Bowersock 1965 remains a classic study of the interplay between literature and politics in this period; Clarke 1999 and Hau 2016 juxtapose several different late Hellenistic historiographical and

The situation is very different for the large volume of publications on what is often described as the Roman 'cultural revolution' of the late Republic. That tends to be seen now as a time of enormous creativity, which saw the development of new, and interconnected intellectual disciplines and approaches in Latin literature and Roman elite culture. Roman engagement with Greek models is viewed as a central part of that process, but generally without much interest in the way in which Greek literature continued to develop in its own right in these centuries, partly, perhaps, because of the silent assumption that Rome had now taken over political as well as cultural leadership from her Greek neighbours.[53] The work of Andrew Wallace-Hadrill is a good example: his monumental account of Roman cultural change in this period, *Rome's Cultural Revolution*, is very subtle and cautious in its account of cultural exchange as a two-way process,[54] but the main object of analysis for him is the cultural production of Latin-speaking Romans.[55] That focus is entirely legitimate, of course, and leads to an enormously rich account, but it means that the Greek literature of this period (much of it itself written in Rome) has often been overshadowed.

Our aim, in response, is to give late Hellenistic Greek literature a more prominent place in scholarship alongside the Latin works of the same period, and in the process to break new ground in our understanding of Greco-Roman interaction. Greek influence on Latin writers has been widely discussed, but the same is not true of the influence of Rome and the emergence of Roman power on Greek authors. Many of the chapters in this volume demonstrate, in fact, that the late Hellenistic expansion of the Roman Empire was a key factor in the evolution of new modes and new scales of literary interactivity: in other words that the new richness and complexity of literary interconnectedness that we chart in the volume was partly a consequence of empire. Those new modes of interactivity went far beyond the well-documented processes whereby Roman writers absorbed and adapted Greek models. They were intertwined with the late Hellenistic and imperial explosion of interest in knowledge-ordering,

---

geographical authors; see also de Jonge 2008: 25–48 for stimulating discussion of the cross-fertilisation between different fields interested in language, esp. grammar, rhetorical theory and philosophy. The chapters collected in Meeus 2018c discuss historical writers from Polybius to Plutarch, but there is not much attempt to bring their texts into dialogue with each other, with the sole exception of Almagor's chapter on Polybius and Plutarch.

[53] See Prag and Quinn 2013b on the equivalent problem for the Hellenistic west.
[54] E.g., Wallace-Hadrill 2008: 16.
[55] See Habinek and Schiesaro 1997 and Moatti 2015 for good parallels.

encyclopaedic projects, which we suggest was similarly stimulated by the new interconnectedness of the Roman empire (although it was rarely in the service of empire or directly dependent on imperial institutions as many knowledge-ordering projects have been in modern European imperial contexts).[56] But that was only one part of a much bigger widening of horizons, which involved a vast expansion in the range of possible reference points available for ancient writers as they sought to enter into dialogue with the world around them.

This takes us to the second of the two kinds of dialogue in which we are interested, that is the dialogue between late Hellenistic and imperial texts (discussed further in the section following). Late Hellenistic Greek literary production was, to a significant extent, fuelled by the engagement with the Romans. Imperial Greek literature is sometimes characterised by contrast as having a tendency to ignore Rome, looking back to the classical past as if to escape from the Roman present.[57] It has become increasingly clear, however, that these later authors too are centrally concerned with the problems of how to engage with Roman power.[58] In that sense they need to be seen in a continuum with their late Hellenistic predecessors. That assumption dovetails with our observations above on the inherent difficulties of defining an end point of 'Hellenistic' literature. The 'dialogues' that we are interested in have a diachronic, as well as synchronic, dimension. Our contributors have therefore been encouraged to see the difficulty of defining a firm end date for 'late Hellenistic' literature as an opportunity which can prompt us to examine not just the interrelations between different kinds of texts from the century and a half leading up to the reign of Augustus, but also their relationship with texts which were written in later decades and later centuries.

How does this 'dialogic' approach play out in practice? The search for interconnections could conceivably be based on a traditional model of literary allusion, of the kind which is so important for our understanding of Alexandrian poetry in particular. Some of the chapters that follow are indeed interested in specific moments of clearly identifiable influence, but we also aim to go beyond that kind of approach through a much a more fluid model of intertextual connectedness. The multi-facetedness of late Hellenistic literature beyond the close-knit circle of Alexandrian poetry requires us to explore different ways of conceptualising textual interplay and interdiscursivity and to move beyond conventional concepts of direct

---

[56] See König and Woolf 2013b; cf. König and Whitmarsh 2007b, esp. 35–8; Most 2011.
[57] See Bowie 1974.   [58] E.g., see Whitmarsh 2001a.

and deliberate influence.⁵⁹ 'Dialogue', as we understand it, does not require an author to have known the work of another and to be making reference to it deliberately. The act of bringing two works or authors into dialogue with each other can be on the readers' initiative; it need not necessarily be a matter of identifying some pre-existing and easily demonstrable contact between the two.⁶⁰ In fact, our awareness of ancient authors' direct knowledge of each other's work – as comforting and encouraging as it might be from a positivist point of view – can also be rather limiting. The knowledge, for example, that Strabo and Dionysius knew Polybius' *Histories* ought not to prompt us to see a discussion of the interrelationship of these three authors as the only meaningful and legitimate way of locating their works within the larger landscape of Hellenistic literature. We do not know, for example, how familiar Dionysius and Polybius were with the flourishing production of contemporary Greek epigram, whether Ovid read Polybius or whether the authors of civic decrees were familiar with Diodorus' *Bibliotheke*. Yet, as the chapters in this volume will demonstrate, much is to be gained from reading their texts in conjunction with each other. Only thus will we begin to see shared preoccupations, ideas and concepts, and shared narrative and literary strategies, that are independent of direct literary dependency or generic convention. It is the way in which these authors reacted to and interacted with their shared cultural and political context across different kinds of texts and genres, and not simply how they interacted with each other directly, that lies at the heart of our approach to late Hellenistic literature in the chapters of this volume. We are thus adopting a deliberately flexible concept of 'dialogue' which owes much to modern concepts of intertextuality and literary interaction as they have been discussed recently with regards to Latin literature: to adopt a helpful phrase from A. König, Langlands and Uden, we use 'dialogue' in the sense of 'a flexible and expansive conception of literary interaction, encompassing many potential

---

⁵⁹ Our attempts to understand late Hellenistic interactivity have been greatly helped by recent work on literary interactions under Nerva, Trajan and Hadrian by A. König and Whitton 2018a and A. König, Langlands and Uden 2020a; see especially A. König and Whitton 2018b: 12: 'the preference for "interactions" over, say, "intertextuality" reflects a desire to encourage fresh scrutiny of tralatitious models of reference and allusion, and to explore the areas which intertextuality, as defined by most Classicists today, can find difficult to reach', with n. 61: 'Or, to put it another way, to restore some of the Kristevan breadth to "intertextuality", a term used in practice by most Latinists as a synonym for "allusion"'.
⁶⁰ This important point was made forcefully for Latin poetry by Hinds 1998: esp. 17–51.

relationships between texts, from salutation, citation, allusion and echo, to omission, occlusion, interdiscursivity and extratextuality'.[61]

Such a flexible concept of 'dialogue', we would argue, also helps address some of its potential problems as identified recently by Hardwick with particular reference to the use of the concept in reception studies.[62] Hardwick notes that 'dialogue' raises questions about 'who sets the agenda; about who participates; about who persuades and how; about agencies; about how and by whom the "dialogue" is situated, conducted and appraised' and that it directs 'attention to problems about whether – and if so then to what extent – the ancient texts themselves (written and material) can be said to have a dialogical agency other than that constructed and refracted by scholars and creative practitioners'.[63] These concerns are valid, but at the same time we would argue that any attempt to separate text and readers and, with it, 'dialogical agency' (supposedly) inherent in the texts and 'dialogue' as constructed by readers creates a false dichotomy. Texts are richer than just their authors' intentions – in fact, as Hinds has argued, authorial intentions are themselves constructed by readers –[64] and cases in which clear semantic and/or linguistic features in one text strongly evoke another need to be considered alongside relationships which stem from different texts drawing on a shared cultural, political and literary background. Whenever literature and texts are involved, there will unavoidably be readers involved as well, and these readers will, to an extent, set their own agendas. It is by encouraging openness about those agendas, and diversity in our approach to texts, we would argue, that we can prevent dialogue from becoming coercive. When it is used flexibly and openly – in a way that corresponds to the flexibility and openness of the literature discussed in this volume – 'dialogue' can, on the contrary, be liberating. It has the potential to free us from traditional modes of reading and interpreting that are often applied without much questioning, setting the texts instead into new and unconventional contexts and in the process allowing us to generate new angles of vision and fresh interpretations.

In line with this open and 'flexible' concept of dialogue, many of the following chapters explore connections between traditions and texts and objects that have not usually been analysed together. The chapters by Kim, Gray and Wiater, for example, bring literary and non-literary texts,

---

[61] König, Langlands and Uden 2020b: 2–3 [62] Hardwick 2020.
[63] Cf. Hardwick 2020: 21 (for the first quote), 28 (for the second quote). [64] Hinds 1998: 49.

especially inscriptions, into dialogue with each other.⁶⁵ Other chapters pay fresh attention to the interplay between Republican Latin writings and their Greek counterparts, especially Connolly, who brings Cicero's engagement with Athens into dialogue with its Greek equivalents.

We also acknowledge the importance of rethinking the phenomenon of cross-cultural interaction by being more ready to see texts from outside the mainstream of Greco-Roman culture as part of the complex fabric of late Hellenistic literature. The interrelations between the Greeks and the Near East have been intensively explored for the archaic and early classical period in particular,⁶⁶ but scholars have only recently begun to examine the complex interrelationship between the different cultures of the West and East in the Hellenistic period.⁶⁷ Hellenistic Jewish literature plays a particularly important role in that story. Jewish authors are still rarely discussed side by side with their Hellenistic Greek counterparts.⁶⁸ There is a large body of material – albeit for the most part in fragmentary form – still awaiting analysis in relation to the wider currents of Hellenistic literature. There have been some first steps, but they remain relatively few. Greensmith's chapter, with its focus on the third Sibylline Oracle, aims to extend that discussion in new directions. Like the author of that text, other Jewish Greek writers too were immersed in Greek culture and Greek *paideia*, often intertwining it with specifically Jewish literary and biblical tradition.⁶⁹ Many of them in the process assert the primacy and antiquity of Jewish culture in relation to Greek. Much of this literature was produced in Alexandria, which was among other things a place associated with literary and cultural translation between Jewish and Greek.⁷⁰ To name only a few, the *Letter of Aristeas* describes the process by which the Jewish law was translated into Greek there in the reign of Ptolemy

---

⁶⁵ Images, on the other hand, are less prominently represented in this volume as 'dialogue partners' of literary texts, apart from some discussion in the chapters by Baumann and Greensmith; a more systematic exploration of the relationship between text and image in late Hellenistic culture remains a desideratum for future study, building on important work on that topic for other periods of classical antiquity (e.g., Squire 2009).

⁶⁶ The classic discussion is Burkert 1984; the most comprehensive treatment is West 1999.

⁶⁷ E.g., Prag and Quinn 2013a; Haubold 2013; most recently, Stevens 2019; for similar studies of cross-cultural interactions in imperial literature, see Whitmarsh and Thomson 2013; A. König, Langlands and Uden 2020a.

⁶⁸ There are occasional exceptions in Gutzwiller 2007: e.g., 122–3 on Ezekiel, or 194–5 on the *Letter of Aristeas*.

⁶⁹ For detailed discussion of all the works mentioned below, see Barclay 1996 and Gruen 1998a; also Bartlett 1985: 1–10 for an overview, followed by translation of a number of key works, accompanied by brief commentary.

⁷⁰ See Bartlett 1985: 5 for a summary.

Philadelphus. The Greek translation of the Book of Esther seems to have been brought to Alexandria by Dositheus in 78–77 BCE. We know of many Jewish historians working in this period, Artapanus and Eupolemus among them. The poet Ezekiel rewrote the Exodus story as a Greek tragedy in his *Exagoge*, drawing on a huge range of precedents from both Greek and Jewish literature to create a novel and powerful revisioning of the biblical narrative.

Recent work on these texts has tended to emphasise, like Greensmith in this volume, the creativeness with which these authors engaged with both the Greek and the Jewish heritage together, often in a way which involved an ingenious balancing act between assimilation with and independence from Greek culture. Some accounts organise Hellenistic Jewish works according to a contrast between works which recommend integration with Greek culture and others which favour cultural resistance.[71] Clearly there was a spectrum of responses, with some works that were much more strident and explicit than others in their hostility to Greek culture. However, it is also increasingly clear that we often find both of those strands in an uneasy tension in individual works. Tim Whitmarsh's work on Ezekiel's *Exagoge* has made that clear, in arguing that this text represents an 'allegorical commentary on contemporary Alexandria', dramatising the tension between conflicting pressures towards acculturation and resistance.[72] Erich Gruen, meanwhile, has brought out the extravagant and often playful inventiveness of Hellenistic Jewish narratives such as the *Letter to Aristeas* and the surviving fragments of the work of Artapanus.[73] That latter account in particular is a playful appropriation of the kind of stories about other Greek and near-eastern culture heroes that we find in Diodorus Books 1–5, as discussed by König in his chapter below;[74] it defies any simplistically confrontational model of the relationship between Greek and Jewish culture in Hellenistic literature.[75] Much more remains to be done on this fascinating area of cultural and literary interactions. We hope that Goldhill's mapping of potential directions for future work in the field, together with Greensmith's case study, will make a significant contribution towards further establishing Greco-Jewish writing as an

---

[71] See esp. Barclay 1996: 125–228.
[72] Whitmarsh 2013c; see also Whitmarsh 2013d along similar lines for the fragments of Hellenistic Jewish epic.
[73] Gruen 1998a: 155–60, 206–22.
[74] On the overlaps with Diodorus, see Barclay 1996: 129 n. 9; Gruen 1998a: 158.
[75] E.g., see Gruen 1998a: xiv–xv.

important presence in the wider landscape of late Hellenistic literature, and in stimulating further study.

Late Hellenistic and Imperial Dialogues

We have focused so far primarily on the dialogue between different kinds of texts produced in the second and first centuries BCE. As already noted, however, we are also interested in the dialogue between late Hellenistic and later imperial texts. The discussion in the second section of this introduction has shown that the conventional end point of the 'Hellenistic period', the battle of Actium, is an artificial one.[76] There is no clear and obvious moment or event that marks the end of the 'Hellenistic' period and the beginning of something radically new and different. Many of the chapters in this volume therefore look beyond the late 30s BCE not just by exploring texts from the late first century BCE and the early first century CE, but also by looking much further ahead to the literature of the second or even early third centuries. In that sense we are interested not just in dialogue within late Hellenistic literature, very broadly defined, but also between late Hellenistic texts and their much later imperial successors.

There is a range of different models for thinking about that relationship: it is common, as we shall see, to imagine a clean break between them; alternatively we might emphasise continuity; or perhaps best a spectrum of gradual change over time that brought both continuities and disjunctions between earlier and later texts.[77] We would argue that it is hazardous to generalise about the value of those different images: no single metaphor or model can sum up the complex relationship between such vast bodies of material, produced over such a long time scale. Polybius and his late Hellenistic successors laid the ground for much of the later Greek writing under Roman rule, and for many of the literary and cultural strategies employed by authors of the imperial period. There has been a tendency, we suggest, to underestimate that influence. In response, however, it is important not to replace that misconception with an equally simplistic narrative of continuity. Our hypothesis is that bringing imperial and late Hellenistic texts into dialogue with each other can open up fresh perspectives on both sides of the comparison, revealing new connections – many distinctively imperial genres and themes actually turn out to be rooted in

---

[76] See above, pp. 7–12.
[77] Cf. Whitmarsh 2017 for discussion along similar lines, with particular reference to the significance of these insights for the way in which we envisage the 'Second Sophistic'.

late Hellenistic literary practices when we look more closely – but also in some cases giving us a new understanding of important differences. Many of the chapters that follow do argue for significant areas of common ground in the preoccupations of the two 'periods' we are dealing with, in ways which suggest that the notion of a disjunction or a gap between them has been overstated. Others, by contrast, give more attention to the differences, and also to the way in which ancient authors themselves used concepts related to our own notions of periodisation in their own cultural self-definition (see further below on Philostratus in particular). Either way we aim to emphasise above all the complexity and variety of that relationship: we need to assess it freshly every time we bring a pair of authors or texts into dialogue with each other.

One of the most striking trends in earlier treatments is a tendency to stress the difference between late Hellenistic Greek authors dependent on Roman patronage and engaged with the realities of Roman rule and imperial authors whose greater cultural confidence allowed them to be more stand-offish towards Rome and to look back to the classical Greek world as their main focus. The differences are real, of course, but they may have been overstated. In the second century BCE, and then especially in the first century BCE after the Mithridatic wars, the Greek cities of the east were financially and politically weakened.[78] With the exception of Alexandria, the status of the great Hellenistic capitals as cultural centres was eroded.[79] Greek intellectuals flooded into Rome where they worked under Roman patronage.[80] In other cases, Polybius being, perhaps, the most prominent example, Greek statesmen and intellectuals were brought to Rome as 'hostages' and continued to live and work in the city for some considerable time, forming bonds with members of the Roman elite (e.g., in Polybius' case, the Scipiones). Some of them engaged quite explicitly with the Greek experience of Roman rule.

By the second century CE, by contrast, we see a rather different picture. The Greek cities of the east by then had regained their wealth. In some respects the Greek elite had become much more closely integrated into Roman politics: the numbers of Greeks with membership of the senate and even consulships increases as the second century goes on. But that

---

[78] See Rawson 1985: 7 for a typical assessment: 'the Mithridatic Wars, from Sulla to Pompey, proved in many respects a turning-point'.

[79] See Rawson 1985: 14–15, with reference to Pontus, Bithynia and the Seleucids; also Pergamum, which lost its court in 133, but maintained its library until it was taken to Rome in the mid-first century BCE.

[80] See Rawson 1985: 7–9; Hidber 2011: 122–3 for a list of many of the key authors.

went side by side with a greater cultural confidence and independence, which manifested itself in a highly creative celebration of the Greek cultural heritage without reference to Rome. Simon Swain has expressed that view convincingly as follows:

> The Greeks of the second and first centuries BC ... were not overly prosperous ... Leading Greek intellectuals were drawn to Rome to find Roman patrons. Thus there is a significant difference between the major authors of the late Republican/Augustan period like Philodemus, Diodorus, Nicolaus, Dionysius, Strabo, and others, who did important work in Rome, and the leading writers of the later first century and after, beginning with Plutarch and Dio of Prusa. The dislocation between the two sets reflects a quite different cultural landscape. The leaders of Greek intellectual life in the second sophistic period were part of a world that did not need Rome.[81]

In its broad contours it is hard to quarrel with those claims, but there is perhaps a risk of underestimating the confidence of late Hellenistic Greek literature, and correspondingly underestimating the dependence of later imperial Greek authors, too, on Roman patronage.[82]

Moreover, the new cultural abundance of the second century CE is often described with the image of renaissance, in a way which potentially overstates the extent of its disjunction from its late Hellenistic predecessors.[83] The literary output of that century is part of a wider phenomenon of cultural flourishing, which is visible also in the expansion of the festival calendar, with its athletic and musical competitions. More recently, however, A. J. S. Spawforth has attempted to push back the origins of that renaissance to the reign of Augustus, arguing that Greek culture was self-consciously reinvented during those decades in line with the moral priorities of the new emperor; he then sees a second wave of Roman cultural investment in the Greek east under Hadrian.[84] That argument builds on the observation others have made before about the way in which Greek culture in the Roman Empire was influenced by Roman preferences,[85] but he sees that as a much more self-conscious and concerted process, and his work is in that sense an exception to the trend we drew attention to above whereby Roman cultural revolution has been given attention over its Greek equivalents. It also represents a welcome challenge to the assumption that the Greek 'renaissance' did not begin until the late first century CE. At the same time Spawforth's view risks overestimating the degree of

---

[81] Swain 1996: 2–3. [82] Cf. Whitmarsh 2017: 14. [83] E.g., see Walker and Cameron 1989.
[84] Spawforth 2012. [85] E.g., see Schmitz and Wiater 2011b: 41.

top-down control, and underestimating the degree to which at least some of these phenomena must have emerged organically and chaotically, because of a huge range of different factors, many of them autonomous developments within Greek culture.[86] A focus on Augustan innovations also has the potential to leave pre-Augustan late Hellenistic literature languishing, and to underestimate the continuities we see from Polybius onwards, into the first century CE and beyond (although Spawforth himself looks back to pre-Augustan Roman engagement with Greek culture every so often). As Wiater demonstrates in his chapter, prominent ways of conceptualising the extent of Roman rule over the *oikoumene* that have traditionally been associated with the imperial period are established as early as the second century BCE.

One way of exploring those issues further is through an examination of the increasing interest in classicism from the first century BCE onwards. Imperial Greek literature is characterised by an interest in looking back to the classical Greek past.[87] But classicism was increasingly important for late Hellenistic literature too, as Wiater has shown for Dionysius of Halicarnassus.[88] That said, the classicism of late Hellenistic Greek literature was sometimes inflected rather differently, or in some cases less extensively developed than its later equivalents. The late Hellenistic treatment of Athens is a good example. Athens is central to the imperial Greek imagination, as a place of literary, philosophical and historical memory. But as Schmitz has shown elsewhere, Athens has very little attention in the world history of Diodorus Siculus, written in the mid-first century BCE. In the process he argues that Diodorus shows only relatively muted traces of the classicism that would become so commonplace a century or two later.[89] Even in such a programmatically 'classicising' author as Dionysius of Halicarnassus, Athens is much less present than one would expect, and Dionysius' image of the classical city is far from unambiguous. In his historical work in particular, Athens is criticised heavily, and Dionysius' *Early Roman History* can, in fact, be read as an attempt to overcome the influence of Athens in order to open up the way for the new Greek culture (as Dionysius saw it) of Rome.[90] Athens is widespread, by contrast, in the Latin writing of the late Republic, which anticipates the classicising, universalising visions of Athens that are so powerful in later

---

[86] Cf. Wiater 2011: 8–18 on the problems of a top-down approach to understanding 'Augustan' culture.
[87] See Bowie 1974, who envisages a strong break between the two periods.
[88] Wiater 2011; de Jonge 2008: esp. 9–20.
[89] Schmitz 2011a; cf. Schmitz and Wiater 2011b: 35–42.　　[90] See Wiater 2018c, 2019.

imperial Greek literature, as Connolly shows in this volume. Her argument has a certain amount in common with Spawforth's, in its emphasis on the Roman influence over Greek culture, with the difference that her main focus is well before the reign of Augustus in the writing of Cicero and others.

Alternatively, one might approach the problem by genre. That approach seems particularly promising given that the Greek renaissance of the imperial period has often been associated with generic innovation. Quite a few genres emerge for the first time in this period, or re-emerge in new forms or with particular abundance. Here too it is clear that the distinction between late Hellenistic and imperial has some justification, but also that there is a great danger of oversimplifying, not least because the newly important genres of the imperial period nearly always turn out to have Hellenistic precedents when we begin to look more closely. Moreover, the later authors' willingness to experiment with new genres might in some ways be seen as a continuation of the openness of late Hellenistic authors, in prose as well as poetry, to transgress and experiment with established genre boundaries.

The obvious starting point is sophistic oratory. The idea of a revival for performance oratory in the principate is one that has ancient precedents.[91] Philostratus, in his *Lives of the Sophists*, traces the origins of that movement to the classical Athenian orators of the fourth century BCE, Aeschines in particular:

> We must think of the old variety of the art of sophistry as philosophical rhetoric (Τὴν ἀρχαίαν σοφιστικὴν ῥητορικὴν ... φιλοσοφοῦσαν) ... But the sophistic art that came after it, which is better referred to not as 'new', for it is in itself ancient, but rather 'second', sketched out poor men and rich men, chiefs and tyrants, and famous subjects that history introduces us to. Gorgias of Leontini founded the older type in Thessaly, and Aeschines, son of Atrometus, the second, after he had been exiled from political affairs in Athens and moved to Caria and Rhodes. (*VS* 1.pr, 480–1)

From there Philostratus moves straight to their imperial successors, skating over the Hellenistic period almost entirely, with only the briefest mention of a few figures from that period.[92] To be more specific, he dates the

---

[91] Cf. Baumann in this volume for the argument that Philostratus' work is part of a broader 'trend of re-oralising literature in the imperial period' (pp. 115–17).
[92] E.g., Philostratus the Egyptian at *VS* 1.5, 486, who is said to have been associated with Cleopatra, and Theomnestus of Naucratis at 1.6, 486, who may have been active in Athens in the first century BCE, if he is the philosopher referred to by Plutarch in *Brutus* 24. See Civiletti 2002: 370 for notes

revival of the 'second sophistic' very precisely to the sophist Niketes of Smyrna in the reign of Nero (*VS* 1.19, 511).

When we look more closely, however, there are reasons to doubt Philostratus' account.[93] For one thing we find extensive accounts of performance orators in Rome in the last decades of the first century BCE in the work of the Elder Seneca.[94] Spawforth would like to see these as examples of the imperially sponsored emergence of Greek cultural innovations under Augustus,[95] but performance oratory was, of course, an important part already of Hellenistic rhetoric.[96] There are therefore good reasons for backdating the sophistic renaissance to many decades before the starting point we find in Philostratus and in much late twentieth-century scholarship. Kim in this volume stresses above all the complexity of the evidence, testing out the hypothesis that the 'Asianist' style prominent in Philostratus' account of the sophistic oratory of the second century CE is likely to have had its roots (contrary to Philostratus' own claims) not just in the work of Gorgias but also in late Hellenistic rhetoric, but also showing how difficult that argument is to sustain in the absence of close resemblances between Philostratus' examples and their most obvious late Hellenistic comparison points.

The idea of a disjunction between imperial sophistic and the late Hellenistic world is further complicated by the fact that Philostratus' account has some close similarities with what we find in Dionysius of Halicarnassus' *On the Ancient Orators*. For one thing it is striking that Dionysius' combination of biography with critical, stylistic assessment is an important precedent for what we find in Philostratus, even if Dionysius has a lower proportion of biographical detail than the *Lives of the Sophists*.[97] Even more striking is the similarity between Philostratus' notion of the

---

on both. Both are included by Philostratus in his category of philosophers who were not genuine sophists.

[93] Cf. Whitmarsh 2017: 12–13 for brief discussion along similar lines; Wyss, Hirsch-Luipold and Hirschi 2017 similarly examine the evidence for sophistic activity in the Hellenistic period, although with some lack of clarity about what distinguishes sophists from other intellectuals and about the reasons for the absence of the term 'sophist' in Hellenistic culture.

[94] See Civiletti 2002: 429–30 with n. 5.   [95] See Spawforth 2012: 73–81, 264–70.

[96] Cf. Wiater 2014a: 861–2 with n. 9; von Christ, Schmid and Stählin 1920: I, 455–7.

[97] A possible reason for the less prominent presence of biographical narrative in Dionysius is that Dionysius identifies 'style of life' and 'style of writing'; for that argument see Wiater 2019: 64–5: 'it is not through his biographical sketches that Dionysius intends to illustrate the classical authors' characters and moral and political attitudes' but, rather, 'through the aesthetics of these authors' texts, understood as an immediate, and immediately experienceable, expression of their identity, their characters and moral and political values'. Philostratus harks back to the presence of biographical elements in Dionysius' criticism, but reinterprets them in a more concrete, historical-biographical sense.

decline of a literary movement, grounded in the classical period, followed by its later revival and what we find in Dionysius, although they also use that notion quite differently in some ways.⁹⁸ The key extracts from Dionysius' preface are as follows:

> In the era before our own time, the old and philosophical Rhetoric (ἀρχαία καὶ φιλόσοφος ῥητορική) was mistreated and endured terrible abuse and fell into a decline (προπηλακιζομένη καὶ δεινὰς ὕβρεις ὑπομένουσα κατελύετο). From the death of Alexander of Macedon it began to expire and gradually waste away, and in our generation it had almost entirely disappeared. Another type of rhetoric stole in and took its place, intolerable in its theatrical shamelessness, ill-bred, and having no trace of philosophy or any other field of liberal education. (*The Ancient Orators* 1.2)

Now, however, Dionysius suggests, 'our period ... has allowed the old and sound rhetoric to take back her rightful honour that she previously enjoyed' (2.2). The precise relationship between Dionysius' account and Philostratus' is open to debate, and we do not attempt to solve that problem here (see further discussion in Kim's chapter below). But it seems likely that Philostratus knows Dionysius' version from two centuries or more before and perhaps even that he deliberately reacts against it.⁹⁹ Their shared notion of 'philosophical rhetoric' is the most obvious verbal correspondence.¹⁰⁰ Both of them also choose to represent style in vividly metaphorical terms; Philostratus' monumental imagery stands in contrast with the body imagery of Dionysius, but they share the notion of restriction or confinement: in Philostratus' case the art is 'in desperate straits' (ἐς στενὸν ἀπειλημμένην, *VS* 1.19, 511); in Dionysius it 'began to expire and gradually waste away'. Dionysius values the old philosophical rhetoric (the term covers far more than just speeches and applies to literary production generally) and welcomes its revival. Philostratus gives a perfectly positive assessment of philosophical rhetoric, but he is much more interested in what he describes as the 'second' type of the sophistic art. Whether that second type is intended as a positive version of the degenerate, secondary oratory that Dionysius describes is not clear – the distinction between Atticist and Asianist rhetoric that Dionysius is engaging with does not necessarily map on directly to Philostratus' distinction between 'first' and 'second' sophistic – but it does seem to be the case that

---

⁹⁸ For more detailed analysis of the relationship between their two accounts, see Kim 2017b.
⁹⁹ Cf. Kim 2017b: 238.
¹⁰⁰ On Dionysius' use of that concept, see Hidber 1996: 44–56, 100–3, with brief mention of the Philostratus parallel at 102; cf. Civiletti 2002: 359 n. 12.

Philostratus is making a self-conscious attempt to contrast Dionysius' account with his own more idiosyncratic vision of what kind of rhetoric is to be valued.[101] On the other hand, it is clear that Philostratus' intermediate period of decline roughly corresponds in chronological terms to the Asianist period about which Dionysius is so scathing (although of course it continues beyond the date of Dionysius' work by several decades). And Philostratus' pattern of decline followed by revival, which is what leads him to elide late Hellenistic rhetoric almost entirely, is very close to Dionysius' vision of the contemporary revival of a classical style. In other words, Philostratus' model of development over time is prefigured closely within the late Hellenistic literature he so conspicuously ignores.[102] Philostratus' account thus shows signs of a close engagement with late Hellenistic approaches even as he marks out his own distinctions from them.

Related questions about continuities and differences in the aesthetic and critical evaluation of literature lie at the heart of several chapters in this volume. They allow us to set the question of the relationship between Dionysius and Philostratus into a larger perspective. Kim, as mentioned above, takes a longue-durée view of the debate about 'Attic' and 'Asianist' style. De Jonge examines what 'classicism' meant at different periods by providing a groundbreaking, in-depth study of the relationship between Dionysius', Dio Chrysostom's and Quintilian's concepts of the literary canon. De Jonge thus shines a new light on the changing cultural value of 'canonical' authors such as Menander, Euripides and Homer, under different cultural circumstances. His chapter reminds us that we should see canons as flexible cultural constructs rather than fixed and relatively stable phenomena. We even get a glimpse of the process by which Augustan Rome was itself becoming 'classical' or 'canonical' to Greek intellectuals, as Dio 'recommends reading the orators of Augustan Rome next to those of classical Athens'.[103] The latter observation in particular makes for a fascinating comparison with Philostratus' (virtual) dialogue with Dionysius about the value of literature produced in different periods. Read in conjunction, these authors also provide valuable insights into

---

[101] Cf. Kim 2017b: esp. 242.
[102] For the model of decline followed by revival in Dionysius' preface, see Hidber 1996: 14–25, with mention of a number of parallels from other works, and including brief mention of Philostratus, *VS* 1, 480, at 20; also Whitmarsh 2001a: 67, n. 108 for passing comparison between the two passages; and de Jonge 2008: 10 for the point that the tripartite view of history in this passage of Dionysius is typical of classicism of the first centuries BCE and CE.
[103] de Jonge in this volume below, p. 349.

the different ways in which Greeks sought to integrate literature produced under Roman rule into their critical-interpretive schemes.

For many other genres too, the links between imperial and late Hellenistic are still underexplored. Historiography is an important case. Ewen Bowie has pointed out some of the differences. For example, there seems to be a gap in the production of universal histories in the first century CE; when the genre re-emerges it does so in rather different form, typically either stopping with Alexander the Great or writing world history from a Roman perspective, without much attention to Hellenistic Greek experience.[104] But for all that difference of emphasis it is clear that there are profound and still not fully mapped connections and continuities. Maier in this volume, for example, shows that Plutarch in his *Lives* adapted important techniques from Hellenistic historiography, especially from Polybius, with a particular focus on his acute awareness of the 'swarm of possibilities', the large volume of different possible pathways that his history might have taken. Reading Polybius (history) and Plutarch (biography) side by side in relation to their treatment of contingency also opens up novel ways of understanding the structure of Plutarch's *Lives*: 'By arranging Greek and Roman biographies in pairs, Plutarch not only illustrates the moral virtues and vices which his protagonists have in common, a prominent feature of the *Parallel Lives*. The comparative arrangement also illustrates how similar historical structures had different outcomes, thus inviting the reader to rethink the course of the past with an alternative ending.'[105] Maier's chapter thus also shows how untypical of the realities of Hellenistic and imperial literature Polybius is in advocating a clear-cut boundary between history and biography in his criticism of Theopompus (see above): it is striking that there is a very Polybian approach towards the representation of contingency lying at the heart of Plutarch's biographical innovations.

Plutarch's texts not only stand between history and biography but also raise questions about the development of philosophy. Later imperial philosophy clearly had its own distinctive features, not least in the increasing prominence for Plato, which led ultimately to the growth of neoplatonism, but there are also close connections with the first century BCE. Most importantly, the destruction of the philosophical schools in Athens in the early 80s BCE led to a period of increasing cross-fertilisation between different approaches which carried through right into the second century CE and beyond.[106] Hatzimichali's chapter opens up new ways of

---

[104] Bowie 1974: 175–8.   [105] Maier in this volume, pp. 261–2.   [106] See Trapp 2007: x–xi.

understanding how philosophical ideas were transmitted to later periods outside strictly philosophical channels: she explores the late Hellenistic intensification of interest in the great philosophical texts and authors of classical Greece, which has much in common with the classicism we begin to see in other areas of late Hellenistic intellectual activity too and which was continued and extended through the first few centuries CE.[107] Similarly, the ideas about cosmopolitanism in late Hellenistic writing studied by Gray – which originate in philosophical thinking but also spill out very widely into epigraphical and historiographical discourse – can now be appreciated better also as a bridge between classical and imperial responses, both of which have been much more intensively studied than their late Hellenistic equivalents.

We see a similar picture for other fields and other genres too. The Greek novel is often presented as one of the key literary innovations of the imperial period, but it has long been clear that it has connections with various kinds of late Hellenistic narrative, even if it is hard to trace their development and their influence precisely.[108] Encyclopaedic and miscellanistic writing is similarly often viewed as one of the most important innovations, and one of the most important genres outright, of the imperial period,[109] but it is heavily rooted in Republican and late Hellenistic precedents, including the encyclopaedic historical and geographical work of Strabo and Diodorus and Posidonius, as König argues in his chapter below.[110] Biography and autobiography tend to be presented as genres that flourished particularly in the imperial period,[111] but there is surely a good chance of being misled by the dazzling creativity of Plutarch and Lucian and Philostratus, and by the way in which they dominate the later transmission of biography as a genre. Polybius, as mentioned above, was not only the author of a biography himself but was also concerned with biography as a genre and its relationship to historical narrative (despite his criticisms of Theopompus). To this we

---

[107] See also Trapp 2007: xi for the way in which the revival of interest in Plato and also Aristotle has its roots in the first century BCE, even if it did not develop fully until much later.

[108] Cf. Whitmarsh 2017: 15–18 for general discussion along similar lines, and at more length in Whitmarsh 2013b; also Rohde 1876 for a much earlier, influential attempt to trace the Greek romance back to Hellenistic origins.

[109] See König and Whitmarsh 2007b; König and Woolf 2013b; also Morgan 2011: esp. 54 on the miscellany as one of the key genres of the Roman empire.

[110] Cf. Most 2011.

[111] See Whitmarsh 2005: 74–83, again with further bibliography, and stressing the way in which these claims have been widely linked, following Foucault, with the idea of a new interest in care of the self in the imperial period; König 2009: 86–98.

need to add the huge volume of evidence for non-surviving Hellenistic biographies.[112] If even some of that work survived we would no doubt be more inclined to emphasise continuity rather than disjunction.

Greensmith's chapter, finally, raises new and interesting questions about the interrelations between Hellenistic and imperial receptions of epic poetry. Greensmith shows that there has been a tendency to associate subversive appropriations and rewritings of Homer particularly with imperial prose authors like Lucian and Dio Chrysostom, who playfully shed doubt on his reliability and on his role as a central figure in the Greek tradition. Her discussion demonstrates that we need to go beyond that limited view by putting verse back into the picture – not just the epic of the imperial world, which has started to find more and more readers in the last few decades, but also late Hellenistic verse produced outside the mainstream of Greco-Roman literary culture.

When we start to look for them, then, we see striking continuities which complicate any straightforward narrative of cultural transformation and renaissance. Those continuities are evident not just in generic terms but also in themes and practices that straddle a range of different genres. At the same time, the comparative approach that many of the chapters following employ can also help us to understand even more clearly what makes each of these periods, and the individual texts and authors that we study, distinctive. Hatzimichali, for example, draws parallels between Strabo's intellectual and disciplinary self-definition and equivalent phenomena in later imperial writers, while also pointing out that he is less inclined to insist on a Greek intellectual provenance for the philosophy that he views as so central to his own work. Baumann explores the idea that the imperial period saw a widespread trend towards 're-oralisation', which presents the learned Greek prose literature of this period as part of an oral culture, disguising to some extent its reliance on books as physical objects, in contrast with the late Hellenistic tendency to embrace the realities of reading and writing conspicuously. König sketches out a distinctively approving late Hellenistic approach to the theme of landscape alteration and explores the possibility that this is linked with stereotypical Greek closeness to the Roman empire in the first century CE – although at the same time his chapter aims to complicate that narrative by drawing out the hesitations and ambiguities within individual texts and within late Hellenistic and imperial culture more broadly which make it so hard to generalise about the differences between them. Schmitz too sees similarities

---

[112] See Whitmarsh 2005: 75 for some starting points.

and differences between late Hellenistic epigrams and the literature of the later imperial period in their constructions of geographical space. He sees common ground in their use of geography to make sense of the vastness of the Roman empire, but he also draws attention to the same distinction as König, exploring the possibility that imperial Greeks felt less need to write about Rome and the west as a result of their greater cultural confidence. Wiater notes different ways of representing the *oikoumene* in Polybius and late-Republican and early imperial culture and links these with changes in Romans' and Greeks' 'mental maps' of the Roman empire. De Jonge, finally, argues for significant differences between Dionysius of Halicarnassus and Dio of Prusa in their recommendations about which authors to read: even though they are drawing on the same basic tradition they use it in very different ways and with different emphases.

Intratextual Dialogues: A Road Map to This Volume

As will have become apparent in the preceding sections, the contributions to this volume, just like the texts which they discuss, can be brought into dialogue with each other in many different ways. We have therefore chosen not to divide the volume formally into thematic sections. Broadly speaking the volume opens with a series of chapters that focus on geographical themes (Wiater, Schmitz, Baumann, König); then contributions that explore various kinds of cross-cultural dialogue, for example between local and global, Jewish and Greek, Greek and Roman (Gray, Greensmith, Connolly, Hatzimichali); finally, a set of chapters that take a more close-up view of the changing use of literary procedures, genres and canons over time (Maier, Kim, de Jonge).[113] However, that tripartite categorisation can only scratch the surface of the interconnectedness between these different contributions. Our hope is that readers will find many different points of connection for themselves. In this concluding section, we will merely draw attention to some key examples of generic cross-fertilisation and to some of the overarching themes that recur over and over again in successive chapters, with the aim of offering a (provisional and partial) road map to the volume – a set of suggestions about chapters that can productively be

---

[113] As Goldhill points out in his chapter the boundaries between these sections are not clear-cut: Gray's chapter could equally be included in the first group, given his interest in representations of space, and Maier's in the second group, given his concern with textual authority and cultural tradition, and his interest in alternative perspectives.

read in conjunction with each other for those who wish to explore particular topics.

Our first topic is the way in which a significant proportion of the chapters in the volume explore the intertwining of philosophical, geographical, historical and political discourse. For example, Hatzimichali's chapter investigates with a new degree of comprehensiveness the intricacy of Strabo's engagement with the philosophical culture of his contemporaries, flagged so prominently in the very opening lines of his work. Polybius, too, as Maier reminds us, was concerned with larger philosophical issues such as contingency and human power to influence the course of events that underpinned historical narrative. Gray explores how values prominent in Stoicism were appropriated for civic self-definition in official decrees and inscriptions of Hellenistic *poleis* but also became crucial elements in the self-definition of late Hellenistic historians such as Diodorus. As these chapters show, the boundaries between history-writing, geography and philosophy were much more fluid than modern scholars are often prepared to admit, and a comprehensive understanding of any of the three 'genres' is possible only if we take their interaction seriously. Baumann's discussion of Diodorus' description of the Red Sea engages with related issues: he throws new light on the interplay of landscape description and historical contextualisation in Diodorus' ekphrastic account of the Red Sea, prompting us to see that passage as a space in which different genres (*periplus*, geography, history) interact with the kind of sophisticated vividness and conscious intermediality that is more commonly associated with the Alexandrian poets. His chapter can fruitfully be read alongside Gray's discussion of Diodorus, which uncovers some of the different ways in which Diodorus' narrative resounds with contemporary political and cultural resonances. Gray's chapter, in turn, has many points of contact with Hatzimichali's discussion of Strabo and Stoicism. Moreover, his exploration of the relationship between local and cosmopolitan perspectives, which Diodorus shares with the narratives of the political decrees, recalls Hatzimichali's discussion of different local and global centres in Strabo's geographical narrative. Gray's final section in fact addresses Strabo directly, arguing that he is engaged with local civic life just as much as Diodorus even if more sceptical about its moral qualities.

That dialectic between local and cosmopolitan is part of a broader preoccupation that recurs over and over again in these chapters, that is the late Hellenistic fascination with space, especially imperial space and its representation. The relationship between local and global perspectives, and the ways in which Greek and Romans conceptualised, in a broad range of different media, the impact of Roman power on the structure of the inhabited world lies at the heart of Wiater's discussion of Polybius' image of the *oikoumene* as a body and his verbal 'map of the world', which sets the scene for his description of Hannibal's march over the Alps. By taking a 'bird's-eye view' of the *oikoumene*, Polybius prompts his readers to think in 'global' terms and see Hannibal's march, with its physical movement from one part of the world to another, as a crucial part of the re-ordering and re-formation of the Mediterranean world during the mid-Republican period. Polybius' text evokes contemporary Roman representations of power, including the material fabric of the Roman cityscape but also road building, building inscriptions and milestones. It thus enters into a complex dialogue with non-literary, Roman expressions of space and power, anticipating the concept of the *corpus imperii* that becomes prominent in imperial Latin literature. Wiater's chapter thus adds another element to the exploration of different forms of dialogue between Greek and Roman texts that is key also to Connolly's chapter. It can also be read in conjunction with Hatzimichali's and Gray's discussion of different ways of negotiating global and local perspectives in different kinds of narratives.

The theme of late Hellenistic representation of space ties together many other chapters in this volume too. For example, König draws on recent approaches in the environmental humanities in focusing on the topic of landscape alteration in Hellenistic and imperial culture. He asks how far different authors' attitude to that phenomenon might reflect the political and cultural climate of their times. Is the comparatively positive attitude towards landscape alteration that we find in Strabo and Diodorus an echo of Augustus' deliberate attempt to re-order the world, a way of providing their contemporaries with a mental map of the world in which they lived as a controlled space created and shaped by human beings? And how do Strabo and Diodorus negotiate between this more positive attitude towards landscape alteration and the much more negative one in the 'canonical' narrative of Herodotus, where landscape alteration is regularly associated with *hybris*? Here too, as for Gray, Wiater and others, the tension between local and global perspectives is crucial: ancient historiographical and geographical texts are able to project a global image of human–environment relations by juxtaposing many different local incidents and local cultures on a vast scale. Schmitz brings Hellenistic epigrams into dialogue with the spatial turn and Pierre Nora's concept of *lieux de mémoire*. He reads epigrams as part of the development of an imperial world-view, an attempt to reduce the complexity of the world into a 'harmonious, well-ordered body that is ruled by a rational, civilised power and can be encompassed by a single view from within the centre of this empire'. The epigrams, he argues, 'bring order to the world'.[114] That, Schmitz maintains, makes them precursors to the project of Pausanias almost two centuries later; but it also invites us to read the configuration of space in Hellenistic epigram against and alongside the 'mental maps' of the Roman empire proposed in Polybius (Wiater), Strabo's attitude towards landscape alteration as part of a process of actively ordering and shaping the world (König) and, more generally, Strabo's large-scale project of representing the order of the world under Augustus in literature (Hatzimichali). The complex interrelationship of local and global perspectives along with the concern with configurations and representations of (imperial) space can thus be seen to cut across both poetry and prose of the Hellenistic as well as the imperial period. Schmitz also explores how different ways of representing space in epigram might be a medium to express a range of attitudes towards Roman power (from flattery to subversion), thus endowing the voice of epigram with a political significance similar to that restored to Diodorus' narrative by Gray, and matching the positive and negative strands that we see in König's chapter on landscape alteration.

Other chapters address related issues about Greek heritage and identity through an interest in processes of canonisation and in the role of different forms of classicism and different ways of preserving and engaging with the past. Perhaps surprisingly, Strabo, as discussed by Hatzimichali, has a lot to tell us about such processes not only from a literary and geographical, but also from a philosophical angle: situating himself in relation to the philosophical heritage is a key part of his intellectual self-definition in which knowledge of space is intimately linked with philosophical and literary education. Strabo's work thus not only plays a part in the larger late-Hellenistic negotiations of philosophy and identity explored by Gray in this volume; he also participates in discourses of (literary) education that are the focus of the chapters by de Jonge and Kim. De Jonge shows how reading lists of canonical authors can be presented differently in different texts to project very different views of the Greek literary heritage. Kim challenges oversimplifying assumptions about the influence of classicising styles in Hellenistic (and also imperial) oratory through painstaking stylistic analysis of a series of case studies. In the process he shows, for the first time conclusively, that the prominent opposition between Attic and Asianist style, which was of such fundamental importance to some aspects of Greek cultural

---

[114] Schmitz in this volume below, p. 89 (first quotation), p. 85 (second quotation)

identity, was a cultural construct to begin with (and began much earlier than is often assumed).

In many cases the preoccupations of the authors discussed in this volume – with space, with power, with philosophy, with literary canons and education – are vehicles for coming to terms with Roman power and Roman culture. This is relevant to virtually all contributions to this volume and demonstrates what a stimulating effect the rise and development of Roman power had on Greek literature. Taken together, the chapters brought together here remind us of the role of the Romans not only as a political presence to be reckoned with but as a crucial factor driving Greek literary production and prompting Greeks to rethink, adopt and adapt pre-existing (often 'classical') concepts and ways of thinking and writing. Polybius, Strabo and Dionysius of Halicarnassus are good examples of that, as are some of the authors of Greek epigrams whose impressive political careers were built on Roman patronage won, not least, by their literary production and their command of *paideia*.[115]

The presence of so many recurring preoccupations in these very different texts gives us a glimpse of the remarkable creativity that distinguishes Hellenistic literature. Multiplicity and interconnectivity are key. It will, we hope, become clear that we cannot understand Polybius fully if we classify his work simply (and simplistically) as 'history' or Strabo's as 'geography'; if we think of epigrams in the first instance purely as refined cultural artefacts rather than as active players in much wider cultural, geographical and political discourses; or if we read Diodorus in isolation from contemporary civic practice and inscriptions, to name only a few examples. The Sibylline Oracles provide an important backdrop to the dominating narratives of Roman power in Polybius and Dionysius; and what Strabo is doing with space becomes clearer when it is compared with the role of space in Hellenistic epigram, along with the configuration and representation of space in historical narratives.

Dealing with Hellenistic literature thus challenges us as observers to rethink our methodological preconceptions of literary analysis. Neither narrow concepts of allusion and direct textual dependence nor the confines of generic categorisation provide a suitable basis for any kind of proper understanding of Hellenistic literature in its wider cultural and political context. By offering fresh perspectives on a wide range of different authors and genres – their relationship with each other, and their changing contours over time – we aim to lay the foundations for a revision of the

---

[115] See esp. Whitmarsh 2011.

prevailing view of the literature of the late Hellenistic period. We offer an image of late Hellenistic literary culture as vibrant, sophisticated and innovative; in doing so one of our goals is to challenge prevailing narratives, shaped by Philostratus among others, about the decline of Greek literature in the first and second centuries BCE and its subsequent 'renaissance' in the late first century CE. That is not to say that we aim for a simple view of undifferentiated similarity from Polybius to Philostratus: the picture is an enormously complicated one, and it is crucial to acknowledge differences and shifts of focus as well as points of connection between late Hellenistic authors and their imperial successors. It is only when we delve into the details of individual case studies that we start to see how varied and rich that web of relationships must have been.

CHAPTER I

The Empire Becomes a Body
Power, Space and Movement in Polybius' Histories

Nicolas Wiater

Looking Backwards: From Ovid to Polybius

At around 9 CE, Ovid sent the second book of his *Tristia* to Rome. About halfway into his letter-poem, he addresses the question of his 'guilt', the reason for his exile. Augustus' judgment of his 'foul' character (*turpi carmine*) and corrupting influence on Roman marital values (*Tr.* 2.211–12), Ovid argues, is unfounded because Augustus did not have direct knowledge of his *Ars* – understandably, because 'just as Jupiter, as he watches the gods and the high heavens at the same time, does not have time to attend to small matters, things belonging to the lower spheres escape your preoccupations, as you are holding watch (*circumspicis*) over the circle of the earth (*orbem*) which depends on you (*de te pendentem*)', 215–18). Ovid then goes on to elaborate on this image of Augustus and his relationship to the 'earth' (219–34):

> not thus does the mass (*moles*) of all that is called Roman (*Romani nominis*) press down on you (*urget*), not so light (*leve*) is the weight (*onus*) carried (*fertur*) on your shoulders (*in tuis umeris*), that you could turn away your glance (*lumen*) to foolish games and examine with your eyes (*oculis*) our idle pursuits. Now it is Pannonia that needs subjection (*domanda*), now the Illyrian country, now the Raetian and Thracian weapons cause fears; now the Armenian asks for peace, now the Parthian rider surrenders his bow and the captured standards with fearful hand ... last, not least, for there to be no part (*pars*) in such a great body of empire (*corpore ... inperii*) as has never existed before (*quantum non extitit umquam*), that is faint and shaky (*labet*), the City (*urbs*), too, and the watch over laws and morals, which you have given and wish to be like your own, is taking its toll (*lassat*).[1]

My interest in this chapter is the concept of the Roman empire as a physical, indeed, corporeal entity, which comes through particularly well

---

[1] All translations of ancient and modern texts in this chapter are my own, unless otherwise indicated.

in these lines from Ovid. The empire is all but identified with the *orbis* and Augustus pictured as 'seeing' what is happening in all different parts of the earth-empire from a high vantage point, not unlike Jupiter surveying the heavens and the other gods. Augustus' *imperium* is thus endowed with a concrete, physical quality that can be seen (note the multiple references to sight and eyes) and even touched. The *orbis* 'depends on' Augustus, an image that blends the image of Zeus pulling up all the gods along with the earth and the sea on a golden chord, which illustrates the supreme god's superior strength in *Iliad* 8.19–26 (cf. Ovid's **deos** *caelumque . . . tuenti*), with the image of Augustus holding the (fate of the) entire world 'in balance' on a pair of scales.² The 'mass of all that is called Roman' that is 'pressing down' on him and weighs heavily on his shoulders, on the other hand, recalls Atlas (or Heracles who has taken over from Atlas)³ holding up 'wide heavens' 'with his head and never-tiring hands' (Hes. *Th.* 517–19), while evoking more recent pictorial representations in which the 'heavens' are represented as a globe (*orbis*).⁴

The physical interaction of Augustus with his empire and the *orbis* is taken to its next and final level when Ovid prompts his readers to imagine this *orbis*-wide empire as itself constituting a body (*corpus . . . inperii*) the individual limbs of which are represented by the different peoples that Augustus needs to subject (*domanda, arma . . . metum*), or already has subjected, to Roman power (*petit . . . pacem, porrigit arcus . . . timida captaque signa manu*). Ovid's lines invite the reader to witness the transformation of the *orbis terrarum* into the *corpus inperii* which, slowly but surely, comes to accept its position inferior to the body of its supreme and ever-watchful ruler, Augustus. By mentioning Rome, the *urbs*, last, Ovid not only evokes the word play of *urbs* and *orbis* (which he had used to good effect in the famous phrase *Romanae spatium est Urbis et orbis idem*, *Fast.* 2.684). He also sets Augustus' activities as a legal and moral reformer in Rome apart from his more martial endeavours in the rest of the world, thus recalling the traditional formula *domi militiaeque* and, perhaps, evoking an image similar to that in Horace *Carm.* 4.15.14–15, 21–4,⁵ by which the superior laws and morals – modelled on the person of the *princeps* himself (*similes . . . tuis*) – spread out from the centre of Roman power to even the farthest margins of the empire.

---

² For the latter use of *pendere* see OLD 1322 s.v. 3a.
³ On Heracles and Augustus see Hor. *Carm.* 3.3.9–12; *Epist.* 2.1.10–12.
⁴ Furtwängler 1884–90: 710.
⁵ Cf. 3.5.1–4 for the connection between Augustus' (alleged) successes in Britain and against the Parthians and comparison with Jupiter; Ov. *Fast.* 1.85–6.

The corporeal concept of both the emperor and the world subject (or about to be subject) to his power, chimes with the contemporary representation of Augustus himself. The famous statue of Prima Porta, for example, identifies 'the literal body of the emperor', as Michael Squire put it, 'with a metaphorical *corpus imperii*'. And on the equally famous 'Gemma Augustea' the viewer finds the *princeps* in the company of various female figures representing Rome (seated next to him), *Oikoumene*, who is crowning Augustus with the *corona civica*, and *Italia* seated to the right side of his throne in the company of her children and carrying a *cornucopia* as a symbol of prosperity.[6]

Recent scholarship has done much to trace the development of the concept of the Roman *imperium* as a body and elucidate its significance in Latin imperial literature, in particular the studies of Kienast, Meister and Squire, as well as the earlier work by Béranger.[7] The pre-imperial history of the concept, by contrast, is much less well understood. The passage from Ovid's *Tristia* is usually cited as the first instance of the Roman empire – I am using that term here and throughout this chapter in as neutral a sense as possible, with reference to the geographical extent of Roman power as imagined by contemporaries – being described in terms of a body.[8] For its immediate predecessors, scholars refer to the idea of *corpus rei publicae* found twice in Cicero (*Phil.* 8.15–16; *Off.* 1.85) as well as a passage in which he speaks of Italy in terms of a body and its limbs (*Att.* 8.1.1).[9] As Cicero's predecessors, in turn, scholars identify the metaphor of the city as a body found in the Attic orators, especially the phrase τὸ τῆς πόλεως σῶμα ('the body of the *polis*') that occurs in Dinarchus and Hyperides, along with the larger discourse common in both orators and philosophers, most prominently Plato, that describes the citizen community in terms of a (usually sick) body which it is the philosopher's or politician's task to cure.[10]

As this brief overview shows, the existing discussions of the body metaphor leave a big gap between the end of the fourth and the late first century BCE. It seems unlikely that the political use of the body metaphor,

---

[6] Squire 2015: 311–12, 316–21 (the quote at 321); also Squire 2013b on the Prima Porta statue specifically.
[7] Kienast 1982; Meister 2012: esp. 131–221; Squire 2015; Béranger 1953: esp. 219–43.
[8] E.g., Kienast 1982: 10; Squire 2015: 309.
[9] Kienast 1982: 6–7. For a recent discussion of the body metaphor in Cicero and late-Republican political oratory see Walters 2020; also Meister 2012: 158–63.
[10] See Din. 1.110; Hyp. 5 col. 25, for τὸ τῆς πόλεως σῶμα; cf. Pl. *Resp.* 5, 564b9–c4. The imagery itself goes back at least as far as Solon, see, e.g., fr. 4.17. Full discussion with further references in Brock 2013: 69–82.

which was so popular throughout the late archaic and the classical Greek period, suddenly fell out of use at the end of the fourth century, only to surface two hundred years later in Latin literature, in the works of Cicero. This is an opportunity for a volume such as the present one, which aims to investigate the relationship between Hellenistic and imperial literature, and the dialogue which the works of these periods entered into with each other but also with other, Greek as well as Latin, partners. The starting point of my chapter is the beginning of Polybius' *Histories* where Polybius, in a striking metaphor, uses the body metaphor to conceptualise the effect of the rise of Roman power both on the inhabited world and historical narrative. Polybius is, in fact, the first author – that we know of – to think of the Roman empire in terms of a body.

In the first part of this chapter I will demonstrate that Polybius' use of the body metaphor represents a significant innovation compared to its use in his classical predecessors and is, in many respects, more similar to Ovid than to Plato or Dinarchus. Comparing Polybius' use of the body metaphor to represent the *oikoumene* with late-Republican and Hellenistic representations of the *oikoumene* in contexts of political power, I will also argue that Polybius' peculiar take on the body metaphor, which stresses the functional interrelation of the body's parts (*energeia*) as its defining characteristic, is a reflection of the nature and representation of the expansion of Roman power in the mid-Republican period. Polybius' text thus represents a concrete instance of how intellectual engagement with Roman power, the attempt to come to grips with it by finding appropriate ways to represent it in narrative, prompted Greeks to rethink pre-existing modes of thinking and literary expression. But the discussion will also enable us to see Polybius as part of much larger, Greek as well as Republican and imperial Roman, cultural and literary discourses.

In the second part of this chapter, I argue that the *energeia* which characterises Polybius' view of the reconfiguration of the *oikoumene* through Roman rule is also constitutive of his narrative account of that process. I will argue that the geographical 'digression' (a misnomer, as we will see) inserted into Polybius' account of Hannibal's march, is designed to link Hannibal's march with Polybius' vision of the new interconnectedness of the *oikoumene* brought about by Roman power (the *symploke*). The role of movement in that process has generally been neglected by scholars, who tend to focus on the *symploke*'s temporal aspect instead. Movement, Hannibal's march and Roman power are linked in the 'digression', I suggest, through rich intertextual interactions which link Polybius' text (and Hannibal's march) with texts such as building inscriptions and milestones that represent the expansion of Roman power and the new order established by it.

Polybius thus constitutes the main focus of this chapter, and I will offer novel readings, I hope, of two important but undervalued passages. At the same time, however, I branch out from his text in order to explore the ways in which it participates in larger political and literary discourses, both Greek and Roman, synchronically as well as diachronically. My aim, I should state clearly, is not to claim any direct influence between Polybius and any of the other texts. Our material is too lacunose for that. I rather see Polybius' as well as the other texts as individual expressions of the same larger, underlying complex of concerns, issues and preoccupations about space, power and their representation. Methodologically, my attempt to bring Polybius' text into dialogue with a range of texts in different media, including non-literary texts, and to explore the significance of elements of Polybius' narrative that have often been marginalised in scholarship, is inspired by New Historicism.[11] But similar approaches to ancient literature, without any particular reference to New Historicism, have been proposed by, for example, Nicholas Purcell and Andrew Riggsby.[12]

This chapter addresses themes and topics that are prominent throughout this volume. In its exploration of the 'global' perspective of Polybius' work and the way in which he brings, by way of the geographical 'digression', local and global perspectives into dialogue in his narrative of Hannibal's march, it complements Gray's discussion of local and cosmopolitan perspectives in civic inscriptions and Hellenistic historical writing. But while Gray's chapter is centred on civic values prominent in Hellenistic *poleis*, with particular reference to the influence of Stoicism, my focus is more strongly on Rome as a factor in Greek conceptions and representations of space in narrative. Like Gray, on the other hand, I seek to achieve that aim by bringing literary narratives into dialogue with other kinds of texts, including (Roman) inscriptions. The dialogue between Greek and Roman links my chapter with those of König and Schmitz; with König I share an interest in Roman influence on Greek concepts of space, but his discussion is more specifically focused on changing Greek views of landscape alterations. Like Schmitz, I will be discussing concepts of 'global' space but my focus will be on prose, rather than poetry. My interest in movement, finally, adds an additional perspective to

---

[11] Cf., e.g., Gallagher and Greenblatt 2000: 1–48, esp. 6–7, 13, 26–9, 45.
[12] With Alice König I am currently preparing a volume on representations of war and battle which applies this kind of interdiscursive approach systematically to a range of thematically related texts.

Baumann's discussion of the *periplus*, which plays a role as an intertext also in Polybius' geographical 'digression', but it also dovetails with Schmitz's and König's chapters in both of which movement plays a central role.

The *Oikoumene* as Body: Polybius' Body Metaphor in Context

At the beginning of his historical work, Polybius makes a strong statement. The world under Roman rule is fundamentally different to what it was before (1.1.6; cf. 1.4.1, 2–3). In order to illustrate this new state of the world, and the new kind of history-writing which it requires, Polybius offers the reader a striking image. Anyone attempting to represent this new, unified state of the inhabited world (τὸ τῆς ὅλης οἰκουμένης σχῆμα καὶ τὴν σύμπασαν αὐτῆς θέσιν καὶ τάξιν, 1.4.6; cf. συνόψεσθαι τὰ ὅλα, 1.4.7) by using traditional approaches to historical narrative, approaches, that is, which focus on individual regions, places and events separately (τῆς κατὰ μέρος ἱστορίας, 1.4.7),

> seems to me to suffer the same as when people believe that by looking at the dissevered limbs (διερριμένα τὰ μέρη) of a living and beautiful body (σώματος), they achieve a satisfactory first-hand view (ἱκανῶς αὐτόπται γίνεσθαι) of the living being (τοῦ ζῴου)[13] itself in its functionality (ἐνεργείας)[14] and beauty (καλλωνῆς). For if then somebody put the living being together and made it whole again right there and then in both its outer appearance and live elegance (τῇ τῆς ψυχῆς εὐπρεπείᾳ)[15] and then showed it again to those same people, then, I think, they would all quickly agree that previously they were quite far from the truth/ reality (τῆς ἀληθείας) and like people in a dream. For it is possible to get an impression (ἔννοιαν) of the whole thing from a part, but knowledge and an accurate opinion are impossible to obtain in that way. That is why one needs to be of the opinion that histories of parts (τὴν κατὰ μέρος ἱστορίαν) make but a small contribution to a reliable experience of the whole (τὴν τῶν ὅλων ἐμπειρίαν καὶ πίστιν). Only from everything at once, as it is interwoven with and stands side-by-side each other (ἐκ τῆς ἁπάντων πρὸς ἄλληλα συμπλοκῆς καὶ παραθέσεως), and from the similarities and differences, would one be able to obtain, thanks to the view from above (κατοπτεύσας), the useful as well as the pleasurable from history.

---

[13] The term ζῷον covers all living creatures, including human beings; see LSJ s.v.
[14] A somewhat imperfect translation of ἐνέργεια, but 'functionality' is the best term I can find to capture what Polybius has in mind here; see the discussion below.
[15] τῆς ψυχῆς here harks back to ἐμψύχου 'living'. For the use of ψυχή 'life' see *Polybios-Lexikon* (eds A. Mauersberger et al. 2nd ed. Berlin 2000–4) s.v. 1 ('Lebenshauch, -kraft, Leben'), even though they misclassify the present passage (all the while noting the link of ψυχή with ἐμψύχου) under II.2 'Gesinnung', 'Wesensart, Charakter'.

This passage follows from, and elaborates on, Polybius' earlier statement at 1.3.4, that from the 140th Olympiad (220–216 BCE) onwards, 'history', i.e., the events unfolding all over the *oikoumene*, has become 'body-shaped, as it were' (οἷον σωματοειδῆ), 'as events in Italy and Libya were woven together (συμπλέκεσθαι) with those in Asia and the Greek ones, and everything was moving towards one ending-point (πρὸς ἕν ... τέλος)'.

It has often been noted that Polybius is here identifying the structure of the events of the world, *historia*, with his narrative of them, *historia rerum gestarum*.[16] Adriana Zangara in particular has linked Polybius' image of the body-shaped history and historiography with his stress on the visual quality of his narrative (note συνόψεσθαι, κατοπτεύσας in the above passages), and I have discussed elsewhere the implications of these observations for our understanding of the relationship between aesthetics and truth in Polybius' concept of history(-writing).[17] My interest in this chapter, by contrast, as I said in the introduction, is to uncover links between Polybius' image of the *oikoumene* under Roman rule as a living, beautiful 'body in action' (ἐνεργείας) with other literary and cultural discourses, both Greek and Roman. Walbank already made an important first step in this direction when he related Polybius' image to 'the Platonic-Aristotelian concept of the unity of a literary work', citing, in particular, Plato, *Phdr.* 264c and Aristotle, *Poet.* 23, 1.1459a17–18, the 'novelty' being that Polybius, 'facilitated by his conception of the role of *Tyche*, ... projects the notion of the unity of an historical work upon the objective course of historical events'.[18]

As Walbank rightly saw, the core element of Polybius' image of the *oikoumene* as body is that all individual parts are now related to each other and form a new, complex and functional unity, the body's ἐνέργεια, in which resides also its 'beauty' as a living creature. This is precisely the idea underlying the simile, which then glides into a metaphor, at Plato, *Phdr.* 264c2–5, that

> every speech (λόγος) needs to be composed (συνεστάναι) like a living creature (ζῷον), with its very own body, as it were (σῶμά τι ἔχοντα αὐτὸν αὑτοῦ), so that it is neither without head or feet but has middle parts and extremities (μέσα τε ... καὶ ἄκρα) that are written so as to fit with each other and the whole (πρέποντα ἀλλήλοις καὶ τῷ ὅλῳ).

---

[16] See already Walbank 1957: 43; cf. Zangara 2007: 41; more recently, Grethlein 2013: 230.
[17] Zangara 2007: 41–3; Wiater 2017: 203–5.   [18] Walbank 1957: 43.

As Harvey Yunis well puts it: 'The comparison asserts that as a complex, purposeful entity like the body of a living creature, a speech should possess all and only the parts it needs in order to achieve its purpose ... and the parts should function together to advance that purpose'.[19] Aristotle, in the famous explanation of the (ideal) epic plot by way of comparison with the (ideal) tragic plot, makes a similar point but adds, significantly, the idea that such a successful plot also produces pleasure (ἡδονή) (*Poet.* 23.1459a17–18; tr. Halliwell):

> As regards narrative mimesis in verse [epic], it is clear that plots, as in tragedy, should be constructed dramatically (δραματικούς), that is, around a single, whole, and complete action (περὶ μίαν πρᾶξιν ὅλην καὶ τελείαν), with beginning, middle, and end, so that epic, like a single and whole animal (ὥσπερ ζῷον ἓν ὅλον), may produce the pleasure proper to it (τὴν οἰκείαν ἡδονήν).

Polybius' image features elements common to both Plato and Aristotle, especially in the idea of the essence of the living body consisting in the functional interrelation of its individual parts (Polybius ἐνέργεια; cf. Aristotle's δραματικούς, which similarly implies 'action').[20] It is closer to Aristotle than Plato, however, in the emphasis on the aesthetically pleasing effect that arises from the interrelation of the living being's individual parts: 'its own kind of pleasure' in Aristotle and the καλλωνή 'beauty' in Polybius. The question to what extent Polybius might have had any direct knowledge of Aristotle's works remains a matter of debate, but it is, in light of these similarities, difficult to avoid the conclusion that Polybius' thinking about the nature of the world under Rome and the adequate way of describing it in narrative, are, as Walbank put it, 'ultimately' inspired by Plato and Aristotle, and Walbank might be right that Hellenistic historiography might have been an important intermediary.[21] With reference to Aristotle's passage in particular it is worth noting that Polybius ascribes the same kind of unity and resulting beauty to the new structure of the

---

[19] Yunis 2011 *ad loc.*
[20] Lucas 1968: 214 (on 59b19) links Aristotle's use of δραματικός here with 23 59b10, where the unified, 'dramatic', plot results from the interrelation of its constitutive elements (μέρη).
[21] Cf. also συνορᾶσθαι, 1359b19; εὐσύνοπτος, 1351a4, once again in the context of a comparison of plots with a 'living creature' (ζῷον) and a 'body' (σῶμα), as well as Aristotle's use of the weaving metaphor (Polybius' *symploke*) at 1356a9, 1359a34. Cf. Wiater 2017: 205 n. 14, 207. For recent discussions of the importance of Hellenistic historiography for Polybius see Scardino 2018; Parmeggiani 2018.

oikoumene and its representation in his narrative that Aristotle ascribes to the poetic plot much rather than historical narrative.[22]

While the relationship of Polybius' use of the body metaphor with its uses and occurrences in classical Greek literature is important and will be discussed further below, its full significance becomes apparent only when compared with *later* instances in which the concept is used, as in Polybius, to conceptualise Roman power. A comparison with Ovid's *corpus inperii* in the passage cited and discussed at the beginning of this chapter yields particularly interesting results. Ovid's conception of the Roman extension of power is, like Polybius', but unlike Cicero's concept of the *corpus rei publicae* (see above), fundamentally geographic.[23] Polybius is less specific in the image on the details of the extent of Roman power than Ovid, who specifically mentions individual peoples and regions (I shall come back to this point later).[24] But it is clear from the immediate context, esp. 1.1.5 (ἅπαντα τὰ κατὰ τὴν οἰκουμένην), the strong geographical element of the comparison of the extent of Roman power with that of previous empires (1.2.1–7, esp. 7: οὐ τινὰ μέρη, σχεδὸν δὲ πᾶσαν πεποιημένοι τὴν οἰκουμένην ὑπήκοον αὐτοῖς) as well as the specifically geographical definition of the *symploke* at 1.3.4 (cited above), that Polybius is thinking of Roman power in terms of its geographic extension and that the body metaphor conceptualises the new close relationship of different places all over the Mediterranean through Roman rule. Like Ovid's *corpus inperii*, moreover, but unlike the 'body' of the *polis* in Polybius' classical predecessors (see further below), the 'body' of the *oikoumene* in Polybius is emphatically described as an organic unity of different, interrelated limbs which achieves an almost graphic physicality in Polybius' rather concrete image of the 'living creature's' 'scattered limbs' (διερριμμένα τὰ μέρη, 1.4.7). This is further supported by verbs of vision (συνόψεσθαι, θεώμενοι, αὐτόπται), the adjectives qualifying the aesthetics of the appearance of the ζῷον (ἐμψύχου καὶ καλοῦ) and the kinetic verbs of 'putting' those severed limbs 'back together' to (re-)create the full, functional body of the ζῷον (συνθείς, ἀπεργασάμενος, 1.4.8). As in Ovid, finally, Polybius describes the interrelation of these different parts so as to form the one

---

[22] Cf. Walbank 1957: 43, with references; Wiater 2017: 205 n. 14.

[23] *Pace* Clarke 1999: 124–5, Polybius' image of the *oikoumene* as body has nothing to do with the idea of life cycles of either individuals or states, or the 'biological pattern of birth, development, and decline' (124).

[24] Cf. Weißenberger 2002: 265, who makes the same observation comparing Polybius' preface (without, however, discussing the body metaphor) with Dionysius of Halicarnassus' and Appian's; Richardson 1979: 1–2.

'body' of the *oikoumene* in terms of Roman superiority and conquest.[25] The 'body's' ἐνέργεια, the essential interdependence of its various parts that transforms an unappealing assemblage of severed limbs into a beautiful, living creature, ultimately results from Roman dominance. In his emphasis on the beauty resulting from the new, corporeal unity brought about by Roman power, Polybius comes rather close to one particular aspect of the body metaphor in the Roman empire, in which the idea of the whole and complete body is often used in order to stress the importance of it being kept together by the emperor. What Polybius calls the ἐνέργεια of the body and its resulting beauty, later comes to carry a specific message: 'any separatist tendency, at least in principle, causes outrage. It destroys the balance between the parts and compromises the gratifying arrangement of the whole. It therefore needs to be rejected like an insurrection against reason itself' ('une tendance séparatiste, au moins en principe, scandalise. Elle rompt l'équilibre des parties, compromet le bonheur général. Il faut donc la rejeter comme une insurrection contre la raison').[26] *Pace* Walbank, I find it difficult not to see in Polybius' image, too, at least an implied 'judgment on the rise of Rome'.[27]

The concrete, physical quality of Polybius' image of the *oikoumene* as body and the similarities with Ovid's image of the world under Roman rule, especially the emphasis on the interrelation of its different parts, are worth stressing because it is often held that the body metaphor takes on such a concrete quality, in the sense of 'an image of the organic union of different parts', only in later Republican Latin literature, especially Cicero.[28] Polybius' use of the image, it is true, is not as physical as that of Cicero's *res publica* in some of his speeches, where the *res publica* has wounds (*volnera*, *Leg. agr.* 1.26; *cicatrix*, *Leg. agr.* 3.4), nerves (*Leg. man.* 17), guts (*viscera*, *Cat.* 1.31) and blood (*Dom.* 124).[29] But neither is Ovid's. Polybius' *oikoumene* is, however, much more physically concrete than the image of the city of Athens and the Athenian *chora* as a 'body' (σῶμα τῆς πόλεως) in Dinarchus and Hyperides, the closest classical precedent to Polybius' image of the *oikoumene* under Rome as a living

---

[25] 1.1.5, 2.1, 7, 3.9. Cf. Richardson 1979: 2; Weißenberger 2002: 265. With Richardson 1979: 6 it is important to stress that this does not mean that Polybius and Ovid conceptualised Roman power in the same way.
[26] Béranger 1953: 226–7, with references (the quote at 226).
[27] Walbank 1957: 45. Polybius' view of the quality and future of Roman power had, however, become more complicated by the time he wrote the 'second preface' at the beginning of book three; see Wiater 2016.
[28] E.g., Osborne 2011: 104 (the quote ibid.).
[29] For these and other examples see Knoche 1952: 370–1.

creature.[30] On the one hand, Polybius goes beyond his Greek predecessors and foreshadows, to an extent, Cicero's *corpus rei publicae* by endowing his geopolitical body with a more concrete, physical quality. On the other, he goes beyond both his Greek predecessors and Cicero and foreshadows, to an extent, Ovid's *corpus inperii* by transferring the body metaphor from the individual city/civic community to a 'global' level. While Osborne is, therefore, right that 'there is no body politic in the classical Greek world' in the sense that the classical Greek use of the body metaphor never really amounts to the image of the state as an 'organic union of different parts',[31] he and others are mistaken in identifying late-Republican Latin literature, especially Cicero's concept of the *corpus rei publicae*, as the first manifestation of this change.[32] As our discussion of Polybius' metaphor of the *oikoumene* as body has shown, this process – and the concomitant attempt to find ways to conceptualise the unprecedented impact of Roman power on the inhabited world – began much earlier and is attested at least as early as the mid-second century BCE.

Returning to the passages from Plato and Aristotle cited by Walbank as the ultimate inspiration for Polybius' use of the body metaphor, we see now that matters are somewhat more complex. The body metaphor made sense to describe the *oikoumene* under Roman rule because it already had a well-established history as a political metaphor. But in its pre-existing form, the political body metaphor was not suitable adequately to describe the effect of Roman power on the inhabited world because it was limited to small-scale political entities and, most importantly, it lacked the idea of the body being defined by the interrelation of its individual limbs, a whole greater than the sum of its parts. It is this idea that Polybius found in the literary-critical use of the metaphor in the Platonic-Aristotelian tradition. Literature and politics come together in the metaphor, just as the metaphor itself describes both the political developments and their representation in Polybius' narrative. Narrative composition is crucial in this process

---

[30] This is rightly stressed by Osborne 2011: 104; see further Smith 2011: 17. I will discuss the use of σῶμα in these passages, their relationship to the concept of the citizen community as body as well as their relation to Polybius and subsequent uses of the concept in a separate study.

[31] Osborne 2011: 104.

[32] Osborne cites as the prime example of such an 'organic union' the image of the body in the fable of Menenius Agrippa. The origins of this famous fable, however, remain obscure (despite Nestle 1927). The versions that we have, and to which Osborne refers, are both from the early imperial period (Livy and Dionysius of Halicarnassus) when, as Squire has shown, the idea of the *corpus inperii* was strongly influenced by the visual representation of the physical body of the emperor (see the introduction to this chapter, above, for references). We simply do not know to what extent these early imperial versions reflect possible earlier ones. On Agrippa's fable see further Pieper 2016; Wiater 2018a on Dion. Hal. 6.83.2 (esp. 455 n. 306) and 6.86.

as the *symploke*, and the related image of the *oikoumene* as body, are the central metaphor on which Polybius' narrative of the rise of Roman power is organised. The dialogue between the political and the literary-critical traditions of the use of the body metaphor arises out of the need to find a way to conceptualise, and render manageable, the complexities inherent in the attempt to write *the* history of Rome's rise to power and impact on the world.

The question then arises what might have prompted Polybius to place so much importance on the 'organic' (Osborne's term again) aspect of the body, the dynamic interrelation of individual parts which thus form a new whole. I will argue now that this is a reflection of the nature of the expansion of Roman power and its material representation in mid-Republican Rome. An observation made by different scholars (albeit without reference to the body metaphor) provides a suitable starting point: Polybius' description of the extent of Roman rule remains geographically rather imprecise, especially when compared to the geographical detail in Ovid's *corpus inperii* but also, for example, the preface to Appian's historical work which begins with a lengthy enumeration of 'the boundaries of all the peoples over which the Romans rule' (τοὺς ὅρους ὅσων ἐθνῶν ἄρχουσι Ῥωμαῖοι, 1.pr.1–5, the quote at pr.1). Polybius, by contrast, clearly did not believe that describing the extent of Roman rule in terms of concrete peoples and regions was essential to conceptualising Roman power in the same way as Appian and Ovid did.

Appian's and Ovid's conception of imperial space in terms of a clearly defined number of subject peoples and regions reflects, I would argue, the image of an *orbis terrarum* structured by acknowledged geopolitical units, namely the Roman provinces,[33] and, based on that, the preoccupation with the *fines imperii Romani* and their advancement.[34] It is noteworthy that the peoples and regions named by Ovid (Pannonia, Raetia, Thracia, Illyria, Armenia and the Parthians) are all problematic fringe areas along the eastern/north-eastern border of the Roman sphere of influence. Ovid is

---

[33] On *provinciae* being regarded 'in principle ... as a limited piece of territory' see Lintott 1981: 54. Cf. Richardson 1991, who argues that the term *imperium* changed its meaning from 'right of command within the Roman state, vested in the magistrates and pro-magistrates' to 'an increasingly concrete, territorial sense'; this process was finished by the second half of the first century CE. This does not mean, of course, that the Romans viewed the *imperium Romanum* exclusively in terms of its *provinciae* or as 'coextensive with the provinces'. See Morstein Kallet-Marx 1995: esp. 24 for the quote and further references. The point I wish to make is that the development of the provincial system provided contemporaries with a growing number of increasingly concrete geographical fix-points, as it were, that underpinned their mental map of the extent of Roman power.

[34] On frontiers of the Roman empire cf. Lintott 1981: 64–6; cf. the following notes.

here echoing contemporary political discourse, as the mention of several of these same areas in the *Res Gestae* along with Augustus' claim to have subjected them to Roman power,[35] shows. This chimes with Appian's introduction of his 'survey' of the regions and peoples under Roman rule at the beginning of his work as 'the boundaries' of Roman power (pr.1, cited above).

Such a concept of the Roman *imperium* in terms of a complex of more or less well-defined geographical regions and boundaries, along with a specific way of representing the *oikoumene*, does not become prominent before the mid-first century BCE.[36] Of particular importance here is Pompey's 'cumulative' triumph of 61 BCE which celebrated his achievements in all his military campaigns (ἅπαξ ἀπὸ πάντων τῶν πολέμων) and is described by Cassius Dio (37.21.2).[37] Pompey paraded trophies representing each individual war (καθ' ἕκαστον τῶν ἔργων), followed by 'one big trophy, richly decorated and carrying an inscription, that it was the *oikoumene*'. Nicolet convincingly links this representation of the *oikoumene* with Pompey's *imperium terra marique* in 67 BCE and his 'three triumphs over the three parts of the world (Africa, Europe, and Asia)'.[38] Coming last, the *one* representation of the *oikoumene* at Pompey's triumph in 61 'summed up' his achievements in the concrete individual regions all over the known world: the *oikoumene* is here clearly conceived of as consisting of a specific number of geographical regions now united under Roman rule. This fits with the appearance, at about that same time, of coins showing the *Genius Populi Romani* on the obverse and a sceptre with wreath, globe and rudder on the reverse.[39] The geographical concept of the

---

[35] See esp. Mon. Anc. 30.1–2; cf. 26.1; 27.2–3. Richardson 1991: 6–7 notes that the term *imperium* in its concrete sense of 'dominion, realm, empire' becomes 'especially frequent during and after the Augustan period'.

[36] This development did not, of course, preclude the existence of alternative ways of conceiving of the extent of Roman power even in the late Republic and the principate. See Morstein Kallet-Marx 1995: 24; Richardson 1991: 6–7.

[37] Oddly, Richardson 1991: 7 links the shift of the meaning of *imperium* towards 'a more precisely determined physical entity' only with Caesar and Augustus.

[38] Nicolet 1991: 37. The formula (rule/power) 'by land and sea' was, of course, much older and had Hellenistic precedents which were themselves based on classical precursors; see Momigliano 1942: esp. 62–4. I would argue that the term's significance changed between the second and the mid-to-late first century BCE. That conforms to the conclusions of Momigliano, who identifies Pompey as the first example of 'the celebration of the individual Ruler of Land and Sea' (63). Momigliano, however, does not discuss concepts of Roman power except for the notoriously difficult passages in Lycophron's *Alexandra*.

[39] The first such coin listed by Crawford is RRC 393, a denarius minted by Cn. Lentulus in 76–75 BCE: 'The types associate the Genius populi Romani with domination *terra marique*' (Crawford comm.); cf. Nicolet 1991: 38.

sway of Pompey's power over the world also lies behind the statue group of fourteen *nationes* which he had erected in his theatre – 'the earliest instance of such personifications in Rome'.⁴⁰ These were, probably, complemented by a statue of Pompey himself in heroic nudity, with sword, cloak and a globe in his left hand.⁴¹ The statues of the *nationes* not only expressed Rome's domination in terms of geographical entities; they also made the space subdued by Rome visible and tangible, thus investing it with physical concreteness. This 'tangible' quality of Roman power is then given not too subtle an expression in Pompey's 'handling' the globe (*orbis terrarum*). At the same time, from the first half of the first century onwards, coins begin to appear showing the Roman provinces in the form of female personifications.⁴²

The focus on the representation of the geography of empire in triumphal processions remains key after Pompey. Caesar, for example, appears to have been the first to show personifications of rivers in his triumphal parades in 46,⁴³ as visually effective representations of (perceived) important boundaries that were crossed by the Roman armies,⁴⁴ and 'monuments representing the peoples of the Empire' 'boomed' under Augustus, as demonstrated, for example, by his *Porticus ad nationes*.⁴⁵ Pompey in many ways set the scene for representations of the extent of Roman power by subsequent rulers, especially Caesar and Augustus. Pompey's apparently aniconic representation of the *oikoumene*, in particular, is taken to a new level by a statue of Caesar on the Capitol which showed him 'treading on' (ἐπιβιβασθῆναι) an 'image' (εἰκόνα) of *Oikoumene* (Cassius Dio 43.14.6; cf. 21.2), no doubt a (probably female) personification.⁴⁶ There appears to be a correlation between the increasingly more concrete representation of the *oikoumene* under Roman rule as an actual body and the increasing prominence of individual Roman leaders who were seen, and represented themselves, as rulers over large, geographically concrete stretches of the

---

⁴⁰ Edwards 2003: 65.   ⁴¹ Cf. Nicolet 1991: 38, referring to *Mon. Anc.* 26.1; cf. above, n. 35.
⁴² Östenberg 2009: 222. Östenberg surmises (ibid.) that even if Pompey was not 'the first to show personifications of *gentes* and *nationes* in a triumph', he was 'most likely ... the first to fully exploit their potential, in his processions as on coins and in sculpture'.
⁴³ Östenberg 2009: 230–1.
⁴⁴ Cf. Östenberg 2009: 235–6. On the importance of rivers in the Romans' imaginary topography of power see Purcell 2012.
⁴⁵ Östenberg 2009: 223.
⁴⁶ Nicolet 1991: 39–40, adopting a suggestion of G. Picard. Since Dio also mentions Caesar's chariot, the statue group might have represented Caesar alighting from his chariot onto *Oikoumene*. Cf. Arnaud 1984: 114–15. The marble version of Epitychides' famous statue of the Tyche of Antiochia in the Vatican, which shows the Tyche with her feet resting on an allegorical representation of the river Orontes, might be a good visual parallel (decent-sized photograph in Holliday 2002: 113).

inhabited world. This chimes with Michael Squire's observation, cited in the introduction to this chapter, that the concrete image of the *corpus inperii* in the imperial period is intimately linked with the (representation of the) physical body of the emperor. The material discussed here suggests, however, that in that respect, as in so many others, the Augustan principate was the heir to late-Republican cultural and social developments.

In this context it is important to note that such concrete, corporeal representations of the *oikoumene* as in the statue of Caesar had Hellenistic precedents that would have been known also to Polybius and at least some of his Roman contemporaries. Duris of Samos mentions a painting of Demetrius Poliorcetes that showed him 'driving his chariot on the *oikoumene*' (ἐπὶ τῆς οἰκουμένης ὀχούμενος, FGrH = BNJ 76 F 14), certainly a personification. This very image, Schlachter suggested, might have inspired Caesar's statue.[47] Furthermore, *Oikoumene* is represented as a woman crowning Homer on the famous *Apotheosis of Homer* by Archelaos of Priene, found in Bovillae,[48] and discussed in a different context by Emma Greensmith in this volume (see Figure 6.1, p. 182). The date of the relief remains a matter of contention, with proposals ranging from the late third to the late second century. The Archelaos relief appears, in any case, to be the earliest securely identified personification of *Oikoumene*,[49] but it does not seem as though the artist expects the viewer to be surprised by her appearance. *Oikoumene* on the relief appears as one of several personifications, including Chronos, Myth, History, Poetry, Tragedy and Comedy as well as Physis, Arete, Mneme, Pistis and Sophia. Personifications of places in particular had become increasingly popular since the end of the fifth century, with the 'most inclusive geographical personification known from the Classical period' being Hellas, who is, along with regions and cities, 'embodied as [an] ageless wom[a]n'.[50] After

---

[47] Schlachter 1927: 65 n. 4, followed by Nicolet 1991: 39 n. 42; cf. Arnaud 1984: 114. With Schlachter and Nicolet I think it highly unlikely that the *oikoumene* was represented here as a globe. The latter view was held by, for example, Vogt 1929: 158 n. 22, who is unable, however, to cite any supporting evidence. The decisive point to me seems to be this: why should any Greek have used the term *oikoumene* (as Duris does) to refer to a globe before the Roman period at all? Even when Crates of Mallos created the presumably first globe as a representation of the world (σφαῖραν, Strab. 2.10 C116), he regarded the *oikoumene* as merely one part of, not identical with, it (Strab. ibid.). I would argue that representing the *oikoumene* as a globe only makes sense after the 'inhabited world' had been identified with the Roman concept of *orbis terrarum*, on which see Vogt 1929: 153–4. Neither Jacoby nor Pownall (on BNJ 76) discuss the issue.

[48] Smith 1991: fig. 216; for a recent discussion, with further references, see Newby 2007. I should like to thank Zahra for providing me with an electronic file of her paper when libraries all over the world were closed due to the Covid crisis.

[49] See LIMC s.v. 'Oikoumene' (Canciani). [50] Smith 2011: 91.

Alexander's large-scale empire and the emergence of the empires of his successors, many of which, at least initially, had 'global' ambitions and claimed universal rule, it is not surprising to find concrete representations also of *Oikoumene* along these lines. The connection between political power and specific forms of representation of the *oikoumene* receives further support from the identification of *Oikoumene* on the relief with Arsinoe III and of Chronos, standing next to her, with her husband Ptolemy IV.[51]

This brief overview suggests that different forms of representations of the *oikoumene* are linked with specific kinds of power structures. The Hellenistic material in particular shows that Polybius could have drawn on such female representations to conceptualise the inhabited world under Rome but chose not to. In fact, another century had to go by until a Roman, Caesar, building on the precedent set by Pompey, chose to avail himself of these Hellenistic precedents and represent the *oikoumene* under Roman rule in the form of a female personification. The fact that Polybius chose instead the image of an unspecific 'living creature' defined by the functional interrelation of its parts (ἐνέργεια) lends support to my earlier suggestion that this might be reflective of the specific representation of Roman power in the world at his time. Indeed, as I will argue now, the expansion of Roman power as it presented itself to Polybius and his contemporaries was characterised by a similar impression of individual parts becoming interconnected and gradually forming a new whole, rather than one, comprehensive action as the one claimed by Pompey in his triumph in 61.

The primary means of representing Rome's growing power in mid-Republican Rome were pictorial representations both in temples and during triumphal processions,[52] expositions of booty, statues with inscriptions of successful commanders and public buildings, especially temples, that were vowed during battle and/or erected with the money generated from military success.[53] All of these representations of Rome's expanding power shared the same, key feature – reflecting the intensely competitive nature of mid-Republican society – that each new acquisition of territory was presented as an individual achievement and linked, usually by an

---

[51] Other Hellenistic rulers have been suggested; see the discussion in Newby 2007: 170–2. On political personifications in late classical and Hellenistic art see Messerschmidt 2003.
[52] The most convenient collection of the evidence remains Zinserling 1959–60. For the most recent specialist discussion see Östenberg 2009: 189–261; cf. also Walter 2004: 131–95; Holliday 2002: 22–121.
[53] See Davies 2017 for the best recent treatment.

inscription, to the one specific magistrate who claimed responsibility for it. Collectively, however, all of these individual achievements – which remained clearly marked as such – left their visible imprint on the cityscape of Rome where all these individual processes came together and formed, and were visible, as elements of one, new whole. To cite only one, representative example, in 175, Ti. Sempronius Gracchus set up in the temple of Mater Matuta a painting of Sardinia, presumably a rather schematic outline rather than a geographically and topographically precise map,[54] including representations (*simulacra*) of his battles and accompanied by an explanatory description (Liv. 41.28.8–10, with quotation of the inscription). To commemorate his successes in Sardinia Gracchus chose a place that already strongly symbolised Rome's expanding might: the temple itself had been dedicated by Camillus after the siege of Veii and in 196, L. Stertinius had erected two arches with gilded statues *de manubiis* in front of the temple and its 'twin', the temple of Fortuna, 'the first arches in Rome that might be called triumphal'.[55] By adding his own 'monument' to the pre-existing ones, Sempronius Gracchus inscribed himself into the line of successes of the earlier leaders, just as Atilius Calatinus cast himself as the successor of Duilius when he erected the temple of Spes to commemorate a (probably naval) victory in 254 next to the temple of Janus erected by Duilius shortly after 260 to celebrate his naval victory over the Carthaginians, commemorated also by two famous *columnae rostratae*.[56] To buildings such as these we need to add the *spolia* exhibited, with inscriptions, throughout Rome and, indeed, Latium and other parts of the growing Roman empire.[57]

These buildings and objects have been discussed from several different angles: as important media of Roman *memoria*,[58] as part of aristocratic self-presentation and competition and generally mid-Republican Roman political culture,[59] as important documents for our understanding of the development of Roman art and architecture and Roman attitudes to art more generally,[60] and, most recently, as evidence for social and economic developments.[61] The aspect of these monuments that is most relevant to

---

[54] See Brodersen 2003: 157–8.
[55] Richardson 1992 s.v. 'Mater Matuta, Aedes'; Davies 2017: 121–2, on the *fornices Stertinii* and other arches commemorating military successes.
[56] See Davies 2017: 60; Ziolkowski 1992: 61–2 (Ianus in Foro Holitorio), 152–4 (Spes in Foro Holitorio); on Duilius' columns see Richardson 1992 s.vv. 'Columna Rostrata C. Duilii' (1) and (2); Davies 2017: 65.
[57] Cf. Rawson 1990; Gruen 1992: 84–130; Edwards 2003: 49–57.
[58] E.g., Hölkeskamp 1993; Walter 2004: 131–95.   [59] Hölkeskamp 2001; Davies 2017.
[60] Cf. Gruen 1992: 84–182.   [61] Bernard 2018.

the present discussion, by contrast, has received relatively little scholarly attention, namely the way in which the display of peoples and representations of cities, rivers and landscapes, the permanent paintings of regions subdued by Roman generals, such as Gracchus' 'map' of Sardinia, and the buildings and artwork associated with subjected places near and far shaped the Romans' mental map of the world by shaping the structure of the city. Important exceptions include Kai Brodersen, who argued that the triumph in particular, with its representation of non-Roman peoples and their cities in its various forms, was crucial to the Romans' mental map of the world under their rule. Such representations of subjected regions, places and peoples created 'landmarks', the primary means, according to Brodersen, of perceiving and conceptualising space at the time.[62] And in an important 1990 paper, Nicholas Purcell argued that monuments and buildings created by the Romans in conquered territory were 'focal points' that were 'important in imagining the world', while their inscriptions constituted their own kind of information about the (order of the) world that did not depend on or even require the ability to verify the listed peoples' existence, their geographical location and their actual relationship with the Romans.[63] Representations of Roman power and geographical 'knowledge' of the world under Roman rule were inextricably intertwined.

The point I want to make here is the extent to which the expansion of Roman power in the middle Republic fundamentally shaped the structure and appearance of the city and how that cityscape, in turn, created a specific image of the world under Roman rule and of the nature of Roman power. The growth of Roman power was literally mapped onto the cityscape. This must have been particularly visible in areas where monuments representing individual Roman leaders' military successes formed clusters, for example, along the route of the triumphal processions or in the monumental complex that gradually grew on the *forum Boarium* (see above).[64] The growth and gradual transformation of the cityscape through monuments and buildings associated with specific contributions to the expansion of Roman power by individual members of the Roman elite thus made that expansion experienceable as a gradual, cumulative, step-by-step process.[65] This also shaped spectators' vision of Rome's place

---

[62] Brodersen 2003: 116–37, esp. 118–19, 129–30.   [63] Purcell 1990: 179–80.
[64] Cf. Davies 2017: 65, on the rostrate monuments of Duilius (above) and Maenius 'mark[ing] important phases of Roman hegemony' and 'describ[ing] a narrative of expansion'.
[65] Far from 'eliding' each other (Davies 2017: 60), these individual contributions, as Hölkeskamp 2001: 156 rightly stresses, complemented each other, thus creating a complex of interrelated layers of Roman power by individual achievement inscribed on the physical fabric of the city.

within this growing network of interconnections as with each addition to its cityscape based on a military achievement outside of the city walls, Rome appeared more and more as the reference point where the different strands of military activity literally came together.[66]

Richardson noted 'the absence in Polybius of any Roman concept of *provincia*'. The reason for this, he suggested, is that Polybius conceives of Roman power in terms of the Hellenistic monarchies.[67] While Polybius' Hellenistic background is certainly important, the preceding considerations suggest an alternative view. For the absence of the concept of *provincia* in Polybius also fits well with a political culture in which the Roman empire was not yet fully defined in formal, legal and, we should add, geopolitical categories.[68] *Provinciae* did, of course, exist at Polybius' time. But they were less important as geographically well-defined 'building blocks' of the Roman empire than as concepts that helped define the radius of activity of a magistrate's *imperium*.[69] Polybius' image of the *oikoumene* as a body defined by the newly gained, dynamic interactions of previously unrelated 'limbs' does fit very nicely the image of the expansion of Roman power as a continuous process of increasing, mutual connectivity of Rome and an ever-widening range of places all over the *oikoumene* through subsequent, individual addition of parts to the constantly developing whole. It was this process of the spread of Roman power over an ever larger part of the *oikoumene* which Polybius could observe and, indeed, experience in the very city of Rome and that is reflected, I suggest, in his emphasis on the essence of the *oikoumene*-as-body lying in its *energeia*, the newly established, dynamic interrelation of individual parts resulting in a new, aesthetically pleasing whole. The innovative adaptation of the traditional, political use of the body metaphor in classical Greek literature, which Polybius achieved by bringing it into dialogue with its use in literary criticism, is thus ultimately inspired by and grounded in the materiality of the expansion of power and its representation in mid-Republican Rome.

---

[66] The fundamental importance of space and movement to the nature and experience of mid-Republican Roman power has recently been emphasised – with respect to Roman institutions and administrative processes – by Gargola 2017.
[67] Richardson 1979: 5–6. [68] Cf. Morstein Kallet-Marx 1995: 29.
[69] Cf. Gargola 2017: 69–82. *Provinciae* only seem to take on a more geographical significance from the beginning of the final quarter of the second century; scholars have identified the *lex Porcia* of 123 or the *lex de provinciis praetoriis* of 100 as the earliest evidence for this development. See Gargola 2017: 76, 80–1.

Enacting *Symploke*: Hannibal's March in Context

In the last section I argued that Polybius' image of the *oikoumene* as a 'functional' ('organic') body, rather than a (female) personification, reflects the importance of interconnectivity in the creation, representation and experience of Roman power in the third and second centuries BCE. In this, the final section, I will argue that this perception of Roman power, as it is condensed in Polybius' image of the *oikoumene*-as-body, also informs his narrative of the historical events, where movement, speed and shrinking distances are of crucial importance. Movement and, hence, interconnectivity lie, in fact, at the heart of Polybius' image of the *oikoumene*-as-body, in that *energeia*, the defining feature of Polybius' 'living creature', is associated with 'movement' (*kinesis*) throughout Greek literature. Aristotle even defines 'movement' as 'a kind of *energeia*' (e.g., *De an.* 474a14). Given the close connection between Polybius' image of the *oikoumene* as a body and the *symploke* (1.3.4), the question arises whether we can identify movement as a key factor in realising the interweaving of the different parts of the *oikoumene* also in the actual course of events. Polybius' concept of the *symploke* has, of course, been discussed before. But these discussions have usually focused on macrostructural elements of Polybius' narrative, especially his use of synchronisms and the structure of his work by geographical regions, with particular reference to the problems inherent in these.[70] The preceding discussion of Polybius' body metaphor prompts us to shift the focus and look for the processes 'on the ground', at the micro-level of his narrative, through which the *symploke* is realised.

Hannibal's march suggests itself as a suitable episode to explore the interrelation of movement, interconnectivity and power in Polybius' narrative of how the *oikoumene* became an 'organic' unity under Roman rule. Hannibal's march constitutes the beginning of the Second Punic War, which is identified by Polybius at 1.3.1–2 as one of the three wars that constituted the beginning of the *symploke*. As I will argue, Polybius uses Hannibal's march to illustrate the changing horizons and new interconnectivity of the world brought about by the *symploke*. His march literally connects not only Spain and Italy but even links Italy and Africa. For this part of my argument I will not discuss Polybius' narrative of the march

---

[70] See Walbank 1972; Walbank 1975, but note his brief remark at 211; Quinn 2013; Clarke 1999: 119–23, esp. 119: 'The progressive expansion of Roman rule further contributed to the domination of time over space', even though she rightly stresses at 119 n. 90 that 'Polybius *was* interested in the geographical aspect of Roman rule, in the looser sense of the zones in which domination was exercised'.

itself but will focus on the geographical 'digression' at 3.36–9 that immediately precedes it and which has received very little attention from scholars.[71]

At 3.36, shortly after starting his narrative of Hannibal's march to Italy, when Hannibal is crossing the Pyrenees on his way to the Rhône (35.7–8), Polybius interrupts his account. In order for his readers to get an accurate sense of the locations and route of Hannibal's march, he explains, there is no point in providing so many names of places which readers do not know and which are, therefore, only so many empty words. Instead, a broad perspective is needed that is based on orientation marks known to everybody (36.1–5). Polybius then starts with the most fundamental frame of reference, the compass points in the heavens (the rising and setting of the sun for East and West, 'midday' and 'Ursa Major' for South and North), and maps these onto the outline of the *oikoumene* which he proceeds to describe (37–38.4).[72] Polybius regards the *oikoumene* as consisting of three 'parts' (μέρη):[73] *Asia*,[74] between the river Tanais (Don) and the Nile, *Libye*, between the Nile and the Columns of Heracles, and *Europe*, between the Columns of Heracles and the Tanais river. Each of these he links with one of the compass points, a procedure for he which he was, not unjustly, criticised by Strabo (2.4.7).[75] Polybius, without saying so, clearly assumes a fixed position of the viewer somewhere in the central Mediterranean (τῆς καθ' ἡμᾶς θαλάττης, 37.6). Polybius then 'zooms in' on *Europe* which stretches 'from the rising of the sun to its setting' (37.7) and is subdivided further into a part between the Tanais and the river Narbo (modern Aude), in the area of Massilia, and between Massilia and the Columns of Heracles. Between the Narbo and the Pyrenees live the Celts (37.9), the part between the Pyrenees and the Columns of Heracles is further subdivided into the part bordering the Mediterranean, called 'Iberia', and the part towards the Ocean ('the outer sea'), 'which does not have a commonly agreed-upon name because it has only

---

[71] The best recent discussion is Maier 2010, who links Polybius' geographical descriptions to the didactic purpose of his work; Clarke 1999 remains fundamental on Polybius and geography; Walbank 1948.
[72] Cf. Clarke 1999: 112–13.
[73] The subdivision of the *oikoumene*, as well as the boundaries between the individual 'parts', were contested in antiquity; Polybius' division is the one attributed by Herodotus (2.16.1) to 'the Ionians and Greeks'.
[74] I will use Latinised versions of the Greek terms when referring to the 'parts' of Polybius' image of the *oikoumene*, in order to avoid creating the impression that these are identical with modern geographical/geopolitical subdivisions referred to by the same or similar names.
[75] Cf. Walbank 1972: 118–19; Clarke 1999: 114 offers a more balanced, and more favourable, assessment of Polybius' treatment of geography.

just been explored (προσφάτως κατωπτεῦσθαι) and is in its entirety inhabited by populous barbarian peoples' (37.11). And just as nobody knows where *Asia* and *Libye* connect, the northern part of Europe between Tanais and Narbo 'is, so far, unknown to us, unless we take the initiative (πολυπραγμονοῦντες) in the future and start to make enquiries (ἱστωρήσωμεν)' (38.2).

After having described the structure of the world and the structure of Europe within it, Polybius maps Carthaginian power onto his virtual map of the *oikoumene*, thus gradually returning to his narrative of the march (39.2–5):

> At this time, the Carthaginians were in control of all parts of *Libye* that are oriented towards the inner sea [the Mediterranean], from the Altars of Philaenus ... to the Columns of Heracles. The length of this coastal line is over sixteen thousand *stades*. After crossing the strait at the Columns of Heracles, they had equally subdued also all of Iberia, up to the mountain ridge that constitutes, on the side towards our sea, the end point of the Pyrenees mountains, which separate the Iberians and the Celts. This place is about eight thousand *stades* distant from the straits at the Columns of Heracles.

This brief extract is representative of the nature of the entire chapter 39. Polybius subdivides the route from the Columns of Heracles to Northern Italy into smaller geographical units, providing distances for each of them: Columns of Heracles to Carthago Nova, 'from where Hannibal set off on his invasion (ὁρμήν) of Italy', three thousand *stades*; from Carthago Nova to the Ebro, two thousand six hundred *stades*; from the Ebro to Emporium, one thousand six hundred *stades*; <from Emporium to ***, *c.* six hundred *stades*>;[76] from there to the crossing of the Rhône, *c.* one thousand six hundred *stades*; 'as they [the Carthaginians] were marching (πορευομένοις) from the crossing of the Rhône towards its sources and the ascent of the Alps into Italy' (39.9), *c.* one thousand four hundred; finally, the crossing of the Alps itself, *c.* one thousand two hundred *stades*.[77] 'After he had surpassed (ὑπερβαλών) these [the Alps], he was going to arrive (ἔμελλεν ἥξειν) at the plains of the Po, in Italy' (39.10), with all of these individual stages adding up to around nine thousand *stades*, 'which he had to pass through (διελθεῖν)' (39.11): 'in terms of the distance (μῆκος) of these places, Hannibal had passed through (διεληλύθει) half, but in terms

---

[76] Part of the text is missing here and was supplied by the editors because otherwise Polybius' total of *stades* does not match the individual stations.

[77] For a recent discussion of these distances see Hoyos 2006: 409.

of difficulty, the main part of his march was still left' (39.12). At the beginning of the next chapter, 40.1, we touch base with Hannibal again, as 'he was busy crossing (ἐνεχείρει ταῖς διεκβολαῖς) the Pyrenees mountains'.

While technically a 'digression,' inasmuch as they interrupt Polybius' narrative of Hannibal's march,[78] these chapters are, in fact, an integral element of Polybius' march narrative. This is particularly evident from the sophisticated way in which Polybius inserts them into his account. Polybius embarks on the 'digression' as Hannibal has just started a new phase of his march. He is beginning the crossing of the Pyrenees after having further reduced his troop numbers in order to be able to cross the Alps (38.7–8); it is really only at this point, then, that Hannibal leaves Spain and orients himself fully towards Italy. This is further supported by the passage above, where Polybius identifies the Pyrenees as the boundary of the Carthaginian sphere of influence in Spain. Hannibal is, in fact, in the process of crossing the Pyrenees towards the next significant moment of his march, the crossing of the Rhône. The digression thus fills the time that Hannibal spends marching over the mountains and allows Polybius to make the duration of that part of the march perceivable without giving a detailed narrative of it. The next time we see Hannibal 'in action', consequently, is when he has already arrived at the Rhône and is preparing the crossing of the river (42.1), a particularly challenging and dramatic phase of the march. But Polybius also takes great care in reconnecting the 'digression' with Hannibal's march as he smoothly steers the narrative in stages back from the heavens first to the *oikoumene* as a whole, then one part of the *oikoumene*, *Europe*, then one part within *Europe*, Iberia, and then the concrete stages and distances covered by Hannibal on his march within Spain; this is accompanied by a transition from a general 'bird's eye view' of the world, the *oikoumene*, *Europe*, and Spain to the reintroduction of a human perspective of that space, first, through plural verbs of motion (διαβάντες [*scil.* the Carthaginians], 39.4; πορευομένοις 'as they were marching', 39.9) to Hannibal's perception and interaction with that space in particular towards the end of the 'digression' (λοιπαί, i.e., for Hannibal and his army; ἔμελλεν ἥξειν [Hannibal], 39.10; οὓς ἔδει διελθεῖν αὐτόν, 39.11; αὐτῷ ... ἀπελείπετο, 39.12), followed by the 'name cap' 'Hannibal' at the beginning of 40.1. We also need to be mindful of Polybius' programmatic introduction of the 'digression' which rejects a more topographically detailed narrative as it was offered by other historians (presumably Sosylus and Silenus).[79] Walbank's comment, that Polybius'

---

[78] Cf. Fabrizi 2015: 127–8.   [79] 36.2, with Walbank's note.

'failure adequately to describe πόθεν ὁρμήσας Ἀννίβας ... εἰς ποῖα μέρη κατῆρε τῆς Ἰταλίας is shown by the still inconclusive discussion on which Alpine pass Hannibal used', misses the point: as Polybius makes unmistakably clear, even though he could have given the sort of precise topographical narrative of the march that modern historians keep longing for, he decided not to.[80]

I want to argue here that this decision is linked to his specific conception of the *oikoumene* under Roman rule as discussed in the previous part of this chapter. In fact, Polybius' digression enables readers to see Hannibal's march enacting the process of the 'dispersed limbs' of the 'living being' being linked so as to form a new, interrelated whole. Based on the design of the 'digression' and Polybius' introductory comments, the purpose of these chapters is to dissociate Hannibal's march from its topographical micro-context and inscribe it into a larger, ecumenical perspective. By 'zooming out' from the march and then gradually 'zooming back in', Polybius prompts the reader to see Hannibal's march not as a local, but a 'global' phenomenon.[81] He is translating, as it were, the political and historical significance of the march into geographical perspective: what happens in Spain has repercussions for the entire *oikoumene*. The individual 'parts' (μέρη) of the *oikoumene*, the three, as we would call them, continents, also provide a linguistic link with the 'parts' (μέρη, not, *notabene*, μέλη) of the 'living creature' as which Polybius pictures the world in times of the *symploke*.

This aspect becomes particularly clear in the list of distances in chapter 39. Describing these figures as 'statistics', thus suggesting that somehow they are an end in themselves,[82] is just as mistaken as modern scholars' habit of focusing only on the distances after the Pyrenees, because these might help us figure out which route Hannibal actually took and thus satisfy our obsession with the kind of geographical precision explicitly rejected by Polybius. As Nicholas Purcell reminds us, numbers represent their own type of 'rhetoric', which, just like lists of peoples and places discussed in the previous section, is integral to the representation of power.[83] Numbers create visibility of the initiative, organisation, determination and resources necessary to master and control space. As such, they are a less flashy alternative to representing a ruler like Demetrius of

---

[80] In fact, Polybius does appreciate the importance of more detailed topographical descriptions elsewhere; see, e.g., 1.41.7; 2.14.3; 16.29.3–4, with Clarke 1999: 92–4.
[81] On 'global' perspectives in Polybius, albeit from a very different angle, see also Isayev 2014.
[82] Walbank 1957: 371.   [83] Cf. Purcell 1990: 181 (on Pliny the Elder).

Phaleron riding his chariot over the *oikoumene* (above) and akin to Roman milestones, to which I will return below. As far as Polybius' list of distances is concerned, in narrative terms it is only through the long list of impressive numbers that the reader gets a sense of the enormous scale of Hannibal's undertaking. These numbers, which are impressive even to a modern reader, must have had an even greater effect in antiquity, when the primary means of conceptualising space was the itinerary, space as experienced through movement, rather than the map.[84] Hannibal brings enormous chunks of the *oikoumene* under his control, seemingly unstoppable, as he moves from, and links, segment to segment. The concrete spatial reality, as it were, of Hannibal's march becomes perceivable as Polybius inscribes his progress, stage by stage, from Carthago Nova to the plains of the Po, on the imaginary map of the *oikoumene* which he has created in the previous chapters.

But Polybius' chapter does more than that. The preoccupation with the exact route of Hannibal's march makes it easy to overlook that the segments and distances in chapter 39 are not at all limited to Hannibal's march.[85] On the contrary, they set Hannibal's march into the perspective of continuously expanding Carthaginian imperial space.[86] As mentioned above, Polybius' list of distances does not begin with Carthago Nova or even the Columns of Heracles. In fact, the first sentence of the chapter, which introduces the distances, refers to the comprehensive extent of Carthaginian power (ἐκυρίευον) in *Libye* from the 'Altars of Philaenus' to the Columns of Heracles.[87] He then continues with their crossing (διαβάντες) of the straits at the Columns of Heracles, which, as the reader knows from the previous chapters, marks the boundary between two of the three 'parts' of the *oikoumene*, *Libye* and *Europe*, and reminds the reader that the entire (ἁπάσης) stretch from the Columns to the Pyrenees was already under Carthaginian power (ἐκεκρατήκεισαν, 39.4). Hannibal's march thus appears as the continuation and last stage of a continuous process of the expansion of Carthaginian power that now threatens to

---

[84] The classic study is Janni 1984, who calls this mode of perceiving space 'hodological'; cf. Brodersen 2003, but note Clarke 1999: 103 n. 59, who notes, rightly, that Polybius cannot be pinned down to a conception of space in 'linear terms'.

[85] The prominence of Hannibal's march has informed the view of the chapter even of scholars who are not primarily interested in it, e.g., Clarke 1999: 108: 'In relating Hannibal's invasion of Europe, Polybius maps out *the route from the Pillars of Hercules to the Po valley*' (emphasis mine).

[86] On Carthaginian imperialism (as opposed to the Roman 'right' to rule) as an important topic in Livy's description of Hannibal's march see Fabrizi 2015: esp. 129–36.

[87] As Clarke 1999: 95 points out, Polybius repeats the same phrase when describing Scipio's conquests in Africa (10.40.7).

incorporate also the heartland of *Europe*, Italy, thus creating a long line of Carthaginian power, from the 'Altars of Philaenus' to Rome and, potentially, beyond. This reading of Polybius' distances receives further support from the rich associations of Hannibal's march with the campaigns of the great conquerors of the ancient world, starting with Heracles whose route, the so-called *via Heraclea*, he was following and with whom he associated himself through his coinage and the sacrifice at the sanctuary of Gades at the beginning of the march (Liv. 21.21.9),[88] via Alexander to more ambivalent undertones especially in Polybius' narrative, of near-eastern rulers, including Darius and Xerxes and their invasion of Greece.[89]

Polybius thus invites his reader to view his detailed account of the distances in chapter 39 as part of a larger discourse about movement creating new, potentially permanent power structures across the different parts of the *oikoumene*. Such an association receives further support from the well-known link between the creation of a large-scale, 'global' empire and the measuring of distances in the case of Alexander the Great who famously had *bematistai* measure and record the distances covered by his army.[90] These *bematistai* produced the so-called *Stages of Alexander's March* (Σταθμοί τῆς Ἀλεξάνδρου πορείας) which, judging by the traces they have left in later authors such as Pliny (e.g., *HN* 6.44–5, 61–3 = FGrH 119 F2a), must have looked rather similar to Polybius' chapter, thus, incidentally, reinforcing also the association between Hannibal and Alexander. Polybius' distances thus introduce an implied counterfactual into his narrative: they invite the reader to consider what the world would have looked like if Hannibal had succeeded in integrating *Libye* and most of *Europe*, including Italy and Rome, into the space of Carthaginian power.[91] This counterfactual prompt is strengthened by the similarity of Polybius' chapter with another important kind of text familiar to his readers. The passage from one continent to another along the coast, ordered by landmarks and providing the distances between them, along with Spain as the starting point of Hannibal's march specifically, evoke the *periploi*, which often adopted the same structure.[92]

---

[88] See, e.g., Acquaro 1991: esp. 72–3; Briquel 2004; Fabrizi 2015: 129–36.
[89] On Alexander, see, e.g., Breckenridge 1983; Manfredi 1999; cf. MacDonald 2015: 228, 232, 234–5. I will discuss associations of Hannibal and near-eastern rulers in Polybius in my Oxford commentary on book three and a monograph on the debate about Hannibal's march from antiquity to the twenty-first century, the work on both of which is currently in progress; meanwhile, see Clarke 1999: 99–100 and her index s.v. Xerxes.
[90] See FGrH 119–23 for the fragments. [91] On counterfactuals in history see Maier (this volume).
[92] Cf. Prontera 1984: 220, 230–1. On adaptations of the *periplus* in late Republican and imperial Greek narratives see Baumann (this volume).

Together with the echoes of Alexander's campaign, this intertext suggests the possibility of Hannibal's march to Italy merely being the start of a much larger expedition that might eventually have comprised the entire *oikoumene*. Hannibal did, after all, actively associate himself – or, at the very least, encouraged others to associate him – with (the) other great Hellenistic rulers many of whom such as Demetrius Poliorcetes, Ptolemy II, Ptolemy IV and his wife Arsinoe III and Pyrrhus had gestured towards, or were credited with aspirations to, *oikoumene*-wide rule.[93] In fact, Alexander himself was said to have conceived of the idea of an *oikoumene*-wide rule, including also its western part, at the Temple of Heracles/Melqart at Gades, the same temple visited by Hannibal before embarking on his invasion of Italy in Livy.[94] Hannibal could thus be seen as being in the early stages of creating the kind of 'global' rule which Alexander had planned but failed to realise. Within the *Histories*, moreover, readers are certainly invited to set Hannibal, operating in the West, on a par with Philip V, who was at the same time actively pursuing universal rule (τῆς ὑπὲρ τῶν ὅλων ἐπιβολῆς, 5.101.10) in the eastern part of the Mediterranean.[95]

As Polybius' readers knew, however, ultimately, the interconnection between *Libye* and *Europe* brought about by Hannibal's march benefitted not him but the Romans. In fact, Polybius' text encourages a 'double vision' of Hannibal's march as both a re-enactment, on Hannibal's part, of the great campaigns of Alexander and Heracles, and, with hindsight, an important step in the entanglement of the western part of the Mediterranean with Roman power (*symploke*), by inscribing Hannibal's march into the shifting horizons of the *oikoumene* brought about by the expansion of Roman power. Particularly important in that respect is 37.11 (cited above), where Polybius mentions that the part of Iberia stretching alongside the Ocean (the 'outer sea') lacks 'a commonly agreed-upon name because it has only just been explored'. Ever since Cuntz, this comment

---

[93] Cf. above, pp. 50–1, on Demetrius Poliorcetes and Ptolemy IV and Arsinoe III. The *pompe* held by Ptolemy II in the early third century, 'the visible result of the success of Ptolemaic policy in the south' (Huss 2001: 292), featured, alongside statues of Alexander the Great, Ptolemy I and Arete, personifications of Corinth and the Ionian and Greek cities which had been liberated by Alexander, the latter represented by real women; see Callixinus of Rhodes, FGrH = BNJ 627 F2, with Paul T. Keyser's commentary. On Pyrrhus cf. Plut. *Pyrrh.* 14.4–11. Seibert 1993: 72–3, 76–80, offers a useful review of the most influential scholarly works situating Hannibal in the Hellenistic world; cf. also MacDonald 2015.

[94] Liv. 21.21.9; Curt. 10.1.17–18; cf. Liv. 9.16.19 (Alexander); 21.21.9 (Hannibal at Gades); cf. Cresci Marrone 1993: 100.

[95] On the idea of 'world rule' in the *Histories* cf. Clarke 1999: 117; Walbank 1993.

has been taken, convincingly, to refer to the progress of knowledge of these regions due to Roman military campaigns.[96] Such a connection is made by Polybius explicitly at the famous passage 3.59.3–4, where he states that more precise knowledge even of marginal regions of the *oikoumene* (τῶν περὶ τὰς ἐσχατιὰς τῆς καθ᾽ ἡμᾶς οἰκουμένης, 58.2) has become possible because 'in our time, due to Alexander's reign, the places in *Asia*, and, due to the Romans' supremacy, all other places have become accessible by sea and land (πλωτῶν καὶ πορευτῶν γενομένων)'. The last phrase in particular recalls the formulaic *terra marique*, thus rendering the connection between knowledge and power even more evident. In light of this passage, also Polybius' comment about the possibility to learn more about the as yet unknown northern boundaries of the *oikoumene* at 38.2 might be read as an allusion to the link between knowledge of the *oikoumene* and the expansion of Roman power.[97] Finally, the phrase ἡ καθ᾽ ἡμᾶς θάλαττα, which occurs at 37.6, 37.9 and, twice, 37.10, might introduce a specifically Roman framework of thinking about the world if Dubuisson is right in associating it with the Latin *mare nostrum*.[98]

But the very design of Polybius' chapter, I would argue, also evokes other, much more specific and, moreover, typically Roman kinds of text in which, to no lesser extent than the *Stathmoi* of Alexander's campaigns, movement, space and power are inextricably interlinked. At 39.8, right after the distance of the part of the march immediately before the Rhône, the manuscripts transmit the sentence: 'for this [distance/part of the march] has now been thoroughly measured (βεβημάτισται) and marked with a sign (σεσημείωται) at every eighth *stade* by the Romans'. There is some debate about the authenticity of these words, which have been taken to refer to the opening of the *via Domitia* in 118, when Polybius, who was presumably born shortly before 200, would have been implausibly old. Büttner-Wobst therefore brackets them as a later addition. If authentic, and if reference is to the *via Domitia*, the sentence would have to be taken to be among Polybius' very last additions to his work;[99] alternatively, reference might be not to the *via Domitia* but an earlier *via militaris* that

---

[96] Cuntz (followed by Walbank 1957: 370) suggested the campaign of D. Iunius Callaicus in 138–137, which would imply that this comment was added rather late in Polybius' life. Molin 2004: 50 n. 164 suggests, perhaps more plausibly, the campaigns of L. Mummius in 153 or L. Licinius Lucullus in 151.

[97] Supported by verbal echoes: cf. 38.2: πολυπραγμονοῦντες ἱστορήσωμεν, and 59.4: πολυπραγμονεῖν καὶ φιλομαθεῖν.

[98] Dubuisson 1985: 172–3.   [99] Thus, e.g., Walbank 1957: 373.

already featured milestones.[100] Whether or not the passage was added by Polybius himself is of secondary importance to the present argument. Even if it is a later addition, it gives us a rare glimpse of the effect which Polybius' enumeration of the distances of Hannibal's march had on an ancient reader: in the middle of his description of the distances covered by Hannibal on his invasion of Italy, Polybius' text conjures up the enduring (νῦν; perfect tenses) form of order imposed on the very same route by Roman power.[101]

Roads and the different kinds of texts that came with them should be seen as an integral part of the cumulative acquisition of Roman power that is, as I have argued in the previous section, typical of the third and second centuries BCE. Especially the roads built before the Gracchan reforms were clearly linked with military conquest, the protection of newly won territory, the establishment of *coloniae* and the resulting, fundamental changes to existing social, political and economic structures.[102] Anne Kolb aptly speaks of the 'road-oriented model' of Roman 'spatial assessment' and emphasises its links with the expansion of Roman influence and the 'consolidation and administrative pervasion of [their] global Empire'.[103] Her characterisation of the road system as developing 'piece by piece by incorporating and expanding existing connections, but also by establishing new routes' and as being 'designed to be directly connective' chimes particularly well with the representation of the expansion of Roman power in terms of newly established connections between Rome and other places within and outside of Italy outlined in the previous section.[104] The main textual representations of the road-building activity were building inscriptions, milestones and *itineraria*,[105] all of which, I suggest, are evoked as possible intertexts by Polybius' text. The famous Elogium from Polla, to begin with the first category, which is also the oldest preserved example of this kind of text, was set up at Forum Popillii (Polla) by (probably)

---

[100] Thus Molin 2004: 52 n. 170, with a useful overview of the debate. On *viae militares* as precursors to Roman roads see Nünnerich-Asmus 1993: 122–8, esp. 127 on the *via Heraclea*.
[101] This point has much profited from a conversation with Jonathan Prag.
[102] Cf. Hinrichs 1967: 165, with a list of the ten roads built before 133 BCE on 164–5. Laurence 1999 offers a full-scale discussion of road building and its relation to the expansion of Roman power; also Nünnerich-Asmus 1993; Purcell 2002. On milestones, Schneider 1935 remains excellent; Kolb 2016: 232–5 for a more recent discussion.
[103] Kolb 2016: 223–4; cf. 228: 'The creation of the great state roads ... largely reflects the progress of Roman expansion.'
[104] Kolb 2016: 229 for the quotes. On power and landscape alteration see also König (this volume).
[105] Kolb 2016: 229.

P. Popillius Laenas, the consul of 132,[106] to 'presen[t] the space made accessible by the newly constructed road from Capua to Rhegium' in individual, consecutive segments.[107] The beginning of the inscription in particular shows some fascinating similarities to Polybius' text:

> [P. Popillius, son of Caius, consul] built a road from Rhegium to Capua and set up on that road all bridges, milestones and direction-posts.[108] From here [Forum Popillii] to Nuceria it is 51 miles, to Capua 84, to Muranum 74, to Cosentia 123, to Valentia 180, to Fretum, to [my?] statue, 231, to Regium 237. The sum total from Capua to Regium is 321 miles.

Polybius, it is true, gives the distances from one segment to the other, whereas Popillius gives the distances to each town from the same point of origin, Forum Popillii, first, via Nucera, to the road's starting point, Capua, and then south towards Rhegium.[109] But the principle underlying both texts is the same: the space traversed, or opened up,[110] by one 'leader' (for lack of a better word) has now become part of a larger (power) structure. The link between road building, connectivity and Roman power comes through even more strongly if we think of Popillius' *elogium* (and Polybius' text) in conjunction with the other typically Roman marker of space, the milestone.[111] The distances and place names in the first part of Popillius' inscription recall the design of milestones which typically combine the information about distances with the name or title of the magistrate responsible for the construction of this part of the road.[112] Milestones reconfigured perceptions of space by linking individual places along the road with the nearest regional centre or with both the nearest regional centre and Rome.[113] In that respect they are similar to written

---

[106] Since the beginning of the inscription is missing, the identity of the speaker is a matter of debate; most scholars, however, agree on a second-century date. See Bernard, Damon and Grey 2014: 954 n. 2.
[107] Kolb 2016: 229. For the text see ILLRP 454; Bernard, Damon and Grey 2014, with particular reference to the representation of power; Purcell 2002: 19–20.
[108] For 'direction-posts' see OLD s.v. *tabellarius* 1. Degrassi (ILLRP 454 n. 3) suggests that these were stones subdividing each mile into *stades*. Cf. Bernards, Damon and Grey 2014: 970.
[109] Bernards, Damon and Grey 2014: 871.
[110] Note the emphasis on *primus* in the *elogium*; cf. Bernard, Damon and Grey 2014: 964. It is worth mentioning that there was a tradition, rejected by Polybius (3.48.5–7) but accepted by Nepos (*Hannibal* 3.4), that Hannibal was the first human (after Heracles) to have crossed the Alps with an army and that he rendered the region accessible for the first time (*loca patefecit, itinera muniit*). On ancient attitudes towards alterations of landscape to render places accessible see König (this volume).
[111] Cf. Kolb 2016: 234 on milestones as 'symbols of rule'.
[112] ILLRP 448–66 for numerous examples.
[113] E.g., ILLRP 450, a milestone set up by M. Aemilius Lepidus (consul 187), gives distances to both Bologna and Rome. For an even closer parallel to Popillius' text cf. ILLRP 452, which names the

itineraries which likewise provided 'lists of routes and distances' used by private travellers but also Roman generals when planning their campaigns.[114]

Awareness of the association of Polybius' chapter with the latter kind of text in particular is already implied in Walbank's remark that 'The measurements ... seem to have been taken from coastal journeys, recorded distances along roads and the like', as well as Katherine Clarke's comment that Polybius 'displays the kind of knowledge that might have come from generals' reports or itinerary maps'.[115] Neither of them, however, explored these connections further. On the basis of the above discussion, we can see that Polybius' text, just like his image of the *oikoumene* as a body, resonates with contemporary discourses of Roman power and its representation. Works of historians before Polybius did, of course, feature enumerations of numbers and distances; but Polybius' text, I would argue, takes on particular significance in its Roman context, which so overtly links measuring space with the expansion of power. On the Greek side, the most prominent model, as pointed out above, is probably Alexander the Great, but the link between measuring, ordering and controlling space was much more pervasive in contemporary Roman culture, represented, as it was, on buildings, milestones and itineraries, rather than only in the records of specialists appointed by the Macedonian king. Intentionally or not, Polybius' text becomes a nodal point in which narratives of Hannibal's march, Alexander's campaigns and Roman discourses of measuring and controlling space intersect.

The geographical 'digression' (if we still wish to use that term) thus brings out the full complexity of Hannibal's march before Polybius even embarks on his detailed narrative of it: its link with the expansion of Carthaginian power over large parts of the inhabited world and its potential for Hannibal to become a new Alexander of the West who will bring two out of the three μέρη of the *oikoumene* under the control of one single superpower. More than any explicit authorial statement, the distances make palpable the enormous scale of Hannibal's march, and the extent of Carthaginian power of which it is just the latest stage, as well as the threat which it poses. Or, rather, posed: the link with Roman road building precisely along the route of Hannibal's march – present in the

---

starting and end point of the stretch of road constructed by the consul responsible, the total distance of that stretch and the distance from the milestone to Cremona. On milestones 'accentuat[ing] ... supra-regional connections' with (usually) Rome, see Kolb 2016: 235.
[114] Kolb 2016: 235–7 (the quote at 235), with further literature.
[115] Walbank 1972: 128; Clarke 1999: 108.

transmitted text through the possible interpolation but inherent in the list of distances anyway due to similarities with representations of Roman rule and 'order' through building inscriptions, itineraries and milestones – reminds readers that Hannibal's march ultimately resulted in the expansion and stabilisation of Roman power in Iberia and, eventually, *Libye*.

It has in any case, I hope, become clear that the 'digression' plays an important part in the textual representation of the *symploke*, while furthering our understanding of how Polybius envisaged that process. It showcases the spatial dimension of the 'entanglement' of the different 'limbs' of the *oikoumene* through concrete, large-scale movements 'on the ground'. Moreover, just like his image of the *oikoumene* as body, which, as I argued in the previous part of this chapter, foreshadows imperial ideas of the *corpus inperii*, Polybius' 'digression', and his chapter on the distances in particular, participates in larger discourses of the conceptualisation and representation of Roman power that will come to full fruition only in imperial texts such as the Tiberian *Tabulae Dolabellae* and the *Stadiasmos* monument in Lycia erected under Claudius.[116]

Conclusions

This chapter argues for the need to read Polybius within broader political, cultural and literary discourses, Greek as well as Roman, and to go beyond traditional approaches that focus on (alleged) direct influences (or lack thereof) of other texts on Polybius or of Polybius on other texts. Those discourses, moreover, are represented in a broad range of different kinds of texts, including literary texts and inscriptions but also building programmes and the urban spaces created by them; all of them ought to be considered appropriate 'dialogue partners' for our explorations of Polybius' narrative. Polybius' use of the body metaphor is a case in point. Polybius creatively draws on, and develops further, the use of the body in classical philosophy and oratory by combining its political with literary-critical uses. In so doing he introduces the idea of an 'organic' (Osborne) interrelation of different limbs as crucial to the living body – Polybius calls this *energeia* – into the political metaphor, thus foreshadowing the metaphor of the *corpus inperii* as found in Ovid and later imperial literature. This innovation is prompted by the need to adapt a pre-existing metaphor to the new realities of the world under Roman rule. This makes Polybius the first author, that we know of, to use the body metaphor to conceptualise

[116] Kolb 2016: 230.

the effect of Roman power on the structure and order of the inhabited world. In fact, the very core of Polybius' metaphor, the emphasis on the body's 'organic' unity, its *energeia*, is, I have argued, rooted in the material reality of the nature of the expansion of Roman power and its representation in Rome's cityscape in the middle Republic. A Greek's intellectual engagement with Rome here leads to a significant development of pre-existing modes of thinking and literary expression.

A similar association of Polybius' text with expressions of Roman power is evoked by Polybius' geographical 'digression', and the chapter on the distances of Hannibal's march in particular, that programmatically sets Hannibal's march, I have argued, into a 'global' perspective. The 'digression' fulfils the important narrative function of emphasising the role of movement as part of the *symploke*: it represents Hannibal's march as the last stage of a long-standing process of the expansion of Carthaginian power which – should Hannibal be successful – is about to stretch over two of the *oikoumene*'s three parts from the 'Altars of Philaenus' to the very heart of Italy and, potentially, beyond. Evoking *periploi* and the *Stathmoi* of Alexander's march, the distances prompt readers to contemplate the enormous scale – geographically as well as militarily and politically – of Hannibal's march and ponder its consequences. This counterfactual reading of the march is offset by the intertextual link with typically Roman textual (milestones, building inscriptions) and material representations of power, especially road building, including the Roman road that covers Hannibal's route at the end of the second century BCE: ultimately, and paradoxically, Hannibal's invasion made *Libye* and the western parts of *Europe* part of the Roman, rather than the Carthaginian, empire. Read in conjunction with the body metaphor, however, the 'digression' reveals its crucial function to Polybius' narrative of the *symploke* and the central role played by movement 'on the ground' in that process, as it is the Carthaginians' movement from the 'Altars of Philaenus' into Italy, from *Libye* to *Europe*, that relates two 'parts' of the *oikoumene*'s body with each other. The movement of Hannibal's troops enacts the *energeia* which endows the inhabited world under Roman rule with the new, 'organic' unity that Polybius' body metaphor is designed to illustrate.

CHAPTER 2

Pyrenaean Mountains and Deep-Valleyed Alps
Geography and Empire in the Garland of Philip

Thomas A. Schmitz

In recent years, the term 'spatial turn' has been used in numerous disciplines to describe a renewed attention to space and geography. Many theoretical approaches have begun to promote a new awareness for space as a defining factor of history and of human configurations of the world. Some of the most prominent influences are the French Marxist thinker Henri Lefebvre, the *Annales* school, in particular Fernand Braudel, and postcolonial deconstructions of the binary opposition 'centre/periphery'. The availability of massive amounts of geographical data (for example through geo-tagging) and new methods of making use of this 'big data' have helped develop this new paradigm.[1] Despite the fact that we do not have the same depth of geographical data for the ancient world, many classicists have successfully adapted these new models to our discipline.[2] As is to be expected, periods during which the spatial configuration of the ancient world changed dramatically are the most promising subjects of research. The conquests of Alexander the Great and the Hellenistic globalisation are as prominent in this area of modern scholarship[3] as is the spatial consolidation of the ancient world in the Roman empire. This spatial turn has triggered new interest in the attention to space in a number of ancient writers (such as historians, but also poets and philosophers)[4] and in ancient geographers and travel writers such as Strabo, Dionysius Periegetes, Pausanias, or Pomponius Mela.

This contribution will focus on space in Greek poetic texts of the late Hellenistic and early imperial period; in particular, it will attempt to provide some insights into the ways in which these short poems navigate

---

[1] For examples of these new trends, see the contributions in Warf and Arias 2009 and in Bodenhamer, Corrigan and Harris 2010.
[2] Again, I quote collected volumes as examples: Adams and Laurence 2001, Raaflaub and Talbert 2010; Geus and Rathmann 2013, Schmidt-Hofner 2016.
[3] An excellent reading of 'Alexandrian' geography in Posidippus' epigrams can be found in Bing 2005.
[4] See, e.g., Hadjittofi 2010; Myers 2011.

(an apt metaphor) the tensions between local and global perspectives.[5] Before we can begin to analyse configurations of space in Greek epigram, a few methodological remarks and caveats about the difficulties of the material are in order. First, as I have already noted, the paucity of data points does not allow any meaningful statistical analysis. The epigram collections that will be studied here provide around 200 mentions of geographic entities, and these are rarely straightforward references, but often connected with mythical, poetical, historical and political traditions. A quantitative approach thus seems less useful than a close analysis of the ways in which these geographical names are being used.

Moreover, the nature of the collections of epigrams that I will be studying presents serious problems. One aspect of these difficulties is the complex manuscript transmission of the texts and the confusing arrangement of poems in our manuscripts.[6] More importantly, we often lack contextual information about the writers of these short poems. This contribution will focus on epigrams in the *Garland* (Στέφανος) of Philip of Thessalonica, a collection that was probably put together under Nero, in the middle of the first century CE.[7] While Meleager, in his *Garland*, produced between 90 and 80 BCE, tried to collect a representative sample of epigrammatists active before his time, Philip's collection picks up where Meleager had stopped, integrating poets active between the beginning of the first century BCE and his own time, as Philip emphasises in the introductory poem (*Anth. Pal.* 4.2.5–6 = Philip i 2632–3 Gow and Page):[8]

  ἀντανέπλεξα
τοῖς Μελεαγρείοις ὡς ἴκελον στεφάνοις.
ἀλλὰ παλαιοτέρων εἰδὼς κλέος, ἐσθλὲ Κάμιλλε,
γνῶθι καὶ ὁπλοτέρων τὴν ὀλιγοστιχίην.

I in my turn have woven a garland like Meleager's. You know the fame of older poets, noble Camillus; learn also the brief poems of later men.

Since (most of) the poems in Philip's *Garland* can thus be dated to the period between 100 BCE and 60 CE, they should provide a good starting point for analysing their writers' view of space in a rapidly changing world:

---

[5] See Introduction, pp. 31–3.
[6] Cameron 1993 provides an in-depth study of the difficult material; cf. most recently F. Cairns 2016: 28–30.
[7] On the date of Philip's collection, see Cameron 1993: 56–65, Argentieri 2007: 158–9.
[8] Text and translation of epigrams is quoted from Gow and Page 1968. Where I give page numbers in quotations of their edition, they refer to the commentary in the second volume.

this is the period that taught people in mainland Greece and the Greek east that the Romans were here to stay, that the Greek world was now part of a new empire.⁹ As his poems show, Philip himself was probably active at the imperial court in Rome;¹⁰ he was thus in direct contact with Roman power. The poems collected in his *Garland* thus provide direct testimony of Greek intellectuals and their changing geopolitical outlook.

However, a major problem is our lack of precise knowledge about individual epigrammatists. The tentative and rough dating within the period 100 BCE–60 CE is often the only piece of information about individual texts and authors that we can assume; usually, we have no certainty about the geographical, historical, social, political or ethnic affiliations of writers; in some cases, we cannot even be certain whether the authors were Greeks or Romans writing Greek. The attribution of individual epigrams is notoriously unreliable;¹¹ there are numerous divergences in the manuscript transmission, and there appear to be quite a few poets who shared names. Manuscripts of the *Anthology* sometimes add geographical epithets to distinguish these homonyms, but again, these labels sometimes appear to be mere guesswork and are thus not reliable. Identifying epigrammatists with individuals known from other ancient sources is in most cases pure speculation.¹² This means that it will not be possible to trace any development within the period that the epigrams cover: it would be wonderful if we could see that, for example, attitudes towards Rome and the Romans change over time, but our evidence simply does not allow such conclusions; we have to take the entire *Garland* as a relatively undifferentiated text with several authors.

As it is important to understand the limitations of our knowledge, I will provide an example of a text that resists interpretation because of our lack of contextual information. Here is an epigram by Crinagoras on the city of Corinth and its new inhabitants (*Anth. Pal.* 9.284 = Crinagoras xxxvii 1981–6 Gow and Page):

> Οἴους ἀνθ' οἴων οἰκήτορας, ὦ ἐλεεινή,
>   εὗραο· φεῦ μεγάλης Ἑλλάδος ἀμμορίης·
> αὐτίκα καὶ †γαίη† χθαμαλωτέρη εἴθε, Κόρινθε,
>   κεῖσθαι καὶ Λιβυκῆς ψάμμου ἐρημοτέρη,

---

⁹ See Argentieri 2007: 164: 'The first [*Garland*] was composed in an eastern Mediterranean milieu where the Roman Republic was only one of many contestants in the struggle for supremacy; the second saw the light under the first dynasty of the Roman Empire.'
¹⁰ Several poets whose texts are collected in Philip's *Garland* had connections to the imperial court; cf. Cogitore 2010.
¹¹ See Cameron 1993: 369–76.   ¹² See Argentieri 2007: 160.

ἢ τοίοις διὰ πᾶσα παλιμπρήτοισι δοθεῖσα
θλίβειν ἀρχαίων ὀστέα Βακχιαδῶν.

O pitiable, what dwellers you have found for yourself, and in what others' place! Woe for the misery of great Hellas! O Corinth, I would have you lie more prostrate than ⟨ ⟩, more deserted than the sands of Libya, rather than be surrendered whole to such shop-soiled slaves, and vex the bones of the ancient Bacchiads.

Crinagoras is relatively well known;[13] we have some information about his career and a number of his epigrams. In this poem, he laments the current state of Corinth: it had better be 'more deserted than the sands of Libya' than be inhabited by 'such shop-soiled slaves'. How are we to interpret this text against the background of historical and political circumstances of Corinth in the first century BCE? After the Roman conquest of Greece, Corinth had been destroyed and depopulated in 146 BCE. In 44 BCE, Caesar resettled the city with Roman freedmen. Is Crinagoras' epigram then witness to what one might be tempted to call Greek national indignation against these new (Roman) settlers, who are described as being unworthy of Corinth's former glory? The text seems to suggest this reading. Gow and Page drily remark that such criticism of the new Corinth can be found in several epigrams, 'provided that [the poet] was not dependent on the favour of the Julian family'.[14] This, however, appears to be the case for Crinagoras: he had been on several embassies to Julius Caesar and was connected with Augustus. Gow and Page, after consideration, nevertheless accept that the 'indignation and contempt … reflect the universal emotion of the Greeks';[15] in a similar manner, Bowie calls the poem an 'emotional outburst'.[16] But is it believable that Crinagoras, who was active as a diplomatic envoy on behalf of his city, would forget all restraint and tact at the sight of a city? And do emotional outbursts come in the form of elegiac distichs? Scholars have proposed several solutions to this conundrum: Crinagoras is referring to a small group of inhabitants (rather than to the entire Roman population) who plundered tombs in Corinth to sell the artworks they found, as Strabo (8.6.23) relates.[17] Like all Mytilenaeans, he was a firm supporter of

---

[13] For Crinagoras and his diplomatic and poetical career, see the most recent studies in Bowie 2011 and Gandini 2015.
[14] Gow and Page 1968: 247.   [15] Gow and Page 1968: 247.
[16] Bowie 2011, 192. A similar interpretation is given by Gutzwiller 1998, 257 n. 60.
[17] This had been proposed by Bücheler 1883: 510–11.

Pompey; after Caesar's assassination, he saw an opportunity to vent his hatred against the tyrant by denigrating the city he had founded.[18] His lines demonstrate the condescending attitude of a Greek aristocrat towards Roman freedmen.[19] In the end, we must admit that we do not have enough information to decide the issue. When was the epigram composed? What exactly was Crinagoras' social and political background? How did his relationship with Caesar and Augustus evolve over time? How was the text circulated? Which audience did Crinagoras expect for his poem? How did attitudes towards Corinth change in the tumultuous years of the Roman civil wars? We have no definitive answers to these questions, hence our interpretation of Corinth as a place on the mental map of the Roman empire remains vague: the text may present it as a symbol of Greek humiliation and decadence, but the story may be much more complex than meets the eye.

With these reservations in mind, we will now look at the presentation of geographical data in the *Garland* of Philip. As we will see, the collection provides a fascinating snapshot of Greek attitudes to Rome and the Roman empire, even if we are unable to appreciate the fine distinctions between individual authors' political, historical and local affiliations. What we see here at work is a 'dialogue of texts' as the introduction to this volume defines it:[20] we do not have two individual authors or texts that interact via methods such as allusion or citation, but rather an engagement of individual epigrams with an overarching cultural text, the 'map of the known world' that several centuries of literature and science had drawn. The changing landscape of the late Hellenistic and early imperial eras created tensions between this traditional discourse and a reality that many writers experienced first-hand. Our analyses will show how this new mental map developed and how poets used traditional imagery and descriptions to come to terms with this new world.

From its very beginning, Greek civilisation was in contact with areas all around the Mediterranean. Even in the archaic period, Hesiod, who famously declared that he had never gone to sea except to take the ferry from Euboea to Chalcis (*Op.* 650–1), was the exception; travelling, long-distance trading, and colonial endeavours were part of everyday life for many Greeks. Hence, a fascination with extreme climates, bizarre animals, or the strange customs of faraway regions can be observed in all sorts of

---

[18] A suggestion made by Mommsen 1889: 980–1. For Mytilene's sympathy for Pompey, see Sherk 1963: 151–2.
[19] Meyer and Wirbelauer 2007: 333–4.   [20] Introduction, pp. 12–35.

cultural manifestations since the archaic period. The conquests of Alexander the Great and the establishment of a number of rather unstable states in the east by Alexander's generals brought further enlargements to the Greek view of the world. Seeing oneself as positioned in a vast world encompassing strange regions at a great geographical distance had been part of the Greek experience for many centuries when they became part of the Roman empire. Nevertheless, it became apparent that this new empire brought change, and this change is often reflected in geographical imagery. Here is an epigram that demonstrates this change when it looks at two ancient islands and their fortunes in recent times (*Anth. Pal.* 9.550 = Antipater xciv 603–8 Gow and Page):

> Κλεινὴν οὐκ ἀπόφημι, σὲ γὰρ προπάροιθεν ἔθηκαν
>   κλῄζεσθαι πτηνοί, Τῆνε, Βορηιάδαι.
> ἀλλὰ καὶ Ὀρτυγίην εἶχε κλέος, οὔνομα δ᾽ αὐτῆς
>   ἤρχετο Ῥιπαίων ἄχρις Ὑπερβορέων.
> νῦν δὲ σὺ μὲν ζώεις ἡ δ᾽ οὐκέτι. τίς κεν ἐώλπει
>   ὄψεσθαι Τήνου Δῆλον ἐρημοτέρην;

> Your fame I deny not; the winged sons of Boreas made you celebrated, Tenos, in bygone days. But Ortygia was famous too, and its name travelled as far as the Hyperboreans of Rhipae. And now you are alive, she lives no longer; who would have thought to see Delos more deserted than Tenos?

Tenos is a small island; its only claim to fame is the mythical narrative that the sons of Boreas were killed there by Hercules.[21] Neighbouring Delos, however, used to be famous in archaic and classical times both because of its connections with the myth of Apollo and because of its ritual and political significance. Both islands had suffered during the Mithridatic Wars, but while Tenos recovered after the end of the war, Delos remained depopulated, as Pausanias (8.33.2) tells us in the second century CE.[22] Both islands thus symbolise the radical changes that had taken place in the world. Numerous epigrams use similar geographical symbolism to refer to this new world order:[23] we find descriptions of the ruins of Mycenae (*Anth. Pal.* 9.101 = Alpheus ix 3560–5 Gow and Page), of Thebes (*Anth. Pal.* 9.250 = Honestus vi 2422–7 Gow and Page), or of Sardis (*Anth. Pal.* 9.423 = Bianor xvi 1731–8 Gow and Page).

---

[21] The story can be found in Apollonius Rhodius 1.1302–8 and already in Acusilaus 2 F 31 FGrH = Apollodorus, *Bibl.* 3.15.2.
[22] There are several epigrams lamenting the desertion of Delos: see Ypsilanti 2010.
[23] See Argentieri 2003: 186–7.

It is obvious that these descriptions present a pessimistic view of the fundamental change that the Roman conquest of the east had brought about: places that once were famous and flourishing lie in ruins now. Moreover, Antipater makes use of the topos of an upside-down world: famous Delos is so reduced in importance that it is now inferior even to tiny Tenos. In this context, it is interesting to see that Antipater uses a second geographical symbol to describe the fate that befell Delos: its fame used to reach the most remote parts of the inhabited world, represented by the Hyperboreans. The story that Delos was in contact with this mythical people, who live close to the no less mythical Rhipaean mountains, is related in Herodotus (4.33). Delos thus used to have connections to the ends of the world,[24] but is now reduced to its tiny island. It is thus atypical for a general tendency of the Roman empire: a number of Greek writers emphasise that Roman conquest had made the world more accessible and knowable; one example would be Polybius' description of his own period (4.40.2):[25]

> τοῦτο γὰρ ἴδιόν ἐστι τῶν νῦν καιρῶν, ἐν οἷς πάντων πλωτῶν καὶ πορευτῶν γεγονότων οὐκ ἂν ἔτι πρέπον εἴη ποιηταῖς καὶ μυθογράφοις χρῆσθαι μάρτυσι περὶ τῶν ἀγνοουμένων, ὅπερ οἱ πρὸ ἡμῶν πεποιήκασι περὶ τῶν πλείστων.

> For this is the characteristic of the present age, in which, all parts of the world being accessible by land or sea, it is no longer proper to cite the testimony of poets and mythographers regarding matters of which we are ignorant, as my predecessors have done on most subjects.

While for most inhabitants, the world had opened up, it had been reduced for Delos. In line 4 of the epigram, Antipater describes Delos' fame as 'travelling as far as the Hyperboreans of Rhipae'. While the form ἤρχετο derives from ἔρχομαι 'set out, walk,' one might wonder if Antipater wants to allude to the word ἀρχή:[26] Delos had an 'empire' that extended to the mythical boundaries of the earth, but is now confined to its immediate surrounding.

While Delos is thus a symbol of decline and decentering, other areas of the inhabited world became much more prominent for Greek writers. As is to be expected, this was most visible in the case of Italy. While the south of

---

[24] On the 'edges of the world', see Romm 1992.
[25] On this passage, see Clarke 1999: 95–6; and 312–13 for similar ideas in Strabo's work.
[26] There are around 125 occurrences of the form ἤρχετο in Greek texts until the second century CE; only 15 (12 per cent) derive from ἔρχομαι, and none of these examples occur in poetic texts. Antipater's readers thus were more likely to think of ἄρχω initially.

the peninsula and Sicily had been part of the Greek view of the world since the late archaic period, Italy as whole was a recent addition to the Greek perspective, and it presented a certain challenge to their way of seeing the world. Here is Strabo's analysis of Italy's place (6.4.1; tr. H. L. Jones):

> ἐν μέσῳ δὲ καὶ τῶν ἐθνῶν τῶν μεγίστων οὖσα καὶ τῆς Ἑλλάδος καὶ τῶν ἀρίστων τῆς Ἀσίας μερῶν τῷ μὲν κρατιστεύειν ἐν ἀρετῇ τε καὶ μεγέθει τὰ περιεστῶτα αὐτὴν πρὸς ἡγεμονίαν εὐφυῶς ἔχει, τῷ δ' ἐγγὺς εἶναι τὸ μετὰ ῥᾳστώνης ὑπουργεῖσθαι πεπόρισται.

> Since [Italy] lies intermediate between the largest races on the one hand, and Greece and the best parts of Asia on the other, it not only is naturally well-suited to hegemony, because it surpasses the countries that surround it both in valour of its people and in size, but also can easily avail itself of their services, because it is close to them.

Not only was Italy ruling a huge empire that encompassed most of the civilised world, it had also taken over the position at the centre of the world (ἐν μέσῳ) that had, in classical Greek thought, belonged to Greece.[27] How is this new world order reflected in epigrams? Another epigram by Crinagoras is a good example of the tensions surrounding Italy's place in the world (*Anth. Pal.* 9.559 = Crinagoras xxxii 1955–60 Gow and Page):

> Πλοῦς μοι ἐπ' Ἰταλίην ἐντύνεται· ἐς γὰρ ἑταίρους
>   στέλλομαι, ὧν ἤδη δηρὸν ἄπειμι χρόνον.
> διφέω δ' ἡγητῆρα περίπλοον, ὅς μ' ἐπὶ νήσους
>   Κυκλάδας ἀρχαίην τ' ἄξει ἐπὶ Σχερίην·
> σύν τί μοι ἀλλά, Μένιππε, λάβευ, φίλος, ἵστορα κύκλον
>   γράψας, ὦ πάσης ἴδρι γεωγραφίης.

> I am getting ready to sail to Italy. I am going to join my friends, from whom I have been away so long a time, and I am looking for a circumnavigator-guide to the island Cyclades and ancient Scheria. Now, Menippus, give me a little help, my friend, write me a scholarly Tour, my expert in all geography.

As for many Greeks in this period, travelling to Italy or even living there for an extended period of time had become a normal part of life for Crinagoras.[28] His epigram shows an interesting mixture of familiarity and disorientation: on the one hand, Crinagoras intends to go to Italy to

---

[27] See Clarke 1999: 186–7; Dueck 2000: 107–9.
[28] Bowie 2008: 233–4 is right to remind us that Crinagoras may have travelled to Italy on more occasions than his three embassies; it is thus futile to pinpoint the epigram to a certain date, as Gow and Page 1968: 243–4 attempt to do.

visit friends (whom he calls ἑταίρους, not ξένους), whom he has not seen in a long time (δηρὸν ... χρόνον); this implies that he had been to Italy before and that he had Roman connections. On the other hand, it is obvious that the perspective on Italy that the text adopts is from the outside. Crinagoras is travelling *to* Italy from his home,[29] and he asks his friend, the famous geographer Menippus of Pergamum, for a treatise to help him find his way: even if Italy is somewhat familiar, it is better to take a road map. Of course, this demand is tongue-in-cheek and more a token of friendship and honour for Menippus than a practical request. Nevertheless, we see that Crinagoras expects his readers to share his feeling that Italy is somehow foreign territory, not quite an integral part of the known (Greek) world.

Furthermore, Crinagoras uses two geographical names to signify his journey across the Mediterranean: the Cyclades, and the island Corcyra, which is here identified with the Homeric Scheria, home of the Phaeacians.[30] In the *Odyssey*, Scheria is located on the border between Odysseus' mythical adventures and his return to the real world. When Crinagoras uses the name to refer to Corcyra, he is, in a typically Hellenistic manner, playing with learned interpretations of Homer,[31] which had proposed this identification, but he can also be understood as hinting that he is leaving familiar reality, that he is, like Odysseus, crossing a boundary – only to find himself on the other side in the company of old friends he had not seen in a long time. The epigram is thus an excellent illustration of the Greek ambivalence about Italy's place in the civilised world.

It is not surprising that we find fewer traces of a similar Greek ambivalence about Italy's Roman inhabitants. Most of the poets represented in Philip's *Garland* were writing with an eye on Roman patrons, so we should expect them to be respectful or even deferential to Romans. One of the few instances in which ambivalence about Italians may be perceived is an epigram by Philodemus. In the first lines, the speaker of the poem describes in great detail a girl's perfect body and refined movements which

---

[29] As Bowie 2008: 234 remarks, the poem does not state that Crinagoras' journey began in Mytilene, but the Cyclades as the first step of his route make this assumption plausible, and even if precise references are absent, it is clear that he is travelling from a place 'here' within the Greek world to a place 'there' in Italy.
[30] For the identification, which goes back as far as Thucydides 1.25.4, cf. Garvie 1994: 19–20 (with further bibliography).
[31] See Sistakou 2007.

kindle his passion.³² The last distich delivers the punchline (*Anth. Pal.* 5.132.7–8 = Philodemus xii 3234–5 Gow and Page = *ep.* 12.7–8 Sider):

> εἰ δ' Ὀπικὴ καὶ Φλῶρα καὶ οὐκ ᾄδουσα τὰ Σαπφοῦς,
> καὶ Περσεὺς Ἰνδῆς ἠράσατ' Ἀνδρομέδης.

> What though she be an Oscan, and with a name like Flora unable to sing the verse of Sappho? Did not Perseus love Andromeda, though she was an Indian?

What exactly is implied in the ethnic attribute Ὀπική? In his edition of Philodemus, Sider insists that the word denotes 'neither "barbarous" … nor "Italian" in general, but "Oscan"'.³³ Flora is thus 'a local, uncultured, Campanian girl'. This is certainly right, yet the term has a number of associations and overtones that we should not dismiss. It occurs several times in Latin literature and can be ironically self-deprecating, as in this passage in Aulus Gellius (2.21.4):³⁴

> hic ego ad nostros iuuenes conuertor et 'quin,' inquam 'uos opici dicitis mihi, quare, quod ἅμαξαν Graeci uocant, nos septentriones uocamus?'

> Here I turn to my young companions and say, 'Why don't you *opici* tell me why what the Greeks call ἅμαξα, we call *septentriones*?'

Swain points out that the term has its origin as an ethnic, but was later 'used by Greeks to disparage Romans' and 'developed the sense of a Roman who failed to understand Greek'.³⁵ When Philodemus admires the beauty of a girl that is Ὀπική, his expression can be understood as a wink to fellow Greeks, as an allusion to this entire complex of regional and ethnic prejudice and emotion. This reading is supported by the last words of line 7, which contain a double entendre: if Flora is unable to sing Sappho's songs, this may, on the one hand, indicate that she does not speak Greek and is thus no *docta puella* like Catullus' *Lesbia*; on the other hand, it may also refer to the sexual practice of λεσβιάζειν, oral intercourse:³⁶ this particular service in Flora's repertoire may be less than satisfactory. The epigram thus presents a complex network of social, cultural, ethnic and linguistic references, which challenge the reader's own position in terms of ethnic and cultural identity.

---

³² An interesting, if somewhat speculative, comparison of Philodemus' epigram to a passage in a Qumran text can be found in Cohen 2010: 3–14.
³³ Sider 1997: 108, following Stella 1949: 263 and Gow and Page 1968: 382.
³⁴ Tr. Howley 2014: 177. ³⁵ Swain 2004: 38. See also Dubuisson 1983; Howley 2014: 176–7.
³⁶ On λεσβιάζειν/λεσβίζειν, see Henderson 1991: 183–4.

Of course, this somewhat unflattering depiction of an Italian girl is mitigated by aspects of ethnicity (as we have seen, Ὀπική originally denoted Oscans) and social class (the description of her body shows that she must be a prostitute). In general, depictions of Romans in the epigrams of Philip's *Garland* are accurate reflections of the power balance in the real world: many Greek poets seek protection and sponsorship from their Roman patrons; accordingly, members of the Roman elite are shown in a positive light – critical readers may call this attitude abject flattery. Out of a great number of examples that could be adduced, two will suffice. Antiphilus is a poet about whom we know next to nothing.[37] In one of his epigrams, he lets the island of Rhodes address its local deity, the sun (*Anth. Pal.* 9.178 = Antiphilus vi 815–20 Gow and Page):

Ὡς πάρος Ἀελίου, νῦν Καίσαρος ἁ Ῥόδος εἰμὶ
   νᾶσος, ἴσον δ' αὐχῶ φέγγος ἀπ' ἀμφοτέρων·
ἤδη σβεννυμέναν με νέα κατεφώτισεν ἀκτίς,
   Ἅλιε, καὶ παρὰ σὸν φέγγος ἔλαμψε Νέρων.
πῶς εἴπω, τίνι μᾶλλον ὀφείλομαι; ὃς μὲν ἔδειξεν
   ἐξ ἁλός, ὃς δ' ἤδη ῥύσατο δυομέναν.

I, Rhodes, once the Sun's island, am now Caesar's, and I boast of equal light from both. Just as my fire was dying, a new radiance illumined me: O Sun, surpassing your light, Nero shone forth. How shall I say to whom I owe the more? The one revealed me from the sea, the other rescued me just as I was sinking.

The poem describes the restoration of Rhodian liberties in 53 CE, when the future emperor Nero pleaded their cause in the senate.[38] The praise is extravagant: Nero is compared to and elevated above the god Helios, the mythical founder of Rhodes. Nero, the philhellenic emperor, is thus firmly depicted as part of the Greek world; this integration into Greek values would match Bowie's interpretation that Antiphilus probably wrote for Greek rather than Roman readers.[39] A similar development can be observed in an epigram by Crinagoras describing the triumphal return of M. Claudius Marcellus, the immensely popular nephew of Augustus, who was immortalised in Virgil's *Aeneid* (6.854–92). On arrival in Italy,

---

[37] See Müller 1935: 11–21.
[38] Müller 1935: 14–20 and Cameron 1993: 56–61 have decisively shown that the Νέρων in line 4 must be Nero, not Tiberius, as some scholars have assumed.
[39] Bowie 2008: 229.

Marcellus shaves his beard for the first time (*Anth. Pal.* 6.161 = Crinagoras x 1819–22 Gow and Page):[40]

> Ἑσπερίου Μάρκελλος ἀνερχόμενος πολέμοιο
> σκυλοφόρος κραναῆς τέλσα παρ' Ἰταλίης,
> ξανθὴν πρῶτον ἔκειρε γενειάδα· βούλετο πατρὶς
> οὕτως, καὶ πέμψαι παῖδα καὶ ἄνδρα λαβεῖν.

> Marcellus, returning trophy-laden from the western war to the bounds of craggy Italy, then first cut his flaxen beard. This was his fatherland's desire, to send him out a boy and take him back a man.

In Crinagoras' text, Italy receives the epithet κραναῆς ('craggy'). The word, used almost exclusively of Ithaca in the Homeric epics, is applied to a number of cities and places in post-Homeric poetry.[41] When Crinagoras calls Italy κραναῆς, he is thus inserting it into a familiar Greek landscape. Moreover, the spatial configuration of this epigram is worth exploring: when Marcellus returns from his western war, Italy becomes the centre of the text's perspective, seen against the backdrop of the immense Far West of the Roman empire (ἑσπερίου...πολέμοιο). In this perspective, Italy is the 'fatherland' (πατρίς). Even if the use of this term could be understood as an instance of embedded focalisation (it is Marcellus who sees his journey as a return to his fatherland),[42] Italy clearly is the emotional centre of the epigram. At least in this text, it is not perceived as foreign and 'other', but is considered a part of 'our' world; the reader is invited to adopt a Roman perspective.

It is not surprising that travelling was an important aspect of the new universe that Greeks found themselves inhabiting. This vast new world offered new opportunities, but it was also potentially threatening and dangerous. One topic in epigrams that is repeated in a number of variations is the tomb in a foreign land. Of course, it reflects a reality which must have been an everyday experience in the ancient world: sailors and soldiers, tradesmen and captives would often die and be buried far away from home;[43] hence, this is clearly a theme of literary epigram that derives from actual inscriptions, which mention this fact from the archaic period on.[44] The topic becomes more prominent in Hellenistic epigram, when

---

[40] Schmitzer 2008: 22 points out that the coincidence of the first shaving and of the triumphant return to Rome blends Greek and Roman elements.
[41] Homeric examples: *Il.* 3.201, *Od.* 1.247; Athens: Pind. *Ol.* 7.82; Delos: Pind. *Isth.* 1.3.
[42] This is certainly the case in *Anth. Pal.* 9.59.6 = Antipater xlvi 322 Gow and Page, where Rome is the 'fatherland' of Augustus' grandson.
[43] See Tacoma and Tybout 2016.   [44] See Meyer 2005: 206–8.

the world had opened up and travelling had become even more frequent than before.⁴⁵ In late Hellenistic book epigrams, the distance between home and exotic burial place becomes ever greater and thus signifies a yet bigger world in which people move all over the surface of the earth. In all these cases, the motif of death and burial far away from home is meant to arouse sympathy and pity.⁴⁶ Crinagoras writes this epitaph for one Seleucus who is buried far from his native Lesbos (*Anth. Pal.* 7.376.3–6 = Crinagoras xvi 1855–8 Gow and Page):

> ἦν ὅδε καὶ μύθοισι καὶ ἤθεσι πάντα Σέλευκος
> ἄρτιος, ἀλλ' ἥβης βαιὸν ἐπαυρόμενος
> ὑστατίοις ἐν Ἴβηρσι, τόσον δίχα τηλόθι Λέσβου
> κεῖται ἀμετρήτων ξεῖνος ἐπ' αἰγιαλῶν.

> Here was Seleucus, perfect in all his words and ways; yet, enjoying youth's prime but a brief season, among the outermost Iberians he lies, sundered so far from Lesbos, a stranger on a distant⁴⁷ shore.

Gow and Page may be right in assuming that this Seleucus was a real person, a member of the Mytilenaean embassy who died en route to (or from) Tarragona in 26 or 25 BCE, and that this epigram was composed for a real inscription. When we examine the spatial configuration of these lines, we see that the eccentricity of the burial place is heavily emphasised: Seleucus lies ὑστατίοις ἐν Ἴβηρσι 'among the outermost Iberians', as far away from home as one can imagine; this enormous distance is emphasised by the somewhat redundant expression τόσον δίχα τηλόθι 'sundered so far'. The opposition between this huge distance and Seleucus' short life (βαιόν) is mirrored in the contrast between the 'immeasurable' (ἀμετρήτων) world and the tiny epigrammatic form that encompasses this boundless expanse.⁴⁸ Seleucus' epitaph is thus a perfect symbol of the dangers and the potential disorder entailed by the huge empire and its new horizons.

---

⁴⁵ See Tueller 2010: 51–4 on the increasing use of the term ξένος in Hellenistic epigrams.
⁴⁶ Cf. Gutzwiller 1998: 208–9 and F. Cairns 2016: 265–75 on the related topic of 'cenotaphic *epitymbia*'.
⁴⁷ Gow and Page translate 'untrodden'; their note (1968: 224) on ἀμετρήτων is not quite convincing: 'usually "immeasurable"; "unmeasured", implying "untrodden", seems more suitable here'. I am not quite certain why 'unmeasured' should imply 'untrodden'. Moreover, in epigram, the adjective is applied to the 'immense' sea (*Anth. Pal.* 9.34.1 = Antiphilus xxxii 979 Gow and Page; *Anth. Pal.* 9.362.4; cf. Pind. *Isth.* 1.37; Oppian, *Hal.* 1.179; Dionys. Per. 1171). Here, I would argue that it is transferred to the shore of the immense sea and thus signifies the great distance Seleucus has travelled.
⁴⁸ For this motif, see Elsner 2014: 162–3.

While the motif of 'death away from home' plays a role in the following text, it is outweighed by other thoughts. Crinagoras here describes a heroic Roman legionary who fights in Germany, is left for dead, but then gathers his remaining strength to recapture an eagle standard that had been taken by the enemies, before dying a noble death (*Anth. Pal.* 7.741 = Crinagoras xxi 1883–90 Gow and Page):[49]

Ὀθρυάδην, Σπάρτης τὸ μέγα κλέος, ἢ Κυνέγειρον
ναύμαχον ἢ πάντων ἔργα κάλει πολέμων·
Ἄρεος αἰχμητὴς Ἰταλὸς παρὰ χεύμασι Ῥήνου
κλινθεὶς ἐκ πολλῶν ἡμιθανὴς βελέων
αἰετὸν ἁρπασθέντα φίλου στρατοῦ ὡς ἴδ' ὑπ' ἐχθροῖς,
αὖτις ἀρηιφάτων ἄνθορεν ἐκ νεκύων·
κτείνας δ', ὅς σφ' ἐκόμιζεν, ἑοῖς ἀνεσώσατο ταγοῖς,
μοῦνος ἀήττητον δεξάμενος θάνατον.

Call Othryades to witness, Sparta's great glory, or Cynegeirus the sea-fighter, or the great deeds of any war: an Italian warrior of Ares lay by the Rhine's streams half-dead from many missiles; but when he saw the eagle snatched from his dear legion in the enemy's power, he leapt up once more from the bodies of the battle-slain, killed the man who was carrying it off, and returned it safe to his commanders. He alone got death without defeat.

The Roman soldier in this epigram is integrated into Greek cultural norms. The Spartan and Athenian heroes who serve as a comparison for his exploit are the very essence of Greek cultural identity: the story about Othryades, the sole Spartan survivor of the battle of Thyreae, is told in Herodotus (1.82);[50] Cynegeirus, the brother of the tragic poet Aeschylus, died in the battle of Marathon; both are stock themes in rhetorical exercises.[51] In addition, the Roman soldier receives the Homeric epithet Ἄρεος αἰχμητής 'warrior of Ares'.

These features can be described as an attempt to come to terms with a bigger world and to impose some sort of order on these unknown

---

[49] Bowie 2011: 192–4 discusses this epigram; I follow his textual suggestions in two places where he diverges from Gow and Page 1968: the river named in line 3 is probably the Rhine rather than the Nile, and for the first word in line 3, I follow Bowie in accepting the transmitted text, where Gow and Page adopt Scaliger's conjecture to introduce the name Arrius. My conclusions agree with the interpretation of this epigram in Meyer and Wirbelauer 2007: 334–6.

[50] The battle is a topic in several Hellenistic epigrams; see Fantuzzi and Hunter 2004: 314–16, F. Cairns 2016: 306–13.

[51] In the ironical catalogue at Lucian, *Rh.Pr.* 18, both are included in the list of hackneyed topics that a would-be orator has to treat in his speeches: 'Cap everything with references to Marathon and Cynegeirus, without which you cannot succeed at all. . . . let the inscription of Othryades be deciphered' (tr. A. M. Harmon).

territories. The Roman soldier may have fought in a barbarian country next to the Rhine, but he is depicted as 'one of us', as belonging to a Greek culture and a Greek world, not as some nameless barbarian dying in a cold Nordic country at the end of the earth. Greeks of the early Roman period found themselves part of a bigger universe and perceived this new situation as an intellectual challenge that they had to deal with. They had to come to terms with the fact that they now lived in a huge empire, which contained a number of places that were not anchored in Greek culture or that had been regarded as being located beyond the confines of the civilised world. They had to adjust to the many changes that even familiar places had undergone or were undergoing: they became depopulated like Delos or inhabited by unseemly new settlers like Corinth.

The strategies we have found in our epigrams can be described as a reduction of complexity: against the vastness of this new world, our poets employ a number of poetic and intellectual devices to impose order. They use the structure provided by their Greek *paideia* to appropriate geography and make this world their own, by integrating it into familiar mythical, historical, rhetorical or philosophical frameworks.[52] One further example of this use of literary culture to impose order on space is the use of geographical epithets that are added to names. We may speculate that this habit arose out of pragmatic necessity: given the relatively small number of common Greek names, given the growth of the population that considered itself Greek, it became necessary to distinguish which Philip or Diogenes or Aristides one was referring to, and geographical epithets thus became more and more common. However, in some cases, other mechanisms for these epithets appear to be more important. Here is a variation on a well-known topic, a fictitious epitaph for a famous

---

[52] For an example that shows an opposite strategy, cf. the careful geographical introduction in Polybius 3.36–8: in a lengthy and slow-moving excursus, the historian describes the place of Italy and Spain in the western Mediterranean. He emphasises that merely providing names is of no help to prospective readers: 'I am of the opinion that as regards known countries the mentions of names is of no small assistance in recalling them to our memory, but in the case of unknown lands such citation of names is of just as much value as if they were unintelligible and inarticulate sounds' (3.36.3: οἶμαι δ', ἐπὶ μὲν τῶν γνωριζομένων τόπων οὐ μικρὰ μεγάλα δὲ συμβάλλεσθαι πεποίηκε πρὸς ἀνάμνησιν ἡ τῶν ὀνομάτων παράθεσις· ἐπὶ δὲ τῶν ἀγνοουμένων εἰς τέλος ὁμοίαν ἔχει τὴν δύναμιν ἡ τῶν ὀνομάτων ἐξήγησις ταῖς ἀδιανοήτοις καὶ κρουσματικαῖς λέξεσι. tr. W. R. Paton). For Crinagoras and his readers, neither the Rhine nor (as we will see later) the Alps or the Pyrenees constitute 'unintelligible and inarticulate sounds'. For Polybius' view of the world as a structured body, see Wiater's contribution in this volume.

Greek poet, written by Laurea (*Anth. Pal.* 7.17 = Laurea ix 3909–16 Gow and Page):[53]

Αἰολικὸν παρὰ τύμβον ἰών, ξένε, μή με θανοῦσαν
τὰν Μιτυληναίαν ἔννεπ' ἀοιδοπόλον·
...
γνώσεαι, ὡς Ἀίδεω σκότον ἔκφυγον οὐδέ τις ἔσται
τῆς λυρικῆς Σαπφοῦς νώνυμος ἠέλιος.

> Passing by the Aeolian tomb, stranger, say not that I, the poetess of Mytilene, am dead ... You shall know that I escaped the darkness of Hades, and there shall never be a day that does not name Sappho the lyric poetess.

In this epigram, the name 'Sappho the lyric poet' would have sufficed; no Greek reader would need the 'Aeolian' tomb and the 'Mytilenaean' singer to identify her. But this reassuring use of geographical labels becomes stereotypical for a number of poets named in epigrams: Anacreon is Tean; Sophocles and Aristophanes are connected with Athens; Aeschylus is Athenian, yet lies buried 'far from his native Cecropia'.[54] One may speculate that this type of epigram is also connected with the establishment of literary canons[55] and the beginnings of literary history, for example in Callimachus' *Pinakes*, where identification and differentiation between namesakes became important. We may also wonder if such connections of Greek cities with their most famous classical intellectual figures cater to the expectations of Roman visitors who come to Greece looking for such connections.[56] What is certain: they provide a mnemonic device to establish a cultural map of the Greek world. Mytilene is more than a mere place name, it is the home of Sappho, connected with

---

[53] He may be identical with Cicero's freedman Tullius Laurea, who wrote a Latin epigram quoted in Pliny, *HN* 31.3.6–8.

[54] Anacreon: *Anth. Pal.* 9.239 = Crinagoras vii 1805 Gow and Page; Sophocles: *Anth. Pal.* 7.367 = Erucius xi 2262–6 Gow and Page; Aristophanes: *Anth. Pal.* 9.186 = Antipater ciii 653–4 Gow and Page; Aeschylus: *Anth. Pal.* 7.40 = Diodorus xiii 2166–7 Gow and Page, *Anth. Pal.* 7.39 = Antipater xiii 143 Gow and Page. On the numerous variations of such fictitious epitaphs for classical poets, see Bing 2008: 50–90, Gutzwiller 1998: 259–65.

[55] This interpretation seems apt for an epigram such as *Anth. Pal.* 9.26 = Antipater xix 175–84 Gow and Page, which provides a catalogue of nine female poets.

[56] To quote a prominent example: Cicero is obviously proud when he relates that he searched for Archimedes' grave, 'which was unknown to the Syracusans (as they totally denied its existence), and found it enclosed all round and covered with brambles and thickets; for I remembered certain doggerel lines inscribed, as I had heard, upon his tomb' (*Tusc.* 5.64; tr. J. E. King): he has more knowledge of local tradition than the locals themselves, and his literary knowledge of a verse inscription trumps the ignorance of the Syracusans.

mythical, cultural and historical traditions.⁵⁷ It is not only poets and philosophers who provide such cultural significance to geographical entities in the *Garland* of Philip; we find the same stereotypical connections for historical and mythical figures. To quote just a few examples: numerous epigrams are variations on an inscription for Themistocles' tomb in Magnesia or for Leonidas and his famous 300 Spartans who died at Thermopylae.⁵⁸ They rehearse the connection of cities with their mythical past, sometimes in the forms of long lists, such as this text by Honestus (*Anth. Pal.* 9.216 = Honestus iii 2408–13 Gow and Page):⁵⁹

> Ἁρμονίης ἱερὸν φήσεις γάμον· ἀλλ' ἀθέμιστος
>   Οἰδίποδος. λέξεις Ἀντιγόνην ὁσίην·
> ἀλλὰ κασίγνητοι μιαρώτατοι. ἄμβροτος Ἰνώ·
>   ἀλλ' Ἀθάμας τλήμων. τειχομελὴς κιθάρη·
> ἀλλ' αὐλὸς δύσμουσος. ἴδ', ὡς ἐκεράσσατο Θήβῃ
>   δαίμων, ἐσθλὰ κακοῖς δ' εἰς ἓν ἔμιξεν ἴσα.

> You may call the marriage of Harmonia holy; unlawful was that of Oedipus. You may call Antigone saintly; abominable were her brothers. Immortal was Ino; miserable was Athamas. The lyre was for song-built walls; the flute for ill-omened music. See how Fate has compounded good with evil for Thebes, mixing them equally into a single brew.

Such lists may very well be connected to the education system, providing easily memorisable chunks of knowledge. In terms of a cultural configuration of space, we can say that they populate the map of the earth with familiar names that trigger cultural associations; they bring order to the world. Similar observations could be made for other places such as Athens or Sparta: they are reduced to stereotypical connections and images so they become easily recognisable.⁶⁰ Such cultural associations can come in the form of refined allusions, as is the case in this poem by Euenus,⁶¹

---

⁵⁷ This 'material classicism' became more and more prominent in the second century CE; see Schmitz 2004: 92–3; Schmitz 2007.
⁵⁸ Themistocles: *Anth. Pal.* 7.236 = Antipater cxv 723–4 Gow and Page, *Anth. Pal.* 7.235 = Diodorus xi 2160–4 Gow and Page, *Anth. Pal.* 7.74 = Diodorus xiv 2170–4 Gow and Page, *Anth. Pal.* 7.73 = Geminus i 2342–7 Gow and Page, *Anth. Pal.* 7.237 = Alpheus vi 3542–7 Gow and Page; Thermopylae: *Anth. Pal.* 7.243 = Bassus ii 1591–6 Gow and Page, *Anth. Pal.* 7.279 = Bassus vii 1617–22 Gow and Page, *Anth. Pal.* 7.304 = Parmenion x 2604–7 Gow and Page.
⁵⁹ On Honestus, cf. Jones 2004: 93–5. For a similar list, cf. *Anth. Pal.* 9.253 = Philip xlv 2931–8 Gow and Page.
⁶⁰ For Athens, see *Anth. Plan.* 222 = Parmenion xv 2624–7 Gow and Page, and cf. J. Connolly's contribution in this volume; for Sparta, see *Anth. Pal.* 5.307 = Antiphilus xiii 861–4 Gow and Page, or cf. *Anth. Pal.* 9.58 = Antipater xci 583–90 on Ephesus.
⁶¹ On Euenus, see Geiger 2014a: 82–7.

which criticises a swallow for feeding upon a cicada, even though both are singers (*Anth. Pal.* 9.122.1–2 = Euenus v 2318–19 Gow and Page):

> Ἀτθὶ κόρα, μελίθρεπτε, λάλος λάλον ἁρπάξασα
> τέττιγα πτανοῖς δαῖτα φέρεις τέκεσιν . . .

> Attic maiden, honey-fed, you chirruper seize the chirruper cicada, and carry him to feed your wingless babies . . .

The text addresses a real swallow, an animal, not a mythical creature. Nonetheless, the first words call the animal 'Attic maiden' because of the myth of Philomela and the Thracian king Tereus. In this case, the connection between the swallow and Athens is not explained in the text and requires readers to activate their knowledge about the swallow's mythical story. In other cases, such connections become automatic and end up as rather worn-out clichés. A few examples will suffice: every dedication to Pan is inevitably made by an Arcadian; if an epigram mentions an archer, he must inevitably be Cretan.[62] Such stereotypes can again be read as attempts to convert a vast and confusing world into a tidier, well-ordered structure, in which place names are not simply geographical indications, but loaded with cultural significance: these people behave in expected ways and conform to the transmitted values of Greek culture. At the risk of sounding a bit too Hegelian in assuming a precise direction of historical development, this ideological, stereotyped landscape can be described as a precursor of the project that Pausanias will bring to perfection almost two centuries later, when we see all of Greece transformed into an ideal classical panorama.

For a better understanding of this process, we can refer to Pierre Nora's concept of *lieux de mémoire*. The term describes specific places or objects which come to embody collective memories that are pervaded with emotional values and are considered crucial for a group's social and political identity. Nora has expressed the function of such places as attempts 'to materialize the immaterial'.[63] Our epigrams allow us to witness this attempt; what we see is a transformation of geographical space into a culturally and historically meaningful landscape.

---

[62] Pan and the Arcadians: *Anth. Pal.* 6.109 = Antipater liv 363–72 Gow and Page, *Anth. Pal.* 9.261 = Erucius i 2200–5 Gow and Page; Cretan archers: *Anth. Pal.* 9.265 = Apollonides xix 1231–6 Gow and Page, *Anth. Pal.* 9.223 = Bianor vii 1675–82 Gow and Page.

[63] See Nora and Kritzman 1996–8; the quotation is from Nora's introduction, Vol. 1, 15. The French expression *lieux* provides a more tangible and immediate concept than the English translation 'realms,' hence I prefer to retain the original term. For an attempt to make use of the concept in Classics, see Jung 2006.

Thermopylae becomes forever enshrined as the memorial of the Greek fight for freedom; Xerxes' progress towards Greece as he sails over land and walks across the sea embodies human folly; Themistocles' tomb in Magnesia recalls both the Greeks' greatest historical achievement and the touchy subject of internal strife, which forced this great man into exile.[64] The following text is a good example of this use of geographical names that are loaded with emotional and cultural significance (*Anth. Pal.* 9.288 = Geminus ii 2348–53 Gow and Page):

> Οὗτος ὁ Κεκροπίδῃσι βαρὺς λίθος Ἄρεϊ κεῖμαι,
>   ξεῖνε, Φιλιππείης σύμβολον ἠνορέης,
> ὑβρίζων Μαραθῶνα καὶ ἀγχιάλου Σαλαμῖνος
>   ἔργα Μακηδονίης ἔγχεσι κεκλιμένα.
> ὄμνυε νῦν νέκυας, Δημόσθενες· αὐτὰρ ἔγωγε
>   καὶ ζωοῖς ἔσομαι καὶ φθιμένοισι βαρύς.

> Behold me, stranger, a stone grievous to the sons of Cecrops, dedicated to the War-god, symbol of Philip's valour; I am an insult to Marathon and the deeds of Salamis by the sea, that are humbled by the spear of Macedon. Swear now by your corpses, Demosthenes; yet I shall be grievous to your living and your dead.

The poem is a fictitious epigram for the Athenians who died in the battle of Chaeronea (338 BCE) where they were defeated by king Philip II of Macedon. When this imaginary stone proclaims that it is 'an insult to Marathon and Salamis', the symbolic and emotional associations of these names are obvious: they are not mere geographical references, but indeed *lieux de mémoire*. If the poet Geminus is indeed to be identified with the Roman politician C. Terentius Tullius Geminus, cos. suff. 46 CE and thereafter *legatus* of Moesia,[65] one could even read this epigram as a piece of Roman propaganda (if one wants to use this somewhat anachronistic expression).[66] The Romans had tried to depict their conquest of Greece as a liberation of Greek cities from the brutal Macedonian oppression. Hence, when a Roman poet, writing in Greek, reminds his presumably Greek readers of the shame of Chaeronea, which stands in stark contrast to the places of their greatest successes in their fight for freedom, this can be

---

[64] Thermopylae and Themistocles: above, p. 85; Xerxes: *Anth. Pal.* 9.708 = Philip lvii 3015–16 Gow and Page.
[65] Gow and Page 1968: 295 find the identification 'quite likely'; Bowie 2008: 248 agrees.
[66] The term 'propaganda' is used in Walsh 1996. The clearest formulation of the idea can be found in Plutarch's *Life of Titus Flamininus* 5.6: 'the Romans were come to wage war, not upon the Greeks, but upon the Macedonians in behalf of the Greeks' (tr. B. Perrin); cf. Touloumakos 1971: 23–5; Swain 1996: 148–9. See Meyer and Wirbelauer 2007: 329 on epigrams celebrating Flamininus.

read as a not so subtle reminder that Greece had indeed lost its freedom to the Macedonians and had regained it thanks to the Roman intervention. Geminus' epigram is thus an excellent example of the use of place names that are loaded with emotional significance, just as names such as Agincourt, Verdun or Dunkirk ring bells in Europe, even today, or names such as Lexington, Iwo Jima or Tonkin in the US.

Epigrams in Philip's *Garland* are also testimonies to a Roman effort to create a new *lieu de mémoire* at Actium. After his victory, Augustus founded the new city of Nicopolis; it was given territories from neighbouring towns while their inhabitants were persuaded or forced to move to the newly founded city.[67] In an anonymous epigram, the city itself speaks (*Anth. Pal.* 9.553 = Anonymous Epigrams iv 3512–17 Gow and Page):[68]

Λευκάδος ἀντί με Καῖσαρ ἰδ' Ἀμβρακίης ἐριβώλου
 Θυρρείου τε πέλειν ἀντί τ' Ἀνακτορίου
Ἄργεος Ἀμφιλόχου τε καὶ ὁππόσα ῥαίσατο κύκλῳ
 ἄστε' ἐπιθρῴσκων δουρομανὴς πόλεμος
εἵσατο Νικόπολιν θείην πόλιν, ἀντὶ δὲ νίκης
 Φοῖβος ἄναξ ταύτην δέχνυται Ἀκτιάδος.

To replace Leukas and fertile Ambracia and Thyrrheum and Anactorium and Amphilochian Argos and as many cities as spear-mad war leapt upon and shattered round about, Caesar founded me, Nicopolis, city divine; and lord Phoebus receives this in return for the victory at Actium.

The text depicts the changing landscape and the foundation of the new city in a glorious light: Nicopolis replaces old towns that had been shattered by war. The sanctuary of Apollo at Actium is an obvious point of contact for Greeks and Romans. But while Nicopolis as a city was a success story, Actium as a (Greek) *lieu de mémoire* did not quite take off, and we can speculate on the reasons for this failure: on the one hand, the Roman elite was never quite united in seeing Actium as a triumphant success (for many members of the senatorial elite, the battle still was an important step in the loss of Republican freedom, and the emperor Caligula was a grandson of Mark Antony); on the other hand, Actium held no real collective significance for Greeks – it had not been their battle (if Greeks fought in it, they mostly did so on the losing side).

I have argued that such *lieux de mémoire* are a way to transform a vast and bewildering universe into a coherent cultural landscape; the map of

---

[67] See Bowersock 1965: 93–4; Isager 2001.
[68] Cf. *Anth. Pal.* 6.236 = Philip ii 2642–7 Gow and Page, and *Anth. Pal.* 6.251 = Philip vii 2672–9 Gow and Page.

the world no longer presents huge unknown areas, but an ordered structure whose parts are connected with each other and with history and thus make sense to an educated viewer. Of course, there had always been geographical places in the Greek world that bore a political, social or cultural significance; suffice it to mention Delphi or Plataeae. However, most of these places were familiar or at least accessible and represented a physical reality for many Greeks. This imagined and significant landscape changes when the conquests of Alexander the Great open up a new world, and it is still in flux when the new reality of the Roman empire begins to stabilise. Greek culture under the Antonines will have its own classicising system of *lieux de mémoire*, built upon a selective memory of what is assumed to constitute the quintessence of Greek culture.[69] The epigrams we have studied show important (and not always successful) milestones on the way to this new memorial landscape. Their way of presenting the world can be compared to the late Hellenistic attitude towards landscape alteration analysed in Jason König's contribution to this volume: the landscape (physical and imaginary) is undergoing momentous changes, and Greek writers of this period are willing to see it from a perspective that welcomes these changes and makes them acceptable for their public. Greece and the eastern Mediterranean have not yet finalised their role in this new world order; there is still some ambivalence about a few of these changes. The dominant direction of these texts, however, appears to be towards an imperial view of the world where the reduction of complexity succeeds in transforming even extreme regions of the earth into parts of a harmonious, well-ordered body that is ruled by a rational, civilised power and can be encompassed by a single view from within the centre of this empire.[70]

A striking number of epigrams already display this view of an orderly, rational world that can be encompassed in a single glance. A few examples will illustrate this tendency: *Anth. Pal.* 9.58 = Antipater xci 583–90 Gow and Page gives a complete catalogue of the Seven Wonders of the World; each is set in its particular place, with a succinct description of its features. *Anth. Plan.* 61 = Crinagoras xxviii 1929–34 Gow and Page declares that both the Araxes and the Rhine are now drunk by peoples who are subjects to Rome, thanks to the invincible virtue of (probably) Tiberius. The two

---

[69] See Schmitz 2007; Borg 2011.
[70] For an excellent reading of Dionysius Periegetes as a text that imposes such an 'imperial' order on the world, see Jacob 1991; for the connection between empire and systematisation, see Murphy 2004 and Most 2011.

rivers represent the far East and the far North and allow the reader a view of the boundaries of the earth. But it is not only such lofty topics that display this 'imperial' perspective. In this epigram, Philip denounces a particularly bad wine (*Anth. Pal.* 9.561.1–6 = Philip lv 3001–6 Gow and Page):

Τίς σε πάγος δυσέρημος ἀνήλιος ἐξέθρεψεν
  Βορραίου Σκυθίης ἄμπελον ἀγριάδα
ἢ Κελτῶν νιφοβλῆτες ἀεὶ κρυμώδεες Ἄλπεις
  τῆς τε σιδηροτόκου βῶλος Ἰβηριάδος;
ἢ τοὺς ὀμφακόραγας ἐγείναο, τοὺς ἀπεπάντους
  βότρυας, οἳ στυφελὴν ἐξέχεον σταγόνα.

What desert sunless hill of northern Scythia reared you, a wild vine, or what snow-beaten ever-icy Celtic Alps, or clod of iron-bearing Iberia, you mother of these sour grapes, these unripened clusters that have poured forth their acrid juice?

Philip wonders in what extreme corner of the Roman empire this sour drink originated: in Scythia, or the Celtic Alps, or in Spain. The text presents a clear dichotomy of (named) periphery and (implied) centre; its perspective is again meant to embrace the entire Roman world: the reader understands that these outlandish place names circumscribe the Roman empire.[71]

I want to conclude this overview by examining two epigrams by Crinagoras that contain, in a particularly lively and clear manner, most of the elements we have seen so far. The first praises Augustus and mentions a trip to the Pyrenees that the emperor had taken (*Anth. Pal.* 9.419 = Crinagoras xxix 1935–40 Gow and Page):

Κἢν μυχὸν Ὀρκυναῖον ἢ ἐς πύματον Σολόεντα
  ἔλθῃ καὶ Λιβυκῶν κράσπεδον Ἑσπερίδων
Καῖσαρ ὁ πουλυσέβαστος, ἅμα κλέος εἶσιν ἐκείνῳ
  πάντῃ· Πυρήνης ὕδατα μαρτύρια·
οἷσι γὰρ οὐδὲ πέριξ δρυτόμοι ἀπεφαιδρύναντο
  λουτρὰ καὶ ἠπείρων ἔσσεται ἀμφοτέρων.

Though Caesar the Most August should journey to the depths of Hercynia's forest or outermost Soloeis and the fringe of the Libyan Hesperides, glory shall go with him everywhere. The waters of the Pyrenees are witness: in them not even the neighbouring wood-cutters washed, yet now they shall be baths for both continents.

---

[71] Cf. similar catalogues in *Anth. Pal.* 7.369 = Antipater xlix 337–42 Gow and Page ('both continents,' 'Athens' as well as 'the Nile,' are proud of the accomplishments of the orator Antipater) and *Anth. Pal.* 7.692 = Antipater cvii 675–80 Gow and Page (the wrestler Glycon was successful in Italy, in Hellas, and in Asia).

The text reminds us of plaques that can be found in many obscure places all over Europe, commemorating that some ruler or cultural hero once had a cup of tea in this house; the language is bombastic and the subject anticlimactic.[72] Yet the epigram is again a revealing example of the tendency to use geographical extremes to convey the idea of an ordered world. Augustus' travels to the remotest parts of the Empire are described in terms that convey a clear image of centre and periphery (μυχόν, 'depths'; πύματον, 'outermost'; or κράσπεδον, 'fringe'); the summarising πάντῃ ('everywhere') and the expression ἠπείρων ἀμφοτέρων ('both continents')[73] provide the all-encompassing imperial perspective. The term for Augustus' 'glory' is κλέος, a word that is often used to denote heroic poetry and can here be read as being self-referential: by naming West Africa, Germany and the Pyrenees, the epigram itself is 'travelling' to these locations that Augustus has visited or might visit;[74] κλέος in the form of this epigram is accompanying him. As the emperor's glory, Crinagoras' poetry has made the world its theatre, visiting, describing and thus ordering its farthest ends.

The last example we will examine provides the 'Pyrenaean mountains and deep-valleyed Alps' for the title of this contribution (*Anth. Pal.* 9.283 = Crinagoras xxvi 1917–22 Gow and Page):

> Οὔρεα Πυρηναῖα καὶ αἱ βαθυάγκεες Ἄλπεις,
>   αἵ Ῥήνου προχοὰς ἐγγὺς ἀποβλέπετε,
> μάρτυρες ἀκτίνων, Γερμανικὸς ἃς ἀνέτειλεν
>   ἀστράπτων Κελτοῖς πουλὺν ἐνυάλιον·
> οἱ δ' ἄρα δουπήθησαν ἀολλέες· εἶπε δ' Ἐνυὼ
>   Ἄρεϊ· 'Τοιαύταις χερσὶν ὀφειλόμεθα.'

> Pyrenean mountains and deep-valleyed Alps that face the Rhine's flood nearby, you bear witness to the rays that Germanicus made to dawn with lightnings of mighty battle against the Celts. They in their masses crashed to earth, and Enyo said to Ares: 'To such hands as these our services are due.'

---

[72] Gow and Page 1968, 240 drily remark: 'It is well that there are not many more such epigrams by Crinagoras.'

[73] It occurs also in *Anth. Pal.* 7.240.1 = Adaeus v 22 Gow and Page. Cf. also *Anth. Pal.* 6.235 = Thallus ii 3414–19, which addresses an (unidentified) emperor as 'great joy to the farthest West and East'.

[74] Gow and Page 1968: 240 are rightly sceptical whether Augustus has really visited the Hercynian Forest or Soloeis. Schmitzer 2008: 26–7 has some good remarks on the difference between Greek and Latin poets in the depiction of Augustus.

It is difficult to pinpoint the historical reality to which this poem seems to allude: we can neither identify this 'Germanicus' nor the battles which he may have fought in Germany and Gaul.[75] However, even in the absence of precise references, we see that Crinagoras again uses the strategies we have already analysed to conquer the new spaces of the Roman empire. At least in poetical language and imagination, this vast world has become a Greek world. Just as the Homeric Zeus witnesses the battles of the Trojan war from the heights of Olympus, the reader of this epigram has a commanding view of even the most peripheral and barbarian regions of the world. The Greek war gods may now 'be due' to Roman hands,[76] but the poetic voice of the epigram and its readers will feel proud that they can claim to have a share in this empire.

As I hope to have shown, the epigrams in Philip's *Garland*, despite the uncertainties surrounding their context, provide fascinating and valuable evidence of the ways in which Greek intellectuals came to terms with the new geographical configuration of the world produced by the Roman empire. My contribution can only be a first step towards further explorations of the exciting opportunities that this material opens up. One possible avenue for future research would be by way of comparison: on the one hand, one could compare these early Greek reactions to becoming part of the Roman world with the full-blown Greek Renaissance of the second and third centuries CE. My intuition would be that Greeks in this later period felt more secure in their own culture and heritage and saw less need to look towards Rome and the western part of the Empire, but this question needs to be examined more thoroughly.[77] Another important point of comparison would be Roman intellectuals writing (in Latin) during the same period.[78] A poet such as Ovid can claim: 'The land of other nations has a fixed boundary: the circuit of Rome is the circuit of the

---

[75] Gow and Page 1968: 234–6 give a thorough, but ultimately inconclusive account of the different attempts to find a historical context for the poem. It should also be noted that the poem is attributed to Bassus in part of the manuscript tradition; this is accepted by some scholars (such as Cichorius 1922: 307–9).

[76] The semantic value and syntactic structure of ὀφειλόμεθα in line 6 is unclear; Gow and Page 1968: 236 quote Latin paraphrases from older commentaries, but no parallels. The sense appears to be a vague 'be beholden to,' comparable to the use of ὀφείλομαι in *Anth. Pal.* 9.178.5 = Antiphilus vi 819 Gow and Page, quoted above, p. 79.

[77] For an attempt to analyse Philostratus' 'cultural geography,' see Kemezis 2011; for a tentative comparison of late Hellenistic and imperial Greek constructions of tradition, see Schmitz 2011a.

[78] By way of example, I refer readers to three recent studies of the configuration of space in Lucan's epic: Bexley 2009, Pogorzelski 2011, Myers 2011.

world.'⁷⁹ For Greeks, the situation was more complex. It is easy to imagine that for some of them, who lived as expatriates in Italy,⁸⁰ it would have been difficult to pinpoint the centre of their personal lives. As for the notion of a 'centre of the earth', it is interesting to contrast the accounts of Strabo and of Plutarch. When Strabo describes Delphi, he is quite cautious about its claim to be at this centre (3.9.6): 'it is almost in the centre of Greece taken as a whole, between the country inside the Isthmus and that outside it; and it was also believed to be in the centre of the inhabited world'.⁸¹ When Strabo goes on to tell the myth of the two eagles that met at Delphi, he explicitly calls it a 'fiction' (προσπλάσαντες). Plutarch, on the other hand, relates an event that places Delphi firmly at the centre of a *Roman* world (*De def. or.* 410a):

> a short time before the Pythian games, which were held when Callistratus was in office in our own day, it happened that two revered men coming from opposite ends of the inhabited earth met together at Delphi, Demetrius the grammarian journeying homeward from Britain to Tarsus, and Cleombrotus of Sparta, who had made excursions in Egypt and about the land of the Cave-dwellers, and had sailed beyond the Persian Gulf.⁸²

Again, more research is needed to elucidate these discussions about centre and periphery, with all the emotional and ideological connotations these terms carry.

Travelling the Roman empire via Philip's *Garland* can thus be seen as the first step in a long journey. As I hope to have shown, it is an entertaining and fascinating one and provides unusual insights into the way Greek intellectuals in the Roman empire perceived their world.

---

⁷⁹ *Fast.* 2.683–4: *gentibus est aliis tellus data limite certo:* | *Romanae spatium est urbis et orbis idem* (tr. J. G. Frazier).
⁸⁰ For an overview, see Hidber 2011.
⁸¹ Τῆς γὰρ Ἑλλάδος ἐν μέσῳ πώς ἐστι τῆς συμπάσης, τῆς τε ἐντὸς Ἰσθμοῦ καὶ τῆς ἐκτός, ἐνομίσθη δὲ καὶ τῆς οἰκουμένης; cf. Clarke 1999: 225.
⁸² Ὀλίγον δὲ πρὸ Πυθίων τῶν ἐπὶ Καλλιστράτου καθ' ἡμᾶς ἀπὸ τῶν ἐναντίων τῆς οἰκουμένης περάτων ἔτυχον ἄνδρες ἱεροὶ δύο συνδραμόντες εἰς Δελφούς, Δημήτριος μὲν ὁ γραμματικὸς ἐκ Βρεττανίας εἰς Ταρσὸν ἀνακομιζόμενος οἴκαδε, Κλεόμβροτος δ' ὁ Λακεδαιμόνιος, πολλὰ μὲν ἐν Αἰγύπτῳ καὶ περὶ τὴν Τρωγλοδυτικὴν πεπλανημένος, πόρρω δὲ τῆς Ἐρυθρᾶς θαλάσσης ἀναπεπλευκώς.

CHAPTER 3

Sailing the Sea, Sailing an Image
Periplus *and Mediality in Diodorus'* Bibliotheke
and Philostratus' Imagines

Mario Baumann

This chapter takes up the volume's key notion of 'dialogue' by comparing – and thus bringing into dialogue – two *periploi* from the late Hellenistic and the imperial period, the description of the Red Sea in Diodorus' *Bibliotheke* 3.38–48, from the mid-first century BCE, and the ecphrasis in Philostratus' *Imagines* 2.17, from the early third century CE, which is arranged as a sea voyage, with the speaker and his addressee passing through a group of islands.* With this topic, the chapter complements two important thematic and methodological strands of the volume: it can be read alongside Benjamin Gray's and Jason König's discussions of Diodorus, and it is closely related to the contributions which deal with representations of space, and in particular with travelling (Wiater) and the perception of landscape (König, Schmitz).

To these larger themes, the chapter adds the aspects of mediality and reader response. Focusing on the *periplus* in the *Bibliotheke* in the first section and on *Imagines* 2.17 in the second section, I will show that both texts use a similar ecphrastic technique but differ greatly as to their mediality: the *Bibliotheke* is characterised by a marked 'bookishness' whereas the *Imagines* creates a feigned orality. In the third section, I will turn to the reader's experience of the two *periploi* and contextualise the differences in mediality and reader response within broader trends and discourses: the *Bibliotheke*'s *periplus* situates itself in the contemporary discourse on the pleasures of reading historiography while *Imagines* 2.17 partakes in the trend of re-oralising literature in the imperial period.

Sailing through the Red Sea: Diodorus Siculus, *Bibliotheke* 3.38–48

The greater part of the third book of Diodorus' *Bibliotheke* is dedicated to the geography and ethnography of Ethiopia and the Red

---

* I would like to thank the editors of the volume and Calum Maciver for their helpful comments and suggestions.

Sea (3.1–48).¹ At the end of this section, the narrator gives an extended description of the Red Sea in the form of a *periplus* (Diod. Sic. 3.38–48).² He starts his account with a general overview of the topography of the 'Arabian Gulf' (the modern Red Sea), followed by an explanation of how he will arrange his *periplus* – in two movements, each from North to South, the narrator will describe first the African, then the Arabian side of the Red Sea (3.38.4–6):³

> ὁ δὲ προσαγορευόμενος Ἀράβιος κόλπος ἀνεστόμωται μὲν εἰς τὸν κατὰ μεσημβρίαν κείμενον ὠκεανόν, τῷ μήκει δ' ἐπὶ πολλοὺς πάνυ παρήκων σταδίους τὸν μυχὸν ἔχει περιοριζόμενον ταῖς ἐσχατιαῖς τῆς Ἀραβίας καὶ Τρωγλοδυτικῆς. εὖρος δὲ κατὰ μὲν τὸ στόμα καὶ τὸν μυχὸν ὑπάρχει περὶ ἑκκαίδεκα σταδίους, ἀπὸ δὲ Πανόρμου λιμένος πρὸς τὴν ἀντιπέραν ἤπειρον μακρᾶς νεὼς διωγμὸν ἡμερήσιον. τὸ δὲ μέγιστόν ἐστι διάστημα κατὰ τὸ Τύρκαιον ὄρος καὶ Μακαρίαν νῆσον πελαγίαν ὡς ἂν τῶν ἠπείρων οὐχ ὁρωμένων ἀπ' ἀλλήλων. ἀπὸ δὲ τούτου τὸ πλάτος ἀεὶ μᾶλλον συγκλείεται καὶ τὴν συναγωγὴν ἔχει μέχρι τοῦ στόματος. ὁ δὲ παράπλους αὐτοῦ κατὰ πολλοὺς τόπους ἔχει νήσους μακράς, στενοὺς μὲν διαδρόμους ἐχούσας, ῥοῦν δὲ πολὺν καὶ σφοδρόν. ἡ μὲν οὖν κεφαλαιώδης τοῦ κόλπου τούτου θέσις ὑπάρχει τοιαύτη. ἡμεῖς δ' ἀπὸ τῶν ἐσχάτων [τούτου] τοῦ μυχοῦ τόπων ἀρξάμενοι τὸν ἐφ' ἑκάτερα τὰ μέρη παράπλουν τῶν ἠπείρων καὶ τὰς ἀξιολογωτάτας κατ' αὐτὰς

---

¹ The main source for Diod. Sic. 3.1–48 is the fifth book of Agatharchides of Cnidus' *On the Red Sea*. Agatharchides' treatise itself is lost, but there is an excerpt of its first and fifth book in Photius' *Bibliotheke* which is extant and provides sufficient basis for identifying *On the Red Sea* as Diodorus' source and comparing both accounts. For a detailed analysis of the relationship of the two texts, see Bommelaer 1989: xxiii–xxxi and xlii–xlix; Hau 2018a. Bommelaer convincingly shows that Diodorus 'a su compléter sa source, la préciser, voire la rajeunir, et la développer' (xxx) and points out that his *Bibliotheke* is highly original in its 'sens du pittoresque' (xliii) and its 'expression de l'émotion' (xlv). For a detailed *Sachkommentar* on Agatharchides' treatise, see Woelk 1966 and Burstein 1989.

² An extract of Agatharchides' periplus of the Red Sea, which Diod. Sic. 3.38–48 is based on, is found in Photius, *cod.* 250, *p.* 456a33–460a7. Both Agatharchides and Diodorus use a textual macrostructure which emphasises the actual sailing through the Red Sea: having discussed the regions and peoples in the hinterland of the Red Sea in the previous chapters (cf. Diod. Sic. 3.15–37 and Photius, *cod.* 250, *p.* 449a11–456a32), they focus solely on the coasts of the Red Sea and their geography, ethnography and history. Strabo, on the other hand, quotes Artemidorus of Ephesus to inform his readers about the Red Sea and the neighbouring regions (16.4.5–20). While Artemidorus' account is thought to be based on Agatharchides' *On the Red Sea* (cf. Radt 2002–11: vol. VIII, 344–5), its structure is quite different: the *periplus* proper is interrupted several times to integrate detailed passages on the hinterland which seem to take centre stage. It is therefore no accident that Agatharchides/ Diodorus present a much more vivid account of what a sailor of the Red Sea sees and feels, thus creating what narratologists call 'experientiality' (cf. below in the third section of this chapter, esp. n. 31), while Artemidorus/ Strabo give a more 'neutral' description which highlights the topography as such rather than its perception by a passing seafarer.

³ Here as elsewhere in this chapter I quote Oldfather's translation of the *Bibliotheke*. Bommelaer 1989: xxix rightly points out that, 'quant à la description du golfe d'Arabie [i.e., Diod. Sic. 3.38.4–6], qui est sans équivalent chez Agatharchidès, elle ne ressemble en rien non plus à celles que l'on trouve chez Strabon (XVI, 2, 30 et XVI, 4, 2 et 4), dans des passages qui proviennent d'Ératosthène'.

ἰδιότητας διέξιμεν· πρῶτον δὲ ληψόμεθα τὸ δεξιὸν μέρος, οὗ τὴν παραλίαν τῶν Τρωγλοδυτῶν ἔθνη νέμεται μέχρι τῆς ἐρήμου.

But the Arabian Gulf, as it is called, opens into the ocean which lies to the south, and its innermost recess, which stretches over a distance of very many stades in length, is enclosed by the farthermost borders of Arabia and the Troglodyte country. Its width at the mouth and at the innermost recess is about sixteen stades, but from the harbour of Panormus to the opposite mainland is a day's run for a warship. And its greatest width is at the Tyrcaeus mountain and Macaria, an island out at sea, the mainlands there being out of sight of each other. But from this point the width steadily decreases more and more and continually tapers as far as the entrance. And as a man sails along the coast he comes in many places upon long islands with narrow passages between them, where the current rises full and strong. Such, then, is the setting, in general terms, of this gulf. But for our part, we shall make our beginning with the farthest regions of the innermost recess and then sail along its two sides past the mainlands, in connection with which we shall describe what is peculiar to them and most deserving of discussion; and first of all we shall take the right side, the coast of which is inhabited by tribes of the Troglodytes as far inland as the desert.

According to his own words, the narrator in his description will focus on τὰς ἀξιολογωτάτας ἰδιότητας, 'the peculiarities that are most worthy of mention'. What does he mean by that? A glance at the first proper section of his *periplus* shows that, first of all, he highlights geographical traits of the coastline which stand out because of their perceptible qualities (Diod. Sic. 3.39.1):

Ἀπὸ πόλεως τοίνυν Ἀρσινόης κομιζομένοις παρὰ τὴν δεξιὰν ἤπειρον ἐκπίπτει κατὰ πολλοὺς τόπους ἐκ πέτρας εἰς θάλατταν ὕδατα πολλά, πικρᾶς ἁλμυρίδος ἔχοντα γεῦσιν. παραδραμόντι δὲ τὰς πηγὰς ταύτας ὑπέρκειται μεγάλου πεδίου μιλτώδη χρόαν ἔχον ὄρος καὶ τὴν ὅρασιν τῶν ἐπὶ πλεῖον ἀτενιζόντων εἰς αὐτὸ λυμαινόμενον. ὑπὸ δὲ τὰς ἐσχατιὰς τῆς ὑπωρείας κεῖται λιμὴν σκολιὸν ἔχων τὸν εἴσπλουν, ἐπώνυμος Ἀφροδίτης.

In the course of the journey, then, from the city of Arsinoe along the right mainland, in many places numerous streams, which have a bitter salty taste, drop from the cliffs into the sea. And after a man has passed these waters, above a great plain there towers a mountain whose colour is like red ochre and blinds the sight of any who gaze steadfastly upon it for some time. Moreover, at the edge of the skirts of the mountain there lies a harbour, known as Aphrodite's Harbour, which has a winding entrance.

The one single feature of the streams that is mentioned is the bitter taste of their water, while the mountain literally stands out from the surrounding plain because of its specific colour. It is noteworthy that the narrator explicitly describes the strong sensual, even destructive effect of the mountain's visual appearance on the beholder: throughout the *periplus* the narrator points out the dangers of that region faced by the sailors and emphasises the impact of the Red Sea's ἰδιότητες ('peculiarities') on their senses.[4]

Moreover, the narrator often stresses that a traveller of the Red Sea encounters θαυμάσια, 'wonders'. An example is the topaz, a stone of wondrous colour quarried on the 'Snake Island' off the Egyptian coast (3.39.4–6):[5]

> παρακομισθέντι δὲ τοὺς τόπους τούτους κεῖται νῆσος πελαγία μὲν τῷ διαστήματι, τὸ δὲ μῆκος εἰς ὀγδοήκοντα σταδίους παρεκτείνουσα, καλουμένη δὲ Ὀφιώδης, ἣ τὸ μὲν παλαιὸν ὑπῆρχε πλήρης παντοδαπῶν καὶ φοβερῶν ἑρπετῶν, ἀφ' ὧν καὶ ταύτης ἔτυχε τῆς προσηγορίας, ἐν δὲ τοῖς μεταγενεστέροις χρόνοις ὑπὸ τῶν κατὰ τὴν Ἀλεξάνδρειαν βασιλέων οὕτως ἐξημερώθη φιλοτίμως ὥστε μηδὲν ἔτι κατ' αὐτὴν ὁρᾶσθαι τῶν προϋπαρξάντων ζῴων. οὐ παραλειπτέον δ' ἡμῖν οὐδὲ τὴν αἰτίαν τῆς περὶ τὴν ἡμέρωσιν φιλοτιμίας. εὑρίσκεται γὰρ ἐν τῇ νήσῳ ταύτῃ τὸ καλούμενον τοπάζιον, ὅπερ ἐστὶ λίθος διαφαινόμενος ἐπιτερπής, ὑάλῳ παρεμφερὴς καὶ θαυμαστὴν ἔγχρυσον πρόσοψιν παρεχόμενος. διόπερ ἀνεπίβατος τοῖς ἄλλοις τηρεῖται, θανατουμένου παντὸς τοῦ προσπλεύσαντος ὑπὸ τῶν καθεσταμένων ἐπ' αὐτῆς φυλάκων.

> And as a man coasts along these regions he comes to an island which lies at a distance out in the open sea and stretches for a length of eighty stades; the name of it is Ophiodes and it was formerly full of fearful serpents of every

---

[4] The most elaborate descriptions of dangers occur in Diod. Sic. 3.40.4–8 (sailors shipwrecked in a shallow spot of the Red Sea) and 3.44.4–5 (dangerous cliffs and currents frighten the passing seamen): cf. the detailed discussion in section three below. 3.46 gives the most detailed account of a sensual experience in Diodorus' *periplus* by evoking the exotic scents of 'Happy Arabia' (see Baumann 2020: 146–52). That this emphasis on sensual perception is a characteristic (and specific) trait of Diodorus' literary technique is shown by a comparison with Agatharchides' and Strabo's accounts. In Agatharchides' *periplus* as excerpted by Photius, there is either no equivalent passage (this is the case for 3.44.4–5, cf. Bommelaer 1989: xxvii–iii) or the respective descriptions are much shorter and/or less vivid (contrast 3.40.4–8 and 3.46 with Photius, *cod*. 250, *p*. 456b39–457a10 and 458a35–458b15; cf. Bommelaer 1989: xlvi). In Strabo 16.4.5 (cf. Diod. Sic. 3.39.1) no spectator is mentioned at all. Moreover, Diod. Sic. 3.40.4–8 (shipwreck description) has no equivalent in Strabo (cf. 16.4.7–8). In Strabo 16.4.18 (cf. Diod. Sic. 3.44.4–5) there is a passing reference to the danger of the cliffs, but no elaboration comparable to Diodorus' description. Likewise, Strabo 16.4.19 touches on the scents of 'Happy Arabia' without aiming to give a vivid description.

[5] Other conspicuous examples include 3.43.3 (the coast, divided by many large mountains, 'affords a marvellous spectacle (θαυμαστὴν θέαν) to those who sail past it'), 3.47.6–7 (marvellous wealth of the Sabaeans) and 3.48.1–4 (τὰ κατὰ τὸν οὐρανὸν ὁρώμενα παράδοξα ἐν τοῖς τόποις, 'the strange phenomena which are seen in the heavens in these regions'). The focus on θαυμάσια and παράδοξα is a characteristic trait of the *Bibliotheke*'s first pentad: cf. De Morais Mota 2010: 49–111; Trevisan 2010: 282–6; Baumann 2018; Baumann 2020: 25–114.

variety, which was in fact the reason why it received this name, but in later times the kings at Alexandria have laboured so diligently on the reclaiming of it that not one of the animals which were formerly there is any longer to be seen on the island. However, we should not pass over the reason why the kings showed diligence in the reclamation of the island. For there is found on it the topaz, as it is called, which is a pleasing transparent stone, similar to glass, and of a marvellous golden hue. Consequently no unauthorised person may set foot upon the island and it is closely guarded, every man who has approached it being put to death by the guards who are stationed there.

The description of that stone is part of a narrative which once again conveys a sense of danger, both of a historical and of a present kind: it once *was* dangerous to enter that island because of the many snakes; presently, the snakes have been removed, but approaching the island still *is* dangerous, even lethal, because of the guardians of the topaz. This episode shows that the narrator not only strives for a vivid depiction of what can actually be seen, but also aims to expose what could be seen in the past. By doing so he becomes an overt narrator who makes his presence felt: it is the narrating historian who informs the reader about the actions of the Ptolemies on the 'Snake Island' and about the reason for their efforts, and the presence of his voice is explicitly marked here by the self-referential ἡμεῖς, 'we' (3.39.5).[6]

In a similar vein, the narrator's presence is palpable when he gives *aitia* of the names of places,[7] explains why a place is worshipped,[8] or names the natural causes of visible phenomena, as he does at 3.40.2–3:

ἀπὸ δὲ τούτων τῶν μερῶν ἄρχεται συναγωγὴν λαμβάνειν ὁ κόλπος καὶ τὴν ἐπιστροφὴν ἐπὶ τὰ κατὰ τὴν Ἀραβίαν μέρη ποιεῖσθαι. καὶ τὴν φύσιν δὲ τῆς χώρας καὶ θαλάττης ἀλλοίαν εἶναι συμβέβηκε διὰ τὴν ἰδιότητα τῶν τόπων· ἥ τε γὰρ ἤπειρος ταπεινὴ καθορᾶται, μηδαμόθεν ἀναστήματος ὑπερκειμένου, ἥ τε θάλαττα τεναγώδης οὖσα τὸ βάθος οὐ πλεῖον

---

[6] οὐ παραλειπτέον δ' ἡμῖν οὐδὲ τὴν αἰτίαν τῆς περὶ τὴν ἡμέρωσιν φιλοτιμίας, 'However, *we* should not pass over the reason why the kings showed diligence in the reclamation of the island.' The narrating historian also gains some presence in the corresponding passage of Photius' excerpt of Agatharchides, but to a significantly lesser degree ([νῆσον] πρότερον μὲν γέμουσαν παντοίων ἑρπετῶν, ἐφ' ἡμῶν δὲ ἐλευθέραν τούτων, '[an island] once full of snakes of all kinds, but in *our* days free of them', Photius, *cod.* 250, *p.* 456b14). There is no self-referential 'we' in the equivalent section of Strabo's quotation of Artemidorus (16.4.6). Apart from that, the present danger to everyone who approaches the island is only mentioned by Diodorus. See Hau 2018b: 280–3, for an overview of the different forms of narratorial interventions in the *Bibliotheke*.

[7] Cf., e.g., 3.40.1 ('Harbour of Soteria') and 3.42.1 ('Poseideion').

[8] Cf. 3.42.3 (an oasis has been made a sacred place because it is the sole spot in a desert which provides food).

εὑρίσκεται τριῶν ὀργυιῶν, καὶ τῇ χρόᾳ παντελῶς ὑπάρχει χλωρά. τοῦτο δ' αὐτῇ φασι συμβαίνειν οὐ διὰ τὸ τὴν τῶν ὑγρῶν φύσιν εἶναι τοιαύτην, ἀλλὰ διὰ τὸ πλῆθος τοῦ διαφαινομένου καθ' ὕδατος μνίου καὶ φύκους.

From this region onwards the gulf begins to become contracted and to curve toward Arabia. And here it is found that the nature of the country and of the sea has altered by reason of the peculiar characteristic of the region; for the mainland appears to be low as seen from the sea, no elevation rising above it, and the sea, which runs to shoals, is found to have a depth of no more than three fathoms, while in colour it is altogether green. The reason for this is, they say, not because the water is naturally of that colour, but because of the mass of seaweed and tangle which shows from under water.

Thus, the narrator not only provides the reader with an ecphrastic *enargeia* of perceptible features, but also with interpretations of what can be seen or experienced by someone sailing past these coasts.[9]

From chapter 42, the narrator turns to the other, that is, the Arabian side of the Red Sea. Here, too, he combines vivid description with historical contextualisation, as is illustrated by 3.44.7–8:

μετὰ δὲ τούτους[10] ὁρᾶται χερρόνησος καὶ λιμὴν κάλλιστος τῶν εἰς ἱστορίαν πεπτωκότων, ὀνομαζόμενος Χαρμούθας. ὑπὸ γὰρ χηλὴν ἐξαίσιον κεκλιμένην πρὸς ζέφυρον κόλπος ἐστὶν οὐ μόνον κατὰ τὴν ἰδέαν θαυμαστός, ἀλλὰ καὶ κατὰ τὴν εὐχρηστίαν πολὺ τοὺς ἄλλους ὑπερέχων· παρήκει γὰρ αὐτὸν ὄρος συνηρεφές, κυκλούμενον πανταχόθεν ἐπὶ σταδίους ἑκατόν, εἴσπλουν δ' ἔχει δίπλεθρον, ναυσὶ δισχιλίαις ἄκλυστον λιμένα παρεχόμενος. χωρὶς δὲ τούτων εὔυδρός τ' ἐστὶ καθ' ὑπερβολήν, ποταμοῦ μείζονος εἰς αὐτὸν ἐμβάλλοντος, καὶ κατὰ μέσον ἔχει νῆσον εὔυδρον καὶ δυναμένην ἔχειν κηπεύματα. καθόλου δ' ἐμφερέστατός ἐστι τῷ κατὰ τὴν Καρχηδόνα λιμένι, προσαγορευομένῳ δὲ Κώθωνι, περὶ οὗ τὰς κατὰ μέρος εὐχρηστίας ἐν τοῖς οἰκείοις χρόνοις πειρασόμεθα διελθεῖν.

Beyond them a neck of land is to be seen and a harbour, the fairest of any which have come to be included in history, called Charmuthas. For behind an extraordinary natural breakwater which slants towards the west there lies a gulf which not only is marvellous in its form but far surpasses all others in the advantages it offers; for a thickly wooded mountain stretches along it, enclosing it on all sides in a ring one hundred stades long; its entrance is two plethra wide, and it provides a harbour undisturbed by the waves sufficient for two thousand vessels. Furthermore, it is exceptionally well supplied with water, since a river, larger than ordinary, empties into it, and it contains in its centre an island which is abundantly watered and capable of supporting

---

[9] For *enargeia* as defined by ancient rhetorical theory, see Lausberg 2008: §§810–18; Webb 2009: 87–106.
[10] *Scil.* the ἀέριοι θῖνες ἄμμου, the 'sand dunes' described in the preceding paragraph.

gardens. In general, it resembles most closely the harbour of Carthage, which is known as Cothon, of the advantages of which we shall endeavour to give a detailed discussion in connection with the appropriate time.

After describing the marvellous beauty and utility of Charmuthas, the narrator draws an explicit comparison between this place and Carthage.[11] In doing so, he employs a double strategy of contextualisation: first, he connects distant parts of the *oikoumene* and helps the reader to appreciate the qualities of Charmuthas by offering a point of reference. That reference is particularly helpful because Graeco-Roman readers have probably heard of the ports of Carthage, whereas Charmuthas might well be unknown to them. But even a reader who has no (or no significant) previous knowledge of 'Cothon' can profit from the second aspect of the narrator's strategy of contextualisation, namely from the cross-reference to a later part of the *Bibliotheke* at the very end of the quoted passage.[12] This reference enables, and motivates, the reader to look up the more detailed description of 'Cothon' in the *Bibliotheke*, thus turning the abstract link between two geographical places ('Charmuthas resembles Cothon') into a concrete, tangible connection of two passages in the *Bibliotheke* as a physical book. By explicitly naming and establishing such a connection, the *Bibliotheke* highlights its own 'bookishness', which is an important – and specific – aspect of the *Bibliotheke*'s self-referentiality and mediality as will become clear from the comparison with Philostratus' *Imagines*.[13]

---

[11] 3.44.8 is not the only instance of this technique in the *periplus*. Cf. 3.44.6 where the narrator compares some scattered islands off the Arabian coast to the so-called Echinades in the Ionian Sea (cf. Bommelaer 1989: 65 n. 2). Neither of these comparisons appears in Photius' excerpt of Agatharchides (cf. Bommelaer 1989: xxvii–xxviii) or in Strabo's quotation of Artemidorus (16.4.18).

[12] Due to the *Bibliotheke*'s fragmentary state we do not know for certain what passage the narrator refers to here, but it is at least probable that the detailed description of 'Cothon' was part of book 32 (cf. Rubincam 1989: 54–5).

[13] In her detailed analysis of cross-references in the *Bibliotheke*, Rubincam points out that Diodorus' technique of cross-referencing shows three specific traits which differ from what may tentatively be described as the 'standard' of ancient literature (Rubincam 1989: 46–51): (a) the high number of forward cross-references in the *Bibliotheke* (fifty-three of a total of ninety-five in the extant parts of the work); (b) the high degree of specificity, mainly by allusion to some obvious principle of organisation, i.e., by use of phrases like 'will be discussed at its proper time (ἐν τοῖς οἰκείοις χρόνοις)'; (c) the long distance across which many references carry (cf. the distance of twenty-nine books probably traversed by the forward reference of 3.44.8). All these traits contribute to a strategy of making full use of the *Bibliotheke*'s bookishness and of communicating the potentials of this mediality to the reader. See König in this volume on other forms of interlinking in the *Bibliotheke*, esp. by repeated motifs and repeated vocabulary. On the role of reading and the written word for the *Bibliotheke*'s educational and cosmopolitan ambitions, see Liddel 2018 and Gray in this volume. On the *Bibliotheke*'s didacticism in general, cf. Hau 2016: 73–123.

To sum up the observations made so far: the narrator of the *Bibliotheke* combines in his *periplus* of the Red Sea descriptive vividness with historical contextualisation and interpretation. He focuses in particular on the marvels and dangers experienced by the sailors in these regions. He presents himself as an overt narrator by explicitly referring to himself and his historiographical text whose 'bookishness' he strongly marks by connecting distant passages of the *Bibliotheke*. All this makes Diodorus Siculus 3.38–48 a striking example of the interlinking and intertwining of genres and discourses (in particular historiography, geography and paradoxography) which the editors of this volume emphasise as a characteristic feature of late Hellenistic literature.[14]

Sailing through an Image: Philostratus the Elder, *Imagines* 2.17

Turning now to the *Imagines* of the Elder Philostratus, I take the question of the narrator's overtness as the starting point for my discussion. In the *Imagines* the reader encounters a voice which is even more present than the *Bibliotheke*'s narrator. The *Imagines* consists of sixty-four descriptions of paintings, and all these ecphrases are presented as *impromptu* speeches given in front of the pictures. The speaker of the ecphrases introduces himself in the proem where he describes the context of his improvised performances: the paintings, he says, belong to a gallery near Naples, and his speeches are addressed to the young son of the owner of that gallery (*Imag*. pr. 4–5).[15] Throughout the *Imagines*, the speaker foregrounds this situation by directly addressing the boy. That is precisely what happens at the beginning of *Imagines* 2.17 – the longest description in the *Imagines* and the only one that takes the form of a *periplus* (2.17.1):[16]

> Βούλει, ὦ παῖ, καθάπερ ἀπὸ νεὼς διαλεγώμεθα περὶ τουτωνὶ τῶν νήσων, οἷον περιπλέοντες αὐτὰς τοῦ ἦρος, ὅτε Ζέφυρος ἱλαρὰν ἐργάζεται θάλατταν προσπνέων τῆς ἑαυτοῦ αὔρας; ἀλλ' ὅπως ἑκὼν λελήσῃ τῆς γῆς, καὶ θάλαττά σοι ταυτὶ δόξει μήτ' ἐξηρμένη καὶ ἀναχαιτίζουσα μήθ' ὑπτία καὶ γαληνή, πλωτὴ δέ τις καὶ οἷον ἔμπνους. ἰδοὺ ἐμβεβλήκαμεν· ξυγχωρεῖς γάρ που; καὶ ὑπὲρ τοῦ παιδὸς ἀποκρίνασθαι· "ξυγχωρῶ καὶ πλέωμεν". ἡ μὲν θάλαττα, ὡς ὁρᾷς, πολλή, νῆσοι δ' ἐν αὐτῇ μὰ Δί' οὐ

---

[14] Cf. the introduction to this volume.
[15] There is a broad consensus nowadays among scholars that the paintings as well as the performance context the *Imagines* refers to are fictional; cf. Bowie 1994; Webb 2006; Giuliani 2007; Baumann 2011: 103–5; Primavesi and Giuliani 2012: 45–8; Bachmann 2015: 49–52.
[16] Here as elsewhere in this chapter I quote Fairbanks' translation of the *Imagines*.

Λέσβος οὐδ' Ἴμβρος ἢ Λῆμνος, ἀλλ' ἀγελαῖαι καὶ μικραί, καθάπερ κῶμαί τινες ἢ σταθμοὶ ἢ νὴ Δία ἐπαύλια τῆς θαλάττης.

> Would you like, my boy, to have us discourse about those islands just as if from a ship, as though we were sailing in and out among them in the spring-time, when Zephyrus makes the sea glad by breathing his own breeze upon it? But you must be willing to forget the land and to accept this as the sea, not roused and turbulent nor yet flat and calm, but a sea fit for sailing and as it were alive and breathing. Lo, we have embarked; for no doubt you agree? Answer for the boy: 'I agree, let us go sailing.' You perceive that the sea is large, and the islands in it are not, by Zeus, Lesbos, nor yet Imbros or Lemnos, but small islands herding together like hamlets or cattle-folds or, by Zeus, like farm-buildings on the sea-shore.

The speaker not only addresses the boy, he explicitly negotiates with him. The basic communicative process of the *Imagines* is here foregrounded to such a degree that the text even includes the boy's own voice. Thus, the speaker's ecphrasis temporarily turns into a dialogue. Furthermore, the *periplus* here is not treated as a given, but as something the speaker and his primary addressee need to agree upon, as something that needs to be (and actually is) constructed – and this very constructedness is laid bare by the speaker. We find here, then, an overt and self-conscious speaker, but it is an overtness and self-referentiality that differs from the one displayed by the *Bibliotheke*'s narrator in his *periplus* of the Red Sea: there is no primary addressee distinct from the reader in the *Bibliotheke*, nor any direct dialogue in the *periplus* of the Red Sea, and the description from the perspective of a seafarer is not explicitly negotiated or openly shown to be constructed by the narrator; he simply 'gives' a periplus.

These differences go hand in hand with an apparent divergence in the mediality of both texts: the speaker of *Imagines* 2.17 describes a painting, that is, a visual representation of the sea and islands, whereas the *Bibliotheke*'s narrator 'directly' describes the shores of the Red Sea.[17] This means that in the case of *Imagines* 2.17 an ecphrasis in the form of a continuous *periplus* entails crossing the boundary between two media: the speaker, together with his primary addressee, enters the picture and, in this verbal performance, 'sails through' the image, as is shown by his

---

[17] The *Imagines* is, in other words, an *intermedial* text: cf. Squire 2009: 297–9 and 416–27. For a useful introduction to intermediality, see Rajewsky 2002: esp. 6–27 (definition of 'intermediality') and 155–80 (forms of intermediality).

introduction to the last island described in *Imagines* 2.17: ἐνταῦθα δέ, ὦ παῖ, καὶ καθώρμισται ἡμῖν, 'on this island, my boy, we have put ashore' (2.17.12). This ecphrasis, then, is based on a metalepsis, in other words 'a deliberate transgression between the world of the telling and the world of the told'.[18] And that metalepsis is closely tied to the dialogicity of *Imagines* 2.17: in fact, the negotiation that takes place at the beginning of the ecphrasis can aptly be described as laying out and discussing the conditions of the metaleptic 'jump' into the painting. By agreeing on these conditions, the speaker and his addressee enter what might be called a 'contract of metalepsis'.

As to their mediality, then, both descriptions show marked differences: whereas the *periplus* of the Red Sea partakes in and contributes to the 'bookishness' of the *Bibliotheke*, the island ecphrasis in the *Imagines* devises a feigned orality, even dialogicity. It is no accident that, contrary to the *Bibliotheke*, there are no explicit cross-references in the *Imagines*. In fact, there are not even any explicit transitions between the ecphrases: one description immediately follows the other, rendering the proem the only paratext in the entire work. Paratextuality is diminished in favour of emphasising the (fictional) immediacy of the speaker's *impromptu* performances.

On the other hand, *Imagines* 2.17 also exhibits features that are similar to the descriptive and interpretative technique of the *Bibliotheke*'s *periplus*, namely, a strategy of contextualisation. This strategy manifests itself already at the beginning of the ecphrasis, when the speaker distinguishes the depicted islands from Lesbos, Imbros and Lemnos. Another even more striking example occurs at 2.17.4 where the speaker turns to a pair of islands:[19]

> αἱ δ' ἐχόμεναι τούτων νῆσοι δύο μία μὲν ἄμφω ποτὲ ἦσαν, ῥαγεῖσα δὲ ὑπὸ τοῦ πελάγους μέση ποταμοῦ εὖρος ἑαυτῆς ἀπηνέχθη. τουτὶ δ' ἔστι σοι καὶ παρὰ τῆς γραφῆς, ὦ παῖ, γινώσκειν· τὰ γὰρ ἐσχισμένα τῆς νήσου παραπλήσιά που ὁρᾷς καὶ ἀλλήλοις ξύμμετρα καὶ οἷα ἐναρμόσαι κοῖλα ἐκκειμένοις. τοῦτο καὶ ἡ Εὐρώπη ποτὲ περὶ τὰ Τέμπη τὰ Θετταλικὰ ἔπαθε· σεισμοὶ γὰρ κἀκείνην ἀναπτύξαντες τὴν ἁρμονίαν τῶν ὀρῶν ἐναπεσημήναντο τοῖς τμήμασι, καὶ πετρῶν τε οἶκοι φανεροὶ ἔτι

---

[18] Pier 2016: no. 1. The term 'metalepsis' was coined as a narratological category by Gérard Genette, cf. Genette 1972: 243–5 and Genette 2004. Its analytic value is not limited to genres or media that are strictly narrative, but extends to transmedial phenomena in a broader sense as Wolf 2005 has shown. For a detailed discussion of metalepsis in Philostratus' *Imagines*, see Baumann 2013: 258–70; cf. also Grethlein 2020: 25–31.

[19] See Robiano 2018: 509–11 for the recurring motif of the bridge which connects *Imag.* 2.17.4 and 1.9.5 and similar links between 2.17 and the other *tableaux de paysage* in the *Imagines*.

παραπλήσιοι ταῖς ἐξηρμοσμέναις σφῶν πέτραις, ὕλη θ', ὁπόσην σχισθέντων τῶν ὀρῶν ἐπισπέσθαι εἰκός, οὔπω ἄδηλος· λείπονται γὰρ δὴ ἔτι αἱ εὐναὶ τῶν δένδρων. τὸ μὲν δὴ τῆς νήσου πάθος τοιοῦτον ἡγώμεθα, ζεῦγμα δὲ ὑπὲρ τοῦ πορθμοῦ βέβληται, ὡς μίαν ὑπ' αὐτοῦ φαίνεσθαι, καὶ τὸ μὲν ὑποπλεῖται τοῦ ζεύγματος, τὸ δὲ ἁμαξεύεται· ὁρᾷς γάρ που τοὺς διαφοιτῶντας αὐτό, ὡς ὁδοιπόροι τέ εἰσι καὶ ναῦται.

The two islands next to these were formerly both joined in one; but having been broken apart in the middle by the sea its two parts have become separated by the width of a river. This you might know from the painting, my boy; for you doubtless see that the two severed portions of the island are similar, and correspond to each other, and are so shaped that concave parts fit those that project. Europe once suffered the same experience in the region of the Thessalian Tempe; for when earthquakes laid open that land, they indicated on the fractures the correspondence of the mountains once to the other, and even today there are visible cavities where rocks once were, which correspond to the rocks torn from them, and, moreover, traces have not yet disappeared of the heavy forest growth that must have followed the mountain sides when they split apart; for the beds of the trees are still left. So we may consider that some such thing happened to this island; but a bridge has been thrown over the channel, with the result that the two islands look like one; and while ships sail under the bridge, wagons go over it; in fact you doubtless see the men making the passage, that they are both wayfarers and sailors.

The speaker again makes reference to the geography of the Mediterranean, but here the reference is part of a more complex hermeneutic strategy: by closely examining the present shape of the islands the speaker infers what they looked like in the past, and this conclusion is corroborated by the analogy of Tempe. What was said above about the narrator of the *Bibliotheke*, that he not only strives for a vivid depiction of what can actually be seen but also aims to expose what could be seen in the past (cf. the account of the 'Snake Island' in Diod. Sic. 3.39.4–6), thus also holds true for the speaker of the *Imagines*.[20] In contrast to the *Bibliotheke*'s *periplus*, however, the primary focus here is on the process of inference made explicit by the speaker who, once more, strongly asserts his presence and his virtuosity in interpreting the painting.

---

[20] See Squire 2013a: 108 on Philostratus' 'concern with visibility and invisibility' and its implications for the self-referentiality of the *Imagines*.

A further similarity to the *Bibliotheke*'s *periplus* is the emphasis on marvels. A case in point is *Imagines* 2.17.5, the paragraph which immediately follows the description of the double island:[21]

τὴν δὲ νῆσον, ὦ παῖ, τὴν πλησίον θαῦμα ἡγώμεθα· πῦρ γὰρ δὴ ὑποτύφει αὐτὴν πᾶσαν σήραγγάς τε καὶ μυχοὺς ὑποδεδυκὸς τῆς νήσου, δι' ὧν ὥσπερ αὐλῶν ἡ φλὸξ διεκπαίει ῥύακάς τε ἐργάζεται δεινούς, παρ' ὧν ἐκπίπτουσι ποταμοὶ πυρὸς μεγάλοι τε καὶ τῇ θαλάττῃ ἐπικυμαίνοντες. καὶ φιλοσοφεῖν μὲν βουλομένῳ τὰ τοιαῦτα νῆσος ἀσφάλτου καὶ θείου παρεχομένη φύσιν, ἐπειδὰν ὑφ' ἁλὸς ἀνακραθῇ, πολλοῖς ἐκπυροῦται πνεύμασι τὰ τὴν ὕλην ἐξερεθίζοντα παρὰ τῆς θαλάττης ἀνασπῶσα· ἡ γραφὴ δὲ τὰ τῶν ποιητῶν ἐπαινοῦσα καὶ μῦθον τῇ νήσῳ ἐπιγράφει, γίγαντα μὲν βεβλῆσθαί ποτε ἐνταῦθα, δυσθανατοῦντι δ' αὐτῷ τὴν νῆσον ἐπενεχθῆναι δεσμοῦ ἕνεκεν, εἴκειν δὲ μήπω αὐτόν, ἀλλ' ἀναμάχεσθαι ὑπὸ τῇ γῇ ὄντα καὶ τὸ πῦρ τοῦτο σὺν ἀπειλῇ ἐκπνεῖν. τουτὶ δὲ καὶ τὸν Τυφῶ φασιν ἐν Σικελίᾳ βούλεσθαι καὶ τὸν Ἐγκέλαδον ἐν Ἰταλίᾳ ταύτῃ, οὓς ἤπειροί τε καὶ νῆσοι πιέζουσιν οὔπω μὲν τεθνεῶτας, ἀεὶ δὲ ἀποθνήσκοντας. ἔστι δέ σοι, ὦ παῖ, μηδ' ὑπολελεῖφθαι δόξαι τῆς μάχης ἐς τὴν κορυφὴν τοῦ ὄρους ἀποβλέψαντι· τὰ γὰρ ἐπ' αὐτῆς φαινόμενα ὁ Ζεὺς ἀφίησι κεραυνοὺς ἐπὶ τὸν γίγαντα, ὁ δ' ἀπαγορεύει μὲν ἤδη, πιστεύει δὲ τῇ γῇ ἔτι, καὶ ἡ γῆ δὲ ἀπείρηκεν οὐκ ἐῶντος αὐτὴν ἑστάναι τοῦ Ποσειδῶνος. περιβέβληκε δὲ αὐτοῖς ἀχλύν, ὡς ὅμοια γεγονόσι μᾶλλον ἢ γινομένοις φαίνοιτο.

The neighbouring island, my boy, we may consider a marvel; for fire smoulders under the whole of it, having worked its way into underground passages and cavities of the island, through which as through ducts the flames break forth and produce terrific torrents from which pour mighty rivers of fire that run in billows to the sea. If one wishes to speculate about such matters, the island provides natural bitumen and sulphur; and when these are mixed by the sea, the island is fanned into flame by many winds, drawing from the sea that which sets the fuel aflame. But the painting, following the accounts given by the poets, goes farther and ascribes a myth to the island. A giant, namely, was once struck down there, and upon him as he struggled in the death agony the island was placed as a bond to hold him down, and he does not yet yield but from beneath the earth renews the fight and breathes forth this fire as he utters threats. Yonder figure, they say, would represent Typho in Sicily or Enceladus here in Italy, giants that both continents and island are pressing down, not yet dead indeed but always dying. And you, yourself, my boy, will imagine that you have not been left out of the contest, when you look at the peak of the mountain; for what you see there are thunderbolts which Zeus is hurling

---

[21] Another pertinent passage which highlights wonders and marvels is the description of the 'Golden Island', the last island of this ecphrasis (*Imag.* 2.17.12–14).

at the giant, and the giant is already giving up the struggle but still trusts in the earth, but the earth has grown weary because Poseidon does not permit her to remain in place. Poseidon has spread a mist over the contest, so that it resembles what has taken place in the past rather than what is taking place now.

The speaker both stresses the marvellous nature of this island and explains the volcanism.[22] The technique of combining ecphrastic vividness and interpretation is reminiscent of Diodorus Siculus 3.40.2–3, where the narrator explains the physical causes of the peculiar green colour of the water in a certain stretch of the Red Sea (the sea appears green because of the seaweed and tangle: cf. the discussion above). At *Imagines* 2.17.5, however, the speaker offers two explanations, a scientific and a mythological one. The latter, it appears, is the model used by the painter of that image, and this model invites the speaker to contextualise the features which are immediately visible in the painting within the larger narrative of the giants and their struggle with Zeus. In other words, the speaker once more does not restrict himself to the present of the situation depicted by the painter but narrates the past events which preceded that situation, yet another similarity to the *Bibliotheke*'s *periplus* and its use of historical contextualisation. It is noteworthy that the speaker at *Imagines* 2.17.5 points out that this is precisely the goal of the painting, to make the depicted events 'appear more similar to what has taken place in the past than to what is taking place now' (ὡς ὅμοια γεγονόσι μᾶλλον ἢ γινομένοις φαίνοιτο).[23]

Imagines 2.17, in sum, differs from the *Bibliotheke*'s *periplus* because of its specific (inter-)mediality whose main traits are feigned orality, dialogicity and metalepsis. On the other hand, there are many similarities between the two *periploi* as both strive for contextualisation by historicising and narrativising the sensual perceptions of the seafarer and the beholder of the painting, respectively. What are we to make of these

---

[22] This combination of focalising wonders and explaining them forms an integral part of the speaker's hermeneutic strategy and is employed throughout the *Imagines*: cf. Leach 2000: 246–8; Newby 2009: 331–3; Baumann 2011: 21–6. Other instances of scientific explanation provided by the speaker in *Imag.* 2.17 include the account of owl eggs and their effects on children in 2.17.8 and the information about the behaviour and the medicinal value of seagulls in 2.17.11.

[23] We should therefore not interpret the speaker's technique of historicisation and narrativisation as an instance of the paragon or the contest of the arts. The speaker does not simply 'go beyond' the image when he narrates the past in his verbal performance: he rather shows an acute awareness of the complex narrative and hermeneutical potential of these paintings, and his interpretations are effectively very much 'in line' with the images. For a fuller analysis of whether the paragon can serve as an appropriate model for interpreting the *Imagines*, see Baumann 2011: 179–85.

similarities and discrepancies? To answer this question I will turn now to one last difference between the texts which allows us to examine further the poetics of the two *periploi* and interpret them against the backdrop of their cultural contexts. This difference is the treatment of the dangers faced by a seafarer. As noted above, the *Bibliotheke*'s narrator is quick to point out the perils of the Red Sea. In *Imagines* 2.17, however, the speaker never explicitly mentions any danger.

Dangerous Sailing, Secure Reading? Reader Response and Mediality in Both *Periploi*

The dangers of sailing the Red Sea are closely tied to the *Wirkungsästhetik* of the *Bibliotheke*'s *periplus*. For, unlike the sailors of those shores, the reader of the *Bibliotheke* is in a position of safety: his/her life is not threatened by the shallows, cliffs or storms highlighted time and again by the narrator. The reader is in a literal sense far removed from, for instance, the agony of the shipwrecked mariners whose gloomy fate (they die from starvation) is described in detail at Diodorus Siculus 3.40.4–8. It is precisely this distance which allows the reader to enjoy the vivid and even emotional depiction of those dangerous seas.

The *Bibliotheke*'s *periplus* of the Red Sea is thus a prime example of the kind of enjoyment which Thomas Anz in his seminal study of the pleasures of reading called 'die Befriedigung über die eigene Sicherheit' ('satisfaction about one's own safety').[24] From the perspective of the psychology of reading, this kind of pleasure is part of a double movement which characterises the reception of literary accounts of threatening or fearful events: readers allow themselves to be carried away by the descriptive and emotional force of such passages, but they also know that they are just reading a piece of literature and are not actually threatened by whatever is described in the text.[25] That this duality is at play in the *Bibliotheke*'s *periplus* is demonstrated by the following episode which lays open the double dynamics of involving readers and keeping them at a distance (3.44.4–5):

> μετὰ δὲ τὰς νήσους ταύτας αἰγιαλὸς παρήκει κρημνώδης καὶ δυσπαράπλους ἐπὶ σταδίους ὡς χιλίους· οὔτε γὰρ λιμὴν οὔτε σάλος ἐπ' ἀγκύρας ὑπόκειται τοῖς ναυτίλοις, οὐ χηλὴ δυναμένη τοῖς ἀπορουμένοις τῶν πλεόντων τὴν ἀναγκαίαν ὑπόδυσιν παρασχέσθαι. ὄρος δὲ ταύτῃ παράκειται κατὰ μὲν κορυφὴν πέτρας ἀποτομάδας ἔχον καὶ τοῖς ὕψεσι καταπληκτικάς, ὑπὸ δὲ

[24] Anz 1998: 149.   [25] Cf. Anz 1998: 146–7.

τὰς ῥίζας σπιλάδας ὀξείας καὶ πυκνὰς ἐνθαλάττους καὶ κατόπιν αὐτῶν φάραγγας ὑποβεβρωμένας καὶ σκολιάς. συντετρημένων δ' αὐτῶν πρὸς ἀλλήλας, καὶ τῆς θαλάττης βάθος ἐχούσης, ὁ κλύδων ποτὲ μὲν εἰσπίπτων, ποτὲ δὲ παλισσυτῶν βρόμῳ μεγάλῳ παραπλήσιον ἦχον ἐξίησι. τοῦ δὲ κλύδωνος τὸ μὲν πρὸς μεγάλας πέτρας προσαραττόμενον εἰς ὕψος ἵσταται καὶ τὸν ἀφρὸν θαυμαστὸν τὸ πλῆθος κατασκευάζει, τὸ δὲ καταπινόμενον κοιλώμασι σπασμὸν καταπληκτικὸν παρέχει, ὥστε τοὺς ἀκουσίως ἐγγίσαντας τοῖς τόποις διὰ τὸ δέος οἱονεὶ προαποθνήσκειν.

Beyond these islands there extends for about a thousand stades a coast which is precipitous and difficult for ships to sail past; for there is neither harbour beneath the cliffs nor roadstead where sailors may anchor, and no natural breakwater which affords shelter in emergency for mariners in distress. And parallel to the coast here runs a mountain range at whose summit are rocks which are sheer and of a terrifying height, and at its base are sharp undersea ledges in many places and behind them are ravines which are eaten away underneath and turn this way and that. And since these ravines are connected by passages with one another and the sea is deep, the surf, as it at one time rushes in and at another time retreats, gives forth a sound resembling a mighty crash of thunder. At one place the surf, as it breaks upon huge rocks, leaps on high and causes an astonishing mass of foam, at another it is swallowed up within the caverns and creates such a terrifying agitation of the waters that men who unwittingly draw near these places are so frightened that they die, as it were, a first death.

The narrator gives a powerful description of this dangerous coastline. Cliffs and waves are described in detail, as are the sounds which are produced by the surf. All this incites the readers' imagination. Moreover, the text names and emphasises the impact of the sights and sounds on the spectator and hearer: the key words θαυμαστός ('astonishing'), καταπληκτικός ('terrifying') and τὸ δέος ('fear') invite readers to put themselves in the mariners' place.[26]

At the end of the passage, however, the narrator makes it clear that the danger which the seamen face does not materialise: they do not experience

---

[26] As already mentioned above (cf. n. 4), nothing of the kind happens in Agatharchides' or Strabo's descriptions of the Red Sea. In Agatharchides' *periplus* as per Photius' excerpts, there is no equivalent passage, while Strabo 16.4.18 offers a shorter and much less vivid account: ἐφεξῆς δ' ἐστὶν αἰγιαλὸς λιθώδης, καὶ μετὰ τοῦτον τραχεῖα καὶ δυσπαράπλευστος ὅσον χιλίων σταδίων παραλία σπάνει λιμένων καὶ ἀγκυροβολίων· ὄρος γὰρ παρατείνει τραχὺ καὶ ὑψηλόν· εἶθ' ὑπώρειαι σπιλαδώδεις μέχρι τῆς θαλάττης, τοῖς ἐτησίαις μάλιστα καὶ ταῖς τότε ἐπομβρίαις ἀβοήθητον παρέχουσαι τὸν κίνδυνον, 'Next in order one comes to a stony beach, and after that to a stretch of coast about one thousand stadia in length which is rugged and difficult for vessels to pass, for lack of harbours and anchoring-places, since a rugged and lofty mountain stretches along it. Then one comes to foot-hills, which are rocky and extend to the sea; and these, especially at the time of the Etesian winds and the rains, present to sailors a danger that is beyond all help' (tr. Jones).

shipwreck, and none of them dies; they only suffer a quasi-death because of their own fearful anticipation (ὥστε ... διὰ τὸ δέος οἱονεὶ προαποθνῄσκειν). οἱονεί ('as it were') is the decisive word. It is a signal to readers, drawing their attention to both the role of perceptions and expectations and the rhetorical fabric of the whole description. On one level, οἱονεί shows that even those directly affected by the dangers of the sea simply fall victim to a kind of illusion; one could call the sailors' experience a 'near-death out of imagination'. This demonstrates to readers that as to these dangers, there is no 'objective' or 'unmediated' position: there are only experiences of different kinds, and all these experiences are mediated by processes of imagination. This is where the narrator comes into play, the second level on which οἱονεί works. By using this word, the narrator shows that he deliberately employs the rhetorical figure of hyperbole: the mariners do not literally die, but they are so scared that they, *as it were*, die from fear. Thus, the narrator points to himself as the one who shapes his account and, by the same token, the readers' experience.

Taken together, both aspects of οἱονεί prompt readers to reflect on their position vis-à-vis the mariners' fate, but also in relation to the narrator and his descriptive rhetoric. In consequence, the quoted passage combines two dynamics. Readers are invited to put themselves in the mariners' place, but they are also made aware of their actual position: they are outside of the event and not actually threatened by any wave. The combination of these two dynamics, of involvement and distancing, absorption and reflection, is precisely what affords pleasure to readers.

To arrive at this conclusion one does not have to rely solely on modern concepts of the psychology of reading. We find the same idea expressed and described in detail in another text from the first century BCE: Cicero, in his letter to L. Lucceius of 56/55 BCE, develops what could be called a piece of reader-response criticism relating to historiography. He discusses this with his own deeds in mind – the purpose of the letter is to ask Lucceius for a historiographical treatment of Cicero's consulate – but he also makes some very pertinent points on the pleasures of reading historiography in general (Cic. *Fam.* 5.12.4–5):[27]

> multam etiam casus nostri varietatem tibi in scribendo suppeditabunt plenam cuiusdam voluptatis, quae vehementer animos hominum in legendo te scriptore tenere possit. nihil est enim aptius ad delectationem lectoris quam temporum varietates fortunaeque vicissitudines. quae etsi nobis optabiles in experiendo non fuerunt, in legendo tamen erunt

[27] Tr. Shuckburgh.

iucundae. habet enim praeteriti doloris secura recordatio delectationem; ceteris vero nulla perfunctis propria molestia, casus autem alienos sine ullo dolore intuentibus, etiam ipsa misericordia est iucunda. quem enim nostrum ille moriens apud Mantineam Epaminondas non cum quadam miseratione delectat? qui tum denique sibi evelli iubet spiculum postea quam ei percontanti dictum est clipeum esse salvum, ut etiam in vulneris dolore aequo animo cum laude moreretur. cuius studium in legendo non erectum Themistocli fuga redituque retinetur? etenim ordo ipse annalium mediocriter nos retinet quasi enumeratione fastorum; at viri saepe excellentis ancipites variique casus habent admirationem, exspectationem, laetitiam, molestiam, spem, timorem; si vero exitu notabili concluduntur, expletur animus iucundissima lectionis voluptate.

For my vicissitudes will supply you in your composition with much variety, which has in itself a kind of charm, capable of taking a strong hold on the imagination of readers, when you are the writer. For nothing is better fitted to interest a reader than variety of circumstance and vicissitudes of fortune, which, though the reverse of welcome to us in actual experience, will make very pleasant reading: for the untroubled recollection of a past sorrow has a charm of its own. To the rest of the world, indeed, who have had no trouble themselves, and who look upon the misfortunes of others without any suffering of their own, the feeling of pity is itself a source of pleasure. For what man of us is not delighted, though feeling a certain compassion too, with the death-scene of Epaminondas at Mantinea? He, you know, did not allow the dart to be drawn from his body until he had been told, in answer to his question, that his shield was safe, so that in spite of the agony of his wound he died calmly and with glory. Whose interest is not roused and sustained by the banishment and return of Themistocles? Truly the mere chronological record of the annals has very little charm for us – little more than the entries in the fasti: but the doubtful and varied fortunes of a man, frequently of eminent character, involve feelings of wonder, suspense, joy, sorrow, hope, fear: if these fortunes are crowned with a glorious death, the imagination is satisfied with the most fascinating delight which reading can give.

The *Bibliotheke*'s periplus is not devoted to the fortunes of an outstanding individual. Its subject is more of the kind which Cicero discusses in another letter, *QFr.* 2.15, where he expresses his fascination with his brother's account of Caesar's expedition to Britain and in particular with Quintus' description of the ocean and the British coast: *o iucundas mihi tuas de Britannia litteras! timebam Oceanum, timebam litus insulae* ('How glad I was to get your letter from Britain! I was afraid of the ocean, afraid of the coast of the island', 2.15.4). Nevertheless, the principle of *praeteriti doloris secura recordatio* and the portrayal of the readers as *casus alienos sine ullo dolore intuentes* capture very well the dynamics of historiographical accounts like the periplus of the Red Sea.²⁸

Another important aspect of contextualising the *Bibliotheke*'s *periplus* is opened up when one looks at the *Bibliotheke*'s proem where the motif of danger plays a central role (Diod. Sic. 1.1.1–2):

> Τοῖς τὰς κοινὰς ἱστορίας πραγματευσαμένοις μεγάλας χάριτας ἀπονέμειν δίκαιον πάντας ἀνθρώπους, ὅτι τοῖς ἰδίοις πόνοις ὠφελῆσαι τὸν κοινὸν βίον ἐφιλοτιμήθησαν· ἀκίνδυνον γὰρ διδασκαλίαν τοῦ συμφέροντος εἰσηγησάμενοι καλλίστην ἐμπειρίαν διὰ τῆς πραγματείας ταύτης περιποιοῦσι τοῖς ἀναγινώσκουσιν. ἡ μὲν γὰρ ἐκ τῆς πείρας ἑκάστου μάθησις μετὰ πολλῶν πόνων καὶ κινδύνων ποιεῖ τῶν χρησίμων ἕκαστα διαγινώσκειν, καὶ διὰ τοῦτο τῶν ἡρώων ὁ πολυπειρότατος μετὰ μεγάλων ἀτυχημάτων
>
> πολλῶν ἀνθρώπων ἴδεν ἄστεα καὶ νόον ἔγνω·
>
> ἡ δὲ διὰ τῆς ἱστορίας περιγινομένη σύνεσις τῶν ἀλλοτρίων ἀποτευγμάτων τε καὶ κατορθωμάτων ἀπείρατον κακῶν ἔχει τὴν διδασκαλίαν.

> It is fitting that all men should ever accord great gratitude to those writers who have composed universal histories, since they have aspired to help by their individual labours human society as a whole; for by offering a schooling, which entails no danger, in what is advantageous they provide their readers, through such a presentation of events, with a most excellent kind of experience. For although the learning which is acquired by experience in each separate case, with all the attendant toils and dangers, does indeed enable a man to discern in each instance where utility lies – and this is the reason why the most widely experienced of our heroes suffered great misfortunes before he
>
> Of many men the cities saw and learned their thoughts; –
>
> yet the understanding of the failures and successes of other men, which is acquired by the study of history, affords a schooling that is free from actual experience of ills.

Diodorus claims an ἀκίνδυνον διδασκαλίαν, a 'learning without danger' as the main benefit of the *Bibliotheke*. Nicolas Wiater has shown that this claim is part of broader strategy in the proem which sets the *Bibliotheke* apart from Polybius' concept of pragmatic history and self-consciously

---

²⁸ For a detailed discussion of Cic. *Fam.* 5.12 in the context of historiographical theory of the Late Republic, see Pausch 2011: 53–64.

marks the *Bibliotheke* as a work of book history. Compilation, the proem asserts, is the adequate way to produce historiography in Diodorus' time, and 'bookishness' is its main trait – the title *Bibliotheke* is, of course, no accident.[29] The motifs of danger and safety, then, are closely tied to the mediality of the *Bibliotheke* and the status of its reader. The fact that the narrator keeps pointing to the dangers of the Red Sea throughout his *periplus* and that he uses the contrast between these perils and the reader's safety for eliciting a complex response from the reader fits into this picture very well. All the specific benefits offered to the reader by the *Bibliotheke*, in particular learning and pleasure, derive from its decidedly 'bookish' conception of historiography.

In Philostratus' *Imagines*, the situation is quite different. As I have already mentioned, the speaker, throughout *Imagines* 2.17, never points to any danger at all. To be more precise, he does describe one single instance of a potentially dangerous situation, but neither does he himself seem to be threatened by it when he passes this spot on his imaginary ship nor does he evoke any other vessel or crew in distress. The passage I am referring to is the description of the volcanic island already quoted above (2.17.5):

> τὴν δὲ νῆσον, ὦ παῖ, τὴν πλησίον θαῦμα ἡγώμεθα· πῦρ γὰρ δὴ ὑποτύφει αὐτὴν πᾶσαν σήραγγάς τε καὶ μυχοὺς ὑποδεδυκὸς τῆς νήσου, δι' ὧν ὥσπερ αὐλῶν ἡ φλὸξ διεκπαίει ῥύακάς τε ἐργάζεται δεινούς, παρ' ὧν ἐκπίπτουσι ποταμοὶ πυρὸς μεγάλοι τε καὶ τῇ θαλάττῃ ἐπικυμαίνοντες. καὶ φιλοσοφεῖν μὲν βουλομένῳ τὰ τοιαῦτα νῆσος ἀσφάλτου καὶ θείου παρεχομένη φύσιν.

> The neighbouring island, my boy, we may consider a marvel; for fire smoulders under the whole of it, having worked its way into underground passages and cavities of the island, through which as through ducts the flames break forth and produce terrific torrents from which pour mighty rivers of fire that run in billows to the sea. If one wishes to speculate about such matters, the island provides natural bitumen and sulphur.

The flames produce ῥύακας δεινούς, 'terrific torrents', and huge rivers of fire 'run in billows to the sea' (τῇ θαλάττῃ ἐπικυμαίνοντες) – but apart from calling all these phenomena a wonder the speaker does not seem to be in any way affected by them. One could easily imagine here a description in the style of Diodorus Siculus 3.44.4–5, the near-shipwreck account from the *Bibliotheke*'s *periplus*. But nothing of the sort occurs in *Imagines*

---

[29] Cf. Wiater 2006b: esp. 253–60. For other discussions of the *Bibliotheke*'s proem, see Meeus 2018a (with extensive bibliography) and, in this volume, Gray and König.

2.17: after the first sentence, the speaker immediately moves on to his contextualising interpretation which I discussed above. Accordingly, the reader of this description is put in a position that significantly differs from what one experiences when reading the *Bibliotheke*'s *periplus*. Here, there is no contrast between the sailors' danger and the reader's security, for the only seafarers present, the speaker and the boy, appear to be in perfect safety themselves. Nor are there any emotional elements that could move the reader: no one panics and no one dies, or virtually dies, from fear.

Instead, the focus is wholly on the speaker's contextualising interpretation, on his – to quote an expression coined by Jaś Elsner – 'appropriation' of the painting.[30] That is why, compared with the *Bibliotheke*'s *periplus*, *Imagines* 2.17 provides a different kind of what narratologists call 'experientiality'.[31] This ecphrasis hardly makes the reader experience the sea voyage as such. Throughout *Imagines* 2.17 there is virtually no description of the actual passages between the islands. In fact, 2.17.12 is the only case where the passage is explicitly mentioned at all (ἐνταῦθα δέ, ὦ παῖ, καὶ καθώρμισται ἡμῖν, 'on this island, my boy, we have put ashore'), and even at the beginning of the ecphrasis, when the narrator succinctly describes the situation of the islands and the general conditions of the sailing (season, wind, waves), there is no concrete reference to the actual movement of the ship apart from the exclamation ἰδοὺ ἐμβεβλήκαμεν, 'Lo, we have embarked' (Fairbanks), or 'we have laid ourselves to the oars'.[32] The experience of the sea voyage is thus largely reduced to a sequence of views or close-ups of individual islands. The experience of listening to the speaker's words, of attending his virtuoso performance, takes centre stage. This brings us back to a point already made above: the speaker of *Imagines* 2.17 asserts his presence even more strongly than the narrator of the *Bibliotheke*'s *periplus*. And it is this strong presence that shapes the reader's experience of *Imagines* 2.17. Put differently, *Imagines* 2.17 is less about experiencing a sea voyage as such than it is about experiencing the *virtuoso* sophist taking us with him on a cruise through the painting.

---

[30] Elsner 1995: 30–1.
[31] For 'experientiality' as a narratological concept, see Caracciolo 2014. The term was introduced by Monika Fludernik who defined it as 'the quasi-mimetic evocation of "real-life experience"' (Fludernik 1996: 12). Fludernik denies or at least plays down (Fludernik 2010) the presence of experientiality in historiography, a position that has rightly been challenged by Grethlein 2013: 355–64.
[32] Cf. LSJ p. 539 s.v. ἐμβάλλω, II 3.

This specific form of experience is achieved by the feigned orality of the ecphrasis, another trait of *Imagines* 2.17 demonstrated above. It is worth returning briefly to this point, for two reasons: first, it allows us to round off our analysis of the different treatment of (potential) dangers in both *periploi*. For just as the emphasis of the perils of the sea in the *Bibliotheke*'s *periplus* is closely tied to its 'bookishness', the apparent lack of any dangers in *Imagines* 2.17 may be interpreted as one aspect of the constructed orality of that text. *Imagines* 2.17 does not aim to establish and exploit a 'gap in experience' between intra-textual figures and extra-textual reader. Rather than highlighting and using what I called above 'mediation by imagination', Philostratus' ecphrasis strives to recreate in a written text the immediacy that is typical of oral communication: we as readers do not just take the audience's place by imagination, we *are actually made* the audience by the speaker and his performance. We hear the sophist speak, we follow his rhetorical display word by word – by virtue of the performance of the text, we *are* on that boat with him.[33]

Second, the feigned orality of *Imagines* 2.17 provides an 'anchor' for interpreting this ecphrasis against the backdrop of a broader tendency in imperial Greek literature. This is an important point because readers faced with the task of contextualising *Imagines* 2.17 can easily feel lost due to the sheer idiosyncrasy of the *Imagines*. The standard – and perhaps problematic – way of approaching questions of contextualisation is to look for similarities in other texts from the same period on the basis of criteria such as shared genre, recurring motifs and so on, in order to establish valid 'points of reference' that can serve as the basis for a comparative interpretation. This, however, proves difficult in the case of the *Imagines*. What, for example, is the genre of this text? The *Imagines* is narrative to some degree since there is a 'story' of sorts which is told in the proem: 'I was once asked to interpret the paintings of a gallery, and so I started giving speeches in front of the images.' But this potential narrative frame remains implicit and suspended in the rest of the text because of the lack of any paratextual transitions between the individual ecphrases. The speaker and his audience move from image to image, and even though this could have been explicitly narrated ('and then we went on to the next painting'), it is not. Thus, the *Imagines* greatly differs from ecphrases that are embedded

---

[33] Cf. Schirren 2009: 132: 'wir sind als Rezipienten [i.e., of *Imag.* 2.17] eigentlich immer schon eingestiegen und sind immer schon Passagiere auf *sightseeing-tour*, nämlich dadurch, daß wir uns als Rezipierende auf den Text überhaupt einlassen. Das heißt, der Text scheint uns gar keine Wahl lassen zu wollen, ob wir einsteigen wollen oder nicht.'

into larger narratives as, for example, in the ancient novels.³⁴ If one turns to motifs, on the other hand, one might think that the motif of 'moving through space to describe places' forms a valid link with a text like Pausanias' *Periegesis*. But here again, *Imagines* 2.17 proves to be quite a specific case. For, as I pointed out above, *Imagines* 2.17 is based on metalepsis: since the speaker does not directly describe the islands, but rather a painting of this archipelago, an ecphrasis in the form of a continuous movement through space entails crossing the boundary between two media by entering the picture and sailing through the image. This, of course, does not happen in Pausanias, whose descriptions are not based on metalepsis.³⁵

We might therefore want to consider whether the point of the *Imagines* is precisely to create a text that resists any simple comparison and presents itself as incommensurable. If that is true, this strategy can be interpreted in the context of the contemporary culture of παιδεία with its marked competitiveness, that is, as an attempt to surpass and outdo any potential competitor.³⁶ I think, however, that it is possible to find a simpler, albeit tentative, answer to the present question, and this brings us back to the feigned orality of *Imagines* 2.17. It may be difficult to find significant contemporary parallels to *Imagines* 2.17 by focusing on genre and recurring motifs, but as to its mediality, *Imagines* 2.17 actually fits a trend in imperial literature, namely a tendency of re-oralisation in the context of a highly developed and sophisticated book culture.

If one accepts the idea that there was a revival of performance oratory in imperial Graeco-Roman culture, this 'movement' – usually referred to as the 'second sophistic,' as Philostratus calls it (*VS* 1 pr., 481) – is a first case in point. There are good reasons, however, to doubt Philostratus' account of sophistic revival in this period, as, among others, the editors of this volume argue in their introduction.³⁷ Two other cases or 'models' of re-oralising imperial literature bring us on safer ground: the fiction of entering into a dialogue with the authors of the past and the use of metalepsis to merge the qualities of written and oral communication.

---

³⁴ Cf., e.g., the description of the painting of Europa and the bull in Achilles Tatius' *Leucippe and Clitophon* (1.1.2–13). On Philostratus' innovations vis-à-vis the tradition of embedded ecphrasis, see Elsner 2002: 3–9 and 13–14.
³⁵ Likewise, the *Periplus of the Erythraean Sea* from the mid-first century CE (for the date see Casson 1989: 6–7) and the *periplus* section in Arrian's *Indike* (second century CE, but based on Nearchus' earlier account) differ from *Imag.* 2.17 in that they give 'direct' descriptions of the Red Sea and/or the Indian Ocean, comparable (in this respect) to the *Bibliotheke*'s *periplus*.
³⁶ See the discussion in Baumann 2011: 13–14 and 152–8.   ³⁷ See Introduction, pp. 23–6.

The first 'model' was pointed out by Jason König in a recent analysis of Plutarch's *Sympotic Questions*. König shows that this collection of conversations constructs an idealised imagery of an intellectual community which is 'heavily dependent on oral ways of recalling and interacting with the authors of the past'.[38] The characters of the *Sympotic Questions* often refer to classical writers, but almost entirely without mentioning books as physical objects to be read. Rather, Plutarch's imagined community acts as if authors like Plato and Euripides are actually brought into direct dialogue with the symposiasts, for example at *Sympotic Questions* 8.2, 718b–c:[39]

> Ἐκ δὲ τούτου γενομένης σιωπῆς, πάλιν ὁ Διογενιανὸς ἀρξάμενος 'βούλεσθ'' εἶπεν, 'ἐπεὶ λόγοι περὶ θεῶν γεγόνασιν, ἐν τοῖς Πλάτωνος γενεθλίοις αὐτὸν Πλάτωνα κοινωνὸν παραλάβωμεν, ἐπισκεψάμενοι τίνα λαβὼν γνώμην ἀπεφήνατ' ἀεὶ γεωμετρεῖν τὸν θεόν; εἴ γε δὴ θετέον εἶναι τὴν ἀπόφασιν ταύτην Πλάτωνος.'

> After this, when silence had fallen, Diogenianus, making a new start, said, 'Are you willing, since the conversation has turned to the gods, that we should invite in Plato himself as a participant, given that this is Plato's birthday, examining in what sense he intended the claim that "God is always doing geometry"? – if indeed that claim is to be attributed to Plato.'

Terms such as παραλαμβάνω ('invite') and κοινωνός ('participant'), which suggest conversation or other forms of personal contact with the authors of the past, abound throughout the *Sympotic Questions*. This way of portraying intellectual interaction in *symposia* contributes to what König identifies as the basic effect of the *Sympotic Questions* on the readers: 'That style of conversation . . . engages us as readers: we are invited to imagine how we would respond to these questions, almost as though we are participating in the conversation for ourselves.'[40]

Even closer to the mediality of Philostratus' *Imagines* are other cases of metalepsis in imperial literature. Peter von Möllendorff has shown that literary works of that era frequently use metalepsis to combine the advantages of written texts with key qualities of orality. Strategies used to that end often include metalepses which operate on the boundary between texts and images, as for example at the end of Lucian's *De mercede conductis* where the speaker evokes an allegorical image of the way of life he denounces and tells the addressee to consider whether he (the addressee)

---

[38] König 2018: 58.   [39] Tr. König.   [40] König 2018: 56.

should 'enter that image' (προσελθεῖν εἰς τὴν εἰκόνα, *De mercede conductis* 42).[41] The use of metalepsis to re-oralise literature has several effects: it increases the intensity of the communication between speakers and recipients, it gives concrete presence to figures who would otherwise just be literary representations and it bridges the distance that literary communication establishes between narrators/ speakers and their readers. The high degree of communicative complexity that can be achieved by employing metalepses for these purposes is demonstrated by Lucian's twin dialogues *Imagines* and *Pro imaginibus*. There, a book that first appears on the intradiegetic level (Luc. *Im.* 9) is later shown to be identical to the book that is announced and, in a way, performatively created on the extradiegetic level of *Imagines/Pro imaginibus*, thus paradoxically entangling the reader in a structure of repeated readings and intertwined acts of dialogical discussing and writing.[42]

As we have seen, lending immediacy to the communication between speaker and reader and making the speaker's presence felt are also distinctive features of Philostratus' island ecphrasis. Above all, *Imagines* 2.17 quite literally places speaker and reader together in one boat. I would therefore argue that these dynamics of re-oralisation represent a constitutive link between the *Imagines* and the more general tendencies of imperial Greek literature.

Conclusion

In their introduction, the editors of this volume advance the hypothesis that bringing late Hellenistic and imperial texts into dialogue opens up fresh perspectives on both sides of the comparison, revealing striking continuities, not just in generic terms but also in themes and practices that straddle a range of different genres, while at the same time helping us to understand even more clearly what makes each of these periods, and the individual texts and authors that we study, distinctive.[43] The observations made in this chapter corroborate this hypothesis. The comparison of the *periplus* of the Red Sea in Diodorus Siculus, *Bibliotheke* 3.38–48, and the island description 2.17 in Philostratus, *Imagines*, shows how both texts employ a fairly similar ecphrastic technique characterised by contextualisation, historicisation and narrativisation in order to afford their readers quite different experiences. The key elements here are their divergent

---

[41] Cf. von Möllendorff 2013: 365–7.   [42] Cf. von Möllendorff 2013: 372–7.
[43] See Introduction, pp. 19–20.

strategies of mediality: the *Bibliotheke* is characterised by a marked 'bookishness', whereas the *Imagines* strives for re-oralisation. Both strategies have their place in contemporary discourses and contexts, and this is where 'understanding distinctiveness' most of all comes into play. The *Bibliotheke* situates itself in the late Hellenistic debate on writing and reading history, and particularly in the discourse on the pleasures of reading historiographical texts, while the *Imagines* is part of a broader trend of enriching texts with structures and elements of oral communication in the imperial period.

CHAPTER 4

Ecocritical Readings in Late Hellenistic Literature
Landscape Alteration and Hybris in Strabo and Diodorus

Jason König

Introduction: Ecocritical Approaches to Ancient Literature

Human alteration of the landscape was an object of fascination for ancient Greek and Roman culture, as it has been also in the post-classical world. It attracts both positive and negative representations in ancient literature. Sometimes it is portrayed in celebratory terms as a sign of progress towards civilisation and order: cutting through mountains and diverting rivers are portrayed as acts of benefaction. Side by side with that celebratory attitude runs a much more negative strand, where scarring and disrupting the earth's surface is linked with *hybris*, and in some cases viewed even as an offence against the will of the gods. In much of ancient literature the second of those two strands is particularly prominent, not least because the most high-profile acts of landscape alteration were often taken as signs of the tyrannical character of the rulers who sponsored them. My hypothesis in this chapter, however, is that in late Hellenistic and Augustan Greek literature the first, celebratory strand is unusually prominent. We will see that here especially for the opening books of Diodorus Siculus' *Historical Library* and for Strabo's *Geography*. Exploring that hypothesis will involve bringing these two texts into dialogue with each other and with a range of classical, late Hellenistic and imperial equivalents in order to draw out some of the similarities and the differences between them.

I also aim to show, however, just how complex the story of those shifting patterns of representation is. If we want to do justice to ancient responses to landscape, we need to understand the ambiguities that run not only through whole centuries but also even through individual works. And that involves recognising the way in which knowledge-ordering texts like the works of Strabo and Diodorus were designed to be read from end to end, with close attention to their intratextual complexity, even when they were composed largely of material derived from other, earlier works. When we do that we start to see traces of equivocation or hesitation even in these most celebratory portrayals of human resourcefulness.

That argument, I suggest, has important implications for our understanding of the relationship between humans and the environment in the ancient world, and of its significance for modern ways of thinking about human impact on the environment. The last few decades have seen a rapid growth in the environmental humanities. One of the key driving forces for that development has been the cross-disciplinary field of ecocriticism, which focuses on literary representations of the relationship between humans and the environment, often with an interest in challenging the sense of a clear dividing line and a clear hierarchy of value between human culture and the 'more-than-human' world.[1] Those themes of course have resonances with some of the traditional concerns of scholarship on the ancient Mediterranean, but there have nevertheless been relatively few attempts within Classics to engage with the discipline of ecocriticism explicitly. That has begun to change,[2] but the challenge of using ecocritical perspectives to open up new questions about particular genres, regions and periods in the ancient Mediterranean is still a work in progress.[3] Ancient Greek and Roman literature in turn represents a huge untapped resource for our understanding of the long history of human responses to the environment.

One enabling factor for an increase in ecocritical engagement within Classics is the way in which ecocriticism itself has evolved over the last decade or two. In its earliest manifestations ecocriticism tended to focus on non-fictional nature writing about particular places, which was often used as a springboard for quite localised environmental activism, based on an ideal of pristine nature undamaged by human interference. Within that context premodern texts were often ignored – although that is no longer the case for medieval[4] and early modern literature –[5] thanks in part to the widespread assumption that the societies that produced them were just not interested in any sustained engagement with or description of the natural world.[6] More recently, however, the focus of ecocriticism has expanded dramatically to look far beyond the category of nature writing: for example

---

[1] See Clark 2019: 10, 13–14 and 111–36; Schliephake 2017b: 9–10; and Bosak-Schroeder 2020 for a sustained attempt to apply those interests to ancient literature, focusing especially on Herodotus and Diodorus (see further discussion below).
[2] See esp. Schliephake 2017a and 2020.
[3] For a recent example see Burrus 2018 on late antique Christian literature.
[4] E.g., see Rudd 2007 on medieval English literature, and Goldwyn 2018 on Byzantine literature.
[5] See Hallock, Kamps and Raber 2008, among many other examples.
[6] The most notorious example is in the history of human engagement with and representation of mountains: Nicolson 1959 has been very influential in encouraging the view that premodern responses to mountains were nearly universally characterised by fear, distaste and indifference, by contrast with the 'mountain glory' of modern responses from the eighteenth century onwards; for recent challenges see Koelb 2009, Hollis 2019, Hollis and König 2021.

at texts with urban as much as rural settings.⁷ It is widely recognised now that any text can be open to ecocritical questions, with their potential to reveal underlying assumptions about the relations between human culture and the environment even where those assumptions are not explicitly stated. That shift has made it easier to bring classical literature into dialogue with ecocritical themes. Greek and Latin generally do not offer extended set-piece descriptions of the natural world of the kind we are familiar with from Romantic period onwards⁸– although with a partial exception in the *locus amoenus* traditions of describing beautiful landscapes⁹– but if we are ready to read ancient texts from end to end, with attention to their intratextual complexity, we can begin to see that many of them do in fact project very distinctive images of the relations between human culture and the environment, through passages which often seem individually brief and insignificant on first reading, but which between them can have a powerful, cumulative effect.

The classical world also has an important part to play in turn in any attempt to understand where modern environmental attitudes have come from. Some early works of ecological scholarship made sweeping claims about either similarities or differences between past and present environmental challenges and responses;¹⁰ some of those claims are still surprisingly widely accepted. As soon as we look closely, however, it becomes clear that the relationship between past and present is enormously complex. The environmental engagements we find in ancient literature are both familiar in some ways and quite alien to modern experience in others:¹¹ we will see that ancient criticism of landscape alteration has striking resonances with a lot of modern thinking on the subject, while also being quite different in some respects, for example because it is often articulated within frameworks of religious thinking and ideas about political authority which are quite different from our standard ways of engaging with related questions today. Moreover, the classical heritage has been used in a vast range of different ways by post-classical writers and thinkers: we cannot possibly sum up that reception history within a few generalisations.¹²

---

[7] See esp. Armbruster and Wallace 2002, which includes several chapters on premodern authors.
[8] Cf. Schliephake 2017b: 5–6.
[9] See Koelb 2006 for the influence of classical traditions of *ekphrasis* over Romantic place descriptions.
[10] Cf. Schliephake 2017b: 8, with reference to related discussion of that phenomenon in Sonnabend 2005.
[11] See Schliephake 2020: 4–6; also Holmes 2017: xii on the play of similarity and unfamiliarity between ancient and modern in relation to the category of 'nature'.
[12] Cf. Schliephake 2017b: 4.

To be more specific, one of the issues in ancient culture that has had most attention from an environmental perspective is the question of what degree of environmental damage there was in the ancient Mediterranean, and how such damage was viewed. Most of the initial assessments came from studies outside the discipline of Classics; they sought to summarise ancient ideas about the relationship between humans and the environment, often in just a few pages, in order to make an argument about either continuity or disjunction between ancient and modern environmental thinking. Many of these works make wide-ranging generalisations on the basis of simplistic summaries of a few key ancient texts. In some cases, Greek and Roman culture are viewed as the originators of our current willingness to alter the environment for human purposes;[13] in other cases they are taken in exactly opposite terms as examples of environmental respect which was lost, according to one influential narrative, with the advent of early Christianity's more anthropocentric approach to the natural world.[14] The last few decades have seen a series of much more careful studies of ancient environmental thinking. The work of J. Donald Hughes is one example.[15] Hughes still has a tendency, like some of his predecessors, to extract brief quotations from very lengthy and complex works without any acknowledgement of their wider context. That in turn can lead us to ignore the fact that both positive and negative views on landscape change will often stand in tension with each other even within individual ancient texts: we will see examples in what follows. But despite that, he has made progress in demonstrating that both concern about exploitation of the earth's resources and celebrations of human improvement of the natural world existed side by side with each other all the way through the classical tradition.[16] Peter Coates, drawing on Hughes' work, has made similar arguments in setting out the classical background to later thinking about the concept of 'nature'.[17] 'We are hard pressed', he suggests, 'to find a single doctrine of man–nature relations in any era . . . A number of attitudes, notions and orientations invariably coexist in often messy contradiction.'[18] As we shall see, that is the case for the late Hellenistic world just as it is for other periods of ancient Greek and Roman history.[19] Drawing out that complexity, I suggest, can help us

---

[13] E.g., see Sessions 1981. [14] Most influentially White 1967. [15] E.g., see Hughes 2014.
[16] See also Thommen 2012 for summary statement of that view, although without much detailed analysis of particular sources.
[17] Coates 1998: 23–39. [18] Coates 1998: 12.
[19] Cf. Glacken 1969: 13 for brief acknowledgement along similar lines.

towards a much more careful understanding of the long history of the environmental attitudes we encounter in the present.

There are also two other respects, I suggest, in which the texts I examine here might be valuable as resources for contemporary environmental thinking. The first is as repositories of sophisticated ways of presenting the intertwining between local and global environmental concerns. Some prominent recent publications have agonised about the idea that modern literary forms, especially the novel, with its traditional focus on the local and the personal, are not well suited to imagining the way in which environmental damage today is unfolding on a global level.[20] In some ways ancient Greek and Latin literature are more suited to the challenge of imagining the global and the local side by side,[21] not least in ancient historiographical and geographical writing, which as we shall see characteristically juxtapose vast numbers of different localised events and histories in a broad vision of the whole of the inhabited world and invite us to measure them up against each other.

Second, and finally, looking at ancient accounts of landscape alteration from an ecocritical perspective can shed new light on the long history of one aspect of modern environmental thinking in particular, that is the concern with environmental justice. Timothy Clark sums up eloquently the importance of that issue for the environmental humanities: 'For most ecocritics, human abuse of the natural world is best understood as the corollary of unjust or oppressive forms of government and economics, and forms of social organisation ... that both abuse other human beings and which have no hesitation taking a similar stance towards anything else.'[22] It is increasingly clear that the risks associated with climate change tend to have a disproportionately serious impact on disadvantaged populations in many contexts.[23] Environmental justice approaches, with their focus on human consequences, have often been opposed to more ecocentric ways of thinking about environmental change which focus on the balance and health of the environment as a whole, resisting anthropocentric perspectives.[24] Clearly some ancient Greek and Roman thinkers were interested in

---

[20] See Ghosh 2016 for the best known representative of that view; also Buell 2005: 62–96; Heise 2008, esp. 205–10; Clark 2019: 78–110, esp. 97–9.
[21] Cf. Ben Gray's contribution to this volume.
[22] Clark 2019: 3; also Bate 2000: 48: 'ecological exploitation is always coordinate with social exploitation'; Buell 2005: 112–27.
[23] See Clark 2019: 5: 'exposure to environmental risk is not evenly distributed across the world, but tends to victimise people who are already impoverished or side-lined'.
[24] See Buell 2001: 224–42.

images of the cosmos as a coherent system held in a careful equilibrium, which are not so far removed from modern ideas of environmental harmony.[25] But it is striking that ancient writing about landscape alteration tends to be relatively uninterested in that phenomenon, except in the sense that reshaping the land is sometimes viewed as an offence against divine will and divine order,[26] and in that sense it can look a little disappointing when we come to it from modern perspectives on environmental destruction, which tend to be shaped by a much more urgent, activist agenda. What those ancient texts do persistently give attention to, however, is the impact of massive landscape-engineering projects, most of them in imperial contexts, on the populations who lived close to them or who were co-opted to bring them into being. That theme has the potential to complicate even the most celebratory portraits of human alteration of the earth's surface.

Herodotus

Any history of ancient representations of landscape alteration must give Herodotus a prominent role, not just because of the sophistication of his exploration of that theme but also because of his influence. We find both positive and negative accounts of landscape-engineering projects in the *Histories*. The dominant impression, especially in the last three books of the work, is of the hybristic character of Persian attempts to alter the landscapes they encounter in their expeditions against Greece. However, it is important to stress that those incidents are set against a wide spectrum of different possibilities for landscape alteration, which are focalised through a range of different individuals and groups, and that many of these projects are given positive overtones.[27] In that sense Herodotus, like Strabo and Diodorus, offers us a remarkably wide-ranging, even global vision of human interference with the environment, inviting us to compare a series of different cases over space and time.

Some passages in the first half of the work especially portray incidents of landscape manipulation as objects of wonder, or at any rate as examples of

---

[25] E.g., see Usher 2020; also Glacken 1969: 35–79, with Schliephake 2017b: 7.
[26] See Prencipe 2017: 135–7, esp. 136 in relation to the actions of Xerxes discussed further below.
[27] See the excellent, detailed discussions by Clarke 2018: esp. 171–218 and Bosak-Schroeder 2020: 32–56; I came to both of these discussions at a relatively late stage in working on this chapter, but both have helped greatly in refining my views on Herodotus (and on Diodorus, in the case of Bosak-Schroeder: see further below); also Romm 2006: 186–90 for a briefer account along similar lines; and now Schlosser 2020 for other aspects of Herodotus' ecological thinking.

impressive technical accomplishment. At one point, for example, Herodotus praises the people of Samos for digging a passage through a mountain to bring water into their city (the so-called Tunnel of Eupalinos, which can still be visited as a tourist attraction today). It is described as one of three Samian achievements that are 'the greatest of all things achieved by the Greeks' (Herodotus, *Histories* 3.60). Here Herodotus seems to admire the ingenuity of the Samians, without any hint of negative judgement, in line with the declaration of interest in the 'great and marvellous deeds (ἔργα μεγάλα τε καὶ θωμαστά)' (1.pr) of the world's human populations in his preface.[28]

Increasingly as the work goes on, however, more negative versions of that motif come to predominate,[29] although they never completely overpower the possibility of more positive representations. That development is prefigured early on in the story of the Cnidians, who attempted to dig through the isthmus that joined their peninsula to the mainland of Asia Minor. When they noticed that the diggers were getting injured to an unusual degree (literally 'in a rather divine way', θειότερον, 1.174) they sent for advice to the Delphic oracle; the reply – 'Do not fence in the isthmus with towers, and do not dig through it; Zeus would have made it an island had he wanted to' (1.174) – suggests divine disapproval of their alteration of the earth's geography. Landscape alteration also comes to be associated especially with tyranny. Later in Book 3, for example, we hear about a plateau in Asia surrounded by a ring of mountains, with five gorges running through them, each one inhabited by a different tribe. The Persian king has dammed up all five gorges, making the plateau into a sea, and opens the gates only when the desperate, water-starved tribes come to plead with him and bring tribute (3.117).[30] This is a good example of the way in which ancient literature is often interested in the human consequences of landscape alteration. In this case the exercise of power leads to an extreme crisis of human access to resources which has a certain amount in common with modern concerns about environmental justice within marginal communities disproportionately affected by environmental change. The *Histories* in fact dramatises the way in which Persian tyranny over nature is equivalent to and intertwined with their oppression of human populations.[31]

---

[28] Cf. Bosak-Schroeder 2020: 39 on this passage as one of several examples of positive representation of earthworks and waterworks in Herodotus; also Clarke 2018: 151–2.
[29] See Lateiner 1989: 126–35.   [30] See Clarke 2018: 192–3.
[31] See Clarke 2018: esp. 238–46; also Bosak-Schroeder 2020: 33 for the point that Herodotus (and also Diodorus) judges the value of landscape alteration according to its 'consequences to the human community'.

The association between landscape alteration and tyranny comes to a head in the final three books and especially in Book 7, in a series of passages describing Xerxes' attempts to tame and enslave the natural world. First come Xerxes' works on the Athos peninsula,[32] which had been planned for about three years, according to Herodotus, in response to the destruction of the Persian fleet that sailed in the previous invasion just over ten years before, shipwrecked by a great storm on the coasts beneath the mountain, as described at *Histories* 6.44. That initial incident establishes Mt Athos for the Persians as a landscape of fear.[33] Taming it is an enormous task: 'men of all nations who were part of the army worked at digging, under the whip (ὤρυσσον ὑπὸ μαστίγων παντοδαποὶ τῆς στρατιῆς); and the men went to work in turn; also involved in the digging were the people who lived around Athos' (7.22). There is more than a hint of tyrannical behaviour in the detail of the diggers under the lash.[34] Herodotus' closing observation similarly has negative overtones: 'What I find when I make an assessment of this work is that Xerxes ordered the canal to be dug out of arrogance (μεγαλοφροσύνης), and wanting to display his power and leave behind a memorial (μνημόσυνα λιπέσθαι)' (7.24). Herodotus explains that the Persians could perfectly well have dragged their ships across the isthmus, and that they made the channel twice as wide as it needed to be. On that account Xerxes is motivated primarily by a desire for self-aggrandisement, in line with widespread stereotypes of Persian tyranny.[35]

That said, it is important to stress that one might see some positive notes even here.[36] At any rate Xerxes' desire to leave a memorial echoes Herodotus' stated goal in the opening paragraph of the work, already quoted above, of preventing great achievements from losing their glory over time (1.pr). The excavation requires a vast effort of human cooperation in the taming of nature, and one might argue that there is a hint of admiration in some of these details. That becomes particularly clear when he tells us about the difficulty many of the diggers had because of the way in which earth at the top of the channel tended to crumble away as they

---

[32] See Clarke 2018: 198–200.   [33] Cf. della Dora 2011: 26.
[34] See Bridges 2015: 56 on Xerxes as enslaver, and on the way in which that is contrasted in Herodotus' account with the Greek commitment to freedom.
[35] Cf. della Dora 2011: 29 on the way in which Xerxes' canal is associated by Herodotus with Persian otherness, and Athos itself imagined as a boundary between east and west.
[36] See Baragwanath 2008: 254–65 for excellent discussion of the doubleness of Herodotus' account, and particularly of the possibility that there are ways of viewing Xerxes' desire for magnificence as a positive trait; cf. Bridges 2015: 56–7.

dug down, except in the case of the Phoenicians, who 'show wisdom (σοφίην) in their works generally, as they did in this case too' (7.23), and who started digging a trench twice as wide as the eventual channel they were aiming for. There are similar technical details later when Herodotus returns to the subject of the canal a few pages later to describe its completion: 'When ... the works around Mt Athos – both the mounds around the mouths of the channel, which were made because of the breaking of the sea, so that the mouths of the excavation should not be filled up, and the channel itself – were reported to be fully completed ...' (7.37). Here Xerxes' preparation is described as a careful, rational process which runs smoothly and precisely as planned, and resists the natural tendency of the sea towards disruption and disintegration.

Despite those caveats, however, the association of isthmus-cutting with tyranny is hard to ignore, and there are other passages that reinforce that impression in what follows. Most famously of all, Xerxes whips the Hellespont and throws a pair of shackles into it when his first attempt at a pontoon bridge is destroyed in a storm (7.35).[37] This is a fascinating passage partly because Xerxes' actions here treat the Hellespont in humanising terms. That effect contributes to Herodotus' negative portrayal of Xerxes, for example by contributing again to a sense that environmental exploitation is related to the exploitation of human populations.[38] There are many similar incidents later. At one point, for example, Xerxes sets a third of his army to work (an army so vast that it drinks whole rivers dry; Herodotus numbers it above two million men – no doubt an exaggeration, but still ...)[39] in cutting down woods on the Macedonian mountains into the district of Perrhaebia in northern Thessaly to give his army passage (7.131). While they are doing that, he questions his local advisors about the path of the river Peneius, and concludes that the only reason the Thessalians have surrendered to him is their fear that he would have dammed up the river and flooded the whole plain of Thessaly (7.130). Here Xerxes' reputation for landscape alteration in itself enables his project of conquest and oppression. Herodotus' characterisation of Xerxes as a

---

[37] See Clarke 2018: 214–16 on the predominantly negative characterisation of Xerxes' actions here, which nevertheless need not imply a blanket disapproval of this kind of project; also Bosak-Schroeder 2020: 33–5; Romm 2006: 190; and Bridges 2015: 57 and 58–60 on a series of other passages in Herodotus' work where other rivers are tamed and enslaved, esp. 1.189, 3.134 and 4.87.
[38] Cf. Clarke 2018: 240–1.
[39] See Herodotus 7.21.1 for the claim that all but the great rivers were drained by Xerxes' army; also 7.108.2 for the same claim about the river Lisos and 7.109.2 for a lake drained dry by the army's pack animals; and discussion by Bridges 2015: 52.

serial landscape manipulator is part of the wider pattern of overreaching and transgressing that eventually leads to the defeat of the Persian army.

Imperial Responses

The later history of these ideas can be told as a story of continuing ambivalence which is nevertheless dominated by negative responses. Even before Herodotus, Xerxes' encounter with the Hellespont is described in hybristic terms by Aeschylus in his *Persians*.[40] That image is then picked up by a number of fourth-century authors, most stridently by Lysias and Isocrates, who present much less nuanced and subtle accounts of Xerxes than Herodotus in order to serve their own rhetorical purposes.[41] Xerxes is also a negative reference point for many writers, both Greek and Latin, in the Republic and the early empire. For example, Manilius in *Astronomica* 3.19-21 refers in passing to 'the Persian war declared upon the deep, and the sea hidden by a huge fleet, and the channel inserted into the land, and the road on the waves of the sea' as one of the subjects he has chosen not to cover.[42] That text and others like it suggest that the rhetorical commonplaces that we find in Lysias and Isocrates were alive and well even four centuries later.[43] For a Greek example from the decades following one might look at Philo, in his work *On Dreams*, written in the first half of the first century CE. Philo there condemns Xerxes' *hybris* as vehemently as any other ancient author:

> But some people are full of such great foolishness that they are angry if the earth itself does not follow along with their intentions. For this reason Xerxes the king of the Persians, wanting to terrify his enemies, made a display of great achievements, altering nature; for he transformed both the land and the sea, giving land to the sea and sea to the land, by yoking the Hellespont with bridges and breaking up Mt Athos into deep gulfs, which were filled with sea and became a new ocean made by human hands, transformed from its ancient nature. (*On Dreams* 2.117–19)

There is a hint of the agency of the earth itself in the detail about its failure to follow along with human intentions, but that is quickly submerged in

---

[40] See Bridges 2015: esp. 14–16 and 27–8, with reference to *Persians* 71 and 722–52; also Romm 2006: 186–7 on the likelihood that Herodotus knew Aeschylus' play.
[41] For a survey of fourth-century responses, see Bridges 2015: 99–125. The key passages are Lysias, *Funeral Speech* 2.29 and Isocrates, *Panegyricus* 4.89; and see della Dora 2011: 29–30.
[42] See Bridges 2015: 159.
[43] Cf. Bridges 2015: 164–5 on Seneca the Elder, *Suasoriae* 2.3, 5.4 and 5.7.

the rest of the passage: that quasi-human recalcitrance seems to make Xerxes all the more determined to impose his own anthropocentric desires.

Some Latin texts from the late Republic and early empire are more conflicted, reflecting both praise of Rome's conquests of nature and also disapproval.[44] Pliny's *Natural History* is perhaps the most complex example of that phenomenon. In some sections of his work he seems to view Roman engineering works as objects of wonder. Elsewhere he offers quite passionate denunciations of the damage done to the earth's surface by human labour.[45] We find a similarly complex situation when we look at descriptions of villa landscapes in Latin, and also in the visual and architectural record for ancient villa construction. That is a common subject already in Republican Latin literature. Pompey, for example, is said to have accused his rival Lucullus in the 60s BCE of being a *Xerxes togatus* ('Xerxes in a toga') because of his elaborate building programmes, which included cutting through a mountain to channel sea water into his fishponds.[46] There are also much more positive accounts, however. Luxury villas in Roman Italy were often built into the landscape in a way that seems to have celebrated the interplay between building and environment;[47] that assumption is also reflected in depictions of villa buildings and their surrounding landscapes in Roman wall-painting.[48] Statius, writing in the second half of the first century CE, offers celebratory portraits of the elaborate villas of some of his contemporaries and the kinds of landscape alteration which have created them.[49] Most remarkable of all is his depiction of the villa of Pollius Felix in Campania:

> Here there used to be a mountain where now you see level ground, and wilderness where now you enter beneath a roof; where you now see tall woods, there was not even land; the occupier has tamed it, and the land

---

[44] See also Armstrong 2009 on the ambivalence of Augustan verse authors like Propertius and Horace and Virgil towards marvellous artistic and architectural achievements.

[45] E.g., see Pliny, *Natural History* 36.1 for a moralising denunciation of the way in which human greed for marble leads to the destruction of the earth's fabric; later in the same book, however, he praises a series of Roman tunneling and channeling projects at length, at 36.121–5.

[46] E.g., see Velleius Paterculus 2.33.4 and Plutarch, *Lucullus* 39.2–3, with Jolivet 1987; Bridges 2015: 173; Edwards 1993: 143–9 for broad discussion of the association between landscape alteration and excessive luxury in Roman elite building projects, and 145–6 on the Xerxes parallel specifically; Purcell 1987: 190–2 on the way in which these criticisms draw on the widespread link between landscape alteration and tyranny; for a more neutral representation of Lucullus' projects, see Varro *Rust.* 3.17.9; and for more general criticism of practices of landscape alteration in villa building, see Sen. *Controv.* 2.1.13; Sallust, *Catiline* 13.1–2, with Vretska 1976: 1, 238–9.

[47] See Zarmakoupi 2014.   [48] See Hinterhöller-Klein 2015: 329–498.

[49] Other relevant passages include *Silvae* 1.3 on the villa of Manilius Vopiscus at Tibur; 3.1.91–104 for more on Pollius' building projects; and 4.3 on Domitian's construction of the Via Domitiana.

rejoices as he shapes cliffs or destroys them, following his lead. Now see the rocks learning to bear the yoke, and the buildings as they enter, and the mountain which has been ordered to withdraw. (Statius, *Silvae* 2.2.54–9)

On the face of it Statius' representation of these places is celebratory,[50] although his readers would have been well aware that there was a tradition of moralising denunciation of them lying behind his text.[51] Ancient authors in their descriptions of landscape alteration are often quite ready to ascribe agency and quasi-human identity to the land, as Statius is here (we shall see more examples below), but that is rarely developed into anything like a modern ecocritical vision of respect for the value and independence of the more-than-human world. It may be that we are expected to feel uneasy about the ease with which the poet's voice endorses an anthropocentric view – just as we are likely to be uneasy about Xerxes' anthropocentric manipulation of humanising metaphors for landscape at the Hellespont – but there is no attempt to draw attention to that expectation if so, or to articulate what an alternative, more environmentally respectful response might look like.

When we look ahead to the second and third centuries CE we find a striking number of negative judgements of landscape alteration, although they are still interwoven with some positive images. For example, it is easy enough to find passages where praise of the Romans is directed at their feats of engineering and their mastery over the terrain. Aelius Aristides, in his speech *Praise of Rome*, composed in the mid-second century CE, talks about the ease of travel that Roman rule has brought with it in precisely those terms: 'You have measured the whole inhabited world, you have yoked rivers with many different kinds of bridges, you have cut through mountains to make them accessible to traffic' (Aristides 26.100–1).[52] But the dominant approach is a more sceptical one. Xerxes is still a standard example of excessive passion: for example, Plutarch in his work *On the Control of Anger* (455e) describes an angry letter sent by Xerxes to Mt Athos in which he threatens to cut the mountain down and throw it into the sea. Xerxes is also repeatedly associated with bad emperors. One obvious example is Caligula's bridging of the bay of Naples at Baiae, which

---

[50] See Spencer 2010: 104–13; Newby 2012: 353–5; and for a useful collection of passages celebrating landscape alteration from Statius, and also Martial and Pliny the Younger, see Pavlovskis 1973.
[51] As Newby 2012: 353, n. 18 acknowledges.
[52] Cf. the discussion of Roman power, road building and travel in Polybius and mid-Republican texts in Wiater's chapter in this volume.

is equated with Xerxes' mastery of the Hellespont in the work of Cassius Dio, Josephus, Suetonius and Seneca.[53]

Several Greek texts from this period also take a very negative, Herodotean view of Nero's project to cut the Isthmus of Corinth (an enterprise that was originally associated with the tyrant Periander).[54] Cassius Dio goes furthest of all in suggesting divine disapproval:

> As a secondary achievement from his time in Greece, having conceived a desire to dig through the isthmus of the Peloponnese, he made a start on it, even though others shrank from the task. For blood spouted up from the ground when the first people touched it, and groans and bellowing were heard, and many phantoms became visible. And having picked up a mattock himself and having dug a little he compelled the others too to imitate him, and he sent for a great multitude of people from other nations too to carry out the work. (Cassius Dio 62.16)

Here the huge volume of workers could conceivably be given a positive spin, as an example of widespread cooperation in a project for public benefit, but in this case the information that they were 'sent for' is surely intended to hint at a more tyrannical motivation; that detail also recalls the 'men of all nations' who work for Xerxes in Herodotus' account. The details of the blood and the groaning ascribes agency to the land, but in a way which is once again quite different from anything we find in modern environmental writing: in this case they are used to point above all to divine presence in or guardianship over the landscape, rather than to any developed sense of more-than-human value in the environment itself. At the same time this passage does anticipate modern environmental concerns in reinforcing the impression that environmental and human oppression go hand in hand.

Strabo

That story of mixed responses, where negative images of environmental interference never lose their prominence, is disrupted by two remarkably positive visions of landscape alteration from late Hellenistic and Augustan Greek literature, in the works of Diodorus Siculus and Strabo. What stands out is not so much the fact that landscape alteration is open to

---

[53] See Bridges 2015: 171–3.
[54] See Pausanias 2.1.5–6 with Hutton 2005: 47; Ps.-Lucian, *Nero* 2; also by contrast Suetonius, *Nero* 19.2–3 for a more positive view of the Isthmus project as an act of benefaction; and Pettegrew 2016 for an overview.

positive assessment – it is easy enough to find parallels, as we have seen – but rather the fact that that vision is sustained so consistently and at such great length.

Do these two works have any significant connection with each other in their representation of human moulding of the natural environment? Do they between them allow us to speak of a distinctive strand of late Hellenistic and Augustan environmental thinking which stands apart from what comes before and after, connected perhaps with a positive attitude towards Rome's conquests under Pompey and Caesar and Augustus in the late first century BCE and the early first century CE, and with their self-representation as cultural heroes and benefactors moulding the world for the benefit of all in the model of Alexander the Great?[55] Later Greek authors, by contrast, tend to take a much more sceptical or else indifferent view of Rome's achievements and seek their models instead in the classical world and in Herodotus in particular, with his suspicion of tyranny. That way of telling the story is obviously in line with many of the ways in which scholars have thought about the relationship between late Hellenistic culture and the 'Second Sophistic' in recent decades. On that view, the late Hellenistic and Augustan period when Strabo was writing saw many Greek writers working in Rome and dependent on Roman patronage, and still engaged in the project, started by Polybius, of negotiating Greece's place in a new, Roman world.[56] By the second century CE, by contrast, the increased wealth and confidence of the cities of the Greek east made it easier to live without constant reference to Rome; that development went hand in hand with increasing attention to the classical Greek past. For example, a number of recent publications have tended to stress the enormous differences between Strabo and Pausanias – the former more engaged with a global view of the Mediterranean world that seems influenced by imperial ideals,[57] the latter, writing a century and a half later, with a much more local, classicising focus and more hesitant about mentioning or endorsing Roman rule.[58]

---

[55] On Strabo's positive image of Augustus, see Dueck 2000: 96–106, esp. 104 on comparison of Augustus and other Roman generals with Alexander; also 115–22 on Strabo's approving attitude to Roman conquest. On continuities between Pompey, Caesar and Augustus in the representation of the (global) space of Roman power, see Wiater in this volume.

[56] Cf. Hatzimichali below for other aspects of Strabo's closeness to Rome.

[57] E.g., see Nicolet 1991: esp. 47, who sees the *Geography* as one of many examples of the intersection between knowledge and imperial power in Rome in the reign of Augustus and the decades that followed.

[58] See Pretzler 2005; also Cohen 2001.

Alternatively, are there strands of Herodotean ambiguity even in Diodorus and Strabo, once we delve into the detailed texture of their works in more depth, which throw doubt on the validity of any simplistic narrative like the one I have sketched out here? Examining those questions is the main task of the rest of this chapter. I look first of all at Strabo, building on my own earlier work on the *Geography*'s representations of mountain landscapes,[59] before turning in more detail to his predecessor Diodorus.

Strabo in particular is remarkable for the way in which a positive attitude to landscape alteration is threaded right through the work (whereas in Diodorus' case, as we shall see, it clusters above all in the opening books). Over and over again Strabo describes projects which involve the taming of the natural environment. It is at first sight hard to find examples which even hint at the ideas of *hybris* that are so prominent in the Herodotean tradition and in so much later historiographical and geographical writing. Strabo's views are linked among other things with his division of the inhabited world between civilised and uncivilised cultures. Both in different ways tend to live close to the land. Untamed peoples on the edges of empire are affected negatively by their experience of the harsh environments they inhabit. In that sense Strabo is quite typical of ancient thinking on environmental determinism, although he also shows how Augustus in particular has begun to bring these people into a state of civilisation among other things by his refashioning of the landscape.[60] By contrast, and more innovatively, civilised regions like Greece and Italy are shown to have moulded the landscape to their own purposes many centuries before. Strabo is particularly fascinated by the image of cities built into mountains or coastlines, as I have argued elsewhere: there are repeated examples in his account of the urbanised landscapes of Italy in Book 5, and then again in Books 8–9 on mainland Greece, and Books 12–14 on Asia Minor.[61]

The *Geography* is also packed with examples of engineering projects of various types that have brought human benefits. One area where Strabo seems to have had an unusually intricate interest was mining: it has even been suggested that he may have had some kind of specialist mining experience.[62] He tends to avoid criticism of mining, in contrast with the much more negative image of damage to the earth's surface which we find

---

[59] König 2016a.
[60] E.g., see König 2016a: 55–8 on mountain landscapes and mountain peoples; also Dueck 2000: 99 on *Geography* 4.6.6, where Strabo describes Augustus' road-building in the Alps.
[61] See König 2016a: 59–67.   [62] See Roller 2014: 12–13.

just a few decades later in Pliny's *Natural History*. For example in his account of the natural resources of Spain he offers a lengthy account of mining techniques used both there and elsewhere (3.2.8–11). He quotes Posidonius as a precedent for his own positive representation of the mines of Tourdetania and for some of the technical details of his account.[63] At 14.6.5 he even suggests (again quoting a Hellenistic predecessor, this time Eratosthenes) that in Cyprus 'in the old days the plains were overgrown with woods, and all the land was overrun with thickets and not able to be farmed. Mining helped a little with this, since they cut down trees to burn copper and silver.' Remarkably in that case mining is represented not just as a successful example of landscape alteration on a specific site, but also as a practice that contributes more broadly towards conquest of the wilderness (he also mentions shipbuilding and a scheme which allows ownership of land as a reward for clearance).

Waterworks are another important category. In 16.1.9–11, for example, Strabo tells us about the artificial cataracts built by the Persians on the river Euphrates to prevent anyone from sailing up. Alexander dismantles many of them, and renovates the network of canals that dealt with the river's floodwater.[64] For example, one of the canals turns out to be in bad condition, so Alexander 'opened up another new mouth thirty stadia away, having chosen a rocky place, and diverted the stream there' (16.1.11). Here Alexander removes the Persians' engineering projects and undertakes his own, virtuous project of landscape surveillance and alteration, characterised by care and by motives of benefaction – although the impression of moderation is partially undermined in what immediately follows when we hear that the diversion of the stream led him to plans for the conquest of Arabia: 'the truth is that he was reaching out to be master of all' (16.1.11).

Strabo's account of Xerxes similarly strips away much of the negativity of the Herodotean tradition, but without abandoning it entirely: even for Strabo it seems to be hard to escape entirely from the tradition of negative characterisation. He describes the cutting of the Athos peninsula in a very neutral, non-judgemental fashion: 'Here a canal is also visible, in the region around Akanthos, where Xerxes is said to have dug through Athos and brought his fleet from the Strymonic Gulf across the isthmus, by bringing the sea into the canal' (7.F15a). Taken on its own that passage is unremarkable, but it is important to stress that it stands as just one of

---

[63] E.g., 3.2.9. [64] 16.1.9–11; cf. 17.1.3 on regulation of the Nile.

many similar passages in Strabo which presents us with the human achievement of altering the earth's surface: they have a cumulative and largely positive effect. The passage that follows complicates matters a little, however:

> Demetrios the Skepsian does not think that this canal was navigable, for as far as ten stadia he says that it has good soil and has been dug, but then there is a high flat rock almost one stadion in length that could not have been excavated entirely through to the sea. And even if it could have been dug that far it would not have been deep enough to make a navigable passage.

The absence of explicitly negative language here is striking: this passage is typical of the way in which Strabo cites his sources in an impersonal and matter-of-fact way where others might resort to moralising pronouncements. That in turn enhances Strabo's self-representation as an author whose judgement and appreciation of grand engineering schemes is based on careful attention to the on-the-ground realities, rather than sweeping judgements and received traditions. Nevertheless, this postscript does undermine Xerxes' achievement.[65] Is it even perhaps meant, by portraying the Athos canal as an enormous vanity project, or at least a military deception that was never carried through in full, to recall Herodotus' claim that Xerxes was motivated primarily by the appearance of magnificence? For example, we might suspect that it is intended to contrast the illusory nature of Xerxes' achievement with more solid and lasting Greek and Roman dominance over landscape, as in the detail above about Alexander's dismantling of the Persian cataracts.

Diodorus Siculus

Where does Diodorus fit in with that picture? My argument here is that the *Library of History* adds weight to the idea of a distinctively late Hellenistic attitude to landscape alteration, but also that his text, rather more so than Strabo's, has elements of equivocation and ambiguity which complicate that assumption, if we read it from beginning to end. Diodorus' history was widely denigrated during the twentieth century as a second-hand compilation drawn from other writers' histories. That characterisation led until quite recently to a situation where scholars were not prepared to explore the challenge of reading the text from cover to

---

[65] Cf. 9.1.13 for passing mention of Xerxes' failed attempt to construct a mole to Salamis.

cover and looking for thematic continuities and dissonances between different sections. Much has changed within the last two decades or so, and it is now a less uncommon procedure in Diodorus scholarship to draw connections between different sections of the text, as we shall see further in a moment, and to assume an overarching design in the work, shaped in part by Diodorus' own thematic interests and by his own distinctively late Hellenistic concerns.[66] I share those assumptions here.

Those developments in Diodorus scholarship have occurred side by side with a growing attention to the knowledge-ordering and encyclopaedic literature of the Roman imperial world, although the two have not often been explicitly connected.[67] The recent expansion of scholarship on that vast body of literature has made it clear even more than it was before that for ancient readers compilatory writing was highly valued. It has also shown that much of this work is open to consecutive reading, of the kind which allows us to experience developing narratives that thread their way through individual texts.[68] Encyclopaedism and miscellanism in the ancient world, in other words, were narrative modes, or at least were always open to being read as narratives (not that I mean to suggest that they were viewed exclusively in those terms; clearly the intellectual culture of the Roman empire was also feeling its way to the kinds of methodologies of consultative reading that we are familiar with today, albeit surprisingly slowly and tentatively).[69] With that context in mind, the fact that Diodorus is usually viewed as an 'encyclopaedic' historian should be an encouragement to read his work from end to end rather than the opposite.

Diodorus returns over and over again in his first five books to the image of great culture heroes whose deeds, which often include various kinds of engineering projects,[70] earn them a reputation for immortality. In some

---

[66] See Sacks 1990: esp. 3–5 for summary; Sulimani 2011: esp. 55, n. 92; Rathmann 2016; Hau 2016: 73–123; Muntz 2017: 1–26; Hau, Meeus and Sheridan 2018; Morton 2018, incl. 534–5, n. 4 for a fuller list of recent publications 'interested in Diodorus as an author'; Rood 2018; also Palm 1955 for the argument that Diodorus' style is consistent across the work, even between sections generally thought to have been copied from different authors. Cf. also Baumann's chapter in this volume.

[67] The obvious exception is Rubincam 1987, 1989 and 1997. Wiater 2006b argues that Diodorus' choice of a compilatory method is a positive one, and that Diodorus views it as a modern way of writing history in contrast with the outdated insistence on autopsy in earlier historiographers.

[68] E.g., see the essays in König and Whitmarsh 2007a and König and Woolf 2013; also König 2016a on Strabo, and 2016b on Pollux.

[69] See Riggsby 2007 and 2019, although he also stresses ultimately the gap between ancient compilations and modern reference works.

[70] See esp. Sulimani 2011: 246–65 on various kinds of water engineering in Books 1–5; and cf. Dionysius of Halicarnassus, *Roman Antiquities* 1.41.1 for another late Hellenistic discussion along similar lines: he describes the way in which Heracles turned the course of rivers and cut roads

cases these are massive projects involving the diversion of rivers or carving of mountains. Recent work on Diodorus has shown that he, like Herodotus, avoids monolithic value judgement on these projects, that he is repeatedly interested in calculating their costs and benefits, and that he tends to reserve his most positive accounts for those that 'benefit both ruler and ruled' –[71] another example of the way in which ancient assessments of environmental alteration are often very much aware of its impact on human populations. Nevertheless it is also clear that Diodorus, like Strabo, shows relatively little sign of the kinds of strongly negative judgement which are so frequent in much of the post-Herodotean Xerxes tradition. The first examples come in Diodorus' account of Egypt. We hear, for example, about the foundation of Memphis by the Egyptian king Uchoreus, which involved the construction of a vast mound and a lake to protect the city from the waters of the Nile.[72] That is followed by the building of another lake twelve generations later by king Moeris. In this case the language of benefaction is quite explicit: the lake, Diodorus tells us, is 'remarkable for its utility and incredible in the magnitude of the achievement (τῷ ... μεγέθει τῶν ἔργων) ... Who, in trying to calculate the greatness of the structure, would not reasonably ask how many tens of thousands of men (πόσαι μυριάδες ἀνδρῶν) brought this to completion, over how many years?' (1.51.5–6). He makes a similarly positive assessment later: 'as for the usefulness of this lake and its shared benefit to all the inhabitants of Egypt, and as for the ingenuity of the king, no one is capable of praising it in a way which does justice to the truth' (1.51.7). Moeris also builds a canal between the lake and the river, and uses the reservoir to control the water supply to the surrounding farmland, at great expense. A later ruler, Sesoösis, throws up great mounds of earth above the flood plains to build new cities, and constructs an additional network of canals for public benefit (1.57.1–3). In some cases in Books 1–5 achievements of this kind are accompanied by cruel and tyrannical behaviour, but usually that kind of detail is supplemented or even mitigated by generous or even merciful acts. Sesoösis, for example, uses captives to construct a series of temples; they revolt, 'unable to endure the hardships' of the work, but are eventually granted an amnesty and allowed to found their own colony (1.56.3). The idea of landscape alteration as both wonder and benefaction

---

through mountains for the benefit of all; and discussion by McEwen 2003: 130–1, who links this passage of Dionysius with both Diodorus and Vitruvius.
[71] Bosak-Schroeder 2020: 43–7 esp. 45 for that quotation.
[72] Cf. Hdt. 2.99 for a related account, but ascribing this to a different king, Min.

is extended in Diodorus' portrayal of Mesopotamia in Book 2. For example, he describes Semiramis' foundation of Babylon, which is carried out by a vast workforce – 'she gathered together from her entire kingdom two million men to complete the work' (2.7.2) – and involves a massive project of river diversion (2.9).[73] Diodorus then gives a long account of the deeds of Heracles along similar lines in Book 4.[74]

There are also repeated references to similar acts of landscape alteration threaded through his later books, although less frequently so than for Strabo, and it is that later material that I turn to now. Here especially the principle of consecutive reading I outlined above becomes important. The increasing readiness to see connections between different parts of Diodorus' work has led recently to a renewed interest in Books 1–5 and in their significance for the work as a whole.[75] Several scholars have attempted recently to understand the connection between the mythical narratives of benefaction in the opening books and the historical books that follow.[76] In most cases the tendency has been to emphasise the continuities, for example the way in which those mythical benefactors prefigure historical actors who turn up in the later books, Julius Caesar in particular.[77] Some scholars have suggested that contemporary readers could have drawn comparisons with recent examples of Roman conquest of the Mediterranean landscape. Diodorus seems to have been working on the text at least up to 27 BCE. It is clear that he does not go anything like as far as he could have in addressing contemporary Roman history: from his statements on the end date of the work it seems likely that he began writing the work in 46 BCE and originally intended to take that as the finishing point of his history, but that he later changed his mind and finished instead at 60 BCE.[78] Nevertheless, there are clear contemporary

---

[73] For Semiramis' many mountain-cutting projects, see 2.11.4, 2.13.1, 2.13.5 and 2.13.7–8.
[74] See esp. 4.18, 4.19, 4.22.   [75] Cf. Baumann's chapter in this volume as well as Baumann 2020.
[76] Beagon 2013 argues that Pliny in his *Natural History* draws a parallel between his own labour as compiler and the labour of Hercules and other culture heroes; it seems likely that Diodorus intends a similar link in his own case too, not least because of his mention of the benefactions conferred by universal historians, in the opening sentence of the work (1.1.1); and cf. brief discussion along similar lines by Bosak-Schroeder 2020: 37.
[77] E.g., Sacks 1990 has drawn comparisons between Books 1–5 and what follows later (see esp. 71–82 on the benefactions of various rulers and commanders in later books of the work), but without any reference to the theme of landscape alteration especially; cf. Wiater 2006a on the way in which that effect (especially the use of the culture-bringers of Books 1–5 as models for Alexander and Julius Caesar) acts out the goals of universal history writing laid out by Diodorus in his preface to Book 1, especially the connection between peoples of different time periods.
[78] See Sacks 1990: 169–72; Sulimani 2011: 37; and Muntz 2017: 215–47 for an extended reconstruction of the likely progress of Diodorus' writing during the 40s BCE and after.

resonances. Often cited examples include the evidence for Roman irrigation works in Egypt,[79] or Agrippa's alteration of Lake Lucernus and Lake Avernus,[80] acts which are echoed within Diodorus' account of these early culture heroes of Greek civilisation, especially Heracles. Diodorus' description of Heracles' progress over the Alps echoes the interventions of successive Roman commanders in this region, which made the passage of the mountains safe by building and repairing roads and by the conquest of hostile inhabitants.[81] Most importantly, Diodorus repeatedly makes reference to Julius Caesar's deification, and explicitly mentions him in Books 1–5, side by side with those other deified benefactors,[82] although his decision to end the work in 60 BCE rather than 46 BCE means that Caesar's career is largely absent from the work, so he holds back from the opportunity to explore that link in any detail.[83]

Those views of Diodorus' structure are broadly convincing. What I want to stress here, however, is the way in which there are also occasional disjunctions between the opening books and what follows in the rest of the work. Those are not necessarily disjunctions that paint the work's historical actors in a negative light, but they might every so often give us pause before we accept the idea of a clear-cut connection between mythical and historical past. The quasi-heroic protagonists of those earlier books tend to be represented as universal benefactors, who receive divine status as a reward for their deeds. That theme is echoed in many of the historical books: there are some examples of historical actors being rewarded for their benefactions, sometimes even with divine honours, and Iris Sulimani has argued that that motif is unique to Greek and Latin writers of the mid-first century BCE.[84] It is also clear, however, that there are plenty of exceptions. Many of the protagonists of Diodorus' later books tend to act out of much more mundane motivations and with much more mundane outcomes, often within the context of military campaigns,[85] in a way which leaves the impression that the greatness of the mythical benefactors of the early books

---

[79] Sulimani 2011: 246–52.   [80] Sulimani 2011: 259–60.
[81] See Sulimani 2011: 216–20 and 344, stressing especially the way in which Heracles' making-safe of the Alps echoes the exploits of Julius Caesar.
[82] Diodorus 3.38.2–3, 4.19.2, 5.21.2; and see Sacks 1990: 175–84, although he also shows that Diodorus is ambivalent about some aspects of Roman rule, despite his idealisation of Julius Caesar.
[83] See Sacks 1990: 172–3.
[84] See Sulimani 2011: 64–82. On the wider Hellenistic background to the discourse of benefactions and its relationship with contemporary historical writing, including Diodorus and Strabo, see Gray's chapter in this volume.
[85] Examples include 15.12, where the Spartans divert a river to flood the city of Mantineia; 16.49, where Lacrates diverts the river at Pelusium away from the city so that he can bring up siege engines; 15.42, where Nectanebus fortifies the Pelusiac mouth of the Nile and digs channels for defence.

is being echoed only in quite a distant fashion in later events.[86] As soon as we move beyond the end of Book 5, we enter (as one would expect) a different world.

One of the factors that Diodorus uses to prompt his readers to compare the different sections of his work is the repetition of repeated motifs and repeated vocabulary. Most striking for the passages I examine here is the motif of a large labour force. That recurs over and over again in the mythical books, as we have seen: there the size of the labour force is often in itself a source of wonder. It is also a distinctive preoccupation of Diodorus in the later books. One of the vehicles for that motif is the word πολυχειρία ('many-handedness', in the context of a large body of workers). That word occurs fifty-eight times in surviving pre-Christian Greek literature. Nineteen of those occurrences are in the work of Diodorus. In nearly all of those cases it occurs in the context of a description of some military engineering project being brought to completion, often unexpectedly speedy completion, because of the large numbers involved.[87] It is hard to believe that Diodorus has lifted all of these passages from the work of his predecessors, when they are so similar to each other and when that word is so unusual in other surviving historiographical writing, and hard to avoid the conclusion that Diodorus is here tying together his work (whether consciously or otherwise) by imprinting his own distinctive interests on to his source material.[88] That repetition prompts us to make our own comparisons. If we think back to figures like Semiramis and Sesoösis when we read about these huge armies of workers that might quite plausibly prompt us to think of the historical leaders Dionysus describes as heroic benefactor figures. But that is not a foregone conclusion: in principle we might be equally likely to sense difference.

In the rest of this chapter I want to look at two examples in detail: the first is Diodorus' account of Xerxes' Mt Athos canal; the second is Alexander's siege of Tyre. Of all the incidents Diodorus recounts, Xerxes' campaign is the one that we would expect to put most strain on

---

[86] Cf. Muntz 2017: 133–90, who argues that most of the Hellenistic rulers Diodorus describes, including Alexander, are depicted as falling short of the divine honours of the deified culture bringers of the early books.

[87] The relevant passages in Diodorus are 1.31.9, 1.35.10, 1.63.9, 11.2.4, 11.40.2, 13.86.1, 14.18.6, 14.51.1, 14.58.3, 15.68.3, 15.93.3, 17.40.5, 17.41.2, 17.42.7, 17.44.5, 17.85.6, 17.89.6, 18.70.7, 20.92.1.

[88] Cf. Morton 2018: esp. 536–40 for a similar argument on the words ὑπερηφανία, ἐπιείκεια and φιλανθρωπία, which recur repeatedly through the text, often in combination with each other; for example all three terms are used together seven times; the last two are used together in some form thirty-three times (539).

Diodorus' generally positive vision of landscape alteration. Is it possible that even Xerxes' manipulation of the landscape of Greece can be rescued? For the most part Diodorus manages that challenge well. And yet there are little hints, if we think back to the mythical sections of the work, that remind us almost inevitably of the negative side of the Xerxes tradition.

Diodorus' account, for all his debt to Herodotus,[89] strips away much of the detail of that earlier account and turns the whole episode into a very brief one:

> Then, dividing his army, Xerxes sent ahead a sufficient number to bridge the Hellespont and to dig through Athos at the neck of the Cherronesus, making the passage safe and short for his forces (ταῖς δυνάμεσιν ἀσφαλῆ καὶ σύντομον τὴν διέξοδον ποιούμενος) and at the same time also hoping by the greatness of his deeds to terrify the Greeks in advance (τῷ μεγέθει τῶν ἔργων ἐλπίζων προκαταπλήξεσθαι τοὺς Ἕλληνας). The men who had been sent to get these works ready completed them quickly, because of the multitude of people working on them (διὰ τὴν πολυχειρίαν τῶν ἐργαζομένων). (11.2.4)

And then a little later: 'when Xerxes learned that the Hellespont had been bridged and that Athos had been excavated, he set out from Sardis and made his way to the Hellespont; and when he had arrived at Abydos, he led his army over the bridge into Europe' (Diodorus 11.3.6). And then finally at 11.5.1: 'the ships passed through the place where the canal had been cut into the other sea quickly and safely' (συντόμως καὶ ἀσφαλῶς). 11.5.1 repeats the language of 11.2.4 in its reference to the combination of speed with safety, emphasising the success of Xerxes' enterprise.

Where does this account stand on the spectrum between Books 1–5, with their vision of landscape alteration and benefaction, and the tradition stemming from Herodotus which views Xerxes' alterations of the landscape as acts of *hybris*? One way of addressing that question is with reference to Diodorus' representation of the 'many-handedness' (πολυχειρίαν) of those who were doing the work. That word once again presents this as part of a long series of other landscape-alteration scenes in Diodorus. Whether we should emphasise their continuity or disjunction is not clear, however. One might feel that in the case of Xerxes large numbers can hardly help suggesting *hybris*, especially given that Diodorus stresses the size of Xerxes' expedition repeatedly in the pages that come before and

---

[89] On the importance of Herodotus for Diodorus' conception of universal history, see Sulimani 2011: 52; on the similarities between Herodotus and Diodorus in their portrayals of Xerxes, see Bridges 2015: 136.

after the Athos description, in a way which surely for some readers would reactivate stereotypes of Persian military excess and tyranny: that is one feature of Herodotus' account that Diodorus does not dilute. And yet as we have seen, some of the culture heroes of Books 1–5 are also described even more explicitly as tyrannical: that need not automatically be incompatible with their status as benefactors.

Alternatively one might look for ways in which Diodorus resists some of the most distinctive emphases of the Herodotean tradition. For example, his point about the desire to strike terror into the Greeks parallels Herodotus' suggestion that the project was undertaken for show, but reshapes that point so that the canal comes to have a clear military purpose, rather than appearing as a piece of self-indulgent posturing. And even more than Herodotus, Diodorus emphasises the smoothness of the process: the task is completed 'with dispatch'; there is no mention of the problems of crumbling canal walls or the challenge of building embankments to stop the entrances from silting up. Arguably that omission lessens the sense of monumental achievement that we get from Herodotus' account, but it also cuts out any impression of uncertainty about the success of Xerxes' undertaking.[90]

At the same time, however, it is striking that Xerxes' deeds are also different in some respects from what we see in Books 1–5. Diodorus' emphasis on the greatness of Xerxes' deeds ties it very closely to that mythical prehistory. For example, the phrase τῷ μεγέθει τῶν ἔργων exactly repeats 1.51.5 (quoted above), where Diodorus is describing Moeris' construction of the lake at Memphis. What is missing (as for many of the descriptions of landscape engineering in the historical sections of the work) is any mention of benefaction, let along divine status arising from benefaction. Xerxes' making-safe of a mountain route has several parallels in Books 1–5.[91] There is no sense, however, of universal benefaction, or even benefaction towards Xerxes' own people. Instead the 'making safe' is aimed much more narrowly at Xerxes' own forces: 'in this way not only making the passage safe and short for his forces'. Attentive readers will notice, if they think back to the early books of the work, that Xerxes' canal is certainly not being presented here as a universal good. And yet even in

---

[90] Diodorus' relatively positive account of Xerxes' actions here may be linked with his broader tendency to downplay the importance of Athenian victory in the Persian wars, which Schmitz 2011a: 242–3 and 245–6 takes as a sign of the difference between Diodorus' late Hellenistic attitude to the Greek past and the more developed classicism of the later imperial period.

[91] See also Sulimani 2011 on the way in which Xerxes is just one of several figures in the work associated with crossing of the Hellespont (cf. 1.20.1 on Osiris and 3.65.4–6 on Dionysus).

that respect it is hard to see a completely clear dividing line between Xerxes and his mythical predecessors. When Semiramis cuts a road through Mt Zarcaeus we are told that it is for her own benefit – 'she was ambitious both to leave an immortal memorial of herself and at the same time to make her way short (σύντομον)' (2.13.5) – in contrast with Heracles' road over the Alps, which has a more universal impact: 'with the result that it is passable for armies and baggage-trains (ὥστε δύνασθαι στρατοπέδοις καὶ ταῖς τῶν ὑποζυγίων ἀποσκευαῖς βάσιμον εἶναι)' (4.19.3).[92] Even within Books 1–5, in other words, Diodorus is far from consistent in his portrayal of the motivations underlying great achievements.

The siege of Tyre incident in Book 17, my second test case, is one of a series of military engineering and more specifically causeway-building projects in the central books of Diodorus' history. In 13.47, for example, we hear about the Euboean project to connect their island with the mainland, with Boeotian help, as a means of self-defence, prompted by fear of Athens. The building work proceeds quickly: 'for they gave orders not only to the citizens to come out en masse but also to the foreigners who were living there, so that thanks to the large number who came forward to do the work the proposed project was quickly brought to completion' (13.47.4). Here yet again we have the standard motif of a large work force bringing the task to quick completion. This, like the equivalent incidents in Books 1–5, is a much more positive version of the motif of international collaboration that we have seen already as a sign of tyranny in Herodotus and Strabo. But even if it is hard to see any negative intent in this passage it is striking, if we read this with images of Semiramis and Sesoösis still lingering in our minds, that the collaborative nature of the undertaking seems relatively democratic, with no single named benefactor. We find here precisely the kind of shared benefit and contact between different communities that Sesoösis brings about in 1.57, but in this case it arises from civic consensus, or at least from anonymous orders (προσέταξαν) rather than the authority and mastery of an individual. This is a different, more democratic world. Then in 14.48, Diodorus recounts the siege of the island of Motye by Dionysius of Syracuse in 397 BCE. The Motyans breach the artificial causeway that joined their city to the Sicilian mainland, and Dionysius sets out to rebuild it, committing more and more resources (14.49.3). He succeeds finally, and the city falls: 'After Dionysius had completed the causeway by employing a large force of labourers

---

[92] Cf. Muntz 2017: 166 for the point that even Sesoösis and Semiramis do not qualify for the divine status that is earned by acts of universal benefaction.

(τῇ πολυχειρίᾳ τῶν ἐργαζομένων), he brought up war engines of every kind against the walls' (14.51.1). Here we do have a single individual driving the engineering project forwards and directing the vast number of helpers. But once again there are obvious ways in which this differs from the projects of the early books, above all because it would be very hard to view this as an act of benefaction when the inhabitants are sold into slavery, unless Dionysius' generosity to his own soldiers can be viewed in those terms.

The final and most complex example in this series of causeway-building episodes is at 17.40–3, where Diodorus gives a lengthy account of Alexander's famous siege of the city of Tyre in 332 BCE, which similarly involved building a causeway across the water to reach the island. When the Tyrians ban Alexander from entering the city, he takes action immediately:

> εὐθὺς οὖν καθαιρῶν τὴν παλαιὰν λεγομένην Τύρον καὶ πολλῶν μυριάδων κομιζουσῶν τοὺς λίθους χῶμα κατεσκεύαζε δίπλεθρον τῷ πλάτει. πανδημεὶ δὲ προσλαβόμενος τοὺς κατοικοῦντας τὰς πλησίον πόλεις ταχὺ διὰ τὰς πολυχειρίας ἠνύετο τὰ τῶν ἔργων.
>
> Immediately he demolished what was known as Old Tyre and with many tens of thousands of men carrying stones he constructed a mole two plethra in width. He drafted in the entire population of the nearby cities and the building made rapid progress because of the large numbers. (17.40.5)

Once again we see the characteristic emphasis on volume of workers and on rapidity which ties together so many of these different incidents within Diodorus' text. And a little later we hear similarly that the Tyrians were 'outstripped by the large size of Alexander's labour force' (καταταχούμενοι δ' ὑπὸ τῆς πολυχειρίας) (17.41.2). Neither of these mentions of the volume of workers has any equivalent within the parallel account by Quintus Curtius in his *History of Alexander* Book 4, which makes it more likely that they are Diodorus' own addition.

In what follows the question of divine approval is raised repeatedly. The Tyrians sail up to the causeway and ask whether Alexander expects to 'get the better of Poseidon' (17.41.1). Later a sea monster appears[93] and 'both sides interpreted the portent as a sign that Poseidon would help them, inclining in their opinions towards the interpretation most in their own interests' (17.41.5–6). Those details raise the possibility of divine disapproval and *hybris*. They also make it clear that we are in a world where the

---

[93] That detail is also in Curtius, at 4.4.3–5.

value of large-scale projects like these is far from clear-cut; in Books 1–5, by contrast, that is never in doubt. The possibility of *hybris* is then raised again when a gale damages a large part of the causeway, in a way which depicts Alexander's building project as a struggle against nature.[94] In response, Alexander brings huge trees down from the mountains and 'blocked the force of the waves' (ἐνέφραξε τὴν βίαν τοῦ κλύδωνος) (17.42.6).[95] Much of this account recalls Herodotus' description of Xerxes crossing the Hellespont: there too a storm destroys the bridge, which then needs to be strengthened with the addition of wood.[96] Those echoes are not necessarily Diodorus' additions: Alexander was regularly contrasted with Xerxes by later historians, but often in a way that did not rule out the possibility of associations and similarities between them too.[97] Diodorus too, for all his overwhelmingly positive portrayal of Alexander, has not suppressed those associations entirely.

Conclusions

This chapter has explored the possibility that late Hellenistic and early imperial culture were particularly open to positive views of landscape alteration, partly in response to the imperial conquests of Alexander and of his Roman successors. The works of Diodorus and Strabo certainly point in that direction: that connection between the two, and the degree to which they stand out from most other ancient treatments of the same subject, have not to my knowledge been discussed at length before. Their work also offers at least partial confirmation of the stereotype of late Hellenistic writers expressing sympathy with the Roman imperial project, by contrast with their later imperial successors who tend to take a more stand-offish view of Roman rule in their writings.[98]

It is also clear, however, that we have to be very careful about any generalising account of late Hellenistic attitudes, or even of the attitudes of either of these authors individually. Even Strabo and Diodorus maintain traces of the deep-rooted negativity about environmental alteration that is so prominent in earlier and later sources. Moreover, when we look more closely, there are significant differences between them as well as

---

[94] In Curtius 4.3.2–7 the main cause of destruction is a fire started by the Tyrians (not mentioned by Diodorus); the gale is just an additional hazard; however, see Curtius 4.3.16–18 for another storm which nearly sinks Alexander's fleet
[95] No equivalent phrase in Curtius.   [96] Herodotus 7.34–6.
[97] See Bridges 2015: 119–25; cf. Harrison 2005: esp. 32.
[98] See Swain 1996: 2–3, and further discussion in the introduction to this volume.

similarities. Strabo in particular is remarkable for the way in which his positive views about landscape alteration are spread quite evenly throughout the work, with only very muted qualifications and hesitations. He is also often explicit in his approval for the civilising mission of Rome and of Augustus in particular. For Diodorus, by contrast, Rome is a much more shadowy presence (although partly because of what is missing from his published work). His views of landscape alteration too are less straightforward than Strabo's. Occasionally he allows Herodotean overtones of *hybris* to work their way into his account. There are also elements of disjunction between his opening, mythical books and what follows. When we see acts of landscape alteration in the later books it is surely hard not to be aware that they are different from what comes before, less able to be counted straightforwardly as acts of benefaction aimed at universal human benefit than the mythical works of Semiramis and Sesoösis and others. That is all the more striking given that those later passages often recall the language of Books 1–5, especially in their emphasis on the size of the labour forces involved.

At the same time, even if these two authors are ultimately slightly different from each other in their representation of landscape alteration, they do share a common approach to knowledge-ordering as an intratextually challenging exercise, where environmental (and other) themes are threaded through their works in ways which invite us to read actively and to draw comparisons for ourselves between successive passages. The complex relationship between Books 1–5 of Diodorus and the rest of the work is just one of many signs that Diodorus was crafting his sources carefully into a narrative designed to be read consecutively, as Strabo was too, rather than just reproducing them passively. Those shared assumptions also bring them closer to their later imperial successors, as well as to each other. In other words, they may differ from those later authors in some aspects of their presentation of human–environment relations, but in that vision of encyclopaedism as a narrative enterprise, where knowledge-ordering texts are intended to be read from end to end with attention to their intratextual complexity and their cumulative force, they are firmly in line with what we find for later imperial Greek culture too.

What implications does all of that have, finally, for ecocritical approaches to the literature and cultures of the ancient Mediterranean? Many of the texts we have looked at do have striking resonances with present-day environmental concerns, although that impression of familiarity is also complicated by features that are quite alien to present-day discourse. Perhaps most importantly, ancient writing on landscape alteration often takes an interest in the way in which it affects human communities, especially marginal or disempowered communities. Not only that, but authors like Strabo and Diodorus are able, through the geographical scope and the cumulative, compilatory structures of their works, to project a global vision of the range of ways in which the phenomenon of landscape alteration can manifest itself. They present us with a series of examples, some of which are presented as more problematic and some less. That kind of global perspective, which on some accounts can be frustratingly difficult to achieve in modern literary genres like the novel, comes naturally to ancient geographical and historiographical writing. At the same time, despite those resonances with present-day ecocritical concerns, some features of these texts offer quite defamiliarising versions of present-day environmental preoccupations. It is striking, for example, that ancient exploration of the impact of environmental alteration on human populations is usually contextualised in relation to distinctively Greek and Roman worries about the tyrannical behaviour of individual rulers who often coerce whole populations directly, rather than in relation to a vision of global structural inequalities which bring indirect environmental consequences, as it increasingly is in environmental scholarship today. The texts we have looked at also often ascribe agency to the land, and as in modern ecocritical work that insight can be used to project a negative view of human alteration of the natural world. At the same time, however, it is often tied up with a distinctively ancient religious framework, whereby the violation of the land is represented as an act of impiety,[99] and it is rarely if ever developed into a sustained argument for the inextricable intertwining of humans and their environment, or for the respectful co-existence of human populations with the more-than-human world.

We have also seen something of the complexity of ancient engagements with issues of environmental damage. Diodorus and Strabo do both represent a relatively anthropocentric strand in ancient thinking, in their predominantly positive representations of landscape alteration. Those kinds of anthropocentric views from ancient literature have clearly influenced post-classical thinking about the environment in some respects. We have also seen, however, that their engagement with those issues is enormously complex and conflicted even within their works individually, and that it needs to be set against the backdrop of a wide spectrum of different views in ancient literature generally. In that context, generalising about the

---

[99] Cf. Walter 2017 on the way in which religious responses to natural disaster in the ancient world may have parallels with and lessons for modern ecological discourse.

idea that ancient culture anticipates or stands in contrast with modern anthropocentrism – or indeed modern ecological rejection of anthropocentrism and environmental damage – in the service of convenient narratives about the long history of environmental thinking is always likely to lead one to very misleading conclusions. Apart from anything else, there is something about the topic of landscape alteration in ancient culture that seems to bring an almost inevitable doubleness: the traces of centuries-old traditions of both positive and negative representation are almost impossible to erase entirely; they tend to resurface in even the most one-sided of assessments. Ancient ideas about the relationship between humans and the environment were often far more multivocal than we give them credit for.

CHAPTER 5

Civic and Counter-Civic Cosmopolitanism
Diodorus, Strabo and the Later Hellenistic Polis

Benjamin Gray

Cosmopolitan and Civic Perspectives in the Later Hellenistic World

Later Hellenistic prose literature about politics might easily be perceived as divided between two different worlds, which have tended to attract different modern scholarly approaches and methods, though both are central to this volume.* On the one hand, many later Hellenistic intellectuals who wrote on politics self-consciously embraced a thoroughly universalist or cosmopolitan perspective, of the kind explored here in the chapters by Connolly, Hatzimichali, König and Wiater. According to these thinkers, social relations and intellectual horizons should not be limited to any one city or region but should rove across the newly integrated Roman Mediterranean. The aim of political interaction and thinking should be to identify and reinforce commonalities in this new expanded 'world city'. For other later Hellenistic writers on political themes, however, the local context – either a region or even a single *polis* – remained the principal focus, even if the interlinking of separate areas or city-states was recognised or embraced. This chapter explores the complex interconnections between these two approaches in the later Hellenistic world, with an emphasis on the dialogue between them. This is intended as a contribution to many of the themes raised in the introduction to this volume, including the complex interlocking of local and cosmopolitan perspectives, but also of historical, geographical, philosophical and political discourses, in the later Hellenistic world.

Many Stoic philosophers adopted the former, universalising approach, developing earlier Stoic cosmopolitan thinking,[1] but also gaining ideas and support from their allies in the Roman elite; like other later Hellenistic

---

* I would like to thank the editors and peer reviewers of this volume, as well as participants in the Classical Association of Scotland annual conference in St Andrews in 2015 and in a workshop on the later Hellenistic world at Columbia in 2017 for their help with this chapter. I am also very grateful to the Alexander von Humboldt-Stiftung for the research fellowship during which it was written.
[1] See Erskine 1990; Schofield 1999; Vogt 2008; Richter 2011: esp. 55–86.

cosmopolitans, they were in dialogue with the new forms of universalism advocated by Roman thinkers in this period (see Connolly, this volume). As well as being promoted by certain philosophers, this perspective was also favoured by the best preserved later Hellenistic prose authors, all central to this volume:[2] the historians of the new integrated *oikoumenē* Polybius (compare Wiater, this volume) and Diodorus Siculus (König and Baumann, this volume) and its geographer Strabo (Hatzimichali and König, this volume). These three wrote monumental works seeking to integrate the history and geography of the whole world within a single literary work and conceptual scheme. Their works were based on the assumption that the world is a complex, unified whole, whose nature demands appropriately synoptic intellectual attempts at understanding and political attempts at action and leadership.[3] Stoicism and Stoic cosmopolitanism were important factors in shaping these thinkers' approaches: for Diodorus and Strabo,[4] in particular, the lost works of the leading first-century BCE Stoic Posidonius would have shown how a Stoic theorist of the role of *logos* in structuring and integrating the whole cosmos handled writing about the historical and geographical dimensions of that process.[5]

This broad intellectual approach was in part a reflection of the lifestyles and social experience of relevant thinkers. Many lived very mobile lives, spending time working in the new 'world city' of Rome, but also moving between Greek cities and exploring the wider world.[6] The new opportunities for mobility coalesced with the disruptive effects of political instability in the old Greek intellectual centres of Athens and Alexandria, which broke up existing physical institutions such as the Athenian philosophical schools, whose members were dispersed around the Mediterranean by Sulla's sack of Athens in 86 BCE (compare Hatzimichali, this volume). The result was a far-flung diaspora of Greek intellectuals, among whom long-range communication through the written word, including commentaries on canonical classical texts, took on special importance.[7]

---

[2] Compare Schmitz, this volume, for parallel tendencies in verse, in later Hellenistic epigrams which engage with an expanded vision of a unified imperial Mediterranean.

[3] See the foundational work on this line of argument of Reinhardt 1926; more recently, Clarke 1999 offers a full study of it.

[4] On Strabo's philosophical and Stoic inspirations, see Hatzimichali, this volume.

[5] See Clarke 1999: 129–92; and Kidd 1988–99 for commentary on the surviving fragments of Posidonius' works.

[6] For the mobility of elite citizens of Greek *poleis* in this period, see the papers in Heller and Pont 2012.

[7] For the social context of philosophy in the later Hellenistic world, see the introduction to Schofield 2013; compare Rawson 1985: 3–18.

The resulting style of long-range, interconnected intellectual exchange would have mirrored the nature of political communication across the Empire, giving an added impetus to intellectual projects of cosmopolitan interpretation.[8]

This might all seem fundamentally removed from the other major camp of later Hellenistic writers and thinkers on politics. This latter camp was made up principally of the active citizens and teachers who reflected about, but also actively sustained, the continuing civic life of the many small and medium-sized Greek cities across the Aegean world and beyond. Their main preserved form of expression was the inscribed civic document. Continuing a long tradition, the later Hellenistic cities inscribed for long-term public display their most important civic decisions. Very prominent among the preserved later Hellenistic corpus of civic inscriptions are honorary decrees passed by cities in honour of their major benefactors, both outsiders and citizens. Many such decrees from the period after *c.* 150 BCE are particularly vivid and intricate in their rhetoric,[9] as also demonstrated by Kim's analysis (this volume) of the style and prose rhythm of selected later Hellenistic inscriptions (including a civic honorary decree from Mantineia). Relevant inscriptions use that rhetoric to build up complex 'biographies'[10] of the honoured individuals, which link their virtues and achievements to the local civic context. These complex texts, of which some examples are studied in the sections below on Diodorus and Strabo, deserve to be treated as important contributions to the 'later Hellenistic literature' studied in this volume (compare Kim's chapter). They were obviously also very different from the other works studied in this volume: they had a complex multiple authorship, the product of interaction between the honoured individual, his or her supporters, and the *dēmos* as a whole, within the decision-making institutions of the relevant *polis*, especially the assembly.[11] This itself contributed to their richness and interesting ambiguity.[12]

---

[8] Compare the discussions of the interactions between knowledge, texts and imperial order in König and Whitmarsh 2007a. On the broader Roman background to the developments surveyed here, see Ferrary 1988; Spawforth 2012.
[9] See, for example, Robert 1960: 213; 1967: 12, n. 1; also now Forster 2018.
[10] On honorary decrees as biographies, compare Rosen 1987: esp. 284–7; Errington 2002: esp. 20–8.
[11] On the whole complex negotiation, see Ma 2013: esp. 15–63. On the role of civic elites in formulating proposals, which had to be ratified by the *demos*, compare Errington 2002: 25–6; Fröhlich 2005: 255, with n. 118.
[12] On Hellenistic decrees as important parts of the surviving corpus of Hellenistic rhetoric: Chaniotis 2013a.

The principal political and ideological focus of civic inscriptions, including honorary decrees, was, unsurprisingly, the local city context: the close-knit, particularist interactions among citizens, and some honoured outsiders, which sustained local civic community, institutions and prosperity. The later Hellenistic cities were undergoing major social and political changes, including expanding Roman control; new powers and freedoms from scrutiny for narrowing local elites, who interacted with enduring democratic institutions in new ways;[13] and changes in the balance within civic life between, first, narrow politics and war and, second, culture and education, which had always been prominent in the *polis* but now took on an even greater role at the heart of the citizen ideal.[14] Nonetheless, despite these pressures, later Hellenistic citizens sustained local participatory institutions of self-government, together with accompanying civic styles of rhetoric, ideology and interaction, with modifications to accommodate changing conditions.[15] Central to this was the use of the honorific process to emphasise benefactors' strong, particular, patriotic attachment to the honouring city and its citizens, expressed in concrete actions.[16]

Enduring local civic patriotism and engagement were sustained, not only by the day-to-day workings of civic institutions and dialogue, but also by culture and education themselves. Formal education in rhetoric and philosophy played an important role. Demand for such education created an opening for intellectuals and teachers interested in continuing to promote a more civic than cosmopolitan approach to life and virtue. The Hellenistic Peripatetics as a school appear to have carved out a role for themselves as local teachers of civic rhetoric, imbuing citizens with the ideals and skills needed to sustain civic life.[17] This was in keeping with the Peripatetics' continuing doctrinal interest, derived from their founder

---

[13] These changes are emphasised in Quaß 1993; Veyne 1976 sees them already well-established in the earlier Hellenistic period.

[14] For changes in the civic life and political culture of the later Hellenistic cities, see, for example, Gauthier 1985, e.g., 56–9; Robert and Robert 1989; Fröhlich and Müller 2005; Grieb 2008, e.g., 196–8 (on Cos) and 260–1 (on Miletus); Alston 2011; Hamon 2012, together with the other papers in Mann and Scholz 2012; Müller 2014. On the special importance of the cultural and educational institution of the gymnasium in the Hellenistic cities, see Kah and Scholz 2004; on later Hellenistic developments in Greek culture and historical identity, see Schmitz and Wiater 2011a.

[15] The collections edited by Fröhlich and Müller 2005 and Mann and Scholz 2012 reveal many later Hellenistic continuities in civic life, as well as ruptures. For the role of honorific processes and decrees in sustaining civic consciousness and culture in the later Hellenistic world, see Ma 2013: esp. 45–62; compare Gray 2013a.

[16] For later Hellenistic decrees' picture of benefactor citizens as '*polis* fanatics', see Wörrle 1995.

[17] Compare Cic. *De or.* 1.43, 3.57–76, esp. 62; *Brut.* 119–20; *Tusc.* 2.9, with Griffin 1997: 9–10; Wiater 2011: 33–40; Inwood 2014: 75; Gray 2018.

Aristotle, in the small-scale participatory city as an ideal context for a virtuous and fulfilled human life.[18] There seems in general to have been a revival in interest in the later Hellenistic world in the pre-Hellenistic philosophies of Plato, Aristotle and the Pythagoreans.[19] Those older schools and their new adherents treated the *polis* as a much more central concern than the Hellenistic Stoics, Epicureans or Sceptics tended to do, even though many members of those Hellenistic schools had remained attached to a *polis* lifestyle and accompanying ideals.

The Peripatetics were certainly not alone in offering rhetorical and philosophical education tailored to the needs of civic elites focused on local political leadership. The Stoic Panaetius in his *On Duty*, the inspiration for Cicero's *De officiis*, and Dionysius of Halicarnassus in his rhetorical works were both partly addressing the educational needs of the Roman elite; Dionysius, at least, was based in Rome. Nonetheless, their focus on how to live and operate within a republican political system and culture was almost certainly also addressed to the citizens and leaders of the very many still vibrant Greek cities, who needed guides to rhetoric and action to inform both internal civic interaction and their negotiation of their cities' prerogatives with powerful Romans.[20] Dionysius promoted as central to an education in *politikē philosophia* the oratory of those inextricably civic figures, the classical Attic orators.[21] Civic life beyond the assembly and formal institutions also created opportunities for writers and intellectuals who wished to champion the continuing relevance of the traditional small-scale *polis*: the world of local historians and ethnographers attested in Jacoby's *Fragmente der griechischen Historiker*, many dating to the later Hellenistic period, reveals the continuing vitality of prose writing about the past which took a particular city or region as its focus.[22] Civic inscriptions and the writings of city-focused philosophers, rhetoricians and historians display a strong shared interest in the intricacies of particular places, as well as their distinctive identities, local knowledge[23] and cultural

---

[18] See the summary of Hellenistic Peripatetic ethics preserved in Stobaeus, usually attributed to Arius Didymus, which concludes with a summary of the Peripatetic approach to political theory, centred on *paideia* and solidarity in a small-scale *polis*, inherited from Aristotle's *Politics*: see Sharples 2010: text 15A, esp. sections 45–52.
[19] Compare Sedley 2012; Schofield 2013.
[20] For this view of Panaetius, see Wiemer 2016; for Dionysius, compare Delcourt 2005: e.g., 66–7; also Wiater 2011: e.g., 360.
[21] Dion. Hal. *Orat. vett.*, section 4.
[22] Compare, for example, Clarke 2008: 245–369; Thomas 2019.
[23] See the papers in Whitmarsh 2010a for this theme.

traditions. A related shared concern is the question of how those local particularities can be given a political and institutional form which can be nurtured and developed through local political participation and debate.

Despite the gulf between these two broad tendencies in later Hellenistic political thought and literature, the cosmopolitan and the civic, they were, as suggested above, bound together in a complex interrelationship, the focus of this chapter. Scholars have emphasised that conceptions of the local and the imperial, and corresponding local and 'world' identities, were defined and redefined in dialogue with each other in the eastern Roman Empire.[24] This chapter argues, for the later Hellenistic world, that this process was much more than simply one of opposition and mutual counter-definition. Rather, it also involved each side's close attention to, and often co-option of, the perspectives, arguments and even institutions of its rival. The two camps sketched here were part of a broad, complex, border-crossing Mediterranean public sphere, whose participants subjected the social, political and cultural changes of the later Hellenistic world to intense scrutiny and debate.

Civic-minded later Hellenistic Greeks revealed a keen awareness of cosmopolitan and universalising perspectives. Some cities used their inscribed honorary decrees to respond to the cosmopolitan challenge to the primacy of the small city as a form of life, by alternately co-opting and resisting pressures to open the *polis*' closed structures and ideology to outsiders. The results were complex adaptations of Greek republican and egalitarian theory and practice to accommodate or defuse cosmopolitan imperatives. At the institutional level, citizenship and civic privileges and activities often became more fluid and open to outsiders.[25] At the level of ideology, as I have argued elsewhere, many later Hellenistic decrees came to give a new prominence to the intrinsically universalistic virtue of *philanthrōpia* ('humanity'). They praised citizens for showing *philanthrōpia* even in their relations with fellow citizens, with whom only more particularist, visceral relations would earlier have been expected.[26] This tendency was mirrored, among civic-focused literary authors, in the work of Dionysius of Halicarnassus, where *philanthrōpia* also emerges as a central civic virtue, a key to Rome's success.[27] Even the intensely civic-minded Peripatetics had by the later Hellenistic period taken on board Stoic universalism, in some cases seeking to adapt Peripatetic ethical

---

[24] See, for example, Whitmarsh 2010b: e.g., 2.
[25] See Heller and Pont 2012; Martzavou 2014; Müller 2014.   [26] Gray 2013b.
[27] See Delcourt 2005: 170–2.

teaching to give weight both to civic commitment and to wider humane attachments.[28]

In this chapter I discuss, for context at the end of the sections on Diodorus and Strabo below, one epigraphic example of this side of the dialogue: the first-century BCE honorary decrees of Priene for A. Aemilius Zosimus, a naturalised Prienian as well as a Roman citizen.[29] Those inscriptions' complex rhetoric and ideas make them particularly worthy of study as contributions to later Hellenistic literature. However, my focus in this chapter is on the other side of the exchange: universalising literary authors who show a close familiarity and engagement with the Greek small-*polis* tradition, as well as its contemporary expression in the later Hellenistic *polis* world. Diodorus does so in a way sympathetic to the small *polis* and its traditions, whereas Strabo uses his familiarity with civic thinking often against the civic model itself. Both use their familiarity with civic ideals, rhetoric and institutions to structure and refine their competing cosmopolitan visions of the world. Whereas contemporary Romans tended to focus on the particular city of Athens to shape their universalist outlook (see Connolly, this volume), these Greek authors drew on a wider range of cities and civic models, going beyond a partly imaginary Athens.

This chapter is intended partly as an example of the altered perspective gained by integrating epigraphic evidence more closely into the picture of later Hellenistic literature and political thought, and using it to place literary texts within a wider later Hellenistic dialogue. Integrating epigraphic evidence helps to show what was distinctive, complex and urgent about the particular kinds of cosmopolitan thinking and expression which were central to later Hellenistic culture and thought. Later Hellenistic cosmopolitan ideas and practices were a bridge between the utopian, quite generic cosmopolitanism of the fourth century and early Hellenistic period, especially early Stoicism, on the one hand, and the developed cosmopolitanism of the High Roman Empire. Both the earlier and later developments have been very well and intensively studied, not least in Richter 2011, which draws explicit links between the early (fourth century BCE) and later (Roman imperial) stages, but pays much less attention to intervening mid- and later Hellenistic debates and experimentation. This chapter seeks to bring into focus examples of those debates and that

---

[28] See Annas 1995; compare Schofield 2012 and Tsouni 2019 for Antiochus of Ascalum's contribution to this process.
[29] *I.Priene*² 68–70, new editions of *I.Priene* 112–14.

experimentation, which extended from the intellectual centres of Rome and Alexandria to the public sphere of smaller cities such as Iasos or Priene, attested in inscriptions.

Background: The Stoics, Polybius and Hellenistic Cosmopolitanism

The cosmopolitan ideal was, by its very nature, a response to the *polis* as an ideal and reality; fourth-century and early Hellenistic Cynics and Stoics had transformed the *polis* into a metaphor for the structure of their ideal world community of the virtuous and wise.[30] This abstract Stoic form of cosmopolitanism was a live and prominent philosophical option in the later Hellenistic world, as is clear from Cicero's *De finibus*. Cicero's Marcus Cato there appeals to the city partly as one rung on the ladder of natural and necessary human ethical attachments, extending from love between parents and children to membership of a cosmic community of both gods and men; but he also uses it as a metaphor for that cosmic community itself.[31]

As this chapter will show, later Hellenistic cosmopolitan historians and geographers developed and refined this style of engagement with the *polis* as a political model and metaphor, in order to articulate their own subtle, detailed, more concrete accounts of the workings of a cosmopolitan order across the Mediterranean.[32] Scholars have demonstrated well the powerful influence of *poleis* and other small communities on Polybius' political thought and historical vision, including his conception of a united Mediterranean world entangled in one joint historical process (see Wiater, this volume, for detailed analysis).

As F. Millar argued, Polybius saw himself as part of a continuum of civic Greek politics and historiography stretching back to the Persian Wars; this helped to shape many of his central political concerns, such as his insistence on civic autonomy and the rule of law.[33] At the same time, Polybius was well capable of seizing upon civic concepts and institutions in order better to conceptualise and understand larger-scale political units. This is very clear in his polemical praise for his home state, the federal Achaean League of Peloponnesian cities, which he presents as almost a single

---

[30] See Erskine 1990; Schofield 1999; Vogt 2008; Richter 2011: esp. 55–86.
[31] See Cic. *Fin.* 3.62–4.
[32] On the straddling of local, Roman and cosmopolitan perspectives by later Hellenistic writers of history, compare Yarrow 2006.
[33] Millar 1987: esp. 94–6, 105. For Polybius' ethical and political conservatism, compare Eckstein 1995; for his interest in civic values of freedom and community, compare Champion 2004.

pan-Peloponnesian *polis* at its second-century high point. He even claims that it would not be possible to find a purer democratic system – something more readily associated with a single *polis* – than the federal constitution of the League, with its guarantees of freedom and equality for all members.[34] This was a comprehensible extension of the thinking behind Polybius' home city of Megalopolis itself, a composite Arcadian city foundation of the fourth century BCE which was intended both to preserve and to transcend the small-scale, exclusive *polis* model. Polybius' facility in adapting Greek political theory and institutional concepts to different, larger political forms also underpins his analysis of the Roman constitution, and the expanding Roman empire.[35]

Diodorus Siculus' Preface: The World as a Later Hellenistic *Polis*

The tendency identified in Polybius' work was considerably developed by his first-century BCE successor Diodorus Siculus. Scholars have studied in detail how Diodorus develops a monumental vision of a united Mediterranean, with an intertwined past and present.[36] Despite this overarching perspective, Diodorus' familiarity with small-city virtues, institutions and practices is clear throughout his work, especially from his detailed discussions of the internal politics and diplomatic relations of historical Greek cities. His presentation of past cities is partly coloured by the contemporary civic world: for example, by an emphasis on gentle virtues, such as *philanthrōpia* (humanity) and *epieikeia* (decency),[37] which were gaining increasing prominence, as mentioned in the introduction, in the civic discourse of the later Hellenistic cities themselves.

Importantly for the concerns of this chapter, Diodorus' own embedding in civic consciousness and structures even provides the framework for his most explicit articulation of his cosmopolitan vision, in his preface in praise of historians of the world, also discussed in the chapters by Baumann, Hatzimichali and König in this volume. According to Diodorus, historians of the world have striven to bring all humans under one order (ἐφιλοτιμήθησαν ὑπὸ μίαν καὶ τὴν αὐτὴν σύνταξιν ἀγαγεῖν), recognising their common kinship as humans, despite their distance in time and space. In writing the history of the world as if of one city (τὰς κοινὰς τῆς οἰκουμένης πράξεις καθάπερ μιᾶς πόλεως ἀναγράψαντες),

---

[34] Polyb. 2.37.9–11, 38.6.   [35] Compare Henderson 2001; Quinn 2013.
[36] See, for example, Sacks 1990: esp. 55–82; Clarke 1999: 80, 114–15; Rathmann 2016: 273–95.
[37] Compare Muntz 2017: 11–13, citing earlier bibliography.

they have emulated the role of divine providence (*pronoia*) in bringing the stars and men into a common, ongoing structure.³⁸ This preface is now widely recognised as Diodorus' own work, consonant (for example) with his wider interest in heroic benefactors of humanity (compare König, this volume). The preface was, however, of course also marked by wider later Hellenistic language and themes, as well as by older historiographical and philosophical influences.³⁹ Among the later Hellenistic influences was the later Hellenistic *polis* reality, which helped to give definition and substance to Diodorus' metaphorical conception of the *oikoumenē* as like 'one city'.

Diodorus' preface opens as follows:

> Τοῖς τὰς κοινὰς ἱστορίας πραγματευσαμένοις μεγάλας χάριτας ἀπονέμειν δίκαιον πάντας ἀνθρώπους, ὅτι τοῖς ἰδίοις πόνοις ὠφελῆσαι τὸν κοινὸν βίον ἐφιλοτιμήθησαν· ἀκίνδυνον γὰρ διδασκαλίαν τοῦ συμφέροντος εἰσηγησάμενοι καλλίστην ἐμπειρίαν διὰ τῆς πραγματείας ταύτης περιποιοῦσι τοῖς ἀναγινώσκουσιν·
>
> It is just that all humans should assign great gratitude to those who have written common histories, because they have striven to assist common life with their individual efforts; for by introducing a danger-free education in what is beneficial they provide the finest experience, through this enterprise, for their readers.⁴⁰

These opening lines would have called to mind many intertexts for later Hellenistic readers. Not least, they would have placed Diodorus immediately in the tradition of Greek moralising historiography.⁴¹ They would also have demonstrated his facility with the conventions of Greek panegyrical rhetoric in general. Nonetheless, they would also have evoked strongly one particular type of Hellenistic panegyric: the honorary decree containing intricate rhetoric of praise. Almost all inscribed examples of such decrees contain some form of so-called 'hortatory clause', explaining the general principle that benefactions to the common good by individuals should be rewarded with honours and gratitude (*charis* or *charites*, as in Diodorus) and often also explicitly exhorting other potential benefactors to emulate the particular benefactor being honoured.

A basic formula very close to that used and elaborated by Diodorus is found, for example, in a second-century BCE decree of the city of

---

³⁸ Diod. Sic. 1.1.3. For interpretation, see Burton 1972: 35–8; Sacks 1990: 79–81; Clarke 1999: 80, 114–15; Rathmann 2016: 292–3; Muntz 2017: 7–8.
³⁹ E.g., Burton 1972: 38; Sacks 1990: 11. Other recent work has emphasised Diodorus' engagement with his contemporary world: e.g., Muntz 2017 on Diodorus and the Roman Republic.
⁴⁰ Diod. Sic. 1.1.1.
⁴¹ See recently, on this tradition and Diodorus' place in it, Sheridan 2010; Hau 2016: esp. 73–123.

Apollonia Salbake in Caria for Pamphilus, who had served as an important envoy: 'it is just that good men should obtain suitable gratitude for their benefactions' (δίκαιον δέ ἐστιν τοὺς ἀγαθοὺς τῶν ἀνδρῶν καταξίας χάριτας κομίζεσθαι τῶν εὐε[ρ]γετημάτων).[42] This formula was applied *ad hominem* in a later Hellenistic decree passed by the magistrates and councillors of Akraiphia in Boeotia in honour of an agonothete, Aischriondas: 'it is just that he should receive for these [contributions] good gratitude of the fitting sort' (δίκαιον δέ ἐστιν τυγχάνειν αὐτὸν ἐπὶ τούτοις εὐχαριστίας τῆς προσηκούσης).[43] The honouring people (*dēmos*) or group could also be explicitly identified as the active bestower of *charis* for benefactions to the common good, the role envisaged for 'all humans' in Diodorus. In a late Hellenistic decree of the *polis* of Delphi for King Nicomedes and Queen Laodice of Bithynia, the hortatory clause claims that the purpose of the honorary decree is that the *polis* 'should be seen to accord [ἀπονέμειν, also Diodorus' verb] suitable gratitude to those who choose to make benefactions to it' (ὅπως [οὖν καὶ ἁ πόλις φανε]ρὰ γίνηται καταξίας ἀπονέμουσα [χ]άριτας τοῖς εὐεργε[τεῖν αὐτὰν προαι]ρειμένοις).[44] In an educational context, a later second-century BCE Athenian decree for Eudoxus, a teacher and supervisor (*kosmētēs*) of the ephebes, prefaces its own honours by saying that the ephebes themselves crowned him, because they wanted to accord appropriate *charis* to him, in accordance with duty (οἱ ἔφηβοι βουλόμενοι κατὰ τὸ καθῆκον ἀπονέμειν αὐτῷ καταξίας χάριτας ἐστεφάνωσαν αὐτόν).[45] As Diodorus' 'all humans' were supposed to do, the ephebes, and subsequently the Athenian people, recognised with honours this man's public-spirited contribution to *paideia*, recognised to be of common benefit.

The particular services for which Diodorus thought all men should honour authors of 'common histories' of the world also chime closely with the formulae and ethical framework of later Hellenistic honorary decrees. Diodorus praises historians of the world for striving through love of honour (ἐφιλοτιμήθησαν) to benefit common life (ὠφελῆσαι τὸν κοινὸν βίον) with their individual labours (τοῖς ἰδίοις πόνοις). Each element of this formulation evokes characteristic features of honorary decrees. 'Love of honour' or *philotimia* is almost ubiquitous in honorary decrees as a quality of good benefactors.[46] Moreover, decrees always stress, like Diodorus, that

---

[42] Robert and Robert 1954, II: no. 167, ll. 28–30.   [43] *IG* VII 4148, ll. 5–6.
[44] *FD* III 4.77, ll. 24–6; compare, for example, *SEG* 14.544 (Karthaia on Keos), ll. 16–18.
[45] *IG* II² 1011, ll. 42–3. Cf. *IG* II² 1008, ll. 61–2.
[46] See recently on this virtue Ferrucci 2013. For use of Diodorus' form ἐφιλοτιμήθησαν itself to describe a whole city's aspiration to do good to another, see *I.Erythrai* 122, ll. 21–2.

this striving for honour is channelled into dedicated service and benefactions to the community. This was brought out very explicitly in the opening of the highly rhetorical later Hellenistic decree of Sestos for the citizen benefactor and envoy Menas:

ἐ[πειδὴ Μηνᾶς Μένητος] ὑπ[. … ἐκ τῆς] [π]ρώτης ἡλικίας κάλλιστον ἡγησάμενος εἶναι τὸ [τῆ πατρ]ίδι χρήσι[μο]ν ἑα[υτὸν] [π]αρέχεσθαι, οὔτε δαπάνης καὶ χορηγίας οὐδεμιᾶς φειδόμενος, οὔτε κακοπαθία[ν] (l. 5) [κ]αὶ κίνδυνον ἐκκλίνων οὔτε τὴν ἀπαντωμένην καταφθορὰν τῶν ἰδίων τοῖς ὑπὲρ τῆς πόλεως πρεσβεύουσιν ὑπολογιζόμενος, πάντα δὲ ταῦθ᾽ ἡγούμενος δεύτερα καὶ πρὸ πλείστου θέμενος τὸ πρὸς τὴν πατρίδα γνήσιον καὶ ἐκτενές, βουλόμενός τε τῷ μὲν δήμῳ διὰ τῆς ἰδίας σπουδῆς ἀεί τι τῶν χρησίμων κατασκευάζειν, ἑαυτῷ δὲ καὶ τοῖς ἐξ ἑαυτοῦ διὰ τῆς ἀπαντωμένης ἐκ τοῦ πλήθους εὐχαριστίας δόξαν ἀίμνηστον (l. 10) περιποεῖν …

> Since Menas son of Menes has from his earliest youth thought it the finest thing to make himself useful for his country, not sparing any expense or contribution, nor avoiding any hardship or danger, nor taking into account the damage to his private resources arising through those making embassies on behalf of the *polis*, but thinking all of these things secondary and considering of most importance sincerity and assiduousness towards his country; and wishing through his individual effort always to secure for the people something useful, and to achieve for himself and his descendants an immortal reputation, through the good gratitude coming from the people …[47]

Like Diodorus' historians of the world, Menas expressed his love of glory and aspirations to long-term reputation through individual effort (διὰ τῆς ἰδίας σπουδῆς, compare Diodorus' τοῖς ἰδίοις πόνοις) which achieved goods of benefit to all, the most important kind. Diodorus' notion that the community has a 'common life' which benefactors can promote is explicitly expressed in decrees for another major later Hellenistic benefactor: the honorary decrees of Priene in western Asia Minor for A. Aemilius Zosimus, mentioned in the introduction. In both the first and second decrees for him, Zosimus is praised for benefactions – first, more secure financial record-keeping and, second, the upkeep of civic sacrifices – which secured the life (*bios*) both of individuals and of the whole *polis*.[48]

To give an idea of how these different elements of later Hellenistic honorary decrees fit together, it is worth quoting an example in full. The following is a decree of the city of Iasos in Caria, passed for the young man

[47] *I.Sestos* 1, ll. 1–10.   [48] *I.Priene*² 68, ll. 23–7; *I.Priene*² 69, ll. 68–70.

and ephebarch Melanion. I have selected this example partly because it is relatively concise and also because it is strongly cultural in its focus, which raises further interesting comparisons with Diodorus' preface:

> ἐπειδὴ Μελανίων Θεοδώρου προγόνων ὑπάρχων εὐεργετῶν τῆς πόλεως, ἄξια πράσσων τῆς ἐκείνων ἀρετῆς ἐμ πᾶσιν καλοκἀγαθικῶς ἀναστρεφόμενος ἀνὴρ καλὸς (l. 5) κἀγαθός ἐστιν καὶ εὐσεβῶς μὲμ πρὸς τὸ θεῖον διάκειται, φιλοστόργως δὲ καὶ ὡς πρέπον ἐστὶν ἀνδρὶ σώφρονι καὶ πεπαιδευμένῳ προσφέρεται τοῖς γονεῦσιγ καὶ τοῖς λοιποῖς συγγενέσιν, εὐνοϊκῶς δὲ καὶ φιλοδόξως καὶ πρὸς (l. 10) πάντας τοὺς πολίτας ὑπεξάγει, ἀπό τε τῆς πρώτης ἡλικίας ζηλωτὴς τῶν καλλίστων γινόμενος ἀνέστραπται ἐν τῷ γυμνασίῳ φιλοπονῶν καὶ φιλομαθῶν καὶ ἐπὶ τὰ κάλλιστα ἐπιδιδοὺς ἑαυτόν, ἔν τε τοῖς οἰκείοις τῆς ἡλικίας παιδεύμασιγ (l. 15) καταγινόμενος καὶ ἐν τοῖς κατὰ φιλοσοφίαν λόγοις ἱκανὴν ἕξιγ καὶ προκοπὴν ἐσχηκὼς ἀναστρέφεται σωφρόνως καὶ ἀξιοζηλώτως καλὸν ὑπόδειγμα τῆς ἰδίας προαιρέσεως καταβαλλόμενος, καθόλου τε καὶ λέγων καὶ πράσσων τὰ (l. 20) κάλλιστα καὶ ἐνδοξότατα διατελεῖ ἐμ πᾶσιν στοιχῶν τῇ τε ἰδίᾳ ἀρετῇ καὶ δόξῃ καὶ τῇ {ι} διὰ προγόνων ὑπαρχούσῃ αὐτῳ καλοκαγαθίᾳ· ἀποδειχθεὶς δὲ καὶ ἐφήβαρχος προΐσταται τοῦ γυμνασίου καὶ τῆς τῶν ἐφήβων καὶ νέων εὐκοσμίας ἀξίως (l. 25) ἀναστρεφόμενος τοῦ τε πατρὸς καὶ τῶν νέων καὶ τοῦ σύμπαντος δήμου· καλῶς δὲ ἔχον ἐστὶν τοὺς ἀγαθοὺς ἄνδρας τῆς καλλίστης ἀποδοχῆς κ[α]ὶ προτιμῆς διὰ παντὸς τυγχάνειν, ὅπως [καὶ οἱ] λοιποὶ θεωροῦντες τ[ὴν τοῦ] (l. 30) πλήθους εὔ[νοι]αν ἐκ τενεῖς καὶ προ[θύμους] ἑαυτοὺς πα[ρέχωντα]ι τῷ δήμῳ· διὸ καὶ [ἔδοξεν] ἐπῃνῆσθαι Μ[ελανίωνα Θ]εοδώρου ἐπί τε [τῇ ἀρετῇ] καὶ καλοκἀγα[θίᾳ καὶ ᾗ ἔχ]ει πρὸς πάντας το[ὺς πολίτας] εὐνοίᾳ· καὶ σ[τεφανῶσ]αι αὐτὸν χρυσῷ [στεφάνῳ] (l. 35) ἀριστείῳ· [στῆσαι δ]ὲ αὐτοῦ καὶ εἰκόν[α γραπτὴν] ἐν τῷ γυμ[νασίῳ τῷ] Πτολεμαιείῳ ἐ[ν ὅπλῳ ἐπι]χρύσῳ, στ[ῆσαι δὲ αὐτο]ῦ καὶ εἰ[κό]να χα[λκῆν καὶ εἰ]κόνα χρυσ[ῆν ἐν τῷ ἐπιφανεστάτ]ῳ [ὅπου ἂν βού]ληται τόπ[ῳ ... εἰκ]όνα...] (l. 40) δὲ αὐτοῦ [....] ἀ[ναγράψαι δὲ ...] ἐφ' ἑκάστ[ης ...]

Since Melanion son of Theodorus, descended from ancestors who were benefactors of the city, doing things worthy of their virtue, and in all cases behaving in a fine and good way, is a fine and good man; and is piously disposed to the divine; and behaves in a loving way and as befits a self-controlled and educated man towards his parents and his other relatives; and is disposed with good-will and love of glory towards all the other citizens; and, having been from his earliest youth a striver after the finest things, has conducted himself in the gymnasium as a lover of effort and a lover of learning and dedicated himself to the finest pursuits; and busying himself in the educational activities appropriate to his age, and having had, in his rational education in philosophy, a suitable disposition and made suitable progress, conducts himself temperately and in a way worthy of emulation, giving a fine example of his own moral purpose; and in general continues to do and say the finest and most honourable things, conforming with his own virtue and reputation and with the nobility belonging to him from his ancestors. Having been appointed ephebarch, he takes charge of the gymnasium and the good discipline of the ephebes and the young men, behaving worthily of his father, the young men and the whole people. It is excellent that the good men should always receive the finest reception and honour, so that the rest, seeing the good-will of the majority, make themselves assiduous and enthusiastic towards the people.[49] For this reason it was resolved to praise Melanion, son of Theodorus, for his virtue and excellence and his good-will towards all the citizens. And crown him with a gold crown (l. 35) of excellence; and set up a painted statue of him in the Ptolemaic Gymnasium in gold-plated arms; and set up a bronze statue of him and a gold statue in the most prominent place he chooses ... statue (l. 40) of him ... and inscribe it ... on each ...

This decree can stand as an example of the 'biographical' cast of many later Hellenistic decrees: highly rhetorical documents which survey the life of a benefactor, embedding it in its civic and moral context. Chronologically organised praise leads up to a hortatory clause stating that it is 'fine' (καλῶς δὲ ἔχον ἐστίν, compare Diodorus' δίκαιον [sc. ἐστίν]) that good men should receive the best recognition and honour, to encourage emulation. The decree builds up a picture of Melanion's ethical and educational achievements, which involve interactions with different groups (family, fellow youth, all fellow citizens), on whose welfare and psychology Melanion has an important influence.[50] The distinction between the young, aspirant citizens, ephebes and *neoi*, and the wider adult citizen-body is particularly important.[51]

This template mirrors that of a later part of Diodorus' preface, where he praises the specific educational influence of historians on different parts of a broad reading community,[52] including different age groups:

διὸ καὶ πρὸς ἁπάσας τὰς τοῦ βίου περιστάσεις χρησιμωτάτην ἄν τις εἶναι νομίσειε τὴν ταύτης ἀνάληψιν. τοῖς μὲν γὰρ νεωτέροις τὴν τῶν γεγηρακότων περιποιεῖ σύνεσιν, τοῖς δὲ πρεσβυτέροις πολλαπλασιάζει τὴν ὑπάρχουσαν ἐμπειρίαν, καὶ τοὺς μὲν ἰδιώτας ἀξίους ἡγεμονίας κατασκευάζει, τοὺς δ' ἡγεμόνας τῷ διὰ τῆς δόξης ἀθανατισμῷ

---

[49] *I.Iasos* 98.
[50] For description of a benefactor's different circles of ethical relationships in a later Hellenistic decree, compare *I.Priene*² 64 (new edition of *I.Priene* 108), ll. 15–18.
[51] On the complex relationships between these groups in the Hellenistic *polis*, see Fröhlich 2013; Kennell 2013; van Bremen 2013.
[52] On its breadth, compare Rathmann 2016: 271–2.

προτρέπεται τοῖς καλλίστοις τῶν ἔργων ἐπιχειρεῖν, χωρὶς δὲ τούτων τοὺς μὲν στρατιώτας τοῖς μετὰ τὴν τελευτὴν ἐπαίνοις ἑτοιμοτέρους κατασκευάζει πρὸς τοὺς ὑπὲρ τῆς πατρίδος κινδύνους, τοὺς δὲ πονηροὺς τῶν ἀνθρώπων ταῖς αἰωνίοις βλασφημίαις ἀποτρέπει τῆς ἐπὶ τὴν κακίαν ὁρμῆς.

> For this reason one would think that the gaining of [historical knowledge] is most useful for all circumstances of life. For it bestows on the younger men the understanding of those who have grown old; it multiplies the existing experience of older men; and it makes private individuals worthy of leadership; and it urges leaders to the finest deeds through the prospect of immortality through reputation; and, apart from these things, it makes soldiers, through its posthumous praise, more ready to face dangers on behalf of their country; and it deflects the wicked among men, through eternal invective, from the urge towards evil.[53]

As well as mirroring decrees' tendency carefully to enumerate the benefactor's benefactions, including their particular relevance for different subgroups, this section of Diodorus' preface also recalls later Hellenistic decrees' interest in ethical education and exhortation. In particular, the claim that history-writing can urge (προτρέπεσθαι) leaders towards 'the finest things' echoes decrees' interest in the educational power of both good citizens and decrees themselves: later Hellenistic benefactors could be praised for educating and inspiring fellow citizens using this same verb, which also features in hortatory clauses, where its role is to describe decrees' own educational and galvanising influence.[54] For Diodorus, both the work of the historians whom he praises and his own 'honorary decree' for them can have a similar effect on the politically active. Indeed, according to Diodorus, history's ethical exhortation draws leaders towards 'the finest things' (τὰ κάλλιστα). In similar fashion, the young civic leader Melanion of Iasos, for example (compare above), was praised for continuing in general to say and do the finest things (καθόλου τε καὶ λέγων καὶ πράσσων τὰ κάλλιστα), guided by his civic education, during which he had also dedicated himself to the finest things (ἐπὶ τὰ κάλλιστα).[55]

To sum up, as a result of Diodorus' deep awareness of contemporary civic culture, his image of a world *polis* crossing both space and time is perhaps surprisingly concrete and well-developed. According to Diodorus' ideal, it should resemble a contemporary, later Hellenistic *polis*: it should

---

[53] Diod. Sic. 1.1.4–5.
[54] Compare Robert 1960: 213; 1967: 12, n. 1. The epigraphic usage of προτρέπεσθαι is discussed in Gray 2013a: 248–53.
[55] *I.Iasos* 98, ll. 10–20.

have a broad citizenry ('all men') which possesses a strong sense of its common interests and culture, and can find a common voice to honour its benefactors using accepted panegyrical tropes. At the same time, it can also be divided into sub-groups: young and old, or leaders and private individuals. Moreover, like later Hellenistic citizens such as the Athenian ephebes or the Iasian *dēmos*, the citizens of Diodorus' cosmopolis should be particularly appreciative of the contributions of intellectuals and teachers, who make a distinctive major contribution to their welfare through *paideia*.

Diodorus remains sensitive to the differences between *polis* and cosmopolis. For example, he explicitly stresses the role of reading and the written word in mediating the educational relationships of his cosmopolis.[56] This would not have been impossible in a local *polis* context: an honorary decree from Olbia on the Black Sea, dating to the Imperial period, overlaps closely with Diodorus' approach in explicitly referring to its exhortation (προτροπή) of its own *readers* (οἱ ἀναγεινώσκοντε[ς]) to imitate the life praised in the decree.[57] Nonetheless, cities' decrees tended to preserve an impression of face-to-face exhortation and *paideia*: the Iasians, for example, were expected directly to observe (θεωροῦντες) the people's rewarding of Melanion's virtue. Diodorus' changes to his civic model are, however, an inevitable part of his careful, detailed adaptation of small-city rhetoric and virtues to suit the nature of the wider world, in which reading of written works and commentaries did take on increasing importance (see my introduction and other contributions here). Perhaps sensitive to the discrepancy, Diodorus implies that the written records produced by historians do, in fact, have a civic correlate: for him, historians' works are a 'common archive' (κοινὸν χρηματιστήριον) of past achievements for the information and education of the world *polis*,[58] perhaps analogous to actual *poleis*' civic archives (χρηματιστήρια), in which testimonies of benefactor citizens' generosity could be stored in a later Hellenistic city.[59] Diodorus' *Bibliotheke*, like those of his fellow world historians, is thus not only a metaphorical museum,[60] but also a metaphorical civic archive.

---

[56] On Diodorus' close attention to his text's relationship with its readers, see Baumann, this volume.
[57] *IOSPE* I² 39 (Olbia), ll. 36–9 (ἀνατεθῆναι δὲ τὸ ψήφισμα ἐν ἐπισήμῳ τόπῳ, ἵνα οἱ ἀναγεινώσκοντε[ς] προτροπὴν ἔχωσιν εἰς τὸ μειμεῖσθαι βίον ἐπαινούμενον).
[58] Diod. Sic. 1.1.3.
[59] *SEG* 39.1243 (Colophon, later second century BCE), col. III, ll. 43–7: debtors relieved of burdens by Polemaeus' generosity left testimonies of his humanity in the civic archives (ἐ<ν> τοῖς δημοσίοις χρηματιστηρίοις).
[60] Wiater 2006a.

It would not be quite right, however, to suggest that Diodorus single-handedly himself transplants to the world scale the civic forms of the later Hellenistic *poleis*. In fact, his embedding in contemporary civic culture is deeper than that: his 'civic cosmopolitanism' can itself be seen as part of a common tendency, also evident in some later Hellenistic *poleis* themselves, to fuse civic and cosmopolitan ideas and institutions (compare my introduction). A striking example from a *polis* comes from the Prienian decrees for A. Aemilius Zosimus already briefly mentioned, which date to the first century BCE.[61] Zosimus was a Roman citizen who was also naturalised as a citizen of Priene, and went on to play a prominent role in Prienian civic life. His origins are unclear, though it is perhaps unlikely that he was an elite Greek of Asia Minor who had gained Roman citizenship: a promising hypothesis is that he was a freedman who had gained Roman citizenship on manumission, and subsequently been integrated into the Prienian civic community.[62]

The first honorary decree for him, passed after he had served as gymnasiarch, includes explicit reflections about his outsider status and the changing, increasingly fluid character of the Prienian civic community. This involves an attempt to adapt civic honorific institutions and ideals in a cosmopolitan direction, not unlike that of Diodorus' preface. There is some traditional civic particularism: Zosimus is said to have been devoted to Priene as if it were his own *polis*, showing the concern of a 'genuine citizen'.[63] This claim does at least, however, allow for the possibility of civic patriotism on the part of outsiders to the ethnic civic community. This more open approach is made explicit in the claim that Zosimus 'never pursues his private enjoyment in a way showing ignorance of what is excellent, knowing that virtue alone brings the greatest fruits and gratitude from foreigners and citizens who hold the fine in honour' (ἐν οὐδενὶ δὲ τὴν ἰδίαν ἀπιροκάλω[ς διώκων ἀπόλαυ]σιν συνιδὼν δ' ὅτι μόνη μεγίστους ἀποδίδωσιν ἡ ἀρετὴ καρποὺς καὶ χάριτας π[αρὰ ξένοις κ]αὶ ἀστοῖς τὸ καλὸν ἐν τιμῇ θεμένοις).[64] The honorific community envisaged here, like Diodorus' imagined community of 'all men' honouring world historians, is a broad and heterogeneous one, which is unified by shared appreciation of abstract moral virtue ('the fine'), rather than particular bonds of kinship or religion.

---

[61] The precise dating is disputed; for discussion of the arguments, see Kah 2012: 63. For detailed discussion of the Zosimus decrees: Forster 2018: 302–12.
[62] See Kah 2012: 62–3, with discussion of earlier views.   [63] *I.Priene*² 68, l. 17.
[64] *I.Priene*² 68, ll. 13–14. For the restoration χάριτας π[αρὰ ξένοις κ]αὶ ἀστοῖς, compare, for example, Maiuri 1925: no. 19, col. II, ll. 6–8.

Later in this first decree, the Prienians honour Zosimus for his educational contributions to the *polis* as gymnasiarch. They describe in detail the bodily and psychological effects of his contributions to the education of the ephebes: he provided 'also round boxing-gloves and weapons and the grammatical teacher of the ephebes for the philological branch [of learning], wishing through the former to make their bodies unhesitating and through the latter to lead their souls towards virtue and humane emotion' (ἔτι δὲ σφαίρας καὶ ὅπλα καὶ τὸν ἐπιστά[τησοντ]α τῶν ἐφήβων τοῖς ἐκ φιλολογίας γραμματικόν, δι' [ὧν μὲν] τὸ σῶμα βουλόμενος ἀοκνο[ν] τυγχάνειν, δι' ὧν δὲ τ[ὰς ψυχ]ὰς πρὸς ἀρετὴν καὶ πάθος ἀνθρώπινον προάγεσθαι).[65] Like Diodorus' imagined appreciative quasi-civic community of all humans, therefore, the Prienians honoured Zosimus for cultural and educational contributions which themselves contributed to building a broad humane community: whereas Diodorus' ideal historians helped to bring the world into a unity through history-writing and reading, Zosimus' provision of a philological tutor within the civic gymnasium helped to endow the young ephebes with the kind of 'humane emotion' or 'human emotion' (πάθος ἀνθρώπινον), presumably including sympathy for all fellow humans as humans, which would be required in a stable cosmopolis. Diodorus' cosmopolis thus tapped into the political culture of the later Hellenistic *poleis*, not only in its use of widespread civic honorific and educational forms but also in its aspirations to adapt those forms to create a broader human community, unified by learning and virtue alone.

Strabo's Counter-Civic Cosmopolitanism and Its Civic Context

Diodorus' preface is, therefore, a place where the civic and cosmopolitan perspectives meet and interact fruitfully to produce a complex hybrid manner of speaking and thinking. This was not the only possible way for them to interact in a large-scale later Hellenistic work. The distinctiveness and force of Diodorus' approach emerge further through the contrast with the geographer Strabo's approach. Whereas Diodorus takes the (later Hellenistic) *polis* as the model for his cosmopolis, Strabo, in his own methodological preface, presents a Mediterranean-wide system[66] which is distinguished more by hierarchy and the power of the governing elite than by quasi-civic notions of the common good and collective political

---

[65] *I.Priene*² 68, ll. 73–6.
[66] See, for example, Engels 1999; Dueck 2000; Pothecary 2005; compare also König, this volume.

participation across long distances (compare Hatzimichali and König, this volume, for analysis of the distinctive cast of Strabo's universalist outlook). Strabo explicitly addresses his work to the leaders of this new world, expressing particular admiration for the commanders who have brought the world under a single political order (εἰς μίαν ἐξουσίαν καὶ διοίκησιν πολιτικήν).[67]

Even Strabo, however, is deeply embedded in civic ways of thinking. This is clear from his polemical defence of geography as the ideal discipline for educating the leaders of this new world. According to Strabo, geography shares with political and ethical philosophy a focus on 'the lives and needs of rulers' (τοὺς ἡγεμονικοὺς βίους καὶ τὰς χρείας), but it can outdo those other disciplines because of its more practical focus. To justify his claim that political and ethical philosophy are really concerned with the lives of rulers, and their specific needs, Strabo makes a somewhat tendentious argument: political philosophy has always defined political regimes by the nature of the ruling element (*monarchia*, *aristokratia*, *dēmokratia*); by consequence, it has inevitably focused its attention on the rulers.[68]

This immediately shows Strabo's familiarity with the Greek civic tradition, perhaps partly due to his Peripatetic teachers, whom he had followed before turning to at least a loose affiliation with Stoicism.[69] The engagement with philosophical traditions is also consistent with Strabo's aspirations to emphasise the philosophical qualities of his own project, studied in this volume by M. Hatzimichali. At the same time, Strabo's claim at this point also clearly reveals his aspiration to change radically the emphasis of the civic and philosophical tradition he had inherited, or to expose an underlying, unrecognised alternative focus which that tradition had possessed all along. Contrary to the impression Strabo gives, Greek political philosophy in the tradition of Plato and Aristotle had long, in fact, focused on the common good and justice for whole cities, and the duties and entitlements of all citizens, rather than on any one element within the city. Aristotle had argued, for example, that legitimate political regimes always look to the welfare of the whole *polis*, rather than to the interests of the rulers; focus on the latter is a sign of despotism, not a free city.[70] Accordingly, philosophy of politics, in Aristotle's view, should concern itself with defining the moral *telos* of civic life, which provides standards of

---

[67] See especially Strabo 1.1.16; compare Clarke 1999: 203.
[68] Strabo 1.1.18. For Strabo's shift of focus from collective participation to power and leadership in defining political life, compare 16.2.38: the Jews are a political group (*politikoi*) because they live according to a common authority (ἀπὸ προστάγματος κοινοῦ).
[69] See Dueck 2000: 11; compare Hatzimichali, this volume. [70] E.g., Arist. *Pol.* 1279a17–21.

good and bad for all;[71] this *telos* is elsewhere defined as the good life of virtue for all citizens.[72]

In fact, Strabo has a particular, controversial alternative inspiration in mind: that notorious anti-civic symbol, the Thrasymachus of Book 1 of Plato's *Republic*. It is from Thrasymachus that Strabo draws his argument about the implications of the names of different constitutions (see above), as well as the aside to which this builds up (1.1.18): 'for this reason also some said that justice is the advantage of the stronger' (διὰ τοῦτο δὲ καὶ τὸ δίκαιον εἶπόν τινες τὸ τοῦ κρείττονος συμφέρον). This is an allusion to the wording and content of Thrasymachus' famous argument that moral standards of justice are in fact determined by the dominant power in any given society, which designs them in its own interest, to enable exploitation of the weaker party.[73] The truly strong and admirable are those who can burst through the demands of conventional justice.

Strabo thus seems to latch on to one of the most famous attacks within the Greek civic tradition itself on core civic ideals of justice, equality, law and virtuous cooperation. Although Strabo does not directly endorse the claim that 'justice is the advantage of the stronger', his toying with this most infamous slogan of the anti-civic, amoral challenge in classical Athens raises the possibility that the moral and civic ideals emphasised by Diodorus and others are no more than an illusory superstructure, which diverts attention from true power dynamics. Strabo's whole defence of geography confirms that he himself wants to focus on those underlying dynamics: to burst the bounds of traditional Greek ethics and intellectual life focused on the individual small *polis* of free equals, in order to offer more utilitarian, practical advice to the bold leaders of the new world order, who soar above conventional moral or local concerns. It required an intimate familiarity with the Greek civic tradition to attack it at this most fundamental point. This adds weight to the main thesis of this chapter: even Strabo, the most critical of the Greek civic tradition among the later Hellenistic authors surveyed here, reveals that tradition's inescapable influence on later Hellenistic cosmopolitan perspectives.

The relevant part of Plato's *Republic* – perhaps the whole of Book 1 as a school text – may well have been stock reading material, and a stock point of reference, for those engaged in politics and political thought in the later Hellenistic world. A civic decree from the city of Mylasa in Caria appears to allude to Socrates' riposte to Thrasymachus. This is a first-century BCE

---

[71] Arist. *Eth. Nic.* 1152b1–3.   [72] Arist. *Pol.* 1280b31–40.
[73] Compare Pl. *Resp.* 338c2–339a4. Radt 2002–11: vol. v, 67, notes the allusion in Strabo.

decree passed by the Mylasan civic subdivision of the Otorkondeis. It praises a benefactor, Iatrocles, on the grounds that he has shown financial generosity and flexibility to individuals concerning difficult debt repayments, 'thinking that justice is more beneficial than injustice' (λυσιτελεστέραν ἡγούμενος τὴν δικαιοσύ[νην] τῆς ἀδικίας).[74] This is almost a quotation of Socrates' response to Thrasymachus: injustice is never more beneficial than justice (οὐδέποτ᾽ ἄρα, ὦ μακάριε Θρασύμαχε, λυσιτελέστερον ἀδικία δικαιοσύνης])[75] – the thesis which Socrates elaborates and defends in the rest of the *Republic*. For the Otorkondeis, unlike Strabo, Book 1 of Plato's *Republic* offers a bolster to ideals of strong civic community, justice and solidarity, against the competing attractions of elite self-assertion. This decree and Strabo's introduction can thus be seen as competing contributions to a dynamic late Hellenistic public sphere, sustained by complex arguments and texts in both epigraphic and literary form, each engaging with the classical canon.[76]

Strabo was certainly deeply familiar with the intricacies of the civic life of the Greek cities, especially in Asia Minor. He details their geography and history, giving a prominent place, as the late Hellenistic cities themselves did, to each city's leading cultural and literary figures.[77] He also weaves the cities into his broader monumental cosmopolitan vision.[78] He does, however, also often betray a cosmopolitan and unsentimentally power-oriented distrust or even contempt for small cities and their civic life, singling out some for stupidity or philistinism.[79] For example, he ridicules the Iasians for abandoning a musical performance *en masse* when the arrival of the fishing boats in the harbour is announced. This gives a rather different impression of the Iasians' level of cultural sophistication from that implied in their own decrees, such as the decree for Melanion quoted in the previous section.[80]

Strabo's cosmopolitan scepticism about local civic life emerges perhaps most clearly in his discussion of the first-century BCE civic life of Tarsus in south-eastern Asia Minor (also mentioned in Hatzimichali's chapter here).[81] Strabo praises the philosophical and rhetorical schools of Tarsus, which he thinks can rival even those of Athens and Alexandria. There is, however, a significant difference: most of the students are locals, and they

---

[74] *I.Mylasa* 109, ll. 4–10.   [75] Pl. *Resp.* 353e7–354a9; compare 354b7; 360c8.
[76] On the role of philosophy in Hellenistic civic life, see Long 2006: 3–39; Haake 2007.
[77] See Engels 2005; the chapters in Biraschi and Salmeri 2000 survey Strabo's discussions of the cities of Asia Minor.
[78] Compare Clarke 1999: 314–15.   [79] E.g., Strabo 13.3.6 (Kyme).
[80] E.g., Strabo 14.2.21 (Iasos); contrast *I.Iasos* 98.   [81] Strabo 14.5.12–15.

tend to travel abroad for their further education and to live their lives. Strabo perhaps saw this as weakening the local political life of the city, which had recently needed rescue through the intervention of one of the city's returning emigré intellectuals, the Stoic Athenodorus Cananites. This Athenodorus originated from an obscure village, but became a very successful Stoic philosopher, a teacher of Octavian. Athenodorus returned to his home city of Tarsus as an old man and removed the illegitimate regime of a certain Boethus, who had gained power by demagoguery, as a protégé of Antony.

In telling this story, Strabo once again reveals his deep engagement with the later Hellenistic *polis* world towards which he can also express such scepticism. He shows his familiarity with increasingly cultural conceptions of civic life and citizenship by describing the demagogue Boethus as a 'bad poet and a bad citizen' (κακοῦ μὲν ποιητοῦ κακοῦ δὲ πολίτου). Boethus engaged with panhellenic cultural traditions, but in the wrong way: he used Homeric poetry to praise Antony for his victories in the East, for which Antony rewarded him with illegitimate political power. Strabo is also sufficiently conversant with the values, institutions and honorific practices of later Hellenistic cities to satirise Boethus for inverting the good citizen's stereotypical habits of euergetism: rather than donating olive oil to the gymnasium, a benefaction very often praised in Hellenistic civic inscriptions,[82] he was caught stealing the oil.

For Strabo, Tarsus' debased civic life could be redeemed only through the intervention of a Stoic doctrinal cosmopolitan and world citizen with a better grasp of culture, philosophy and ethics. In Strabo's account, Athenodorus' intervention was met with hostility from some Tarsians, who resorted to informal epigraphy: they wrote satirical and vulgar hexameter graffiti attacking Athenodorus ('actions for young men, deliberation for middle-aged men, and flatulence for old men', ἔργα νέων, βουλαὶ δὲ μέσων, πορδαὶ δὲ γερόντων). Athenodorus responded by adapting the hexameter ('thunder for old men', βρονταὶ δὲ γερόντων) and calling for concord, showing the culture, mildness and intelligence otherwise lacking from Tarsus' civic life. In a final display of civic degeneracy, an incontinent citizen then soiled Athenodorus' own house. Strabo portrays Athenodorus, in his response, displaying a deep embedding in the Greek civic tradition, by drawing an analogy between sickness (*nosos*) and the disorder and unrest of the city as a whole: this was a very old

---

[82] E.g., *I.Priene*² 68, ll. 57–65; for many further examples, see Curty 2015.

and well-known Greek political metaphor.[83] The cosmopolitan Stoic Athenodorus, like Strabo himself in his methodological preface, thus uses the very resources of traditional Greek civic ideology in order to attack the shortcomings of inward-looking *polis* life.

Strabo's account of Tarsian politics shows particularly clearly that he was so familiar with the later Hellenistic *poleis* that he could even put his finger on their inherent contradictions, including the tensions between civic and cosmopolitan ideals themselves. These tensions are also documented in the first-century BCE Prienian decrees for A. Aemilius Zosimus, first discussed in detail at the end of the previous section, which suggest a civic environment not unlike Strabo's Tarsus. The first decree for Zosimus, discussed in the previous section, tends to fuse together the civic and cosmopolitan perspectives, in a seemingly harmonious hybrid ideology similar to Diodorus': Zosimus aspires to be honoured by a diverse quasi-civic community including outsiders, and he employs a literary tutor to help make the ephebes humane in their souls. However, other parts of that first decree, and especially the second decree for him, distil the elements of this synthesis into competing perspectives.

Already in the first decree, Zosimus is praised for certain unconditional, universal benefactions which sit uncomfortably with the civic tradition of drawing and reinforcing complex distinctions of personal status and belonging.[84] For example, he sponsored participation in the gymnasium and baths for all unconditionally, including generic 'foreigners' and Romans.[85] Zosimus' promotion of a form of cosmopolitan universalism which overrode civic status distinctions and structures is made explicit in the second decree for him, passed, with a different proposer (the adoptive brother of the first proposer), after Zosimus had held the principal Prienian magistracy, the stephanephorate. On his first day in that office, he invited all in the city to a celebratory breakfast at his house, 'making his first day of office a common day [of celebration] for all on equal terms, on which the chance fate of the slave and the formal status of the foreigner were to be deemed of the least importance' (τὴ[ν π]ρώτην τ[ῆς ἀρχῆς ἡμέρ]αν κοινοποησάμενος πᾶσιν ἐπ' ἴσον, ἐν ᾗ καὶ δούλου τύχη[ν] καὶ ξένου χρ[ηματισμὸ]ν ἦν ἐν ἐλαχίστῳ τίθεσθαι).[86] The way in which this sentence is expressed suggests some thoroughgoing scepticism about the

---

[83] See Brock 2013: 69–82.
[84] See Kamen 2013 for classical Athens; Purcell 2005: 87, for the later Hellenistic period (and the Zosimus dossier).
[85] *I.Priene*² 68, ll. 57–65, 76–80.   [86] *I.Priene*² 69, ll. 55–6.

validity of key civic status distinctions, of the kind normally associated with the Stoics or even the Cynics:[87] slave status may be really a matter of chance, and the status of foreigner only a bureaucratic formality. This is perhaps understandable on the part of Zosimus, himself possibly a former slave or descendant of slaves and certainly a foreigner who had gained citizenship in Priene by special grant. At this point in the decree, Zosimus emerges playing a similar role to Strabo's Athenodorus at Tarsus: the cosmopolitan outsider who injects enlightened humanity into a local civic environment still marked by petty status distinctions, rivalries and particularism.

This more extreme, counter-civic form of cosmopolitanism would still have to have secured the approval of the broader Prienian civic community, which endorsed these decrees. That was perhaps only achieved, however, through a complex negotiation, traces of which are preserved in other parts of this second decree. At the same time as praising Zosimus for his unconditional humanity, including towards slaves and foreigners, the second decree also lays strong emphasis on Zosimus' more traditional civic contributions, focused on the exclusive civic community and its particular honoured associates. He ensured that traditional civic sacrifices continued to be carried out, securing the traditional civic ideal of the concord (*homonoia*) of the *polis*. He also fulfilled a promise to hold a civic banquet for the whole citizen-body ([πάνδ]ημον εὐωχία[ν]), organised by traditional civic subdivision (*phylē*), for the first time 'since the war'.[88] In this case the invitations would have been far more selective. Full citizens, members of the *phylai*, this time took centre stage. They were accompanied by outsiders with a particular claim to affinity with the *dēmos*: non-citizens who had passed through ephebic training and citizens of cities with particularly close and honoured links with Priene (Rome, Athens, Thebes, Rhodes, Miletus, Magnesia, Samos, Ephesus and Tralles).[89]

This 'banquet for the whole *dēmos*' was probably accompanied or followed by extravagant theatrical entertainment:

[βουληθ]εὶς? δὲ μὴ μόνον τὰ πρὸς ἡδον[ὴν καὶ..., ἀλλὰ καὶ τὰ πρ]ὸς ἀπάτην χορηγῆσαι, [ἀκροάματα (?)] (l. 65) μὲν ἀπὸ τῆς [ξένης μι]σθωσάμενος καὶ τὸν δυνάμενον τῇ τ[έχνῃ ψυχα]γωγῆσαι παντόμιμ[ο]ν [Πλ]ουτογένην, ἐπιδιξάμενος δ' αὐτὸν ἐπὶ τ[έσσερας?] ἡμέρας ἀβέβηλον καὶ τῆς τοιαύτης ἐπιθυμίας τὸν {τε} καιρὸν [ἐποίησε].[90]

---

[87] Compare Hamon 2012: 70–2.
[88] Perhaps the First Mithridatic War, or the war of Labienus (see Kah 2012: 63).
[89] *I.Priene*² 69, ll. 39–45, 58–70.
[90] *I.Priene*² 69, ll. 63–7, with textual restorations and discussion in Robert 1930: 114–17.

because he wanted to provide not only the things conducive to [bodily] pleasure (*hēdonē*), but also those conducive to entertainment (*apatē*), he hired entertainments (?) (l. 65) from abroad, including the pantomime artist Plutogenes, who is able to beguile men's souls (*psychagōgein*) through his art; by arranging for him to perform for four (?) days, he ensured that the moment did not go by without being blessed (?) with this kind of desire (*epithymia*) also.

The description of this entertainment, and its psychological effects, is far less straight-laced than most other such accounts in Hellenistic inscriptions: whereas those tend to stress the skill and controlled beauty of the performances,[91] this decree stresses entertainment, bewitching of souls (*psychagōgia*) and desire. These concepts and words often had negative connotations of lack of seriousness, self-control, morality, cultivation or utility in Greek discussions of ethics and literature. The word *psychagōgia* is the most striking. Socrates uses it twice in Plato's *Phaedrus* to describe the power of rhetoric over individual souls, which, he shows in the rest of the dialogue, must be counteracted with the enlightening force of true philosophy.[92] It could have more neutral or even positive meanings in the Hellenistic period,[93] but the disparaging usage was still current. Contemporary with this inscription, Strabo himself rejects Eratosthenes' claim that poets necessarily aim at *psychagōgia* rather than teaching (*didaskalia*); poetry can, in fact, offer 'first philosophy'.[94] Indeed, according to Strabo, the Greek cities educate their young through poetry, not in the name of trivial *psychagōgia*, but for the sake of improving their self-control (οὐ ψυχαγωγίας χάριν δήπουθεν ψιλῆς, ἀλλὰ σωφρονισμοῦ).[95] The word *apatē*, though it might have come to mean only 'entertainment', probably preserved for most hearers at least a trace of its original meaning of 'deception', gesturing towards the idea that entertaining mimetic art is dangerously misleading, made famous by Plato; Polybius and Dionysius of Halicarnassus use it in that way, to refer to music and non-Thucydidean history-writing respectively.[96] The word *epithymia* also evokes basic, raw desire, as opposed to cultivated artistic appreciation.

---

[91] See the inscriptions surveyed in Chaniotis 2009; but the psychology of *SEG* 35.744 (Kalindoia AD 1), ll. 15–26 (on entertainment at civic banquets and festivals) is much closer to this text. On the broader theatrical dimensions of Hellenistic public life, see also Chaniotis 1997.
[92] See Pl. *Phdr.* 261a7–b2; 271c10–d1. Compare the strongly negative use at Pl. *Leg.* 909b2–3.
[93] E.g., Polyb. 6.2.8; 31.29.5; 38.5.3.   [94] Strabo 1.1.10.   [95] Strabo 1.2.3.
[96] Polyb. 4.20.5; Dion. Hal. *Thuc.* 6 and 7 (Thucydides aims instead for 'utility', ὠφέλεια). For disparaging reference to the *psychagōgia* and *apatē* (used together) of performances, contrasted with public speech for the common good, see Dio Chr. *Or.* 32.5.

The likelihood that this part of the second decree was intended to portray the pantomimist's entertainment as markedly unserious, and detached from the sober concern for morality and virtue so prominent elsewhere in these decrees, is greatly increased by these lines' striking intertextual allusion to the lines about education in the gymnasium in the first decree. In that first decree, the tutor in literature (φιλολογία) employed by Zosimus was said to have been engaged to 'lead the souls' (τ[ὰς ψυχ]ὰς ... προάγεσθαι) of the young men towards virtue and humane emotion; here, the pantomimist is said also to have been skilled in 'leading souls' ([ψυχα]γωγῆσαι), but through the very different method of deceptive entertainment, stimulating the very different psychological response of desire (*epithymia*). The contrast rests partly on the fact that, whereas the philological tutor was, by the nature of his field, concerned mainly with words (*logos*), the pantomimist, by the nature of his art, largely dispensed with words in favour of gestures and movement, though he could have been accompanied by words sung by a singer.[97]

This complex intertextual relationship between the two decrees attests to the literary sophistication of the public language of the Prienian *polis*. It is all the more remarkable for being the product of multiple, complex authorship, involving the processes of negotiation between benefactors and *demos* mentioned above. From one angle, the passage about the pantomimist, and its allusion to the earlier account of literary education in the gymnasium, might be seen as a further expression of counter-civic cosmopolitan haughtiness by Zosimus and his associates, comparable to that of Strabo's Athenodorus of Tarsus: condescension to feed the less refined appetites of the *polis*-bound citizens who have not come to appreciate fully the new cosmopolitan culture. On this possible hypothesis about the force these lines would have possessed for some Prienians, the underlying idea would have been a modification of the outlook made famous by the three-class system of Plato's *Republic*: whereas a more cosmopolitan elite can benefit from rational, literate education, including in the Prienian gymnasium, the souls of most of the *dēmos* have to be fed and led through more crude forms of *psychagōgia*. This hypothesis is not meant to rely on any intrinsic connection between pantomime and less educated or less mobile social groups,[98] but rather on this particular text's implied antithesis with literary education in the gymnasium and focus in its presentation of

---

[97] See Webb 2012: 221.
[98] On the complex role of pantomime in ancient society and literature, including other ancient reflections on its psychological effects: Hall and Wyles 2008; Webb 2012.

pantomime on immediate pleasure and desire within a bounded, local civic community. The main sign of this boundedness is the pantomime's apparent association with the civic banquet also organised by Zosimus (see above), which was not open to all like some of his other benefactions.[99]

Even if it has some truth, however, this hypothesis cannot account fully for these lines: Zosimus and his supporters would have had to gain the support of the Prienian *demos* also for this part of the decree. Members of the *demos* perhaps accepted, or even helped to shape, these lines because it was possible to give them a markedly different interpretation and force. If educated cosmopolitans had usurped reason and language (*logos* and *philologia*) as their medium, civic-minded citizens with a strongly local consciousness might have best asserted their rival claims by finding an alternative medium. They might have presented localised, face-to-face civic life as the ideal context for more visceral forms of emotion, shared experience and solidarity, of the kinds celebrated in these lines on the bounded civic banquet and the pantomimist. Such intense collective experience would not be possible in a worldwide cosmopolis dependent only on civilised literate communication. Perhaps some Prienians, partly resembling the authors of the anti-Athenodorus graffiti in Strabo's Tarsus, embraced effervescent celebration of pleasure-seeking and the body as the best counter-discourse to cosmopolitan rationality.

It is, of course, impossible to be sure what meaning the lines on pantomime had for different members of the Prienian audience. However, their complex ambiguity, placed in the wider context of the decrees for Zosimus, helps to reveal some of the complex tensions between civic, counter-civic and cosmopolitan voices in a later Hellenistic city, negotiated in its own public rhetoric. To return to Strabo, not the least striking aspect of his political outlook is his deep engagement with those tensions at civic level. That engagement helped to shape the polemical character of Strabo's own cosmopolitanism, not only in his detailed accounts of local politics, but also in his attacks on small-*polis* thinking in his methodological theorising. In that theorising, with which this

---

[99] The reference to a moment (*kairos*) which was enhanced by the pantomime makes it likely that Zosimus hired this entertainment in conjunction with the special occasion of the first civic banquet 'since the war', described in the immediately preceding lines; that more discrete event is a more probable reference for *kairos* than Zosimus' whole first period of office. Even if these performances were open to a wider section of the population than the banquet, the fact that they are described at this point in the decree – in between the accounts of the civic banquet and of Zosimus' civic sacrifices – associates them with the more traditional civic elements of Zosimus' benefactions.

section began, Strabo marked his hostile distance, not only from traditional civic ideology, but also from the Stoicising style of highly moral counter-civic cosmopolitanism evident in places in the Zosimus decrees: the view that unconditional, universal humanity renders civic boundaries and status distinctions meaningless, or harmful. With his Stoic leanings, Strabo must have been aware of that critique, but formulated his own more radical attack on civic perspectives and morality: they are a form of false, constraining consciousness whose emphasis on virtuous, just cooperation distracts attention from the realities of power. Since Strabo toys with the idea that it is really the strong who set the rules of 'justice', readers could have inferred that even the more idealistic forms of cosmopolitan universalism were themselves a useful tool of a new Roman elite. The practical implication was that those who wanted to participate in true politics should put less stress on civilised cooperation in a *polis* or civic cosmopolis, in order to join the new power-focused imperial elite, guided by Strabo's geographical education. Even within the counter-civic cosmopolitan camp there were varied and competing approaches, rival contributions to a single dialogue which cut across literary and epigraphic texts.

Conclusion: A Unified Literary and Public Sphere of Debate about *Polis* and Cosmopolis

This chapter has sought to portray a complex, sophisticated later Hellenistic public sphere, incorporating both literary texts and civic inscriptions. That varied public sphere encouraged debate about the nature of the newly interlocking Mediterranean, as well as the continuing relevance of the traditional small-scale city-state. Cosmopolitan literary authors, the main focus of this chapter, can be interpreted in a different light when seen as participants in these wide-ranging debates.

Diodorus and Strabo contributed to these debates in contrasting ways. Diodorus, for his part, pursued an optimistic approach to the possibility of reconciling traditional *polis* and new cosmopolis: for him, the later Hellenistic *polis* model, especially its honorific institutions, could be quite seamlessly expanded to cover the whole cosmopolis. This was in keeping with the aspirations of some civic Greeks and their cities to reconcile *polis* and cosmopolis. On the other hand, in many cities tensions and contradictions arose: new forms of social universalism and ethical ideals of humanity, based on a strict insistence on universal rational standards of thought and behaviour, were not always easy to reconcile with civic emphasis on the rewards of moral engagement with a particular place, community and tradition. This led to the complex negotiations and power dynamics, involving mobile cosmopolitan rulers and intellectuals in dialogue with local *polis* citizens, discussed in the previous section.

Strabo was much more explicitly conscious than Diodorus of these tensions and realities of power. This led him to develop a much more unsentimental, power-oriented form of cosmopolitanism, which was 'counter-civic' especially in its close critical engagement with local civic ideals and public life, which sometimes drew on counter-civic voices at city level. Indeed, the subtlety and persuasive force of both authors' literary articulation of their contrasting forms of cosmopolitanism owed much to their engagement with the sophisticated public discourse of the later Hellenistic cities, preserved now in the often complex – even literary – texts of their public inscriptions.

CHAPTER 6

The Wrath of the Sibyl
Homeric Reception and Contested Identities in the Sibylline Oracles 3

Emma Greensmith

Introduction

At some time in (perhaps) the first century BCE, in (perhaps) Alexandria, an anonymous poet adopts the voice of the Sibyl to rage against Homer. In fiery, spluttering hexameters, this Sibyl attacks the famous bard and exposes his woeful insufficiencies: he is old, a liar, a thief, and a false later imposter of her poetic craft:

(420) καί τις ψευδογράφος πρέσβυς βροτὸς ἔσσεται αὖτις
ψευδόπατρις· δύσει δὲ φάος ἐν ὀπῆσιν ἑῆσιν·
νοῦν δὲ πολὺν καὶ ἔπος διανοίαις ἔμμετρον ἕξει,
οὐνόμασιν δυσὶ μισγόμενον· Χῖον δὲ καλέσσει
αὐτὸν καὶ γράψει τὰ κατ' Ἴλιον, οὐ μὲν ἀληθῶς,
(425) ἀλλὰ σοφῶς· ἐπέων γὰρ ἐμῶν μέτρων τε κρατήσει·
πρῶτος γὰρ χείρεσσιν ἐμὰς βίβλους ἀναπλώσει·
αὐτὸς δ' αὖ μάλα κοσμήσει πολέμοιο κορυστάς,
Ἕκτορα Πριαμίδην καὶ Ἀχιλλέα Πηλείωνα
τούς τ' ἄλλους, ὁπόσοις πολέμια ἔργα μέμηλεν.
καί γε θεοὺς τούτοισι παρίστασθαί γε ποιήσει,
(430) ψευδογραφῶν κατὰ πάντα τρόπον, μέροπας κενοκράνους.
καὶ θανέειν μᾶλλον τοῖσιν κλέος ἔσσεται εὐρύ
Ἰλίῳ· ἀλλὰ καὶ αὐτὸς ἀμοιβαῖα δέξεται ἔργα.

And then there will be a certain false writer, an old mortal, who has a false fatherland. The light in his eyes will go out. He will be very smart and have a speech suitable for his thoughts which will be joined under two names. He will call himself an inhabitant of Chios. He will write the story of Ilium, not truthfully, but cleverly. For he will have mastered my verses and metres, since he will be the first to open my books with his hands. He will highly embellish the helmed men of war, Hector, son of Priam, Achilles, son of Peleus, and others, as many as cared for warfare. And he will make gods, in fact empty-headed people, to stand by them, writing falsely in every respect.

And it will be a great glory for them to die at Troy. But he will also receive retribution.

(*Or. Sib.* 3.419–32)[1]

To the classicist interested in the reception of Homer in later Greco-Roman antiquity – a topic which has certainly found no shortage of enthusiasts in recent years – this tirade is a treasure chest of material. The Sibyl's words display a number of familiar patterns of Homeric reading, reception and rejection. She[2] unpicks aspects of Homer's biography – his birthplace, genealogy and physiognomy; she challenges the veracity of his epic tales; and she puts forward a reading of literary time which sees Homer, the font of Greek learning and education, as secondary, belated and derivative. In a few angry lines, notions of Homeric truth, fiction, originality and temporality are boldly articulated. And yet the oracle has received no mention in recent scholarly literature on the reception of Homer in the Hellenistic or imperial Greek worlds, nor in the studies exploring the links between these two epochs. I begin with this fact not to perform the usual move of decrying critical neglect of an underexplored work, but because it provides fundamental grounding for this chapter's central topic. For this absence is significant; but, when we consider the text's provenance, perhaps not wholly surprising.

The passage is taken from the third book of the Sibylline Oracles: the oldest, mostly Jewish, book of a vast compilation of eschatological utterances attributed to the Sibyl's voice.[3] Ranging in date from the second century BCE to second century CE, these oracles make moralising, sometimes apocalyptic[4] pronouncements, and they give elongated genealogies about the starts of the world and premonitions about the end of it, including the fall of Rome, the great superpower which will one day be brought down by its own vices. The passage, the book and the entire

---

[1] The text of *Or. Sib.* 3 is taken from Geffcken 1902 and the translations adapted from Buitenwerf 2003.
[2] The issue of the authorship of the Sibylline Oracles is perennially contentious: see below, 'The Sibyl and Sibyllina: A Tradition of Plurality'. In full acknowledgement of these issues, I shall refer throughout this chapter to the poet of Book 3 as 'she', partly as a means of circumventing the thorny and unsolvable question of who really wrote this work, and partly as a nod to the feminine identity of the poetic voice being appropriated (on this aspect, see Levine 1995, who reads the Oracles as part of a feminist commentary on scriptural and intertestamental literature).
[3] There are fifteen books, the last of which does not survive. For editions, commentaries and scholarship on individual books (predominantly 1–2, 3 and 5, on which scholarly work has focused), see discussion and references below, 'The Sibyl and Sibyllina: A Tradition of Plurality'.
[4] On how far the oracles can rightly be deemed apocalyptic, see Collins 1974 and 1986 with discussion in Lightfoot 2007: 111–14.

collection are extremely difficult to contextualise: each book, and often each oracle, contains a mixture not only of dates, but also of cultural and religious politics – some are pagan, some Jewish, some Christian, some an elusive mixture of all three. The oracles' literary sources are hard to track, and their poetic sophistication is dubious and often disparaged. As a result, the collection has tended to slip into the precarious critical space between Classics and theology departments. Jane Lightfoot begins her monumental edition of the first two books of the Oracles[5] by outlining this problem: 'The Sibylline Oracles are still a relatively unexplored area. They are just that bit too classical for students of the Jewish or Christian apocrypha to feel really comfortable handling them. For classicists, their origins in the byways of . . . Jewish or early Christian culture may serve to counteract the familiarity of their classical literary form.'[6] And yet, Lightfoot proceeds with cautious optimism, everyone who has worked on the Oracles agrees just 'how interesting they are'.[7] This passage from Book 3 is from the outset highly 'interesting' to the classical scholar of late Hellenistic Homer, not only because of the issues and themes that it raises, but also because of the form that it takes. By writing in epic hexameters, the conventional metre of oracles, the author is also able to attack Homer using his own medium and textual fabric.

In this chapter, I shall take this passage as my focus, to make the case for the Oracles' significant engagement with later Hellenistic literary culture. In her attack on Homer in Book 3, the Sibyl uses her poetry to reflect, distort and disrupt notions of Homeric authority and exegesis for a new and distinctive agenda. I begin with two frameworks to contextualise this reading: firstly, the expanded authority of and investment in Homer beginning in late Hellenistic culture and reaching its zenith in the 'Second Sophistic'; and secondly, the long-stretching ancient traditions surrounding the figure and books of the Sibyl, which also intensified in late Hellenistic and early imperial times. In both discussions, we shall see how issues of competitive authority, diverse traditions, and contested points of origin emerge over and again – issues which bring the figures of Homer and the Sibyl into a provocative dialogue. The third part of this chapter brings these two frameworks together. The Sibyl of *Or. Sib.* 3, I argue, acknowledges and manipulates these shared contentious aspects of

---

[5] Lightfoot 2007. Lightfoot's study (which has much to say about the third book in relation to these later sections: see especially 94–152) has itself done much to usher the collection out of the critical wilderness it once inhabited.
[6] Lightfoot 2007: vii.   [7] Lightfoot 2007: vii.

Homeric and Sibylline receptions to construct herself as a rival (not just a parallel) literary authority to Homer, the avatar of Greek *paideia*. Through this undertaking, the author of this passage stands as a remarkable witness to the ways in which Homeric poetry and its criticism could be used and inverted by Hellenistic Jews of the time.

A central aim of this volume is to pursue more rigorously the potential connections between late Hellenistic and imperial Greek literature and culture.[8] This oracle offers a fascinating route for tracing such links. Seated on the cusp of the Hellenistic and imperial worlds,[9] this Jewish poetic work displays in its response to Homer and the literary tradition themes and techniques predominantly associated with classicising imperial prose. Pulling its reader forwards and backwards in time, the Sibyl's competitive self-modelling provides an instructive bridge between the literary politics of the late Hellenistic period and those of the Second Sophistic, and recasts Homeric criticism onto the most cosmic, trans-temporal of scales.

Homeric Reception, Imperial Prose

In 'Visions and Revisions of Homer', a widely read and cited piece on the reception of Homer in the Second Sophistic, Froma Zeitlin begins with an image drawn from earlier in Greek history. A Hellenistic marble votive relief from the late third/mid-second century BCE, signed by Archelaos of Priene, found in Italy but originally from Alexandria, offers for Zeitlin 'a remarkable visual witness to the expansion and consolidation of Homer's prestige in the post-classical era' (Figure 6.1).[10] The sculpture depicts the *apotheosis* of Homer: the bard is figured as one of the gods, and then receiving sacrifice, honoured with an altar and shrine. In the lowest zone, Homer is seated in splendour, being crowned on a throne, holding a sceptre and a book roll.[11] He is surrounded by personified figures such as Poetry, Tragedy and Comedy, and with two small kneeling figures before him representing the *Iliad* and *Odyssey*, and two crawling mice at his feet

---

[8] On this 'second type of dialogue', see the Introduction to this volume.
[9] On the dating of the book, see below, 'The Sibyl and Sibyllina: A Tradition of Plurality', and for the date of our central passage within it, see 'The Sibyl vs Homer: Oracular Confrontations'.
[10] Zeitlin 2001: 197. Whilst my discussion here focuses on Zeitlin's piece, it also draws on other important art historical scholarship on the relief and its dynamics: see especially Pinkwart 1965 and Onians 1979, with further bibliography in Ridgway, 1990: 257–68.
[11] Homer also appears (in all likelihood) on the top section of the relief, where he is residing on a mountain peak with the Olympians, and placed (literally) on a pedestal.

Figure 6.1 Marble relief showing the *apotheosis* of Homer, Archelaos of Priene; c. 200 BCE; from Bovillae; height 1.15 m. London, British Museum.
© The Trustees of the British Museum

indicating the *Batrachomyomachia* – a parodic work in Homerising hexameters which, in earlier phases of literary history, was occasionally attributed to Homer himself.[12] An overt and ornate reflection of Homer's canonised and hyper-literary status (the scrolls suggest the bookish culture of

[12] See Graziosi 2002; Peirano 2012: 36–73.

Alexandrian libraries), the relief also depicts a sacred shrine to the epic poet which, it has been suggested, is modelled on the Homereion, a temple which as Aelian later describes it, depicted in its own tableau Homer surrounded by all the cities which 'claimed [him] as their own.' (*Varia Historia* 13.22). The places are not named, but they could have included Chios, Smyrna, Ionia, Argos, Athens, Babylon, Rome and even Egypt, all of which laid claim to being Homer's birthplace, and in the case of Chios, Smyrna, Ionia and Argos had initiated cults specifically dedicated to the poet.

Part of a wider culture of material responses to Homer from the late Hellenistic and early imperial periods, including the much-discussed *Tabulae Iliacae* (one of which, the Tabula Capitolina, appears to be from the same villa as this relief, the Messer Paolo at Bovillae), the Archelaos imagery provides an intense and powerful vignette of the allure and authority of Homer, and the multiplicity of forms that such authority could take. This is a figure of awe, fleshed out, personified (and accompanied by personifications) and deified, of intense competition (poetic contests and geographical ones), and of textual and material literary status.[13] Homer's perennial importance, present in all phases of ancient Greek culture, is here concretised and concentrated. For Zeitlin, however, this Hellenistic illustration serves as a 'prologue' (her term) to the article's central area of enquiry: the 'seeds of investment' in Homer displayed here in the late centuries BCE, she argues, expanded to their fullest only in what happened next. In the wake of Alexander the Great's conquest of the Persian Empire and the subsequent expansion of Greek rule throughout the eastern Mediterranean, through an enlarged and diverse population and the consolidation of a 'remarkably standardized' educational system throughout the Hellenistic world[14] (of which Homer's epics stood at the centre), it was in the imperial period that the weight of Homeric prestige could exert its most 'persistently pervasive influence'.[15]

Therefore after the enticement of this Hellenistic prelude, the remainder of Zeitlin's analysis focuses on examples drawn from imperial Greek literature in the early centuries CE: specifically, the prose declamations and witty treatises of Lucian, Philostratus and Dio Chrysostom, which use close encounters with Homer and his heroes, deep textual engagement with his epics, and ironic correction of his plots, to claim a space for the

---

[13] On the *Tabulae Iliacae* see the seminal work by Squire 2011 and Petrain 2014.
[14] See particularly Morgan 1998, Cribiore 2001, Too 2001. 'Remarkably standardized' is from Kim 2010: 7.
[15] Thus Zeitlin 2001: 203.

authority of Greek culture 'under' Roman rule.[16] Other scholars of post-classical Greek reception of Homer reveal a similar focus. J.F. Kindstrand's study examines Dio, Aristides and Maximus of Tyre;[17] Robert Lamberton considers the appropriation of Homer by Neoplatonist writers;[18] and Félix Buffière treats mainly the allegorical tradition.[19] In *Homer between History and Fiction*, Larry Kim treats three works from the Second Sophistic which make sustained efforts to argue against the poet and to challenge the historical truth of his account of what happened at Troy: Dio's *Trojan Oration*, Lucian's *True Histories* and Philostratus' *Heroicus* (alongside which is discussed the *Vita Apollonii*).[20] However, Kim goes so far as to argue that these texts form a *distinct* group within the field of Homeric rewritings owing to their shared interest in the historical 'truth' of Homer's account, explicit and detailed discussion of Homeric poetry, and centralisation of the figure of Homer himself. Thus Dio's *Trojan Oration* insists, following Herodotus, on the alleged testimony of an Egyptian priest that Helen was rightfully married to Paris, Hector killed Achilles, and Troy actually won the war. In the second book of Lucian's *True Histories*, Lucian actually meets the bard himself, during a stay on the Island of the Blessed, and interviews him on the truth about his life and works: this ghostly Homer 'sets the record straight' on matters of Alexandrian criticism like which of the *Iliad* and *Odyssey* came first, why he started the *Iliad* in the middle, and from which city he really came (*Ver. hist.* 2.20). And in the *Heroicus* it is revealed via the storytelling vine-dresser that 'Homer knew the truth but changed much of it to suit the subject he had chosen' (*Her.* 43.16); covering up, for instance, Odysseus' role in the murder of Palamedes as the result of a necromantic bargain struck with Odysseus himself. Through such scholarly treatments, these stars of the Second Sophistic have emerged as those who use Homer most sophisticatedly to assert their affinity to Greece in the Roman world.

This narrative is, of course, a highly familiar one. I have retraced its tenets not to provide another overview of the role of and reactions to Homer in the imperial period, but rather to stress how the gap between Zeitlin's 'prologue' and her analysis has yet to be entirely filled.[21] These types of challenge to Homer's authority are now naturally associated with

---

[16] 'Under' reflects the title of the volume in which Zeitlin's piece appears: Goldhill 2001, *Being Greek under Rome: Cultural Identity, the Second Sophistic and the Development of Empire*.
[17] Kindstrand 1973. [18] Lamberton 1986. [19] Buffière 1956. [20] Kim 2010.
[21] On the Hellenistic cultural politics of the relief itself, and its reflection of or engagement with Alexandrian 'institution fabric' see Pollitt 1986 and Stewart 1990: 218. Zeitlin herself uses Alexander and his phil-Homerism, and Hellenistic epigrams (many of which also attest to the

Second Sophistic *paideia*; 'the fascinating cultural work of visioning and revisioning the bard'[22] is seen as the central (even exclusive) domain of imperial prose. And yet the Archelaos relief provides a crucial reminder of how the walls of this periodisation must not be constructed too solidly. The growth of this discourse of Homeric reception can be charted more diversely; and a meaningful dialogue can be created between the responses to Homer beginning in later Hellenistic culture, and the boisterous reworkings of the Second Sophistic.

There is however a further layer to this dialogue. The figure of Poetry on the Archelaos relief, the scrolls representing the Homeric text, and the representations of the *Iliad*, *Odyssey* and *Batrachomyomachia*, alongside the texts in both prose *and verse* found on many of the *Tabulae Iliacae* all suggest that poetry – both Homer's own verse and poetic works written in response to it – must feature strongly in assessments of later Greek strategies of Homeric response. The earliest centuries CE were for a long time considered to be an era where, in terms of literary culture, poetry was 'annexed' by prose.[23] The situation is now very different. Verse is increasingly recognised as having offered a living medium of expression in imperial Greek culture; and epic in particular, the continued apex in the hierarchy of genres during this period, is rightly seen as a powerful vehicle through which traditional language and themes were renegotiated.[24] But despite some excellent studies on individual imperial poets,[25] poetry has still not yet been fully amalgamated into the wider literary-cultural picture. In that complex, liminal space between the Hellenistic and imperial periods, the role of poetry, and particularly epic, in articulating Greek self-positioning remains under-interrogated.

My initial point therefore is a simple one. The question of how the authority of Homer was moulded and manipulated in later Greek literary culture can be posed differently. The terms of enquiry must be widened:

---

competitions regarding Homer's birthplace) as further 'points of departure and return' from her main imperial foci.

[22] Zeitlin 2001: 196.

[23] See Bowie 1989a and 1990 for further bibliography. More recently, König's introductory study (2009) of imperial Greek literature includes only a coda on poetry, suggesting how embedded this attitude to the forms still is.

[24] See the bibliography compiled by Cuypers for an overview of the volume of work done on these poets: https://sites.google.com/ site/ hellenisticbibliography/ empire (last accessed 17 March 2021).

[25] See, e.g., on Quintus, Baumbach and Bär 2007, which instigated the 'Second Sophistic' reading of the poem, Maciver 2012 and Greensmith 2020, and on Nonnus, Shorrock 2011, Spanoudakis 2014 and Accorinti 2016. Cameron 2016 considers various aspects of poetic and philosophical culture in the fourth to sixth centuries CE, though he is chiefly concerned, in his own words, 'less with poetry and philosophy than with poets and philosophers' (xi).

both in terms of period and in terms of form – from Hellenistic to imperial; poetry and prose. My strategy in what follows is to offer one, rather unconventional way of reformulating this question. Rather than offering a brief survey of the response to Homer in late Hellenistic and early imperial poetic works, I shall explore these ideas through the detailed reading of one text – the 'anti-Homer' section of the Third Sibylline Oracle – where issues of Homeric authority and poetic textuality are highly insistent. On the one hand, this text takes us far away from the milieu of the Second Sophistic authors and their Homerising games. And yet on the other, it mirrors a number of the strategies of Homeric reading and criticism displayed in and associated with these works. It therefore offers a significant opportunity to consider the different uses to which subversive approaches to Homer could be put. The passage reveals a poetic voice fully immersed in Greek 'Homer-mania', but who uses it to articulate a Jewish form of Hellenic identity: one that is self-consciously othering, programmatically obscure and proudly temporally shifty.

The Sibyl and Sibyllina: A Tradition of Plurality

From this brief resumé of responses to Homer displayed on the Archelaos relief and pursued by 'groups' of texts from the Second Sophistic, we may highlight, for all the variety, a number of recurrent themes: questions centred on where Homer was from; what he was 'like' (the divinised god receiving worship on the Archelaos relief, the ghostly spectre on Lucian's island, or a figure in the underworld in the *Heroicus*, communicating with his own heroic characters), and the nature and structure of his works. Before we turn to what the author of this passage of the Sibylline Oracles has to say about these sorts of Homeric questions, we must first address the Sibyl's own identity: her life and her works as conceived in the Hellenistic and imperial imagination. Here too we find a tradition built upon a driving sense of elusiveness: the Sibyl emerges as an obscure, compound figure, who could belong to everyone and to no one; who was the subject of competition and contention, and who occupies a number of difficult interval spaces – between human and divine; truth and falsehood; atemporal and localised identities; oral and written verse.

The Sibylline Oracles must be understood within a long and disparate tradition in Greek and Roman antiquity concerning the Sibyl as a figure and her prophecies and books. Sibyls or inspired prophetesses were well known in the Greco-Roman world: always portrayed as an old woman, the Sibyl was credited with having given oracles at the time of the Trojan

Wars, at the dawn of Greek history. Plutarch's quotation of Heraclitus (500 BCE) is taken to be the earliest reference to the figure: here we find a frenzied, garrulous voice-piece whose words have no literary or textual value, but which convey a transcendent divine mediation, and grant eternal fame:[26] 'Σίβυλλα δὲ μαινομένῳ στόματι' καθ' Ἡράκλειτον 'ἀγέλαστα καὶ ἀκαλλώπιστα καὶ ἀμύριστα φθεγγομένη, χιλίων ἐτῶν ἐξικνεῖται τῇ φωνῇ διὰ τὸν θεόν' ('"But the Sibyl with frenzied lips," as Heraclitus has it, "uttering words mirthless, unembellished, unperfumed, yet reaches to a thousand years with her voice through the god"') (Plutarch, *De Pythiae oraculis* 397a).[27] Two plays of Aristophanes, the 'first clear testimony that the sibyl ever existed',[28] offer a different but equally ambivalent picture: in *Knights* (424 BCE) he uses the verb σιβυλλιάω as a synonym for ἀείδω χρησμούς (31). Like Plato in the *Phaedrus*, who makes the Sibyl akin to the soothsayer (the 'Sibyl and others, who by practising heavenly inspired divination have foretold many future things accurately', 244b), the emphasis is on the utility and exactitude of the Sibyl's words. In the *Peace*, however, Aristophanes ridicules the oracle-monger Hierocles, and by transferal the very practice of sibylline consultation, as meretricious and insincere, because he attends to oracles only to get a good meal.[29]

The bulk of evidence concerning the spread and use of Sibylline oracles comes from the Greco-Roman period, where a number of sources attest to traditions of both public and private consultation of the Sibyl, who prophesied events of unconditional misery (earthquakes, floods, upheavals and war) or explained phenomena as portents of catastrophes. The oracles officially preserved at Rome were consulted by a college of priests (the *quindecemviri sacris faciundis*) at the command of the Senate at serious political crises. They were all destroyed when the Capitol was burnt in 83 BCE, but a new collection was formed in 12 CE and deposited by Augustus in the temple of Apollo on the Palatine hill, where they lasted until the fifth century.[30] The content of these books does not survive, but evidence reveals both the reverence in which they were held, and the suspicion

---

[26] Unsurprisingly, there is no consensus on what in this description comes from Plutarch and what is Heraclitus (see Lightfoot 2007: 4, n. 4 for full references on the scholarly debate).
[27] Translation via Buitenwerf 2003: 93.   [28] Buitenwerf 2003: 94.
[29] There is also some evidence that Euripides also mentioned the Sibyl in a play now lost: see Parke 1998: 104–5 and Buitenwerf 2003: 93.
[30] Prudentius, *Apotheosis* 439–42, in the latter half of the fourth century CE wrote that 'no longer does a priest possessed utter with foaming mouth and panting breath fates drawn from Sibylline book … Cumae is dumb and mourns for its oracles.' For more detail on the decline in the consultation of the Oracles, possibly (though not necessarily, given the mixture of religious politics evinced in the

which they attracted. Cassius Dio, for instance, records how the consuls in 19 CE were troubled by a particular oracle: 'when thrice three hundred revolving years have run their course, destruction shall bring civil strife upon Rome, and the folly of Sybaris too'. Tiberius declared the verses false and gave orders to examine all existing prophetic books: some were declared worthless and others preserved as genuine. People, however, did not forget this oracle, and when in 64 CE a huge part of Rome was destroyed by fire, they claimed that this sibylline prophecy – which was now deemed apocryphal, found nowhere in the sacred books – had indeed foretold the destruction that was now coming true (Cass. Dio 62.18.3). In terms of form, it is clear that these books were all written in hexameter verse, the metre also used in historical oracle centres, at Delphi and in Asia Minor, and for the literary depiction of legendary prophecy (Orpheus, Musaeus, Linus, Bacis and Epimenides). These were, therefore, popular, public and *poetic* predictions.

Our sources also affirm the fluctuating status of the Sibyl as a particular prophetess or many prophetesses with a generic name. Plutarch's Heraclitus sees the Sibyl as a lone ranger, without time or any clear place, her voice resonating throughout the ages: she is cast as an extra-temporal figure, 'almost a disembodied voice'.[31] And yet other earlier Sibyls were much more geographically centred, and in the later Hellenistic and early imperial periods, they proliferated further and became associated with specific places, which resulted in the growth of a number of key Sibylline sites. Varro in 47 CE published a catalogue of ten Sibyls, preserved by Lactantius, including the Sibyl of Persia, Libya, Delphi, Phrygia, Erythrae and (the one which receives the fullest attention) Cumae – the most famous Sibyl of Rome. Pausanias (*Periegesis* 10.12) also associated the Sibyl with Delphi, Delos, Erythrae, Marpessus and Alexandria in the Troad (where he describes her tomb beside the images of nymphs and statues of Hermes: 10.12.6) and details a competition between Erythrae and Marpessus over which place can really claim the status of being her birth town (10.12.3 and 10.12.7). The Erythraean Sibyl – a point to which we shall return – was particularly tied to Trojan premonitions: Pausanias (10.12.2) says that the Erythraean Sibyl predicted that 'Helen would be brought to Sparta to be the ruin of Asia and Europe, and that for her sake the Greeks would capture Troy', and in Varro's list as quoted by

---

surviving collection) in connection with the Christianisation of the Empire, see Buitenwerf 2003: 104–5, with further references.

[31] Lightfoot 2007: 4.

Lactantius, it is the Erythraean Sibyl who calls Homer's writings 'lies' (*Div. inst.* 1.6.9). The particular association with Erythrae is also strikingly displayed on a grotto built or renovated on the occasion of a visit to the town (on the west coast of Asia Minor) by Lucius Verus in 162 CE. In an epigram carved on the gate-post, the Sibyl speaks of her parents (her mother here is the nymph Nais) and confidently asserts that whilst she has prophesied all over the world, she has only one true birthright and burial place:

> I am Sibyl, uttering oracles, the servant of Phoebus
> The first-born daughter of a nymph, a Naiad.
> Erythrae is my only home town
> And Theodore was my mortal father
> The (mountain) Kissotas carried my birth, the place where I left
> The womb and immediately spoke oracles to mortals
> While I was sitting on this rock
> I sang for the mortals predictions of future sufferings.
> I lived for three times 300 years
> I, an unwedded virgin, and I travelled all over the world.
> But now I am again sitting here on my dear rock,
> Delighted by this charming spring.
> I am glad that the time of which I spoke has now come true,
> The time in which, according to my prophecy, Erythrae will flourish again
> And will enjoy good order, wealth, and fame,
> Through a young Erythrean who comes to his beloved home.[32]

The inscription confirms the impression given by Pausanias of an agonistic attitude amongst cities towards the Sibyl's genealogy. As David Potter has argued, the Sibyl could be adopted by local communities as a celebrated and actively honoured figure.[33] These literary and inscriptional testimonies thus show how the Sibyl had become part of the complex dialogue in late Hellenistic culture between cosmopolitan and local perspectives,[34] and by the imperial period was part of a well-established practice by local communities of seizing upon sources of mythical and literary prestige and making them their own.

What therefore emerges from this nebulous tradition is the recurring preoccupation with the Sibyl's liminality, ambiguity and multiplicity. One Sibyl or many? Extra-spatial or geographically specific? True or false

---

[32] For the Greek text, see *IGRom.* IV, 1540; Engelmann and Merkelbach 1973: inscription 224. See also Buresch 1892: 16–36; Buitenwerf 2003: 118–19.
[33] Potter 1990.
[34] As explored productively in the contributions to this volume by Gray and Hatzimichali.

prophecies? Mortal or divine?³⁵ Written, book-bound poetry or oral frenzy? Her identity is formed around such questions. These sorts of issues were of course a standard prospect for Homer himself. As Barbara Graziosi and others have well illustrated, the debates over authorship, the contents of the Homeric canon and even discussions about where Homer was from all stretch back to the sixth century. Thus the *Homeric Hymn to Apollo*, the *Margites* and the *Hymn to Artemis* – all often attributed to Homer until the final reduction of the corpus to the *Iliad* and *Odyssey* – can all be read as alluding to a special connection between Homer and a particular place: respectively Chios, Colophon or Smyrna.³⁶ The *Hymn to Apollo* provides the boldest and most famous early endeavour in this vein – embodying facets of Homeric biography, the poet claims to be singing as Homer himself:

μνήσασθ', ὁππότε κέν τις ἐπιχθονίων ἀνθρώπων
ἐνθάδ' ἀνείρηται ξεῖνος ταλαπείριος ἐλθών·
'ὦ κοῦραι, τίς δ' ὔμμιν ἀνὴρ ἥδιστος ἀοιδῶν
ἐνθάδε πωλεῖται, καὶ τέωι τέρπεσθε μάλιστα;'
ὑμεῖς δ' εὖ μάλα πᾶσαι ὑποκρίνασθαι ἀφήμως·
'τυφλὸς ἀνήρ, οἰκεῖ δὲ Χίωι ἔνι παιπαλοέσσηι·'

If ever some long-suffering stranger comes here and asks, 'O Maidens, which is your favourite singer who visits here, and who do you enjoy most?' Then you must all answer with one voice (?), 'It is a blind man, and he lives in rocky Chios.
(*Homeric Hymn to Apollo* (3) 167–72)

It was precisely this long tradition that enabled the Hellenistic and imperial writers to pose such questions about Homer again, with fresh energy and cynicism. These sources suggest parallel developments in the 'invention' of Homer and the Sibyl: beginning in the archaic period, these creation narratives amplify in the late Hellenistic and Roman times; so that at exactly the time that Homer's identity politics were being used to assert the Greek world's own status and cultural standing, the Sibyl and her sayings were being analogously canonised, proliferated and criticised.³⁷

---

³⁵ See below under 'Final Roar: The Sibyl's Self-Disclosure' for further discussion of this question.
³⁶ Graziosi 2002.
³⁷ The connections between these traditions have been noted, most insightfully by West 1999: 364–92, who aligns the 'inventions' of the figures of Homer and the Sibyl (and others such as Orpheus and Pythagoras) from as far back as the fifth and sixth centuries BCE. See also the recent contribution by Faraone (2019), who argues that Circe's instructions to Odysseus can be read as 'an early sibylline oracle': he suggests that Homer borrows from the speech acts of hexametric oracles and 'echoes closely' traits of the archaic tradition of the Sibyl. My aim in what follows is to suggest how the Sibyl's claims about Homer in Book 3 mobilise these ideas in light of the cultural preoccupations and reading strategies of her own, later time.

Book 3 of the Sibylline Oracles displays an intense awareness of this reception story; and, as we shall see, inventively develops the potential Homeric analogy.[38] Let us now turn to consider this book in more depth. This is the book of the Sibylline collection which has received the most critical attention, and scholars have been keenly interested in the socio-religious history which it displays: how and why Hellenistic Jews took up this traditional and diverse figure of the Sibyl as the vehicle for their prophecies.[39] As Olivia Stewart well puts it, these Jewish authors and editors both exploit and control the Sibyl's traditional power, 'bringing her into their own authoritative stories and recasting her as a servant of their god'.[40] The specific questions asked of this book, however, have been largely – almost exclusively – historical. What sort of events can be reconstructed in which the book might have originated? What is the author's or authors' attitude towards their fellow Greek inhabitants on the one hand, and the 'Roman conquerors' on the other? What was these Oracles' place in society? Who were their intended addresses? What light can they shed on the religious and ethical topics preoccupying Jews at this time?[41] Like the ancient cities who claimed her singular birthright, modern critics are driven by the paradoxical impulse to locate this wandering, mobile prophetess: to contain her, via cultural context, into one specific space.

Whilst such questions are compelling, when applied to this text, their answers are inevitably elliptical. If one enquires about the historical events reflected in the work, one is forced first to confront the issue of when exactly 'it' was composed. If the question is instead about the author's attitudes, audience and relationships in his society, then we must know first who he was, and of which 'society' he formed a part. This is all

---

[38] For the purpose of concision and in order to preserve the focal points of this chapter's argument, I do not provide any overall introduction and overview to the Sibylline Oracles collection. Such an outline – a mammoth task in itself, for material as diverse and inconsistent as this – has been well and fully given elsewhere. Particularly useful starting points for orientation are Lightfoot 2007, Collins 1997, Parke 1998, with shorter overviews in Levine 1995 and Bartlett 2010, each with further bibliography. In the readings to follow, I shall reference the structure, conventions and issues in the other books where they are most relevant to the themes of Book 3.

[39] For the structure and contents of Book 3, see Lightfoot 2007: 94–5; Buitenwerf 2003: 139–43. I provide my own overview of the contents of the final sections of the book below under 'The Sibyl vs Homer'.

[40] Stewart 2017: 1233.

[41] Thus for Buitenwerf 2003: 303 in his extensive study of Book 3, 'The most important question ... is what its function was in the social context of its author.' And for Bartlett 2010: 39, who takes *Or. Sib* 3 and 5 as two of the central texts to address his monograph's topic, 'Jews in the Hellenistic world', 'these oracles [reveal that] Hellenised Jews [were] happy to write in the hexameter verse made famous by Homer and studied throughout the Greek speaking world'. Collins 1974 is another example of a historically-inflected approach.

information which we cannot definitively pin down. Whilst (to summarise absurdly, but necessarily, the detailed scholarly standpoints on the matter) most estimates now date the main corpus of the book to the middle second/ early first century BCE, with a number of later-added sections from the imperial period,[42] the oracles' deliberately obfuscating nature, and the difficulty therefore of discerning whether a prophecy is *ex eventu* or eschatological mean that any historical foothold is inherently unsteady. So too with the issue of authorship. As demonstrated by the trenchant debates between critics – who envisage the author or compiler as, variously, one 'literary' man from Asia Minor,[43] a succession or series of authors from Alexandria or elsewhere in Egypt,[44] or a patchwork of material assembled from earlier sources (in their modern textual-transmission traditions too, Homer and the Sibyl have much in common ...) – it is clear that the act of historical reconstruction can only ever be partially successful.

And yet in spite of – or perhaps because of – the persistent focus on this reconstruction, far less attention has been paid to the *literary* engagements within the text.[45] This taciturnity is at least in part due to the fact that the poetic quality of the whole collection has been poorly regarded. If Heraclitus' view of the Sibyl sees her words as artless and charmless (and

---

[42] The main corpus is traditionally considered to be (in the most maximalist reading) lines 97–349 and 489–end: thus Collins 1974, with a full survey of evidence. In regard to dating this corpus, it is the conventional consensus that references to Ptolemaic kingdoms with no apparent indication that they will ever end suggest 31 BCE as a reasonable *terminus ante quem*. Collins 1974: 32–3 takes the reference to the seventh king (*Or. Sib.* 3.162–95) as a firm historical marker, and thus 'we must conclude that the main corpus of the third book of sibylline oracles ... was compiled in the middle of the second century BC' (33). Compare, however, Nikiprowetzky 1970, who 'ingeniously' (thus Collins) attempts to suggest that this 'seventh' actually refers to a queen, Cleopatra; and Buitenwerf 2003, who thinks that the reference is better taken to refer to events belonging in the author's future and views the ordinal 7 as probably a symbolic number (as does Gruen 1998a: 272–7), and who thus suggests instead a dating range between 80 and 31 BCE. My own approach in the final sections of this chapter is to accept Collins' (and the still generally accepted) dating parameters, to locate my focus-passages within them using their own internal cues, and to consider connections between different passages in the book as a productive possibility. I thus treat the text, in its final condition, as a 'literary unity' whose characteristics, however, can only be understood against the background of its disparate origins and transmission.

[43] Buitenwerf 2003.

[44] Collins 1974: 21–35. Bartlett 2010 thinks that the oracles derive either from Alexandria or 'possibly' the Jewish military colony Tell-el-Yahudiya in Leontopolis (though he does not discuss at any length why).

[45] There has certainly been some interest in the metre, lexicon and style of, particularly, the first three books: special mention should be made of Lightfoot 2007: 153–202 on the language, style and poetics of *Or. Sib.* 1–2, and Nikiprowetzky 1970 on these aspects of Book 3. In terms of source criticism, Hornblower 2015 has recently attempted to pursue the possible links between *Or. Sib.* 3 and Lycophron's *Alexandra*, albeit with tentative conclusions. However, in general the larger questions – in terms of the work's engagement with whole literary worlds and systems of reading – have not been consistently posed.

it was notorious that the oracles were often written in defective verse), and, like Ovid's image of the floating voice in the *Metamorphoses*, denies or ignores any textual component to her oracles,[46] then modern criticism of the Sibyllina, and of Book 3 in particular, has been similarly coarse in its judgements. The book's structure, it is claimed, is disorganised and chaotic, and its poetic diction unimpressive and at times even sloppy. If such features mirror (intentionally or otherwise) the defective metrics and 'frenzied' tone of the oracular mode, it seems from such verdicts that *Or. Sib.* 3 has done the job a little too well.[47] In general, it has also proven hard to identify firm literary sources in the text, as the non-surviving canon of Sibylline books is deemed to be one of its main influences. Rieuwerd Buitenwerf's assessment of the work's allusive range is reflective of such sentiments. Whilst he, like all readers and commentators, acknowledges that 'the [surviving] source which the author is generally believed to have used more intensively than any other consists of the works of Homer', and notes the author's borrowing of many words and phrasing from Homeric vocabulary, his final verdict is decidedly underwhelmed:

> The author was aware that his hexameters linguistically and stylistically resemble the writings of Homer. Still, this does not prove that the author actually had a copy of Homer's works at his disposal as he wrote. In the passage referring to Homer, he scarcely goes further than summarizing common knowledge about the Trojan war. He does not mention any specific detail from either the *Iliad* or *Odyssey*. Everything seems to indicate that the author used Homeric phrases because that was the way he had learned to write hexameters at school.[48]

Other scholars go further. Yehoshua Amir argues that the author of Book 3 intentionally mixed Homeric and biblical traditions in order to advocate biblical ideas, and that he makes them more attractive by rephrasing them in Homeric style and adding parts of Homeric verses which his audience were supposed to recognise.[49] Erich Gruen likewise believes that *Or. Sib* 3, like Ezekiel and the tragedian Eupolemus, was designed to bring the sentiments of Greek thinkers in line with the Torah: the author's

---

[46] Cf. Lightfoot 2007: 16.
[47] Amir 1985 views the book as a popular work of poor literary quality. Buitenwerf 2003, as discussed below, views the author's engagement with classical and biblical literature as superficial, not close or even necessarily direct. For a more positive view, see Nikiprowetzky 1970: 278–80.
[48] Buitenwerf 2003: 324–31, quotation at 325. On other literary sources for the collection (particularly Hesiod and the Hebrew Bible), which this chapter conceptually engages with but cannot pursue in depth, see Lightfoot 2007: 203–56 and, for Book 3 in particular, Nikiprowetzky 1970 *passim*, each with further references.
[49] Amir 1985.

engagement with Homer 'ultimately serves to enable Jews to present their traditions in Greek disguise'.[50] However, the conception of the text's Homeric engagement in itself as superficial and unsophisticated[51] has obscured the precise nature of the self-constructed relationship between Sibylline and Homeric poetics which it conveys.

In the final sections of this chapter, I want to return afresh to the most self-consciously Homeric passage of this most self-consciously textual book. Reading the passage in tandem with the later Second Sophistic treatments of Homer – texts which, unlike *Or. Sib.* 3, are habitually lauded as complex and 'sophisticated' in their Homeric reworkings – will reveal this Sibyl's deep engagement with Homer's works, and with highly 'specific' aspects of his reception: this poetic conversation is more sustained and subversive than previous readings have allowed. In the manoeuvres undertaken in these lines, well-known features of the sibylline tradition are transformed into acts of combative, critical, *Homeric* self-posturing: the oracular mode, in its Jewish refashioning, is now made to profess openly epic ambitions.

Such a literary focus can add a further dimension to the 'Jewishness' of this Third-Oracle Sibyl. A number of scholars of Hellenistic Judaism have revealed crucial and sustained intersections between Jewish exegetical works produced in Alexandria and the larger discourse concerning the reception and interpretation of the Homeric epics in the last few centuries BCE. To take an extensive example, Maren Niehoff has read a number of strands of Jewish biblical interpretation as displaying either positive or polemical connections with Homeric scholarship, surrounding both large philosophical ideas and close-focus textual problems. Thus, for instance, Demetrius' concern with contradictions between various biblical passages reflects similar desires for Homeric non-contradiction, particularly in Aristotle's influential *Aporemata Homerica*; whereas the author of the *Letter of Aristeas* actively opposes such Homeric hermeneutic techniques, 'react[ing] to the activity of his colleagues by offering an authentic Greek text of the Bible, which must be protected against such critical work'.[52] And Philo, whom Niehoff and others have analysed most comprehensively, launches a sustained rejection of the whole comparative, universalising style of reading, which held the Bible and Homer's epics to be the same

---

[50] Gruen 1998a: 288–91 and 1998b.
[51] Both Amir and Gruen share Buitenwerf's judgements, for the most part, about the lack of intertextual depth in the Sibyl's use of Homer: see Buitenwerf 2003: 325 for the three scholars in dialogue.
[52] On textual problems, see Niehoff 2011 (this quotation p. 27) and 2012.

kind of literary work, to advance his complex reformulation of scriptural interpretation.[53] This Sibylline Oracle, re-read with an eye to its deeper engagement with Homer, can take its place in this wider culture of cross-fertilisation between scriptural and Homeric reading strategies. However, by making its points as a *poem* (all of the Jewish texts cited here are prose) it also takes things further. Pairing the idea of a literary parity between Scripture and Homer with a biographical parity between Homer and the Sibyl, this author works aspects of accumulating, evolving interpretation traditions not into exegetical prose, but into new Homerising verse.

The Sibyl vs Homer: Oracular Confrontations

The Sibyl's *agon* with Homer is staged in the middle of the Third Oracle as it is now compiled. The section (295–488)[54] contains variously loosely connected prophecies against foreign nations, centred on punishment and destruction, temporary triumphs before falls.[55] A number of the initial predictions are grounded in a firm biblical or historical setting – for instance, the punishment of the Babylonians for the destruction of the Temple; the devastation of Asia during and after the Mithridatic wars (350–80); the rise and fall of Alexander the Great and his empire (388–400). The Sibyl then moves suddenly to foretell a deeper and more elusive past. She predicts that Phrygia, and especially the Phrygian town Dorylaeum, will suffer from severe earthquakes (401–10), signs which presage an even worse event: the destruction of Troy by the Greeks:

> σήματα δ' οὐκ ἀγαθοῖο, κακοῖο δὲ φύσεται ἀρχή. (410)
> παμφύλου πολέμοιο δαήμονας ἕξει ἄνακτας,
> Αἰνεάδας *διδούς* αὐτόχθονος, ἐγγενὲς αἷμα.
> ἀλλὰ μεταῦτις ἕλωρ ἔσῃ ἀνθρώποισιν ἐρασταῖς.
> Ἴλιον, οἰκτείρω σε· κατὰ Σπάρτην γὰρ Ἐρινὺς
> βλαστήσει περικαλλὲς ἀείφατον ἔρνος ἄριστον (415)

---

[53] See especially Niehoff 2011: 75–130; also Niehoff 2001 and now Niehoff 2018; and Runia 1990, Calabi 2008, Cohen 1995, Winston 1990, with much useful material in the handbook by Seland 2014.

[54] Thus, according to Buitenwerf's thematic subdivisions, these comprise the 'oracles against foreign nations.' Lightfoot 2007: 95 groups verses 300–519 along similar lines.

[55] Thus, to give the briefest scene setting: God will punish Babylonians for destroying the temple; Egypt will suffer until the seventh generation of Kings, as will Gog, Magog and Libya. Rome (the 'daughters of the west') will be punished for their destruction of the temple, and there will be many portents of catastrophe and many cities in Europe, Asia and Egypt will be destroyed. Asia will take revenge on Rome, and will have a peaceful period; Macedonia will conquer the world – its most important King, Alexander the Great, will subdue Asia, but his empire will be destroyed.

Ἀσίδος Εὐρώπης τε πολυσπερὲς οἶδμα λιποῦσα·
σοὶ δὲ μάλιστα γόους μόχθους στοναχάς τε φέρουσα
θήσει· ἀγήρατον δ' ἔσται κλέος ἐσσομένοισιν.

These signs will be the beginning of misery, and not of good. It will have princes skilled in the warfare of many tribes, and will bring forth the Aeneadae, people originating from this very country, born of the same blood. But after that you will be a prey of people in love. Ilium, I weep for you! A fury will sprout in Sparta, a very beautiful, famous, excellent shoot. She will leave the wide bay of Asia and Europe, and she will bring you the worst weeping, distress and groans. However, there will be never-ending fame among future generations.

(*Or. Sib.* 3.410–18)

The lines, and the Homeric prophecy which follows them, are considered to be one of the later, supplementary sections of the book, appended of course after Rome's conquest of Greece.[56] However, it is clear that the sibylline voice also thematises her simultaneous earliness *and* lateness in this section, and marks her special position as straddling different parts of mythic history. The prophecy itself begins chiastically: the opening verse (410) runs good into evil, and ends with a beginning, expressing in its linguistic texture an explicit sense of contradiction in time. Equally explicit is the emphasis on reverse genealogies: the fall of Troy and the Romans who will rise from its ashes (412). Almost every word in this verse conveys the intermeshed identity of these races: Troy produces Aeneas' people 'from this very country' (αὐτόχθονος), and they are 'born of the same blood' (ἐγγενὲς αἷμα). Troy and Rome, it is stressed, are always already a double act: their origins, falls and identities are structurally inverted, formed as retrospective analogies of one another. This type of layered temporal structuring must affect how we read the whole passage and its approach to Homer in the lines to come.[57]

Indeed, just as Rome's rise precedes Troy's fall, so too does Troy appear in this prophecy before Homer, the poet who gave it its glory. Before the bard is 'identified' physically, he is summoned intertextually: this depiction

---

[56] I broadly agree with the estimations of Collins 1974: 27–8, who uses the connections to the Erythraean Sibyl and the wider references in the section (namely the Roman civil war at lines 464–9, the 'man who will come to Asia' at 388–400, generally identified as Alexander, and general gestures to Rome and the Aeneadae) to date this passage between 146 and 84 BCE.

[57] This approach will determine my own stance on the relative dating of this passage within *Or. Sib.* 3 as a whole. Whilst it falls outside of the 'main corpus' of the book, whose date, as we have seen, is usually set at 250–100 BCE, I shall treat the section as self-consciously positioning itself *within* this corpus; in that sense its later (possibly early imperial) dating makes it perfectly suited to articulate the connections between the earlier (Hellenistic) sections and later (imperial) preoccupations and themes.

of Troy's downfall contains engagement with the Homeric text which goes far beyond Buitenwerf's conception of an author vaguely recalling his classroom learning. The reason for the fall (414) is singular and categorical: Helen, identified but not named here, via tragedy rather than epic, as the 'Fury' from Sparta.[58] Homer's ambivalence towards Helen and her status as the *aitia* of the war is frequently expressed in the *Iliad* and *Odyssey*: debated and discussed by the chieftains at the Trojan wall and in her own self-deprecating – and self-exculpatory – narrations.[59] Her role, however, also became a staple feature of the revisionist tradition of Homeric critique. From Herodotus to Gorgias to Euripides, Helen's status in the Trojan story is used as a launchpad for undermining Homer's version of events: Helen never went to Troy, or a ghost went in her place – the Homeric tale is based on a spectre, a misrecognition, or even a *lie*. This style of reading was continued by the Second Sophistic wave of this trend. Dio's *Trojan Oration* insists, as part of its 'historical' reversal of Homer's tale,[60] that Helen was rightfully married to Paris; and Lucian reworks the motif of Helen as phantom to imagine her lingering, along with a host of heroes and villains including Homer himself, on the ghostly Island of the Blessed (*Ver. hist.* 2.25). In Lucian's account, she attempts to run off once again, this time with one of Lucian's time-travelling companions, but is captured and catapulted back to her rightful place by Menelaus' side, in what has been read as a new take on the recurring possibility of a different, counterfactual outcome for Helen in Homer and the Epic Cycle: mythic literature 'repeating itself as a farce'.[61]

In her categorical blaming of Helen, the Sibyl first marks her clear engagement with, and standpoint on, these sorts of causation debates. However in the lines to follow, she takes this question of Helen's real role in the Trojan narrative and gives it a decisively Homeric refraction. For despite the misery that Helen will cause, there will, she foretells, 'be never-ending *kleos* for future generations' (418). Now this verse replays a

---

[58] Helen's identification as a Fury offers a nod to the tragic reception of her tale. In Aeschylus, the coming of Paris to Troy with Helen as his bride is described as the arrival of an Erinys, one of the administrators of Zeus's justice. Cf. also Cassandra's self-identification as an Erinys in Eur. *Tro.* 457. In a fragment of Ennius' *Alexandros* (likely a close adaptation, even a translation, of Euripides' lost play of the same name), Helen is also termed 'one of the Furiae' (*quo iudicio, Lacedaemonia mulier, Furiarum una, adveniet*: R³ 1.7.56 = *TRF* 11.151.18). In this image system, Helen is not merely a ghost (as in the Herodotean motif), but a nightmarish, vengeful spirit.
[59] The famous and most extensive examples are the *Teichoscopia* of *Iliad* 3 and Helen's speeches at *Il.* 6.312–68 and *Od.* 4.220–80.
[60] On the dynamics of this reversal more broadly, see particularly Hunter 2009a.
[61] Bompaire 1958: 671–2; Kim 2010: 169.

'prophecy' from the *Iliad*, where it is Helen herself who makes this sort of claim: she remarks, with metapoetic foresight, on the future fame that she and her fellow Trojan war participants will share: οἷσιν ἐπὶ Ζεὺς θῆκε κακὸν μόρον, ὡς καὶ ὀπίσσω / ἀνθρώποισι πελώμεθ' ἀοίδιμοι ἐσσομένοισι ('Zeus has brought an evil fate upon us, but in days to come we shall be a song for those yet to be born') (Homer, *Il.* 6.357–8). This Sibylline author, who apparently does not have the text of Homer in his hand or even really in his head, in fact cues this Homeric passge closely. Where Homer's Helen imagines Zeus 'placing' (θῆκε) evil fate upon the Trojans, here the Sibyl makes Helen perform the same action, with the same verb (θήσει). And as Helen's Iliadic prediction ends with the bold and affirmative ἐσσομένοισι – the future substantive participle in the dative – so the Sibyl signs off with the same word-form, in the same position. This verse, linguistically as well as thematically, begins and ends with Homer. It could be countered that these are perfectly common words and phrases: τίθημι in isolation would seem inconsequential as an intertext, and ἐσσομένοισι πυθέσθαι / καὶ ἐσσομένοισιν ἀοιδήν is a motif picked up frequently in sepulchral epigram. Indeed, this same book of oracles uses a similar phrase again later on in its prophecies – ἐσσομένοισι πυθέσθαι, 774. And yet in a passage so centred on Homer and his characters, the possibility for a more directed use of 'clichéd' language is strong. In other words, this Helen must be taken, on some levels, as *Homer's* Helen, whose Homeric function and language becomes entwined with that of the Sibyl: it is now the Sibyl, not Helen, who 'weeps for Ilium' and predicts its future fame. The Sibyl thus does not only pre-empt and predict the Helen of the *Iliad*. She pre-emptively appropriates her role, and takes a sentiment famously spoken by her character and turns it into a refracted premonition *about* her, in the deep past before she was born. In a bold redrafting of futuricity and prophecy, the source of *kleos* is thus transferred from internal Homeric characters to the status of the Homeric *text*. Such techniques pave the way for the more aggressive (and the most ludic) section of the passage, where the Sibyl tests the limits of this style of Homeric critique.

The prophecy about Homer (419–32) startlingly literalises this topsy-turvy nature of the Sibylline relationship to the poet. The text's primary literary influence is summoned as a figure of the future, not named but described with clear references to his biographical tradition, and subjected to an amazing series of refractions. Homer is 'introduced' first as καί τις (419). He is not only anonymous (τις, 'someone', nods to his famous lack of self-disclosure in his poetry), but, with καί ('and'), literally, supplementary: he and his text come after 'his' story – Helen and her *kleos*, which the

Sibyl has now already told. With ἔσσεται he is put directly into the future tense; but this prolepsis is also knowingly undermined by the backward glance of αὖτις[62] and in the antiquity of πρέσβυς. The notion of Homer as an old man, of course, taps into the idea common by the late Hellenistic and imperial era of picturing Homer as perennially old (he is bearded on the depiction on the Archelaos relief): a physical maturity to match his canonical ancientness. However, the next noun to describe him undermines this compliment. Because this old man is *mortal* (βροτός). Now, the Archelaos relief also illustrated how by the late Hellenistic period Homer was so canonical that he could be deified. In this emphatic assertion of Homeric *mortality*, the Jewish Sibyl tears this deification down.

The following prediction that light will fade from Homer's eyes can function as an elaboration of this mortality – a shorthand metaphor for his death.[63] It also, however, addresses another common strand of Homeric biography: to think of Homer as blind. Where Lucian uses his own sight to deny Homer's sightlessness – as an eyewitness on the Island of the Blessed, he can see for himself that Homer is not blind – the Sibyl is even more provocative in her deflation: mixing the literalism of blindness with the imagery of the darkness of death, she gives Homer sight in order to take it away. In a single line, this poetic voice succinctly asserts its rivalry both with Homer *and* with existing lines of his reception.

The next descriptive markers continue this two-pronged attack. Homer is now defined by what he is not: he is a false writer (ψευδογράφος, 419) with a false fatherland (ψευδόπατρις, 420). Both terms are promptly expanded and glossed: Homer will say (καλέσσει) that he is from Chios (423). We have already glanced at the long history of claims about Homer's birthplace. The *Homeric Hymn to Apollo* has 'Homer' tell the world that he is from Chios, and the *Hymn to Artemis* posits an alternative location: the reference to the river Meles could hint at the story that

---

[62] Which can mean, of course, either 'in turn' sequentially or 'again' temporally – both of which work nicely here.

[63] The metaphorical use of light and darkness as expressions of life and death is commonplace in Greek myth and literature (see the survey of Greek and Indo-European versions of this trope in Giannakis 2001; with relevant discussion also in Horn 2018 and Cairns 2016). In a slightly different image, the interplay between the eyes, seeing, and death (as non-seeing) is also frequently attested in the surviving Greek canon: to take two examples, in *Odyssey* 11.93, where the blind Teiresias wonders why Odysseus left the sunlight in order to journey to the world of Hades, and in Sophocles' *Ajax*, as Athena blinds the eyes of the hero she is about to destroy. The Sibyl here seems to be merging these two strands of metaphor (and weaving in the common Homeric use of δύω to denote the movement in death down to Hades: e.g., ἔδυν δόμον Ἄϊδος εἴσω, *Il.* 11.263; δύσομαι εἰς Ἀΐδαο, *Od.* 12.383) so as to play on Homer's double status as blind and mortal/immortal.

Homer was born on this river in Smyrna, so as to imply a geographical connection between Artemis and Homer, goddess and bard:[64] Ἄρτεμιν ὕμνει Μοῦσα κασιγνήτην Ἑκάτοιο, / παρθένον ἰοχέαιραν, ὁμότροφον Ἀπόλλωνος, / ἥ θ' ἵππους ἄρσασα βαθυσχοίνοιο Μέλητος / ῥίμφα διὰ Σμύρνης ... ('Sing, Muse, of Artemis, sister of the far-shooter, the virgin pourer of arrows, reared with Apollo, who after watering her horses at the reedy Meles drives her chariot all of gold swiftly through Smyrna ...') (*Homeric Hymn to Artemis* (9) 1–4). We have also seen how such debates intensified in the Hellenistic and imperial periods, as different countries and cities vied to hold the status of being Homer's home town. Many other Hellenistic and Roman sources reflect this pointed uncertainty about Homer's origins: several ancient epigrams deal with the subject, and two school texts have been found which also discuss the issue, showing how it was explored at all levels of literary society.[65] Some authors attempt to cut through such debates by consulting the poet himself. Lucian's Homer gives a direct and surprising answer during his interview: he was originally a Babylonian named Tigranes.[66] And a Hellenistic epigram attributed to Alcaeus (*Anth. Pal.* 1.22) ventriloquises Homer to have him claim, as the earlier *Hymn to Apollo* does, that he is a Chian. However, the Sibyl's innovation here is not to make Homer settle this location debate by telling the 'truth' about where he was from, but rather to conjure him, in the future, as the author of one of these *lying* biographical claims. In their references to Chios, earlier 'Homers' like that of the *Homeric Hymn to Apollo* and the pseudo-Alcaeus epigram have thus misled posterity about themselves. Redrafting the trope of genealogical ambiguity into a personal Homeric fault, the prophecy brings together two strands of contention in Homer's biographical tradition – the 'truth' of his origin and the veracity of his work – into a singular stinging insult.

The term 'false writer' (ψευδογράφος; repeated again in 430, ψευδογραφῶν) then explicitly acknowledges the more conventional sense in which Homer was considered 'false': in terms of the historical accuracy of his account of Troy. He will write about Ilium οὐ μὲν ἀληθῶς, / ἀλλὰ σοφῶς (423–4). This idea of Homer as crafty and mendacious as well as

---

[64] For the possibility that this reference could indeed be taken as a link to Homer's birthplace, see Graziosi 2002: 72–7 with related discussion in Greensmith 2018: 262.
[65] On these school texts, see Tait and Preaux 1955: 387 (= *Ostr.Bodl.* 2.2174) and Cribiore 1996: 46, 215 and 219.
[66] See Kim 2010: 164–5 for the wider context of this passage, and the interesting suggestion that Homer's biography here reflects Lucian's own journey from Syria and his assimilation into Greek culture.

simply incorrect on the one hand evokes a fundamental tenet of later Second Sophistic preoccupations: the Sibyl's phrases here could work as a pithy proleptic summary of the stance held by the 'group' of texts which Kim defines as special in their attack on Homer's poetic deceptiveness. The precise wording of the oracle here is also reminiscent of ancient debates on the attributes of Homeric characters: Plato, for instance, draws the contrast between Achilles as truthful and simple (ἀληθής τε καὶ ἁπλοῦς), versus Odysseus as 'polytropic and lying' (πολύτροπός τε καὶ ψευδής, *Hp. mi.* 365b).[67] In this reformulation, Homer himself is destined to become a slippery, Odyssean liar.

However, the reason for Homer's lying is given a remarkable and personal physicality, which takes the Sibyl far beyond these revisionist manoeuvres which she otherwise foreshadows and echoes: ἐπέων γὰρ ἐμῶν μέτρων τε κρατήσει· πρῶτος γὰρ χείρεσσιν ἐμὰς βίβλους ἀναπλώσει ('for he will have mastered *my* verses and metres, since he will be the first to open my books with his hands', *Or. Sib.* 3.424–5). The Sibyl here surpasses the authoritative knowledge of the Herodotean eyewitness or Lucianic interviewer: she knows that Homer lied because he stole his material from *her*. Homer the supplementary καί τις is now πρῶτος; but he is primary only in his theft – the original literary imposter. Now, the notion that the Sibyl predicted the Trojan war before Homer turned it into song, and thus deemed him a liar, is, as we have seen, an established part of the Erythraean strand of the sibylline tradition. The related idea that Homer imitated the Sibyl's style also finds precedent in, for example, Diodorus Siculus 4.66, where Homer is said to have copied many of the verses of the Delphian Sibyl, identified as Daphne, the daughter of Teiresias. However, set within this poetic passage of close Homeric allusion, these claims are reasserted with a new and highly textual edge. Firstly, the image of Homer's theft is rooted in a double materiality: the physical book and Homer's rapacious hands. With χείρεσσιν the Sibyl drives home her fleshy, embodied vision of the elusive poet. Like the bearded figure – man turned to god – on the Archelaos frieze, and the ghostly but recognisable character on Lucian's island and in Philostratus' underworld, the

---

[67] Cf. also the Platonic debate on which character truly deserves the epithet *sophos* (for Hippias it is Nestor, not Odysseus: σοφώτατον δὲ Νέστορα, *Hp. Min* 364c4–7), in contrast with, e.g., Eustathius' later discussion of σοφία as a relevant term for Odysseus too: in the *Iliad* Odysseus was not yet 'wiser' (σοφώτερος) than Nestor, but his great wanderings after the war brought him huge ἐμπειρία, 'experience', which allowed him to surpass even Nestor (*Commentary on Homer's Odyssey* 1381.61–1382.2).

Sibyl's Homer is a 'real-life' character, whose crime is a literal one: he handles her books and opens them. The choice of verb in ἀναπλώσει, however, can also have a more conceptual sense: as well as meaning 'open', ἀναπλόω can mean 'explain' 'interpret' or 'simplify'. Under this second system of meaning, Homer is also conceived of as an exegete, doing to the Sibyl's verses what the Hellenistic scholia and Second Sophistic authors did to him. Likewise with βίβλους the Sibyl moves Homer from an oral poet of *epos* to the canonical literary author of contemporary Greek conceptions. Her premonitions of the Homeric poems themselves (421–2) already foreground this shift: the *Iliad* and *Odyssey* (like Homer, clearly identified but not explicitly named) are described first as the product of Homer's internal mind (his *dianoia* – the poet's 'intention' or, again, his interpretation or meaning), but then as an assembled (ἔμμετρον) and compartmentalised canon – 'joined together under two names'.[68]

The emphasis on Homer as a book reflects the scrolls so prominent on the Archelaos *apotheosis* (Homer is deified with, and because of, his 'written' word) and the highly 'Alexandrian' Homer on Lucian's island who, after his interview, composes new material as a 'writer', just as the Sibyl's Homer *writes* (γράψει, 423) poetry which is so clever but so wrong: 'An account of this battle was written by Homer, and as I was leaving he gave me the book to take to the people at home' (ἔγραψεν δὲ καὶ ταύτην τὴν μάχην Ὅμηρος καὶ ἀπιόντι μοι ἔδωκεν τὰ βιβλία κομίζειν τοῖς παρ' ἡμῖν ἀνθρώποις) (Lucian, *Ver. hist.* 2.24). However, here this is turned into a sibylline motif. As the doubling personal pronouns (ἐμῶν μέτρων ... ἐμὰς βίβλους) make bitingly clear, the Homeric metre and the canonical books of his poetry always already belonged to her. Acknowledging the conventional metre of oracular prophecy and the double image of the Sibyl's utterances as floating voices and edited books, the Sibyl here takes the features which she and Homer already had in common and transforms them into material for competition and literary self-betterment: matching and then transcending key features of Homer's constructed identity.

The Sibyl ends her Homeric premonition by pointing out the two major errors that the poet will make (3.426–30). That Homer is wrong

---

[68] ἔμμετρον can also, of course, mean 'metrical' (cf. LSJ s.v. ἔμμετρος, III), so the choice of adjective allows for a witty double meaning: alluding to the fixed and assembled nature of Homeric poetry, and also its metrical properties which align it so closely with the sibylline voice.

to praise the heroes of war accords with the general attitude advanced in *Or. Sib* 3: war, it is repeatedly stated, is the result of immoral behaviour, and will lead to punishment and destruction.[69] However, at the start of this prophecy, the Sibyl spoke complimentarily of the Aeneadae who will spring from Troy's ashes; and this praise was based precisely on their diverse skills in warfare (411). It is not, therefore, praise of heroes in war itself that is wrong: it is praise in the wrong coating, written in the wrong books, devoid of the correct moral framework which this oracular text is expounding. Just as with the pre-Iliadic, wholly Iliadic Helen, the Sibyl here glosses the Homeric reappropriation which her verses perform. Her very words take over and adapt Homer's act of heroic narration. In Ἀχιλλέα Πηλείωνα the *Iliad*'s first name and epithet is retained but shifted: Hector now comes before Achilles. And then in lieu of an extended narrative or catalogue of heroes, the remainder of the Homeric cast is reduced into the infinitely pluralised, tauntingly indefinite τούς τ' ἄλλους. Oracular poetics is thus proclaimed as the proper, truthful way of singing of arms and men.

So too with Homer's second error: his mistakes about the gods, who are mere inventions, or actually (a *hapax* compound) 'empty-headed people' (429).[70] Here the well-established tradition of criticising and challenging the Homeric divine system[71] is retold from this particular religious perspective. Homer's gods are no longer problematic because they are anthropomorphic and flawed. They are, like the poet himself, problematic because they are men, not gods at all. Now, elsewhere in this book, the oracles make frequent reference to the theme of false gods: in the opening sections, the Sibyl elaborates on various forms of false religion (including idolatry and zoolatry), before affirming the worship of the true God, in imagery well known from the Hebrew Bible.[72] Soon after this Homeric prophecy, the Greeks are further denounced for their false religious practice: they 'trust in mortal leaders' and 'give idle presents to the deceased' and 'sacrifices to images' (3.545–50). So in our passage, the wider theology of this oracular text is mobilised as material for Homeric critique; and, in

---

[69] E.g., see 3.204–5.
[70] On μέροψ and its dubious meaning in Homer see LSJ s.v. μέροψ. Its potential connection to speech is usually grounded in the phrase μερίζοντες τὴν ὄπα. The Sibyl elsewhere in this book uses it thus: for example, in her excursus on the genealogy of men and the division of speech the tenth race are twice described as μερόπων ἀνθρώπων (cf. *Or. Sib.* 3.108).
[71] On this long and wide-ranging tradition, the best synthesis remains Feeney 1991.
[72] See esp. 3.20–8.

reverse, well-known challenges to Homer's gods are deployed as evidence for the text's religious agenda.

This agenda continues into Homer's own afterlife. For all of his crimes, this poetic ψευδογράφος will receive retribution (ἀμοιβαῖα δέξεται ἔργα, 432). Many versions of Homer's life-story provide their own unsavoury endings, imagining him in scenarios very different from the celestial heights carved by Archelaos. In the *Certamen Homeri et Hesiodi*, to take one early imperial example[73] (and a version of events also reflected in other sources) after his loss in the competition, Homer meets a bathos-filled demise, dying by slipping on some mud and falling on a stone.[74] And both Lucian and Philostratus envision a static, eerie aftermath for the poet after death.[75] This prophecy once again goes a step further: rather than just narrating Homer's fall from grace in the future, the Sibyl also enacts her predicted punishment in the present, by the very poetry she is composing. Homer's ἀμοιβαῖα ἔργα are received *now*, in the unveiling of this oracle. With ἀμοιβαῖα also hinting at a sense of antiphonic, melic competition, Homer's *amoibaion* now gets its true *responsion*, as the Sibyl 'exchanges' his poetry and all of its power and grandeur for her own.

This oracle thus presents a reading of Homer which is wholly recognisable from 'pagan' Hellenistic sources, and the proleptic links with Second Sophistic twists on these motifs emphasise just how immersed in such approaches to Homer this author really is. But this immersion, in turn, can affect the tone in which we take the wider religious manoeuvres at play. For a significant move found in some of the prose Jewish Alexandrian works which we have previously discussed was to make renowned Greek authors and thinkers dependent on Jewish tradition. So for instance the pseudographic 'Testament of Orpheus' contains a text that called on Orpheus as a witness to monotheism.[76] And Aristobulus, at the forefront of this style of interpretation, made a huge range of Greek philosophers and poets directly indebted to Moses. Thus for example Socrates' famous

---

[73] The surviving text is dated to the second century CE but almost certainly had earlier precedent in some form: see references in n. 74.

[74] *Certamen* 323–38. See also Proclus, *Life of Homer* 5; Tzetz. *Alleg.* 89–92 Boissonade; Tzetz. *H.* 123–42 Colonna. On the *Certamen*, see the recent critical edition and commentary in Bassino 2013. For more on the biographical facets which this work brings to light see the lucid remarks in Graziosi 2002: esp. 83–4, 172–3 and 211–12.

[75] Cf., e.g., Luc. *Ver. hist.* 2.2, where Lucian describes the island, filled with shadowy, ethereal heroes and celebrities plucked from the classical canon, who never grow old, but wander 'like shadows . . . upright and dark'.

[76] See Charlesworth 1985: 831–2.

'divine voice' puts him in the company of Pythagoras and Plato, who claimed that they heard the voice of God when they observed the form of the universe so meticulously created and sustained, and used Moses' words to affirm this point. And Homer too 'took significant material from [Moses] and was admired accordingly'; as evidenced by, for example, the fact that he and Hesiod, 'having taken information from our books, say clearly that the seventh day is holy' (Euseb. *Praep. evang.* 13.12.13).[77] As Gruen observes, by making such claims, Aristobulus 'needed to be creative': for 'unless [Homer and co.] miraculously gained a command of Hebrew, they could hardly have had access to the laws of Moses'.[78] Aristobulus' solution lies in compounding a fiction: Greek translations of at least parts of the Bible had been available some centuries before the compilation of the Septuagint.[79] The Sibyl's story of Homer's theft – a 'fiction' enabled precisely and only by the connections between the figure of Homer and her own poetic persona – thus shows her creative participation in these debates within Hellenistic Judaism about cultural priority and the origins of knowledge.

The Sibyl's Homeric feud, then, is fundamentally based on a *relationship*: between two poets, figures and sources of epic revelation; but also between two exegetical traditions, critical traditions and religious frameworks. Like Rome and Troy in the oracle's opening, Homer and the Sibyl cannot escape from one another: the prophetess' rivalry with her world-famous imitator is based on a similarity (books and metre), an overlap (Trojan topic) and a claustrophobic closeness which strains against all professions of distance. This agonistic attachment does not end here. The book's final oracle moves to make the links between the classical Homer and the Jewish Sibyl more drastic and direct, and their competitive relationship reaches its climax.

Final Roar: The Sibyl's Self-Disclosure

The Homeric oracle implicitly manipulates connections between the Homeric and sibylline traditions, and their shared liminal status between different conceptual modes: mortal/divine; song/book; old/

---

[77] For the use of allegorical readings of the poets to support these readings (focusing, for instance, on lines of Homer where he seems to give some importance to the seventh day) and for Aristobulus' use of spurious or false Homeric quotations, see, e.g., Dawson 1991: 74–82 and, most recently, Mülke 2018: 61–124.
[78] Gruen 2016: 145.   [79] Gruen 2016: 145.

ageless. *Or. Sib.* 3 ends with another take on this analogy, which provides a crucial coda to the Sibyl's pre-Homeric poetics.

(810)
ταῦτά σοι Ἀσσυρίης Βαβυλώνια τείχεα μακρά
οἰστρομανὴς προλιποῦσα, ἐς Ἑλλάδα πεμπόμενον πῦρ
πᾶσι προφητεύουσα θεοῦ μηνύματα θνητοῖς

———————————————

ὥστε προφητεῦσαί με βροτοῖς αἰνίγματα θεῖα.
καὶ καλέσουσι βροτοί με καθ' Ἑλλάδα πατρίδος ἄλλης,
ἐξ Ἐρυθρῆς γεγαυῖαν ἀναιδέα· οἳ δέ με Κίρκης
(815) μητρὸς καὶ Γνωστοῖο πατρὸς φήσουσι Σίβυλλαν
μαινομένην ψεύστειραν. ἐπὴν δὲ γένηται ἅπαντα,
τηνίκα μου μνήμην ποιήσετε κοὐκέτι μ' οὐδεὶς
μαινομένην φήσειε, θεοῦ μεγάλοιο προφῆτιν.
οὐ γὰρ ἐμοὶ δήλωσεν, ἃ πρὶν γενετῆρσιν ἐμοῖσιν·
(820) ὅσσα δὲ πρῶτ' ἐγένοντο, τά μοι *θεὸς* κατέλεξε
τῶν μετέπειτα δὲ πάντα θεὸς νόῳ ἐγκατέθηκεν,
ὥστε προφητεύειν με τά τ' ἐσσόμενα πρό τ' ἐόντα
καὶ λέξαι θνητοῖς. ὅτε γὰρ κατεκλύζετο κόσμος
ὕδασι, καί τις ἀνὴρ μόνος εὐδοκίμητος ἐλείφθη
(825) ὑλοτόμῳ ἐνὶ οἴκῳ ἐπιπλώσας ὑδάτεσσιν
σὺν θηρσὶν πτηνοῖσί θ', ἵν' ἐμπλησθῇ πάλι κόσμος·
τοῦ μὲν ἐγὼ νύμφη καὶ ἀφ' αἵματος αὐτοῦ ἐτύχθην,
τῷ τὰ πρῶτ' ἐγένοντο· τὰ δ' ἔσχατα πάντ' ἀπεδείχθη·
ὥστ' ἀπ' ἐμοῦ στόματος τάδ' ἀληθινὰ πάντα λελέχθω.

These things (I say) to you, after I left the long Babylonian walls of Assyria in a rage, I, a fire sent to Greece. I prophesy revelations of God to all mortals,

———————————————

so that I prophesy divine riddles to the mortals. Throughout Greece, mortals will say that I am from another fatherland, and that I am a shameless one, born in Erythrae. Others will call me raging, lying Sibyl, whose mother is Circe and whose father is The Knowing One. But when all these things happen, then you will remember me. Nobody will call me raging anymore – me, a prophetess of the great God. For he did not reveal to me the things he revealed previously to my parents. God (?) passed on all the things to me that happened first, and God put into my mind all things that would happen later, so that I can prophesy both future and past and tell them to mortals. For when the world was inundated with waters, and a certain man, a single famous person, survived by sailing upon the waters in a wooden house, together with the beasts and birds, so that the world would be filled again ... his relative am I, and I am of his blood. To him the first things occurred, and the last things were revealed. So let all that is uttered from my mouth be taken as true.

(*Or Sib.* 3.809–29)

In this passage – which is likely to be earlier than the Homer prophecy in its date of composition,[80] but placed so as to come after it in this compilation – the Sibyl defines not Homer, but herself. In the prophecy about Homer, Homer remained unnamed, and was subjected to a series of lies, speculation and false claims. Here the Sibyl, by contrast, is able to self-identify – to name herself, to acknowledge in the first person all of the lies which have also been told about her (the scorn and mistrust which, from Aristophanes' *Pax* to Tiberius' ban, we know her prophecies could attract) and to put them right in her own voice.

The first objection raised against the Sibyl is that she is a foreigner – Greece is not her native country (πατρίδος ἄλλης, 813). We have seen how various sources in the Hellenistic and imperial periods attest to the debated issue of the Sibyl's birthplace. Now the Sibyl ventriloquises her own version of this contested history of belonging. But this particular version is focused specifically on Erythrae, where people will falsely claim that she is from.[81] As Buitenwerf remarks, 'we can infer from these lines that the author of Book 3 took the famous Sibyl of Erythrae as his model'.[82] He is right, but there is another aspect to this modelling. We have seen how in Varro and Pausanias it was specifically the Erythraean Sibyl whose story was increasingly associated with Homer's.[83] By focusing on this location, the Sibyl gives valence to this association, encouraging the reader to pursue the similarities between Homer's tradition and her own. Read as a double act with the later-composed tirade against Homer, we can see how in both passages, the Sibyl activates and pushes the possible connections between their legends and reception, carving out her identity using carefully selected raw material from their traditions.

As a hinge between the two oracles, Erythrae thus allows us to read the Sibyl's self-definition here in polemical contrast with Homer.[84] Let us conclude by briefly considering the points in this contrast, as they are

---

[80] This argument is, as per the dating parameters sketched above, taking the passage as part of the main corpus of the text.
[81] The Greek wording on the Erythraean inscription discussed above (πατρίς δ' οὐκ ἄλλη, 'Erythrae is my only home town') is in fact reminiscent of line 813.
[82] Buitenwerf 2003: 297–8; he also points rightly to the plural βίβλους in 425 showing that the author knows of the existence of several such Sibylline books.
[83] Cf. also Lightfoot 2007: 12: 'it is a particularly intriguing suggestion by Jacoby that at some point, perhaps in the works of Apollodorus of Erythrae ... the Homeric legends had in fact crossed over into and begun to influence those of the Sibyl, at least, of the Erythraean sibyl, whose wanderings were modelled on Homer'.
[84] We can even consider the possibility that the Homeric oracle was composed with this earlier passage of the collection already in mind, intentionally positioning itself within the Erythraean discourse, and making explicit the anti-Homeric sentiments which are connected to this strand of the Sibyl's

developed in this closing passage of the book. For it is here that the Sibyl's *Jewish* identity makes her conquer her epic rival once and for all. Whereas Homer is emphatically mortal, the Sibyl here flaunts her slippery status between human interlocutor and divine truth-giver. The slanderous claim that her mother is Circe – an unusual and otherwise unattested genealogy –[85] evokes one of Homer's most famous mystical non-humans, seen here as an attempt by the Sibyl's critics to disqualify her as a prophetess via such a greedy, licentious association.[86] In contrast, she asserts her actual authority through two strands. First, this authority is rooted in the nature of her words – her prophecies are both 'riddles' (αἰνίγματα), a nod to the famous obscurity of oracles, but also perhaps to the long-standing allegorical interpretations of epic poetry, as a means of confronting problematic 'surface' meanings,[87] and θεοῦ μηνύματα (revelations or evocations of [or from] God).[88] And secondly, it comes from the status of her informants (823–8): with a Hesiodic flourish,[89] she asserts how the knowledge of the past and future was revealed to her not by the Muses, but by God.

In this section of the book where the author is most focused on asserting this sibylline 'biography', he also stands most firmly on his monotheistic religious source. This religiosity is continued in the affiliation with Noah (823–8). Noah is presented in terms very similar to Homer: another anonymous καί τις, easily identifiable through the ensuing description. However, whereas the non-name-games in the Homer oracle are designed to undermine this false pretender who has trampled on the Sibyl's Trojan territory, the Sibyl here celebrates her closeness to this 'man' (ἀνήρ) and pushes it as far as possible: she makes herself a kinswoman of Noah, and claims to have entered the ark with him.[90]

---

biography. On the identification of *Or. Sib.* 3.419–32 with the Erythraean Sibyl, see also Collins 1974: 27–8.

[85] This relationship may also add valence to the hypothesis of Faraone 2019 that the Homeric Circe is indebted to sibylline traditions and speech forms. The author of this much later oracle could be showing once again how the relationship works both ways.

[86] On Circe's negative associations with luxuriousness and greed in Greco-Roman ethics, see among others Hor. *Epist.* 1.2.17–31, with the phrase 'drinking from Circe's goblets.'

[87] On this tradition and its pronounced relationship to Homer's poetry, see particularly Keaney and Lamberton 1996; Buffière 1996; Lamberton 1986 and Struck 2004.

[88] The text here is problematic: see Geffcken 1902 and Buitenwerf 2003: 296. I agree with Buitenwerf, *pace* those editors who print, e.g., μηνίματα, that μηνύματα makes better sense and that there is little reason to emend it.

[89] ὥστε προφητεύειν με τά τ' ἐσσόμενα πρό τ' ἐόντα (822); cf. Hes. *Theog.* 38: εἰρεῦσαι τά τ' ἐόντα τά τ' ἐσσόμενα πρό τ' ἐόντα.

[90] At *Or. Sib.* 1.287–90 the family ties between Noah and Sibyl are made more explicit – there she is cited as his daughter-in-law, in what is probably 'an exposition of, and elaboration on this line' (Buitenwerf 2003: 300).

These claims thus become all the more telling if read as part of the Sibyl's anti-Homeric self-positioning.[91] Epic poets themselves, of course, offer models for human-divine interaction through poetic revelation: Hesiod's *Theogony* 22–8 presents the meeting of a humble shepherd with the Muses in all their awe-inspiring glory; and in his famous second Muse-call before the catalogue of ships, Homer himself expresses his awe and wonder at the Muses whose information he must transmit into song (*Il.* 2.484–92). The Sibyl mixes her connection to the Pentateuchal patriarch Noah with her Homeric-Hesiodic qualities to show how through her Jewishness, she can become something more than these gentile poets could ever hope to be. Harnessing a number of features of knowledge-transmission from *both* epic *and* scriptural traditions, this oracle presents the Sibyl as the true, fully realised epic bard; capitalising on the *topoi* of epic inspiration to inscribe this alternative revelation of the real, singular divine truth.

Coda: Literary Bridges

At least five centuries after the composition of the anti-Homer oracle, another epic poet claims in a brazen aside that Homer got it wrong. In the *Dionysiaca*, set in the midst of the Indian war, Nonnus of Panopolis names Homer, conceives of his work as a 'book', and corrects one of his famous gnomic truths: γυναιμανέοντι δὲ μούνῳ / οὐ κόρος ἐστὶ πόθων· ἐψεύσατο βίβλος Ὁμήρου ('But only the man mad for women never has enough of longing. Homer's book lied!') (*Dion.* 42.180–81; cf. *Il.* 13.636–9). This is the only other surviving passage of Greek epic which accuses Homer of lying in this way. Both the (probably) Christian Nonnus[92] and the Jewish Sibyl attack a bookish Homer in Homerising hexameter, in a mythical setting which predates his narratives. An extreme version of Alexandrian 'contrast imitation', and a close encounter more intense and entwined than the sophists of imperial prose, both poets at once reveal their deeply exegetical, culturally inflected modes of Homeric inheritance and constantly deny the linear temporality on which this inheritance is based.

The Homeric oracle of *Or. Sib.* 3 as this chapter has read it can thus represent a crucial interlocutor in these Homeric discussions, standing before and linking between the prose treatises of the first and second

---

[91] This connection also provides a route through a perceived incongruity here: that the Sibyl's claims here to a mixed descent (through Circe and Noah) rub awkwardly against her status as a monotheistic voice-piece of God, which has led to the unnecessary hypothesis that this section was borrowed from an earlier pagan treatment of the Erythraean Sibyl (see Buitenwerf 2003: 300).

[92] For overviews on the vast debate surrounding Nonnus' religion, see Shorrock 2011 and Accorinti 2016.

centuries CE and Nonnus' vast poetic novelty in the fifth. And yet in viewing it in this way, it may be countered, do we risk veering into ahistoricism; replacing the excessive contextualisation of previous assessments of the oracles with a literary circularity, which ignores the cultural, social and religious factors which must render distinct, say, the Archelaos relief from the Jewish Sibyllina from Lucian?

By taking seriously Book 3's literary complexity, we can perceive how these divides are as false and unhelpful as the disciplinary binaries ('Theology vs Classics departments') that held back the study of this material for so long. The oracles' Homeric interactions, illuminated by recourse to a broader range of Hellenistic and imperial comparisons, must be viewed as *part of* their cultural strategy: this sophisticated and subversive self-position functions not as a counterpart or concession to 'mainstream' Greek erudite culture, but a move fully embedded within it. The attempt to appropriate the Sibyl as a figure for Jewish (and later, Christian) prophecy on the one hand, and to attack the foundational text of 'Greekness' on the other must form part of a double act of redrafting the prophetic and apocalyptic tradition to assert the primacy and power of Hellenistic Judaism. And this passage attempts this reappropriation not from a textual and critical distance, like the Second Sophistic treatises, Demetrius' chronicles or Aristobulus and Philo's theses, but by assuming Homer's original literary mode. Vision and revision of Homer, then, is not just a matter for 'Greek' second sophistry, but also Jewish religiosity; and not just for prose, but for poetics. The result, as conveyed so strongly in this oracle, is not merely the 'dressing up' of Jewish material in a Homeric-exegetical, classicising disguise. Rather, it leaves us with a fierce demonstration of how both traditions – Hellenistic Judaism and imperial Greekness – are characterised by ambiguity, elasticity and fluidity, but also irony, mischievousness and wit,[93] as this text shows how it is not only the later-born Lucian, Philostratus and Nonnus who can cynically confront Homer on his own terms. Through mythology, through prophecy and through poetry, the Jewish Sibyl has the last laugh.

---

[93] An instructive parallel can be found in Gruen's approach to the *Letter of Aristeas* 'not just as evidence for a foundation myth about the origins of the Septuagint but as a repository of light comedy', and the assertion by the Jewish writer Artapanus that Moses introduced to the Egyptians their distinctive worship of animal gods as 'a product of mischievous wit' (Gruen 2016: quotation from Martin Goodman's introduction, p. 3).

CHAPTER 7

Imagining Belonging
The Use of Athens in Hellenistic Rome
Joy Connolly

Over the past fifty years a number of scholars (myself included) have argued that activities associated with the pursuit of an 'Attic' ideal – speaking Greek in the linguistic idiom of Athens, adopting a certain rhetorical style, reading literary texts and even wearing clothing associated with Athens in the fifth and fourth centuries BCE – in the five centuries following the death of Alexander were tactics primarily adopted to reinforce 'Greek identity'. In this period Greek literature was spreading to regions where Greek was neither the primary language nor primary cultural identifier just as the Roman empire conquered those regions, so (the argument goes) memorialisation of past cultural glories could help compensate for the political subordination of the Roman imperial present.[1] As an explanation of what has seemed obviously a Greek cultural phenomenon, it might appear sensible to be content with a Greek-centred narrative about the significance of Athens and Atticism from the fourth century BCE onward.

But just as the modern words 'classical' and 'Hellenistic' are defined by the political and cultural pressures of eighteenth and nineteenth century Europe and are thus best used with caution, as Jason König and Nicolas Wiater remind us in the introduction to this volume, so we should reconsider the assumption that the Hellenistic (and Second Sophistic) investment in Athens arises primarily from and shapes itself around 'Greek' objectives. Better, I argue, to see Hellenistic literature as a plural phenomenon, best understood as shaped and sustained by competing Mediterranean and eventually Roman concerns. At the beginning of his

---

[1] Imagine quotation marks around the terms 'classical', 'Attic,' 'Greek' and 'Roman' throughout this essay, not because the terms lack meaning but in order to underline the fact that these terms are under investigation here. The fifty years of scholarship I refer to begins with Ewen Bowie's influential essay 'Greeks and their past in the second sophistic', Bowie 1974 (revised from an earlier version first published in 1970); see also Swain 1996, Connolly 2001a, Connolly 2001b, Whitmarsh 2001b, Connolly 2003.

Roman Antiquities Dionysius of Halicarnassus famously promises to show that Romans in fact 'were Greeks' (1.5.1). Tendentious as his claim is, we will see how Cicero experiments with thinking along similar lines.

In this essay I consider Hellenistic literature from a Roman angle. I see the preoccupation with the emerging Greek canon (heavily Athenian in its orientation) in both Greek and Latin Hellenistic authors as a significant factor in the history of conceptualising forms of group belonging that transcend boundaries of language, ethnicity and what we might call 'birth culture'.[2] Identifying Athens as the pinnacle of human achievement, particularly in the manifestations of its drama, philosophy and oratory – through which Greek literature became a marker of the knowledge proper to a free man – was a habit learned Romans embraced through acclamation and advanced through creative imitation. I will ask: to what end do Hellenistic writers in Rome claim a special status for and a special relationship to the Greek canon? What is it possible to say about the psychological texture and political implications of that relationship? Inspired by scholarship on contemporary fandom, I conclude that Cicero makes knowledge of Attic style and canonical works the basis of a passionate communal identification that transcends legal definitions of citizenship. Because I write at a moment where the putative cultural content of citizenship is hotly contested, I hope my discussion will draw attention to several ethical and political questions that Cicero's move raises for scholars of Greek and Roman literature and culture today.

Structures of Feeling in Cicero's *De finibus*

A generation before Dionysius claimed that Romans were Greeks, Cicero vividly described his first encounter with Athens as a young man in the preface to the fifth and final book of *De finibus*. Whether this 'memory' is authentic or fictional, its nuanced revelation of the structures of feeling animating Cicero's investment in canonical Greek literature deserves a close reading.[3]

> Cum audissem Antiochum, Brute, ut solebam, cum M.Pisone in eo gymnasio, quod Ptolomaeum vocatur, unaque nobiscum Q. frater et T. Pomponius Luciusque Cicero, frater noster cognatione patruelis, amore

---

[2] On the changing nature of the canon, see de Jonge on Dionysius, Quintilian and Dio Chrysostom in this volume.

[3] For the concept of 'structures of feeling', see Williams 1977; for a study of how it helps illuminate Dionysius of Halicarnassus' thinking, see Wiater 2019.

germanus, constituimus inter nos ut ambulationem postmeridianam conficeremus in Academia, maxime quod is locus ab omni turba id temporis vacuus esset. Itaque ad tempus ad Pisonem omnes. Inde sermone vario sex illa a Dipylo stadia confecimus. Cum autem venissemus in Academiae non sine causa nobilitata spatia, solitudo erat ea, **quam volueramus**.

Once when I was listening to Antiochus, as I used to do, with Marcus Piso, in the gymnasium called the Ptolemaeum, together with us were my brother Quintus, Titus Pomponius, and Lucius Cicero, my fraternal first cousin but really my brother, given our love. We agreed to take our afternoon walk in the Academy, mainly because the place would be free of all crowds at that time. So at that time we all met at Piso's place. From there we covered the six stadia from the Dipylon Gate with conversation on various subjects. When we reached the open spaces of the Academy, held in high esteem, not without reason, there was the solitude **that we had wished for**. (*De finibus* 5.1.1; tr. Rackham, adapted)

Readers familiar with the history of the Romans in Athens will remark on the significance of 79 BCE, the year of Cicero's visit to the city. Sulla had destroyed the Academy in his aggressive siege of Athens during the Mithridatic war just a few years earlier, in 86. The timing complicates Cicero's description of the Academy as a place of solitude (*solitudo*) – 'just as they had wished it to be' (*quam volueramus*, 5.1.1). Perhaps the place is quiet thanks to the afternoon siesta; but Cicero elsewhere in his writing tends to use *solitudo* in negative terms, in conjunction with words like *uiduitas* ('bereavement') and *inopia* ('scarcity'). This ominously suggests that the Academy is a deserted field of rubble: a place signifying lack, 'widowed' of its great men by the passage of time, a site in need of the energetic imagination the learned young Romans are poised to bring to it. We will return to this ambiguity later.

> Tum Piso: Naturane nobis hoc, inquit, datum dicam an errore quodam, ut, cum ea loca videamus, in quibus memoria dignos viros acceperimus multum esse versatos, magis moveamur, quam si quando eorum ipsorum aut facta audiamus aut scriptum aliquod legamus? Velut ego nunc moveor. Venit enim mihi Platonis in mentem, quem accepimus primum hic disputare solitum; cuius etiam illi hortuli propinqui non memoriam solum mihi afferunt, sed ipsum videntur in conspectu meo ponere. Hic Speusippus, hic Xenocrates, hic eius auditor Polemo, cuius illa ipsa sessio fuit, quam videmus. Equidem etiam curiam nostram – Hostiliam dico, non hanc novam, quae minor mihi esse videtur, posteaquam est maior – solebam intuens Scipionem, Catonem, Laelium, nostrum vero in primis avum cogitare; tanta vis admonitionis inest in locis; ut non sine causa ex iis memoriae ducta sit disciplina.

Then Piso said: 'Shall I say it is granted to us by nature or by some wandering of mind, that when we see the very places we know men worthy of memory spent much of their time, we are more powerfully moved than if we hear about their deeds or read their writings? Right now I am moved just in this way. Plato comes to my mind, whom we have taken to be the first to make a habit of philosophical argument here in this place; whose gardens close at hand there not only recall his memory but seem to bring the actual man before my gaze. Here was Speusippus, here Xenocrates, and here Xenocrates' pupil Polemo, who used to sit on the very seat we see over there. To be sure, gazing even at our senate-house – I mean the Curia Hostilia, not this new building, which to me seems smaller since its enlargement – I used to think about Scipio, Cato, Laelius, and most of all, my grandfather; so much force of suggestion abides in places; not without reason is the training of the memory derived from them'. (*De finibus* 5.1.2)

Piso is the first to express what turns out to be a feeling everyone shares. The Academy moves him. He sees great Greek thinkers in what he imagines to be their accustomed – we might almost call them 'autochthonous' – places: Plato, Speusippus, Xenocrates, Polemo. He compares these Greeks to the great Romans whom the sight of the Curia Hostilia summons up, back in Rome: Scipio, Cato, Laelius, his own grandfather Piso. Piso links his intense visual experience (*ipsum*) to the originally Greek *disciplina* of oratorical education, specifically Simonides' trick of training the memory by linking facts and arguments to images of places. Anticipating the pairings of Greeks and Romans in Valerius Maximus and Plutarch, Piso makes great men of the past into heroic peers, while keeping them physically separate from one another in his mind's eye, one group in the Academy, one group in the Curia.

Tum Quintus: Est plane, Piso, ut dicis, inquit. nam me ipsum huc modo venientem convertebat ad sese Coloneus ille locus, cuius incola Sophocles ob oculos versabatur, quem scis quam admirer quemque eo delecter. **Me quidem ad altiorem memoriam Oedipodis huc venientis et illo mollissimo carmine quaenam essent ipsa haec loca requirentis species quaedam commovit, inaniter scilicet, sed commovit tamen.**

'Yes indeed, Piso', rejoined Quintus. 'I myself on the way here just now noticed the village of Colonus over there, whose resident Sophocles came before my eyes; as you know I greatly admire and delight in him. **Indeed something about the appearance of the place pushed me deeper into my memory of Oedipus coming right here and asking in the most pleasing of verses what place this is – an empty fancy perhaps, yet nonetheless it moved me**'. (*De finibus* 5.1.3)

Cicero's brother Quintus also imagines figures from the past. His characters hail from the world of Attic drama, and he adds a striking aural element to Piso's use of visual imagery. A glimpse of Colonus from afar prompts him to recollect a scene from Sophocles where Oedipus speaks verses Quintus summarises, as though he, Quintus, were briefly playing Oedipus in Latin. Like Piso, though he knows the whole scene is a figment of his imagination, he is deeply moved (*inaniter scilicet, commovit tamen*).

> Tum Pomponius: At ego, quem vos ut deditum Epicuro insectari soletis, sum **multum equidem cum Phaedro, quem unice diligo**, ut scitis, in Epicuri hortis, quos modo praeteribamus, sed veteris proverbii admonitu vivorum memini, nec tamen Epicuri licet oblivisci, si cupiam, cuius imaginem non modo in tabulis nostri familiares, sed etiam in poculis et in anulis habent.

> Then Pomponius said, 'I too, whom you often attack as a devotee of Epicurus, am **very often in the company of Phaedrus, whom as you know I love dearly**, in Epicurus' Gardens which we passed just now; although thanks to the old proverb, I 'am mindful of the living', nonetheless I could not forget Epicurus even if I wished to, whose image our friends keep not only in paintings but also on their drinking-cups and rings'. (*De finibus* 5.1.3)

Another Roman who speaks Greek now speaks up, seconding Quintus' emotions: Cicero's friend Titus Pomponius, not yet called Atticus. He dwells on the affection he feels and the esteem in which he holds Greek friends and Greek learning. Noting Piso's customary criticism (*insectari soletis*), he defends his habit of talking with his friend Phaedrus in the gardens of Epicurus. He translates Piso's majestic images of long-dead Greeks into small beloved things, the cups and jewellery by which the philosopher's followers admiringly commemorate him.

> Hic ego: Pomponius quidem, inquam, noster iocari videtur, et fortasse suo iure. **Ita enim se Athenis collocavit, ut sit paene unus ex Atticis, ut id etiam cognomen videatur habiturus**. Ego autem tibi, Piso, assentior usu hoc venire, ut acrius aliquanto et attentius de claris viris locorum admonitu cogitemus. Scis enim me quodam tempore Metapontum venisse tecum neque ad hospitem ante devertisse, quam Pythagorae ipsum illum locum, ubi vitam ediderat, sedemque viderim. Hoc autem tempore, etsi multa in omni parte Athenarum sunt in ipsis locis indicia summorum virorum, tamen ego illa moveor exhedra. **Modo enim fuit Carneadis, quem videre videor – est enim nota imago – a sedeque ipsa tanta ingenii magnitudine orbata desiderari illam vocem puto.**

> And I [Cicero] said: 'As for our friend Pomponius, I think he's joking, and perhaps appropriately so. **For he has so settled himself down in Athens that he is almost one of the Athenians, that I expect he will in future have the cognomen Atticus**. But I agree with you, Piso, that by the suggestive effect of places we tend to think more vividly and in a more concentrated way about famous men. For you know how I once came with you to Metapontum, and I would not go to the guest-house until I had seen the very place where Pythagoras lived out his life, even where he sat. All over Athens, I know, there are many reminders of eminent men in the actual place where they lived; but right now I am moved by that alcove over there. For it once belonged to Carneades, whom **I seem to see now – for his likeness is well known – and I think that his very voice is dearly missed by that very seat, widowed of such a great intellect**'. (*De finibus* 5.2.4)

Pomponius' remarks prompt the young Cicero to predict, teasingly, that his friend will receive the cognomen Atticus: he loves Athens so much that he is almost (*paene*) an Athenian himself. Reminding Piso that they had made a pilgrimage to the house of Pythagoras, Cicero is brought by his surroundings to recall the Academic philosopher Carneades. He returns to his brother's emphasis on the grain of the voice, and remarks that Carneades' loss has left the Academy, and by extension the young Romans standing in it, widowed (*orbata*, 4). Athenians and Romans alike long for the dead philosopher whose face, familiar to the learned just like Epicurus', haunts the place.

> Tum Piso: Quoniam igitur aliquid omnes, quid Lucius noster? inquit. An eum locum libenter invisit, ubi Demosthenes et Aeschines inter se decertare soliti sunt? Suo enim quisque studio maxime ducitur. Et ille, cum erubuisset: Noli, inquit, ex me quaerere, qui in Phalericum etiam descenderim, quo in loco ad fluctum aiunt declamare solitum Demosthenen, ut fremitum assuesceret voce vincere. Modo etiam paulum ad dexteram de via declinavi, ut ad Pericli sepulcrum accederem. Quamquam id quidem infinitum est in hac urbe; quacumque enim ingredimur, in aliqua historia vestigium ponimus.

> 'Well,' said Piso, 'since we all have something to say, what about our Lucius? Does he enjoy visiting the spot where Demosthenes and Aeschines used to fight with one another? For each of us is drawn by our own favourite study.' 'Don't ask me,' answered Lucius, blushing; 'I have actually gone down to the Bay of Phalerum, where they say Demosthenes used to practise declaiming on the beach, to learn to pitch his voice so as to overcome an uproar. And only just now I turned off the road a little way on the right, to visit the tomb of Pericles. But in fact this is without end in this city; wherever we walk, we place our steps into some historical narrative or other.' (*De finibus* 5.2.5)

Imagining Belonging 217

Piso acknowledges the common love of Athens and its literature that links the group in order to encourage the shy young Lucius Cicero to speak about his attraction to Attic oratory. Lucius underscores the importance of the sound of the orator's voice by confessing that he visited the spot where Demosthenes trained himself to speak over the roar of the waves. Inspired and excited by his visit, Lucius sees Athens as *infinitum*, peculiarly open to the play of historical memory and imagination.

What is the attraction of Plato's Academy to these men, in Cicero's sketch? It is a quiet refuge – which reminds us that Cicero himself sought refuge in Greece as an exile, as Marcellus will flee Caesar, and Brutus and Cassius their opponents after the Ides of March. It is 'just as they wished it to be': it is a fulfilment of their desires. The Academy is also a place that unleashes the imagination, a place where a Republican Roman wants to be – not just physically, like Atticus or Marcellus or Brutus and Cassius, but figuratively, imaginatively, in poetry, philosophical dialogue, or the dramatic stage. It is a place where Greeks and Romans exist in company: the exemplars of the Athenian past, both historical and fictional, and their Attic voices, line up in Piso's imagination alongside great Romans like Scipio Aemilianus. Pomponius' affection for his friend Phaedrus is a living example of his friends' love of long-dead Athenian writers and speakers.

For these reasons, as we hear again and again, the Academy moves them. It summons up emotion-laden memories of images and voices, providing an image- and sound-repertoire that inspires their thoughts and deepens their affections to one another and to their Greek friends, and to the place itself. These men have not so much planted themselves on the Athenian landscape as they have created what Homi Bhabha calls an 'inscape' which is at once Roman, Greek, and somehow beyond the limitations of both.[4] Their Athens is a sublime place, lifting the men outside themselves.

There is what we might call a 'meta-ethopoetic' element at work in the passage. It is ethopoetic, because these Romans walking in the Academy engage themselves in a dialogue that re-enacts the dialogues of Plato: Quintus' reference to Oedipus speaking Sophocles' verses draws our attention to the dramatic aspects of the scene. For a moment, Cicero and his friends are the Romans that Dionysius of Halicarnassus will imagine a generation later, when he claims in *Roman Antiquities* that 'no one will find a nation that is more ancient and more Greek' (1.89.2). It is

---

[4] Bhabha 1994: 205. In his analysis of the 'recurrent metaphor of landscape as the inscape of national identity', Bhabha tracks how humans invest emotion, memory and historical associations with terrestrial places.

meta-ethopoetic, because the young men's theme is the power of place or location to summon up images and sounds that are a blend of memory and imagination – and we the readers experience the same effect as the characters themselves.

But these flights of imagination, identification, and emotion must not obscure the ambiguity of the Academy's *solitudo*, its deserted silence. Plutarch recalls the Roman siege that destroyed it as a dark moment in Athenian history:

> δεινὸς γάρ τις ἄρα καὶ ἀπαραίτητος εἶχεν αὐτὸν ἔρως ἑλεῖν τὰς Ἀθήνας, εἴτε ζήλῳ τινὶ πρὸς τὴν πάλαι σκιαμαχοῦντα τῆς πόλεως δόξαν, εἴτε θυμῷ τὰ σκώμματα φέροντα καὶ τὰς βωμολοχίας, αἷς αὐτόν τε καὶ τὴν Μετέλλαν ἀπὸ τῶν τειχῶν ἑκάστοτε γεφυρίζων καὶ κατορχούμενος ἐξηρέθιζεν ὁ τύραννος Ἀριστίων . . .

> For some awful and inexorable passion to capture Athens possessed him, either because he was fighting with a sort of ardour against the shadow of the city's former glory, or because he was provoked to anger by the scurrilous abuse which had been showered from the walls upon himself and Metella by the tyrant Aristion, who always danced in mockery as he scoffed . . . (Plut. *Sull.* 13.1; tr. Perrin, adapted)

A generation later, Strabo's story of Sulla's acquisition of the books of Aristotle and Theophrastus after the capture of Athens adds another twist to Cicero's silence. As Strabo tells it, Aristotle's successor as leader of the Peripatetic school, Theophrastus, handed down the collection to his own student, Neleus. Neleus' heirs allowed the books to moulder, ignorantly burying them in a trench when they learned the Attalids were seeking additions to their library at Pergamon, until the family sold the books to Apellicon of Teos for a large profit. When Sulla carried off the library to Rome, it fell into the hands of unscrupulous grammarians and book dealers, whom Strabo blames for additional corruptions to the already mouldy and moth-eaten texts (13.1.54). Here Athens is the repository of Greek texts brought there in tatters, neglected by Greeks who viewed them only in terms of monetary value, a scene re-enacted in the new Athens, Rome, where the books suffer again at the hands of greedy Greeks.

Conscious or not, Cicero's reference to the Academy's silence bespeaks his and his contemporaries' participation in the system of aggression and co-optation that is an inescapable part of Roman encounters with Greece. There is no way to disentangle Roman habits of identification with and attachment to Greek culture from the context of the violent conquest of Greece. Nicolas Wiater, in his study of Dionysius' treatment of Greek ethnicity, suggests that he handles that tension by fashioning Rome as a new political and ethical paradigm that 'combines the strengths of its Greek and Roman components while overcoming their weaknesses'.[5] The anthropologist Renato Rosaldo would argue that 'mourning for what one has destroyed' is a crucial element in dominant societies: so now the Global North draws a line between the profane (industrialised civilisation) and the sacred (nature and non-industrialised people) and then worships the very thing the 'civilising' process is destroying.[6]

Athens as Greece, Greece as the World, the World in the Voice

Part of the appeal of feeling a sense of belonging in Athens, as Lucius Cicero hints, derives from what he and his peers see as Athens' distinctive place in human history. This view is of course not a Roman invention. Early in the fourth century BCE, Athenian writers began to represent their city as a model for all of Greece and beyond, for all humans. Thucydides and Isocrates are key sources for the interrelated themes of Athenian exceptionalism and universalism later adopted by Hellenistic writers in Rome like Dionysius of Halicarnassus and Strabo and by imperial sophists circulating around the Roman empire in the first through the third centuries CE.[7]

For Dionysius, Athens is an exemplum of universalisable knowledge for the global community. As Casper de Jonge and Lawrence Kim show in this volume, its literary canon shapes the genres and styles of the future. Athens leaves not only the legacy of Demosthenes or Aeschines, but all of oratory; not just Socrates and Plato, but philosophy; not just Sophocles and Euripides, but tragedy. Thucydides competes with Herodotus for the founding of history. 'Attic' gives its name to a dominant approved oratorical style. Dionysius reinforces the Athenians' self-identification as the leaders and the teachers of Greece described in Pericles' vision in the funeral oration in Thucydides and Isocrates' in his *Panegyricus*. He grounds his argument on behalf of the ethnic Hellenicity of the Romans in the claim that the Roman empire is the realisation of the Greek *oikoumene* (1.89.2). The habit of seeing Athens in classicised and classicising, universalised and universalising terms – already incipient in fifth- and fourth-century Attic texts – gains traction in Greek texts written in Rome

---

[5] Wiater 2019: 231. [6] Rosaldo 1989: 107–22.
[7] Cf. Gray in this volume on the related concept of 'cosmopolitanism'; Wiater on the idea of the *oikoumene* unified under Roman rule.

by Diodorus Siculus, Nicolaus of Damascus, poets in the *Garland*, and through the second century CE.[8] Aelius Aristides remakes Athens into a παράδειγμα of the *pax Romana* (*Panathenaicus* 13.98 Jebb), using the word Thucydides puts in Pericles' mouth to describe his city (2.37.1). Like Isocrates, Aristides praises Athens as the 'common guard' of all, the city-state that anticipates Roman imperial generosity by giving gifts of land and citizen rights to many men. Where Isocrates praised Athenian colonisation as a panhellenic enterprise and salvation for the Greeks (*Paneg.* 34.7), Aristides sees it as a model for the universal dominion of Rome.[9]

I have argued elsewhere that the universalist construction of Athens created an immensely useful heuristic for the Romans once they had conquered the Mediterranean.[10] If Athens could be claimed as the model for refined human culture on a global scale, it was Roman military might that preserved its memory and made its continued circulation around the world possible. Reverence for the learning symbolised by the Athenian *polis* helped residents of the Roman empire unite in the face of social, linguistic, religious and political division. Through the canon-based education advocated by Cicero, Dionysius of Halicarnassus, Quintilian, Dio and Plutarch,[11] Athens became a meeting point in the imagination for Greeks, Romans, Celts, Syrians and others. The habits of thought and practice advocated by Atticising Hellenism, especially the rule-encoded *ars rhetorica*, purist ideals of language and Stoic-style cosmopolitan thought, promoted a universalist world-view peculiarly favourable to imperial government and its claims to provide security.[12] By the Roman period, speaking pure Greek or Latin in an 'Attic' mode had come to embody itself in a set of cultural practices (like doing rhetoric or philosophy) theoretically accessible to all educated men, regardless of 'native' ethnicity or language.[13]

The canonisation of Athens enabled in turn another kind of imagination that served Roman interests. Because Romans are preservers of ancient Athens, Aristides remarked in his speech in praise of Rome, they are licensed to consider themselves 'lovers of the people' who lived in 'the democracy of the whole world' (*On Rome* 60), the 'only empire to rule over men who are truly free' (36). Dionysius' and Aristides' laudations of this Greek Rome are examples of the ways Atticising culture not only

---

[8] See Schmitz and Wiater 2011b.
[9] Compare Aristides on Athens as the *koine phylax* of the Greeks (*Panathenaicus* 197, 228, *passim*, Behr). See further Saïd 2006: 53; Oudot 2008.
[10] Connolly 2007. [11] Cf. de Jonge in this volume.
[12] Cf. further Gray and Kim in this volume.
[13] On the contested linguistic aspects of 'Atticism' over time, see Kim in this volume.

accommodated itself to the demands of empire, but further, became a common constructed heritage that justified and celebrated empire while leaving enough room (as effective ideological apparatuses must always do) for varied shades of self-definition and even fights over rightful cultural ownership.

Against this talk of rules and systematic practices, we must not lose sight of the emotions and sensations at the level of the individual, so lucidly and significantly bared by the preface to *De finibus* Book 5. Investing in a canon – acquiring a new language, polishing an accent, memorising passages, learning the secondary discourse of taste and judgement – is a complex, embodied process that involves both solitary study and engagement with others. It is best interpreted in phenomenological terms as a process encompassing new and different perspectives on historical time and space, new self-understanding and external identifications.[14] As James Porter points out in his essay 'Feeling classical', there is a whole 'realm of pleasures' in the practices of 'classicism'.[15] Porter's fine-grained treatment of 'feeling classical' illuminates how Hellenistic writers in Rome could take pleasure in 'feeling Roman' in a way that is simultaneously 'feeling Greek'.

The sound of the voice, so important in Cicero's and Dionysius' representation of how the student absorbs and enacts the canon he studies, is central to the individual experience of feeling. Speaking properly is a test of whether Attic learning is fully informing the mind and heart as well as the tongue, and is thus an excellent holistic test of belonging to the virtuous community, depending on whether one is judged to be a properly 'Attic' or 'Asian' speaker – in Dionysius' comparison, a modest wife or a prostitute (Cicero, *Brut.* 51, 314–16, 325–7; *Orat.* 25, 27, 212, 230–1; Dionysius, *Ancient Orators* 1).

Hence the utility of specific rules in rhetorical discourse that govern the formation and expression of voice and label it with ethnic terms symbolising a set of values and norms. It seems unlikely to be a coincidence that Cicero encourages his readers to judge their Latinity by Greek standards at the end of his life, just as he recognised that the traditional structures of the Republic were falling apart. His treatise *Orator*, written in 45 BCE, expresses his desire to regenerate the state by reinforcing linguistic rules and resonances that maintain authority over all facets of life, including the voice itself, that bundle of emotion, reason, and physicality.

But the complexity of the voice and its physiological resistance to perfect control means that it resists singular categorisations, definitions,

---

[14] Somers 1994: 605–49.   [15] Porter 2006: 310.

and judgements. The same applies to Atticism and Asianism themselves. Near the beginning of his treatise *Orator* (28) Cicero praises men 'who adapt themselves to the refined and scrupulous ears of an Athenian audience' as having authentically 'Attic' voices – whose qualities turn out to be virtually impossible to pin down:

> Ad Atticorum igitur auris teretes et religiosas qui se accommodant, ei sunt existimandi Attice dicere. Quorum genera plura sunt; hi unum modo quale sit suspicantur. Putant enim qui horride inculteque dicat, modo id eleganter enucleateque faciat, eum solum Attice dicere. Errant, quod solum; quod Attice, non falluntur.

> So those men who adapt themselves to the smoothly polished and conscientious ears of the Athenians are the men who ought to be considered as speaking 'Attic'. There are many types of 'Attic' speakers; the men here [i.e., Cicero's critics in Rome; cf. 23] believe there is only one type, and of this they merely have a vague idea. For they think that a man who speaks in an aggressive and unadorned fashion, so long as he speaks gracefully and plainly, is the only one to speak Attic. They err, thinking that this is the only [kind of Attic style]; that this is one [Attic style], they are not deceived.

What is Attic? It is everything, in a way: 'brusque and fierce, provided that [the speaker] uses elegant and well-turned expressions' – something simple but not neat, that is not over-heavy but acts like 'thunder and lightning'. What it is not, as Lawrence Kim shows elsewhere in this volume, is linked to its geographical origin. It has become a floating marker of belonging.

Communities of Fans

Canonical knowledge circulated among groups with shared tastes deepens affective ties and creates new modes of identification and belonging. Svetlana Boym, a scholar of the role of canonical knowledge in the formation of twentieth-century groups, shows that in parts of the ex-Soviet Union and other places experiencing mass displacement of peoples and values, individual longing (particularly for a place one can call home and where one can form relationships of trust) is transformed into a collective belonging by the sharing in an aesthetics that transcends individual memories: talking a certain way, walking a certain way, wearing a certain style of coat or shoe and, above all, knowing certain things.[16] The American novelist Jonathan Lethem is a well-known example of a writer who explores how human relationships develop on the basis of shared love

[16] Boym 2001.

of canonical comic books or 1970s music. Films like *High Fidelity* or *Trekkers* do the same work.

These books and films reveal how communities are born out of 'fanon', fan knowledge of the canon. Fandom is the expression of readers' and viewers' sense of collective identity that arises from common familiarities and common knowledge, the mastery of which produces pleasures experienced in common. Scholars and consumers of fandom describe it as a refuge from 'real-life' identity markers such as gender, ethnicity and nationality that fans find repressive. To fans, fandom is a platform for intriguing new forms of collective imagination.

The origins of fandom are debated. Etymologically, 'fan' (which appears in English for the first time in the late seventeenth century) derives from *fanaticus*, a word Cicero and Livy use to describe a temple devotee, itself derived from *fanum*, sacred ground or temple. The role of the fans' agency – specifically their active engagement in producing material of their own supplementary to the original canon – is central to most versions of fandom history. In 1893, readers began to feed their mania for Sherlock Holmes, after Arthur Conan Doyle had killed off the character, by writing their own stories about the detective. In 1901, Conan Doyle finally capitulated to fan pressure and wrote more Holmes stories. Contemporary fan-fiction or fanfic was created in the late 1960s by fans of *Star Trek*: like the hopeful readers of Conan Doyle, *Star Trek* fans first mobilised to keep the series alive when it faced cancellation after its first season, and later sustained their community with newsletters and meetings that evolved into fan-fiction magazines and large regular conventions. With the emergence of the internet, fandom achieved global reach and a global community.

Fandom expresses itself multi-generically. The internet features novels and short stories in various subgenres such as letters and diaries, poetry, comics, songs and fan-made videos recutting scenes from film or television or game footage. These artworks, in their creation of new plots, involve fans in the creative extension of the canon. They often explore a particular relationship in depth, especially homoerotic ones in a substantial subgenre called 'slash fiction' (Sherlock seduces Watson, or in crossover slash, Harry Potter). The scale of the engagement is suggested by the fact that in early 2021 there are nearly 120,000 fan-produced novels, stories, songs, and poems in dozens of languages about the Sherlock Holmes BBC series *alone* on a single website.[17]

---

[17] See archiveofourown.org (accessed 1 December 2021), indexed by date, genre, language and other searchable terms.

We could interpret Roman texts as expressions of fandom according to a strict definition, reading, for example, Catullus 65 or Virgil's *Aeneid* as an elaboration of non-central figures in Homer (in keeping with the popular fanfic trope), or Senecan plays as rewritten versions of Athenian tragedy. We could identify Cicero's *De finibus* with a subgenre of fan-fiction popular on YouTube where fans film themselves in recreated sets, sometimes stepping out of character to comment on (for instance) the satisfaction of 'being' on the bridge of a Federation starship. But for my purposes, I want to adopt a broader approach, learning from contemporary scholarship what fandom is perceived to do: specifically, what emotions it summons up, the knowledge that sustains it and that it generates in turn, and most of all, the imagined communities it creates.

Studies of the construction of the fan community reveal that it is multi- and trans-national: fan-fiction written in English on the Internet is translated almost instantly into Italian, Spanish, Mandarin, Korean, Japanese and many more languages. Scholars and fans themselves see fandom as heterogeneous, with patterns of popularity and creative imitation that are difficult to predict accurately. Kristina Busse speaks of the 'ambiguous space' created in the fandom where identity (gender, sexual orientation, nationality, politics) shifts 'almost completely into the realm of fantasy'.[18] Whether it is true that writers of homoerotic slash fiction are mostly straight white women (a belief taken for granted online), the community emerges out of self-recognition that to a certain extent leaves conventional markers of identity behind. Knowledge of canonical material, by which fans are 'drawn in' (to quote Piso, *ducitur*) is what unites the community. Knowledge, combined with the desire to join a group where common taste itself is the primary identifier – rather than the usual markers of gender, ethnicity, nationality or religion – makes the group.

In the preface to his *Tusculan Disputations*, Cicero declares that Romans are better than Greeks at everything but culture (*doctrina*), and that is only because the Romans have not put in the necessary effort – until Cicero throws himself into the fray, investing himself in knowledge of Greek learning across philosophy, drama, poetry, history and oratory. Responding to this passage, Andrew Wallace-Hadrill notes how curious it is that in spite of Cicero's rehearsal of the elder Cato's complaints about the corrupting effects of Greek culture, 'the transformation of Roman structures of knowledge through *paideia* passes with remarkably little comment ... [T]hough the annexation of new disciplines adds provinces

---

[18] Busse 2006: 208–9. See further Jenkins 1992 and 2002; Gray, Sandvoss and Harrington 2007.

to the Roman intellectual empire, it is not perceived as changing its structure.'[19] Wallace-Hadrill sees late Republican intellectuals using Greek learning to advance the *scientia* of which they were traditional custodians.[20] Romans like Cicero and Varro 'annexed' Greek learning, and made affiliation with Greek texts one part of what it is to be an elite Roman. The Hellenistic canon becomes useful material for a way of belonging as a Roman, at the same time masterful and imitative.

De finibus is creative material produced by a fan for the fandom. Where the writer of a *Star Trek* slash novel reorients canon in a way that responds to her desires, *De finibus* is the product of an emotionally invested practice of reading that reorients a canonical set of texts, Athenian philosophy, drama and oratory, around Cicero's interests and desires. Cicero's text awakens us to the potency of the fantasy into which the Roman fan of Greek literature enters. It is a fantasy of transportation out of oneself, out of daily life, out of local constraints, out of local identities. *De finibus* suggests that Hellenistic learning offers a way to feel Roman that transcends the conventional ethnic and territorial markers of Romanness.

Scholars of fandom have documented the pleasures of companionship nourished by common familiarity with well-known texts; there is the pleasure of transcendence as friends identify with an alien world, created by Jane Austen, Gene Roddenberry or J. K. Rowling. In these communities, cultural artefacts – a jazz tune, a television episode – accrue a crust of factoids, biographical sketches, lists. Accuracy of knowledge becomes a test of group belonging on a par with recognising good 'Attic' style. In his analysis of Hellenistic Roman writing, Feeney speaks of a 'new determination to "get it right" in transposing from the model culture' in the Latin works of the 230s BCE onwards.[21]

The modality of transmitting this cultural information is a flattening out, an elaboration that is also a simplification – the latter partly due to the multi-chrome cultures of fandom, who speak different languages and come from different cultural settings. This explains the flattened representations of Greek characters in Dionysius, Diodorus Siculus or, to take a Roman example, Cornelius Nepos – all examples of Roman fandom. Dionysius lays very little emphasis on Athens as a historical place. On the contrary, Thomas Schmitz and Nicolas Wiater observe, 'in Dionysius, "the classical past" is, in fact, an abstract, placeless entity that exists in and is preserved

---

[19] Wallace-Hadrill 1998a: 9, 14.   [20] See also Gruen 1992.
[21] Feeney 2005: 230. See further Feeney 2016.

through language'.²² As contemporary fans would say, lists, summaries and simple biographies are the stuff of easy-to-test knowledge, ways to ensure the coherence of the fan community and provide it with material for enjoyment and debate. This shines a different light on arguments that place the systematisation of knowledge in Roman and Greek writing in the late first century BCE – an Augustan phenomenon, as Glenn Most argues, where the rule of a single man drove the universalisation and systematisation of knowledge. Most himself admits that this conclusion forces him to treat writers like Varro and Diodorus Siculus unconvincingly as predecessors anticipating the Augustan movement. Rather than seeing the rule of Augustus as signifying the formation of a new era, we should see it as the end of one.²³

With this in mind, consider Cicero's imagined Athens – a place that seems to encourage voluntary affective affiliation with others who stand at a distance from one's local kin-group or linguistic community. By immersing themselves in the visual and aural space of the Academy, Cicero's fellow Roman fans of Greek literature, philosophy and culture create an intensely felt affective affiliation. Each, as he delights in the company of others or the memory of a text, changes in his own eyes and in the eyes of his friends. Cicero had introduced this idea early on, when he suggested that one can love a person to such a degree that the conventional boundaries defining relationships do not apply. In his first reference to Lucius Cicero he says he loves him like a brother, though he was only a cousin (*frater noster cognatione patruelis, amore germanus*, *Fin.* 5.1). In Athens, then, you can love your cousin like a blood brother and a Greek like your best friend, as Pomponius loves his Platonically named Phaedrus (*unice diligo*, 5.3). Atticus loves Athens so much he will supplement his Latin name with the city's name.

As each man identifies Greek writers or orators for whom they feel a special affinity, Athens tugs these Romans out of their local frame, out of exclusively Roman identifications and affiliations. The Americanist Lauren Berlant calls this 'the citizen's erotics', 'to feel infinite because abstract, and passionate in collective self-transcendence'.²⁴ She argues that the 'fantasy-work' involved in community membership has the capacity to escape the microspaces of linguistic, family and even national bonds by translating individuals into an 'Imaginary realm of ideality' which hosts a larger inscape of transcendent identification.²⁵

---

²² Schmitz and Wiater 2011b: 36–9, the quote at 39; cf. also Wiater 2018c, 2019.
²³ Most 2011; see also Schmitz 2011a, on Diodorus' image of Athens.   ²⁴ Berlant 1991: 191.
²⁵ Fanon 1963: 148. See further Cheah and Robbins 1998.

Cultural Identity as a Form of Citizenship

Hannah Arendt declares that the Romans understood a cultivated person to be 'one who knows how to choose his company among men, among things, among thoughts, in the present as well as the past'.[26] The preface to *De finibus* 5 gives us a picture of men, having carefully chosen their present company, choosing their company in the past – thereby, as Arendt would put it, creating the mode of belonging we call 'culture'. Their comments weave several different modes of attachment – friendship, literary taste, shared knowledge of intellectual and political history – into the distinctive sense of belonging they experience at Athens. Frantz Fanon viewed these attachments, which he called the 'passionate' aspect of belonging to a community, as crucial building blocks in the formation of meaningful political sensibility.

While Isocrates, Dionysius, and Aristides conceived Athens and Atticism as a universally appealing cultural phenomenon, they did not make Athenian cultural practice into the basis for arguments to extend political citizenship or 'identity'.[27] The general infrequency of granting Roman citizenship to Greeks and vice versa seems to be the result of combined Roman and Greek reluctance. The Roman enfranchisement of Greeks was virtually non-existent until the first century, when Sulla, and then Octavian and Mark Antony began granting Roman citizenship to Greeks on terms that allowed the recipients to retain their local citizen status if they wished.[28]

Just as the legal enfranchisement of Greeks began to grow more common, in fits and starts, Cicero praises Greek culture in his *Pro Archia* of 62 BCE:

> Qua re, si res eae quas gessimus orbis terrae regionibus definiuntur, cupere debemus, quo hominum nostrorum tela pervenerint, eodem gloriam famamque penetrare, quod cum ipsis populis de quorum rebus scribitur haec ampla sunt, tum eis certe qui de vita gloriae causa dimicant hoc maximum et periculorum incitamentum est et laborum.
>
> So if these deeds that we have done are defined within the territories of the whole world, we ought to wish that wherever the force of our arms has

---

[26] Arendt 1963: 222.
[27] Wiater 2018c insightfully discusses the tension in Dionysius of Halicarnassus' account of early Republican Roman debates over the nature of Rome: a tension between the implicit representation of Athens as a universal model polity and the historical city's policy of reserving citizenship (at least from the middle of the fifth century) to those of both patrilinear and matrilinear descent (213).
[28] Sherwin-White 1980: 308.

> reached, our glory and fame should reach as well. Not only are these ample rewards for those peoples whose achievements are recorded in writing, but for those men who struggle for the sake of glory this is the greatest spur for risks and labours. (*Arch.* 23)

The main thrust of Cicero's defence of Archias' rightful possession of Roman citizenship is that the poet's cultural achievements make him a universalising figure worthy of the Roman *civitas*: his Greek poems about Roman power reach all corners of the civilised world. Cicero nods to the legal standard by which his listeners might evaluate his claims for Archias, but his argument is clearly more focused on justifying Archias' *belonging* in Rome in a way that cross-cuts conventional notions of blood or native affiliations than on the thin legal evidence, which occupies less than a quarter of the speech. Archias' skill as a poet gives Cicero material for his speeches and exemplary inspiration for his own deeds; and it guarantees immortality. Universal reach and appeal, as we have already seen, place poets like Archias in a unique position to communicate Rome's exploits to the whole world, now and forever (Cic. *Arch.* 30). The combination of admiration, desire, pleasure and hope for Rome's imperial future (not only as a political entity but as a permanent artefact of human memory, thanks to poetry) manifest in the *Pro Archia* also characterises writings like *De finibus*, where Cicero describes Rome as the lover, inheritor, transmitter and improver of Greek culture.

Scholarship on contemporary fandom, we have seen, has documented the power of community formation through shared fantasy of transcendent transport. When we view Cicero through the lens of fandom, we can see the forces of identification and desire that made it possible for him to think of Roman citizenship as a purely cultural, transmissible property. Cicero's passions in the *Pro Archia* are strong – a point worth taking seriously. Along with Dionysius and later Greek writers of the second century CE who attested to the essential suitability of the Greek canon for the Roman empire, the feelings Cicero brings to the appropriations of Greek literature, systems of knowledge and habits of thought unlock his civic imagination. Archias deserves citizenship because he produces the literature that Cicero sees as engendering a passionate communal identification that at once crystallises and transcends what it means to be Roman. We see in Cicero's argument the emergence of the idea that individuals are capable of belonging, through voluntary affection, canonical knowledge and proper style, to a group that is not their native-born one.

Cicero, Brutus, Marcellus, Horace and other Romans treat Greece as a refuge both corporeal and psychological – a place to flee to in times of political strife and a place that nourishes creative impulses: collecting Greek art, reading and composing poetry inspired by Greek models, doing Greek philosophy in Latin. The pleasure and transcendence late Republicans like Cicero found in Athens – pre-dating by over half a century Augustus' consolidation of autocratic power and the change in legal and governmental treatment of the eastern provinces under the principate – represents an important step in Cicero's ability to understand Rome as a world empire and its citizens as citizens of a global world. It sheds suggestive light on how, over the next two centuries leading up to the granting of universal citizenship, individual identifications with an extraordinarily large territory, the 'Roman empire', might have operated. Seeing Greek culture as the property of Romanness has the effect of making Greekness properly Roman, and making Romanness something to be viewed as available first to the educated or the wealthy, and then ultimately thinkable as a universal (if by then watered-down) state of being. Read in the light of the *Pro Archia*, Cicero's *De finibus* discloses the affective identifications that are the basis of a cultural form of citizenship.

If Cicero's investment in the Greek fanon allows him to begin to articulate a new mode of citizenship, I want to emphasise that it holds for us as readers both the stimulating promise of how to envision transnational cultural community through common tastes and practice – a promise self-identifying queer communities have explored in recent years – and clear warnings about the entitlement members of dominant groups feel to reimagine themselves and about the violence that enables and accompanies acts of imperial appropriation. Cicero's image of Greece as safe haven and source of both intellectual pleasure and transcendent affective affiliations pulls Athens' political teeth, transforming *polis* citizenship into a looser concept of cultural citizenship, theoretically accessible to all but practically open only to those with the proper (pure) education. Cicero's writing augments the Greeks' own canon, which invites others to join in celebrating the universal appeal of Attic language and culture, but it reorients its original themes toward Roman interests.

The appeal of the fantasy of transcendence is surely part of the appeal of the fandom represented by Greek and Roman studies as the field has evolved over the past six hundred years. To master Greek and Latin is to become a citizen of another state, putatively linked to other citizens by taste and knowledge, an identification that obscures the markers of class and gender and race that gatekeep access to knowledge. This is a fantasy worthy of further exploration.

Fifteen years ago, in his celebrated book *The Ethics of Identity*, the philosopher Kwame Anthony Appiah worried that the term 'identity' ignores a crucial distinction between external and internal identifications – that is, whether one actively self-identifies as a member of a group or is identified by another as a member of a group.[29] Considering both cases, Appiah probes the 'disconcerting ease' with which positive signs of identity can become negative limitations. To be black or to speak good Yiddish is to manifest external signs of internal identifications with groups that may signify a bid for individual dignity or an effort to gain access to some social in-group; but blackness and Yiddishness are also categories that function as instruments of subordination or constraints upon autonomy. Some identities, of course, become identifiable as such only in tandem with the establishment of classificatory systems for social policing; but even when they are treated as handicaps that may be 'remedied' by antidiscrimination laws or other measures, some members of the identity group may not welcome this mandated form of recognition. As the political theorist Patchen Markell brilliantly argues, being identified as a member of a certain group can enable acts of recognition that are empowering or liberating, but it can as easily enable recognitions that lead to violence or a sense of entrapment on the part of the identified – even if the identifier's intention is celebration, congratulation or welcome.[30] To find a way forward from this dilemma, Appiah turns to the ill-defined arenas of personal taste and imagination. He sees these as keys to ways of being and being seen in the world – ways that are responsive to others' views and judgements but that also allow for some individual sense of self-creation.

With this reading of Cicero's *De finibus*, I have argued that the Roman investment in Hellenistic learning makes possible an experiment in political imagination that anticipates Appiah's turn. The dialogue illuminates the political psychology behind and before the Roman Hellenistic investment in Athenian texts and the legal fact of thinking a 'universal' way of belonging in if not to the Roman empire. Roman imaginings of Athens, Roman desires for Athens, open up a way of belonging in the Greek-Roman empire that, precisely because it never deceives itself as being free from the violent reality of imperial conquest, represents an experiment in imagination worth understanding today.

---

[29] Appiah 2005: esp. 111–13.   [30] Markell 2003: 36.

CHAPTER 8

Philosophical Self-Definition in Strabo's Geography

Myrto Hatzimichali

Greek Philosophers in a Roman World

Strabo's *Geography* is one of the monumental texts that display the characteristic traits of late Hellenistic literary production, from classicism to intense preoccupation with the role of Rome as the new centre of political and cultural power, and cross-fertilisation between different genres within one text. One way in which Strabo negotiates these themes is through his self-definition, which is complex and indirect in two different ways that will form the main focus of this chapter. On the one hand, Strabo seeks to inscribe himself in a tradition of Greek intellectuals, referenced through subtle chronological indications and located geographically mainly in Asia Minor. On the other hand, Strabo has a programmatic interest in associating his project with philosophy, and his particular take on certain philosophical themes is another important defining feature that will be explored in this chapter, after some remarks on the broader picture of late Hellenistic philosophy.

Our period was a time of critical transformations in the field of philosophy; they were driven to a large extent by historical circumstances, in the aftermath of Sulla's violent siege of Athens in 89 BCE that spelled the end for the traditional Hellenistic schools of the Stoa, the Epicurean Garden, the Peripatos and the Academy as organised institutions. The distinct identity of each school had been hitherto marked by a recognised line of succession of leaders or scholarchs, by the location of each school at specific premises within the city of Athens or just outside the walls, and, finally, by the acceptance of a set of doctrines (or lack thereof in the case of the Academic sceptics) that were defended in frequent cross-school polemics. This picture started to disintegrate in the early first century BCE, with lines of succession broken and philosophers abandoning Athens for destinations such as Rome, Alexandria or Rhodes.[1] Most

---

[1] For this 'decentralisation' see Sedley 2003, with further references.

crucially, the 'purity' of doctrinal systems was challenged, with Stoics becoming 'lovers' of Plato and Aristotle, and Academics claiming that the Stoics were right about certain things, or that Plato, Aristotle and the Stoics were saying the same things all along.[2] In the later imperial period these renegotiated philosophical identities were crystallised once more, as we can see from the establishment of the four chairs at Athens by Marcus Aurelius,[3] while the ancient authorities of Plato and Aristotle never again receded from the forefront of Greek philosophy.

In the first century BCE, however, as a result of the dispersal of philosophers to different cultural centres, philosophical activity could no longer consist in public performance in the form of lectures or debates, but concentrated increasingly on texts and the recovery of authoritative opinions attributable to 'the ancients'. This transition from a 'civic' to a literary 'cosmopolitan' way of doing philosophy[4] coincided with the phenomenon of classicism that was shared across different genres in the late Hellenistic period: as Michael Frede pointed out, this attitude can be traced back to the Stoics Panaetius and Posidonius (late second/ early first century BCE), and is therefore not solely the outcome of the violent disruption at Athens.[5] What was significant with Panaetius and Posidonius was their renewed interest in the 'classics', Plato and Aristotle, who were now treated as authorities: according to Panaetius, Plato was 'the divine, the wisest, the most venerable, the Homer of philosophers' (Cic. *Tusc.* 1.79). The canon of authoritative ancients also included Pythagoras and his early followers, but here the recovery of ancient wisdom from written texts had to take an alternative route: given the lack of surviving texts, the late Hellenistic period saw the production of a substantial corpus of pseudepigrapha aimed at supplying the missing material.[6]

These classicist tendencies in philosophy were accompanied by a disapproving attitude towards the intervening Hellenistic period, comparable to the picture of rhetoric that emerges from the pages of Dionysius of Halicarnassus.[7] In Dionysius' case, the main 'battleground' was the literary and stylistic imitation of fifth- and fourth-century Athenian orators, which in turn implied a return to moral and political values thought to have been abandoned during the decline of the Hellenistic period.[8] Even Dionysius

---

[2] The main representative of these Academic tendencies was Antiochus of Ascalon: see Sedley 2012.
[3] There were publicly funded chairs for each of the Platonic, Peripatetic, Stoic and Epicurean sects: see Luc. *Eun.* 3; Philostr. *VS* 2.2 566.
[4] See Gray in this volume for the distinction.   [5] Frede 1999: 783–7.
[6] On these texts see Centrone 2014.   [7] See the introduction to this volume, pp. 24–6.
[8] Wiater 2011: esp. 65–77; Hidber 1996: 50; de Jonge 2008: 13–14.

in a few cases extends his classicising outlook to include philosophy, by showing respect towards the authorities of Plato and Aristotle, in contrast to his disparaging treatment of Chrysippus and his purported contributions to the theory of literary composition (*Comp.* 4.16–20). The authority of Aristotle's text is deployed against the unhistorical claims of a later Peripatetic (*Amm.* 1.6), while Plato is admired because he is a great man, despite some deficiencies in his style (*Dem.* 6). This privileging of older authorities over their Hellenistic epigones is especially evident in the pages of Strabo's *Geography*, where an explicit connection is drawn between the decline of the Hellenistic Peripatos and the lack of engagement with Aristotle's original texts, which he ascribes to actual loss and unavailability:[9]

> It was the case that the old Peripatetics who came after Theophrastus, not having access to the books at all, apart from a few mainly exoteric ones, were not able to produce any real philosophy, but were declaiming commonplaces (μηδὲν ἔχειν φιλοσοφεῖν πραγματικῶς, ἀλλὰ θέσεις ληκυθίζειν). The later Peripatetics, however, after these books came to light, philosophised better and were closer to Aristotle's tradition (ἄμεινον μὲν ἐκείνων φιλοσοφεῖν καὶ ἀριστοτελίζειν), but were forced to speak mainly in probabilities because of the large number of errors. (Str. 13.1.54)

Even if we do not accept the whole story at face value (in the preceding lines Strabo has spoken about Aristotle's books lying in a ditch in Asia Minor for two centuries until they were sold to the disreputable bibliophile Apellicon of Teos), it is hard to deny its significance for late Hellenistic perceptions about the 'right' way to philosophise, namely through proper attention to the master's words.[10]

Strabo was in fact close to several individuals who must have been among those who tried to put this into practice but, as Strabo claims, faced difficulties due to problems with the text. He studied with the grammarian Tyrannio (12.3.16), who had some involvement in the restoration of the Aristotelian manuscripts, as well as with the Peripatetics Xenarchus of Seleuceia (14.5.4) and Boethus of Sidon (16.2.24).[11]

---

[9] Strabo is similarly dismissive of Hellenistic achievements in his description of India, where he favours Megasthenes over later (and arguably better informed) sources, cf. Str. 15.1.72 and Dihle 2011: 51–2.
[10] An illuminating discussion of the transition of Peripatetic philosophical practice from public performance and debate to textual commentary may be found in Hahm 2007: esp. 88–101. On Strabo's account see also Barnes 1997 and Hatzimichali 2013.
[11] The wording of his reference to Boethus ('we studied Aristotelian philosophy together') does not make it clear whether he was a pupil or a fellow student of the Sidonian. He also knew of Aristo of

These references to his teachers form part of a large cluster of passages that, as scholars have shown, play a very important part in Strabo's self-representation. In comparison to the strong autobiographical flavour that pervades many texts of the high empire,[12] including scientific ones, Strabo's self-representation offers on the whole rather slim pickings. Given the marked absence of the first person from most of the *Geography* (and crucially from its opening, as we shall see below), particular attention is drawn to those limited occasions where it does make an appearance: Katherine Clarke noted the use of the temporal expression 'in our time' (καθ' ἡμᾶς) in a range of references to Greek intellectuals that go well beyond Strabo's plausible lifespan. She concluded that such references were less about indicating a set of dates and much more about inserting Strabo into a particular intellectual sphere, one dominated by 'notable men' hailing from his native Asia Minor.[13]

This is why these references also have a strong geographical focus:[14] in the entire *Geography*, of the sixty-six cities whose description is accompanied by lists of intellectuals born there, fifty-two are in Asia Minor, compared to only seven in mainland Greece and the Cyclades, while the three cultural centres that would spring most readily to mind in terms of the late Hellenistic and early Roman period, namely Athens, Alexandria and Rome, are not accompanied by such a list at all![15] Strabo's references to prominent intellectuals thus create a privileged space of intellectual excellence centred on Asia Minor. It is significant that the focus is not on Athens, as we would expect, perhaps, from more straightforwardly classicising accounts that place their emphasis on the fifth and fourth centuries BCE.[16] On the other hand, the absence of a list of notables from Alexandria is consistent with the sidestepping of the achievements of the early Hellenistic period.[17] Interestingly, Rome comes to occupy a much

---

Alexandria, who is named among the early commentators on Aristotle's *Categories* alongside Boethus.

[12] See König 2011.   [13] Clarke 1997: 108; see also Clarke 1999: 289–92.

[14] This 'spatial definition' of Strabo's authorial role, noted by Clarke 1997: 108, is further supported by the parallel (and even more frequent) use of καθ' ἡμᾶς to demarcate Strabo's world as the part of the earth centred around the Mediterranean (there are numerous references to ἡ καθ' ἡμᾶς θάλαττα, 'our sea': e.g., 3.4.1; even ἡ καθ' ἡμᾶς οἰκουμένη γῆ, 'our side of the inhabited world': 2.5.18).

[15] See Dueck 2000: 79–80 for a list of all the cities that are accompanied by catalogues of their 'famous men', and the discussion in Engels 2005.

[16] The 'marginality' of Athens in Late Hellenistic authors, compared with the trends of the Second Sophistic, is noted by Schmitz and Wiater 2011b: 35–7.

[17] On these geographical imbalances and a more detailed discussion of the lists of famous men, see Engels 2005.

more significant position on the cultural map once we move past the static picture created by the lists of famous names to consider what Strabo has to say about the more dynamic question of the careers and professional activities of these individuals. Thus, we find Strabo making frequent reference to teacher–pupil relationships that were at the centre of connections of patronage between Greek 'wise advisers' and powerful Romans.[18] The Greek teachers in question are often, but not exclusively, philosophers, as we can see from the following examples:

> [Illustrious natives of Nysa include] Sostratus, the brother of Aristodemus, as well as another Aristodemus, his cousin, who tutored Pompey the Great, [who] were all distinguished grammarians. (14.1.48)

> Xenarchus, on the other hand, who was my teacher, did not spend much time in his homeland [Seleuceia], but [stayed] in Alexandria and Athens and lately in Rome, having chosen the life of a teacher. Having enjoyed the friendship both of Arius and later of Caesar Augustus, he was held in honour until his old age. (14.5.4)

> [Illustrious natives of Tarsus include] two men called Athenodorus (Ἀθηνόδωροι δύο), of whom the one that was called Cordylion lived with Marcus Cato and died at his house; the other one, the son of Sandon, whom they call Cananites after some village, was Caesar's teacher and gained great honour[19] ... my contemporary Nestor (Νέστωρ ὁ καθ' ἡμᾶς) was an Academic, the one who taught Marcellus the son of Octavia, Caesar's sister. He too was head of government having succeeded Athenodorus and he continued to be honoured both by the leading men and in the city. (14.5.14)[20]

This preoccupation with Rome's power, and with its implications for Greek intellectuals as educators par excellence remained a central feature in Greek literary production for many centuries.[21] However, compared to the very personal and individual relationships of patronage described

---

[18] Cf. Ael. *VH* 12.25: 'Lucullus derived some advantage from Antiochus of Ascalon, Maecenas from Arius, Cicero from Apollonius and Augustus from Athenodorus', and Rawson 1989.
[19] Strabo adds here a fair amount of detail about how Athenodorus saved the city of Tarsus from the depredations of a certain Boethus (a 'bad poet and bad citizen') who had been Antony's favourite.
[20] Cf. also 13.4.3 on Apollodorus of Pergamum, who taught Augustus rhetoric. There are also several references to Greek intellectuals becoming 'friends' and receiving honours from Roman notables, e.g., 13.2.3 on Theophanes of Mytilene and Pompey; 14.2.15 on Theopompus of Cnidus and Caesar. See also Rawson 1985: 66–99; Dueck 2000: 130–44; Hidber 2011. For more analysis of the dynamics operating in relationships of patronage between Greek poets and prominent Romans see Whitmarsh 2011.
[21] See the introduction to this volume, pp. 13–14.

above, in the later imperial period the dialogue between Greek philosophy and Roman power was played out at a higher, more centralised level. As a result, texts from that period speak both of resistance against imperial power by philosophers and subsequent persecution at the hands of the emperor, but also of emperors who chose a more 'Hellenised' self-representation and turned to Greek teachers, especially since Trajan.[22] While such connections enhance the image of the Greeks as teachers and mentors of the Romans, they also point very clearly to the undisputed position of Rome as the ultimate centre to which the flow of intellectual capital is directed.[23] In Strabo's text, the movement of intellectual capital does not concern only personnel: even Aristotle's books allegedly remained for a long time in Asia Minor, but eventually they too ended up in Rome, giving rise to both scholarly and commercial activity:

> Rome played an important part in all this; immediately after the death of Apellicon, Sulla, who conquered Athens, took Apellicon's library. When it came here Tyrannion the grammarian, being an admirer of Aristotle's, handled the books from his position in the service of the librarian (διεχειρίσατο φιλαριστοτέλης ὤν, θεραπεύσας τὸν ἐπὶ τῆς βιβλιοθήκης),[24] (as did) some booksellers who used bad scribes and did not collate the texts – the sort of thing that happens also with other books that are copied for selling, both here and in Alexandria. (13.1.54)[25]

A remarkable passage on the city of Tarsus (14.5.13) offers a very illuminating picture of cultural dynamics and migration patterns, in a sustained comparison with practices elsewhere: we learn that philosophical and other education (ἐγκύκλιος παιδεία) in Tarsus has surpassed Athens and Alexandria, but does not attract any foreigners, only natives. Even the natives tend to leave Tarsus for further study and careers abroad. Many other cities attract foreigners for educational purposes, but their natives are not interested in learning. Finally, Strabo claims, the Alexandrians both receive foreigners and send many of their own citizens abroad. This passage on Tarsus brings to the fore many of the parameters outlined above: Strabo's preferential treatment of Asia Minor (involving a likely

---

[22] Whitmarsh 2001a: 133–80 concentrates on the figures of Musonius Rufus and Dio Chrysostom, who fell foul of Nero and Domitian respectively, but used even their exile as a means of constructing identity. Dio's *Kingship* orations, on the other hand, return to the theme of the philosophic adviser/ educator, while Marcus Aurelius represents a unique union between Greek philosophy and imperial power.

[23] For a developed account of Rome as Strabo's ultimate centre see Clarke 1999: 210–28.

[24] Translators often detect a pejorative tone here and translate along the following lines: 'Tyrannio got his hands on the books having buttered up/cultivated the librarian.'

[25] Also discussed by Connolly in this volume, p. 218.

exaggeration about the superiority of the philosophical schools at Tarsus); his parallel admission that local talent cannot flourish fully without making the most of foreign, more developed cultural centres; the idea that these greater centres both benefit and are benefitted by the immigrants from cities like Tarsus. Rome is not mentioned explicitly as one of the destinations, but it is made clear enough from the careers of men like the two Athenodoruses (quoted above) and by Strabo's remark a few lines later: 'above all Rome can demonstrate the number of men of letters coming from this city; for it is full of Tarsians and Alexandrians' (14.5.15).[26]

It appears, therefore, that Strabo's response to the pressing question concerning the place of Greek intellectuals in a Roman world involves stressing the superior credentials of the Greeks, but also linking their attainments to Roman support and patronage. This would place Strabo (as well as Dionysius of Halicarnassus, who opts for a similar approach) firmly in the tradition of negotiating Greek identity in terms of intellectual excellence. Strabo is closer to later imperial authors in advertising proudly his local connections to Asia Minor,[27] which is portrayed as the cradle of excellence, in stark contrast to Dionysius' condemnation of the same geographical area as the source of corruption and intellectual decline (*Orat. Vett.* 1–2).[28] He equally inserts himself among the beneficiaries of the knowledge that was flowing into the imperial capital in another set of autobiographical remarks, where we learn about his sojourn at Rome and the activities he undertook under Roman patronage, such as his travels in Egypt with his friend Aelius, the provincial governor.[29]

Philosophy as a Programmatic Claim

In order to explore more fully how Strabo positions himself and his work within the rich Augustan-Tiberian intellectual scene, we need to go beyond his general assessment of Greek intellectuals and their contribution, and turn to examine in detail his programmatic statements concerning his project. It is significant that the traces of self-identification that we noted thus far scattered in the body of the *Geography* are missing from its

---

[26] Gray in this volume discusses Strabo's account of Tarsus from a very important political perspective.
[27] For the importance of local connections (as opposed to a 'monolithic' Hellenism), sometimes with a prominent role reserved for Asia Minor, see Jones 2004, discussing Aelius Aristides (Oration 23) and Pausanias, and Bowersock 2004, discussing Artemidorus (the author of the *Oneirocritica*).
[28] See Wiater 2011: 60–5; de Jonge 2008: 9–12. Asia as a source of decadence and corruption from luxurious pleasures was almost a cliché among Roman authors, cf. Cic. *Mur.* 11–12; Sall. *Cat.* 13.
[29] Dueck 2000: 85–96.

opening. Katherine Clarke has drawn particular attention to the fact that there is no self-introductory prologue giving the author's name and city of origin, as we famously find in Herodotus and Thucydides.[30] Among Strabo's contemporaries, Dionysius of Halicarnassus in his *Roman Antiquities* expresses a reluctance to engage in 'the customary accounts' reserved for proems (*Ant. Rom.* 1.1.1), but does maintain a very strong first-person presence throughout his introduction, which seeks to establish the value of studying Rome as the greatest global empire, not least because of its Greek origins (1.2.1; 1.3.3; 1.5.1). He reserves his formal introduction for the end of his proem: 'I, the author of this history, am Dionysius of Halicarnassus, the son of Alexander' (1.8.4). Conversely, Polybius expressed himself strongly against the intrusion of personal references, but his was a special case arising from his participation in some of the events he described (Polyb. 36.12).

What is especially interesting in Strabo's case is that the opening of his work amounts to a programmatic description and definition of his geographical project in terms of philosophy. Instead of introducing himself, Strabo introduces geography itself,[31] and proceeds to offer arguments which in his view will make obvious the reasons why geography should be treated as part of the philosopher's business: 'I believe that the study of geography, which I now propose to investigate, is part of the philosopher's concerns (τῆς τοῦ φιλοσόφου πραγματείας) as much as any other [study]. The fact that my belief is not false is obvious from many considerations' (1.1.1). This dialogue with philosophy is present also in the proem of Diodorus' *Library of History*, who similarly omits to introduce himself by name, although he refers to Agyrium in Sicily as his place of origin (1.4.4): the main purpose of Diodorus' proem is to establish the utility of history, especially from a moral perspective.[32] History promotes virtue and uncovers vice, which makes it a primary cause of human flourishing/happiness (*eudaimonia*), and can thus claim a place as 'the prophetess of truth, she who is, as it were, the mother-city of philosophy as a whole' (τὴν προφῆτιν τῆς ἀληθείας ἱστορίαν, τῆς ὅλης φιλοσοφίας οἱονεὶ μητρόπολιν

---

[30] Clarke 1997: 94–5.
[31] See Clarke 1997: 96. Her main parallel for this tactic is the Byzantine historian Theophylact Simocatta, who began with a dialogue between Philosophy and History, both personified. See also French 1994: 123–5 for how Strabo 'constructs' the subject of geography.
[32] For an analysis of Diodorus' moral didacticism see now Hau 2016: 73–123. Hau shows how moralising is linked to ambitions for the improvement of readers' characters and actions, especially in the programmatic passages, and she also provides a sustained examination of Diodorus' use of ethical ideas on the individual virtues and vices.

οὖσαν), fostering piety, justice and nobility of character (καλοκἀγαθία, 1.2.1–3). In this context, philosophy amounts to the human knowledge that guides us to the happy life through virtuous activity.

While Diodorus envisages history as the ultimate source of (and therefore prior/ superior to) philosophy as a whole,[33] the picture in Strabo is more complex. In stating that geography belongs in the philosopher's concerns, Strabo leaves the hierarchical question open, while creating further question marks over the identity of the philosopher: what sort of attainments and range of expertise does he envisage for this ideal intellectual? Before tackling these questions through a more detailed examination of Strabo's text, some further elucidation of the practice of enhancing one's own discipline by appeal to philosophy can be found in the comparable strategies employed by other scientists.

First of all, there is a eulogy of the science of geography, which may or may not be the proem to the second book of the *Geographoumena* by Artemidorus of Ephesus (late second/ early first century BCE), partly preserved on a papyrus which has been dated to the early first century CE.[34] This builds an analogy between the geographer and the philosopher, casting philosophy as intellectual geography with the philosopher 'spreading his soul' across all cognitive territory in the same way as the geographer surveys the earth.[35] The author insists on geography's affinity (παραπλήσιον) with 'most divine philosophy' (Col. 1, 13–15), a move that is more radical than Strabo's approach, which seeks to present geography as a philosophical concern, presumably one of many, and not as a separate field of analogous intellectual standing.[36]

An alternative tactic is to treat philosophy as the necessary intellectual background to one's own science. Vitruvius, for instance, asserts that the best architect will have devoted substantial study to philosophy (*philosophos diligenter audierit*, 1.1.3). Like Diodorus, he locates philosophy's remit mainly in the preservation of good character, and he also treats it as the stepping stone for getting acquainted with subjects like physiology, mathematics, medicine, astronomy, all of which are important to the *artifex*

---

[33] See Kidd 1989: 40–1 on how this creates a significant contrast with Posidonius.
[34] On the philosophical aspects of this text see Sedley 2009.
[35] Sedley 2009: 36. Sedley goes on to argue that the author's attitude and arguments stem from an authentic commitment to the Academic tradition.
[36] On the differences between Artemidorus and Strabo in terms of their approach to philosophy see also Engels 2012: 145–6.

(1.1.7–10).³⁷ A couple of centuries later, Galen will insist again on philosophical credentials, this time for the doctor who aspires to be a true heir of Hippocrates, most notably in his work entitled *The Best Doctor Is Also a Philosopher*. For Galen, close acquaintance with all three fields of philosophy is necessary:³⁸ logic, because medicine requires the ability to construct classifications and demonstrations (*Med.Phil.* 1, 59–60 K); physics, because the doctor needs a certain degree of familiarity with astronomy, geometry, theory of elements and their mixtures, 53 and 60 K); and ethics, because the doctor must have a developed sense of virtues such as self-control/temperance (σωφροσύνη) and justice, and not be motivated by money (60–1 K).

In order to gain an understanding of philosophy's role in Strabo's own disciplinary self-definition, we must take a closer look at the arguments he gives in support of the notion that geography forms part of the philosopher's interests. The first one is an appeal to tradition that amounts to an invention of a history for the discipline of geography:³⁹

> The fact that my belief [that geography is a philosophical enterprise] is not false is obvious from many considerations. For those who first ventured to touch upon this subject were philosophers of a kind (οἵ τε γὰρ πρῶτοι θαρρήσαντες αὐτῆς ἅψασθαι τοιοῦτοί τινες ὑπῆρξαν), namely Homer and Anaximander of Miletus and Hecataeus his fellow-citizen, as Eratosthenes also points out; also Democritus, Eudoxus, Dicaearchus and many others, and moreover those who came after them, Eratosthenes and Polybius and Posidonius, all of whom were philosophers (ἄνδρες φιλόσοφοι). (1.1.1)

Strabo divides his predecessors into three groups: the ancient pioneers (Homer, Anaximander and Hecataeus) were already highlighted by Eratosthenes as geography's earliest exponents.⁴⁰ The presence of Homer at the top of the list is striking but hardly surprising: for Strabo, this association provides venerable pedigree and a direct link to the very fountain of Greek culture and wisdom. In fact, Strabo's further elaboration⁴¹ of his argument from tradition consists almost entirely of a lengthy

---

³⁷ See Most 2011: 174–5, who reasonably questions the relevance of much of this material for the architect.
³⁸ It should be noted that Galen meant this quite literally and had thorough philosophical training himself, to the extent that on one occasion he had to persuade his patient that he really was a doctor and not a philosopher dabbling in medicine (*On Prognosis* XIV, 608 K, cf. 603–5).
³⁹ French 1994: 124.
⁴⁰ See Prontera 1984. Eratosthenes is cited again for information on Anaximander and Hecataeus at 1.1.11, where he characterises them as 'notable men and familiar with philosophy' (ἀξιόλογοι καὶ οἰκεῖοι φιλοσοφίας).
⁴¹ At 1.1.2 he announces: 'but let us go back and consider each of the points made in greater detail'.

vindication of Homer's geographical expertise in order to justify his inclusion as the founder of geography (1.1.2–10).[42] In that section there is no justification for the names included in the second and third groups, but references in the rest of the *Geography*, and especially in the introductory/ methodological Books 1 and 2 offer clear support for the impression given by the list, namely that Strabo considers the last three authors (Eratosthenes, Polybius and Posidonius) as his immediate and most respected forerunners.

The second point in support of the idea that geography is a philosophical pursuit is based on the skills involved and the means of achieving excellence in both subjects: 'Moreover, wide learning (πολυμάθεια), through which alone it is possible to undertake this work successfully, is the characteristic of no one other than the man who surveys the divine and the human (τοῦ τὰ θεῖα καὶ τὰ ἀνθρώπεια ἐπιβλέποντος); and philosophy, as they say, is the knowledge of these very things' (1.1.1). For Strabo this reference to 'surveying all things divine and human' may be a Stoic echo,[43] but it can also be linked to claims made about the value of universal knowledge by authors of large-scale works from the Hellenistic period.[44] Here geography and philosophy are linked in virtue of the fact that they both involve an active interest in all things divine and human. This, in turn, characterises the possessor of 'wide learning', which is presented as a prerequisite for a successful engagement with geography. The appeal to this educational standard is highly reminiscent of the value placed on *paideia* in a broad range of texts that are preoccupied with the position and identity of Greek subjects in a world that is dominated politically by Rome, most notably from the Second Sophistic. Strabo's insistence on *polymatheia* as a prerequisite for the geographer could lead him to prejudicial rejections of sources that he deemed lacking in this respect, such as the explorer Pytheas of Massilia, who had only empirical observations to offer (1.4.3, 2.5.8). Pytheas spoke of temperate climate conditions in Britain and human habitation in Iceland, which Strabo treated as entirely unbelievable just because they contradicted the learned scientific consensus according to which the same climate must prevail in the same latitude from east to west.[45] Strabo does not offer any further

---

[42] Kim 2007 shows how this vindication is centred on the implicit claim that Homer embodies the ideals of ὠφέλεια (benefit) and πολυμάθεια (wide learning), highlighted in Strabo's second and third arguments. See also Lightfoot 2017.
[43] See below, p. 244.   [44] Cf. Diod. Sic. 1.4.6; Polyb. 1.4.6–11; 5.33.1–8.
[45] Strabo and his sources were of course unaware of the effects of the Gulf Stream. See Roseman 2005: 34–5.

reasons for rejecting Pytheas,[46] but opts for a dismissive tone that draws an unfavourable comparison with his other sources ('but in the other writers I have found no such thing', 2.5.8), and contrasts his 'conjurer's fabrications' with the failings of Posidonius that are all the more serious because he was a 'philosopher and fond of demonstration' (2.3.5).[47]

When Strabo comes to elaborate on the contents of the 'wide learning' required for geography at 1.1.12–15, he appears to have in mind a quite specific body of knowledge, which Pytheas lacked, primarily astronomical and geometrical facts that inform the geographer's calculations of longitudes and latitudes. This is not the whole story, of course, since geography 'unites terrestrial and celestial matters' (1.1.15) in its concern with the earth and its inhabited part (*oikoumene*) in particular. This transition towards the geographer's more detailed knowledge of the *oikoumene* from 1.1.16 onwards (animals and plants, land and sea, knowledge gained through travels) picks up on claims made in the final point of Strabo's opening argument, which focuses on utility in a way that is reminiscent of Diodorus' claims about the philosophical utility of history:

> At the same time, the benefit which is manifold (ὠφέλεια ποικίλη τις οὖσα) and concerns, on the one hand, politics and the activities of commanders and, on the other, knowledge about the heavens and about animals, plants and fruits found in land and sea, and about other things which can be seen in each place, is indicative of the same sort of man, the one who cares about the art of living (περὶ τὸν βίον τέχνη) and happiness. (1.1.1)

Strabo's claim is that the same twofold benefit arises from both geography and philosophy, and it is both practical/political and theoretical. Geography's practical benefit is obvious in hunts and military expeditions, representing small-scale and large-scale examples respectively (1.1.17), but Strabo also makes a less well-defined attempt to place geography alongside political philosophy on the grounds that they are equally beneficial to rulers and men of affairs.[48] This theme of utility is prominent in Polybius, too, although he does not try to draw the philosophical connection.[49] The more Strabo develops his point on utility, the more he reveals a tension

---

[46] He does cite, however, Polybius' doubts as to whether a private man of limited means could have travelled as far as Britain and beyond (Str. 2.4.1).
[47] See also Engels 2007: 550.
[48] Gray in this volume emphasises this aspect of utility, and argues for a strongly pragmatic and power-oriented practical focus on Strabo's part.
[49] See Polyb. 7.11.2; 9.1 with Wiater 2016: 251. In this regard, the *Geography* serves similar purposes and is addressed to the same audience (prominent men) as Strabo's historical work (Ἱστορικὰ ὑπομνήματα, 1.1.23), which was a continuation of Polybius.

between the theoretical and practical concerns of his discipline, whereby what is useful for the statesman/ reader does not always coincide with what is of interest to the philosopher:

> But there are certain things that he [*sc.* the geographer] should not concern himself with at all, unless for the sake of philosophical contemplation (θέας φιλοσόφου χάριν); and others that he should accept on trust, even if he does not see the cause (τὸ διὰ τί). For this [*sc.* the cause] is a matter for the philosopher (φιλοσοφῶν), whereas the statesman (πολιτικός) does not have enough free time for this sort of thing, or not always. (1.1.21; cf. 1.1.4, 2.5.34)

This analysis of the programmatic claims from Strabo's proem has brought to the fore the three key aspects he sought to emphasise in his disciplinary self-definition: (i) the link to Greece's past, which is shown to go all the way back to Homer; (ii) the emphasis on wisdom and 'wide learning', which was an important pathway towards enhancing the status of a Greek subject under Roman rule; (iii) the political dimension, evident in the claims about the discipline's usefulness for rulers and men of affairs. All three aspects are united by means of the recurring appeals to philosophy, in a manner that offers a partial reflection of some of the philosophical developments that we noted at the outset, such as the idealisation of the past and the teaching/ advisory role of the Greek philosopher vis-à-vis the Roman aristocracy. At the same time, Strabo's philosophical self-definition, like that of Diodorus and Vitruvius, is subject to the challenge issued by Glenn Most, to the effect that it is all rhetorical posturing, and lacks any substance that could come from a serious engagement with actual philosophical concepts and doctrines emanating from the main Greek schools. For Most, introductions such as Strabo's were aimed at luring general readers who would be impressed by the reflected veneer of seriousness and importance associated with philosophy, particularly since they would not be able to distinguish it from 'real' philosophy.[50] In response to Most, it is first of all necessary to acknowledge that Strabo and like-minded authors were indeed operating with a more 'diluted' sense of what qualifies as philosophy, not restricting it to the well-documented intellectual achievements of the major Greek schools. The fact that Strabo uses the term 'philosophy' for the moral precepts of the Druids in Gaul (4.4.4), the astronomy practised by Chaldeans and Egyptian priests (16.1.6; 17.1.3; 17.1.46) and the wisdom of the Brahmans in India (15.1.59; 15.1.70)

---

[50] Most 2011: esp. 165–6. He uses the term 'pseudo-philosophization' for this tactic.

indicates that he did not consider it an essentially *Greek* pursuit either.[51] This places Strabo at odds with attempts made by authors of the later imperial period to assert the Greek provenance and 'ownership' of philosophy, such as Diogenes Laertius, who opens his *Lives of the Philosophers* with a refutation of the view that 'the business of philosophy began with the barbarians' (Diog. Laert. 1.1). The barbarians in question are reminiscent of Strabo: Persian magi, Babylonian Chaldeans, Indian gymnosophists and Druids among the Gauls and Celts.[52]

Despite these qualifications that must be placed upon Strabo's references to 'philosophy', it remains pertinent to examine whether there are any traces of genuine commitment to philosophical ideas underpinning Strabo's programmatic claims, as well as the rest of the *Geography*.

Strabo's Philosophy and Stoicism

As we attempt to trace 'real' philosophical influences in Strabo's work,[53] it is important to draw attention to another aspect of his self-definition, namely that he explicitly identifies himself as a Stoic.[54] This consists of two references to 'my people' or 'our people' (οἱ ἡμέτεροι) meaning the Stoics (1.2.3; 2.3.8), and two more to Zeno, the founder of the Stoic school, as 'my Zeno' or 'our Zeno' (Ζήνων ὁ ἡμέτερος, 1.2.34; 16.4.27). It is therefore legitimate to look for traces of Stoic doctrine in the *Geography*, starting from the programmatic statements themselves. It quickly becomes apparent that the statements quoted above contain echoes of well-known Stoic ideas that are found in the doxographical tradition. For instance, 'surveying the divine and the human'[55] is in fact the goal of philosophy according to the Stoics:[56]

> The Stoics said that wisdom is scientific knowledge of the divine and the human, and that philosophy is the practice of a fitting expertise (ἄσκησιν ἐπιτηδείου τέχνης).[57] Virtue singly and at its highest is what is fitting, and virtues, at their most generic, are three – the physical one, the ethical one, and the logical one. (Aët. 1, Pr. 2 = SVF II 35, from [Plut.], *Placita*)[58]

[51] See also French 1994: 126–30. [52] See Warren 2007: 140–4.
[53] On what follows see also Hatzimichali 2017 and Laurent 2008, who offers a more detailed survey of prominent Stoic views, showing that most of them are absent from Strabo's work.
[54] This is picked up by the lexicographer Stephanus of Byzantium, who refers to 'Strabo the Stoic philosopher' (not the geographer) in his entry on Strabo's home town of Amaseia (α 261 Billerbeck).
[55] See above, p. 241.
[56] Note that for Strabo the distinction between wisdom and its pursuit has been elided.
[57] For an alternative construal of the Greek as shorthand for περὶ τοῦ ἐπιτηδείου τέχνη, giving the translation 'expertise in utility' see Long and Sedley 1987: Vol. 2, 163 (on text 26A).
[58] Compare Cic. *Off.* 1.153; 2.5; *Tusc.* 4.57; Sen. *Ep.* 89.5.

Strabo was also familiar with the treatment of the three branches of philosophy (physics, ethics, logic) as the three 'most generic' virtues, even though at 1.1.12–15 he gives a distinctly geographical flavour to the 'divine and the human', equating it with celestial and terrestrial observations and measurements rather than with physics and ethics respectively. At 2.5.2 he makes a point about the sequence of sciences, whereby the geographer relies on the results of the geometers, who rely on astronomers, and they in turn on the physicists. Physics, however, does not rely on any other science and in that sense it is a 'virtue': 'physics is a sort of virtue; and they say[59] that virtues do not operate with hypotheses (ἀνυποθέτους) but depend upon themselves, having their principles within themselves, as well as the proofs thereof' (2.5.2).[60] It is also worth noting that the interdependence of sciences presented here by Strabo resembles the views expressed by Posidonius, who was the most prominent Stoic of the first century BCE (Fr. 18 and Fr. 90 Edelstein-Kidd) and one of Strabo's main sources. Posidonius was mainly arguing for the priority of physics over mathematics and astronomy; he also emphasised the fact that physics does not rely on hypotheses and has a self-sufficient set of principles. Strabo was thus able to build on this hierarchical scale and forge a place for geography within the scheme, one step after geometry.

The reference to the 'art of living' (περὶ τὸν βίον τέχνη)[61] is another Stoic echo that has many parallels in the polemics of Sextus Empiricus against the Stoics (e.g., *Math.* 11.170; cf. *Pyr.* 3.239–41). The expression also occurs in the Stoic section of the doxography ascribed to (Arius) Didymus,[62] as preserved by Stobaeus:

> They thought that the doctrine on the wise man's doing everything well follows from the fact that he does everything in accordance with right reason and as in accordance with virtue, which is an expertise concerning the whole of life (περὶ ὅλον οὖσαν τὸν βίον τέχνην). By analogy, the bad man does everything he does badly and in accordance with all the vices. (Stob. *Ecl.* 2.7.5^{b10})

The parallels cited here from the doxographical sources indicate that for the Stoics virtue was the pinnacle of what is fitting/useful, and could be treated as a self-sufficient art of living, embracing the whole of

---

[59] This must be a reference to the Stoics, parallel to the 'they say' at 1.1.1 (above, p. 241).
[60] Other Stoic sources for physics as a virtue (e.g., Cic. *Fin.* 3.72–3) place more emphasis on its contribution towards the good life, which is life in accordance with nature (see also Diog. Laert. 7.87). This aspect is developed in detail in Menn 1997.
[61] See above, p. 242. [62] On this text see Hahm 1990.

philosophy.[63] The conception of philosophy itself as 'the art of life' proved useful for safeguarding and clarifying philosophy's broad remit in the face of increasingly divided and specialised fields of knowledge from the Hellenistic period onwards;[64] for instance, Plutarch used it to back up his view that philosophy is relevant everywhere, even at drinking parties (*Quaest. conv.* 1.1, 613b). It could also be harnessed in support of the philosophical claims made by Strabo and other authors like Vitruvius and Galen, on the grounds that their field, too, contributes to the same 'art of life'.

Other than the use of popular Stoic slogans and concepts, a lot of weight in the assessment of Strabo's adherence to Stoicism has been placed by scholars on his deployment of the notion of *pronoia*, '(divine) providence' or 'forethought'.[65] For the Stoics, providence was a manifestation of divine reason, permeating and governing the whole world.[66] This controlling rational power was indistinguishable from nature, the source of order and beauty in the universe:

> Zeno the Stoic in his work *On Nature* [says that fate (εἱμαρμένη) is] a force that causes matter to change in the same respects and in the same way, and it makes no difference if it is called providence (πρόνοια) and nature (φύσις). (Aët. 1 27.5 = SVF 1 176)[67]

A survey of the *Geography* reveals that for Strabo there was a different conception of *pronoia* at work. Most importantly, in nine out of the fourteen cases where Strabo employs the word *pronoia*, he uses it to denote *human* forethought and initiative.[68] This human forethought is systematically juxtaposed with nature (φύσις), drawing the distinction between natural and man-made environment. At 5.3.8 it is particularly interesting that the agents of human forethought are the Romans, in clear distinction from the Greeks, who were successful at hitting targets and making decisions and selections, but without actively shaping their own luck in the same way.[69]

> The nature of the land (ἡ φύσις τῆς χώρας), then, offers these advantages to the city, but the Romans added the [works] of forethought (καὶ τὰ ἐκ τῆς προνοίας). For while the Greeks are thought to have been successful in the foundation of cities because they paid attention to the beauty and strength

---

[63] Long and Sedley 1987: 1, 383.   [64] On this development see Dihle 1986: 185–98.
[65] For a survey see Dueck 2000: 62–9.   [66] See Diog. Laert. 7.138.
[67] Such passages form part of the debate on fate and determinism, which does not seem to have concerned Strabo directly in the *Geography*, although he was familiar with books on the subject, cf. 4.1.7.
[68] E.g., see 2.5.26; 5.3.8; 17.1.6.   [69] On this material see also König in this volume, pp. 131–5.

of their sites, their proximity to some port, and the fineness of the country, the Romans took great care of things that the Greeks neglected, such as road paving and aqueducts and sewers. (5.3.8)[70]

The human providence exercised here by the Romans shapes and orders the geographical landscape in the same way that cosmic providence is responsible for the orderliness and regularity of the world as a whole.

There are also certain passages where Strabo refers to divine providence, albeit applicable to specific circumstances or events rather than a cosmic benevolent programme.[71] In this respect, Strabo's approach is sharply distinguishable from the explicit references to a Divine Providence or forethought that directs the world in Dionysius and Diodorus.[72] The one passage in Strabo where there is clear reference to *pronoia* at a cosmic level is in fact the most puzzling (and interesting) of all: in the final book of his work Strabo tries to demonstrate that certain parts of Egypt, such as the temple of Amun at the Siwa oasis and the area of lake Moeris, were once sea. He claims that such exchanges between land and sea are part of a normal process of constant change that is necessary in order to regulate the world. The cosmological processes that make these massive changes possible involve different roles and tasks (ἔργα) for nature and *pronoia* respectively. This is most striking because, as we have seen, in Stoicism nature and providence are one and the same or, when Strabo distinguished nature from *pronoia*, the latter referred to human initiative intervening upon the raw natural environment.[73]

> Now I must comment briefly on the work of both nature and providence, bringing them together (εἰς ἓν συμφέροντας). On the one hand, the work of nature (τὸ μὲν τῆς φύσεως) is as follows: of all the things that converge to one point, the centre of the universe, and form a sphere around it, earth is the densest and most central, and water is less dense and comes next in order. Each one is a sphere, the former solid, the latter hollow, having the earth inside it. On the other hand, the work of providence (τὸ δὲ τῆς προνοίας) is the following: given that she is a sort of decorator and creator of countless works, she too has wished among its foremost works to beget animals as something far superior to everything else, and as the most excellent among them gods and men, for the sake of whom the rest is

---

[70] Cf. 12.3.11; 12.3.39.   [71] E.g., see 13.4.14; 13.1.69.
[72] E.g., *Ant. Rom.* 3.5.1; 3.13.3; 5.7.1; 5.54.1; Diod. Sic. 1.1.3; 2.30.1; 16.92.2.
[73] Clarke 1999: 216 refers to the passage under discussion here, but does not acknowledge the separate roles of nature and providence ('for Strabo, nature was providence'). She uses the equation between providence and fate (nowhere explicit in Strabo himself) to make a point about the 'forces of fate and history' converging with physical forces towards Rome, which is portrayed as the centre of the cosmos.

formed ... But since water encompasses the earth, and man is not an aquatic, but a land animal, living in the air, and requiring much light, providence formed many eminences and cavities in the earth, so that these cavities should receive the whole or a great part of the water, covering the land beneath it; and at the eminences the earth should rise and conceal the water beneath it, except so much as was necessary for the use of the human race and the animals and plants around it. (17.1.36)

Even though the two cosmic forces are not in conflict with each other and there is emphasis on 'bringing them together', the assignment of separate roles is distinctly un-Stoic, with nature's responsibility restricted merely to the centripetal force drawing everything towards the centre of the universe. Providence as 'a sort of decorator' has furnished all elaborations and variations found in the world, and is solely responsible for the fact that humans and the animals and plants created for their sake have a place to live. There are clear Stoic echoes in this anthropocentric emphasis and in the privileged treatment of gods and men, which rests on the fact that they share in reason, an all-important aspect of providence (Cic. *Nat. D.* 2.133). However, this does not resolve the problem of the distinction between nature and providence, which creates questions as to how and why Strabo came up with this odd, from a Stoic point of view, division of labour.

The parallels to which one may turn in attempting to address this question include a very close Stoic parallel for the description of the world in terms of layered spheres which, however, contains no hint that this is the work of nature as opposed to providence (Diog. Laert. 7.155). There are also traces of a subdivision of the Stoic active principle (which is canonically God, juxtaposed with matter) in Posidonius: '[fate is] third from Zeus; for first there is Zeus,[74] second nature and third fate' (Aët. 1 28.5 = Posidonius Fr. 103 Edelstein-Kidd, cf. Fr. 107). This move by Posidonius has been interpreted as a Platonist influence, exemplifying the loosening of barriers between schools described in the beginning of this chapter,[75] but it does not amount to Strabo's radical distinction between the roles of nature and providence. A further Platonist parallel may be found in Plutarch's criticism of the Stoic account of providence and nature on the grounds that nature alone cannot guarantee cosmic order (things do enter into 'unnatural' states), otherwise providence would be redundant (Plut. *De fac.* 927 a–b). These parallels and comparanda for Strabo's unorthodox move on providence provide us with limited similarities only,

---

[74] Zeus, the provident God, occupies here the role of providence.
[75] See Kidd 1988–99: II, 415–17; Reydams-Schils 1997.

as Strabo is not interested in fate like Posidonius, nor does he posit a state of unnatural disorder as the counterpart to providential arrangement like Plutarch's Platonist.

I would suggest that the liberties taken with Stoic orthodoxy do presuppose the loosening of doctrinal barriers that characterised the late Hellenistic period and carried on well into the imperial period, to the extent that it is often very hard to locate precisely where the orthodoxy lies. For example, Marcus Aurelius (who does not self-identify explicitly as a Stoic) offers a very 'unorthodox' approach to the issue of divine providence, by listing 'a necessity and inescapable order of fate, or placable Providence, or a random leaderless confusion' as equally valid world-views, his point being that the virtuous should not be intimidated in any of these cases (*Meditations* 12.14).[76] What is of particular interest in Strabo's case is not the simple fact that he presents an unusual account of providence, but that his doctrinal 'aberration' seems to arise not so much out of philosophical considerations as out of the internal priorities of his geographical project. For example, at 17.1.36 the role ascribed to providence is geared towards an explanation of large-scale cosmic changes, which will in turn support his point that certain lands in Egypt were previously covered by sea, and lead to the correct explanation of change in land and water masses. Furthermore, cosmic *pronoia* at 17.1.36 operates in much the same way as human forethought in 5.3.8, by intervening and improving an environment that is already ordered by nature but not quite to the greatest human advantage. The fact that the Romans were the prime agents of forethought in the earlier passage could lead us to connect the beneficial role of divine providence with the controlling care exercised upon the inhabited world by the Roman empire, since they both are seen to improve upon nature without, however, creating anything *ab initio*. The idea that the Roman empire exercised advantageous and benevolent control upon the inhabited world, and perhaps had by its very rise enacted the plan of divine providence, is by no means unique to Strabo, as there are traces of it in both Dionysius of Halicarnassus and later in Plutarch.[77] In Strabo's case, these views are in keeping with his spatially as well as politically romanocentric conception of the *oikoumene*.

---

[76] See also 6.10; 12.24, and Gill 2003: 50. Orthodoxy was equally elusive in the other philosophical schools of the imperial period; see Dillon 1988 for the situation among Platonists.
[77] The main references are: Dion. Hal. *Ant. Rom.* 5.7.1; 5.54.1; 10.10.2; Plut. *Brut.* 47.7; *Phil.* 17.2; *Flam.* 12.10; *De fort. Rom.* esp. 1–2. See Swain 1989.

Conclusions

We have seen that the major force guiding Strabo's self-definition was his aspiration to belong in the Greek intellectual elite, whose special connection to Asia Minor he deliberately emphasised. At the same time, being a Greek intellectual in the late Hellenistic period involved a relationship of mutual benefit and advantage with the Roman political elite, and the dynamics of this relationship can be traced in many chapters of the *Geography*. It is the same twin preoccupations with intellectual distinction and political utility that underpin Strabo's programmatic validation of his discipline, both clearly present in his appeal to philosophy. A comparison between Strabo's claims of allegiance to the Stoic school with his treatment of the key Stoic concept of cosmic *pronoia* reinforces the suspicion that, despite the fact that he was well-informed and educated in both Stoic and Peripatetic philosophy, Strabo's philosophical self-definition does not rest on substantive doctrinal commitments but on philosophy's identification with 'wide learning' and the beneficial 'art of life'. The equation of 'philosophy' with diverse, preferably ancient, wisdom that is beneficial for the conduct of political life may be a broad generalisation, but it is not a deliberate attempt to create false impressions about the content of the *Geography* and its seriousness. In fact, compared with Strabo's questionable account of *pronoia*, this all-encompassing view of philosophy would have a much better chance of meeting with the approval of his Stoic heroes.

CHAPTER 9

Narrating 'the Swarm of Possibilities'
Plutarch, Polybius and the Idea of Contingency in History

Felix K. Maier

Between Narrative and History: Counterfactuals and Sideshadowing

In Philip Roth's novel *The Counterlife* the protagonist Henry Zuckerman, a suburban dentist from New Jersey, dies in the aftermath of heart surgery, which he had to undergo to cure his impotence. However, in the second chapter, the narrative undermines everything that happened before: Henry is still alive, having survived the surgery, and he chose to abandon his former life at the side of his wife, living in a West Bank settlement instead. The third chapter continues the account of the second, but in section four, it is Henry's brother Nathan who suffers from a serious heart condition. He also undergoes surgery and dies. Chapter five resumes the narrative of parts two and three and merges them with the last chapter. Nathan is living with his girlfriend Maria in England, just as he had wanted in chapter four.

The Counterlife is a fascinating, experimental novel that plays with and undermines the reader's anticipation of a logical plot. All five chapters contradict each other, and events that happened in one chapter are presumed not to have happened in subsequent chapters. By adopting such an unconventional structure, Roth – according to his own statement – wanted to provide an example of a novel that would resist any closure and display the 'swarm of possibilities' in life.[1] Roth's text is an intriguing novel that endeavours to prove wrong all philologists who claim that it is not possible to produce a text which reveals the contingent structure of its plot, that is, the fact that events could have happened differently.[2]

---

[1] Roth 1986, quoted in Bernstein 1994: 4: 'Life can go this way or life can go that way. The alternative, the alternative or the alternative, etc.' For the quote, see Bernstein 1994: 98, commenting on Robert Musil's *Man without Qualities*: 'The entire novel swarms with projections of contradictory possibilities.'

[2] Other authors who explore that issue include Jorge Borges, Georges Perec, Italo Calvino, Vladimir Nabokov or John Ashbery. Roberto Calasso 1993: 22, pointed out that it was perhaps the Greek myths with their different storylines that perfectly presented the openness of time and action:

In his book *Narrative and Freedom* Gary Saul Morson studies this dilemma, that narration and life have different structures and that there is a limit to the capacity of texts to portray contingency. Morson is pointing to an apparently inevitable frame that constrains every narrative:

> Lives include all sorts of extraneous details leading nowhere, but good stories do not. Narratives are more successful if they display a structure, which it is hard to find in life ... And stories have a real closure, in which all loose ends are tied up; but there is no privileged point in life comparable to the ending of a novel.[3]

In Morson's view, all narratives are arranged according to a teleological structure that leads towards a specific closure; they focus only on characters and occurrences that are important to the development of the story and often leave out stalemates or dead ends that proved irrelevant *e posteriori*. In short, narratives are characterised by hindsight, even if there is no allusion to the outcome in the course of the story. Consequently, Morson called narratives and life 'anisomorphic', that is, fundamentally different in their basic structures.[4]

Morson's observations raise important questions about historiography, given that most historians use narrative when writing about the past. Historians, too, are confronted with the same dilemma as novelists, and Morson points to the particular difficulties inherent in the attempt to produce a text that does not evoke the impression of a determined past. As historians must stick to the 'truth', they cannot allow themselves to dwell extensively on alternative routes history might have taken.[5] They are bound to present a concise plot, without too many ramifications or too much consideration of unrealised ways of history. For the same reason, they cannot introduce many characters who could have changed the course

---

'Mythical figures live many lives, die many deaths, and in this they differ from the characters we find in novels, who can never go beyond a single gesture. But in each of these lives and deaths all the others are present, and we can hear their echo.' Cf. also Griffin 1993: 25–6: 'The novel, restricted to a single version, makes it more dense, more detailed – to compensate for its lost variants ... [But some modern novels] struggle to reclaim that openness, to regain indeterminacy; in the novel such antiquarianism is regarded as experimental, avant-garde. The reader is dizzied by the variants, just as "the mythographer lives in a permanent state of chronological vertigo."'

[3] Morson 1994: 20.   [4] Morson 1994: 20.
[5] This would result in counterfactual history, which – despite its rising impact in recent theory of historiography – has not (yet) become a stock feature of historical narrative. See Demandt 2001: 16–23 and Ferguson's groundbreaking introduction to his 1998 book *Virtual History*. Recent scholarship attaches more and more importance to the idea of counterfactual thoughts: e.g., see Tellenbach 1994; Olson, Roese and Deibert 1996; Tetlok and Belkin 1996; Cowley 1999; Bulhof 1999; Squire 1999; Brodersen 2000; Rosenstein 2005; Evans 2014 and Prendergast 2019, as well as many other articles published in *History and Theory*.

of history but did not.[6] Additionally, a historian ought to present a concise plot with a clear beginning and closure. Whereas Spanish poet Javier Marías says about his own novels that he does not know what will happen to a protagonist, whom he introduces on page five, on page two hundred, a historian is not free to do the same.[7] But perhaps the most serious problem historians face is of a structural type. Everyone expects a historian to come up with reasons why a certain event happened. No one wants to be told that everything was accidental or that no cause can be found. But this leads to serious misunderstandings, as Isaiah Berlin once put it: 'The more inevitable an event or an action or a character can be exhibited as being, the better it has been understood, the profounder the researcher's insight, the nearer we are to the one ultimate truth.'[8] Thus, history appears to be determined to an extent, as accumulating causes creates the impression of a past that followed a pattern of necessity: 'The more causes and reasons we bring to bear on what it is that we want to explain, the more difficult it is to see how the decline could have turned out to be other than it was.'[9] As a consequence, narrative options for bringing out the contingency of the past stand in contradiction to the historian's task of explaining a past event by identifying causes, both of which have to been balanced carefully against each other. It is precisely this dilemma that once prompted the German philosopher Friedrich Schlegel to characterise the historian as a 'backward-looking prophet'[10] because they 'predict' in their narratives exactly those events which they know took place. Schlegel, of course, was deeply ironic, attributing to the 'prophets' a skill that they owe only

---

[6] Such a narrative device would increase the contingency within the narrative, as Leo Tolstoy very subtly does in *War and Peace*. Tolstoy exploits this technique by introducing Prince Adam Czartoryski, who is said to be one of those men 'who decide the fate of nations'. But every reader expecting Prince Adam to play an important role in the story will be disappointed, because nothing of the sort happens. This makes the reader recognise the contingency of the narrative. Morson 1994: 160, coined the term 'aesthetic potentiality' for this narrative technique, as a contrast to Mikhail Bakhtin's 'aesthetic necessity'.

[7] Marías 2015: 14: 'That's why I have so often said that when I write, I apply the same principle of knowledge that rules life ... so I write what I write on page five of a novel with no idea if this will prove to have been a good idea when I reach page two hundred, and far from writing a second or third version, adapting page five to what I later find out will appear on page two hundred, I don't change a word, I stand by what I wrote at the very beginning – tentatively and intuitively, accidentally or capriciously.'

[8] Berlin 1976: 130.

[9] Hawthorn 1991: 13; see also Carr 1986: 90: 'Historians, like any other people, sometimes fall into rhetorical language and speak of an occurrence as "inevitable" when they mean merely the conjunction of factors leading one to expect it was overwhelmingly strong.' Carr deleted every such phrase from his own texts, criticising himself for not having done justice to the contingency of history: 'No doubt, it would have been wise to say "extremely probable."'

[10] Schlegel 1974 [1802]: 176.

to their hindsight. This knowledge has another serious implication, as a historian also runs the risk of evaluating past events in retrospect, attributing to them a teleological structure which they actually lacked.[11] But is there no way out of this dilemma? Is every narrative of past events doomed to display a determined structure and the narrator, the historian, bound to prove themselves backward-looking prophets?

Fortunately, the situation is not quite so bleak. Even Morson is convinced that narratives can be written in a way that affords readers a glimpse of the contingency of specific moments in history. He coined the term 'sideshadowing' to refer to all narrative techniques used by authors to counteract our tendency to frame later events as the predictable result of what happened before. He thus prompts us to explore possible alternative courses of action and possible different developments of events: 'Sideshadowing restores the possibility of possibility. Its most fundamental lesson is: to understand a moment is to grasp not only what did happen, but also what else might have happened.'[12] Morson presents some examples, mostly drawn from Slavic literature, of narrative devices that implement sideshadowing. Among others, he refers to Tolstoy introducing characters who – against all expectations – do not play any significant role afterwards.[13] Another strategy discussed by Morson is the author deliberately leaving out the causes of a certain event, in a way which renders the narrative more contingent for the reader.[14] Bernstein, on the other hand, explores the ways in which an author might present the characters'

---

[11] Bernstein 1994: 99: 'Only because we know which of these projected futures came to pass are we tempted to privilege that one at the moment of its first articulation.'

[12] Morson 1994: 118. At the same time, Bernstein 1994: 3, invented the term 'backshadowing' in order to counter deterministic narratives and concepts such as those of Marxism or Christian teleology: 'Sideshadowing's attention to the unfulfilled or unrealized possibilities of the past is a way of disrupting the affirmations of a triumphalist, unidirectional view of history in which whatever has perished is condemned because it has been found wanting by some irresistible historico-logical dynamic ... It rejects the conviction that a particular code, law, or pattern exists, waiting to be uncovered beneath the heterogeneity of human existence ... Sideshadowing stresses the significance of random, haphazard, and unassimilable contingencies.'

[13] Cf. n. 6 above. Morson's description (1994: 159) of the reader's usual expectations of plot development, though based on examples drawn from novels, also applies to historical narratives: 'Readers of novels are trained to seek significance. When at the beginning of *Great Expectations*, Pip gives a pie to a convict, the reader knows that this event must have some significance, or it would have not been narrated. The fact that the work is known to be an artifact, an aesthetic structure planned in advance, guarantees significance.'

[14] Another example from *War and Peace* discussed by Morson 1994: 161, is Prince Andrej's change of mind: 'It is neither the oak itself, nor the visit to Natasha, nor his conversation with Pierre, nor any other event close in time to his thoughts about the tree that has caused the process of change in Andrej, though all of these allow us to be aware of its ongoing activity. Because its causes are hidden, the change does not seem inevitable.'

intentions, plans, tactics and strategies, in order to prompt readers to reconstruct the original, open-ended circumstances within which these characters were operating. The more detailed an author's description of such plans or intentions, the more the reader will be prone to believe that these constituted real alternative developments to what actually happened.[15] Many more examples could be added to this list. These narrative techniques are not as extreme as Roth's plot structure in *The Counterlife*, but they do allow the author to make contingency an integral part of their story. All authors who, like Tolstoy and Roth, apply such techniques, strongly believe in the contingency of the past. Their aim is to emphasise that the course of the events which they narrate was not predetermined, thus prompting their readers to imagine alternative developments of the events that might equally well have happened.

In this chapter, I would like to build on these considerations and explore awareness of contingency and its significance in ancient historical narratives. Methodologically, this is a difficult task because, as Morson has pointed out, the constraints placed on narratives generally by the inherently teleological character of texts, and the problems of the structure of historical texts specifically (see above), make it difficult to determine whether a narrator did consider events to be contingent and foreseeable. Historians can, of course, make explicit comments to point out possible alternative developments ('this was just one course of events, but others were equally likely or even more probable'). But such remarks are, in fact, rare in historical narratives, and we cannot even blame the historians for that, given that their task is traditionally to determine what happened and why, not identify alternative courses of action. The way to work around this difficulty is to focus on the presence of sideshadowing in historical narrative. If we can trace sideshadowing in a narrative this allows us to conclude that an author conceived of the past as contingent and aimed to display the undetermined character of what happened at those specific moments of the past. By uncovering narrative strategies of sideshadowing, we get a sense of whether and how historians considered the courses of

---

[15] Bernstein 1994: 98, again refers to Musil's *Man without Qualities*, in which the protagonist Ulrich has to organize the seventieth anniversary of the Emperor Franz Joseph's coronation, scheduled to take place on 2 December 1918. Although the reader knows that this event will never happen – Franz Joseph dies in 1916 – Musil undermines this knowledge by presenting a plethora of different hopes and expectations of his characters: 'Because it is impossible for the reader to suspend his knowledge of the book's historical aftermath, the narrator will play upon that knowledge not in order to exploit it for the emotional intensities it might add to the story, but rather to undermine that readerly self-confidence.' The effect is akin to counterfactual history: see Bernstein 1994: 116.

events they describe to be only one of many possible outcomes rather than the predetermined result of its circumstances, even though they might not explicitly state that.

Plutarch seems a particularly suitable ancient author on whom to test these assumptions, since he is considered to be a historian who regards *tyche* as the main cause of his protagonists' successes or failures and believes in history being guided by providence.[16] Morson's considerations provide a particularly helpful interpretive framework for such an analysis. Some Greek historians certainly did believe in the contingent nature of history and were, therefore, confronted with the same problem of dealing with the constraints inherent in narrative which I outlined above with regard to modern historians. I propose to demonstrate that despite all these constraints, Plutarch did find different ways of emphasising contingency in his narrative.[17] In the first part of this chapter, I will explore various strategies through which Plutarch managed to avoid the seemingly unavoidable fate of narratives of the past, namely, to present the course of events as predetermined. In the second part, I will show that in so doing, Plutarch resorted to narrative devices that had already been established in Greek historiography at least as early as the time of Polybius. Bringing Plutarch into dialogue with Polybius will enable us to see the continuity of the concept of narrating the 'swarm of possibilities' (Bernstein) from the Hellenistic period to the early empire.[18]

Roads Not Taken: Alternative Pasts in Plutarch's *Lives*

At first sight, Plutarch's *Parallel Lives* appear to describe a determined past. This is suggested by both explicit statements and implicit allusions. In the *Life of Caesar*, for example, Plutarch comments on Caesar's death occurring right next to the statue of Pompey: 'The place ... made it wholly clear that it was the work of some heavenly power which was calling and guiding

---

[16] Particularly, Swain 1989: 272–302; Babut 1969: 479–81; Barrow 1967, 129; Jones 1971: 69; Brenk 1977; Aalders 1982: 58–9; Hoffmann 1907: 88; Tatum 2010: 449 and 458. For different views on the role of *tyche* in Plutarch see Titchener 2014 and, recently, Eckholdt 2019.

[17] I will mainly draw upon passages from the *Parallel Lives*. The chapters by Larmour 2014, Geiger 2014b, van der Stockt 2014, Duff 2014, Nikolaidis 2014 and Titchener 2014 provide a helpful overview of recent scholarship on various aspects of Plutarch's works; see further Pelling 2002 and Scardigli 1995. Grethlein 2013: 92–130, offers some interesting insight, albeit with a different emphasis.

[18] On the problem of whether Plutarch should be seen as part of the 'Second Sophistic', see Schmitz 2014, Roskam 2012. For a recent discussion of Plutarch's relationship with Polybius, with particular emphasis on Plutarch's explicit references to Polybius and Plutarch's role as narrator, see Almagor 2018.

the action thither' (παντάπασιν ἀπέφαινε δαίμονός τινος ὑφηγουμένου καὶ καλοῦντος ἐκεῖ τὴν πρᾶξιν ἔργον γεγονέναι, *Caes*. 66; tr. Perrin). Only a few chapters before, when summing up the events leading to Caesar's death, another remark suggests a similar interpretation: 'But destiny, it would seem, is not so much unexpected as it is unavoidable' (ἀλλ' ἔοικεν οὐχ οὕτως ἀπροσδόκητον ὡς ἀφύλακτον εἶναι τὸ πεπρωμένον, 63). In addition to such explicit comments, Plutarch's narrative often creates the impression of a teleological past also on a more implicit level, thus allowing him, or so it seems, to avoid raising awareness of the contingent character of particular historical moments and the full range of their potential, tremendous consequences.

In the *Life of Alexander*, while describing the events of 330 BCE, Plutarch mentions only in passing that the Macedonian king had been hit previously by an arrow in the leg below the knee (*Alex.* 45.5). This incident, which might have had deadly consequences for Alexander and would in this case certainly have changed the course of events significantly, is not mentioned when it occurred and is included fleetingly here seemingly for the sake of completeness alone. Plutarch could have chosen not to include that information at all – but he did. Plutarch then adds a similar episode: 'At another time he was smitten in the neck with a stone so severely that his eye-sight was clouded and remained so for some time' (ibid.). Being informed about these accidents all of which could have led to a different outcome and could have ended Alexander's campaign right away, the reader gets the impression that Plutarch does not attach much importance to them, as though the course of Alexander's life was guided by destiny anyway and could not have been altered by such incidents. But it is not quite as simple as that. There are many instances of Plutarch subtly reminding us of the contingency of history, and these put passages such as those in the *Life of Alexander* into a larger perspective. The reader sees them in a different light, thinking about possible different outcomes and consequences of individual events.

I will now discuss some of the narrative techniques which Plutarch frequently uses to that effect and which are rather similar to the concept of *sideshadowing*. I will then explore to what extent these techniques affect the assumption that Plutarch is presenting the lives of his protagonists, and the course of history in general, as predetermined.

The first narrative technique used by Plutarch in order to emphasise the contingency of the past is an increase of complexity. Plutarch does this by embedding side-plots within the main plot. This kind of narrative strategy is very conspicuous as Plutarch usually does not jump from one plot to another, but rather follows the course of events, mostly from his protagonist's perspective. There are some passages, however, in which he significantly increases his *dramatis personae*, with important consequences for our purposes. To mention yet another example from the *Life of Alexander*: within a digression on the internal conflicts within Alexander's army, Plutarch splits up his plot into different branches. The resulting interplay between subplots has an unexpected but crucial impact on the main plot, making the reader realise the contingent nature of the events. First, Plutarch informs us about a certain Macedonian named Limnus, from Chalaestra, who planned an attack on Alexander's life. Plutarch then adds another level, reporting that Limnus invited a certain Nicomachus, one of the young men with whom he was involved in an amorous relationship, to take part in the conspiracy. After that, further complexity is added when Nicomachus does not accept the invitation himself. Instead, he tells his brother Cebalinus about the attempt which, in turn, leads to the fourth level: Cebalinus contacts Philotas, asking him to give him and his brother access to Alexander in order to warn him. But Philotas, 'for whatever reason, would not let them in ... and he did this twice'. Nicomachus and Cebalinus are thus forced to find a different way to prevent the attack but eventually do manage to inform Alexander (*Alex.* 49.2–4).

The reader is not confronted with a drama-style plot structure of only two or three characters on stage pursuing their goals; instead, several protagonists suddenly and in quick succession join the action, each one of them with different intents and purposes. Their complex interaction has consequences: since many key players influence the course of action, the 'historical entropy' increases and the reasons behind many of the events sometimes seem beyond human comprehension.[19] The actions of Limnus, Nicomachus, Cebalinus and Philotas affect one another several times in ways not intended or foreseen by the individual agents; by triggering further events, they also directly or indirectly influence Alexander's situation. The reader realises that the increase in the number of protagonists increases the number of different paths which history could have taken.

---

[19] In physics, entropy serves as a quantitative measure for disorder in thermodynamic systems. Higher entropy indicates an increased degree of randomness and disorder due to a larger amount of interacting particles: see, e.g., Sasse 1979, 14–15. I am aware that the scientific term entropy does not fully match the historical constellation I have outlined above, but the term nevertheless seems helpful as a shorthand that encapsulates the increase of the complexity of the situation and its consequences for the author's and readers' ability to understand the factors that influenced the course of events.

Moreover, since all the protagonists follow different plans but Plutarch sometimes keeps their motivations in the dark, the consequences of their actions appear contingent, as there is no real explanation why something actually happened in the way it did. Thus, within this dense net of possible ramifications, the boundaries between what happened and what might have happened become blurred and the reader realises that the conspiracy was, for quite some time, just as, and, perhaps, even more, likely to succeed as fail.

Closely connected with this kind of sideshadowing is another narrative strategy which was used to great effect by Xenophon in his *Anabasis*: the unexpected entrance of a protagonist who significantly influences the course of events. Xenophon marked his own appearance in the *Anabasis* with the conspicuous phrase ἦν δέ τις ἐν τῇ στρατιᾷ Ξενοφῶν Ἀθηναῖος.[20] Plutarch skilfully plays with this phrase: in nearly every case, it deliberately contrasts the coincidental nature of a new agent's appearance, and thus retrospectively emphasises their crucial influence on the course of history.[21] Before recounting the battle of Issus, Plutarch describes at length an important incident which could have changed the course of the past. He begins his account with the introduction of a certain Amyntas: ἦν δέ τις ἐν τῷ Δαρείου στρατῷ πεφευγὼς ἐκ Μακεδονίας ἀνὴρ Μακεδών ('there was a man in the army of Darius, a Macedonian, fugitive from Macedon').[22] Amyntas, who was well acquainted with the nature and tactics of Alexander, begs king Darius not to fight a battle with the Macedonian king in the narrow passes of the mountains. Instead, he advises him to attack Alexander in the broad and spacious plains which would allow him fully to avail himself of the vastly superior number of his forces against the smaller army of the invader. But Darius did not listen to Amyntas and so suffered a humiliating defeat.[23] It is remarkable how much emphasis Plutarch puts on this incident and how prominently he introduces a man who appears out of nowhere only to disappear again, but whose fleeting appearance is intimately connected to the outcome of one of the most decisive battles of Hellenistic history. The reader is thus prompted to see Amyntas as someone who *almost* prevented the Persians' devastating defeat, with the phrase ἦν δέ τις ἐν τῷ Δαρείου στρατῷ

---

[20] Xen. *An.* 3.1.4; cf. Hdt. 7.143.1 (ἦν δὲ τῶν τις Ἀθηναίων ἀνήρ, introducing Themistocles). Huitink and Rood 2019 *ad loc.* also note Homeric precedents. The unexpected nature of this character's presence is marked in Greek by the enclitic indefinite pronoun τις, the inconspicuous syntactic construction of which reinforces the 'out-of-nowhere' effect of the sudden introduction of Xenophon. An important predecessor to Plutarch's use of this device is Polybius; see further below.
[21] Cf. Plut. *Alc.* 9.6. [22] Plut. *Alex.* 20.1. [23] Plut. *Alex.* 20.2–3.

conjuring up the image of a certain Athenian called Xenophon, who *did* change the fate of a beaten army and significantly alter history.

A similar case is the encounter of Antony and the Egyptian seer. When describing the events following the treaty of Misenum (39 BCE), Plutarch tells us that Antony happened to meet an Egyptian seer who advised him to put as much distance as possible between himself and Octavian. At first glance, this story does not seem very important and appears to be yet another example of Plutarch's preference for trivial episodes. But there is more to it than just that. As in the similar episode discussed above, Plutarch lends additional weight to the encounter by commenting that Antony should have listened to the seer: 'for we are told that whenever they were casting lots for fun in whatever situation they happened to be engaged in at the time, or throw dice, Antony came off worsted. They would often match cocks, and often fighting quails, but Caesar's would always win' (λέγεται γὰρ ὅτι κληρουμένων μετὰ παιδιᾶς ἐφ' ὅτῳ τύχοιεν ἑκάστοτε καὶ κυβευόντων ἔλαττον ἔχων ὁ Ἀντώνιος ἀπῄει. πολλάκις δὲ συμβαλόντων ἀλεκτρυόνας, πολλάκις δὲ μαχίμους ὄρτυγας, ἐνίκων οἱ Καίσαρος, *Ant.* 33.2–3). Two points about this concluding comment of the episode are noteworthy: first, Plutarch does not refer to fortune, or fate, as responsible for Octavian's victory. He rather compares Antony's lot to an undecided game of dice, or animal fights, thus reminding the reader that history could have taken a different path if Caesar's former general had heeded the seer's advice. Second, Plutarch uses the same formula as in the Amyntas episode to introduce the Egyptian seer (ἦν γάρ τις ἀνὴρ σὺν αὐτῷ μαντικὸς ἀπ' Αἰγύπτου, 33.2). He thus prompts the reader to identify a pattern of instances in the past when a course of events that would have altered the past considerably was not realised because a historical agent chose to ignore important advice.

I will now turn to another narrative technique which Plutarch often employs and which supports the suggestion that he was interested in making the reader aware of the contingent character of history. Although this technique might look like foreshadowing, it lacks the inevitability and determinism of conventional foreshadowing, evoking rather a large range of sideshadowed possibilities. My first example is from the *Life of Pompey*, where Plutarch introduces Pompey by way of a description of his father's reputation: 'never have the Romans manifested so strong and fierce a hatred towards a general as they did towards Strabo, the father of Pompey'. After thus alluding to what might have caused a difficulty for Pompey's career, Plutarch tells us that, in stark contrast to what one might have expected, Pompey did manage to win the appreciation and support of his father's troops, which, in turn, constituted the most important factor in his literally unprecedented rise to power (*Pomp.* 1.1–2). By reminding us of this, Plutarch emphasises that there is no simple and straightforward connection between Pompey's youth and his success as a general afterwards. Mentioning Strabo's dubious position at such a prominent point of his work, Plutarch makes us realise that the conditions for Pompey's career were by far less advantageous than we might be inclined to imagine based on his subsequent success.

A similar interpretation is suggested by a substantial remark of Plutarch at the beginning of the *Life of Coriolanus*, where he explicitly criticises our tendency to transform the past into a coherent story. Telling us that Coriolanus grew up without his father, Plutarch lays emphasis on the contingency of history: 'He [Coriolanus] showed ... that such loss of a father, although otherwise bad for a boy, need not prevent him from becoming a worthy and excellent man, and that it is wrong for worthless men to lay upon it the blame for their perverted nature' (*Cor.* 1.2).[24] By alluding to a different course of action – namely that Coriolanus' life might have been determined negatively by the significant loss in his childhood – Plutarch emphasises that Coriolanus' nature and particular situation did not predetermine his later life. On the contrary, Coriolanus' family situation made his later career seem very unlikely. Plutarch thus reminds us that our longing for a direct, rational and necessary explanation is at odds with the way in which history actually develops. His implicit counterfactual prompts us to consider what might have happened, but did not.[25]

Plutarch's use of implicit counterfactuals to underline the contingent nature of the past is by no means limited to explicit statements. He also subtly uses the particular structure of his works to achieve the same effect. By arranging Greek and Roman biographies in pairs, Plutarch not only illustrates the moral virtues and vices which his protagonists have in common, a prominent feature of the *Parallel Lives*.[26] The comparative arrangement also illustrates how similar historical structures had different outcomes, thus inviting the reader to rethink the course of the past with an

---

[24] Plutarch makes this point quite explicit in the following statement: 'on the other hand, the same Marcius bore witness for those who hold that a generous and noble nature, if it lack discipline, is apt to produce much that is worthless along with its better fruits, like a rich soil deprived of the husbandman's culture'.
[25] Counterfactuals, either implicit or explicit, are indications that the author perceives the world and its history as contingent; see Prendergast 2019.
[26] See Larmour 2014; Duff 1999: 287–309; Pelling 1986; Jones 1971: 106–7.

alternative ending. An intriguing example of this technique is found in the *Lives of Alexander* and *Caesar*. Plutarch tells us about a serious problem which Alexander faced in India. The battle with Porus, an Indian king of the territory of modern-day Punjab, discouraged his Macedonian troops and stayed their advance into India. The troops violently opposed Alexander when he insisted on crossing the river Ganges. At first, Alexander closed himself in his tent, feeling no satisfaction with what he had already achieved unless he should cross the Ganges, and regarding retreat as an admission of defeat. Plutarch elaborates on that passage, describing in detail why Alexander's soldiers did not want to continue and how their refusal affected his plans. As part of this description Plutarch introduces Androcottus, a dangerous enemy, who at that time was already well known for his power and subsequently became even more powerful by marching through the whole of India with a mighty army (*Alex.* 62.1–9). By bringing Androcottus into the picture, Plutarch prompts us to imagine what would have happened if Alexander had been able to advance.

Against this background, Plutarch creates the image of an alternative fate Alexander could have encountered. He does so, however, not in the *Life of Alexander*, but in its companion, the *Life of Caesar*. Plutarch reports how Caesar, too, faced an uprising of his soldiers during his campaign against Pompey. Despite the different historical circumstances, the structural similarity (especially the way in which both situations are oriented around a *peripeteia*, the decision on whether to continue or turn back) and the comparable setting (mutiny of the troops) of this and Alexander's situation in India encourage the reader to bring both episodes into dialogue with each other.[27] Having crossed the Adria on his way to Apollonia, Caesar's troops 'since they were now past their physical prime and worn out with their multitudinous wars murmured against Caesar'. Plutarch has the soldiers utter their complaints, relating all their objections. Their reluctance seems to turn the tide but Caesar's determined advance changed their mind (37.5–8). By juxtaposing what happened to Alexander and what happened to Caesar, the reader imagines how either campaign might have ended differently. At both points history could have followed a completely different path. The description of the event in one *Life* thus constitutes a virtual alternative outcome of its counterpart in the other:

---

[27] Similarities between the speeches of Alexander's and Caesar's soldiers enhance this effect: Caesar's men raise some of the same objections with which Alexander was confronted.

what would have happened if Alexander's soldiers had changed their mind, or if Caesar's troops had been as persistent as Alexander's?

I will bring this section to a close by citing one final example of this technique. Both Pericles and Fabius Maximus faced the challenge of implementing an unpopular strategy. Pericles had to convince the Athenians to keep up a defensive plan, Fabius did everything to persuade both the Senate and the people of Rome not to engage with Hannibal in combat. But while Pericles eventually lost his position as general, Fabius partly succeeded in his plan and prevented his fellow generals from engaging the Carthaginians in battle. Here, too, the reader is prompted to imagine what might have happened if Pericles had been as successful as Fabius, or if the Roman general had been as unsuccessful as his Athenian counterpart.[28]

The passages discussed above show how Plutarch confronts his readers with a swarm of alternative paths which history might have taken. Cutting across the narratives of the two biographies of the same pair, Plutarch's use of this technique throws new light on the complex ways in which two *Lives* of a pair interact with each other well beyond the explicit points of comparison made in the *synkriseis*. It also shows that Plutarch did not have a deterministic vision of the past: at several, crucial junctures of his accounts, Plutarch prompts us to imagine how lives of his protagonist could have gone in different directions. The past as it develops in Plutarch's *Lives* is a contingent process in which failure or success of the protagonists are not simply due to fate (*tyche*), but to certain key moments in their lives and the decisions made at these key moments. In the following, and final, section, I will address the question of the origins or, at least, the prehistory, of Plutarch's concept of sideshadowing. A case can be made, I believe, that the various narrative techniques that Plutarch employs to bring out contingency within his narrative, adopt several key elements of the narrative of Polybius.[29] Bringing these two authors into dialogue with each other sheds further light on Plutarch's narrative techniques and so also on an important element of continuity from the Hellenistic to the early imperial period.

---

[28] Cf. particularly Plut. *Per.* 18.1, 22.1; *Fab.* 2.4–5, 5–7.
[29] I do not mean to deny that Plutarch was strongly influenced also by other historians such as Herodotus, Thucydides and Xenophon. But it seems to me that, on the whole, Plutarch's sideshadowing is particularly close to the narrative strategies employed by Polybius to emphasise the contingent character of the past.

264   Felix K. Maier

Looking Backwards: From Plutarch to Polybius

I shall start with the technique of what I have suggested we call 'increasing the entropy' (above). Here, there are some remarkable similarities between the narrative designs of the two authors.[30] In the preface to Book 3, where Polybius identifies the most important historical agents of the events he is going to narrate, we get a clear idea of his view of history. It is no longer a drama with a limited set of characters but rather a 'collision' of many actors: the Romans, the Carthaginians, Philip, Antiochus, Ptolemy, the Rhodians, Prusias, Attalus, the Aetolians, the Galates, Eumenes, Ariarathes, Pharnaces. Such a long list of key players by itself indicates the far-reaching and complicated consequences implied in such an interaction of events in the field of world politics. All of a sudden, the number of the *personae* of history increases, their numerous plans and intentions cross, everything becomes part of one large-scale development and history becomes unpredictable and accidental.

Polybius' account of the conflict over Seleucia between Ptolemy IV and Antiochus III during the Fourth Syrian War (219–217 BCE) in book five vividly illustrates this. At the end of the episode, both Ptolemy and Antiochus seem to be in complete control during the battle of Raphia. Prudently commanding their troops, they act like *petteutai* 'draught-players', shaping the course of events according to their plans and tactics.[31] Before the battle breaks out, however, Polybius suddenly mentions a whole range of 'supporting actors' (the Spartan king Cleomenes, Ptolemy's advisor Sosibius, his acquaintance Nicagoras, among others) who significantly affect the historical process at different levels. The reader realises that Ptolemy's success cannot, in the end, be attributed to the brilliance of the king but ought rather to be considered as a random series of different

---

[30] It is without doubt personal experience that shaped Polybius' concept of history and influenced his idea of contingency in relation to the *symploke* – the 'weaving together' of different political stages along with the Roman conquest of the Mediterranean area. Polybius' concept of the *symploke* has often been analysed by modern scholarship, but usually with regard to his idea of history and its methodological, rather than narrative, implications; see, e.g., Ziegler 1952: 1515–19; Pédech 1964: 496; Walbank 1975; Mohm 1977: 68–91; Roveri 1982: 56–9. For different approaches see Miltsios 2013; Maier 2018 and Wiater in this volume.

[31] Both Ptolemy and Antiochus find the right place for setting up camp a few days prior to the battle (5.80.1–7). Polybius then goes on to describe their battle formation (5.82.1–13), which evokes the impression of a duel between the two kings without any external involvement. Finally, Ptolemy's important role with reference to the outcome of the battle is highlighted and recognised in a summary (5.85.8, 86.1).

interventions on the part of several protagonists.³² The actions of many key players intersect across different levels and affect one another, thus leading to accidental occurrences that directly or indirectly influence Ptolemy's situation. Ptolemy, in stark contrast, is not mentioned in the text, which is noteworthy in itself. Looking at the interplay at all levels of the narrative, it becomes apparent that the number of protagonists involved in the action increases with the gamut of different paths that history *could* have followed.

The role of increased entropy in Polybius' narrative shows some significant similarities to that in Plutarch's works. A key role is played, once again, by the conspicuous phrase ἦν δέ τις, which was discussed in the previous section. The phrase itself and its variations go back to Herodotus and his introduction of Themistocles at 7.143.1 (and ultimately, via Herodotus, to Homer). The most prominent instance, as pointed out above, is perhaps Xenophon's reference to himself at *Anabasis* 3.1.4. Polybius, too, makes use of that phrase. In his text it always creates the impression that someone appeared completely unexpectedly. A well-known example is the slave Spendius. This historical agent is introduced out of the blue with ἦν δέ τις Καμπανός. The consequence of his actions, however, turn out to be considerable: Spendius is presented as responsible for triggering – for purely personal reasons – the mercenary war which pushed Carthage to the brink of destruction (Polyb. 1.69.4–5). By using this well-established phrase, the casual character of which contrasts effectively with the importance of the historical agent,³³ Polybius increases the entropy of history in his text and emphasises again the contingent character of historical processes. If someone like Spendius, who does not play in the first league, as it were, of history, but rather emerges from the lower ranks, is able to shape history to such an extent, it becomes clear to the reader that the number of factors that have the power to influence the course of events is potentially infinite, making the future development of events impossible to foresee.

---

³² Polyb. 5.35–7. By way of this subtle narrative technique, Polybius intimates that the Egyptian king succeeded in keeping his power not so much thanks to any praiseworthy ability to lead (which Ptolemy did, however, demonstrate at Raphia and which Polybius duly emphasised) as due to accidental events the interference of which eventually secured his reign; see Maier 2012b: 173–6.

³³ The historical agent is introduced merely by an enclitic, the smallest grammatical entity. However, precisely because this phrase was so well known, the reader also perceives it as significant and as foreshadowing an important event, because they know that the phrase ἦν δέ τις introduces a person who will later become significant.

But there are also striking differences between Plutarch and Polybius. Whereas people introduced by ἦν γάρ τις in Polybius (as in Xenophon's *Anabasis*) strongly influence the course of events, they do not do so in Plutarch. The episode with Antony and the Egyptian seer, as well as the episode of Darius and Amyntas, both of which were discussed in the previous section and both of which featured the introductory phrase, are good examples. Both represent key moments that *could* have turned the course of events upside down, but did not.[34] Readers familiar with the use of the phrase in previous authors, especially Polybius and Xenophon, are likely to read similar episodes in Plutarch with the expectation that the two characters introduced by the phrase ἦν γάρ τις will have a significant effect on the course of the past. By deliberately disappointing these expectations, Plutarch is, implicitly, making a point about the predictability of events, or, rather, the impossibility of predicting events: in his *Lives*, history does actually *not* happen according to patterns of anticipation established by previous historical narratives. Plutarch startles his readers, who are familiar with classical and Hellenistic historiography, by applying an established narrative device but using it in an entirely different way and to an entirely different effect. By way of his innovative use of the familiar phrase ἦν γάρ τις, he introduces an element of surprise into his narrative. Plutarch's narrative thus allows readers to experience the contingency of the past – our inability to know what is next – with which the historical agents were faced, despite the fact that they already know exactly the future development of events.[35] In so doing, Plutarch considerably reduces the gap separating the historical agents' and the readers' experience of the past.

A comparison of Polybius and Plutarch is equally profitable with regard to counterfactual remarks. Counterfactuals had a long tradition in ancient literature, including historiography.[36] From Homer onwards, many authors prompted their readers to think about alternative outcomes, and they applied different techniques of alluding to what might have been. Herodotus and Thucydides both mostly used explicit counterfactuals although implicit techniques to refer to a different course of events are also found in their narratives. Plutarch, however, resorts to counterfactuals in a way that is interestingly different from that of his predecessors and similar to the way in which Polybius used *virtual history*.

---

[34] See Maier 2012b: 153–5. Cf. also Plut. *Lys.* 10,4; 15.2–3, and esp. Plut. *Alex.* 20, the Amyntas episode, discussed above.

[35] This, too, is similar in Polybius, as Miltsios 2013 has demonstrated.

[36] Much work has been done on counterfactuals in Homer, e.g., Nesselrath 1992; de Jong 1987; recently, Flatt 2017. See further Lang 1989; Morrison 1992; Louden 1993.

Instead of simply recounting what happened, Polybius quite often raises the question of what *might* have happened, and he does so far more often than Herodotus or Thucydides. For example, he often explicitly alludes to possible alternatives using the phrase 'if x had not been the case, y would have followed'.[37] In the third book of his *Histories*, Polybius explains the causes (αἰτίαι) of the Second Punic War. As 'first cause' (πρώτη αἰτία) he identifies Hamilcar's anger, which continued beyond the Carthaginian defeat in the first war. Despite the peace treaty, Hamilcar immediately embarked on preparations for a new war. Answering the implicit question of why this new war did not break out earlier, Polybius comments: 'had not the mutinous outbreak among the mercenaries occurred, he [Hamilcar] would very soon, as far as it lay in his power, have created some other means and other resources for resuming the contest' (εἰ μὲν οὖν μὴ τὸ περὶ τοὺς ξένους ἐγένετο κίνημα τοῖς Καρχηδονίοις, εὐθέως ἂν ἄλλην ἀρχὴν ἐποιεῖτο καὶ παρασκευὴν πραγμάτων, ὅσον ἐπ' ἐκείνῳ, 3.9.8; tr. Paton). Thus, Polybius challenges the idea of a predetermined course of events at a significant point in the past by prompting the reader to consider the consequences that Hamilcar's intentions *could* have had if the Mercenary War had not interfered.[38] But *virtual history* in Polybius' work is perhaps even more interesting when he employs narrative strategies that hint at what might have happened without mentioning it explicitly. Polybius applies a large spectrum of different techniques: the plans and speeches of his protagonists, for example, present courses of events that could have taken place as well.[39] The increased entropy of history, too, which was discussed above, is a kind of sideshadowing inasmuch as it makes the reader realise how unstable and 'accidental' history is.[40]

Against this background, it is noteworthy that Plutarch, as we saw above, considered *virtual history* an essential part of his historical writing

---

[37] See Maier 2012b: 103–39 for examples; de Jong 2001: 586 speaks of 'if-not situations'.

[38] The reader is prompted to consider different alternative future developments: would Hamilcar, for example, have led the Carthaginians to victory against Rome? If not, what would have happened to Rome afterwards? Would there have been another Hannibalic War anyway?

[39] Maier 2012b: 119–29. See, e.g., the speeches of Hannibal and Scipio before the battle at the Trebia (Polyb. 3.63–4), where Polybius shows that Scipio's envisaged outcome, Roman victory, was more likely to happen than the outcome projected by Hannibal in his speech, i.e., Carthaginian victory. See also the famous debate between the Aetolian Chlaeneas and the Acarnanian Lyciscus in Book 9. Whereas Lyciscus warns about Rome being ready to interfere with and dominate Greek affairs, Chlaeneas omits any mention of Rome and thus presents a future scenario entirely without the presence of the new power from the West.

[40] See Maier 2012b: 117–38 for more counterfactual techniques. See further Wiater's discussion in this volume of how intertextual references in Polybius' narrative of Hannibal's march introduce counterfactual elements into Polybius' text.

and adopted some characteristic features of Polybius' sideshadowing. But he went beyond the methods of his Hellenistic predecessor. He developed his own technique of triggering a process of permanent counterfactual thinking in his readers by structuring his biographies in parallel pairs. Through comparing similar biographies and therefore similar situations with different outcomes in each pair, Plutarch continuously prompts the reader to think about the course of events in one life in terms of the other and, thus, consider possible alternative outcomes. Plutarch, in so doing, emphasises the contingency of history without the need for such explicit remarks as those found in Polybius. This feature is all Plutarch's, who made the experience of 'sideshadowing' a constituent part of his *Parallel Lives*.

A final aspect that throws light on Plutarch's adaptation and modification of Hellenistic techniques of historical narrative is the role of *tyche* in history. Beginning with the speeches of the Attic orators in the fourth century, *tyche* is an unpredictable deity whose actions seem to be incomprehensible to humans, who are powerless and entirely exposed to her will.[41] In Hellenistic times, *tyche* becomes an all-powerful goddess who often thwarts human plans while remaining impenetrable as to her own designs.[42] Polybius, at first glance, seems to take up this idea of *tyche* as the overwhelming and almighty force in history. It is true that he refers to *tyche* more than one hundred and fifty times in his history, sometimes in the context of very prominent events. On the other hand, he vehemently criticises other historians for awarding *tyche* too much importance in their explanation of causes.[43] At a closer look, we see that his references to *tyche* actually serve either to emphasise unexpected and astonishing historical incidents or to reflect the perspective of the protagonists.[44] Thus, Polybius' references to *tyche* should not be considered as an explanatory device employed by the historian but rather a narrative strategy designed to bring

---

[41] See Eckholdt 2019: 72; cf. Dem. 18.192–5; Herzog-Hauser 1948.
[42] Gasparro 1997: 90 links this prominence of *tyche* in the Hellenistic period to 'the turbulences of that age, in politics, society, culture and religion' which 'certainly encouraged the rise of belief in the idea of the power with sway over the universe as a whole'.
[43] Polybius' criticism is directed against the so-called 'tragic' or 'mimetic' historiography, in particular Phylarchus. Instead of ascribing everything to the will of *tyche*, historians should look for alternative causes of events: Polyb. 2.16.13–15; 2.56–63; 3.47.6–48.12, 58.9; 7.7; 10.27.8; 12.24.5; 15.34–6. For discussion see Walbank 2007; Hau 2011; Krewet 2017.
[44] E.g., at 1.4, 57; 2.70. Also, adding ὥσπερ removes all divine associations of *tyche*, as in phrases such as 'as if *tyche* was orchestrating the occurrence' (e.g., 1.86.7, 29.19.2); for *tyche* as a means of referring to different perspectives of the historical protagonists see 1.59.2–4; 10.40.6; Maier 2012b: 210–47.

out different perspectives on events, especially in those cases where *tyche* is referred to by historical agents.[45]

Plutarch seems to have adopted a similar approach concerning the role of *tyche*. By emphasising what *might* have happened instead of the actual course of events, Plutarch does not present the past as a predetermined process subdued to the will of *tyche* or the reign of providence. Even if he sometimes appears to believe in a world in which everything happens according to the plan of a destiny that governs all human action, the results of the discussion in the previous section show that this is not representative of his idea of history. The great care which Plutarch took to signal possible alternative outcomes of specific events shows that he regarded these potential different outcomes as highly probable and serious alternatives to the actual course of history. Contingency is a permanently and prominently embedded aspect of his view of the past. Consequently, his protagonists' biographies do not follow an inevitable, predestined path to success, failure or tragic death. Plutarch sharpens our awareness of the role of contingency in each and every one of his *Lives*. We are confronted not only with what really happened but also with a swarm of possibilities whose exact consequences are left to our imagination. Although Plutarch does refer several times to *tyche* in his texts, there is, therefore, evidence that he did not think that the lives of his protagonists were in any way determined to happen as they did. *Tyche* might have played a certain role, sporadically influencing the course of events. But Coriolanus, Alexander, Caesar and all the other politicians and generals had it in their power to shape their fate and gain control over their destiny to a certain extent.

A quick glance at Plutarch's treatise *On the Fortune or the Virtue of Alexander* supports this view. Here, Plutarch elaborates on his concept of *tyche* as a factor in history, discussing whether Alexander owed his success only to *tyche* or to his outstanding skills as a general, politician and – perhaps surprisingly – philosopher. Plutarch points out that there is no need or justification for denying *tyche*'s influence on Alexander's career (*De Alex. fort.* 336d). But he also emphasises that *tyche* played only a minor role and that her impact on Alexander's success is exaggerated by too many people (339a). Moreover, Plutarch endeavours to demonstrate that *tyche* was jealous of Alexander and – in stark contrast to Athena protecting Menelaus – did not prevent the Macedonian king from being seriously wounded many times during his campaigns (340–5): 'if Alexander's spirit ... had not refused to submit to defeat in its wrestling with

[45] Hau 2011.

Fortune', in Plutarch's view, he would certainly have been doomed to failure (341e–f).[46] Plutarch concludes his considerations by emphasising that Alexander, when fighting against the people of Oxydrace, survived only because of his *arete*, not thanks to *tyche*.

It is this concept of *tyche* in history which Plutarch appears to have adopted from Polybius and some Hellenistic philosophical concepts. In Book 9, Polybius emphasises that 'success is in every case possible if the steps we take to carry out our plan are soundly reasoned out' (9.12.1).[47] He even goes a step further and states that there are examples of 'those who have succeeded in bringing their designs to a conclusion, and even when fortune has been adverse to them, have compensated for deficiency in ardour by the exercise of reason' (16.28.2). Polybius encourages his readers – primarily political and military leaders – to take control of their fate and not to surrender to the complexity of reality (9.9.9–10):

> I have offered these remarks … for the sake of the leaders of all, no matter where, who shall be charged with the conduct of public affairs, so that by memory or actual sight of such actions as these, they be moved to emulation, and not shrink from undertaking designs, which may seem indeed to be fraught with risk and peril, but on the contrary are courageous without being hazardous, … always provided that all that is done is the result of sound reasoning.

We find similar concepts in other Hellenistic works, especially Menander's comedies. *Tyche*, it is true, is often presented in his works as an all-powerful figure that controls everything and seems to influence the action according to her will.[48] But this view is offset by another one that gives more power to the individual and their actions. For Menander's comedies also teach us that the protagonists – if they are ambitious and do everything they can to achieve their goals – can win *tyche* over to their side. The more eagerly the characters seek to accomplish their goal, and the better they plan, the more *tyche* is likely to intervene in their favour:[49] 'whoever stands out by sound reasoning will have everything'.[50]

---

[46] Plutarch goes on to say that it was Alexander's fiercest enemy, Darius, who was protected by *tyche*, who, at that time, had grown tired of the Macedonian king (344a–b).
[47] See also 6.2.8; 12.25b.3. At 9.12.1–3 Polybius makes it clear that failure might be more often the case than success due to the overwhelming number of factors that have to be taken into account; cf. also 9.12.10: 'so true is it that nature makes a single trivial error sufficient to cause failure in a design, but correctness in every detail barely enough for success'.
[48] See Men. fr. 372 K.-A.: Τύχη κυβερνᾷ πάντα; cf. Men. *Aspis* 146–8; frr. 682, 860 K.-A.
[49] Vogt-Spira 1992: 69. In the *Dyscolus*, for example, *tyche*'s help (Cnemon falling into the well) would not have had any effect if Sostratus himself had not been so eager to marry Cnemon's daughter.
[50] Men. fr. 191 K.-A.: ὁ λογισμῷ διαφέρων πάντ' ἔχει.

Menander, Polybius and Plutarch thus share similar ideas about the influence of *tyche* on human life and the interaction of human and superhuman forces. Their concept significantly differs from that of other Hellenistic authors such as those criticised by Polybius for writing so-called 'tragic' historiography. Polybius blames those historians for presenting *tyche* as an overwhelming power, leaving almost nothing to human capacity, and Plutarch would have agreed.[51] Against the 'nihilistic' concept of the past of those 'tragic' historians, Polybius sets a programmatically different perspective. His *Histories* is designed to demonstrate how we can achieve our goals *and* cope with a contingent reality, a reality which, to be sure, is incredibly complex but also offers a wide range of unforeseen opportunities waiting to be used by those who are prepared for it.[52] And Plutarch, while perhaps not sharing Polybius' strong didactic intentions, certainly shares his concept of a contingent, not a predetermined, past.

Concluding Remarks

Although Plutarch is often regarded as a historian who believes in the power of providence and its influence on the lives of his protagonists, there is, as I hope to have demonstrated, considerable evidence that his concept of history was more complex. His *Parallel Lives* feature numerous techniques of sideshadowing which confront the reader with the idea of history as a contingent, not a determined process. These narrative strategies, by means of which Plutarch frequently alludes to different possible outcomes of past events, offer short glimpses on what else might have happened. Plutarch was not, as Schlegel thought, a backward-looking prophet, because the past in his narrative swarms with possibilities. A comparison with Polybius shows that Plutarch drew upon concepts and techniques for presenting a contingent past which had already been established in Hellenistic times. But he did not simply copy these techniques, as we can see when we set him side by side with Polybius; he developed them further and took them to another level by adapting them to the needs of his comparative approach to the lives of famous Greeks and Romans.

[51] Polyb. 2.56.   [52] Polyb. 15.36.4.

CHAPTER 10

'Asianist' Style in Hellenistic Oratory and Philostratus' Lives of the Sophists

Lawrence Kim

Introduction

If there is one thing that scholars of the so-called 'Second Sophistic' can agree upon, it is that the 'movement' ushered in nothing fundamentally new as far as Greek orators or oratory were concerned.* Ulrich von Wilamowitz-Möllendorff had already said as much in 1900, when he spoke of 'the continuity of oratorical practice' ('die Continuität der rhetorischen Praxis') from Gorgias to Philostratus and beyond; what characterised the Second Sophistic was only an increase in 'the self-confidence and social prestige of the orators of the imperial period' ('das Selbstgefühl und die sociale Geltung der Rhetoren der Kaiserzeit').[1] Variations on this formulation have been repeated ever since, sometimes with the additional observation that 'display oratory' also 'gained a new prominence and prestige' in the Second Sophistic.[2] But declamation, rhetorical performances before public audiences, wealthy and politically active orators – these had all existed in the Hellenistic period and arguably in the classical as well.

My purpose here is not to question these assertions, which are certainly correct. Instead, I want to address an aspect of 'sophistic' oratory that has been neglected in recent iterations of the 'continuity' argument: prose

---

* This article has evolved considerably in the years since the St Andrews conference. The bulk of new research was conducted in Heidelberg (2013–14, 2015–16), funded by a generous fellowship from the Alexander von Humboldt Foundation; I have also benefited from the comments and corrections of Sira Schulz, the Cambridge University Press referees, and audience members at lectures in Leiden and Oxford (both 2014) and Boston (at the 2018 Society for Classical Studies Annual Meeting). A preliminary overview of some of the material covered in this chapter appears in Kim 2017a: 41–2; 53–60.
[1] Wilamowitz 1900a: 15.
[2] König 2015: 113; cf. 2009: 41. For similar 'continuity' arguments, see Boulanger 1923: 70: 'Or ce ne sont pas les sophistes qui ont changé, mais bien les conditions d'existence et le public'; Bowersock 1969: 10; Anderson 1989: 82–7; 1993: 17–20; Brunt 1994: 26–7; Schmitz 1997: 15; 2011b: 305; Pernot 2017: 212–13.

style. This is somewhat ironic, given that Wilamowitz, as well as the nineteenth-century scholars to whom he was responding, focused almost exclusively on style in their debates about the distinctiveness (or lack thereof) of the Second Sophistic. In particular, Erwin Rohde and his student Wilhelm Schmid, authors, respectively, of *Der griechische Roman* (1876) and *Der Atticismus* (1887–97) – both founding works of Second Sophistic scholarship – had posited a close relation between *Asianismus*, that is, the so-called *asianisch* ('Asianist') style allegedly practised by Hellenistic Greek orators, and that of their Second Sophistic descendants.[3] As Rohde put it in an 1886 article:

> Die wahren Vorväter und Lehrmeister der neuen Sophistik waren die Rhetoren der asianischen Manier ... und so steht er denn vor uns, der Sprössling des Asianismus, die zweite Sophistik, alle Spuren natürlicher Vererbung im Gesicht tragend, τοῦ πατρὸς τὸ παιδίον.[4]

> The true ancestors and instructors of the new Sophistic were the Asianist orators ... what we have in front of us, then, is the offspring of Asianism, the Second Sophistic, whose face shows all the signs of its lineage, τοῦ πατρὸς τὸ παιδίον ['the child of its father'].

A little over a decade later, Eduard Norden in *Die antike Kunstprosa* (1898) drew upon Rohde's ideas while constructing his grand narrative history of Greek and Latin prose. Norden also saw a connection between Hellenistic and Second Sophistic style, but traced the origins of both back to the artistic prose of the *classical* period, particularly that of the sophists and their students. As part of his thesis that the history of Greek prose was characterised by a continuous struggle between adherents of two fundamentally opposed styles – an 'old' and a 'new' ('der alte und der neue Stil') – he drew a direct line of descent from Gorgias and his school through the 'Asianist' orators of the Hellenistic age to the imperial sophists. Under the Empire, he claims:

> Es standen sich gegenüber die Archaisten und Neoteriker des Stils (zwischen beiden suchte eine dritte Richtung zu vermitteln), jene anknüpfend an die attischen Klassiker, diese an die Sophisten der

---

[3] Rohde 1876: 290, n. 1; Schmid 1887–97, Vol. 1: 28–32, 45–7. I translate *asianisch* as 'Asianist' rather than 'Asian' because both are neologisms referring specifically to style rather than geographical or ethnic origin (which would be *asiatisch* in German, 'Asian' or 'Asiatic' in English: see n. 8 below).
[4] Rohde 1886: 190. Rohde's Second Sophistic heirs of 'Asianist' style include Polemo, Achilles Tatius, Longus, Aelian, Philostratus, the sophists mentioned in his *Lives*, and the historians quoted by Lucian in *How to Write History*.

platonischen Zeit und die mit diesen ihrerseits verwandte asianische
Rhetorik [der hellenistischen Zeit].[5]

The opponents were the representatives of the Archaic and those of the
Neoteric style (a third group tried to mediate between those two); the
former harked back to the classical Attic authors, the latter to the sophists
from the time of Plato and their close relative, the Asianist oratory [of the
Hellenistic period].

I find it striking that such claims about the connections between
Hellenistic and imperial Greek style have largely disappeared from recent
discussions of the Second Sophistic.[6] One significant reason, of course, was
that Wilamowitz's article in 1900 authoritatively demonstrated that the
Latin and Greek terms *Asianus, Asiaticus* and Ἀσιανός were (1) pejorative
and never adopted by any ancient orator to describe his own style and (2)
current only for a brief period, from about 50 BCE to 20 CE.[7] Modern
scholars, he warned, should thus be wary of using *asianisch* or *Asianismus*
inappropriately, as if they referred to a movement or school, and anach-
ronistically, in reference to the Second Sophistic.[8] But this critique was
directed toward the improper application of the *term*; far from denying the

---

[5] Norden 1898: 392. Norden's 'neoterics' include those mentioned by Rohde (with the exception of Polemo, whom he places in the third in-between category), but also Favorinus, Iamblichus and the authors of several lesser known works.

[6] The primary exceptions are found in Francophone scholarship, which has never abandoned the term or the concept. Boulanger 1923: 83–108, sees certain imperial sophists, like Nicetes and Polemo, as practising a 'style asiatique' or embodied by 'l'esprit asiatique' (108) inherited from 'l'éloquence asiatique' (77) of the Hellenistic period. Subsequent discussions of imperial rhetoric in French, such as Bompaire 1958: 99–121 and Reardon 1971: 77–96, rely on Boulanger's account, and speak of 'Asianisme' in the Second Sophistic; Romilly 1975: 75–88 sees the 'short-lived Asianism' of the imperial sophists as hearkening back to Gorgias (cf. Guez 2012: 198–203); the essential treatment in Pernot 1993 is discussed below.

[7] Wilamowitz 1900a: 1–8. *Asianus* as a stylistic term was probably first used in Latin in the 50s BCE by the Roman *Attici* to describe Cicero (who prefers *Asiaticus*, e.g., *Brut.* 51; 325); the first reference in Greek to 'Asianist' oratory is in the 20s BCE by Dionysius of Halicarnassus, who mentions 'the [muse] from Asia' (ἡ [μοῦσα] . . . τῆς Ἀσίας: *Orat. Vett.* preface), unless Caecilius of Caleacte's lost treatise *How the Attic and Asian Styles Differ* (Τίνι διαφέρει ὁ Ἀττικὸς ζῆλος τοῦ Ἀσιανοῦ: *Suda* s.v. Καικίλιος) was earlier. The latest ancient orators described as *Asianus* (by Seneca the Elder, *Controv.* 1.2.23.6, 10.5.21.8; *ex Asianis*: 9.1.12.14, 9.6.16.6) were active early in the reign of Tiberius (14–37 CE). References to 'Asian' oratory in the first and early second centuries CE all look back to the Hellenistic or late Republican era: Strabo (τοῦ . . . Ἀσιανοῦ χαρακτῆρος: 13.1.66; τοῦ Ἀσιανοῦ λεγομένου ζήλου: 14.1.41), Petronius (*loquacitas . . . ex Asia*: *Sat.* 2), Quintilian (*Asianos, Asiana gens* [*orationis*], etc.: *Inst.* 12.10.12–13), Suetonius (*Asiaticorum oratorum*: *Aug.* 86), Plutarch (τῷ καλουμένῳ . . . Ἀσιανῷ ζήλῳ τῶν λόγων: *Ant.* 2.4), and Theon (τῶν Ἀσιανῶν καλουμένων ῥητόρων: *Prog.* 71, Spengel, *Rhet.*) The authors listed in this footnote are the only ones before the third century CE who explicitly reference 'Asianist' oratory.

[8] Moreover, they imply nothing about the geographical origin or ethnicity of their practitioners; while some of the orators called 'Asian' in antiquity came from Asia, others like Cicero, Hortensius, or Timaeus of Tauromenium did not. The 'Asia' in question is not the continent, but *provincia Asia*

existence of the *style* that Rohde, Schmid and Norden postulated for the imperial era, Wilamowitz affirmed it: 'Asianist rhetoric lives on in the rhetoric of Nicetes and Polemon' ('die asianische Beredsamkeit in der des Niketes und Polemon lebt').⁹ At the most, he nuanced Norden's model, pointing out that genre or other considerations might influence an orator's choice of style,¹⁰ and thus to speak of a conflict or struggle between advocates of 'old' and 'new' styles was too schematic. For Wilamowitz, the primary change introduced in the Second Sophistic was the phenomenon of linguistic Atticism, which came to the fore in the second century CE.

Wilamowitz's demonstration of the modern misuse of the terms *Asianismus* and *asianisch* appears, however, to have led later scholars to suppose that the style or styles that they were used to describe were no longer current in the imperial era, particularly in the second century CE, when the linguistic Atticist movement became dominant. As a result, while 'Asianist' style in the Hellenistic period (mostly in connection with Latin oratory) has attracted some scholarly attention,¹¹ the only recent in-depth analysis of the ostensibly similar styles found in the imperial era is that of Laurent Pernot in a sub-section of his magisterial two-volume *La rhétorique d'éloge*, published nearly thirty years ago.¹² While Pernot acknowledges the over-schematic nature of Norden's stylistic model and reiterates Wilamowitz's observation that a given author might avail himself of a more sober or flamboyant style as the situation or genre demanded, he nevertheless observes that Norden was basically right:

(Wilamowitz 1900a: 7): the western region of Asia Minor, comprising Caria, Lydia, Mysia and Phrygia (cf. Cic. *Orat.* 25; Dion. Hal. *Orat.Vett.* preface).

⁹ Wilamowitz 1900a: 14. He also affirmed the connection between the classical sophists and *Asianismus*: 'Allein [Norden] will bewiesen haben, dass "der Asianismus der alten Zeit [i.e., the Hellenistic and imperial eras] eine naturgemässe Weiterentwicklung der sophistischen Kunstprosa der platonischen Zeit ist": das unterschreibe ich auch' (21).

¹⁰ Wilamowitz 1900a: 25–7. Also critiqued was Norden's haste to label any elaborated style as *asianisch*: 'Was Norden asianisch nennt, ist meistens das süsse oder blumige oder auch das erhabene' (26). Cf. Norden's concession in Norden 1915: Nachträge, 11.

¹¹ From this point on, I use the adjective 'Asianist' to refer to the style of the Hellenistic Greek authors and texts called 'Asian' by *modern* scholars; the scare quotes are meant as a reminder that the label was not adopted by the authors themselves (see further pp. 289–91 below); I use 'Asian', with quotes, when I am referring to an ancient source's explicit labeling of a style or a writer as such. On Hellenistic Greek 'Asianist' oratory, see Calboli 1986, 1987, 1988; Winterbottom 1982, 1983, 1988; and Papanikolaou 2009, 2012a.

¹² Pernot 1993: 371–94, who stands in the tradition of Francophone scholarship outlined above in n. 6. Winterbottom 1988: 9–10 and 18–19, has pertinent remarks on Hellenistic and imperial declamatory style. See also the idiosyncratic account of Papanikolaou 2012b.

> Norden avait compris que l'asianisme n'est pas un épiphénomène éphémère, mais que derrière cette étiquette se cache une tendance attestée à toutes les époques de la prose d'art antique.[13]
>
> Norden had understood that Asianism was not a short-lived epiphenomenon but that this label covered a tendency found throughout all periods of ancient literary prose.

Moreover, Pernot provides an excellent analysis of these stylistic tendencies as they were instantiated in the imperial era, centred on Favorinus' *On Fortune* and *Corinthian Oration*, and Aristides' *Monody to Smyrna* and *Rhodian Oration*.[14] But this valuable account has not had the impact on non-Francophone scholarship that it deserves. Studies devoted to individual imperial authors may include the occasional mention of stylistic characteristics reminiscent of 'Asianist' oratory, but in more general work on Second Sophistic literature there is rarely any hint that authors like Polemo, Favorinus, Achilles Tatius, Longus, or Maximus of Tyre wrote in a completely different style from that of 'classicisers' like Dio of Prusa, Plutarch, or Lucian.[15]

Part of my goal in this chapter, then, is simply to call attention to the fact that, despite the much-noted overarching classicism of the period, many imperial authors write in a rather *un*-classical style, employing, for example, short clauses of similar length, series of phrases with parallel syntax, liberal use of rhyme and other figures of sound. More substantively, I want to reassess the claims made, in different ways, by Rohde, Schmid and Norden (among others) and to reopen the question of the relationship between the non-classicising styles popular in the Second Sophistic and the so-called 'Asianist' styles of the Hellenistic period. Are

---

[13] Pernot 1993: 379. Cf. Adamietz 1992: col. 1119.

[14] Pernot 1993: 386–93. Although Pernot calls 'cette tendance, ou plûtot ce faisceau de tendances' *virtuosité* (379), he freely uses *asianisme* of imperial style (e.g., 'l'asianisme proprement dit': 386), arguing (unpersuasively) that the term was still in use (377). Also problematic is his subsequent identification (378, expanding on Kennedy 1972: 563) of two types of Second Sophistic *asianisme* – *tragique* and *rythmique*.

[15] The only general works on the Second Sophistic to (briefly) mention 'Asianist'-like styles are Anderson 1993: 95–8 and Whitmarsh 2005: 49–52. Aside from my chapter (Kim 2017a), there is no reference to Greek prose style of any kind in Richter and Johnson 2017. For analysis of individual imperial authors' un-classical styles, see Amato 2005: 86–106 on Favorinus ('l'évident asianisme de ses ouvrages': 86); Trapp 1997: 1960–4 on Maximus of Tyre ('[the *Dialexeis*] exemplify one version of that stylistic tendency known … as Asianism': 1964); Hunter 1983: 84–90 on Longus; Favreau-Linder 2004: 117–21 on Polemo; Laplace 2007: 365–410, Hutchinson 2018: 291–304 and Whitmarsh 2020: 36–40 on Achilles Tatius. On the Greek novel and 'Asianism', see the preliminary remarks of Billault 1995; less useful are Smith 2007: 134–7 and Doulamis 2011: 33–41 (both on Chariton).

they really the same? And what do both of these post-classical styles owe to Gorgias and the sophists of the classical period, with whom they have often been linked?

These are difficult questions, and my aim here is only to offer some tentative answers, based on a comparison of the styles of an admittedly limited selection of extant Hellenistic and imperial texts.[16] Of the latter, I have restricted myself to a very small sample of imperial 'sophistic' prose: five of the longest excerpts quoted in Philostratus' *Lives*, from speeches by Isaeus of Assyria, Apollonius of Athens, Onomarchus of Andros and Pollux of Naucratis.[17] I first compare the style of these passages to that of Gorgias, as exemplified in his *Helen* and *Epitaphios Logos*, and then turn to the Hellenistic period, where I analyse the primary surviving examples of 'Asianist' style: the fragments of the third-century BCE historian and 'sophist' Hegesias of Magnesia (called 'Asian' in some ancient sources), as well as three late Hellenistic inscriptions – the first from Nemrud Dağ in Commagene (*OGIS* 383), which Norden identified as an example of what he called the *bombastisch* ('bombastic') type of 'Asianist' oratory,[18] the second from Mantineia in Arcadia (*IG* v.2.268), described as *asianisch* by Wilamowitz,[19] and the third from Maroneia in Thrace (*SEG* 26, no. 821), discovered in 1969 and linked to the other two inscriptions by its editors and others on stylistic grounds.[20] As far as I can tell, this is relatively uncharted ground: while the style of the inscriptions, Hegesias, and some imperial sophists have each been treated separately, I know of no previous attempt to compare the prose of Hellenistic 'Asianist' authors with that of their imperial sophistic successors. In what follows, I hope to demonstrate

---

[16] I focus on the style of extant texts, rather than on ancient comments *about* style. I thus refrain from discussing ancient descriptions of 'Asian' oratory (listed in n. 7) or 'bad' style in general (e.g., κακοζηλία [texts collected in Jocelyn 1979: 77–109] or *corrupta eloquentia*). Of course, such evidence needs to be considered in any comprehensive account of 'Asianist' oratory or Second Sophistic style (e.g., Norden 1898: 126–49; 270–300; 367–86; Pernot 1993: 373–80), but I prefer to analyse the style of actual extant prose before hypothesising about what that style must have been like based on the vague, hostile and polemical comments of the ancient sources (cf. Pernot 1993: 379–80 on the difficulty of making sense of the subjective judgements of ancient critics on 'corrupt' style). I make a partial exception for Philostratus, since he is the source of my imperial texts.

[17] For reasons of space, I set a – somewhat arbitrary – limit in analysing all passages longer than forty words except for one (by Philagrus: *VS* 2.32.3 = II.8 (580)). Norden quotes the excerpts of Apollonius, Onomarchus, and of Pollux (as well as that of Philagrus), at 1898: 410–15, but does not submit them to any detailed analysis. Guast 2019: 175–6 has a brief treatment of the 'Asian' style of Philostratus' shorter excerpts.

[18] Norden 1898: 140.   [19] Wilamowitz 1900b: 537.

[20] Grandjean 1975; Cf. Winterbottom 2011: 275. Pernot 2005: 80 discusses the inscription but not its style. Papanikolaou 2009 and 2012a examine the two latter inscriptions, respectively; I have not been able to see his 2008 dissertation.

that, although the passages of Hellenistic and imperial 'sophists' undeniably share a broad stylistic similarity that sets them apart from 'classical' or 'classicising' oratory like that of Lysias, Demosthenes, or Dio of Prusa, the differences between them, especially regarding their relation to Gorgianic prose and their preferences for rhythmical clausulae, are perhaps more significant.

The Style of Philostratus' Sophists: *Paromoeosis*, Lists and Repetition

Isaeus of Assyria (fl. 65–110 CE?)

Let us begin with Isaeus of Assyria, active in the second half of the first century CE.[21] Philostratus speaks of Isaeus' ability to 'condense his whole argument into something brief (πᾶσαν τὴν ὑπόθεσιν συνελεῖν ἐς βραχύ: *VS* 1.50.2 = 1.20, 514) and as an example, gives the following excerpt, from a declamation accusing Philip II of Macedon's agent in Athens, Python of Byzantium, of treason after Philip's departure from the city (1.50.5 = 1.20, 514). The passage is arranged below according to cola, with number of syllables and translation.[22]

1. ἐλέγχω Πύθωνα προδεδωκότα — 11 — I find Python guilty of treason
2. τῷ χρήσαντι θεῷ, — 6 — by the god who prophesied
3. τῷ δήσαντι δήμῳ, — 6 — by the people who imprisoned [him]
4. τῷ ἀναζεύξαντι Φιλίππῳ· — 9 — by Philip who departed;
5. ὁ μὲν γὰρ οὐκ ἂν ἔχρησεν, — 8 — For [the god] would not have prophesied
6. εἰ μή τις ἦν, — 4 — unless there was a [traitor];
7. ὁ δὲ οὐκ ἂν ἔδησεν, — 7 — they would not have imprisoned [him]
8. εἰ μὴ τοιοῦτος ἦν, — 6 — unless he was that sort of man;
9. ὁ δ' οὐκ ἂν ἀνέζευξεν, — 7 — and [Philip] would not have departed
10. εἰ μή, δι' ὃν ἦλθεν, οὐχ εὗρεν. — 11 — unless he had not found the man for whom he had come.

The excerpt comprises two sentences, broken up into ten short cola in a carefully balanced structure.[23] The first sentence consists of a main

---

[21] On Isaeus, aside from Philostratus, see Plin. *Ep.* 2.3; Juv. *Sat.* 3.73–80.
[22] Here and for subsequent passages of *VS*, the text is that of Stefec 2016, translations are my own; repeated words are underlined and repeated word endings are in boldface.
[23] Wright 1921: 71, n. 3 notes the 'antithesis combined with ἰσόκωλα'.

introductory clause, followed by three phrases (2, 3, 4) that each possess the same syntactical structure and word-endings: τῷ, -σαντι, -ῷ. The sentence that follows consists of three conditional clauses (5–6, 7–8, 9–10), the apodoses of which (5, 7, 9) are nearly identical (ὁ ... οὐκ ἄν, –ησεν); the verb in each of these corresponds to that in 2 (χρήσαντι – ἔχρησεν), 3 (δήσαντι – ἔδησεν) and 4 (ἀναζεύξαντι – ἀνέζευξεν) respectively. The first two protases (6, 8) are also structurally the same (εἰ μὴ ... ἦν), while the last (10) varies the formula slightly to round off the sentence, although even there the two verb endings (ἦλθ-**εν**, εὗρ-**εν**) pick up the –εν ends of 5, 7 and 9. In essence, then we see short, balanced clauses, parallel in structure and often length (*isocolon* in 2–3, 7 and 9), reinforced by *anaphora*, *homoeoteleuton*, as well as the repetition of word-endings within the clause.

Such attention to parallelism of sound – *paromoeosis* – is characteristic of the prose style of Gorgias.[24] Compare the following passage from *Encomium to Helen* (7):[25]

1.	εἰ δὲ βίᾳ ἡρπά**σθη**	7	But if she was by violence raped
2.	καὶ ἀνόμ**ως** ἐβιά**σθη**	8	and lawlessly forced
3.	καὶ ἀδίκ**ως** ὑβρί**σθη**,	7	and unjustly outraged,
4.	δῆλον ὅτι ὁ <μὲν> ἁρπάσας ὡς ὑβρίσας ἠδίκ**ησεν**,	9 17	it is plain that the rapist as the outrager, did the injustice
5.	ἡ δὲ ἁρπασθεῖσα ὡς ὑβρισθεῖσα ἐδυστύχ**ησεν**.	16	and the raped, as the outraged, did the suffering.
6.	ἄξιος οὖν ὁ μὲν ἐπιχειρήσας βάρβαρος βάρβαρον ἐπιχείρημα	22	It is thus right for the barbarian who undertook a barbaric undertaking
7.	καὶ λόγ**ῳ** καὶ νόμ**ῳ** καὶ ἔργ**ῳ**	9	in word and law and deed
8.	λόγ**ῳ** μὲν αἰτ**ίας**,	6	to meet with blame in word,
9.	νόμ**ῳ** δὲ ἀτιμ**ίας**,	7	exclusion in law,
10.	ἔργ**ῳ** δὲ ζημ**ίας** τυχεῖν·	8	and punishment in deed.

Gorgias, like Isaeus, employs two sets of three clauses with identical syntactical structures (1–3, 8–10), *homoeoteleuton* (1–3: -σθη, 8-10: -ίας) and repetition of internal word-endings (2–3: -ως; 8-10: -ῳ). Isaeus' balanced repetition of words is matched by Gorgias as well: the verbs ἡρπάσθη and ὑβρίσθη from 1 and 3 are repeated in lines 4 (ἁρπάσας, ὑβρίσας) and 5 (ἁρπασθεῖσα, ὑβρισθεῖσα); and the first words of lines

---

[24] As Noël 1999: 198 puts it: 'L'antithèse, la parisoses et l'homéotéleute semblent donc bien constituer l'élément essentiel du style de Gorgias selon les Anciens'; cf. Diod. Sic. 12.53.4. For fuller accounts of Gorgias' style, see Blass 1887: 63–71; Drerup 1901: 257–74; Denniston 1952: 10–12; Zucker 1956.

[25] Text: Most and Laks 2016: 166–84 = F D24 (B11 DK). My translation.

8–10 repeat, in order, each of the three that appear in line 7 (λόγῳ, νόμῳ, ἔργῳ). One also notes the *homoeoteleuton* of -ησεν in lines 4–5, and the internal rhymes of -σας in 4, -θεῖσα in 5 and -ῳ in 7.[26] Gorgias' excerpt might strike the reader as a denser and more extreme example of *paromoeosis* than Isaeus', but the similarities are undeniable.

I would, however, also like to point out some features of Gorgias' prose that do not have a parallel in Isaeus and occur relatively rarely in the other sophistic excerpts from Philostratus. First, his penchant for *paronomasia*, or word play, and the specific variant called *polyptoton* or *figura etymologica*, which involves using a different form of the same word in close proximity. Note βίᾳ and ἐβιάσθη in 1–2, and especially line 6, where an odd repetitive effect is achieved by the placement of words of similar derivation in close juxtapostion: ἐπιχειρήσας βάρβαρος βάρβαρον ἐπιχείρημα ('the barbarian who undertook a barbaric undertaking'). Second, antithesis. While antithesis is a general characteristic of much Greek prose, Gorgias often uses it in a particular way, closely conjoined with the other figures of parallelism and sound: e.g., ὁ <μὲν> ἁρπάσας vs ἡ δὲ ἁρπασθεῖσα or ὡς ὑβρίσας vs ὡς ὑβρισθεῖσα.[27] Neither this nor word play feature much in Philostratus' sophistic excerpts: a reminder that while they may feature several elements of Gorgianic style, they by no means reproduce all of them.

Pollux of Naucratis (138–195 CE?)

My next example (*VS* 2.47.4 = 11.12, 593) comes from a *dialexis*, or introductory speech, by the sophist Pollux of Naucratis, active in the second half of the second century CE:[28]

1. ὁ Πρωτεὺς ὁ Φάριος,	7 Proteus the Pharian
2. τὸ θαῦμα τὸ Ὁμηρικόν,	8 the Homeric marvel
3. πολλαὶ μὲν αὐτοῦ καὶ πολυειδεῖς αἱ μορφαί,	13 many and manifold are his forms
4. καὶ γὰρ ἐς ὕδωρ αἴρεται	8 for he rises up into water

---

[26] I use the more specific term 'internal rhymes' rather than *parechesis* (the repetition of sound within the colon or clause) because the latter includes figures such as alliteration, which is not common in Gorgias' prose.

[27] Cf. the *polyptoton* in *Hel.* 19: ὃς εἰ μὲν θεὸς <ὢν ἔχει> θεῶν θείαν δύναμιν. For more examples of Gorgianic antithesis, see below, pp. 292–3.

[28] I follow the convincing interpretation of the term διάλεξις as *Einleitungsrede* by Rothe 1989: 146. Wright 1921 (discourse), Civiletti 2002 (*dissertazioni*) and Brodersen 2014 (*Vorträge*) prefer less specific terms. On Pollux' sophistic (as opposed to lexicographical) career, see Rothe 1989: 142–54.

5. καὶ ἐς πῦρ ἅπτε**ται**	6 and blazes into a fire
6. καὶ ἐς λέοντα θυμοῦ**ται**	8 and rages into a lion
7. καὶ ἐς σῦν ὁρμᾷ	5 and rushes into a boar
8. καὶ ἐς δράκοντα χωρεῖ	7 and crawls into a serpent
9. καὶ ἐς πάρδαλιν ᾄττει	7 and darts into a panther
10. καὶ δένδρον ἢν γένη**ται**, κομᾷ.	9 and when he becomes a tree, blooms.

Like the previous passage, this one can be easily broken up into ten short cola, frequently of similar length (three contain seven syllables, three contain eight). The structure, however, is different: the opening lines consist of three sets of substantives and predicates, each set in apposition to each other, with no expressed verb. The last seven lines contain seven different descriptions of Proteus' metamorphoses, and are an example of what Michael Winterbottom has named the 'list-style', popular in declamation and epideictic oratory:[29] seven parallel clauses with identical syntax (slightly varied in the seventh) and *homoeoteleuton* (-ει in 8–9, -**ται** in 4–6, picked up by -ᾷ in 7 and 10; and note γένη-**ται** in 10 and μορφ-**αί** at the end of 3).

The same 'list' construction allied with a care for *paromoeosis* can be seen in the following passage from Gorgias' *Funeral Oration*:[30]

1. μαρτύρια δὲ τούτων τρόπαια ἐστήσαντο τῶν πολεμίων,	19 In testimony to which [qualities] they raised trophies over their enemies:
2. Διὸς μὲν <u>ἀγάλ**ματα**</u>,	7 for Zeus, consecrations;
3. ἑαυτῶν δὲ <u>ἀναθή**ματα**</u>,	9 for themselves, dedications;
4. οὐκ ἄπειροι	4 strangers neither to
5. οὔτε ἐμφύτου ἄρεος	8 the fire of battle in the blood,
6. οὔτε νομίμων ἐρώτων	8 nor chaste loves,
7. οὔτε ἐνοπλίου ἔριδος	9 nor armor-clad strife,
8. οὔτε φιλοκάλου εἰρήνης,	9 nor beauty-loving peace,
9. σεμνοὶ μὲν <u>πρὸς τοὺς θεοὺς</u> τῷ δικαίῳ,	11 showing reverence to the gods through justice,
10. ὅσιοι δὲ <u>πρὸς τοὺς</u> τοκέας τῇ θεραπείᾳ,	14 devotion to parents through care,
11. δίκαιοι δὲ <u>πρὸς τοὺς ἀστοὺς</u> τῷ ἴσῳ,	11 justice to fellow-countrymen through fairness
12. εὐσεβεῖς δὲ <u>πρὸς τοὺς φίλους</u> τῇ πίστει.	11 respect to friends through faith.

---

[29] Winterbottom 1988: 10, where a line from this passage is cited and the style's Gorgianic roots noted. Further comments in Rothe 1989: 146–7. Cf. Bethe 1918: col. 774, on Pollux' *VS* excerpts, which 'gehören formell zum Manieriertesten, inhaltlich zum Leersten'.

[30] Text: Most and Laks 2016: 244–6 = F D28 (B 6 DK). Translation: Cole 1991: 72.

In lines 2–3, 5–8 and 9–12 of this excerpt (one long sentence, like Pollux') we see 'lists' of attributes similar to that presented by Pollux, linked by *homoeoteleuton* (-ματα: 2–3), internal repetitions and rhymes (-οι, πρὸς τοὺς, -οὺς: 9–12; the five initial letters ἐ- in 5–8), or simply parallel syntax (5–8). We can also see a care for *isocolon*: eleven syllables in 9, 11, 12; eight in 5–6, nine in 7–8. Again, the Gorgias passage is more extreme than the imperial sophist's version; it packs three 'lists' in close succession, each with its own particular internal structure. Nevertheless, the basic resemblance between the two is apparent.

Isaeus and Pollux thus employ the same range of techniques that we find in Gorgias' work – short cola (often of similar or equal length), simple syntax, the 'list' style, syntactical parallelism of clauses, repetition of words, and the rhyming of sounds at the ends of words and clauses – and toward the same end, *paromoeosis*, or parallelism between clauses through sound effects. It is in this sense that their style could be called 'Gorgianic', even if other conspicuous features of Gorgias' prose, such as *paronomasia* and antithesis, are not so prominent.

The Style of Philostratus' Sophists: Rhythm

If we turn now to the three other passages quoted by Philostratus, we see the same basic arsenal of techniques I have just outlined: sound effects, repetition of words, short clauses, simple syntax. But these excerpts, which are longer, show another feature that was not apparent in the passages discussed in the last section: a strong preference for rhythmical clausulae ending in a cretic ($-\cup-$).[31]

Apollonius of Athens (fl. 185–235 CE)

The best example is the quotation from a declamation entitled 'Callias tries to dissuade the Athenians from burning the dead' (ἐπὶ τοῦ Καλλίου, ὃς ἀπαγορεύει τοῖς Ἀθηναίοις πυρὶ μὴ θάπτειν) by Apollonius of Athens

---

[31] On Gorgias' rhythmic practice, I follow Drerup 1901: 263–7, who analyses the clausulae of the *Funeral Oration* and concludes that Gorgias is conscious of rhythmic effects but follows no discernible pattern (similar conclusions: Röllmann 1910: 13–18). In general, the study of Gorgias' rhythm is rendered difficult by uncertainty as to how to handle hiatus, which is relatively frequent in *Helen* (itself a sign that rhythm was not important to the author) but avoided in *Palamedes*. The statistics for Gorgias' clausulae at Groot 1921: 105, which show idiosyncratic preferences for certain rhythms as well as a wide variation between their use in *Helen* and *Palamedes* (discussed at 59–60), should thus be used with caution, since no information is provided on the procedures for obtaining these numbers.

(VS 2.58.2–3 = 11.20, 601–2).³² The cola are followed by columns providing number of syllables, scansion of clausulae, type of clausula, and translation.³³

1.	ὑψηλὴν ἆρον, ἄνθρωπε, τὴν δᾷδα.	11	– ⏑ – | – ×	c-t	Raise the torch high, man.
2.	τί βιάζῃ καὶ κατάγεις κάτω	10	– ⏑ ⏑ | – ⏑ ×	d-c	Why do you do violence and lead down
3.	καὶ βασανίζεις τὸ πῦρ;	7	– ⏑ ⏑ – | – ⏑ ×	ch-c	and torment the fire?
4.	οὐράνιόν ἐστιν,	6	– ⏑ ⏑ ⏑ | – ×	c²-t	It is heavenly,
5.	αἰθέριόν ἐστιν,	6	– ⏑ ⏑ ⏑ | – ×	c²-t	it is ethereal,
6.	πρὸς τὸ ξυγγενὲς ἔρχεται.	8	– ⏑ ⏑ | – ⏑ ×	d-c	it comes to its kin.
7.	τοῦτο τὸ πῦρ οὐ κατάγει νεκρούς,	10	– ⏑ ⏑ | – ⏑ ×	d-c	This fire does not lead corpses down,
8.	ἀλλ' ἀνάγει θεούς.	6	– ⏑ ⏑ | – ⏑ ×	d-c	but leads gods up.
9.	ἰὼ Προμηθεῦ δᾳδοῦχε καὶ πυρφόρε,	12	– ⏑ – | – ⏑ ×	c-c	Alas, Prometheus, torch-bearer and fire-bringer
10.	οἷά σου τὸ δῶρον ὑβρίζεται·	10	– ⏑ ⏑ | – ⏑ ×	d-c	how your gift is insulted;
11.	νεκροῖς ἀναισθήτοις ἀναμίγνυται.	11	– ⏑ ⏑ | – ⏑ ×	d-c	It is polluted by senseless corpses.
12.	ἐπάρηξον βοήθησον κλέψον, εἰ δυνατόν,	14	– ⏑ – | ⏑ ⏑ ×	c-t¹	Come to its help, give it aid, steal, if possible
13.	κἀκεῖθεν τὸ πῦρ.	5	– – | – ⏑ ×	-c	the fire even from there.

The passage consists of seven short sentences, none longer than ten words, which I have broken up into thirteen clauses. The same features that we noticed above recur here: *isocolon* (identical number of syllables [six] in lines 4, 5 and 8), *homoeoteleuton* (identical, rhyming, word-endings: -εις (2–3), -ιόν (4–5), -άγει and ούς (7–8), -ται (10–11), -ον (four times in line 12)), repetition of words (κατάγει/ς (2, 7); τὸ πῦρ (3, 7, 13);

---

³² On this excerpt, Rothe 1989: 192–3, without reference to the style; on Apollonius generally: 183–95.
³³ Clausulae are given both for 'strong' closes, i.e., those at periods, question marks and semicolons (underlined) and for 'weak' ones, i.e., those at the end of cola. I use the following abbreviations: **c** = cretic (– ⏑ –); **c¹** = cretic with first long resolved into two shorts (⏑ ⏑ ⏑ –); **c²** = cretic with second long resolved into two shorts (– ⏑ ⏑ ⏑); **ch** = choriamb (– ⏑ ⏑ –); **d** = dactyl (– ⏑ ⏑); **m** = molossus (– – –); **m¹** = molossus with first long resolved into two shorts (⏑ ⏑ – –, = 'ionic'); **p** = fourth paeon (⏑ ⏑ ⏑ ×); **s** = spondee (– –); **t** = trochee (– ⏑). Since the last syllable is considered indifferent, what I refer to as a final cretic could also be termed a dactyl; final trochees and spondees are also equivalent, but I prefer trochee, except for the clausula (– ⏑ ⏑ | – ×), which I refer to as 'dactyl-spondee' to retain the association with the hexameter. I adhere to the following principles of scansion: vowels before *muta-cum-liquida* are short (i.e., Attic correption), long vowels/diphthongs before another vowel remain long, no elision at hiatus.

ἐστιν (4–5)) and syntactical parallelism (4–5 and 7–8 [with *antithesis*]). But what marks Apollonius' text as different from the others we have looked at thus far is the rhythm,³⁴ specifically the remarkable consistency of the clausulae: nine of the thirteen lines end in a cretic (– ◡ –), and of those nine, six are preceded by a dactyl (– ◡ ◡).³⁵ Moreover, the four non-cretic endings are variants of a single clausula: the cretic-trochee (– ◡ – | – ×), one in pure form (1), two instances where the second long of the cretic is resolved into two shorts (– ◡ ◡ ◡ | – × : 4–5), and one where the long of the trochee is resolved (– ◡ – | ◡ ◡ × : 12). The severely circumscribed palette of clausulae is noteworthy, as is the frequency with which Apollonius uses the dactyl-cretic clausula (in six of thirteen total endings; and three of seven 'strong' endings). The sample size is admittedly extremely small, and hence not necessarily representative of Apollonius' rhythmic practice, but I nevertheless find the presence of this clausula in almost fifty per cent of this excerpt's endings striking, especially considering its rarity in classical prose: 0.9 per cent in Isocrates, 2.1 per cent in Thucydides and 3.6 per cent in Demosthenes.³⁶

Pollux of Naucratis (138–195 CE?)

We can witness a similar, if not as obvious, rhythmic pattern in a passage from the epilogue of a declamation by Pollux, on the theme 'The islanders who sell their children in order to pay their taxes' (*VS* 2.47.5–6 = II.12, 593):

1. παῖς ἠπειρώτης ἀπὸ Βαβυλῶνος πατρὶ | 19   – ◡ – | – ◡ ×   c-c
   νησιώτῃ γράφει·
   A boy on the mainland writes from Babylon to
      his islander father,
2. δουλεύω βασιλεῖ **δῶρον** | ἐκ σατράπου **δοθείς**,   14   – ◡ ◡ | – ◡ ×   d-c
   'I am a king's slave, given to him as a present
      from a satrap,
3. οὔτε δὲ ἵππ**ον** | ἀναβαίν**ω** Μηδικ**ὸν**   12   ◡ ◡ – – | – ◡ ×   m¹-c
   yet I neither mount a horse of the Medes
4. οὔτε τόξ**ον** | λαμβάν**ω** Περσικ**όν**,   10   – ◡ – | – ◡ ×   c-c
   nor handle a Persian bow,

---

³⁴ Philostratus quotes this passage *because* of its rhythm: 'I have not quoted this passage in order to excuse him for his license in the use of rhythms, but to prove that he also knew how to use the more sober sort' (παρεθέμην δὲ ταῦτα οὐ παραιτούμενος αὐτὸν τῶν ἀκολάστων ῥυθμῶν, ἀλλὰ διδάσκων, ὅτι μηδὲ τοὺς σωφρονεστέρους ῥυθμοὺς ἠγνόει). See Rothe 1989: 193, for a different reading.
³⁵ The colometry and scansion of this passage by Norden 1898: 414, differs slightly from mine.
³⁶ Figures taken from Groot 1919a: chart after p. 196; for more details, see below, n. 63.

5.	ἀλλ' οὐδὲ ἐπὶ πόλεμον ἢ θήραν ὡς ἀνήρ ἐξέρχο**μαι**, no, I do not even go forth to war or to the chase like a man,	18 ⏑ – – | – ⏑ ×	-c
6.	ἐν γυναικωνίτιδι δὲ κάθη**μαι** but I sit in the women's quarters	11 – ⏑ ⏑ ⏑ | – ×	-t
7.	καὶ τὰς βασιλέως | θεραπεύω παλλακάς, and serve the king's concubines,	13 ⏑ ⏑ – – | – ⏑ ×	m¹-c
8.	καὶ βασιλεὺς οὐκ ὀργίζεται, and the king does not resent this,	9 – – – | – ⏑ ×	m-c
9.	εὐνοῦχος γάρ εἰμι. for I am a eunuch.	6 – ⏑ | – ×	<u>t-t</u>
10.	εὐδοκιμῶ δὲ παρ' αὐταῖς θάλατταν Ἑλληνικὴν διηγούμενος And I win their favor by describing to them the seas of Greece	20 – ⏑ – | – ⏑ ×	c-c
11.	καὶ τὰ τῶν Ἑλλήνων μυθολογῶν καλά, and telling them tales of all the fine things that the Greeks do,	12 – ⏑ ⏑ | – ⏑ ×	d-c
12.	πῶς Ἠλεῖ**οι** πανηγυρί**ζουσι**, how the Eleans celebrate their festivals,	10 – ⏑ – | – ×	c-t
13.	πῶς Δελφ**οὶ** θεσπ**ίζουσι**, how the Delphians proclaim their oracles	7 – – | – ×	<u>s-s</u>
14.	τίς ὁ παρ' Ἀθηναίοις Ἐλέου βωμός. and which is the altar of Pity among the Athenians.	12 – ⏑ ⏑ – | – ×	ch-t
15.	ἀλλὰ καὶ σύ, πάτερ μοι, γράφε, But pray, my father, write back and say	9 – ⏑ ⏑ – | – ⏑ ×	ch-c
16.	πότε παρὰ Λακεδαιμονί**οις** Ὑακίνθ**ια** when the Lacedaemonians celebrate the Hyacinthia	15 – ⏑ ⏑ | – ⏑ ×	d-c
17.	καὶ παρὰ Κορινθί**οις** Ἴσθμ**ια** and the Corinthians the Isthmian games,	10 – ⏑ – | – ⏑ ×	c-c
18.	καὶ | παρὰ Δελφ**οῖς** Πύθ**ια** when the Delphians hold the Pythian games	8 ⏑ ⏑ – – | – ⏑ ×	m¹-c
19.	καὶ εἰ νικῶσιν Ἀθηναῖοι ναυμαχοῦντες. and whether the Athenians are winning their naval battles.	13 – ⏑ | – ×	<u>t-t</u>
20.	ἔρρωσο καὶ τὸν ἀδελφόν μοι προσαγόρευσον, Farewell, and greet my brother for me	14 – ⏑ ⏑ ⏑ | – ×	c²-t
21.	εἰ μήπω πέπρᾱται, if he has not yet been sold.'	6 – ⏑ | – ×	<u>t-t</u>

While the first three (of four) sentences in this excerpt are long, their syntax is extremely simple; in the first sentence, there are eight main clauses paratactically arranged (2–9), each with its own indicative verb (seven in the first-person singular!) The sophistic 'list'-form, which incorporates syntactically parallel clauses featuring the repetition of word-endings and clause beginnings (3–4; 12–13; 16–18), is the primary structuring element of the passage, occurring three times (3–6; 12–14; 16–19); a bit of syntactical variation is introduced at the end of the second two lists (14 and 19).[37] The clausulae, however, are what interest me here. While they are by no means as monotonous as in Apollonius, one is struck again by the predominance of cretic endings: thirteen of twenty-one lines, including three dactyl-cretics, four cretic-cretics and three cretics preceded by a molossus with the first syllable resolved (∪ ∪ – –).

Onomarchus of Andros (late 2nd century CE)

The last passage from the *Lives* that I examine is by Onomarchus of Andros, whom Philostratus treats with some ambivalence, noting both that the sophist 'was not greatly admired, yet was evidently not to be despised' (οὐκ ἐθαυμάζετο μέν, οὐ μεμπτὸς δὲ ἐφαίνετο), and that he, 'living as he did so near to the coast of Asia, contracted, as one might opthalmia, the Ionian manner of oratory, which flourished especially at Ephesus' (πρόσοικος δὲ ὢν τῆς Ἀσίας τῆς Ἰωνικῆς ἰδέας οἷον ὀφθαλμίας ἔσπασε, σπουδαζομένης μάλιστα τῇ Ἐφέσῳ: 2.54.1; II.18, 598).[38] But in the end, Philostratus praises Onomarchus' style[39] and illustrates it with an excerpt from his speech 'The man who fell in love with a statue', (*VS* 2.54.2–4 = II.18, 599):[40]

---

[37] On this excerpt, see Rothe 1989: 147–51; brief stylistic remarks at 150: 'besteht fast ganz aus asyndetischen Hauptsätzen ... Hyperbaton und Parallelismus häufen sich'. She speaks also of the *fast tragikomisch* effect of the end of the second sentence, at line 9 above.
[38] Pernot 1993: 377–8 (followed by Billault 1995: 109) takes this and other references in the *Lives* to 'Ionian style' as evidence that a pejoratively termed 'Asianist' style still existed in the Second Sophistic. But the other explicit reference is neutral (2.83.7; II.27, 619: τὸ ἦθος τῆς Ἰωνικῆς ἀκροάσεως, said of Megistias of Smyrna), and in any case, the characteristics of the style are never described; to equate it with the 'Asianist' style of the Hellenistic period is not warranted by the evidence. Cf. Bowie 2004: 65–6, who takes a more agnostic position.
[39] '[F]or though he did corrupt his style to some extent ... nevertheless the opulence of his formulations was like Herodes, and they were pleasing beyond words' (τὸ μὲν γὰρ τῆς ἑρμηνείας παρέφθορεν ... αἱ δὲ ἐπιβολαὶ τῶν νοημάτων Ἡρώδειοί τε καὶ ἀπορρήτως γλυκεῖαι: 2.54.1; II.18, 598). On the translation 'opulence of his formulations' for αἱ ἐπιβολαὶ τῶν νοημάτων, I follow Civiletti 2002: 436, n. 10, who emphasises the connection to richness and luxuriance; νόημα refers to '*thoughts* as expressed in literary form': *LSJ* s.v. I.4.
[40] Winterbottom 1988: 9, refers to it as an *ethopoeia* and thus an example of 'a *progymnasma*, then, and certainly not a *controversia*'.

1.	ὦ κάλλος ἔμψυχον ἐν ἀψύχῳ σώματι,	13	– – – | – ⏑ ×	m-c	Beauty ensouled in a soulless body,
2.	τίς ἄρα σε δαιμόνων ἐδημιούργησε;	13	– ⏑ – | – ×	c-t	what deity fashioned you?
3.	Πειθώ τις ἢ Χάρις ἢ αὐτὸς ὁ Ἔρως,	12	⏑ ⏑ ⏑ ×	p	Some Persuasion, Grace, or Love himself
4.	ὁ τοῦ κάλλους πατήρ;	6	⏑ – – | – ⏑ ×	-c	the father of your beauty?
5.	ὡς πάντα σοι πρόσεστιν ἐν ἀληθείᾳ	12	⏑ ⏑ ⏑ – | – ×	c¹-t	For truly you have everything
6.	προσώπου στάσις	5	⏑ – | – ⏑ ×	-c	the expression of your face
7.	χρόας ἄνθ**ος**	4	⏑ – | – ×	-t	the bloom of your complexion
8.	βλέμματος κέντρ**ον**	5	– ⏑ – | – ×	c-t	the sharpness of your glance
9.	μειδίαμα κεχαρισμέν**ον**	9	– ⏑ ⏑ ⏑ | – ⏑ ×	c²-c	the charming smile
10.	παρειῶν ἔρευθ**ος**	6	⏑ – – ⏑ | – ×	t-t	the blush of your cheeks
11.	ἀκοῆς ἴχν**ος**.	5	⏑ ⏑ | – ⏑ ×	-c	a sign of your listening.
12.	ἔχεις δὲ καὶ φωνὴν μελιτοῦσσαν ἀεί.	12	– ⏑ | – ×	t-t	You even have a voice eternally honeyed.
13.	τάχα τι καὶ λᾰλεῖς,	6	⏑ ⏑ ⏑ | – ⏑ ×	-c	And perhaps you will even speak,
14.	ἀλλ' ἐμοῦ μὴ παρόντος,	7	– ⏑ | – ×	t-t	but when I am not there,
15.	ἀνέραστε καὶ βάσκανε,	8	– ⏑ – | – ⏑ ×	c-c	unloving and baleful woman,
16.	πρὸς πιστὸν ἐραστὴν ἄπιστε.	9	– ⏑ | – ×	t-t	unfaithful to a faithful lover.
17.	οὐδενός μοι μετέδωκας ῥήματος·	11	⏑ ⏑ – – | – ⏑ ×	m¹-c	You have allowed me not a word
18.	τοιγαροῦν τὴν φρῑκωδεστάτην	9	– – – | – ⏑ ×	m-c	Therefore that most frightening curse
19.	ἅπασιν ἀεὶ τοῖς καλοῖς	8	⏑ ⏑ – – | – ⏑ ×	m¹-c	to every beautiful one always
20.	ἀρὰν ἐπὶ σοὶ θήσομαι·	8	– ⏑ ⏑ | – ⏑ ×	ch-c	I will place on you;
21.	εὔχομαί σοι γηρᾶσαι.	7	– – | – ×	s-s	I pray that you grow old.

Despite the extremely short cola, there is less evidence of rhyme or sound effects than in the other sophistic excerpts. The long 'list' (6–11) features some *homoeoteleuton* and a parallel syntactical structure (other than in 9), but not as much internal resonance as in our other examples (although the asyndeton reminds one of Pollux' initial lines on Proteus).

Onomarchus does, however, offer some paradoxical and antithetical word play reminiscent of Gorgias, of the sort which we have not seen in our other authors: ὦ κάλλος ἔμψυχον ἐν ἀψύχῳ σώματι (1–2) and ἀνέραστε καὶ βάσκανε, πρὸς πιστὸν ἐραστὴν ἄπιστε (15–16). In addition, the sententious conclusion has a nice chiastic jingle with repetition of –αι throughout: ἐπὶ σοὶ θήσομαι· εὔχομαί σοι γηρᾶσαι.[41] Stylistically, I judge this passage a bit less Gorgianic than the other passages in some ways (sound effects), more so in others (word play), but recognisably related to them through the extremely short cola, the paratactic syntax and the use of the 'list' style. And while Onomarchus' clausulae are far less consistent than either Apollonius' or Pollux's, the favouring of cretic endings remains noticeable: four of the eight sentence-ends, and eleven of the twenty-one cola.

Conclusion

Despite their individual idiosyncrasies, then, these five passages share enough stylistic characteristics to justify my treating them as a coherent group. Their sentences vary from extremely short to somewhat long, but are usually simple syntactically and constructed from short cola, often similar in length. Nearly all of them seek out *paromoeosis*, or, the balancing of clauses by internal rhymes and *homoeoteleuton*; while sometimes structured in pairs, these clauses more frequently take the form of 'lists' in which each parallel member is expressed in matching syntax. The excerpts generally conclude with an unexpected and witty *sententia*. Other devices such as antithesis or *paronomasia* are not as common, but crop up occasionally.

The style of these excerpts, while not precisely mimicking that of Gorgias, warrants the label 'Gorgianic'; they certainly show more similarities to his style than to that of any other surviving classical author. Finally, while it was difficult to draw any conclusions about clausulae rhythm from the first two, rather brief, passages by Isaeus and Pollux, the three longer

---

[41] This excerpt has often been used to illustrate the excesses of imperial sophistic style: e.g., Norden 1898: 414: 'asianischen Manier'; Kennedy 1972: 563–4: 'an extreme example' of the 'elaborate and ornamented style' practised by some sophists; Anderson 1993: 96–7, briefly analyses the excerpt, notes some Gorgianic features, and calls it 'bizarrely contrived'. These criticisms seem directed at the *content* of the piece, or its conceits, rather than the style itself, which seems restrained in comparison to the other examples we have examined. Pernot 1993: 377 is more sympathetic: 'Dans ce texte, qui en réalité ne manque pas de talent ... Style commatique et asyndétique, énumération, jeux de mots, trait final: c'est bien l'asianisme, agrémenté, dans le lignes qui décrivent la beauté de la statue, d'un soupçon de cette *glukutês* où Onomarchos excellait également.'

excerpts, from Apollonius, Pollux and Onomarchus, suggested a preference for clausulae ending in cretics (nine of thirteen total closes = 69 per cent; thirteen of twenty-one = 62 per cent; eleven of twenty-one = 52 per cent, respectively); sometimes, as in Apollonius, particular clausulae, like the dactyl-cretic, are too prominent to be attributed to anything but concerted effort.

The significance of this fact will become apparent after our discussion of the Hellenistic material below. For now, however, I would like to emphasise how different the style on display in these excerpts is, not only to that of classical Attic authors such as Plato, Xenophon and Demosthenes, but also to that practised by the 'major' writers of the so-called Second Sophistic, like Dio of Prusa, Lucian and Aelius Aristides, not to mention the type of writing recommended by classicising teachers and critics like Dionysius of Halicarnassus and Hermogenes of Tarsus. Philostratus' sophists' diction may be pure Attic, and their speeches often set in the classical period, but their *style* is emphatically *not* classicising; in fact it seems to adhere to principles directly at odds with the tenets of classicism.

'Asianist' Style in the Early Hellenistic Age: Hegesias

If imperial sophistic authors write in a style that resembles Gorgias rather than more traditional 'classical' models, how should this be explained? Are they consciously 'classicising' in their own idiosyncratic way, looking back to the classical period, but to *sophistic* predecessors rather than the Attic orators and philosophers? Or are they simply pursuing the styles that had been considered appropriate for declaimers and orators for centuries? Another way to phrase these questions is to ask whether imperial sophistic style is the direct heir of Hellenistic oratorical style, particularly the brand called 'Asian' by its detractors. As I noted above, Hellenistic 'Asianist' oratory has also been linked to Gorgias, and many of the features we have observed in the imperial sophistic excerpts – short clauses, care for certain rhythmical clausulae, isocolon, parallelism and balance – have been identified as features of 'Asianist' oratory by ancients and moderns alike. Are the imperial sophists then the heirs of Gorgias and the classical sophists as mediated through Hellenistic rhetoric? To answer these questions, I now examine the primary extant examples of Greek 'Asianist' prose from the Hellenistic period in order to clarify its relation with its putative descendants.

Defining 'Asianist'

Before I begin, a few words about my choice of terminology. As I made clear in the introduction, the term 'Asian' is misleading for a number of reasons – in antiquity the words *Asianus*, *Asiaticus* and Ἀσιανός, when used of style, were terms of abuse, did not necessarily describe ethnicity or geographical origin, and were only in use for a short time. I have tried to mitigate these difficulties by employing the neologism 'Asianist', coined as a *stylistic* term, with the scare quotes expressing its use as an externally imposed label.[42] Even this solution, however, does not eliminate a more serious problem, which is that the precise referent of 'Asianist' style(s) is not easily pinned down, either in antiquity or in modern scholarship.[43] At times, the label appears to have been used as a shorthand for Hellenistic Greek oratory in general, at others as the excessive polar opposite to a similarly ambiguously defined 'Attic' style, at others a catch-all for a vague and never properly defined 'corrupt' kind of oratory. As a result even scholars who use the term neutrally are not always careful to define what exactly they mean by it. Is it copious and grand, or sententious and pointed? Is it 'dithyrambic' and inspired, or monotonous and frigid? Is it too poetic or too prosaic? Or is it both, as Norden, following Cicero's famous formulation of two types of the *genus Asiaticum*, asserted? While I am aware of these problems, I continue to employ the term 'Asianist' to refer to the texts I examine in this section because I believe that they, despite considerable internal variation, share certain features that set them apart as a group, and it remains convenient to have a name to refer to these attributes. Alternatives such as baroque, mannerist, sophistic, modern or Hellenistic introduce further difficulties and confusions;[44] for now, 'Asianist' will have to do, with the caveat that my use of the term neither implies that the texts in question were so labelled in antiquity, nor is meant to convey any pejorative, ethnic, or geographic connotation.

Hegesias of Magnesia-on-Sipylus: 'Gorgianic' Style?

There are eleven Greek writers explicitly called 'Asian' in ancient sources with respect to their style. No prose survives from five of them, while the

---

[42] For my use of 'Asianist' as the English equivalent of the German *asianisch*, see n. 3 above.
[43] The scholarship on Hellenistic 'Asianism' is immense but often unreliable. The best succinct treatment of the Roman material is Adamietz 1992; for the Greek side, there is no good summary: one must return to the old treatments of Blass 1865, Norden 1898: 126–52, Wilamowitz 1900a and supplement them with Wooten 1975 and Papanikolaou 2009, 2012a.
[44] For other suggestions, see Wilamowitz 1900a: 51; Pernot 1993: 379; Papanikolaou 2009: 67; on the later use of the term 'Asian', see Robling 1992.

fragments of four others range between one to five lines each.⁴⁵ A bit more – a couple pages of prose – is extant from the remaining two authors, the historian Timaeus of Tauromenium (in Sicily) and the 'sophist' Hegesias of Magnesia-on-Sipylus (in Lydia), both of whom were writing in the early-to-mid third century BCE. Timaeus, however, has never loomed large in discussions of 'Asianist' style; he has no apparent connection to Asia, nor does his style match surviving descriptions of 'Asianist' rhetoric.⁴⁶ Hegesias, on the other hand, who came from Asia, is criticised (although not specifically called 'Asian') on stylistic grounds by Cicero and Dionysius and is known to Strabo as the man who had 'initiated the so-called Asian style, corrupting the established Attic practice' (ὃς ἦρξε μάλιστα τοῦ Ἀσιανοῦ λεγομένου ζήλου παραφθείρας τὸ καθεστὼς ἔθος τὸ Ἀττικόν: Str. 14.1.41).⁴⁷ For modern scholars, therefore, it is Hegesias who has become synonymous with 'Asianist' style in antiquity, and analysis of his fragments is a necessary starting point for any inquiry.⁴⁸

Many modern descriptions of 'Asianist' oratory echo the claim, made long ago by Norden, that Hegesias' style is reminiscent of Gorgias'.⁴⁹ In the previous sections, I identified certain features of Gorgias' style that appear also in the

---

⁴⁵ The first five, active in the late second to the early first century BCE, are Xenocles of Adramyttium (Strabo 13.1.66, cf. 14.2.25 and Cic. *Brut.* 316), Aeschylus of Cnidus and Aeschines of Miletus (Cic. *Brut.* 325), and the brothers Menecles and Hierocles of Alabanda (Cic. *Brut.* 325; *Orat.* 231). The scanty remains of four Augustan-era 'Asian' Greek declaimers are preserved by Seneca the Elder: Adaeus (*rhetor ex Asianis*: *Controv.* 9.1.12), Craton (*professus Asianus*: *Controv.* 10.5.21), Grandaus, and Hybreas of Mylasa (both *Asianus declamator* at *Controv.* 1.2.23).

⁴⁶ Timaeus is named by Cicero as representative of the *[genus] Asiaticae dictionis . . . sententiosum et argutum* at *Brut.* 325 (cf. *De or.* 2.58: *rerum copia et sententiarum varietate abundantissimus*). For brief accounts of Timaeus' style, see Blass 1865: 42 ('sein Stil [wird] ziemlich rein und von Schwulst und Wortpomp frei gewesen sein') and Fairweather 1981: 258, on *FGrH* 566 F 31b ('one searches in vain . . . for anticipation [of this type of Asiatic style]'). I am not aware of any longer analysis of the several relevant fragments (F 22, 31b, 94: all from speeches).

⁴⁷ Hegesias is named as an adherent of 'Asian' style only in this passage; he is closely linked with 'Asian' rhythms at Cic. *Orat.* 230 and Theon *Prog.* 71, line 10 (Spengel, *Rhet.*) but not explicitly said to have used them. Other references criticise Hegesias' faults, but do not use the term 'Asian': Agatharch. *GGM* I, 119–22, Cic. *Brut.* 286, Dion. Hal. *Comp.* 4 and 18, [Longinus], *Subl.* 3.2, Plut. *Alex.* 3. Note that both he and Timaeus date from an era well *before* the term 'Asian' had been invented, and thus only acquired the name centuries after their deaths; according to Cicero (*Brut.* 286), Hegesias saw his rhetorical lineage as stemming from Lysias, that is, as *Attic*.

⁴⁸ On Hegesias in general, see Staab 2004 and Prandi 2016; on his style, Blass 1865: 25–33, Norden 1898: 134–9, Calboli 1987, Winterbottom 1988: 7–8.

⁴⁹ Norden 1898: 138–9; Denniston 1952: 22: 'in Hegesias . . . a recrudescence of the jerky bombast of Gorgias'; Winterbottom 1988: 7: 'we find in the historical fragments of the Asian Hegesias . . . characteristics reminiscent of Gorgias'; Kennedy 1994: 96: 'The effect [of Hegesias' style] is somewhat reminiscent of the style of Gorgias'; Pernot 2005: 82: '[Hegesias] developed and exaggerated stylistic effects harking back to the sophists and the Gorgianic style'; Caragounis 2014: 178: 'Asianism, initiated by Hegesias . . . was . . . ornamented with various Gorgianic figures and wordplay.'

sophistic excerpts in Philostratus: the sentences are broken up into very short units, which often consist of paired clauses (sometimes contrasted with each other: *antithesis*) or longer 'lists', both of which emphasise balance and parallelism of sound (*paromoeosis*) by means of rhyme, matching syntax and identical or near-identical number of syllables (*homoeoteleuton, isocolon/parison*); occasionally, unnecessary words are introduced solely to achieve these effects (*periphrasis*). Gorgias' taste for word play (*paronomasia*) involving the repetition of words in different forms or derivations (*polyptoton, figura etymologica*) was not as much in evidence; also largely absent were examples of *catachresis*, or audacious metaphors – e.g., his notorious description of 'vultures' as 'living tombs' (γῦπες ἔμψυχοι τάφοι: D30b) – for which he was often criticised in antiquity.[50] How then, does this compare with the extant prose of Hegesias?

Among Hegesias' fragments, the most prominent evidence of 'Gorgianic' style is found in a series of *sententiae* that recall Gorgias' penchant for antithetical word play;[51] I present three here, concerning the destruction of Thebes and quoted in the second-century BCE historian Agatharchides' *On the Red Sea* (*GGM* I, 120, ll. 4–5, 12–14; 121, ll. 4–5) in the course of an extended critique of Hegesias' style:[52]

F 6: ὄνομα κατελάβομεν πόλιν καταλιπόντες.   15   – ⏑ ⏑ ⏑ | – × c²-t
      We **found** a name, having **left behind** a city.

F 7: τὸν γὰρ μέγιστα φωνήσαντα τόπον   22   – ⏑ – | – × c-t
      ἄφωνον ἡ συμφορὰ πεποίηκε.
      For the place that **spoke** so loudly,
      misfortune has made **speechless**.

F 14: δεινὸν τὴν χώραν ἄσπορον εἶναι τὴν τοὺς   17   – ⏑ | – × t-t
      Σπαρτοὺς τεκοῦσαν.
      A terrible thing: the land that bore the
      Sown Men is **unsown**.

Compare the following Gorgianic examples that combine antithesis with *paronomasia*:

(1) καὶ ἧκον ἅπαντες ὑπ' ἔρωτός τε <u>φιλονίκου</u> <u>φιλοτιμίας</u> τε ἀνικήτου.

     And they all came because of a **conquer-loving** passion and an **unconquered love** of honour. (*Hel.* 4, 82 B11 D-K; 32 D 24 Most-Laks)

---

[50] [Longinus], *Subl.* 3.2 (in a passage that also mentions Hegesias); cf. Arist. *Rh.* 3.12. In fact, we have very few examples of such metaphors in Gorgias' extant works.
[51] Cf. *FGrH* 142: F 13, 18, 25, 26; Norden 1898: 135: 'Wortwitzeleien besonders gern mit antithetischem Sinn'; Winterbottom 1988: 7 and 16, n. 7 on word play as an 'Asianist' feature, citing the three Hegesias examples quoted above.
[52] Text: *FGrH* 142. Translations of all Hegesias fragments are my own, except where noted.

(2) τοιγαροῦν αὐτῶν ἀποθανόντων ὁ πόθος οὐ συναπέθανεν, ἀλλ' ἀθάνατος οὐκ ἐν ἀθανάτοις σώμασι ζῇ οὐ ζώντων.

> Therefore, though they have **died**, our yearning has **not died** with them, but **undying** in our **not undying** bodies [our yearning] for those **not living, lives**. (*Epitaphios*, 82 B 6 D-K; 32 D 28 Most-Laks)

On the face of it, there are clear similarities between Hegesias and Gorgias' short, compressed sentences: both use etymologically related words contrasted with each other to accentuate a sense of paradox – undying vs not undying; living vs not living; speaking vs speechless, sown vs unsown and so on. But there are also some notable differences. First, Gorgias' word-pairs are grammatically more parallel: two genitive adjectives in sentence 1 (φιλονίκου, ἀνικήτου), two adjectives (ἀθάνατος, οὐκ ἀθανάτοις) and two pairs of verbal forms (ἀποθανόντων, οὐ ζώντων; οὐ συναπέθανεν, ζῇ) in sentence 2. Hegesias, on the other hand, pairs a verb and a participle (from two different words) in F6, a participle and an adjective in F7, and an adjective and a noun in F14. Second, Gorgias' use of *paronomasia* in both examples is part of his broader concern for parallelism and repetition; while Hegesias concentrates his wordplay on the single antithetical pair, Gorgias interweaves his antitheses with others (as in sentence 2) or with other sound-repetitions (φιλο- in sentence 1) in order to give coherence and structure to his prose. As a point of comparison, recall the only antithesis of this sort in our Philostratean excerpts – Onomarchus' ἀνέραστε καὶ βάσκανε, πρὸς πιστὸν ἐραστὴν ἄπιστε (15–16) – which weaves four words together in a more Gorgianic than Hegesian manner. Moreover, Hegesias is not content to cleverly juxtapose a word and its opposite ('sown' vs 'unsown'); he seeks to heighten the *pathos* and increase the effect of the phrase by using the words in a bold metaphorical way, as we saw him doing above: where Thebes once stood, 'we found a name'; Thebes 'spoke' but is now 'speechless'; Thebes is now 'unsown'.[53] In this respect, although these Hegesian *bons mots* are undoubtedly related to Gorgianic antitheses, the way in which they are used reflect a fundamental difference between their styles.[54] Hegesias' distance from the imperial

---

[53] Agatharchides (*GGM* I, 120, l. 19; 121, ll. 10–12) refers to Hegesias' τοὺς ἀστεϊσμούς, or 'witticisms' and complains that he 'takes his antithesis from words, not from facts' (ἐκ τῶν ὀνομάτων τὴν ἐναντίωσιν εἴληφεν, οὐκ ἐκ τοῦ πράγματος).

[54] To be sure, Gorgias describes ὁ πόθος as 'dying' and 'living', but the metaphor is not nearly as audacious as those of Hegesias. The latter's tendency to rely on puns, plays on names, and jokes with words is perhaps why he was connected to Timaeus, who was often excoriated for the same thing (Blass 1865: 41–3; Norden 1898: 148 n. 3): compare the historian's pun on Hermocrates, son

sophists, who rarely deploy these sort of puns or plays on words, is even greater.

The other Hegesian fragment that appears 'Gorgianic' is quoted by Strabo in the course of a description of Athens:[55]

1. ὁρῶ τὴν ἀκρόπολιν	7	∪ ∪ ∪ ×	p
I see the acropolis,			
2. καὶ τὰ περὶ τῆς τριαίνης ἔχει τι σημεῖον.	14	– ∪ – | – ×	c-t
and the story of the trident has a mark;			
3. ὁρῶ τὴν Ἐλευσῖνα	7	– ∪ – | – ×	c-t
I see Eleusis,			
4. καὶ τῶν ἱερῶν γέγονα μύστης·	10	– ∪ ∪ ∪ | – ×	c²-t
and I have become an initiate into its mysteries;			
5. ἐκεῖνο Λεωκόριον	8	∪ ∪ – ∪ ∪ ×	X
there Leokorion,			
6. τοῦτο Θησεῖον·	5	– ∪ – | – ×	c-t
here Theseion;			
7. οὐ δύναμαι δηλῶσαι καθ' ἓν ἕκαστον·	12	– ∪ ∪ ∪ | – ×	c²-t
I cannot point them out one by one;			

As in Gorgias' prose, the excerpt features brief, syntactically simple sentences and clauses and achieves its balanced structure not just by the similar lengths of clauses but also by the repetition of words, syntax and sound: the parallel sentence structure of lines 1–4 (including the pair of four-syllable accusative nouns ending lines 1 and 3); in lines 5–6 the antithesis of τοῦτο and ἐκεῖνο and the rhyming –ον endings (cf. also δύναμαι δηλῶσαι in 7).

On the evidence of the fragments that we have quoted, then, one can see why Hegesias' style has been thought to resemble that of Gorgias: both use short syntactically balanced sentences or clauses, repetition of sounds and antithetical word play (albeit in slightly different ways).[56] In fact, every scholarly assertion of Hegesias' 'Gorgianic' tendencies, from Norden onward, has been based on F 24 on Athens and the *sententiae*. Rarely

---

of Hermon avenging the mutilations of statues of Hermes (*FGrH* 566 F102a–b). Lucarini 2015: 14 argues that Timaeus was only considered an 'Asian' orator by Cicero (*Brut.* 325) because he used *sententiae* of this kind.

[55] F 24 = Str. 9.1.16. I use the text of Radt 2002–11, Vol. 3, who emends line 2; the ms reads: καὶ τὸ περιττῆς τριαίνης ἐκεῖθι σημεῖον. Radt's emendation changes neither the syllable count nor the clausula. The quotation continues for another sentence or so, but the text is corrupt. Strabo appears to know the passage well, and there is no hint of the disparagement of Hegesias we saw in 14.1.41. Cola from Blass 1905: 21; cf. Norden 1898: 136–7 (who places additional colon breaks after τριαίνης (line 2) and δηλῶσαι (6)).

[56] The use of *anaphora* (as seen in Hegesias' Athens fragment: ὁρῶ τὴν in 1 and 3) is not, however, a characteristic of Gorgias' style.

mentioned in these accounts, however, is the curious and problematic fact that Hegesias' two most extensive fragments, both much longer than the twenty-nine words on Athens quoted above, display almost no 'Gorgianic' characteristics other than the brevity of the cola and sentences. This raises the suspicion that Hegesias' style may owe its peculiarities to something other than imitation of Gorgias.

Let us turn to these two long passages. The first, also quoted by Agatharchides (GGM I, 120, ll. 35–42), comes from a speech concerning Alexander the Great's destruction of Thebes.[57]

1. ὅμοιον πεποίηκας, Ἀλέξανδρε, Θήβας   17   – ᴗ – | – ×   c-t
   κατασκάψας,
   When you razed Thebes to the ground,
   Alexander, you did the same thing
2. ὡς ἂν εἰ ὁ Ζεὺς ἐκ τῆς κατ' οὐρανὸν   21   – ᴗ – | – ᴗ | – ×   c-t-t
   μερίδος ἐκβάλοι τὴν σελήνην·
   that Zeus would have if he cast the moon
   out of its place in heaven;
3. ὑπολείπομαι γὰρ τὸν ἥλιον ταῖς Ἀθήναις.   13   – ᴗ – | – ᴗ | – ×   c-t-t
   for I leave the sun to Athens.
4. δύο γὰρ αὗται πόλεις τῆς Ἑλλάδος ἦσαν   15   – ᴗ | – ×   t-t
   ὄψεις.
   These two cities were the eyes of Greece.
5. διὸ καὶ περὶ τῆς ἑτέρας ἀγωνιῶ νῦν·   14   – ᴗ | – ×   t-t
   I fear now for the other;
6. ὁ μὲν γὰρ εἷς αὐτῶν ὀφθαλμὸς ἡ Θηβαίων   19   – ᴗ – | – ᴗ ×   c-c
   ἐκκέκοπται πόλις.
   for one eye, the city of Thebes, has been
   cut out.

As in the other fragments, the sentences (other than the first one) are extremely brief. While the first line, with its pair of identical-length phrases (ὅμοιον πεποίηκας vs Θήβας κατασκάψας) and triple –ας endings, raises expectations of subsequent Gorgianic fireworks, in the rest of the passage we look in vain for some of the other features noticed as characteristic of Gorgias: no rhymes (except perhaps πόλεις - ὄψεις in line 4?), no syntactical parallelism between clauses, no *polyptoton* or repetition of words. Instead we find some strikingly odd word order (e.g., lines 5 and 6), a remarkably consistent set of clausulae rhythms (lines 2–5 each end with a

---

[57] Text: FGrH 142 F 12. Translation adapted from Russell 1981: 175. For cola, I follow Blass 1905: 18–19; for other variations, see Norden 1898: 136 (also breaks after Ἀλέξανδρε in line 1, Ζεύς (2), μερίδος (2), πόλεις (4)); Groot 1919b: 6 (μερίδος in line 2); cf. Groot 1926: 34.

double trochee: – ⏑ | – ×), and a series of audacious metaphors – Athens and Thebes as the 'sun' and 'moon' and the 'eyes of Greece' – that lend the passage an over-the-top quality.[58] As we saw above, Gorgias too favoured short cola or sentences and was said to have used metaphors that overstepped the bounds of good taste (although hyperbaton is rare and his clausulae not rhythmic).[59] But the most conspicuous features of his prose – the so-called 'Gorgianic figures' for which he was so famous in antiquity and which were also evident in Hegesias' description of Athens and the imperial excerpts – are missing here. In this respect it is interesting to note that while Hegesias' passage is filled with *conceptual* contrasts (Alexander vs Zeus; one eye cut out, fear for the other; the moon cast down, the sun remains), these are not exploited to create any syntactic parallelisms or paired, rhyming, antitheses, as they might have been by Gorgias.

The absence of 'Gorgianic' *paromoeosis* is even more obvious in Hegesias' longest fragment, detailing the cruel torture and grisly execution of the barbarian king Baetis by Alexander the Great, and quoted by Dionysius as an example of Hegesias' word arrangement (described by him at *Comp.* 4.11 as 'degraded and effeminate' (ἀγεννές, μαλθακόν)). The passage is quite long; I quote only the opening four sentences:[60]

1. ὁ δὲ βασιλεὺς ἔχων τὸ σύνταγμα   15   – ⏑ ⏑ – | – ×   ch-t
   προηγεῖτο.
   The king advanced, leading his division.
2. καί πως ἐβεβούλευτο τῶν πολεμίων τοῖς   23   – ⏑ | – ×   t-t
   ἀρίστοις ἀπαντᾶν εἰσιόντι·
   Some plan had been formed by the enemy
   commanders to meet him as he
   approached;
3. τοῦτο γὰρ ἔγνωστο κρατήσασιν ἑνός   20   – ⏑ – | – ⏑ | – ×   c-t-t
   συνεκβαλεῖν καὶ τὸ πλῆθος.
   for they had realized that, if they overcame this
   one man, they would also rout his host.
4. ἡ μὲν οὖν ἐλπὶς αὕτη συνέδραμεν εἰς τὸ 15   – ⏑ | – ×   t-t
   τολμᾶν,
   This hope led them on to daring,

---

[58] Winterbottom 1988: 7, refers to the passage's 'bombast'.
[59] One might also point to *periphrasis* as a shared feature: e.g., ἐκ τῆς κατ' οὐρανὸν μερίδος in line 2.
[60] F 5 = Dion. Hal. *Comp.* 18.26. Text from Aujac and Lebel 1981; my translation. Cola from Blass 1865: 19–21, with two exceptions: I do not see ἀπαντᾶν εἰσιόντι (line 2) and τοῦτο γὰρ ἔγνωστο (line 3) as separate cola. On the textual difficulties of this fragment (which only occasionally affect scansion of the clausulae) see Spina 1989; Donadi 2000; Prandi 2016 (s.v. F 5); for discussion of the style, Calboli 1987: 36–40; 1988: 219–20.

5. ὥστ' Ἀλέξανδρον μηδέποτε κινδυνεῦσαι   18   – ⏑ ⏑ ⏑ | – ×   c²-t
   πρότερον οὕτως.
   so that never before had Alexander been in
   such danger.
6. ἀνὴρ γὰρ τῶν πολεμίων εἰς γόνατα   15   ⏑ ⏑ ⏑ – | – ×   c¹-t
   συγκαμφθείς
   For one of the enemy fell on his knees,
7. ἔδοξε τοῦτ' Ἀλεξάνδρῳ τῆς ἱκετείας ἕνεκα   18   – ⏑ ⏑ ⏑ | – ×   c²-t
   πρᾶξαι.
   and Alexander thought he had done so in
   order to ask for mercy.

The sentences and clauses are longer than in the other passages, and it is difficult to find much in the way of rhyme, parallelism, or repetition here. Rather one notices the sometimes strained syntax (line 2, 6–7), odd phrasing (4: εἰς τὸ τολμᾶν) and unusual word order (5: μηδέποτε κινδυνεῦσαι πρότερον οὕτως). The frequent change of subject (different in every line) lends the passage a stuttering feel. The most significant factor, however, is the consistency of the clausulae rhythm: every line ends with a penultimate long syllable. Moreover, lines 2–4 show the same concluding double-trochee pattern (– ⏑ | – ×) that we saw in the last passage, and lines 5 and 7, which both have eighteen syllables and end with periods, feature the same six-syllable clausula (– ⏑ ⏑ ⏑ | – ×). I will talk more about Hegesias' rhythm later, but I think these passages make it clear that many of the peculiarities of Hegesias' style – word order, vocabulary, syntax – results from his dependence on rhythm to structure and balance his prose, in contrast to Gorgias' employment of figures of sound, balance and parallelism.[61]

We are left in somewhat of a quandary: in the shorter fragments we glanced at, Hegesias adopts *some* Gorgianic mannerisms – short clauses of similar length, punning antitheses, bold metaphors, occasional repetition of words and sounds – but in the two longest, only the short, balanced-length clauses and metaphors are present, and we look in vain for the 'Gorgianic' devices used often in the excerpts of Philostratus' sophists: rhyming, lists, *homoeoteleuta*, parallel syntax.[62] Hegesias' style is clearly not

---

[61] Calboli 1987: 32–40 has a similar explanation, but perhaps overstates the 'Gorgianic' nature of Hegesias' prose.
[62] It is presumably for this reason that Blass 1865: 25–33, the first and arguably still the best treatment of Hegesias' style, does not link Hegesias to Gorgias. Even Norden, despite his claims of Gorgianic influence on Hegesias, makes no mention of the so-called 'Gorgianic figures' in his discussion of Hegesias' style.

like that of Lysias, Isocrates, or Demosthenes, but it is not quite Gorgianic or 'sophistic' either. He may occasionally use Gorgianic techniques for rhetorical effect, but the dominant characteristics of his prose are his short clauses, his peculiar word order, and his rhythm. Taken as a whole, his fragments do not very much resemble the five Philostratean passages I analysed in the previous section. One could argue that the tone, conceits and striving for effect are similar, but that the means by which those are achieved are not.

Prose Rhythm: The Hellenistic Canon

Hegesias of Magnesia-on-Sipylus: Rhythm

The longer Hegesian passages are notable not only for their short, balanced clauses but also for their odd word order, *outré* vocabulary, extravagant metaphors and peculiar expressions. As I suggested above, the reason for the prevalence of these features almost certainly lies in what is the most noteworthy feature of Hegesias' prose: his employment of an extremely limited number of rhythmical clausulae at the end of his sentences (and cola). A glance back at the clausulae of the passages I quoted above reveals their remarkable consistency. First of all, only three of the twenty-three total lines do *not* end in a trochee (– x). Even more striking is the dominance of just four clausulae; the cretic-trochee (and two of its resolutions) and trochee-trochee account for 83 per cent (nineteen of twenty-three) of Hegesias' clausulae in these excerpts: five 'pure' cretic-trochees (– ᴗ – | – ×), five resolved cretic-trochees of the *esse videatur* type (– ᴗ ᴗ ᴗ | – ×), one with the first long of the cretic resolved (ᴗ ᴗ ᴗ – | – ×), and eight double trochees (– ᴗ | – ×), of which three are preceded by a cretic (– ᴗ – | – ᴗ | – ×). To demonstrate how unusual Hegesias' practice is, we can compare the frequency of these clausulae in his extant corpus with that of representative samples from three classical Greek authors, given in the following table:[63]

---

[63] The figures for Hegesias are based on my own calculations. I count forty-one 'strong closes' or sentence ends (which include periods, colons, question marks) and twenty-eight additional 'weak closes', i.e., cola endings within the sentence. The statistics for the classical authors include only 'strong closes', but given the small sample size I include the figures for the total of Hegesias' sixty-nine strong and weak closes to show the consistency of his preferences. The percentages for the other authors are those given by Groot 1919a: chart after p. 196, and are based on calculations of all 'strong' clausulae in Isocrates' *Panegyricus* (=338), Thuc. 1.1–52, 2.1–52, 3.1–52, 4.1–52, 5, 6.1–98 (=2000), and Dem. *Orr.* 1–6, 8–9, 13 (=898). The figures for c-t-t are in italics to indicate that they are included in the totals given for the t-t category and thus do not count toward the total percentages. All figures are rounded to the first decimal place.

		Percentage of All 'Strong' Clausulae				
Clausulae		Thuc.	Demosth.	Isocrat.	Hegesias	Heg. (+weak)
– ⏑ | – ×	t-t	14.2	18.9	17.0	**26.8**	24.6
– ⏑ – | – ⏑ | – ×	c-t-t	2.3	3.0	n/a	**12.2**	8.7
– ⏑ – | – ×	c-t	9.4	8.0	12.5	12.2	11.6
⏑ ⏑ ⏑ – | – ×	c¹-t	3.1	0.8	3.3	**4.9**	8.7
– ⏑ ⏑ ⏑ | – ×	c²-t	3.5	1.2	6.0	**29.3**	23.2
Troch. end. Tot.		30.3	28.9	38.8	**73.2**	68.1
– ⏑ ⏑ | – ×	d-s	7.9	11.7	11.3	4.9	4.3
– – | – ×	s-s	18.3	18.7	18.5	0.0	4.3
Avoided Tot.		26.2	30.4	29.8	4.9	8.7
– ⏑ – | – ⏑ ×	c-c	2.6	4.0	1.8	2.4	1.4
– ⏑ ⏑ | – ⏑ ×	d-c	2.1	2.1	2.1	2.4	1.4
– – – | – ⏑ ×	m-c	3.4	4.8	3.3	0.0	1.4
Cret. end. Tot.		8.1	10.9	7.2	4.8	4.2
⏑ ⏑ ⏑ ×	p	8.5	2.6	5.0	2.4	7.2

The percentages for Thucydides' clausulae are very close to what one would predict for Greek prose written with no concern for rhythm;[64] in this chart, then, his figures are a rough benchmark for the frequency of a given clausula in literary, but unrhythmic Greek.[65] Isocrates and Demosthenes (not to mention other classical authors) did have rhythmic preferences, but the variation between the percentages of their clausulae and that of Thucydides is small compared to that between Hegesias and all three of the classical authors.[66] Hegesias prefers two clausulae at a far greater percentage than the Thucydidean 'norm': first, the **double trochee** (– ⏑ | – ×),[67] which appears in 26.8 per cent of his sentence-ends, compared to 14.2 per cent in Thucydides. Even more remarkable is that

---

[64] Groot 1915, although the validity of this presumption has been questioned.
[65] Groot 1919a: 22–5 (cf. Hutchinson 2018: 23); Shewring 1931 slightly modifies the percentages for two clausulae that I do not discuss.
[66] Isocrates appears to consistently strive for a penultimate long syllable in his clausulae, as can be seen on the chart, while Demosthenes' avoidance of series of three or more short syllables *anywhere* in his sentences is well known (the so-called Blass' Law, from Blass 1893: 105–12). In general, see Blass 1901.
[67] Cic. *Orat.* 212 calls this the *dichoreus*, and singles it out as the clausula 'Asia very much pursues': *unum est secuta Asia maxime, qui dichoreus vocatur*.

the subset of the **double trochee preceded by a cretic** ($-\cup-\mid-\cup\mid-\times$) occurs in 12.2 per cent of Hegesias' sentence-ends, far more than the 2.3 per cent in Thucydides and 3.0 per cent in Demosthenes. The second clausula favoured overwhelmingly by Hegesias is the *esse videatur* **resolution of the cretic-trochee** ($-\cup\cup\cup\mid-\times$), which appears an extraordinary 29.3 per cent of the time in his sentence endings (23.2 per cent in his total endings); the next highest figure is Isocrates' 6.0 per cent.[68]

The other conspicuous feature of Hegesias' usage is his conscious *avoidance* of two particular forms that are very common in unrhythmic Greek, as well as in classical authors. First, the so-called 'heroic' clausula, the dactyl-spondee ($-\cup\cup\mid-\times$ = hexameter ending), which appears in 4.9 per cent of Hegesias' 'strong' clausulae as opposed to 7.9 per cent, 11.7 per cent and 11.3 per cent, respectively, in the classical authors. Second, the double spondaic ending ($--\mid-\times$), which is the most common clausula in Thucydides, appearing around 18 per cent of the time, with similar percentages in Isocrates and Demosthenes. In Hegesias, however, this clausula *does not occur at all* among the forty-one 'strong' endings we have, and appears only three times in the sixty-nine strong+weak endings (4.3 per cent). All in all, just four rhythms – the double trochee, the cretic-trochee and two of its resolutions – account for 73.2 per cent of Hegesias' sentence endings, while the two avoided rhythms comprise a mere 4.9 per cent. The corresponding percentages in Thucydides are 30.3 vs 26.2 per cent, in Demosthenes 28.9 vs 30.4 per cent, and in Isocrates 38.8 vs 29.8 per cent. Of course, the sample size of Hegesias' extant clausulae is very small, and the percentages would likely not be so extreme if more of his corpus had survived. But even accounting for this, it seems clear that Hegesias is consciously restricting himself to a very limited set of clausulae that he considers suitable for his prose rhythm.

While Gorgias relies on the repetition of words, word-endings and parallel syntax to achieve balance between his clauses, Hegesias prefers to use the consistency and recurrence of certain rhythmic closes to achieve the same end. His eagerness to do so leads him to make other stylistic decisions, such as shortening his clauses, choosing unusual vocabulary and ordering his words in peculiar ways. Hegesias' care for prose rhythm functions as a better explanation for many of the quirks of his style than any attempt to imitate the sophists of the fifth and early fourth centuries. It also sets him apart from the rhythmic preferences I outlined in the

---

[68] Even Cicero, whose dependence on this clausula was noted in antiquity (e.g., Tac. *Dial.* 23), employs it in only 4.7 per cent of his clausulae. Note how rarely it appears in Demosthenes: 0.8 per cent.

previous section. There, from the limited samples I took of imperial sophistic prose, it appeared that clausulae ending in cretics, rather than trochees, were preferred; they represented around fifty per cent of clausulae, which is far more than in Hegesias, who seems to actively avoid cretic endings (only 8.7 per cent of his sentence and cola endings; 7.3 per cent of his sentences).

Late Hellenistic 'Asianist' vs Imperial Sophistic Rhythm

The rhythmic preferences that we see in Hegesias, whether 'invented' by him or not, represent a major shift in Greek prose style from that of the classical period. Whereas classical authors seem to have had their own particular tastes in terms of clausulae and rhythm, there are very few tendencies common to a set of authors or to particular prose genres.[69] In the Hellenistic period by contrast, there arose a 'canon' of clausulae, for which Hegesias is our earliest witness.[70] The primary evidence for this is the close correspondence of Hegesias' rhythmic preferences with those of Cicero, who favours many of the same clausulae, and who had presumably adapted pre-existing Greek practice to Latin prose (and was called *Asianus* by his opponents, the *Attici*, partly because of his rhythm).[71] But we also see signs of such a 'canon' in Greek prose, most prominently in three 'Asianist' inscriptions of the late Hellenistic period, whose fondness for particular clausulae and distaste for others is nearly identical to that of Hegesias, as the following chart demonstrates:[72]

---

[69] Groot 1921: 28–62; Hutchinson 2018: 23 on classical authors' lack of adherence to the later rhythmic system; and Vatri 2020, who posits a more fundamental difference between the 'musical' understanding of prose rhythm in the classical era ('Attic') and the 'metrical', clausulae-centered one adopted in the 'Asianic' system.

[70] The clausulae belonging to this 'canon' vary depending on the scholar, but there is general agreement (with which I take issue below) that it includes the double-trochee, cretic-trochee and cretic-cretic, along with some of their resolutions. See Norden 1898: 917; Wilamowitz 1900a: 35; Blass 1905: 27 (adds the choriamb-trochee); Heibges 1911: 7 (adds the hypodochmiac); Groot 1919a: 128 (adds the fourth paeon); Winterbottom 2011: 266; Hutchinson 2015: 789 and 2018: 11–12 (adds the molossus-cretic and the hypodochmiac, and considers *all* possible resolutions of his listed clausulae as rhythmic, which he calculates would account for 60.5 per cent of clausulae even in non-rhythmic authors). In a recent digital analysis of Latin prose rhythm, Keeline and Kirby 2019: 164 adopt Hutchinson's clausulae but permit only one resolution per clausula, which results in fifteen different 'artistic' rhythms. For overviews, see the two different accounts of Groot 1921: 62–8 ('Die hellenistische Zeit' on Philo, Hegesias, Nemrud Dağ and Mantineia) and 1926: 34–5 (on 'Le canon métrique' which extends from Hegesias to Longus); more reader-friendly is Hutchinson 2018: 1–19.

[71] On Cicero's central role in the adoption of the Hegesian system into Latin prose, see Blass 1905: 17–39; Hutchinson 2013: 233–5. Cf. Winterbottom 2011: 271 for the suggestion that Cicero developed his preferences from listening to contemporary Greek oratory.

[72] For the sake of consistency, I only cite figures for strong closes; percentages including weak closes are not as extreme, but similar (see n. 74, below). Figures for Isis (=*SEG* 26.281) derived from

Clausulae		Thuc. 2,000	Hegesias 41	Isis 26	Mantineia 11	Nemr. Dağ 30	Cicero[73] 1,000
$-\cup\mid-\times$	t-t	14.2	*26.8*	*26.9*	*27.3*	*23.3*	*25.3*
$-\cup-\mid-\cup\mid-\times$	c-t-t	2.3	*12.2*	7.4	0.0	*6.7*	*5.0*
$-\cup-\mid-\times$	c-t	9.4	*12.2*	*50.0*	*36.4*	*26.7*	*16.2*
$\cup\cup\cup-\mid-\times$	c^1-t	3.1	4.9	*11.5*	0.0	0.0	2.9
$-\cup\cup\cup\mid-\times$	c^2-t	3.5	*29.3*	*11.5*	*36.4*	*16.7*	*4.7*
Troch. end. Tot.		30.3	*73.2*	*100.0*	*100.0*	*66.7*	*49.1*
$-\cup\cup\mid-\times$	d-s	7.9	<u>4.9</u>	<u>0.0</u>	<u>0.0</u>	<u>3.3</u>	<u>1.9</u>
$--\mid-\times$	s-s	18.3	<u>0.0</u>	<u>0.0</u>	<u>0.0</u>	<u>3.3</u>	<u>6.4</u>
Avoided Tot.		26.2	<u>4.9</u>	<u>0.0</u>	<u>0.0</u>	<u>6.7</u>	<u>8.3</u>
$-\cup-\mid-\cup\times$	c-c	2.6	2.4	0.0	0.0	*6.7*	*8.3*
$-\cup\cup\mid-\cup\times$	d-c	2.1	2.4	0.0	0.0	0.0	1.0
$---\mid-\cup\times$	m-c	3.4	0.0	0.0	0.0	3.3	*9.7*
Cret. end. Tot.		8.1	<u>4.8</u>	0.0	0.0	10.0	*19.0*
$\cup\cup\cup\times$	p	8.5	<u>2.4</u>	0.0	0.0	<u>3.3</u>	1.4

As one can see, the Isis and Mantineia inscriptions adhere to the 'canon' even more strictly than Hegesias: the same four clausulae favoured by Hegesias now account for every single one of the former's twenty-six and the latter's eleven strong closes. The Nemrud Dağ author has a more varied palette, but the four clausulae still constitute two-thirds of his

---

Grandjean 1975: 108, 115–17, cf. the slightly different analysis of Papanikolaou 2009 and Winterbottom 2011: 275. For Mantineia (=*IG* v.2.268) cola and scansion based on Wilamowitz 1900b: 536–42, with some modifications adapted from Groot 1921: 67–8, and Papanikolaou 2012a. For Nemrud Dağ (=*OGIS* 383), cola and scansion from Waldis 1920, supplemented by Groot 1921: 64–7, and Diggle 2005: 66–7.

[73] Figures for Cicero (from Shewring 1931) are included only to show the similarity with the 'Asianist' system; see Hutchinson 1995 for Cicero's practice and Keeline and Kirby 2019 for Latin prose rhythm in general, both with bibliography. Cicero's preferences should be compared to the frequency of clausulae in unrhythmic *Latin* prose, which are slightly different from the Greek: percentages for the favoured trochaic rhythms = 17.2, 7.4, 1.9, 2.4, total: 28.9; for avoided rhythms = 8.3, 23.5, total: 31.8; for the cretic rhythms = 2.9, 2.1, 5.4, total 10.4; and 4.4 for the fourth paeon (for criticisms of the methods used to obtain these figures, see Keeline and Kirby 2019: 184–5). Note the high frequency in Cicero's usage of the cretic-trochee, its *esse videatur* resolution, the double-cretic and the molossus-cretic, which are at around twice the expected percentages; the double-trochee and c^1-t are also high. Conversely, the dactyl-spondee, double-spondee, fourth paeon and dactyl-cretic are conspicuously avoided.

sentence-ends, close to Hegesias' 73.2 per cent and more than double Thucydides' 'unrhythmic' figure of 30.3 per cent.[74] And just as Hegesias had, all three inscriptions rigorously reject the dactyl-spondee and double-spondee clausulae, in striking contrast to Thucydides.

The *only* clausulae strongly preferred in all of the texts are the double trochee, the cretic-trochee and the *esse videatur* resolution of the cretic-trochee (c^2-t); if one had to posit an 'Asianist' 'canon', these three clausulae would form its core. But in every standard account of 'Asianist' or Hellenistic rhythm, from Blass onward, the double-cretic is added to this group, despite the fact that in Hegesias' fragments, the clausula occurs only once in sixty-nine strong+weak endings, and not a single time in two of the other inscriptions (Isis: fifty-eight strong+weak endings; Mantineia: thirty-seven).[75] To be sure, the double-cretic is relatively frequent in Cicero's prose (8.3 per cent, compared to 2.9 per cent in unrhythmic Latin) and in the Nemrud Dağ inscription (6.7 per cent vs 2.6 per cent). But it seems to me that Cicero's and the Nemrud Dağ composer's practice must be later variations on an original Hegesian scheme that privileged clausulae ending with trochees, often preceded by a cretic.

Imperial Developments

One reason for believing this is the fact that in the early imperial period, clausulae ending in cretics (the double-cretic, molossus-cretic and especially the dactyl-cretic) become part of the rhythmic 'system', alongside the trochaic ones popular in the Hellenistic period. Philo, Chariton and Josephus all favour this wider range of 'Asianist' endings, while continuing to avoid the dactyl-spondee and double-spondee.[76] In light of this evidence, one could see Cicero and Nemrud Dağ as early adopters of what would become mainstream rhythmic practice in the first century CE.

---

[74] Even if we extend the figures to include 'weak' endings, the predominance of these clausulae remains significant: Hegesias (sixty-nine strong+weak endings, of which the four clausulae constitute 68.1 per cent); Isis (fifty-eight, 87.9 per cent); Mantineia (thirty-seven, 62.1 per cent); Nemrud Dağ (111, 59.1 per cent). In fact, the Mantineia and Nemrud Dağ clausulae are *more* restricted than Hegesias': both conspicuously *avoid* the c^1-t variation (⏑ ⏑ ⏑ − | − ×) of the cretic-trochee, which was slightly favoured by Hegesias (strong endings (0 per cent), strong+weak endings (Mant.: 2.7 per cent; Nemr. Dağ: 0.9 per cent).

[75] Groot 1919b: 5–7 concludes from this fact that Cicero could not have taken over his rhythmic practice from Hegesias, and speculates that his Greek teachers had taught him a different system; in 1919a: 126–31, however, he posits dependence of Cicero on Hegesias, and in 1921: 64 mystifyingly includes the double-cretic as one of Hegesias' preferred clausulae.

[76] Groot, 1919a: 130: 'the main characteristics of later Greek prose-metre appear for the first time clearly in Philo', who combines the double-trochee and cretic-trochee (and fourth paeon) with the dactyl-cretic and the cretic-cretic. See below for more specifics.

In the second century CE, however, there is an observable movement away from trochaic endings and towards cretic endings.[77] We saw this in all three of the 'rhythmic' sophistic excerpts from Philostratus we looked at above, but statistics compiled for other 'sophistic' writers point the same way. In the chart below, one can observe the development from the first century CE, when *both* trochaic and cretic endings are favoured, to the second century CE, when writers are either indifferent to or avoid trochaic endings and prefer cretic endings.[78]

	1st century CE			2nd century CE				
	Thuc.	Philo	Charit.	Polem.	Favor.	Hadr.	T. Long.	Max.
Clausulae	2,000	500	866	898	355	53	all	1,000
−υ|−× t-t	14.2	18.1	21.3	15.0	11.8	11.3	17.8	n/a
−υ−|−× c-t	9.4	16.0	17.6	9.1	5.4	5.7	7.5	2.8
υυυ−|−× c^1-t	3.1	4.6	1.4	1.1	1.2	1.9	n/a	n/a
−υυυ|−× c^2-t	3.5	6.2	3.7	1.4	3.4	1.9	n/a	1.4
Troch. end. Tot.	*30.3*	*44.9*	*44.0*	*26.6*	*21.8*	*20.75*	*25.3+*	—
−υυ|−× d-s	7.9	2.0	2.0	1.7	2.8	1.9	n/a	1.6
−−|−× s-s	18.3	4.6	3.1	4.1	7.0	1.9	n/a	13.3
Avoided Tot.	*26.2*	*6.6*	*5.1*	*5.8*	*9.8*	*3.8*	n/a	*14.9*
−υ−|−υ× c-c	2.6	4.6	7.2	10.5	8.6	17.0	9.0	7.4
−υυ|−υ× d-c	2.1	6.2	5.9	11.6	7.0	10.8	9.1	n/a
−−−|−υ× m-c	3.4	5.4	4.1	7.8	9.5	9.4	5.7	10.1
Cret. end. Tot.	*8.1*	*16.2*	*17.2*	*29.9*	*25.1*	*37.2*	*23.8*	*17.5+*

---

[77] Groot 1919a: 131: 'Nor can it be said that − υ \| − υ, − υ − \| − υ, and − υ − \| − υ − [double-trochee, cretic-trochee, cretic-cretic] are the clausulae of the later prose'; the dactyl-cretic is 'a more typical later Greek form'. Groot also points out that the statistics disprove Wilamowitz' assertion (1900a: 37) that the Atticist reaction drove out rhythmic prose in the second century CE.

[78] Clausulae numbers for Philo (opening of *De humanitate*), Chariton (Books 1–2, 4, 6), and Longus (number unknown, but covering the complete work) include strong closes only; strong+weak closes for Polemo (*Decl.* 1 and 2), Favorinus (*De fortuna* = Dio Chrys. *Or.* 63), Hadrian of Tyre (*Decl.* 1 and 2), and Maximus (unspecified sample). Percentages for Philo taken from Groot 1919a: 196; Chariton from Groot 1915 and 1919a: chart following p. 196 (using data from Heibges 1911); Polemo and Favorinus from my calculations based on the data in Heibges 1911: 83–6 and Goggin 1951: 162–87, respectively; Hadrian of Tyre from my scansion (text: Amato 2009: 70–3); Longus from Hunter 1983: 84–5; Maximus of Tyre from Trapp 1997: 1963–4. Hunter and Trapp report only a selection of clausula percentages, which explains the gaps in the table; the sign (+) thus indicates that the percentage for the total is based only on available figures and is likely higher.

Both sets of imperial authors could be called 'Asianist' in their rhythm since they refrain from using the traditionally avoided clausulae, but the range of preferred endings narrows for many 'sophistic' writers in the later period. This shift in the practice of prose rhythm, although it has not been noticed in any study of which I am aware, is a crucial piece of evidence in evaluating the relationship between the 'Asianist' prose of the Hellenistic era and that of the imperial sophists of the second century CE. Hegesias and other Hellenistic 'Asianists' adhere to a narrow set of clausulae primarily ending in trochees and avoid those ending in cretics; Philostratus' sophists, on the other hand, prefer rhythms ending in cretics and avoid those ending in trochees. Although the reasons for this change are unclear, rhythm is one of the stylistic elements that sets Hellenistic and imperial authors apart, not only from Gorgias and the sophists of the classical period but also from each other.[79]

The Style of Late Hellenistic 'Asianist' Inscriptions

The inscriptions' adherence to a fairly homogenous set of rhythmical guidelines ally them with Hegesias and set them apart from the imperial sophistic texts. What about their style? Dimitrios Papanikolaou has made a case for seeing all three inscriptions as examples of what he calls Hellenistic 'sophistic' oratory, sharing the same attitude not only toward prose rhythm, but also toward style in general: 'a type of gorgianising and dithyrambic oratory which was cultivated by the type of orator who was called "sophist" during the Hellenistic ages'.[80] On the one hand, it is no surprise that the search for specific clausulae leads to some of the same side-effects in the inscriptions as in Hegesias' prose – e.g., hyperbaton and odd vocabulary. There are also other stylistic characteristics common to all three inscriptions, such as isocolon, occasional interest in parallel constructions, and a tendency toward periphrasis. Nevertheless, each of them has an individual style that sets them apart, not only from Hegesias *and* the imperial sophists, but also from each other.[81]

Encomium of Isis, Maroneia (Thrace) (SEG 26.821, c. 150–100 BCE)

The 'Asianist' inscription closest in time to that of Hegesias is an encomium of the goddess Isis, found in 1969 at Maroneia in Thrace and

---

[79] Shewring 1934, who discusses the similar tendencies of Lucian, calls attention to the practice of Plato, who is one of the few classical authors to prefer cretic endings and eschew the cretic-trochee. Did his rhythmic choices influence Second Sophistic writers?
[80] Papanikolaou 2009: 67; cf. 2012a: 149, where the main links are drawn between Mantineia and Nemrud Dağ, with much less emphasis on the Isis inscription.
[81] I record the clausulae only to illustrate their consistency, as discussed in the previous section.

dating to the late second or early first century BCE. I quote eight lines (6–13) of the surviving forty-four lines of the inscription, arranged into twelve cola:[82]

1.	ὥσπερ οὖν ἐπὶ τῶν ὀμμάτων, Ἴσι, So, just as with my eyes, Isis,	11	$- \cup - \mid - \times$	c-t
2.	ταῖς εὐχαῖς ∣[ἐπήκο]υσας, you listened to my prayers,	7	$- \cup - \mid - \times$	c-t
3.	ἐλθὲ τοῖς ἐπαίνοις καὶ⌒ἐπὶ δευτέραν εὐχήν· ∣ come for your praises and to my second prayer;	13	$- \cup - \mid - \times$	c-t
4.	[κα]ὶ γὰρ τὸ σὸν ἐγκώμιον τῶν ὀμμάτων ἐστὶ κρεῖσσον∣ for the praise of you is more important than my eyes,	16	$- \cup - \mid - \cup \mid - \times$	c-t-t
5.	[ὅτ]αν, οἷς ἔβλεψα τὸν ἥλιον τούτοις whenever, with the same eyes with which I saw the sun,	11	$- \cup - \mid - \times$	c-t
6.	καὶ τὸν σὸν βλέπω κόσμον· ∣ I also see your world.	7	$- \cup - \mid - \times$	c-t
7.	πείθομαι δὲ πάντως σε παρέσεσθαι. I am completely confident that you will come again.	11	$- \cup \cup \cup \mid - \times$	c²-t
8.	εἰ γὰρ ὑπὲρ τῆς ἐμῆς καλουμέ∣νη σωτηρίας ἦλθες, For since you, when called, came for my salvation,	17	$- \cup - \mid - \times$	c-t
9.	πῶς ὑπὲρ τῆς ἰδίας τιμῆς οὐκ ἂν ἔλθοις; how would you not come for your own honour?	13	$- \cup \mid - \times$	t-t
10.	θαρ∣ρῶν οὖν πορεύομαι πρὸς τὰ λοιπά, So taking heart I proceed to what remains,	11	$- \cup - \mid - \cup \mid - \times$	c-t-t
11.	γινώσκων ὅτι τὸ⌒ἐγκώμιον∣ knowing that this encomium	9	$- \cup \cup - \mid - \cup \times$	ch-c
12.	νοῦς μὲν θεοῦ, χεῖρες δὲ γράφουσιν ἀνθρώπου. is written by the mind of a god, but also by the hands of a man.	13	$- \cup - \mid - \times$	c-t

[82] Text is that of Grandjean 1975: 115–17, with the exception of 7, where I accept the emendation of [ὅτ]αν, οἷς in place of Grandjean's [πλ]άνοις (see Horsley 1981: 11; Danker 1982: 182; Papanikolaou 2009: 67–8). Clausulae according to Grandjean, except for 3 and 4, where I combine Grandjean's two cola into one; cf. the slightly different colometry in Papanikolaou 2009. Translation adapted from Horsley (different translation in Danker 1982: 180–1).

Like Hegesias, the author breaks up his sentences into very short clauses, avoids hiatus (exceptions in 3 and 11) and employs hyperbaton (in 6, 8 and 12), presumably to aid in maintaining the consistency of the rhythm, which we have already noted is particularly rigorous (note that ten of fifteen clausulae are cretic-trochees). The antitheses in Hegesias' *sententiae* also find their counterparts in 8–9 and 12, albeit in less audacious form. But one is also struck by the way in which the repetition of certain key words in close succession – ὀμμάτα, εὐχή, βλέπω, ὑπέρ, ἦλθον – contribute to a sense of balance between clauses that is more reminiscent of Gorgias. The antitheses perform a similar function, as can be seen more clearly in the following sentence:[83]

13.	αὕτη τῶν ἀνθρώπων οἷς μὲν βάρβαρον,	6	– – – | – ∪ ×	m-c
	She, for some men a non-Greek,			
14.	οἷς δ' ἑλλη|νίδα διάλεκτον ἔστησεν,	12	– ∪ – | – ×	c-t
	for others a Greek language, has established,			
15.	ἵν' ἦι τὸ γένος διαλλάσσον	9	– ∪ – | – ×	c-t
	so that the race might be differentiated			
16.	μὴ μό|νον ἀνδράσιν πρὸς γυναῖκας,	10	– ∪ – | – ∪ | – ×	c-t-t
	not only as between men and women,			
17.	ἀλλὰ καὶ πᾶσι πρὸς πάντας·|	8	– ∪ – | – ×	<u>c-t</u>
	but also as between everyone and everyone.			

The antitheses themselves are more modest and less playful than those of Gorgias, but the care with which our author has constructed this text from the building blocks associated with Gorgias and sophistic *Kunstprosa* – short clauses, antitheses, repetition of words, balance and parallelism – is evident.[84] In this respect, the style of the Isis encomium, despite its adherence to the 'Asianist' rhythmic canon, stands closer to the imperial sophistic texts than to Hegesias, as do the inscription's relative lack of periphrasis, metaphorical expressions and unusual words. But the overall effect is far more restrained, primarily because the aspects of 'Gorgianic' style that were so conspicuous in the imperial texts – their continuous emphasis on echoes of sound (*paromoeosis*) and the taste for series of parallel clauses (or 'lists') – are largely absent.[85]

---

[83] Lines 26–8; cf. 22–4.
[84] According to Grandjean 1975: 108–9, the inscription's style is characterised by purity of language (very little *koine* influence), avoidance of hiatus, frequent use of *anaphora* and assonance, variety of syntactical constructions, and alternation between simple and complex periods.
[85] Papanikolaou 2009 speaks of 'Gorgianic word-play', but he refers only to 'isocolon and parallelism' (60) and repetition of words. The only example of Gorgianic *paronomasia* occurs in lines 30–1: οὐ τὴν βίαν νομικὸν ἀλλὰ [τ]ὸν νόμον ἀβίαστον εὑροῦσαι ('[cities], having discovered not violence legalised, but law without violence').

Mantineia-Antigoneia (Arcadia) IG v.2.268 (c. 27 BCE–15 CE)

The next inscription, dated to the reign of Augustus and found in the Peloponnese, is also an encomium – of an aristocrat, Euphrosynos, and his wife, Epigone. The following passage (= lines 32–42 of the inscription) is characteristic of the forty-five-line fragment:[86]

1.	ἐζεύγνυν|το γὰρ βιό[τοι]ς [κ]αὶ σώμασιν ψυχαὶ They were yoked together, life to life, and in spirit and body,	14	– ⏑ – | – ×	c-t
2.	καὶ παρ' ἀμφοτέροις | ἀμέρι[στος ὁ]μόνοια. and on both sides there was indivisible harmony.	14	[– ⏑ ⏑] ⏑ | – ×	c²-t
3.	φθάνοντες δ' ἀλλήλους ταῖς εἰς | εὐ-[ποΐας] ἐπινοίαις They vied with each other in thinking up bene[factions],	16	–] ⏑ ⏑ | – ×	d-s
4.	ναοὺς μὲν ἤγειραν εἰς ἔδαφος ἠ-|ρε[ιμμέν]ους they constructed temples fixed on foundations,	14	⏑ ⏑ ⏑ – | [– ⏑] ×	c¹-c
5.	δειπνιστήριά τε προσεμήκυναν δειπνι-|[στη]ρίοις they added dining-halls to dining-halls,	16	– – – | [–] ⏑ ×	m-c
6.	καὶ ταμεῖα συνόδοις ἐχαρίσαντο, and they graced associations with treasuries,	12	– ⏑ ⏑ ⏑ | – ×	c²-t
7.	παρεχόμε|[νοι] μὴ μόνον θεοῖς εὐσέβειαν, showing not only piety to the gods,	14	– ⏑ – – ⏑ | – ×	c-t-t
8.	ἀλλὰ καὶ τόποις κόσμον·| but also beauty to places.	7	– ⏑ – | – ×	c-t
9.	ἥ τε σεμνοτάτη καὶ φίλανδρος Ἐπιγόνη The respectable and husband-loving Epigone,	14	⏑ ⏑ ⏑ ×	p
10.	μειμησαμέ|νη τὸν γαμήσαντα καὶ αὐτή, too, imitating her husband,	13	– ⏑ – | – ×	c-t

---

[86] Text: *IG* v.2.268; translation: Bremen 1996: 274–5. Colometry: Papanikolaou 2012a: 138 (exception: he adds a division after βιό[τοι]ς in line 1); cf. the different colometry of Wilamowitz 1900b: 538 and the comments of Groot 1921: 67–8.

11.	πάσῃ θεῷ τὴν ἀνεπίτα|{τα}κτον ἱερωσύνην ἀναλαβοῦσα having taken on the priesthood of every deity, out of her own free will	21	– ∪ ∪ ∪ | – ×	c²-t
12.	μετὰ πάσης δαπά|νης πολυτελοῦς, at great cost,	11	∪ ∪ ∪ ×	p
13.	**τοὺς** μὲν **θεοὺς** ἐθρήσκευσεν εὐ|σεβ**ῶς**, worshipped the gods piously,	11	– ∪ | – ∪ ×	t-c
14.	**τοὺς** δ' ἀνθρώπ**ους** εὐώχησε πανδήμ**ως**. and feasted the people as a whole.	11	– ∪ – | – ×	c-t

Although the sentences here are considerably longer than those in the Isis inscription, the syntax is less varied (dominated by participial phrases), and the balancing of the clauses through *isocolon* even more remarkable: note 12–14, each with eleven syllables; 1, 2, 4, 7 and 9, each with fourteen; 3 and 5 each with sixteen. There are some antithetical flourishes (underlined at 7–8 and 13–14 with their parallel syntax and *homoeoteleuta*), but these are relatively uncommon in the inscription as a whole.[87] Overall, one has the impression of careful, balanced arrangement, but the parallel clauses so fundamental to the Isis encomium are less prominent here, as is the Gorgianic emphasis on sound, rhyme and lists. On the other hand, we do see here some periphrasis, unusual word choice and usage of the kind that appear in Hegesias' prose (though not in the Isis inscription), as well as the canonical clausulae, hyperbaton and strict avoidance of hiatus common to all of the Hellenistic 'Asianist' texts.[88] But what sets this inscription apart from the texts we have examined so far are the long, effusive sentences, conveying a richness that contrasts sharply with the abrupter styles of Hegesias and the Isis encomium.[89]

Nemrud Dağ (before 31 BCE)

The final inscription, a proclamation by Antiochus I the king of Commagene, set up at Nemrud Dağ in the middle of the first century BCE, is without a doubt the most famous of the three. In his *Die antike Kunstprosa*, Norden quoted it in full as a specimen of what he called *die*

---

[87] The use of antithesis is a bit clumsy; the clauses rhyme and are syntactically parallel, but the words employed – εὐώχησε πανδήμως (14) and παρεχόμενοι ... τόποις κόσμον (7–8) – are unnatural, and seem to have been chosen solely to achieve the antithetical effect.
[88] Wilamowitz 1900b: 541–2; Papanikolaou 2012a: 139–40.
[89] Cf. Wilamowitz 1900b: 542: 'es ist etwas wesentlich anderes als die gorgianische Rede, die doch mit coordinirten Gliedern operirt, aber seine Herkunft aus der vorisokratischen Kunstprosa verläugnet dieser "Asianismus" nicht'.

zweite asianische Stilart ('the second type of Asianist style'), following Cicero's well-known 'definition' of two *genera Asiatica* (*Brut.* 226).[90] Here is a typical excerpt (lines 105–19, tr. Dörner 1996):

1. διαμονῆς δὲ τούτων ἕνεκεν, | ἣν ἐμφρονίμοις ἀνδράσι εὐσεβὲς | ἀεὶ τηρεῖν,   – ⏑ – | – ×   c-t
   Now that these regulations have been established, to be observed continually as the pious duty of men of understanding,
2. οὐ μόνον εἰς τιμὴν ἡμετέραν | ἀλλὰ καὶ μακαριστὰς ἐλπίδας ἰδίας ἑ|κάστου τύχης ἐγὼ καθοσιώσας,   – ⏑ ⏑ ⏑ | – ×   c²-t
   not only in my honour but also in the blessed hope of their good fortune, I, in obedience
3. ἐν στή|λ[α]ις ἀσύλοις ἐχάραξα γνώμηι θεῶν | ἱερὸν νόμον,   – ⏑ ⏑ | – ⏑ ×   d-c
   to the inspiration of the gods, have ordered to be inscribed upon inviolable stelae a holy law,
4. ὃν θέμις ἀνθρώπων | γενεαῖς ἀπάντων,   – ⏑ | – ×   t-t
   which it shall be binding upon all generations of mankind
5. οὓς ἂν χρόνος | ἄπειρος εἰς διαδοχὴν | χώρας ταύτης ἰδίαι βίου μοῖραι καταστή|σῃ,   – ⏑ – | – ×   c-t
   who in the immeasurable course of time, through their special lot in life, shall successively be destined to dwell in this land,
6. τηρεῖν ἄσυλον,   – ⏑ | – ×   t-t
   to observe without violation,
7. εἰδότας ὡς χαλεπὴ νέ|μεσις βασιλικῶν δαιμόνων τιμωρὸς ὁμοί|ως ἀμελίας τε καὶ ὕβρεως ἀσέβειαν διώκει, | – ⏑ | – ×   t-t
   knowing that the stern penalty of the deified royal ancestors will pursue equally the impiety caused by neglect as that occasioned by folly,
8. καθωσιωμένων τε ἡρώων ἀτειμασθεὶς νόμος | ἀνειλάτους ἔχει ποινάς.   – ⏑ – | – ×   <u>c-t</u>
   and that disregard of the law decreed for the honor of the heroes brings with it inexorable penalties.

It should be immediately obvious that the prose style of this inscription, despite its avoidance of hiatus, frequent recourse to hyperbaton (e.g., lines 4 and 8) and adherence to the 'Asianist' canon of clausulae, is quite unlike

---

[90] On the language and style of this inscription (not discussed in Versluys 2017), see Waldis 1920; Dörrie 1964: 138–70; Waldmann 1973.

anything we have been examining thus far: instead of the clipped, staccato syntax of Hegesias or the short cola and relatively straightforward language of the Isis inscription, we have here one extremely long sentence, composed of cola much longer than in our other examples and written in a style characterised by verbosity (lines 7 and 8), unfamiliar words (e.g., διαμονῆς in line 1, ἀνειλάτους in line 8) and contorted syntax (line 5), and a generally grandiose tone.[91] As in the Mantineia inscription, which also featured, albeit in a more restrained fashion, periphrases, rare vocabulary and long sentences, the Nemrud Dağ author inserts the occasional parallel antithesis into his prose; for instance at lines 11–14:[92]

1. ἐγὼ πάντων ἀγαθῶν <u>οὐ μόνον</u> | κτῆσιν   22   – υ – | υ υ ×   c-t¹
   βεβαιοτάτην,
   That piety of all good things is not only the
       most secure possession
2. <u>ἀλλὰ καὶ ἀπόλαυ</u>|σιν ἡδίστην ἀνθρώποις   22   – υ | – ×   t-t
   ἐνόμισα τὴν | εὐσέβειαν ...
   but also the sweetest enjoyment for mankind,
       I have come to believe ...

But any resemblances to the Mantineia text are eclipsed by the effect of the drawn-out sentences that resist division into cola and revel in their elaborate circumlocution (the same idea or concept is expressed multiple times using different vocabulary) and monotonous syntax (which rejects subordination in favour of a dependence on relative and participial clauses).[93] The Nemrud Dağ composer, like Hegesias and the authors of the other inscriptions, wrote a careful, rhetorically polished prose and took great care to achieve certain clausulae, but he did so in a style quite different from his Hellenistic counterparts.[94]

Conclusion

The three inscriptions have a number of features in common: they pursue the same 'canon' of clausulae as Hegesias and also employ techniques permitting them to achieve those clausulae, such as the avoidance of hiatus

---

[91] Cf. Grandjean 1975: 109, n. 20 on the stark differences between the style of the Isis and Nemrud Dağ inscriptions.
[92] Cf. lines 20–3: καὶ κινδύνους μεγάλους παραδόξως διέφυγον || καὶ πράξεων δυσελπίστων εὐμηχάνως ἐπεκράτησα || καὶ βίου πολυετοῦς μακαριστῶς ἐπληρώθην ('I have unexpectedly escaped great perils, I have easily mastered hopeless situations, and I have blessedly fulfilled a many-yeared life'). In general, however, antitheses of this sort are rare.
[93] Dörrie 1964: 144.
[94] Cf. Winterbottom 1988: 16, n. 11: 'Its sentence structure is more like Isocrates' than Hegesias'...'

and the frequent use of hyperbaton. In other respects, however, their styles are quite varied. The Isis inscription has medium-length sentences built with short cola of varied syntax, the Mantineia author prefers long paratactic sentences, reliant primarily on participles, while those in the Nemrud Dağ are extended to even more extravagant lengths by the liberal use of circumlocution and relative clauses. Poetic and unusual vocabulary, rare in Isis, are more common in Nemrud Dağ and Mantineia; the former is also partial to periphrasis and metaphorical expressions, which are less evident in the latter, and virtually absent in the Isis encomium. While all three tend to steer clear of the Gorgianic *paromoeosis* so popular in the imperial sophistic excerpts, each has examples of parallel, sometimes antithetical, sometimes rhyming clauses, but these are more fundamental to the prose of the Isis author than to that of the other two, who use them sparingly. *Paronomasia*, whether of the Gorgianic or Hegesianic kind, is very uncommon in all three inscriptions.[95]

One way to explain the differences between these inscriptions would be to fall back on Cicero's idea of two 'Asian' styles, both of which Norden argued had their origins in sophistic *Kunstprosa*. On this scheme, Nemrud Dağ would fall under the rubric of the aforementioned *bombastische Stilart* ('bombastic style'), while the encomium of Isis would represent *die zierliche Stilart* – 'the affected style' – that Norden illustrated with the fragments of Hegesias.[96] If we adopt this distinction, we could speak of a short, choppy style structured with parallel clauses and antithesis (Isis) and a long, copious one filled with poeticisms, unusual words and circumlocutions (Nemrud Dağ); common to both are certain 'Asianist' rhythmic tendencies with their stylistic side-effects.

One difficulty, however, is that the Mantineia encomium appears to lie somewhere between these two stylistic poles: in some respects, its prose is a milder version of Nemrud Dağ's, but its elegance and balanced clauses recall the Isis encomium. Even more problematic is Hegesias' relationship to this bipartite model: although Norden saw him as predominantly a practitioner of the 'affected' style because of his short cola and his love for antithetical *sententiae*, he claims that he practised the 'bombastic' style as well (presumably because of his taste for metaphorical expressions,

---

[95] Papanikolaou 2012a: 141.
[96] Norden 1898: 133–49. Since Norden never explicitly contrasts the two styles, it is hard to determine how he defines each; many 'Asianist' traits – frigid metaphors, periphrasis, rhythm, bad taste – appear to belong to both styles. The only aspect unique to *die zierliche Stilart* is, as far as I can tell, that it is composed of short cola (or *kommata*); in fact, Norden even considers 'die Zierlichkeit' as a property of *die bombastische Stilart* (145)!

periphrases and unusual words). Yet none of Hegesias' fragments strikes me as especially close to the style of *any* of the inscriptions, except of course in their rhythmic preferences. There may be some heuristic value in recognising that 'Asianist' prose could take very different forms, but we should be wary of hypostatising an observation of Cicero into two stylistic 'schools'.[97] While all of the 'Asianist' Hellenistic texts that I have analysed are artificial, highly rhetorical pieces of prose and should be classed together because of their shared practice of adhering to a narrow 'canon' of clausulae, to attribute other specific stylistic characteristics to them *as a group* would be misleading.

Conclusion: Imperial 'Asianist' Oratory?

What response, then, can we give to the nineteenth- and early twentieth-century claims of a 'continuity' of rhetorical style linking the classical sophists, the Hellenistic 'Asianists' and Philostratus' declaimers? In terms of prose rhythm, the (necessarily limited) evidence analysed suggests the following outline: Gorgias and the classical sophists most likely had individual rhythmic preferences, but their surviving work demonstrates no discernible pattern of preferred or avoided rhythms, much less any correspondence with the Hellenistic 'canon'. The imperial sophists, on the other hand, are concerned with avoiding the same clausulae as the Hellenistic 'Asianists' did – the double-spondee and dactyl-spondee – but they no longer restrict themselves to the preferred Hellenistic clausulae of the double trochee and the cretic-trochee (and its resolutions). Instead, cretic endings seem to become the clausulae of choice, both for the sophists whose excerpts we examined (an admittedly small sample) and for other second-century CE 'sophistic' writers whose practice is better documented (e.g., Polemo, Hadrian of Tyre, Longus, Maximus of Tyre). In fact the latter appear to prefer cretic endings not merely *in addition* to trochaic endings, as first-century CE writers like Philo and Chariton had, but rather *instead* of them, rejecting the very 'Asianist' clausulae that were so popular in the Hellenistic period.

The standard accounts of the development of ancient prose rhythm are thus not incorrect: the relationship between Hellenistic 'Asianist' rhythmic practice and that of their imperial counterparts can be characterised as one of continuity, broadly speaking, inasmuch as both groups of orators are

---

[97] See Lucarini 2015: 11–19 for detailed discussion of the two 'Asian' styles, a division invented, according to him, by Cicero.

collectively distinguished from their classical predecessors by their shared *repudiation* of certain common clausulae. Previous scholars have, however, overlooked the significant variation between the *preferences* of each group, a fact that perhaps reflects a change in rhythmic tastes or styles during the imperial era, when earlier practice, if remembered at all, might have struck sophists as unfashionable, overly monotonous, or simply unpleasant. Given our lack of evidence, it is virtually impossible to determine *why* this development occurred or to understand what effect such a change might have had on the audiences of sophistic performances or readers of sophistic writing (the same could be said of the codification of the Hellenistic rhythmic system). Nevertheless, the fact that there was a change remains significant. Prose rhythm was an extremely important element of Hellenistic and imperial oratory, both Greek and Roman, and the care which many writers took to end their clauses and sentences in a particular way was one of the most significant differences distinguishing post-classical Greek prose from its classical models.[98] The point I want to emphasise, however, is that even here imperial 'sophistic' writing appears to have charted a different path than the Hellenistic 'Asianists' before them.

Describing the more general stylistic relationship between the classical, Hellenistic and imperial texts is more difficult. While the Philostratean sophists are more or less homogenous stylistically and employ recognisably 'Gorgianic' figures that link their prose with that of the classical sophists, the Hellenistic texts feature a variety of different stylistic tendencies. On the one hand, all of the Hellenistic 'Asianist' texts are written in what could be called a broadly 'sophistic' style distinguishing them from other authors of surviving Hellenistic literary prose – e.g., Polybius, Diodorus, Dionysius of Halicarnassus. The penchant for shorter balanced clauses and relatively simple syntax that we see in Hegesias, Isis and Mantineia was part of a trend that probably began in the late classical and early Hellenistic periods (and is perhaps ultimately traceable to Gorgias).[99] There are indeed a few 'sophistic' or 'Gorgianic' features in some of these texts: Hegesias' *sententiae* make use of punning antitheses that bear a passable

---

[98] Cf. the classic discussions of Cic. *Orat.* 168–236, Dion. Hal. *Comp.* 17–19 and Quint. *Inst.* 9.4.45–111, which illustrate both how important prose rhythm was to oratory and how difficult its principles or effects were to explain.

[99] See Wooten 1975. The frequency with which Hegesias is still mentioned (albeit unflatteringly) by writers in the first centuries BCE and CE such as Philodemus, Dionysius, Cicero and Longinus, indicates that he most likely played a central role in this development. Cf. also the use of illustrative examples quoted from Hegesias' speeches in Rutilius Lupus' abridged Latin translation of the first-century BCE Greek rhetor Gorgias' *On Figures* (Brooks 1970).

resemblance to those found in Gorgias and (occasionally) in the imperial sophists. The Athens fragment of Hegesias, as well as the encomia of Isis and of Euphrosynos and Epigone, share certain features – short balanced isocola, repetition of words, the occasional antithesis, and some parallel clauses – that place them in the same rough category of 'sophistic' prose as Gorgias' speeches and the excerpts quoted by Philostratus. But in comparison to these 'sophistic' texts, the Hellenistic ones appear more subdued; they use only sparingly the striking stylistic devices of 'Gorgianic' *paromoeosis* – internal rhymes, *homoeoteleuta* and 'lists' – that are deployed with such abandon by the imperial sophists: Pollux' catalogue of Proteus' seven metamorphoses, the two sets of four-clause lists in his letter of the eunuch boy, Apollonius' series of varied but relentless contrasts, echoes and *homoeoteleuta* in the speech of Callias, or the carefully constructed rhyming and repeating scheme of the quotation from Isaeus.[100]

An even greater contrast is presented by the other Hellenistic texts, which appear starkly different from both their sophistic predecessors and descendants. For instance, in his two longest fragments Hegesias, despite using short and syntactically straightforward clauses, exhibits a fondness for hyperbaton, periphrasis, metaphorical expression and unusual vocabulary that is generally absent from both Gorgias' surviving prose and the Philostratean excerpts. The Nemrud Dağ composer employs the same devices as Hegesias, but takes the latter's abrupt, jerky prose and lengthens the sentences, makes the language more elaborate, and adds some flourishes of Gorgianic parallelism and antithesis, but only as part of a larger arsenal of grand and lofty stylistic devices. The presence of double-cretics in the inscription might be a hint of clausulae preference developments to come in the imperial period, when cretic endings become popular, but in stylistic terms I do not see much evidence of either Hegesias' or Nemrud Dağ's 'Asianist' style in *any* Second Sophistic rhetorical or literary prose, much less those I looked at from Philostratus' *Lives*.[101] There are thus

---

[100] Might genre have something to do with this? While the Hellenistic 'Asianist' texts that I have examined belong technically to epideictic genres, they are not necessarily an exact match to the *ethopoeiai*, funeral orations and *dialexeis* quoted by Philostratus. Were the speeches of the early first-century BCE 'Asianists' mentioned by Cicero (e.g., Aeschines of Miletus, or Hierocles and Menecles of Alabanda) more similar to those of the imperial sophists? The only evidence we have are fragments of Augustan and Tiberian-era Greek declaimers quoted by Seneca the Elder (see Migliario 2012); they are nearly all *sententiae* (like the one-line fragments of Hegesias) and hence not necessarily representative, but a systematic analysis might be illuminating (provisional results: Winterbottom 1988: 8).

[101] Cf. Wilamowitz 1900a: 39, who puts it in a different way: 'Nordens sogenannte Neoteriker der Kaiserzeit schreiben freilich ein eben so buntes Griechisch wie Hegesias in dem Bruchstücke seiner Geschichte oder Antiochos von Kommagene; gleichwohl ist es eine ganz andere Buntheit.'

certainly points of stylistic contact between Hellenistic 'Asianist' oratory and that of the imperial sophists, but the stylistic differences between the two sets of authors, to judge from the texts I have examined, appear more evident than the similarities.

Seen from the perspective of 'classical' or 'classicising' prose, our sample of Gorgianic, Hellenistic 'Asianist' and imperial 'sophistic' texts certainly could be considered as stylistically similar – examples of *un*-classical (Gorgias) and *non*-classicising rhetorical prose easily distinguishable from the writing of canonical Athenian authors like Lysias, Plato, or Demosthenes or classicising ones like Lucian of Samosata or Dio of Prusa. This affinity led Norden to imagine a continuous thread of 'neoteric' style spanning the vast expanse of time from classical Athens to imperial Rome and beyond. But my analysis suggests a different relationship between the three instantiations of 'new' or 'sophistic' prose. On the one hand, there does seem to be a strong resemblance between the style of Philostratus' sophists in the imperial era and that of Gorgias in the classical. Hellenistic 'Asianist' oratory, however, employs a variety of 'artificial' styles that render it distinct both from the putative sophistic ancestors and descendants whom it is supposed to link together. Rather than a continuity between Hellenistic and imperial sophistic style, then, there seems to have been something of a break, at least to the extent that the most striking 'Asianist' styles, like that of Hegesias and Nemrud Dağ, appear not to have been adopted by Philostratus' sophists. Instead, the style of Philostratus' sophists, far from being a continuation of the 'Asianist' style of the Hellenistic period, could be seen as a conscious 'return' to the prose of Gorgias and the classical sophists (albeit under the influence of post-classical interests in rhythm). Philostratus explicitly notes that several imperial sophists – Scopelian of Clazomenae (*VS* 1.55.5; 1.21, 518), Herodes Atticus (*VS* 2.18.3; II.1, 564), Hadrian of Tyre (*VS* 2.43.1; II.10, 590) and Proclus of Naucratis (*VS* 2.61.3; II.21, 604) – studied or imitated the style of Gorgias, Hippias, Critias, or the 'ancient' sophists in general. Such an imperial sophistic 'return' to their classical counterparts could be seen as a move analogous to that practised by 'classicising' authors and critics of the Second Sophistic – an attempt to forge a direct link to the fifth and fourth century BCE that downplays and dismisses the developments of the intervening centuries. Such a reading would be supported by Philostratus' notorious characterisation of the entire period between Aeschines in the late fourth century BCE and Nicetes of Smyrna in the late first century CE – corresponding roughly to the Hellenistic age – as devoid of any notable sophists (*VS* 1.45.1; 1.19, 511).

'Asianist' Style in Hellenistic Oratory   317

A more nuanced approach might call attention to Philostratus' role in shaping this vision of Greek rhetorical history. The landscape of imperial Greek 'sophistic' prose was quite varied.[102] When one surveys the extant writing of the sophists mentioned by Philostratus, one can certainly find similarly Gorgianic, rhythmic prose – e.g., Polemo's declamations or some of Favorinus' speeches – but there are also counter-examples, written in a more restrained style, such as the orations of Dio of Prusa and the declamations of Aristides, not to mention the rather different, albeit equally mannered style on display in Philostratus' own *Imagines* and the works of Aelian. The specific passages I have examined and identified as 'Gorgianic' were selected by Philostratus, and possibly reflect his implicit bias in favour of this style. After all, Philostratus asserts Gorgias' primacy as the 'father' of the sophistic art in the *Lives*, and is one of the only ancient Greek literary critics to consistently praise his style.[103] His choice of excerpts is certainly idiosyncratic: why, for example, quote *two* lengthy passages of Pollux? Why provide quotations from lesser known sophists like Apollonius and Onomarchus, but almost nothing from the much more celebrated Polemo, Herodes Atticus, or Hadrian of Tyre?[104]

Regardless of Philostratus' motives and manipulations, there are other indications suggesting a lack of continuity between Hellenistic and imperial sophistic style. It appears that very little Hellenistic oratory had survived the classicising turn of the early Empire; Philostratus' disparagement of the Hellenistic sophistic tradition (and, by extension, style) could have been due less to antipathy, than to a simple lack of knowledge. In a cultural milieu dominated by classical models, it makes sense that those seeking out a more 'sophistic', artificial style would find their inspiration in the surviving works of the classical sophists rather than those of the lesser valued and largely forgotten orators of the Hellenistic age. And, as I have mentioned, while one is hard pressed to find any imperial prose in the style of Hegesias or the Nemrud Dağ sophist, there are certainly Second Sophistic authors whose surviving work displays the 'Gorgianic' features that I have analysed in the excerpts taken from Philostratus' *Lives* – e.g., Longus, Maximus of Tyre, Favorinus and Achilles Tatius (in Latin: Apuleius). Moreover, even works written by otherwise 'classicising' authors – Dio's *On Law* (*Or.* 75), Lucian's *On the Hall*, Aristides' *Monody on Smyrna* and

---

[102] See the introduction in this volume and above, pp. 272–6, for further discussion.
[103] Cf. Philostr. *Ep.* 73, addressed to Julia Domna, in which he defends Gorgias' reputation.
[104] On Philostratus' role in shaping and warping our idea of Greek imperial declamation, see Guast 2019.

Rhodian Discourse (if genuine) – reveal similar stylistic tendencies, supporting Wilamowitz' claim that orators could adopt so-called 'Asianist' styles when they so desired.[105]

Of course, these conclusions are only preliminary and provisional, given the necessarily narrow range of texts on which I have focused my attention. Much more work on the style and rhythm of Hellenistic and imperial prose remains to be done: e.g., stylistic analyses, both of the few other 'sophistic' texts from the Hellenistic period, such as Epicurus' *Letter to Menoeceus* and the fragments of Heraclides Criticus' *Periegesis*,[106] and of the allegedly 'Asianist' imperial texts (including a host of inscriptions) collected, but only cursorily analysed, by Norden;[107] systematic examination of the clausulae preferred by individual authors;[108] and more expansive overviews of the styles of the imperial 'Gorgianic' authors listed above, which have been studied individually, but not compared or contrasted with each other in any detail.[109] The results of such inquiries would no doubt shed more light on the development of rhetorical prose in the period. For now, however, I conclude that while Hellenistic 'Asianist' rhetoric may have developed a rhythmic 'canon', the sophists excerpted by Philostratus seem to have modified their forebears' rhythmical practice by privileging different clausulae. And they took their stylistic inspiration, not from the Hellenistic orators, but from *classical* sophists like Gorgias.

---

[105] Wilamowitz 1900a: 25–7; Pernot 1993: 388–92.
[106] On Epicurus' text, see Heßler 2014: 71–99; on Heraclides, the brief comments of Pasquali 1913: 216–19.
[107] Norden 1898 on *der neue Stil*: literary texts at 407–43, inscriptions at 443–50; brief remarks in Winterbottom 2011: 263–4. Cf. Wilamowitz 1902: 258–9 and Jones 2000 on the sophistic and 'Asianist' style of Nero's speech declaring freedom for Achaea (*IG* 7.2713, from 67 CE).
[108] Hutchinson 2018: 19–32 provides figures from samples taken from authors of imperial Greek prose.
[109] The only attempt known to me is Pernot 1993: 381–94.

CHAPTER 11

Greek Reading Lists from Dionysius to Dio
Rhetorical Imitation in the Augustan Age and the Second Sophistic

Casper C. de Jonge

Introduction

The books that we read shape who we are. Do we prefer Shakespeare or Beckett? Françoise Sagan or Virginia Woolf? Eichendorff or Hesse? *Alice in Wonderland* or *Winnie-the-Pooh*? Young readers develop their own preferences, while being guided by the recommendations of their parents and teachers. This was not different in ancient times. Hellenistic and Roman rhetoricians made use of extensive reading lists that ranked the best authors of each genre. The selected authors of the past were not just to be read and studied, but also to be imitated in writing and speaking: *mimesis* (μίμησις) thus became a defining aspect of the literature of the Hellenistic and Roman world. It was the eclectic imitation and emulation of selected writers from the rich tradition that helped Greek and Roman speakers and authors to construct their own literary identity.[1] The reservoir of models to be imitated was abundant: a 'classic' poet like Homer was always admired, but the appreciation of authors like Xenophon, Theopompus or Isaeus fluctuated considerably through the centuries: different periods had different preferences, and individual teachers and students could also develop their own literary tastes. Reading lists were indispensable for students who wished to acquire a basic overview of literary styles, from which they could make their own choices, depending on their age, their abilities and the purpose of imitation. Depending on the stylistic qualities needed – clear language, realistic characterisation, rhythmical composition and so on – one could choose one's preferred models of inspiration: Sophocles or Euripides, Herodotus or Xenophon, Sappho or Pindar, Demosthenes or Aeschines, Aristophanes or Menander. This chapter will compare two ancient reading lists of Greek literature, one of them produced in the Augustan Age, the other one in

---

[1] On imitation in Greek imperial literature, see Whitmarsh 2001a: esp. 41–89. For the wide-ranging ancient concept of μίμησις, see Halliwell 2002.

the Flavian Age. The authors of the two reading lists are Dionysius of Halicarnassus and Dio of Prusa (also known as Dio Chrysostom).

Dionysius and Dio have many things in common. Both were learned intellectuals from Asia Minor; both men published a substantial number of writings in Greek; both authors went to Rome at important moments in their careers; and both were in touch with influential Romans of their time. Both men could be called rhetoricians; one was primarily a man of theory, the other one a man of practice. The two authors are separated by approximately a century. Dionysius (born before 55 BCE) came to Rome in 30 BCE, where he wrote a history of early Rome and several rhetorical letters, essays and treatises; among his addressees are both Greek intellectuals and Roman aristocrats.[2] Dio of Prusa (c. 45–115 CE) travelled through the Roman world of Vespasian, Titus, Domitian, Nerva and Trajan.[3] Although Dionysius and Dio have a lot in common, their works are not usually discussed in close connection. Dionysius is considered to be the main representative of Greek classicism of the Augustan world, whereas Dio is regarded as a leading figure of the Second Sophistic. The authors of both periods were deeply engaged with the culture of classical Greece: they strongly believed that the intensive reading and creative imitation of classical literature should form the basis of eloquence and writing.[4] But does classicism mean the same thing for Dionysius and for Dio? Are these two authors interested in the same classical orators, historians and poets? And what is the purpose of their literary recommendations? In exploring the 'dialogue' between Dionysius and Dio, this chapter contributes to the two main aims of this volume: to examine the connections between different genres (in this case rhetorical treatises and letters), and to explore the processes of change and continuity between late Hellenistic and imperial texts.[5]

Dionysius' reading list was part of his work *On Imitation* (Περὶ μιμήσεως), of which only fragments and an epitome (perhaps from the third century CE) have been preserved.[6] The second book of the work

---

[2] On Dionysius' life and works, see Hidber 1996: 1–8; on his addressees, patrons and colleagues in Rome, de Jonge 2008: 25–34; on Dionysius and Augustan Rome, see Hunter and de Jonge 2019a.
[3] On Dio's life and works, see von Arnim 1898, Russell 1992: 1–8, and Swain 2000: 1–10. On Dio as a literary critic, see Valgimigli 1912 and Russell 1989: 299–302.
[4] On classicism in Dionysius, see Wiater 2011. On the politics of imitation in Dio, see Whitmarsh 2001a: 133–46.
[5] See König and Wiater in the introduction to this volume. I am here adopting their flexible use of the term 'dialogue', and drawing on their reflections on the range of ways in which we use terms like 'Hellenistic' and 'imperial': Dionysius and Dio are both writers of 'imperial literature', and both could be categorised as 'late Hellenistic'; however, Dionysius is usually considered an 'Augustan' author (e.g., Hunter and de Jonge 2019a), whereas Dio is framed as a Flavian author (e.g., Sidebottom 1996) or an author of the Second Sophistic (e.g., Swain 2000).
[6] For the fragments and the epitome I will follow the edition by Aujac 1992. Battisti 1997 provides an edition with commentary. On the date of the epitome, see Usener 1889: 7. Translations of Dionysius in this chapter are based on Usher 1974 and 1985.

contained a survey of the most important poets, historians, philosophers and orators of classical Greece: our knowledge of this part of the text largely depends on the epitome, but Dionysius' discussion of the historians (Herodotus, Thucydides, Xenophon, Philistus, Theopompus) has also been preserved in his *Letter to Pompeius*, where he cites extensively from *On Imitation*.[7] Dio presents his reading list in *Oration* 18, which is the only text within the corpus Dioneum that takes the form of a letter. Its traditional title is *On Training for Public Speaking* (Περὶ λόγου ἀσκήσεως).[8] There were of course more ancient reading lists, some of which have also survived. The survey of Greek literature in Quintilian's *Institutio oratoria* book 10 was roughly contemporary with Dio's letter and was probably inspired by Dionysius' *On Imitation*, unless the similarities between Dionysius and Quintilian must be explained by the use of a common source.[9] In the second century CE Hermogenes concluded his *On Types of Style* with another reading list.[10] Some of these lists may have been based on the recommendations of Alexandrian scholars of the early Hellenistic period. Quintilian indeed refers to 'the grammarians' list' (*ordinem a grammaticis datum, Inst.* 10.1.54), and he points out that Aristarchus and Aristophanes of Byzantium did not list their own contemporaries.[11]

Scholars who have examined the ancient lists of Greek literature have argued that they are all very similar. More particularly, commentators have

---

[7] Dion. Hal. *Pomp.* 3.2–6.11 cites from *De imit.* Book 2 (fr. 7 Aujac = fr. 5 Battisti): see Weaire 2002.
[8] Edition by von Arnim 1896. Translations of Dio 18 in this chapter are based on Cohoon 1939.
[9] On Quintilian's reading list in book 10, see Tavernini 1953, Steinmetz 1964, Citroni 2006a, Citroni 2006b and Schippers 2019. Usener 1889: 110–11 asserts that Dionysius and Quintilian used the same source. Russell 2001: 246 states that Quintilian's reading list 'appears to be heavily dependent' on Dionysius. Battisti 1997: 35 leaves the question open. Below I will note some important differences between Quintilian and Dionysius: in some cases Quintilian agrees with Dio, while contradicting Dionysius.
[10] Hermog. *Id.* 2.10–12 (Patillon 2012) (= 380–413 Rabe). See Rutherford 1998: 37–9; Wooten 1987 provides a translation.
[11] The reading lists in rhetorical treatises and letters (Dionysius, Dio, Quintilian, Hermogenes) were far more restrictive than the library catalogues of Hellenistic gymnasium libraries. A fragmentary inscription tells us that the gymnasium library of Rhodes (second century BCE) contained works of (among others) Demetrius of Phalerum, Hegesias, Theopompus, Dionysius, Diodotus, Damoclides and Eratosthenes: see Segre 1935 and Rosamilia 2014: 355–60. Of these writers, the historian Theopompus is also included in the reading lists of Dionysius, Dio and Quintilian (see below). Demetrius of Phalerum is included in Quintilian's list of preferred orators, but ignored by Dionysius and Dio, at least in their reading lists (see de Jonge 2021). Hegesias, whose works were present in the gymnasium library of Rhodes, was rejected by Dionysius and other classicising rhetoricians as the worst writer ever, the epitome of the 'Asianist' style: see Ooms 2019 and Kim in this volume. The gymnasium library of Tauromenium (second century BCE) had names of authors painted on the wall (*SEG* 26.1123), including those of the historians Callisthenes of Olynthus, an unknown writer from Elis, Quintus Fabius Pictor, and Philistus of Syracuse, and the philosopher Anaximander of Miletus: see Battistoni 2006. Of these writers, Philistus is the only one who appears in the reading lists of Dionysius and Quintilian. The evidence from Rhodes and Tauromenium thus suggests that gymnasium libraries included much more material than the selective reading lists that were used in rhetorical education. Dionysius and Dio made a very limited selection from the wide range of authors and books that were available in some Hellenistic libraries.

repeatedly claimed that there is a general correspondence between Dio's selection of Greek authors and the reading lists in Dionysius of Halicarnassus' *On Imitation* and Quintilian's *Institutio oratoria*. Lemarchand states that 'there is almost nothing in oration 18 that cannot be found in Dionysius or Quintilian: these are the current prescriptions, the traditional methods that all the handbooks of rhetoric contained'.[12] Cohoon points out that '[t]he fact that there are no great divergences in these lists gives the impression that there was general agreement in the ancient schools as to which were the best authors for students'.[13] More recently, Rutherford has again emphasised the parallels between the reading lists of Dionysius, Dio and Quintilian: he concludes that all these lists distinguish the same genres (namely poetry, history, oratory and philosophy) and that in all versions poetry comes first, followed by the prose categories.[14] Alain Billault has offered a more nuanced interpretation. Although he asserts that there are no 'substantial' differences between the reading lists in Dio, Dionysius and Quintilian, he rightly draws attention to the conciseness of Dio's list and to his emphasis on 'usefulness', which Billault explains by reference to the addressee of the letter (whose identity I will discuss below).[15]

In this chapter I will argue that Dio's reading list is in fact fundamentally different from that of Dionysius. Their surveys will be shown to share only a few superficial characteristics, like the distinction of poetry and three prose genres. But on closer inspection Dio's reading list radically turns away from that of Dionysius, not only in form (as rightly seen by Billault) but also in substance, that is, in the choice of models to be imitated. Among the authors that Dionysius prefers, Homer, Aeschylus, Sophocles, Herodotus and Demosthenes stand out; Dio on the other hand recommends his addressee to study Menander, Euripides, Xenophon and Aeschines. A systematic comparison between the reading lists in Dionysius and Dio will reveal the many differences between their preferences in poetry, historiography, philosophy and oratory. I will offer three explanations for these differences. First, Dionysius and Dio have different

---

[12] Lemarchand 1926: 10: 'Comme on le voit, il n'y a à peu rien dans la lettre XVIII qui ne se retrouve chez Denys d'Halicarnasse et Quintilien. Ce sont les recettes courantes, les procédés traditionnels que contenaient tous les manuels d'art oratoire.'

[13] Cohoon 1939: 209.

[14] Rutherford 1998: 43: 'To summarize, the pre-Hermogean lists share the following points in common: (1) Poetry and prose are distinguished, and prose is divided into the three main genres of history, rhetoric and philosophy. (2) Within this arrangement poetry indisputably comes first and the prose categories come later in variable order.'

[15] Billault 2004: 505. Again, Bost-Pouderon 2008: 45 points out that Dio uses the same categories ('les mêmes catégories') that we find in Dionysius and Quintilian. Mérot 2017 offers a more subtle interpretation of Dio's 'canon épistolaire', inspired by previous versions of the present chapter.

addressees and purposes: their intended audiences need different kinds of advice. Second, their choices to a large extent reflect the preferences of the Augustan Age and the Flavian Age respectively. Although Quintilian follows the order of Dionysius' list rather closely, it is striking that he agrees in essential points with his contemporary Dio. Quintilian's reading list thus confirms that the differences between Dionysius and Dio are not just related to their rhetorical purposes and audiences but also to the evolution of education (παιδεία), perhaps even the dynamics of a changing school curriculum. Combining the evidence from Dionysius, Dio and Quintilian thus allows us to draw a few conclusions about the development of literary preferences (at least in educational contexts) between the late Hellenistic period and the Second Sophistic. Third, Dionysius and Dio adopt a different tone, which is related to the genres of their works: a rhetorical treatise versus a literary letter: whereas Dionysius presents himself as a stern professor with a serious message, Dio adopts a more modest and more relaxed attitude; we will see that he consciously reverses some of the conventional points of the handbooks on imitation, producing what in some cases appears to be a light-hearted and humoristic pastiche of traditional rhetorical teaching.

Dionysius' *On Imitation*

Dionysius dedicated his treatise *On Imitation* to the unknown Greek Demetrius, but his intended audience consisted of all those 'who intend to become good writers and speakers' (τοῖς προαιρουμένοις γράφειν τε καὶ λέγειν εὖ, *On Thucydides* 1.1.). In the *Letter to Pompeius* (3.1) Dionysius summarises the contents of 'the essays that I addressed to Demetrius on the subject of imitation' (τοῖς εἰς Δημήτριον ὑπομνηματισμοῖς περὶ μιμήσεως):

> τούτων ὁ μὲν πρῶτος αὐτὴν περιείληφε τὴν περὶ τῆς μιμήσεως ζήτησιν, ὁ δὲ δεύτερος περὶ τοῦ τίνας ἄνδρας μιμεῖσθαι δεῖ ποιητάς τε καὶ φιλοσόφους, ἱστοριογράφους <τε> καὶ ῥήτορας, ὁ δὲ τρίτος περὶ τοῦ πῶς δεῖ μιμεῖσθαι μέχρι τοῦδε ἀτελής.

> The first of these contains an enquiry into the nature of imitation itself. The second discusses the question of which particular poets and philosophers, historians and orators, should be imitated. The third, in which the question of how imitation should be done, is as yet incomplete.

The epitomised version of the second book starts with two stories (*On Imitation* 1.1–5). The protagonist of the first anecdote (1.2–3) is an ugly farmer who wishes to have beautiful children. Having fashioned beautiful images (εἰκόνας εὐπρεπεῖς), he asks his wife to look at them regularly. He then sleeps with her and so ensures that his children obtain 'the beauty of the images' (τὸ κάλλος τῶν εἰκόνων). The painter Zeuxis of Croton plays the leading role in the second story (1.4). When he is planning to make a painting of the naked Helen, the citizens of Croton send their daughters to the painter, so that he can see them naked. The girls are not all beautiful (καλαί), but it was not plausible that they were altogether ugly (αἰσχραί). Zeuxis selects the most beautiful features of each of them and brings them together into a single bodily image.

The two stories illustrate various aspects of Dionysius' views on the imitation and emulation of classical models. The first story in particular suggests that the intensive contemplation of beautiful models can result in the birth of new masterpieces, even if the 'father' of the text is himself not that beautiful: Dionysius (or his student) may not be a Homer, a Sophocles or a Demosthenes, but he will nevertheless be able to produce excellent texts if he allows his composition to be inspired by the classical models. The second narration makes it clear that μίμησις must be understood as the eclectic imitation of the best qualities of many different models: a new composition may, for example, combine the best qualities of Lysias, Isocrates, Lycurgus, Aeschines and Hyperides. None of these orators was perfect, but each of them had his specific qualities; brought together in the right balance these qualities will produce an excellent composition. Two scholars have recently identified some important themes in these stories: Richard Hunter has analysed Dionysius' language of pregnancy and birth, which invites a Platonic reading of his views on literary mimesis.[16] Nicolas Wiater has rightly drawn attention to the metaphors of body and visual perception that are prominent in both stories. As Wiater points out, the terms of seeing and looking indicate that reading classical texts is an activity of close observation, by which the student must 'absorb the beauty' of the models.[17] This is a fortunate formulation, which I would like to take one step further. The theme of 'beauty' (κάλλος) plays a crucial role in the two anecdotes: the ugly farmer wishes to have beautiful children, and therefore he shows his wife beautiful images. Zeuxis hopes to reproduce Helen, who is universally known as the most beautiful woman, and so he brings together the most beautiful parts of the girls of Croton.

---

[16] Hunter 2009b: 107–26. [17] Wiater 2011: 78–83.

I suggest that this focus on beauty can to a large extent help us to understand Dionysius' selection of authors in the reading list that followed the two stories in *On Imitation* book 2: many of the authors listed in this (epitomised) canon are indeed recommended for the aesthetic qualities of their style, like beauty of expression (καλλιλογία), grandeur (μεγαλοπρέπεια), sublimity (ὕψος) and charm (ἡδονή). One of the qualities of Herodotus and Thucydides is their beauty of language (καλλιλογία, epitome 3.2); grandeur (μεγαλοπρέπεια) is a quality of style that one can learn not only from these two historians, but also from Pindar and Stesichorus; Aeschylus is sublime (ὑψηλός, 2.10), Hesiod and Herodotus took care of charm (ἡδονή, 2.2, 3.3). It is true that the characteristics attributed to a few other writers are more down to earth: the eloquence of Lysias, for example, is a sufficient guide for 'the useful and necessary' (τὸ χρήσιμον καὶ ἀναγκαῖον): he is simple, plain and elegant, and his narratives are clear and detailed (5.2). But overall Dionysius' reading list puts a remarkable emphasis on the aesthetic qualities of high literature, partly represented by poets of lyrical poems in exotic dialects, the practical imitation of which will not have been easy for the average student in Augustan Rome. It is plausible that one could learn something from Lysias' clarity and Demosthenes' vigour; but to write a persuasive speech while integrating Alcaeus' lofty genius (τὸ μεγαλοφυές), Pindar's grandeur (μεγαλοπρέπεια) and Aeschylus' sublimity (ὕψος) must have required a lot of talent, guidance and hard work, the three elements that Dionysius regards as indispensable for students who aim at perfection in eloquence (*On Imitation* fr. 1): skilful nature (φύσις δεξιά), accurate instruction (μάθησις ἀκριβής) and toilsome exercise (ἄσκησις ἐπίπονος).[18]

So how practical were Dionysius' recommendations? In his work *On Thucydides* (1.1), he tells us that he presented the reading list in *On Imitation* 'in order that those who intend to become good writers and speakers should have beautiful and approved standards':

> Ἐν τοῖς προεκδοθεῖσι περὶ τῆς μιμήσεως ὑπομνηματισμοῖς ἐπεληλυθὼς οὓς ὑπελάμβανον ἐπιφανεστάτους εἶναι ποιητάς τε καὶ συγγραφεῖς, ὦ Κόιντε Αἴλιε Τουβέρων, καὶ δεδηλωκὼς ἐν ὀλίγοις, τίνας ἕκαστος αὐτῶν εἰσφέρεται πραγματικάς τε καὶ λεκτικὰς ἀρετάς, καὶ πῇ μάλιστα χείρων ἑαυτοῦ γίνεται κατὰ τὰς ἀποτυχίας, εἴ τε τῆς προαιρέσεως οὐχ ἅπαντα

---

[18] The triad ἄσκησις (or μελέτη), φύσις and τέχνη is already mentioned in Pl. *Phdr.* 269d, Isoc. 13.14–15 and 15.187: Diogenes Laertius 5.18 attributes the same doctrine to Aristotle. See also Cic. *Inv. rhet.* 1.1.2 and *Brut.* 25; Quint. *Inst.* 3.5.1. Cf. Kraus 1996: 71.

κατὰ τὸν ἀκριβέστατον λογισμὸν ὁρώσης εἴ τε τῆς δυνάμεως οὐκ ἐν ἅπασι τοῖς ἔργοις κατορθούσης, ἵνα τοῖς προαιρουμένοις γράφειν τε καὶ λέγειν εὖ καλοὶ καὶ δεδοκιμασμένοι κανόνες ὦσιν, ἐφ' ὧν ποιήσονται τὰς κατὰ μέρος γυμνασίας μὴ πάντα μιμούμενοι τὰ παρ' ἐκείνοις κείμενα τοῖς ἀνδράσιν, ἀλλὰ τὰς μὲν ἀρετὰς αὐτῶν λαμβάνοντες, τὰς δ' ἀποτυχίας φυλαττόμενοι.

In the treatise *On Imitation*, which I published earlier, Quintus Aelius Tubero, I discussed those poets and prose authors whom I considered to be outstanding. I indicated briefly the good qualities of content and style contributed by each, and where his failings caused him to fall furthest below his own standards, either because his purpose did not enable him to grasp the scope of his subject in the fullest detail, or because his literary powers did not measure up to it throughout the whole of his work. I did this in order that those who intend to become good writers and speakers should have beautiful and approved standards by which to carry out their individual exercises, not imitating all the qualities of these authors, but adopting their good qualities and guarding against their failings.

Dionysius is quite clear about the practical purpose of his reading list: students will profit from the classical models while doing their exercises (γυμνασίας). They will adopt various stylistic qualities from a number of models and avoid their mistakes. On a different level, however, Dionysius may be said to be less practically-minded: his comments on the classical authors concentrate on aesthetic qualities rather than on their practical usefulness for political or juridical practice. There are no references to the specific skills needed in the Roman courts or political institutions. Dionysius is more interested in the aesthetic qualities of pure beauty: in claiming that the literary models presented in *On Imitation* are 'beautiful and approved standards' (καλοὶ καὶ δεδοκιμασμένοι κανόνες) Dionysius makes it clear that his selection of classical authors is to a large extent based on the aesthetic appreciation of the literature of a distant past rather than on the practical considerations required by public speech performances in Augustan Rome.

Dio's *On Training for Public Speaking*

Dio Chrysostom's *Oration* 18 presents itself as a letter to an anonymous politician, who wishes to acquire training in public speaking. Dio adopts the role of the young instructor of a rich, busy and powerful statesman, who has for unclear reasons not received a systematic rhetorical education. The date of the work is uncertain; most scholars believe that it is a relatively early composition, written before Dio's exile, perhaps between

60 and 80 CE.[19] The epistolary form and the person of the addressee are crucial to our understanding of the reading list in this oration, for Dio's recommendations are directly relevant and tailored to the recipient of the letter.[20] This is not an objective overview of great authors valued for their own qualities; it is a practical list for a mature statesman who is not very familiar with Greek literature. Dio explicitly states that he would offer a different programme to a lad (μειράκιον) or to a young man who was to withdraw from political life (18.5). The selection of authors presented here exclusively aims to guide a busy statesman (ἀνὴρ πολιτικός) who has no time for laborious training. Dio's point of departure is thus fundamentally different from that of Dionysius in *On Imitation*, and this, as we will see, results in a number of unconventional choices and judgements.

Who is Dio's addressee? Is he Roman or Greek, and what is his political status? Is he real or imaginary? These questions have been answered in different ways. Dio adopts a remarkably humble, almost subservient tone in the introduction of his letter (18.1):

> Πολλάκις ἐπαινέσας τὸν σὸν τρόπον ὡς ἀνδρὸς ἀγαθοῦ καὶ ἀξίου πρωτεύειν ἐν τοῖς ἀρίστοις, οὐδέποτε πρότερον ἐθαύμασα ὡς νῦν. τὸ γὰρ ἡλικίας τε ἐν τῷ ἀκμαιοτάτῳ ὄντα καὶ δυνάμει οὐδενὸς λειπόμενον καὶ ἄφθονα κεκτημένον, καὶ πάσης ἐξουσίας οὔσης δι' ἡμέρας καὶ νυκτὸς τρυφᾶν, ὅμως ἔτι παιδείας ὀρέγεσθαι καὶ φιλοκαλεῖν περὶ τὴν τῶν λόγων ἐμπειρίαν καὶ μὴ ὀκνεῖν, μηδὲ εἰ πονεῖν δέοι, σφόδρα μοι ἔδοξε γενναίας ψυχῆς καὶ οὐ φιλοτίμου μόνον, ἀλλὰ τῷ ὄντι φιλοσόφου ἔργον εἶναι.

> Although I had often praised your character as that of a good man who is worthy to be first among the best, yet I never admired it before as I do now. For that a man in the very prime of life and second to no one in influence, who possesses great wealth and has every opportunity to live in luxury by day and night, should in spite of all this reach out for education also and be eager to acquire training in eloquent speaking, and should display no hesitation even if it should cost toil, seems to me to give proof of an extraordinarily noble soul and one not only ambitious, but in very truth devoted to wisdom.

Various scholars have suggested that this man, 'second to none in influence' (δυνάμει οὐδενὸς λειπόμενον) could be nobody else than Nerva

---

[19] See von Arnim 1898: 139; Moles 1978: 93, n. 122.
[20] Bost-Pouderon 2008 rightly draws attention to the epistolary form of the text: she briefly compares Dio's letter with Dionysius' *Letter to Pompeius* and the two *Letters to Ammaeus*, and with Pliny's letters on literary topics; she concludes (p. 46) that *On Training for Public Speaking* is primarily a letter and not a miniature treatise.

before he became emperor (i.e., before 96 CE).[21] Other scholars prefer to identify the man as Titus before he became emperor (i.e., before 79 CE).[22] On the other hand, it has been argued that the addressee is a Greek man who has an important political function in one of the cities of Asia Minor.[23] Finally, there are scholars who believe that the addressee was not a real person at all: *On Training for Public Speaking* would be a rhetorical 'school exercise' that Dio wrote when he was young.[24]

Two issues should be distinguished here: the opposition real/fictive and the opposition Greek/Roman. Even if he did not actually exist, the addressee could still be portrayed as Greek or Roman. To start with the latter issue, it seems highly improbable that a mature and influential Greek officer active in Asia Minor would not be familiar with Homer, Euripides, Xenophon and the Attic orators. For members of the Roman nobility of the first century CE the situation is slightly different. Many of them studied with a Greek rhetorician, but such training could be either a basic instruction or a more advanced education. Titus, who has been thought to be the addressee, enjoyed a thorough education in Greek rhetoric. According to Suetonius, Titus 'had a ready fluency in both Latin and Greek to such a degree that he could make a speech or compose a poem without preparation'.[25] As a mature man this (future) emperor definitely did not need Dio's basic instructions and can thus be ruled out as the addressee of *On Training for Public Speaking*.[26] But not every Roman

---

[21] Valgimigli 1912: 72; Münscher 1920: 115; von Christ, Stählin and Schmid 1920: 363: 'Nerva vor seiner Thronbesteigung?'; Brancacci 2000: 244, n. 8. For Dio's relationship with the Flavian dynasty, see Sidebottom 1996. On Dio's attitude towards Rome, see Jones 1978 and Swain 1996: 187–241.

[22] Desideri 1978: 137–42; Billault 2004: 515–18. Arguments against Titus are offered in Sidebottom 1996: 450.

[23] Von Arnim 1898: 140: 'Das Schreiben ist also vermutlich an einen höheren Gemeinde-beamten einer der grossen Griechenstädte Asiens gerichtet'; Moles 1978: 93 agrees ('probably Greek'), as does Sidebottom 1996: 450: 'an important local Greek official in a large Greek city of Asia Minor'.

[24] Hammer 1898: 838: 'eine bloße Schulleistung des schon frühe eitlen Dio'; Lemarchand 1926: 6: 'un exercice de rhétorique'; more cautiously de Budé 1948: 12.

[25] Suet. *Tit*. 3. Eutropius 7.21 refers to Titus' Greek poems. Plin. *HN* pref. 5 praises Titus' eloquence and poetry. On Titus' rhetorical education, see Jones 1984: 7–11.

[26] Billault 2004: 516 cites Suetonius' information about Titus' eloquence and poetic skills in order to support his argument that Titus was Dio's student and the addressee of *On Training for Public Speaking*. I cannot agree with this, because Suetonius' description of Titus does not at all fit Dio's portrait of his statesman. Titus had a thorough rhetorical education *when he was a boy*. Suetonius praises his fluency in Greek and Latin in the third chapter of his biography, which deals with Titus' youth (3). The statesman in Dio's letter, on the other hand, did not receive sufficient literary education when he was young. Dio writes to a mature and mighty politician who is gifted (18.4) but has had very little training so far and is only now preparing himself for public speaking (18.6); he has not yet read Menander, Euripides and Homer (18.7), nor Lysias or Xenophon (18.11, 18.14).

statesman will have studied Euripides and Xenophon, let alone Aeschines or Hyperides. We know much less, for example, about Nerva's familiarity with Greek literature. Von Arnim has argued that Dio's addressee was Greek because Dio tells him that Xenophon could be a helpful guide both in the senate and before the people (καὶ ἐν βουλῇ καὶ ἐν δήμῳ, 18.17). According to von Arnim this advice must be directed to a Greek, because Romans would only turn to Greek rhetoric for intellectual development, not for practical usefulness.[27] This argument is not persuasive: Quintilian – Dio's contemporary – does actually point out that Greek literature can be practically useful for men who are active in Roman society. Euripides for example will be more useful than Sophocles 'to persons preparing themselves to plead in court'.[28] Hence, Dio's emphasis on political usefulness does not rule out the possibility that he wrote for a Roman friend, and some of his formulations do in fact suggest that we should think of a Roman rather than a Greek addressee. The useful guidance that Dio's addressee is supposed to find in Xenophon's *Anabasis* seems especially relevant to a man who is in charge of both generals (στρατηγοί) and soldiers (πλῆθος) and is closely connected to the members of royal families (βασιλικοί) (18.16–17):

> καὶ ἀπορρήτοις δὲ λόγοις ὡς προσήκει χρήσασθαι καὶ πρὸς στρατηγοὺς ἄνευ πλήθους καὶ πρὸς πλῆθος κατὰ[29] ταὐτό, καὶ βασιλικοῖς τίνα τρόπον διαλεχθῆναι, καὶ ἐξαπατῆσαι ὅπως πολεμίους μὲν ἐπὶ βλάβῃ, φίλους δ' ἐπὶ τῷ συμφέροντι, καὶ μάτην ταραττομένοις ἀλύπως τἀληθὲς καὶ πιστῶς εἰπεῖν, καὶ τὸ μὴ ῥᾳδίως πιστεύειν τοῖς ὑπερέχουσι, καὶ οἷς ἐξαπατῶσιν οἱ ὑπερέχοντες καὶ οἷς καταστρατηγοῦσι καὶ καταστρατηγοῦνται ἄνθρωποι, πάντα ταῦτα ἱκανῶς τὸ σύνταγμα περιέχει.

> How to hold secret conferences both with generals apart from the common soldiers and with the soldiers in the same way [i.e., apart from the generals]; the proper manner of conversing with kings and princes; how to deceive enemies to their hurt and friends for their own benefit; how to tell the plain truth to those who are needlessly disturbed without giving offence, and to make them believe it; how not to trust too readily those in authority over you, and the means by which such persons deceive their inferiors, and the way in which men outwit and are outwitted – on all these points Xenophon's treatise gives adequate information.

---

[27] Von Arnim 1898: 140: 'Wenn ein Römer sich mit griechischer Rhetorik befast, so thut er es zum Zweck formaler Geistesbildung.'
[28] Quint. *Inst.* 10.1.67: *iis qui se ad agendum comparant utiliorem longe fore Euripiden.*
[29] Here I follow the text of Cohoon 1939; von Arnim inserts the negation οὐ before κατά.

This brings us to the second issue. If Dio does indeed suggest that his addressee is an influential Roman politician, how real is his letter? Neither the beginning nor the end of the letter has a salutation, which might make us suspicious.[30] More important, however, are the remarkable formulations of praise and admiration that Dio uses when addressing his mighty friend.[31] As we have seen, Dio extensively commends his addressee for not displaying any hesitation in his eagerness to acquire training, 'even if it should cost toil' (μηδὲ εἰ πονεῖν δέοι): for Dio, this lack of hesitation is proof of a soul that is not only extraordinarily noble and ambitious, but even 'philosophical' (18.1). This is a rather limited understanding of philosophy, to say the least. As we have seen, Dionysius of Halicarnassus tells his readers that talent, instruction and hard work are indispensable – this is of course the standard view in rhetorical teaching.[32] Dio, on the other hand, claims that not being afraid of toil (πόνος) reveals a philosophical nature. The contrast between the two positions becomes even more apparent when Dio (18.6) formulates his first and foremost piece of advice, which is unheard of in rhetorical teaching:

> τοῦτο μὲν δὴ πρῶτον ἴσθι, ὅτι οὐ δεῖ σοι πόνου καὶ ταλαιπωρίας – τῷ μὲν γὰρ ἐπὶ πολὺ ἀσκήσαντι ταῦτα ἐπὶ πλεῖστον προάγει, τῷ δὲ ἐπ' ὀλίγον χρησαμένῳ συλλήψει τὴν ψυχὴν καὶ ὀκνηρὰν ποιεῖ προσφέρεσθαι, καθάπερ τοὺς ἀσυνήθεις περὶ σώματος ἄσκησιν εἴ τις κοπώσειε βαρυτέροις γυμνασίοις, ἀσθενεστέρους ἐποίησεν – ἀλλὰ ὥσπερ τοῖς ἀήθεσι <τοῦ> πονεῖν σώμασιν ἀλείψεως δεῖ μᾶλλον καὶ κινήσεως συμμέτρου ἢ γυμνασίας, οὕτω σοὶ περὶ τοὺς λόγους ἐπιμελείας ἐστὶ χρεία μᾶλλον ἡδονῇ μεμιγμένης ἢ ἀσκήσεως καὶ πόνου.

> First of all, you should know that you have no need of toil or exacting labour; for although, when a man has already undergone a great deal of training, these contribute very greatly to his progress, yet if he has had only a little, they will lessen his confidence and make him diffident about getting into action; just as with athletes who are unaccustomed to the training of the body, such training weakens them if they become fatigued by exercises which are too severe.

No laborious training, therefore, and no difficult texts; instead, Dio offers a list of authors who are relatively accessible and directly relevant to a politician of the first century CE. In addressing a non-specialist, politically engaged reader, Dio's letter agrees with contemporary scholarly and

---

[30] Cf. Bost-Pouderon 2008: 41. The form of the letter is in fact only articulated by the use of the second person singular (σύ, passim) and the use of the verb γράφειν (to write) in 18.19 and 18.20.
[31] E.g., Dio 18.3: ἐπαινῶ σε καὶ θαυμάζω σε, 'I praise you and admire you'.
[32] See Kraus 1996 on *exercitatio*.

philosophical works of the imperial period: one might for example compare the approach of Plutarch, who 'presents his elite readership with a very practical, unsystematic, and non-rigorous kind of philosophy'.[33] The relaxed, practical and down to earth approach to παιδεία that characterises both Dio and Plutarch clearly differs from the more rigorous and serious tone that Dionysius adopts in his rhetorical treatises – a contrast that seems to reflect a difference between (late) Hellenistic and imperial literature. Dio's advice not to work too hard has been taken seriously by modern scholars – and we cannot entirely exclude the possibility that there was indeed a Roman statesman who requested a shortcut to *paideia*. In a different context Lucian draws a similar comparison between readers and athletes, pointing out that in training one should alternate between hard exercise and relaxation.[34] But although Dio's advice does not stand alone, we can be quite sure that his ancient audience enjoyed his playful reversal of the traditional emphasis on hard work. This remarkable reversal is in line with other aspects of his letter, which is highly unusual and innovative: Dio transforms the traditional reading list of classical highlights, as represented by Dionysius' *On Imitation*, into a survey that is practically relevant to the specific needs of a politician of his age. In doing so he portrays himself as quite different from the stern professors of rhetoric. Dio's deviations from the rhetorical tradition invite us to read *On Training for Public Speaking* as a fanciful adaptation of the genre of rhetorical imitation.

The Poets

Let us now turn to the actual reading lists in the epitome of *On Imitation* and *On Training for Public Speaking*. It will be helpful to compare Quintilian's list of Greek literature (*Institutio oratoria* 10.1.46–84) as a point of reference: on the one hand, Quintilian was familiar with some of Dionysius' rhetorical works (and possibly with the reading list in *On Imitation*); on the other hand, he was a contemporary of Dio.[35] Where Dio and Quintilian agree and differ from Dionysius, their agreement could

---

[33] Van Hoof 2010: 41. On Plutarch's intended readers, see van Hoof 2010: 19–40.
[34] Lucian, *Ver. hist.* 1.1: 'Men interested in athletics and in the care of their bodies think not only of condition and exercise but also of relaxation in season; in fact, they consider this the principal part of training. In like manner, students, I think, after much reading of serious works may profitably relax their minds and put them in better trim for future labour.' Lucian, of course, is advertising his own *True Stories*.
[35] On the relationship between Dionysius' *On Imitation* and Quintilian book 10, see the references in n. 9 above.

be explained by the development of literary taste between the Augustan Age and the Flavian Age (although other explanations must also be taken into consideration). The three authors use the same categories and they roughly present them in the same order: first comes poetry, then the prose genres; in Dionysius the order is historiography, philosophy, oratory; in Dio and Quintilian the order is historiography, oratory, philosophy.[36]

According to the epitome (2.1–14), Dionysius recommends four epic poets (Homer, Hesiod, Antimachus and Panyasis), four lyrical poets (Pindar, Simonides, Stesichorus and Alcaeus), three tragedians (Aeschylus, Sophocles and Euripides) and the comedians, of whom only Menander is mentioned by name. Quintilian (10.1.46–72) offers a similar but extended list: his epic poets and tragedians are identical with those of Dionysius, but he adds a number of poets (mostly Hellenistic) whom Dionysius left out (Apollonius, Aratus, Theocritus, Nicander, Euphorion, Tyrtaeus, Callimachus, Philetas);[37] furthermore, he mentions Archilochus instead of Pindar, and he adds the names of Aristophanes, Eupolis and Cratinus to that of Menander, who 'alone would be sufficient'. Menander is the very first poet mentioned in Dio's reading list, followed by Euripides and Homer (18.6–8). For Dio, that is all: his politician will have no time for lyric and elegiac poetry, iambics or dithyrambs (18.8).

The enormous difference between Dionysius and Dio is self-evident. But a closer look at their comments will further illuminate their distinct approaches. Dionysius starts with Homer, who immediately is presented as an exception: where other authors must be imitated for a specific quality, Homeric poetry must be imitated in its entirety (2.1), 'character, emotion, grandeur, distribution and all other qualities'.[38] Having discussed the other epic poets and lyric poets, he focuses on the three tragedians: here Aeschylus is mentioned first (2.10), and this position corresponds to his superior status:

---

[36] Cf. Rutherford 1998: 43.
[37] Quintilian (10.1.54) remarks that the Alexandrian grammarians ignored their contemporaries. This observation might suggest that Dionysius, who also leaves out the Hellenistic poets, was following an Alexandrian reading list. But it is also natural for Dionysius not to include Hellenistic authors: from the perspective of Dionysian classicism, the period after Alexander (and Demosthenes) was an age of literary decline, dominated by 'Asian' influence: see Hidber 1996 and de Jonge 2014. Cf. Kim in this volume.
[38] The same qualities of Homer's poetry are praised and discussed in the scholia. See Nünlist 2009: 139–49 for scholia commenting on Homer's emotional effects (139–49), on styles and registers (219–21) and on characterisation (238–56). Nünlist 2009: 224 points out that the observations on Homeric style in the scholia on the *Iliad* and the *Odyssey* presumably aimed not only at interpretation but also at imitation. The rhetorical and the exegetical traditions of literary criticism are thus closely connected.

Ὁ δ' οὖν Αἰσχύλος πρῶτος ὑψηλός τε καὶ τῆς μεγαλοπρεπείας ἐχόμενος, καὶ ἠθῶν καὶ παθῶν τὸ πρέπον εἰδώς, καὶ τῇ τροπικῇ καὶ τῇ κυρίᾳ λέξει διαφερόντως κεκοσμημένος, πολλαχοῦ δὲ καὶ αὐτὸς δημιουργὸς καὶ ποιητὴς ἰδίων ὀνομάτων καὶ πραγμάτων, Εὐριπίδου δὲ καὶ Σοφοκλέους καὶ ποικιλώτερος ταῖς τῶν προσώπων ἐπεισαγωγαῖς.

Aeschylus, who comes first, is sublime and possesses grandeur; he knows propriety in the use of character and emotion, he excels in adorning himself with figurative as well as common vocabulary, and he is often himself also a creator and maker of words and things; he shows more variety than Sophocles and Euripides in the introductions of new characters.

In the next section (2.11–13) Dionysius presents a comparison between Sophocles and Euripides. Both have their own qualities, but Dionysius seems to have more sympathy for Sophocles, who excels in painting character and emotion; he preserves the dignity (ἀξίωμα) of characters, and he uses poetic vocabulary, although he often falls from grandeur (μέγεθος) into empty boasting. Euripides, on the other hand, likes complete reality and what is close to actual life (τῷ βίῳ τῷ νῦν). In the rest of the section Euripides is mainly described in negative terms: he does *not* preserve propriety and modesty; he is *less* successful than Sophocles in painting noble characters and emotions; he accurately represents what is undignified, unmanly and mean (ἄσεμνον καὶ ἄνανδρον καὶ ταπεινόν); and finally he is neither sublime (ὑψηλός) nor plain (λιτός), as he uses the mixed style. It is clear that the whole σύγκρισις of Sophocles and Euripides builds on the schematic contrast between high and low: sublime versus plain style, elevated versus low characters, and heroic versus realistic subject matter. A very short reference to comedy finally includes the name of Menander, whom Dionysius – like Quintilian and Dio – admires for his content as well as his style.

Turning now to Dio, the first thing to notice is of course that his list is much shorter, as it contains only three names. Dio regards Menander and Euripides as the most useful poets for his addressee (18.6):

τῶν μὲν δὴ ποιητῶν συμβουλεύσαιμ' ἄν σοι Μενάνδρῳ τε τῶν κωμικῶν μὴ παρέργως ἐντυγχάνειν καὶ Εὐριπίδῃ τῶν τραγικῶν, καὶ τούτοις μὴ οὕτως, αὐτὸν ἀναγιγνώσκοντα, ἀλλὰ δι' ἑτέρων ἐπισταμένων μάλιστα μὲν καὶ ἡδέως, εἰ δ' οὖν, ἀλύπως ὑποκρίνασθαι· πλείων γὰρ ἡ αἴσθησις ἀπαλλαγέντι τῆς περὶ τὸ ἀναγιγνώσκειν ἀσχολίας.

So let us consider the poets: I would counsel you to read Menander of the writers of comedy quite carefully, and Euripides of the writers of tragedy, and to do so, not casually by reading them to yourself, but by having them read to you by others, preferably by men who know how to render the lines pleasurably, but at any rate so as not to offend. For the effect is enhanced when one is relieved of the preoccupation of reading.

Dio's list literally reverses Dionysius' advice: Menander is the last poet to be mentioned in *On Imitation*, but he is the first one mentioned in *On Training for Public Speaking*. Whereas Dionysius portrays Aeschylus as the best tragedian and presents Sophocles as superior to Euripides, Dio recommends Euripides alone.[39] Even more striking is Dio's remarkable advice not to read these poets but to have them recited by somebody else: this recommendation flagrantly contradicts the traditional view that students should be actively engaged and involved in the reading process. Let us compare Quintilian's advice (10.1.19):

> Lectio libera est nec ut actionis impetu transcurrit, sed repetere saepius licet, sive dubites sive memoriae penitus adfigere velis. Repetamus autem et tractemus.
>
> Reading is independent: it does not pass over us with the speed of a performance, and you can go back over it again and again if you have any doubts or if you want to fix it firmly in your memory. Let us go over the text again and work on it.

Quintilian's instruction represents the traditional perspective of the teacher of rhetoric who knows what is good for his students.[40] Dio gives his mighty politician the opposite advice. This is another remarkable reversal of rhetorical teaching that might be interpreted as a piece of irony, which contributes to the light-hearted character of Dio's letter.

Only after Menander and Euripides is Homer mentioned, as the third poet to be read: 'Homer comes first and in the middle and last' ("Ομηρος δὲ καὶ πρῶτος καὶ μέσος καὶ ὕστατος, 18.7). To be sure, this laudatory statement expresses a sentiment that Dio shares with his contemporaries, as Lawrence Kim has observed.[41] But the irony is of course that Homer comes neither first nor in the middle, but indeed *last* in Dio's list of poets, after Menander and Euripides. As we have seen, Dionysius and Quintilian

---

[39] In *Oration* 52 Dio adopts a very different attitude to Greek tragedy: there Aeschylus, Sophocles and Euripides (and their *Philoctetes* plays) are equally admired; the difference between the two orations is explained by the purpose of *Oration* 18 and its addressee, who needs only those authors who are practically useful for political eloquence. *Oration* 52 on the other hand evaluates literature in its own terms and for its own sake. On *Oration* 52, see Luzzatto 1983.

[40] See also Dion. Hal. *De imit.* 5.7 (epitome).

[41] Cf. Kim 2010: 5. The usefulness of Homer as a model for rhetorical imitation is not only indicated in rhetorical treatises, but also in ancient commentaries. For observations on Homeric speeches in the scholia, see Nünlist 2009: 316–26.

start their reading lists with Homer, who was widely regarded as the source of all Greek literature. Dio's formulation pays tribute to Homer, but the order in which he ranks his three preferred poets strongly suggests that he finds the plays of Euripides and Menander more useful guides for a politician than the Homeric epics.[42]

The discussion of Menander and Euripides is important for our purpose, because Dio here acknowledges that his advice does not correspond to that of other critics (18.7):

> καὶ μηδεὶς τῶν σοφωτέρων αἰτιάσηταί με ὡς προκρίναντα τῆς ἀρχαίας κωμῳδίας τὴν Μενάνδρου ἢ τῶν ἀρχαίων τραγῳδῶν Εὐριπίδην· οὐδὲ γὰρ οἱ ἰατροὶ τὰς πολυτελεστάτας τροφὰς συντάττουσι τοῖς θεραπείας δεομένοις, ἀλλὰ τὰς ὠφελίμους. πολὺ δ' ἂν ἔργον εἴη τὸ λέγειν ὅσα ἀπὸ τούτων χρήσιμα· ἥ τε γὰρ τοῦ Μενάνδρου μίμησις ἅπαντος ἤθους καὶ χάριτος πᾶσαν ὑπερβέβληκε τὴν δεινότητα τῶν παλαιῶν κωμικῶν, ἥ τε Εὐριπίδου προσήνεια καὶ πιθανότης τοῦ μὲν τραγικοῦ ἀπαθανατισμοῦ καὶ ἀξιώματος τυχὸν οὐκ ἂν τελέως ἐφικνοῖτο, πολιτικῷ δὲ ἀνδρὶ πάνυ ὠφέλιμος, ἔτι δὲ ἤθη καὶ πάθη δεινὸς πληρῶσαι, καὶ γνώμας πρὸς ἅπαντα ὠφελίμους καταμίγνυσι τοῖς ποιήμασιν, ἅτε φιλοσοφίας οὐκ ἄπειρος ὤν.

> And let no one of the more 'advanced' critics chide me for selecting Menander's plays in preference to the old comedy, or Euripides in preference to the early writers of tragedy. For physicians do not prescribe the most costly (πολυτελεστάτας) nourishments for their patients, but those which are salutary (ὠφελίμους). Now it would be a long task to enumerate all the advantages (χρήσιμα) to be derived from these writers; indeed not only has Menander's portrayal of every character and every charming trait surpassed all the skill of the early writers of comedy, but the suavity and plausibility of Euripides, while perhaps not completely attaining to the grandeur of the tragic poet's way of deifying his characters, or to his high dignity, are very useful (ὠφέλιμος) for the man in public life; and furthermore, he cleverly fills his plays with an abundance of characters and moving incidents, and strews them with maxims useful (ὠφελίμους) on all occasions, since he was not without acquaintance of philosophy.

Dio's consistent emphasis on the usefulness of Menander and Euripides stands in sharp contrast to Dionysius' discussion of tragedy and comedy. We have seen that, for Dionysius, the sublime Aeschylus comes first, followed by Sophocles and Euripides. It is possible, then, that Dionysius – or the teachers of rhetoric who agreed with his views – could be counted among the anonymous 'more advanced critics' (σοφώτεροι)

---

[42] Dio's challenging of Homer thus fits into the patterns of Hellenistic and imperial reception of Homer discussed by Greensmith in this volume.

from whom Dio distances himself. His evaluation of the Greek tragedians seems to reflect the taste of his age: Quintilian (10.1.67–8) agrees with Dio that Euripides is more useful, and he responds to the supporters of Sophocles (like Dionysius) in terms that echo Dio's defence of Euripides:

> Sed longe clarius inlustraverunt hoc opus Sophocles atque Euripides, quorum in dispari dicendi via uter sit poeta melior inter plurimos quaeritur. Idque ego sane, quoniam ad praesentem materiam nihil pertinet, iniudicatum relinquo. Illud quidem nemo non fateatur necesse est, iis qui se ad agendum comparant utiliorem longe fore Euripiden. Namque is et sermone (quod ipsum reprehendunt quibus gravitas et coturnus et sonus Sophocli videtur esse sublimior) magis accedit oratorio generi, et sententiis densus, et in iis quae a sapientibus tradita sunt paene ipsis par, et in dicendo ac respondendo cuilibet eorum qui fuerunt in foro diserti comparandus.

> But far more distinction was brought to this genre by Sophocles and Euripides. Their styles are very different, and there is much dispute as to which is the better poet. I leave this question unresolved, because it has nothing to do with my present subject. What everybody must admit is that Euripides will be the more useful to persons preparing themselves to plead in court. His language (censured by some who find Sophocles' dignity, tragic grandeur and resonance more sublime) is closer to the norm of oratory; he is full of striking thoughts (*sententiae*), and almost a match for the philosophers in expressing their teaching; his technique of speech and debate is comparable to that of anyone who has been famous for eloquence in the courts.

Here Quintilian sides with Dio against Dionysius, or perhaps we should formulate it like this: Dio and Quintilian represent a more practical perspective on Greek literature that turns away from the purely aesthetic approach of their colleague who lived a century earlier. Both Quintilian and Dio emphasise that the discussion should not be about sublimity or grandeur, but about usefulness; and both regard Euripides as the most useful tragedian for political speakers, praising the philosophical quality of his sayings (γνῶμαι, *sententiae*).[43] Quintilian also agrees with Dio on the exemplarity of Menander, one of the first imitators of Euripides (10.1.69):[44]

> hunc et admiratus maxime est, ut saepe testatur, et secutus, quamquam in opere diverso, Menander, qui vel unus meo quidem iudicio diligenter lectus

---

[43] Dio 18.7; Quint. *Inst.* 10.1.68.
[44] Russell 1989: 299 notes the agreement between Dio and Quintilian concerning the usefulness of Euripides and Menander.

> ad cuncta quae praecipimus effingenda sufficiat: ita omnem vitae imaginem expressit, tanta in eo inveniendi copia et eloquendi facultas, ita est omnibus rebus personis adfectibus accommodatus.
>
> Menander, as he often testifies, admired Euripides greatly and indeed imitated him, though in a different genre. And a careful reading of Menander alone would, in my judgement be sufficient to develop all the qualities I am recommending: so complete is his representation of life, so rich his invention and so fluent his style, so perfectly does he adapt himself to every circumstance, character and emotion.

The enthusiasm for Menander and Euripides in Dio and Quintilian seems typical of the period in which these authors were writing. The plays of the two poets were composed in clear and relatively accessible language (as opposed to those of Aeschylus, for example) and they contained lots of quotable maxims. The poetry of Menander, with its light humour and morally unproblematic erotic scenes, was indeed often recited at symposia throughout the Roman Empire.[45] Plutarch, contemporary with Dio, frequently cites lines from both Euripides and Menander in his *Table-Talk*.[46] In one of the conversations Menander is specifically presented as providing the most appropriate entertainment at dinner: 'New Comedy has become so completely a part of the symposium that we could chart our course more easily without wine than without Menander'.[47]

As far as their reading lists of poets are concerned, it turns out that there is no beginning of an agreement between Dionysius and Dio. Where Dionysius recommends a series of twelve poets with various qualities, Dio mentions only three names. Dionysius' list starts with Homer and ends with Menander, Dio's list starts with Menander and ends with Homer. In some respects Dio's preferences seem to reflect the taste of his age: both Quintilian and Dio focus on usefulness and hence prefer Euripides and Menander to Aeschylus and Sophocles. It is plausible that Dionysius' list represents a traditional Greek approach, whereas Dio and Quintilian display a more modern taste that is tailored to the needs of Roman society. For Roman readers Euripides was more accessible than

---

[45] On 'Menander at dinner parties', see Nervegna 2013: 120–200. Plutarch mentions readings of Menander at banquets at Plut. *Quaest. conv.* 5, 673b; 7.8, 712b; and *Comp. Ar. et Men.* 854b.

[46] Menander is quoted in Plut. *Quaest. conv.* 3.6, 654d; 4.3, 666f; 7.5, 706b; 9.5, 739f; Euripides is quoted in *Quaest. conv.* 1, 612d; 1.2, 615d; 1.4, 622a; 1.5, 622c; 2.1, 630b, 630 e; 2.10, 643f; 2.10, 644d; 4.1, 661b; 661f; 4.2, 665c; 4.2; 666c; 7.1, 699a; 7.8, 713d; 7.10, 716b; 8.1, 718a; 9.1, 737a; 9.15, 747d.

[47] Plut. *Quaest. conv.* 7.8, 712b. Translation Minar in Minar, Sandbach and Helmbold 1961. On the ancient reception of Euripides and Menander as poets of 'common Greek', see Nervegna 2013: 110–16.

Aeschylus or Sophocles; and we should not forget that Menander was widely appreciated as the great inspirer of Roman comedy.

In the evaluation of drama, then, there is correspondence between Dio and Quintilian (contra Dionysius), which seems to reflect the preferences of the Flavian Age as opposed to the Augustan Age. In other respects, however, Dio radically turns away from all traditional rhetoric, departing not only from Dionysius but also from the contemporary position of Quintilian: Homer comes last, listening to a recitation is better than reading a poem, and hard work should be avoided. Dio's reading list, then, is not only more practical than Dionysius' *On Imitation*, but also more unconventional, more surprising and more amusing for readers who are familiar with the clichés of rhetorical education.

The Historians

For Dionysius' treatment of the historians we do not depend on the epitome (3.1–12), because he cites this part of *On Imitation* in the *Letter to Pompeius* (3.2–6.11).[48] Dionysius offers an extensive comparison of Herodotus and Thucydides; he then adds Xenophon and Philistus, and finally Theopompus.[49] Quintilian (10.1.73–5) lists the same Greek historians, but he leaves out Xenophon, whom he includes among the philosophers (10.1.82, see below); instead he briefly and critically touches on the names of Ephorus and Clitarchus and, with more appreciation, Timagenes (Augustan Age), 'born long after these' (*longo post intervallo temporis natus*).[50] Dio (18.10) mentions four historians: Herodotus, Thucydides, Theopompus and Ephorus. However, only two of these four are explicitly recommended for imitation: the active politician should read Thucydides and Theopompus; Herodotus is merely enjoyable, while Ephorus is tedious and careless. Like Quintilian, Dio postpones the discussion of

---

[48] *De imit.* fr. 7 (Aujac 1992) = fr. 5 (Battisti 1997): on the connection between the two texts, see Heath 1989a and Weaire 2002.

[49] Philistus of Syracuse (*c.* 430–356 BCE, *FGrH* 556) wrote a *History of Sicily*; he was the advisor of Dionysius I and II. Theopompus of Chios (fourth century BCE, *FGrH* 115) wrote an *Epitome of Herodotus* in two books and a *Hellenika* in twelve books. Philistus was included in the inscriptional remains of the 'catalogue' of the gymnasium library at Tauromenium; Theopompus in that of the gymnasium library at Rhodes: see n. 11 above.

[50] Ephorus of Cyme (*c.* 405–330 BCE, *FGrH* 70) wrote a *History* in thirty books, covering both Greek and eastern history. Clitarchus of Colophon (fourth/third century BCE, *FGrH* 137) wrote about Alexander. Timagenes of Alexandria (*FGrH* 88) came to Rome as a captive in 55 BCE; he wrote *On Kings*, a universal history from the earliest times down to the period of Caesar.

Xenophon to the category of 'the Socratics' (18.13–17): Xenophon alone gets more space than all other authors together.

The differences between Dionysius and Dio are enormous. In Dionysius' discussion, two points are made very clear: Herodotus is superior to Thucydides because of the more uplifting and more enjoyable contents of his works; and Xenophon is good, but only as far as he imitates Herodotus, who is stylistically superior. Dionysius' top ranking of historians is therefore (1) Herodotus, (2) Thucydides and (3) Xenophon. Dio, on the other hand, claims that Thucydides is more useful than the pleasant Herodotus, and he regards Xenophon as by far the most useful author in the entire corpus of Greek texts. In other words, Dio's ranking of these three authors would be the complete reverse of Dionysius' podium: (1) Xenophon, (2) Thucydides and (3) Herodotus; but as Dio counts Xenophon among the Socratic philosophers, there is no direct comparison of Xenophon with Herodotus and Thucydides.

Let us look more closely at Dionysius' comments on the Greek historiographers. In his σύγκρισις of Herodotus and Thucydides, he draws a distinction between subject matter and style.[51] In the discussion of style (*Pomp.* 3.16–21), the two historians divide the points. Thucydides is superior in conciseness, the representation of emotions, and force and intensity; Herodotus is to be imitated for the portrayal of character, persuasion and delight, and propriety; the two historians divide the points for purity of language (Ionic versus Attic dialect), vividness, and grandeur and impressiveness. In the discussion of subject matter (*Pomp.* 3.2–15) Herodotus is the clear winner: he has a more uplifting and profitable subject, a better beginning and ending of his history, and a more appropriate selection of events; Herodotus is also superior in the distribution of his material and in the attitude that he adopts towards the events and characters.[52] After this extensive comparison, Dionysius introduces Xenophon and Philistus, who are presented as the followers of Herodotus and Thucydides respectively. The fact that they are presented as later imitators suggests that they are inferior to their predecessors (4.1–3):

> Ξενοφῶν δὲ καὶ Φίλιστος οἱ τούτοις ἐπακμάσαντες οὔτε φύσεις ὁμοίας εἶχον οὔτε προαιρέσεις. Ξενοφῶν μὲν γὰρ Ἡροδότου ζηλωτὴς ἐγένετο κατ' ἀμφοτέρους τοὺς χαρακτῆρας, τόν τε πραγματικὸν καὶ τὸν λεκτικόν ...

---

[51] On Dionysius' comparison of Herodotus and Thucydides (*Pomp.* 3.2–21), see Heath 1989b: 71–89, Wiater 2011: 132–49 and de Jonge 2017.
[52] Wiater 2011: 147–8 rightly explains Dionysius' preference for Herodotus over Thucydides as resulting from his concept of classicism.

ὁ δὲ λεκτικὸς πῇ μὲν ὅμοιος Ἡροδότου, πῇ δὲ ἐνδεέστερος. καθαρὸς μὲν γὰρ τοῖς ὀνόμασιν ἱκανῶς καὶ σαφὴς <καὶ ἐναργὴς> καθάπερ ἐκεῖνος· ἐκλέγει δὲ ὀνόματα συνήθη τε καὶ προσφυῆ τοῖς πράγμασι, καὶ συντίθησιν αὐτὰ ἡδέως πάνυ καὶ κεχαρισμένως οὐχ ἧττον Ἡροδότου. ὕψος δὲ καὶ κάλλος καὶ μεγαλοπρέπειαν καὶ τὸ λεγόμενον ἰδίως πλάσμα ἱστορικὸν Ἡρόδοτος ἔχει.

Xenophon and Philistus, who flourished at a later time than these writers, did not resemble one another either in their nature or in the principles they adopted. Xenophon modelled himself upon Herodotus in both aspects, subject matter and language ... In style he is in some respects similar to Herodotus, and in others inferior. Like him he is decidedly pure and lucid in vocabulary. The words he chooses are familiar and correspond to the nature of the subject, and he puts them together with no less marked attractiveness and charm than Herodotus. But Herodotus also possesses sublimity, beauty and impressiveness, and what is called by the special name of 'the historical cast of style'.

Xenophon is in some respects similar to his model Herodotus, but he is inferior as far as aesthetic qualities like sublimity (ὕψος), beauty (κάλλος) and grandeur (μεγαλοπρέπεια) are concerned. Dionysius adds that in many passages Xenophon 'goes on too long' (μακρότερος γίνεται τοῦ δέοντος) and is inferior to Herodotus in characterisation; on strict examination he is even found to be 'careless' (ὀλιγωρός) in this respect (*Pomp.* 4.4). Philistus imitates Thucydides, but he is inferior in the beauty of his language (καλλιλογία) (*Pomp.* 5). Theopompus, finally, is praised for his subjects, his industry, his philosophical comments and his Isocratean style; but this style is sometimes artificial and his fairytales are childish (*Pomp.* 6).

Like Dionysius, Dio (18.10) starts with Herodotus, who is however immediately disqualified because of his storytelling:

Ἡροδότῳ μὲν οὖν, εἴ ποτε εὐφροσύνης σοι δεῖ, μετὰ πολλῆς ἡσυχίας ἐντεύξῃ. τὸ γὰρ ἀνειμένον καὶ τὸ γλυκὺ τῆς ἀπαγγελίας ὑπόνοιαν παρέξει μυθῶδες μᾶλλον ἢ ἱστορικὸν τὸ σύγγραμμα εἶναι. τῶν δὲ ἄκρων Θουκυδίδης ἐμοὶ δοκεῖ καὶ τῶν δευτέρων Θεόπομπος.

As for Herodotus, if ever you want real enjoyment, you will read him when quite at your ease, for the easy-going manner and charm of his narrative will give the impression that his work deals with stories rather than with actual history. But among the foremost historians I place Thucydides, and among those of second rank Theopompus.

Dio's observation that Herodotus writes myth (μυθῶδες) rather than history (ἱστορικόν) obviously alludes to Thucydides' famous remarks about his own rejection of myth (τὸ μὴ μυθῶδες, 1.22.4). Whereas

Dionysius presents an elaborate comparison between the two classical historians that results in a victory for Herodotus, Dio dismisses Herodotus' historical value in just one sentence and appropriates Thucydides' point of view in using the term μυθῶδες. Theopompus receives mixed praise. Dio asserts that he is useful, because there is 'a rhetorical quality' (ῥητορικόν τι) in the narrations of his speeches, and he is 'neither incompetent nor negligent in expression' (οὐκ ἀδύνατος οὐδὲ ὀλίγωρος περὶ τὴν ἑρμηνείαν). There follows another doubtful compliment: 'the slovenliness of his diction is not so bad as to offend you' (τὸ ῥᾴθυμον περὶ τὰς λέξεις οὐχ οὕτω φαῦλον ὥστε σε λυπῆσαι).

Although Dio assigns Xenophon to the 'Socratics', not to the historians, I will here cite Dio's praise of Xenophon (18.14), in order to bring out the contrast with Dionysius' critical treatment of the same author:

> Ξενοφῶντα δὲ ἔγωγε ἡγοῦμαι ἀνδρὶ πολιτικῷ καὶ μόνον τῶν παλαιῶν ἐξαρκεῖν δύνασθαι· εἴτε ἐν πολέμῳ τις στρατηγῶν εἴτε πόλεως ἀφηγούμενος, εἴτε ἐν δήμῳ λέγων εἴτε ἐν βουλευτηρίῳ, εἴτε καὶ ἐν δικαστηρίῳ μὴ ὡς ῥήτωρ ἐθέλοι μόνον, ἀλλὰ καὶ ὡς πολιτικὸς καὶ βασιλικὸς ἀνὴρ τὰ τῷ τοιούτῳ προσήκοντα ἐν δίκῃ εἰπεῖν· πάντων ἄριστος ἐμοὶ δοκεῖ καὶ λυσιτελέστατος πρὸς ταῦτα πάντα Ξενοφῶν. τά τε γὰρ διανοήματα σαφῆ καὶ ἁπλᾶ καὶ παντὶ ῥᾴδια φαινόμενα, τότε εἶδος τῆς ἀπαγγελίας προσηνὲς καὶ κεχαρισμένον καὶ πειστικόν, πολλὴν μὲν ἔχον πιθανότητα, πολλὴν δὲ χάριν καὶ ἐπιβολήν, ὥστε μὴ λόγων δεινότητι μόνον, ἀλλὰ καὶ γοητείᾳ ἐοικέναι τὴν δύναμιν.

> It is my own opinion that Xenophon, and he alone of the ancients, can satisfy all the requirements of a man in public life. Whether one is commanding an army in time of war, or is guiding the affairs of state, or is addressing a popular assembly or a senate, or even if he were addressing a court of law and desired, not as a professional master of eloquence merely, but as a statesman or a royal prince, to utter sentiments appropriate to such a character at the bar of justice, the best exemplar of all, it seems to me, and the most profitable for all these purposes is Xenophon. For not only are his ideas clear and simple and easy for everyone to grasp, but the character of his narrative style is attractive, pleasing, and convincing, being in a high degree true to life in the representation of character, with much charm also and effectiveness, so that his power suggests not cleverness but actual wizardry.

Dio here contradicts the views of Dionysius. As we have seen, Dionysius criticised Xenophon's characterisation (*Pomp.* 4.4) and his lack of sublimity (*Pomp.* 4.3); Dio on the other hand praises Xenophon's portrayal of characters and his witchcraft (γοητεία), a term that evokes associations with Gorgias' overwhelming rhetoric.[53] Xenophon's impact on Dio is indeed sublime (18.16):[54] ἐμοὶ γοῦν κινεῖται ἡ διάνοια καὶ ἐνίοτε δακρύω μεταξὺ τοσούτων τῶν ἔργων τοῖς λόγοις ἐντυγχάνων ('my own heart, at any rate, is deeply moved and at times I weep even as I read his account of all those deeds of valour'). Dio praises the speeches in the *Anabasis* with their overwhelming force (18.15), and he concludes that Xenophon's work informs the reader on all sorts of political communication (18.16), a passage that I have cited above.[55] To sum up, the contrast between the approaches of Dionysius and Dio could not be more clearly articulated than in their treatment of Xenophon. Where Dionysius criticises Xenophon for failing to reach the high level of Herodotus, Dio regards him as the one and only model who alone can satisfy all the needs of a statesman.[56] Although he does not go as far as Dio, Quintilian agrees with his contemporary that Xenophon is a very useful model of delight and rhetorical persuasiveness (10.1.82):

> Quid ego commemorem Xenophontis illam iucunditatem inadfectatam, sed quam nulla consequi adfectatio possit? – ut ipsae sermonem finxisse Gratiae videantur, et quod de Pericle veteris comoediae testimonium est in hunc transferri iustissime possit, in labris eius sedisse quandam persuadendi deam.

> I need hardly mention Xenophon's charm – effortless, but such as no effort could achieve. The Graces themselves seem to have moulded his style, and we may justly apply to him what a writer of old comedy said of Pericles, that some goddess of Persuasion sat upon his lips.

Both Quintilian and Dio are more positive than Dionysius about Xenophon; above we have seen that they are also more positive about Euripides. In both cases, Dionysius prefers the beauty and sublimity of the earlier authors (Herodotus among the historians, Aeschylus and Sophocles among the tragedians), whereas Dio and Quintilian admire the usefulness of the later author (Xenophon and Euripides). This preference for Xenophon and Euripides (and Menander) in Dio and Quintilian can be explained in two ways.

On the one hand, both Dio and Quintilian are primarily interested in practical usefulness for rhetoricians rather than in aesthetic qualities; it is the latter aspects of Xenophon that Dionysius finds unsatisfactory. Dio

---

[53] Gorg. *Hel.* 10.
[54] The author of *On the Sublime* also wrote a (lost) book *On Xenophon*: see *Subl.* 8.1 and cf. below, p. 343.
[55] See above, p. 329.   [56] On Dio's admiration for Xenophon, see Jones 1978: 8.

and Quintilian emphasise Xenophon's rhetorical persuasiveness, which is directly relevant to a statesman who is training his eloquence. Although Dionysius likewise claims to write for future orators, his actual evaluative comments are less concerned with practical considerations relevant to Roman society than those of his later colleagues.

On the other hand, the agreement between Dio and Quintilian (and their disagreement with Dionysius) also reflects the evolution of literary taste. In the course of the first and second centuries CE Xenophon became indeed very popular in both Greek and Latin literature.[57] On the Greek side, we should first of all think of Arrian (c. 86–160 CE), who emulated Xenophon in his *Anabasis of Alexander* and *Cynegeticus*. Longinus, who probably lived in the first century CE, frequently cites Xenophon in *On the Sublime*, but he also wrote a separate treatise *On Xenophon*.[58] Xenophon is also a primary model of ἀφέλεια (simplicity) and γλυκύτης (sweetness) in Hermogenes' *On Types of Style* (second century CE) and a model of simplicity in Pseudo-Aelius Aristides' *On Simple Discourse* (second century CE).[59] In Latin literature it is especially authors of the first century CE who admire Xenophon: whereas Cicero had still been critical,[60] Quintilian, Tacitus and Frontinus were all fond of Xenophon, whose influence is visible in their works.[61] One reason for his popularity was indeed his sweet 'simplicity' (ἀφέλεια), which was praised by rhetoricians: as Dio states, Xenophon's ideas are 'clear and simple and easy for everyone to grasp' (σαφῆ καὶ ἁπλᾶ καὶ παντὶ ῥᾴδια φαινόμενα, 18.14). Dio's observations on Xenophon's *Anabasis* suggest another reason for the popularity of Xenophon: the world of the *Anabasis* was in some ways closer to the early Roman Empire than the classical Greek world described by Thucydides. As Dio's observations bring out, Xenophon's world is one of secret communication between kings, generals and soldiers; this may

---

[57] On the reception of Xenophon in Rome, see Münscher 1920: 70–106; for his popularity in Greek imperial literature, see Münscher 1920: 106–213 and Patillon 2002: 13–16.

[58] See *Subl.* 8.1. Cf. Porter 2016: 201. Dio 18.16 (cited above) describes the feelings that Xenophon arouses in him in Longinian terms. Russell 1989: 300 notes a connection between Dio 18 and *Subl.* 17.1.

[59] Hermog. *Id.* 2.3.11–20 (Patillon 2012) (= 326–8 Rabe); 2.4.17–18 (Patillon 2012) (= 335 Rabe). Cf. Münscher 1920: 115. Pseudo-Aristid. *Ars* 2. See Patillon 2002: 16: 'Le style de Xénophon avait donc, à l'époque qui nous intéresse, des partisans résolus et il n'y a rien d'étonnant à ce qu'on en a fait, dans son genre, un modèle.'

[60] Cic. *Orat.* 32: Xenophon's style is 'sweeter than honey, but far removed from the wrangling of the forum' (*melle dulcior, sed a forensi strepitu remotissimus*). Cf. also *Orat.* 62: Xenophon's style lacks vigour.

[61] Münscher 1920: 90–5; in the second century CE references to Xenophon in Latin literature become rarer.

indeed have been one of the many appeals of Xenophon's writing in the Roman world.

Dio's praise of the *Anabasis* bears witness to what we may call a Xenophontic revolution: whereas Cicero rejected Xenophon as a rhetorical model and Dionysius was relatively critical, Dio, Longinus, Pseudo-Aelius, Aristides and Quintilian all embrace Xenophon's charm, his simplicity and his sublimity. This remarkable development is reflected in his status: Xenophon is no longer a historian, but a Socratic philosopher.

The Philosophers

Dionysius deals with the philosophers (epitome *On Imitation* 4.1–3) before he concludes his reading list with the orators; in Dio and Quintilian the order of the last two categories is reversed: Dio ends with 'the Socratics' (18.13–17), Quintilian with the philosophers (10.1.81–4). Dio singles out just one Socratic writer: as we have seen above, he extensively praises Xenophon as the most useful author, who 'can satisfy all the requirements of a man in public life'. If the epitome is trustworthy, Xenophon is also the first name mentioned in Dionysius' list of philosophers, followed by Plato, Aristotle and 'his students'.[62] Quintilian is more specific: he adds Aristotle's pupil Theophrastus and presents his philosophers in the following order: Plato, Xenophon, the 'other Socratics', Aristotle, Theophrastus (and the Stoics, who are not to be imitated).

Dionysius praises the charm, elegance and grandeur of Plato and Xenophon, and Aristotle's forcefulness, learning, and clear and pleasing style. Quintilian focuses on Plato's Homeric style and Xenophon's charm (see above), and he praises Aristotle's learning, pleasing style, invention and variety.[63] The brilliance of language in Theophrastus is divine; the eloquence of the early Stoics is criticised (10.1.84). We may conclude that there is considerable overlap between Dionysius and Quintilian in their evaluations of Plato, Xenophon and Aristotle. Quintilian and Dio share an interest in 'Socratic writers' and their graceful style – the term 'Socratics' does not figure in the epitome of *On Imitation*, but the reference to Plato and Xenophon as one pair (4.2) may indicate that Dionysius likewise distinguished a category of Socratic writers.[64] By far the most remarkable element in the three lists of philosophers, however, is Dio's extensive praise

---

[62] The reference to the Pythagoreans in *De imit.* 4.1 is probably corrupt.
[63] For Plato's Homeric style, cf. Longinus, *Subl.* 13.3–4.
[64] In *Comp.* 16.4 Dionysius refers to 'the Socratic Plato'.

of Xenophon,⁶⁵ with the omission of all other philosophers. With another touch of irony, Dio remarks that 'it would be a long task to eulogise the other Socratic writers; even to read them is no light thing' (τοὺς μὲν δὴ ἄλλους μακρὸν ἂν εἴη ἔργον ἐπαινεῖν καὶ ἐντυγχάνειν αὐτοῖς οὐ τὸ τυχόν).

The Orators

Dionysius selects six Attic orators: Lysias, Isocrates, Lycurgus, Demosthenes, Aeschines and Hyperides (epitome *On Imitation* 5.1–7). In his work *On the Ancient Orators*, Isaeus takes the place of Lycurgus; the other five names are identical. The six orators are there presented in two triads, and the order is slightly different: Lysias, Isocrates, Isaeus; Demosthenes, Hyperides, Aeschines.⁶⁶ Quintilian (10.1.76–80) also lists six orators, substituting Demetrius of Phalerum for Lycurgus/Isaeus. Quintilian's order is different, as he starts with the best orators: Demosthenes, Aeschines, Hyperides, Lysias, Isocrates, Demetrius of Phalerum.⁶⁷ The fact that both Dionysius and Quintilian select six orators shows that the 'canon' of Attic orators was not yet fixed or standard in their age: Caecilius of Caleacte, a contemporary of Dionysius, wrote a treatise *On the Style of the Ten Orators*, which may have listed the orators who would in later times be considered the canonical ten: Antiphon, Andocides, Lysias, Isocrates, Isaeus, Demosthenes, Aeschines, Lycurgus, Hyperides, Dinarchus.⁶⁸

Dionysius and Quintilian praise their six orators in emphasising different qualities. Lysias is pure, plain and elegant (and sufficient for the purpose of usefulness, Dionysius adds). Isocrates is polished and graceful, austere and impressive, morally instructive, and more suitable for reading than for speaking in the courts. Dionysius states that Lycurgus is amplificatory and elevated; Quintilian prefers Demetrius, who is the 'last' orator of the Attic school. Demosthenes is energetic and majestic; his grave and

---

⁶⁵ See above, p. 341.
⁶⁶ Dion. Hal. *Orat. Vett.* 4.5. The treatises on Lysias, Isocrates, Isaeus and Demosthenes have been preserved.
⁶⁷ Dionysius cites Demetrius of Phalerum in *Dem.* 5.6. But this orator (born *c.* 350 BCE) lived probably too late to be included in his list of orators, because Dionysius believes that Attic eloquence started to decline after the death of Alexander (*Orat. Vett.* 1). Quintilian, *Inst.* 10.1.80 mentions that Demetrius 'is said to have been the first to set oratory on the downward path' (*is primus inclinasse eloquentiam dicitur*).
⁶⁸ See the fragments of Caecilius (ed. Woerther 2015) and Pseudo-Plutarch, *Vitae decem oratorum*. It is uncertain when the canon of ten Attic orators was first proposed: see Worthington 1994 and Smith 1995. On the canon of the Attic orators and the reading lists of Dionysius, Dio and Quintilian, see de Jonge forthcoming 2022.

gracious style overwhelms the judges (*On Imitation* 5.4), and for Quintilian he is simply 'the greatest' (*princeps*, 10.1.76). In *On Demosthenes* Dionysius likewise presents Demosthenes as the absolute highlight of classical oratory: Demosthenes combines all styles and qualities of his predecessors (8.4). Aeschines is 'less energetic' (ἀτονώτερος) than Demosthenes but impressive, vivid and agreeable; for Quintilian, on the other hand, Aeschines is 'fuller and more expansive' (*plenior et magis fusus*, 10.1.77). Hyperides is goal-oriented (εὔστοχος); he surpasses Lysias in composition, and everyone in invention; his narratives are subtle and balanced. Quintilian is slightly less enthusiastic about this orator: Hyperides has extraordinary charm and point, but 'he is more equal to minor, not to say trivial causes' (10.1.77).

Dio's discussion of orators (18.11) is very different, although he mentions almost all the orators that Dionysius lists, leaving out only Isocrates: Dio's Attic orators are Demosthenes, Lysias, Hyperides, Aeschines and Lycurgus. He acknowledges that Demosthenes and Lysias are the best; and he mentions some of the characteristics that are traditionally connected to these models, including Demosthenes' vigour, forcefulness and copiousness, and Lysias' brevity, simplicity, coherence and concealed cleverness. Nevertheless, for the purpose of his reading list Dio (18.11) prefers three other Attic orators:

> πλὴν οὐκ ἂν ἐγώ σοι συμβουλεύσαιμι τὰ πολλὰ τούτοις ἐντυγχάνειν, ἀλλ' Ὑπερείδῃ τε μᾶλλον καὶ Αἰσχίνῃ. τούτων γὰρ ἁπλούστεραί τε αἱ δυνάμεις καὶ εὐληπτότεραι αἱ κατασκευαὶ καὶ τὸ κάλλος τῶν ὀνομάτων οὐδὲν ἐκείνων λειπόμενον. ἀλλὰ καὶ Λυκούργῳ συμβουλεύσαιμ' ἂν ἐντυγχάνειν σοι, ἐλαφροτέρῳ τούτων ὄντι καὶ ἐμφαίνοντί τινα ἐν τοῖς λόγοις ἁπλότητα καὶ γενναιότητα τοῦ τρόπου.

> However I should not advise you to read these two chiefly [i.e. Demosthenes and Lysias], but Hyperides rather and Aeschines; for the faculties in which they excel are simpler, their rhetorical embellishments easier to grasp, and the beauty of their diction is not one whit inferior to that of the two who are ranked first [Demosthenes and Lysias]. But I should advise you to read Lycurgus as well, since he has a lighter touch than those others and reveals a certain simplicity and nobility of character in his speeches.

This crucial passage brings out the contrast between two essentially different approaches to classical literature: it is the difference between Dionysius' *On Imitation* and Dio's *On Training for Public Speaking*. Demosthenes and Lysias may be the best orators, as Dio acknowledges; but they are not the most useful reading for an active statesman.

Dio's next step is even more revolutionary. We have observed that Dionysius' list includes only authors of the classical period, while ignoring all post-classical writers. The reason for this choice is given in the preface to *On the Ancient Orators* (1.1–7): after the death of Alexander the Great the Attic Muse was replaced by a harlot from Asia, who stands for vulgar and tasteless rhetoric.[69] Therefore, Demosthenes (384–322 BCE) is the last great orator of the classical past, after whom the decline of eloquence sets in.[70] In agreement with this historical framework Dionysius never mentions writers from the third and second centuries BCE except in order to criticise them: he strongly objects to the styles of Hellenistic historians like Phylarchus of Athens, Duris of Samos and Polybius.[71] Dio does not list writers of the third or second century either; but he does recommend four orators who can be dated to the first century BCE (18.12):

> ἐνταῦθα δή φημι δεῖν, κἂν εἴ τις ἐντυχὼν τῇ παραινέσει τῶν πάνυ ἀκριβῶν αἰτιάσεται, μηδὲ τῶν νεωτέρων καὶ ὀλίγον πρὸ ἡμῶν ἀπείρως ἔχειν· λέγω δὲ τῶν περὶ Ἀντίπατρον καὶ Θεόδωρον καὶ Πλουτίωνα καὶ Κόνωνα καὶ τὴν τοιαύτην ὕλην.

> At this point I say it is advisable – even if some one, after reading my recommendation of the consummate masters of oratory, is going to find fault – also not to remain unacquainted with the more recent orators, those who lived a little before our time; I refer to the works of such men as Antipater, Theodorus, Plution, and Conon, and to similar material.

Antipater may be the father of Nicolaus of Damascus (first century BCE); Theodorus of Gadara was the teacher of emperor Tiberius; Plution and the grammarian Conon were probably also active in the Augustan Age.[72] Dio has thus taken the unusual step of including in his reading list four authors who lived shortly before him (and who were the contemporaries of Dionysius), and he anticipates the criticism that his unconventional advice will generate. Indeed, in praising the exemplarity of Greek orators of the first century BCE Dio's letter *On Training* not only stands apart from contemporary Greek rhetoric and literature, which generally looks back to the Attic orators of classical Greece, but also gives an intriguing corrective to the history of rhetoric presented by Flavius Philostratus some 150 years

---

[69] See Hidber 1996 and de Jonge 2014; on Atticism and Asianism, see also the introduction and the chapter by Kim in this volume.
[70] Demosthenes is also the last great author of the classical past in Longinus' *On the Sublime*. On Demosthenes as a model of the sublime in Longinus and Caecilius of Caleacte, see Innes 2002 and Porter 2016: 127–9 and 189.
[71] See *Comp.* 4.15. [72] For Plution, see Sen. *Suas.* 1.11. Conon's Attic style is praised by Photius.

later: in the *Lives of the Sophists*, Philostratus jumps from Aeschines (fourth century BCE) to Nicetes of Smyrna (second half of the first century CE), devoting no single word to the orators who lived in the intermediate ages.[73] Dio's motivation for including more recent orators in the list is intriguing (18.13):

αἱ γὰρ τούτων δυνάμεις καὶ ταύτῃ ἂν εἶεν ἡμῖν ὠφέλιμοι, ᾗ οὐκ ἂν ἐντυγχάνοιμεν αὐτοῖς δεδουλωμένοι τὴν γνώμην, ὥσπερ τοῖς παλαιοῖς. ὑπὸ γὰρ τοῦ δύνασθαί τι τῶν εἰρημένων αἰτιάσασθαι μάλιστα θαρροῦμεν πρὸς τὸ τοῖς αὐτοῖς ἐπιχειρεῖν ἡμεῖς, καὶ ἥδιόν τις παραβάλλει αὐτὸν ᾧ πείθεται συγκρινόμενος οὐ καταδεέστερος, ἐνίοτε δὲ καὶ βελτίων ἂν φαίνεσθαι.

For the powers they [i.e. recent orators] display can be more useful to us, because, when we read them, our judgement is not fettered and enslaved, as it is when we approach the ancients. For when we think that we are able to criticise what was been said, we are most encouraged to attempt the same things ourselves, and we find more pleasure in comparing ourselves with others when we are convinced that in the comparison we should be found not inferior to them, with the chance, occasionally, of being even superior.

The final words of this passage suggest a kind of weariness with the idealising, hardcore classicism of traditional rhetoric. The uncompromising admiration and exclusive imitation of the Attic orators of the fifth and fourth centuries BCE could, as Dio suggests, reduce the student's confidence. The motif of enslavement is remarkable: we could interpret it as a reversal of an argument that we find in other classicising critics. Dionysius and Longinus believe that reading the speeches of Demosthenes can to a certain extent revive the freedom of classical Greece and hence contribute to the feeling of Greekness of their readers.[74] Dio on the other hand points out that our judgement is enslaved when we constantly try to imitate only the orators of classical Athens: one will feel more free, it is suggested, when reading the speeches of the Augustan Age.

Conclusion

Various scholars in the past have stated that there is a general correspondence between the reading lists of Dionysius and Dio. This belief is

---

[73] Philostr. *VS* 1, 510–11. See introduction above, p. 23.
[74] On Dionysius' classicism, see Wiater 2011. The motif of enslavement also figures prominently in the final chapter of Longinus' *On the Sublime* (44). Longinus adduces two explanations for the lack of sublime literature in his own time: a political and a moral explanation. In both cases, people are 'enslaved': they are the slaves of political rulers or of their insolence and shamelessness. Dio 18.12 seems to reverse Longinus' argument: for Dio we are not enslaved by the present, but rather by the classical past.

mistaken. The differences between Dionysius and Dio are in fact strong and numerous. Dio's letter *On Training for Public Speaking* forms a radical departure from Dionysius' reading list, or, to be precise, from the type of lists that Dionysius represents – for we do not know whether Dio was actually familiar with Dionysius' *On Imitation*. Dionysius prefers the sublime Aeschylus and Sophocles; Dio recommends reading Euripides and Menander. Dionysius finds Herodotus superior to Xenophon; Dio regards Xenophon as the most useful of all ancient writers. For Dionysius the Attic orators are sacred; Dio recommends reading the orators of Augustan Rome next to those of classical Athens. In Dionysius' *On Imitation* various authors are praised for their beauty, grandeur and sublimity; Dio, on the other hand, is only interested in practical usefulness and political eloquence. I have explained these discrepancies in three ways.

First there is a difference between the intended audiences of the two works, which implies a difference in purpose. Dionysius writes for all students who wish to develop their skills of writing and teaching. In that sense his *On Imitation* has of course a practical purpose; but as far as we can tell, the work made no reference to the political circumstances of the Roman world and did not discuss the usefulness of classical Greek authors for the types of eloquence that were actually needed by lawyers or politicians of the Augustan world. Dio, on the other hand, instructs an active statesman, whose time for reading books is very limited. Dio's recommendations are therefore directly relevant and tailored to the affairs of an influential politician in the Roman Empire: Xenophon in particular is put forward as the ideal guide for political eloquence and communication with kings, generals and soldiers.

Second, the reading lists of Dionysius and Dio are the products of two different ages. We have seen that in various points Dio and his contemporary Quintilian agree with each other, while contradicting the views of Dionysius. Most importantly Quintilian and Dio agree that Menander and Euripides, very popular in the first century CE, are more useful than Aeschylus or Sophocles, and that Xenophon is a 'Socratic writer' whose persuasive style rewards imitation. Unlike Dionysius, Quintilian and Dio also include post-classical authors in their reading lists. In turning from Dionysius to Dio and Quintilian, we move from one type of classicism to another: from the hardcore, archaising, democratic, idealising classicism of Dionysius, with its emphasis on beauty and sublimity, to the more pragmatic, modern and imperial classicism of Dio, with its emphasis on practical usefulness. The typical models of classical Greece, which are so important for Dionysius' construction of Greek identity (Herodotus,

Thucydides, Aeschylus, Sophocles, Demosthenes), are partly replaced by the models that fit Flavian Rome (Xenophon, Euripides, Menander, Aeschines).

Finally there is a difference in the genres of the two works: a serious rhetorical treatise versus a light-hearted literary letter. This difference is reflected in the roles adopted by the two instructors. Dionysius represents the traditional teacher of rhetoric: in this respect, Quintilian and Dionysius are in one team. Dio, on the other hand, adopts a more relaxed attitude, either because he has to be careful not to overdo his role of teacher in writing to an important statesman who is hierarchically superior; or perhaps because his letter consciously and playfully attempts to depart from the rules of traditional rhetoric. This is most clearly seen in two of Dio's most remarkable pieces of advice. Dionysius and Quintilian want their students to be actively engaged in reading classical literature; Dio on the other hand advises his friend to have the texts read to him by others. Dionysius and Quintilian instruct their students to work hard, but Dio thinks that too much exercise will not be good for his addressee. We may now add a third piece of innovative advice: Dio tells his addressee that he should not write himself, but dictate to a secretary (18.18); Quintilian on the other hand strongly objects to 'the luxury of dictation' (*Institutio oratoria* 10.3.19–21). It is in these unconventional recommendations that Dio's letter explicitly turns away from rhetorical teaching and becomes a more fanciful literary construct, which was perhaps really useful to a historical recipient, but certainly also pleasant and entertaining to a wider audience. *On Training for Public Speaking* is neither a rhetorical treatise nor a school exercise, but a sophisticated literary letter, which ironically engages with the well-known genre of the Greek reading list and turns it into something practical, innovative and enjoyable.

CHAPTER 12

Envoi
To Live in Hellenistic Times
Simon Goldhill

What does it mean to be 'of one's time'? It is the fantasy of some classical scholars that a history of classical scholarship should consist of a roll-call of great men – and, yes, gender matters here – facing and attempting to solve the same textual problems, in conversation with one another across the ages, unburdened by the contingencies and influences of their own present time.[1] These histories may still drone on in some quarters of academia, but such a model, even when still lived up to by modern scholars in the practice of commentaries, has been replaced in intellectual history by the more complex questions of how a scholar should be situated. I write 'situated' to cue the current insistence on moving away from notions of 'context' to a more fluid and contingent understanding of how a scholar relates not just to the time in which he or she lives, but also to the shifting circumstances and networks of personal and professional life.[2] When Eduard Fraenkel sought to analyse Agamemnon's willingness in Aeschylus' *Agamemnon* to step on the tapestries spread for him by his wife, and explained the king's decision as the behaviour of a gentleman, what is at stake in Fraenkel's explanation has now become a broadening issue of personal history, scholarship in exile, gender politics, and the institutional history of the discipline – all topics embedded in my passing remark that 'yes, gender matters'.[3]

This example of Fraenkel, and the heated debate around Fraenkel's behaviour as a (gentle)man, also emphatically underline the degree to which history is a dialogue between the understanding, normative categories, and expected narratives of the present and those of the past. If we turn to evaluate a book such as Wilamowitz's study of Pindar, *Pindaros* (1922),

---

[1] Güthenke 2020 is an excellent rejoinder to Lloyd-Jones 1982 and Pfeiffer 1968, 1976.
[2] Post Classicisms Collective 2020; Haraway 1988 is seminal.
[3] Fraenkel 1950: II, 441. See Elsner 2017; Stray 2015; Beard 2013: 264–71 – which prompted a good deal of journalism and internet traffic.

a different range of intellectual questions impose themselves. On the one hand, since Wilamowitz reads Pindar's poetry through his construction of Pindar's life, the first compelling questions stress the comprehension of biography as a critical tool – how, that is, to write about Pindar's life? What is the relation between the circumstances of a poet, including the environment in which he lived, and his poetry? How is an ancient psychology to be parsed? These are questions about the institution of life-writing in the 1920s and how Wilamowitz constructed his intellectual project: questions central to *Pindaros*, but resolutely avoided in Wilamowitz's own history of classical scholarship, one of the more egregious examples of selective history, which he paused *Pindaros* to write. On the other hand, the book was mercilessly criticised, especially by Wilamowitz's younger colleagues, not least for being 'out of date'. There is an intergenerational and personal story to be broached if we are to understand what this book means or comes to mean. To understand the impact or failed impact of the book also requires us to see how Wilamowitz did and did not speak to his time, and, later, to us.

I start this 'envoi' with these two cases, both of which have received focused attention in recent years, to open some fundamental starting points for what is to be learned from *Late Hellenistic Greek Literature in Dialogue*. The book makes two grounding claims from the off: first, that it is important and necessary to see the works of a particular period *as* products of a time – that speak to their time of production. Second, that to understand this timeliness it is crucial also to set these works in dialogue not just with each other but with works of other periods to calibrate such 'being of one's time'. The second claim is fundamental if the first is not to lurch into a misleadingly inert sense of how a writer inhabits time. Different generations coexist. There are those who look back to a past world and those who look forward to a new world, living and conversing at the same time (the modernists of the 1920s sat at table with those born in the Victorian era, embodying the Victorian values that the modernists in their modernism despised: the great Wilamowitz was scorned as Wilamops by the Georgekreis. It is salutary to recall that T. S. Eliot's super-trendy 'The Wasteland', with its paraded anthropology of Jessie Weston, was published the same year (1922) as Malinowski's *The Argonauts of the Western Pacific*, a seminal text of modern anthropology which would make Jessie Weston seem hopelessly ... Victorian). There are those who are behind the times and those ahead of their times – both in our perceptions of the past and in a community's sense of itself, two sets of evaluations which may not always overlap. Already in the fifth-century BCE city of

Athens, cultural dissent between the younger and older generations was a subject of comedy, as was the trendiness of Euripides and the conservatism of Aeschylus. The force of history is experienced differently by different groups in the same era: what defines the present may be differently articulated by citizens, slaves, women, foreigners, and so on. Nor is it clear what it is to be exemplary of a time. We may take Dickens to be the paradigmatic Victorian novelist, but there were many other writers who sold more and were more praised than Dickens – Marie Corelli or Edward Bulwer Lytton, say – who are largely unread today and largely denigrated if read, but were treated very much as signs of the times, beacons of the age, in their own day. When Theocritus, Callimachus and Apollonius are taken as paradigmatic of Hellenistic culture because of the tight similarity of their poetic projects and shared institutional involvement, are we not also praising the self-assertive avant-garde for their retrospective success, much as museums today enthrone the marginal and unsold works of impressionist artists in their Victorian rooms, rather than the wonderful genre pictures and religious images of the salons and exhibitions that actually *typify* nineteenth-century art – and were valued as such at the time? Theocritus, Callimachus and Apollonius were rediscovered by the Latin poets of the Augustan era, and a tradition of poetics enshrines the Hellenistic poets as the privileged source of a privileged style. If instead we set these poets in dialogue with the Septuagint, Philo or Clement, however, to stay with Alexandrian literary products, the linearity of that tradition starts to look more constructed – a more ideologically loaded history in its exclusion of hugely influential works that have a different imprimatur, a different agenda.

Nobody is *not* a product of their time: everybody is born into a time and formed by the society in which they grow and live, and the writing of any era is informed by the values, expectations and concepts of its time. This is a truism, although it remains a necessary rejoinder to any attempt to deracinate scholars or artists from such temporal situatedness in the name of universalism or any other such ideologically loaded and self-serving detemporalising gesture. Historicise, always historicise is a motto that ought not to be reserved for Marxist critics.[4] Nobody, however, is only a product of their time. The contingencies of self and circumstance, and the vagaries of engagement with the flow of events, also produce a sense of being at odds with one's own time, to stand out against the clichés or dominant normativities of collectivity: the impressionists were also

---

[4] Jameson 1981 – a much-quoted slogan.

nineteenth-century artists. As Nietzsche, one of those classicists not mentioned by Wilamowitz's history of classical scholarship, knew better than anyone, *untimeliness* is also integral to cultural progress.[5] *How* to construct the timeliness of a work in its era, thus, becomes the compelling question. *How* a text is exemplary of its time requires a series of disambiguating moves to clarify whether one means typical, outstanding, retrospectively influential, dull, revelatory – and revelatory of what. If the first grounding hypothesis of the volume insists on historicisation, the second, the turn to dialogue, introduces a necessary dynamism into how each work can speak to its time: the insistence on dialogue recognises that no literary work is an island unto itself. It recognises that *how* a work engages with its era of production, and is remade in its ongoing history, is a multifaceted process of speaking out, being ignored, claiming authority, being appropriated... In short, fully *dialogic*. So, too, how later critics place the work in its time, in the history of literature, is part of how a text is allowed to speak today. The life of a text, like the life of a person, can be told in multiple ways, but it would be inadequate to ignore how, among the many and complex qualities it may have, it is networked, contingent, institutionally embedded – and written by others.

The force of this *dialogic history of the life of a text* is vividly felt in the relations between the first five chapters of this book. The editors carefully mark in the introduction that these pieces are linked by their focus on *space*, though the chapters are not formally organised and titled as a section on topography. Most tellingly, however, each of these chapters, in their own ways, demonstrates how there is no 'view from nowhere'. Even the topography of a map is drawn from a certain place – a political, moral or conceptual vantage point (as the history of imperial cartography demonstrates most vividly). The late Hellenistic period is marked politically by the coming of Rome, and the shifting dynamics of incipient and then increasingly established empire change the framework of self-placement for Greek and Roman writers. The first general question raised by this book, then, is: how do Greek writers articulate a place on the map of this new and transforming topography of Roman-dominated political organisation?

The first five chapters provide a collective and variegated answer to this question. To discuss how Roman space is conceived in Polybius' Greek history is an exercise in understanding how the mental map of the world is reorganised by the political disruptions and new geographical boundaries of empire. To be Greek in this Roman world requires a change in

---

[5] Nietzsche's *Unzeitgemässe Betrachtungen* (1876) is translated in Nietzsche 1997.

perspective – an ability to see oneself otherwise, both within one's own literary and political tradition and as an object in the politics and imaginary of the imperial power. This internal dialogue is integral to what it means to live in the Roman empire as a non-Roman. If Polybius' history is an attempt to explain the rise of Rome, it is also testimony of how the mental map of space is redefined by this effort of shifting perspective. This internal dialogue of historical perspective is itself in dialogue with the recognition that Greek writing about how humans change landscapes, particularly in Strabo and Diodorus, is fissured by conflicting views within even a single writer, and certainly differently evaluated between different authors. The changing landscape also becomes a way of conceiving the possibilities of empire. And of dramatising responses to the violent reorganisation of space that the imposition of imperial rule brings. What is at stake here is not simply discussions of canal-building or the absence of the language of provinces in a historian: what is at stake is how the geographical imaginary of empire is being formulated.

The imaginary of empire demands a recalibration of thinking about scale and affect. This demand is evident in genres where it may at first sight seem less expected. Epigrams – a genre with a long history, nonetheless taken to be especially of its Hellenistic time – are self-conscious exercises in scalar thinking. Epigrams play with their own smallness, and with their own capturing of the moment. They are thus the perfect paradoxical form to discuss the bigness and ever-lastingness of empire – or so they project. Each of the poems which take the empire and its material spectacles as their subject, dramatises the changing perspective of the subject of empire, responding to its immensity from the stance of the epigram's pointed tininess.[6] Ecphrasis is a more familiar trope of power. The monumentality of empire requires the rhetoric of wonder to testify to its projections of glory. The ceremonials, displays and monumental architecture of empire expect an affective response. On display is an architecture and a performance designed to impress its own power and authority on the viewers, and expects awe and a recognition of its majesty. Whether we turn to Statius' *Silvae* or the more cynical Lucian – who notes if the poor didn't watch, the rich wouldn't strut – there are many examples of the anxiety of such interaction with the spectacles of power. As Theocritus already dramatised in his poem of the women going to the festival of Adonis (*Idyll* 15), responses to ceremonial did not always match the ceremonial's self-projection. What, then, of different ecphrastic

---

[6] On scale and empire see Goldhill 2020: 38–70.

descriptions of harbours as a topographical focus? These may seem to be portrayals that have little to do with the dynamics of power; but they are portrayals which dramatise and promote different registers of affect – part of the imperial project of teaching how to look. If we scroll on from Philostratus in the roster of harbour ecphrases, we will come to an amazing passage in Nonnus, where the harbour at Tyre is described with the most intense erotic affect as 'like a swimming girl, who gives her head and breasts and neck into the sea, stretching her hands out in the middle of the sea on either side, whitening her body with foam from the sea next to her' (*Dion.* 40 319–22).[7] This richly emotive language reveals how aggressively *without* affect Diodorus' descriptive style is. This is not just because Diodorus is writing in a very different genre from Nonnus. It also – in dialogue – reminds us that there is a politics as well as an aesthetics of emotion, when it comes to how to respond to the public works of powerful men. The scale of empire and its spectacles of power both demand an affective reaction from the subjects of empire: here too – in the trained rhetorical and poetic performance of response to the spectacles of empire – we see the construction of the imaginary of empire. The history of how ecphrasis grounds the imperial imaginary includes the great procession of Ptolemy II Philadelphus, and Achilles Tatius, say, or Procopius, John of Gaza, and many others. To leave Diodorus in dialogue with Philostratus alone is inevitably to underplay the retrospective pointedness of Diodorus' designedly bald stylistics.

The stimulating contrast between civic and anti-civic cosmopolitanism articulated by Benjamin Gray provides a powerful culmination to this sequence of chapters. His contrast between local engagement in the affairs of a city, and rejection of such engagement in the name of a broader politics or of a philosophy that attempts to reject the messy business of politics altogether, takes the issues of scale and multiple, fissured perspectives, and explores how such self-positioning is articulated in historical texts and, above all, in the public display of inscriptions: brief public statements of recognised grandeur. The record of Aemilius Zosimus in particular reveals with a certain flamboyance the complex possibilities of self-definition in the topography of empire. Aemilius Zosimus, a Roman citizen, is an outsider to Priene but celebrated for his contribution to the central Greek educational institution of the gymnasium: he is praised for what he has done for 'boxing, weapons and philology', a triad to delight Victorian educationalists with their muscular desire for *mens sana in*

---

[7] Chuvin 1991: 224–50.

corpore sano. Yet what makes this inscription so telling is the dialogic contrast with other attempts at fitting into one's time and place in the Hellenistic era. *How to belong* is a mobilising vector of what it means to be of one's time. The very explicitation of strategies of contribution and the civic recognition of such efforts make engagement with the city an area of contestation as well as contribution. Yet the coming of empire changes the lineaments of belonging. Here, too, then, we see how the dialogic reading opens a window onto how 'being of one's time' becomes a self-defining question, when the political geography of empire transforms what *being in place* means.

If the first general lesson I have drawn out from the volume's chapters concerns the geographical and cultural mapping under the new and changing conditions of empire – formulating the imaginary of empire – the second concerns the question of how textual authority and cultural tradition are constructed under such transformative circumstances. The second set of four chapters each concerns writers who parade their struggle to assert their authority over against the *mos maiorum* of the empire elite – or from within its own cultural insecurities. This raises an especially broad and stimulating range of questions, where the multiple and fissured perspectives of the subjects of empire are strikingly in evidence. The Jewish population of Alexandria was especially large and culturally sophisticated – and it is a topic I will return to. The Third Sibylline Oracle was written, it appears, first in this Jewish community, though collected later with an overlay by Christian writers into its current form. Greensmith's superb reading, which emphasises the text's self-conscious appropriative challenge to the authority of Homer in the name of another, older tradition, underlines the complex dynamics of self-assertion through the alibi of the deep past, that is performed by a community excluded both from the privileged cultural tradition of Greek literature and from the privileged political power of Rome. The Greek-speaking Jewish community is a group which can only perform the precarity of its cultural boundaries.

In fascinating dialogue with this picture of a community marginalised by and yet assimilating itself into the Greek culture of Alexandria, Cicero's and other Roman evocations of an imaginary and fantasised Athens of yore provide a counter-model from the other side of the dynamics of power. Whose past – and how appropriated – is to count? How does Empire change the practice of cultural tourism? Roman desire-filled projections of the cultural pinnacles of Athens do not only remind us that the geographical imaginary is integral to the rulers of empire as well as its subjects, but also uncover the role of the other in placing a fault line in Roman cultural self-confidence. From the point of view of contemporary colonial theory, the literature from Rome, the mother of all Empires, is a distinct anomaly. In recent decades, we have learned a great deal about the strategies of the colonised and the cultural dominance of the imperial power. The requirement of the colonised is to mimic, to pass, to write resistance from below. The ability of the subaltern to speak has been questioned, recalibrated and questioned again. The power of the colonisers, by contrast, is to objectify the other in its gaze, to represent empire as the necessary bringing of civilisation and value to an otherwise backwards culture, to exoticise, loot and then display the spectacle of heritage.[8] Yet Rome's relation to Greece, specifically in cultural terms, reverses the expected dynamics of power.[9] As Horace famously wrote (*Epist.* 2.1, 156–7): 'Captured Greece captured its savage conqueror and brought the arts to rustic Latium.' As with Horace's *bon mot* – a piece of knowing historical, national self-placement from the son of a freedman at the court of the newly flourishing Empire – Cicero, a grandee of empire, dramatises himself and his chums wryly performing their longing for another's cultural memory, and their own silencing of their empire's violence to that cultural heritage. If the Sibyl's poetry encodes a certain sharp wit, Cicero's authoritative smile of recognition enacts a different dynamic of power. The Sibyl's Homer is not the same competitive fantasy of the Greek past as Cicero's Athens.

Roman cultural identity, as Cicero's encounters in Rome typify, is repeatedly formulated in dialogue with an idea of Greekness. Cato, we are told, dismissed Greek medicine as a foreign pretentiousness. Such a dismissal is a parade of Cato's celebrated insistence on his Romanness, and it is a story told and re-told as part of Rome's ambivalent relation to Greek cultural authority; but in Plutarch's snide retelling, Cato's rejection of Greek doctors is the cause of his wife's premature death.[10] In dialogue, stories also change their valence. Belonging can be paraded – but the very need to parade belonging underlines how it has become a subject of contestation.

Polybius, Diodorus Siculus, Plutarch, Aelius Aristides and several other authors who are discussed in this volume, are evidently trying – in their

---

[8] Acheraïou 2008 and 2011; Ashcroft, Griffiths and Tiffin 2002; Cronin 2008; Quayson 2000; Spivak 1988; Young 1990, 1995, 2001, and the seminal Bhabha 1990 and 1994.
[9] On Rome and post-colonial theory see Hose 1999; Quinn 2012; Webster and Cooper 1996. More generally, see Gruen 1992, Mattingly 2013 and 2014, Vanacker and Zuiderhoek 2017, Wallace-Hadrill 1998b; Woolf 2000; Feeney 2016.
[10] *Cat. Mai.* 23.3–4, with Goldhill 2002: 259–61.

different ways – to make sense of Rome and the startling rise to power of the Roman state. Yet it is surprising that in the literature of the late Hellenistic period especially, and even in later imperial writers, it is hard to determine precisely how much engagement with Latin and the specifics of Roman culture is taking place. Even Plutarch, who compares and contrasts Roman and Greek Lives, and writes *Greek and Roman Questions*, studiously downplays his knowledge of the Latin language.[11] A book-length study of whether the *Posthomerica* of Quintus of Smyrna knows and engages with Latin poets and Virgil in particular ends in the same complete uncertainty from which it started.[12] This tendency to turn away from Roman intellectual achievements also makes Strabo all the more paradigmatic. Strabo is, of course, central to our understanding of the constructed topography of the world of late Hellenistic Greek-speaking elites, and his engagement with civic political self-positioning is also well brought out in this volume. Yet Strabo's insistence that true intellectual excellence is located in the Greek East of Asia Minor (as Hatzimichali brings out), and his own rather precarious attempts to assert the philosophical credentials of his own geographical project, is a telling test case of how Greek Hellenistic writers turn their heads away from Rome (but look back over their shoulders at the exercise of power). It is a sign of the times.

The third lesson is the least developed in the volume – its final two chapters – but not the least important. If the first lesson was about the geography of cultural mapping and the second about the performative construction of tradition within a culturally conflicted and self-consciously contentious history, the third concerns the material form of such textual and physical gestures of self-definition. What does it feel like, look like, taste like to live through one's time? Proust could make the taste of a madeleine the portal to the rediscovery of times past; for my parents' generation powdered egg and chicory coffee evoke the rationed years after the Second World War; but they could never inhabit a world which expects a coffee cup and a mobile phone to fill the hand on the street. When I taught a course on the representation of war and showed my students the wonderful naval film *In Which We Serve* (1942), they all found it very hard to understand the upper-class accent of Noel Coward (in a very British way, the film sets three classes of sailors against each other to tell the story of the naval contribution to the war). It was not Coward's vocabulary or syntax that was hard for them to follow, but the accent, rhythm and speed of his speech. For them, it was the sound of a lost and

---

[11] Goldhill forthcoming.   [12] Gärtner 2005.

now incomprehensible way of speaking. There may be a technical interest in the metrics of prose, for both Hellenistic and modern theorists, but it has significance only because it constitutes – it changes – what prose sounds like. How to sound as if you are part of a tradition, is how a tradition is actively continued. To speak *properly*, that is, to sound like you *belong*. Sometimes, to be of your time means to see yourself in a longer history of belonging. There is an *infrastructure* to belonging which is articulated not just in how you speak but also in the required reading lists – which are always about the ideology of canonicity, what is proper to have read, to make you *gebildet* ('educated/ cultured/ civilised'), or *en biblois peponēmenē*, 'worked out in and through books'[13] – and in the genres that are performed: there is always an aesthetic politics at work in the normativity of genre ('Reader, I married him'). Genre matters to cultural formation – as the realist novel (for example) is a telling sign of Victorian culture, or theatre of burgeoning Elizabethan London – much as the specific books that become fashionable open a portal onto the imaginary of an era – just as *how* books are circulated and read, the physicality of such activity, changes significantly over time. There is still room for an extended study of how *being Hellenistic* took a material, performative shape: the increasing bilingualism of Roman elites, the styles of dress and leisure activities, the architectural redesign of civic space, the different styles of ceremonial, new affordances of education, the walk of a philosopher, the stride of a Roman soldier, the influx of new foods and exotic objects that empire allows, all contribute to how Greeks and Romans saw themselves inhabiting their changing present.

This notion that cultural transformation is experienced through the changing physicalities of the mundane – and through the self-consciousness of such changes – is one direction in which the arguments of this book could be extended. There are three further questions that need raising. The first concerns the selectivity of sources. It is striking that the single most important and by far the most influential piece of Hellenistic writing is barely mentioned and not discussed in the volume. This book is not alone in such blindness: almost no contemporary classics course includes it in its offerings on Hellenistic history or literature. I am referring (of course) to the *Septuagint*.[14] Now, the editors define the chronological range of the book as 'from Polybius to Strabo', so that at its point of production the Septuagint falls just outside this range. But to mark this is

---

[13] Posidippus *AP* 12.98 (= Posidippus VI, 3076, Gow-Page, *HE*); reference is to a τέττιξ.
[14] Rajak 2009.

to note the prejudice of choosing those two now mainstream Greek prose authors as the bookends. How different a volume would have been produced if the scope had been defined by 'the *Septuagint* to Philo'? To be clear, I am certainly not playing the familiar and tedious classicist game of listing uncited bibliography or sources as a sort of critical one-upmanship, not least because the editors themselves indicate in their introduction that they are aware of this gap, and the chapters duly have no pretension of comprehensiveness. Rather, I want to emphasise how different a picture of Hellenistic culture could have been produced. It would have been necessary to go beyond the Third Sibylline in the recognition of how a community with different cultural affiliations and alignments responded to the cultural matrix of Greek and Roman intellectual and political authority.

The *Letter of Aristeas*, for example, does not merely tell the story of the translation of the *Septuagint* for Ptolemy, but constitutes a performance of cultural translation in itself. Aristaeus lists and describes the extravagant gifts the king sent to Eleazar, the priest of the temple at Jerusalem, along with his request for translators (an ecphrasis thoroughly Greek, and thoroughly unbiblical, in its expression and expectation of a sophisticated sense of realism: Aristaeus' competitiveness is integrally Hellenised).[15] He describes the lavish feast with which the experts are received in the palace at Alexandria, and their individual, brilliant, summary answers to the king's seventy-two profound philosophical questions (Jews cleverer than Greeks . . .). The Jews duly retreat to the island of Pharos, and in seventy-two days produce an agreed text, the absolute accuracy of which an audience of Jewish notables confirmed. The *Letter of Aristeas* is clearly designed, like other texts of the flourishing Alexandrian community of Jews, to project and promote the status of the Jews primarily in their own but also in others' eyes through the celebration and dissemination of its foundational texts. As ever, *translatio* is not just an exercise in rendition but a bid for cultural capital.

Philo was a leading figure of the Alexandrian Jewish community, who led an embassy to Caligula in Rome, a few years the other side of the chronological limit of Strabo.[16] His numerous works read the Hebrew Bible through the lens of Platonic philosophy, often with an extensive

---

[15] Pearce 2013; thanks to Max Leventhal for discussion. For later Jewish visuality, see Neis 2013; Levine 2012.
[16] On Philo, see Niehoff 2018, with extensive further bibliography (also Runia 2012); Lévy 1998; Niehoff 2001; Hadas-Lebel 2003.

allegorical apparatus. Philo declares that Ptolemy had developed an 'ardent passion' (ζῆλον καὶ πόθον) for Jewish laws, and this motivated his commission of a translation. The seventy-two experts from Jerusalem retreat to Pharos because they want to avoid the confusion of Alexandria with its mix of different animals, peoples, sicknesses and noises: they seek a place of tranquillity and purity for their souls – the philosophical symbolism here is patent enough – and they find a place of elemental nature to write of the genesis of nature. The translation emerged 'as if they were inspired, not with each man producing his own scriptural exposition (προεφήτευον), but everyone using the same words and expressions, as if there was an invisible dictation to each of them' (*Mos.* 2.37). Philo writes a full paragraph explaining that the similarity of the Hebrew and Greek language makes the process of translation close to swapping mathematical symbols of geometry: the Hebrew and Greek tongues are 'like sisters' running together 'in the purest spirit' (2.41) – without the variety and treachery usually associated with translation. This truly unconvincing claim – made with a flourish of linguistic science – reveals Philo's deep ideological investment in the harmony of Hellenism and Jewish culture.[17] So, he adds as proof, there is a festival every year in Alexandria to celebrate the day of the completion of the translation, shared by Jews and Greeks alike – an occasion publicly to perform this sisterhood. For Philo, the *Septuagint* is the sign of a fully Hellenised Judaism, and, he hopes, the harbinger of a Judaised Hellenism. *Translatio* – without addition or subtraction – is the mark of the idealised cultural hybridity Philo himself embodies.

To look at the *Septuagint* is not only thus to take the most influential of the period's texts in the future history of the West as another product of its time, but to open a vista on to the importance of translation, of the different modes of negotiating cultural transformation, of the self-defining and self-conscious work of a community in projecting its own value in a period of conflict over status, authority, position. A question of what belonging means in Alexandria. It would also lead inevitably first to so-called intertestamental literature (another chronological set of bookends that distorts Hellenistic Judaism into a misleading teleological narrative). *2 Maccabees*, for example, has a historical style that seems to inform a novelistic narrative such as *Joseph and Aseneth*, a text which may be early enough to fit into this book's chronological scope; *2 Maccabees* provides a text that moves between Jerusalem and Alexandria and creates an aetiology

---

[17] See Niehoff 2001, 2018; for the connection of Homeric and Jewish scholarship, Niehoff 2012; Honigman 2003; crucial background in Nünlist 2009.

for a new festival, Chanukah, which celebrates the Jewish resistance to the Greek culture of the Seleucids, but does so in a text written in Greek, a paradox passed over in silence (and repeated in the later *3 Maccabees*). The book of *Jubilees*, to take another probably Hellenistic text, reveals an obsessive interest with sabbath observance and the chronological structures that underpin it. It is a text that exists in multiple languages, including Greek, which reveals the likelihood of a Jewish community that is also far more aggressively separatist than Philo, but which is still Greek-speaking, with all that this implies.[18] Second, the *Septuagint* would also lead to another set of Jewish texts written shortly after Strabo, namely, the *Letters of Paul*, and then, later, the *Gospels*. That is, the literature of *koinē* and its history in articulating and enabling cultural difference is a strand of Hellenistic culture that is more easily avoided by defining the era as 'from Polybius to Strabo'.

In constructing a history of late Hellenistic literature that gives a significant place only to the hexameter verse of the Third Sibylline Oracle, with its singular engagement with Homer, out of all the variegated richness of Hellenistic Jewish literature, the editors have placed themselves firmly in the history of classical scholarship, which since the later nineteenth century has striven to separate itself from theology and the texts that make up the history of Judaism and the early church.[19] In this, they are of their time. But perhaps the times they are a-changing ...

My second question is about the drama of dialogue. I have already indicated how integral and salient the notion of dialogue is to the volume. But one should never forget that dialogues need staging, and who is allowed to speak and to whom has its protocols. So, I set the *Letter of Aristeas* in dialogue with Philo because they are both texts from Hellenistic Alexandria that discuss the significance of the production of the *Septuagint*. This is a history that could continue through Josephus, who closely paraphrases a significant part of the *Letter of Aristeas* (*AJ* 12.11–118) and who produces his own prose version of Jewish scriptures in his *Antiquitates*; and through a string of Christian writers, for whom the *Septuagint* was the Old Testament, up to Jerome, the translator *par excellence* himself, who sniffily dismisses tales of the miraculous translation.[20] But we could also set Philo against other philosophical traditions in the Hellenistic intellectual milieu,

---

[18] VanderKam 2018 is an extraordinary new commentary on *Jubilees*.
[19] See Conybeare and Goldhill 2020.
[20] Jer. *Praef. Pent.*; *adv. Rufin.* 2.25. See also Euseb. *Praep. evang.* 13.12.2; Clem. Al. *Strom.* 1.22.168; August. *De civ. D.* 18.42; Tert. *Apol.* 18.

a milieu in which he no doubt cared to see himself. In his description of his embassy to Caligula, however, Philo stands also in a different network of writings, of the philosopher before the emperor, as well as the exploration of cultural exoticism through a ruler's questions of the ambassador from elsewhere, or the ambassador's revelatory bafflement at a foreign court – most amusingly constructed in Lucian's later account of what we could call the Anacharsis moment. Scholarship has invested much more in some dialogues than in others, and privileges some partners and some exchanges over others.

There are two interrelated points here. The first is that scholarship constructs the history of literature, its sense of period, its sense of cultural change by dramatising such dialogues, and the gestures of exclusion and inclusion are foundational, and always open to re-drafting. The link between Callimachus, Theocritus, Apollonius and the Latin Republican and imperial poets is not simply a scholarly invention: it is explicit in the writings of the Roman poets. Yet it is a teleological tale of retrospective influence that restricts the possible understanding of the contemporary dialogues of Callimachus and the poets of the library with other contemporary literature of the period, indeed reducing it often to no more than the self-fulfilling restatement of Callimachus' resentment of the so-called Telchines, the apparent opposition to his poetics. Can we recognise and temper our scholarly investment in such inclusions and exclusions? The second point is to note how hard it is to disentangle the networks of conversations in antiquity. Should we imagine that the exclusivity of Callimachean *arte allusive*, his distaste for popular culture, is in dialogue with Philo's haute-intellectual discovery of allegorical meaning in the texts of the Hebrew bible? Are 'the uses of obscurity' a shared sign of the times? And are these 'uses of obscurity' to be set against the rise of *koinē*, which might align Philo closer to Callimachus than to Maccabees? The linearity of the story that sets Callimachus, Theocritus and Apollonius in a straight line of influence with Horace, Virgil and Ovid might need a more networked, a more rhizomatic model, if the richness of what it means to live 'in one's time' is to be appreciated.

My third and final point is the briefest, and follows from the first two. I have already emphasised the importance of the dynamics of belonging in understanding what 'in one's own time' means. I have also extended the sense of belonging to include belonging to a community, belonging to a cultural tradition, belonging to a language group, belonging to a philosophical or religious sect within – and sometimes against – a civic society and an increasingly aware international imperial society. I have also emphasised how such belonging requires performance, which may be dressing or talking in a particular style, or may involve years of study to place oneself properly and competently within an intellectual tradition and so on. Belonging, however, can be more or less precarious, and involve more or less multiple strategies and possible, overlapping frameworks – this is evidenced at one level by the violent assaults against the Jewish community by the other Alexandrians, whatever exercises in Greekness enacted by a Philo; or at another, very different level, by Aemilius Zosimus whose embedding as a foreigner in city life needed memorialisation. It can involve multiple frameworks, in that belonging to a family, a city, a nation, an empire, a school, a profession, a group of friends, a tradition of intellectual activity, can provide competing as well as supportive affiliations. To inhabit a time, to know where and how one is placed in time, is to enact the *process* of belonging, which, of course, always involves the process of *longing*, the desire inherent in social positioning. While it is useful at one level to catalogue the elements that make up the infrastructure of *Bildung* – including the reading lists, the awareness of genre, the making of a prose style – these affordances of cultural belonging only have purchase when the *process* of social *formation* is articulated: which requires attention to failure as well as success, the fragility as well as assertion of belonging, and the desires that drive the interactions of social life.

These questions, provoked by *Late Hellenistic Greek Literature in Dialogue*, go to the heart of the formation of Greek culture in the Roman Empire – and show how complex and fascinating a set of issues is raised by this colonial narrative, and how much this history has to contribute to contemporary thinking about the culture of colonialism – a dialogue between antiquity and modernity that has all too often been bypassed in contemporary debate, but which has so much to offer.

References

Aalders, G. J. D. 1982. *Plutarch's Political Thought*. Amsterdam.
Accorinti, D. (ed.) 2016. *Brill's Companion to Nonnus of Panopolis*. Leiden.
Acheraïou, A. 2008. *Rethinking Postcolonialism: Colonialist Discourse in Modern Literatures and the Legacy of Classical Writers*. Basingstoke.
2011. *Questioning Hybridity, Postcolonialism and Globalization*. London.
Acquaro, E. 1991. 'Le monete di Annibale', in *Le monete puniche in Italia*, eds E. Acquaro, L. I. Manfredi and A. Tusa Cutroni. Rome, 71–5.
Adamietz, J. 1992. 'Asianismus', in Ueding (ed.), 1: A–Bib, 1114–20.
Adams, C. E. P., and Laurence, R. (eds) 2001. *Travel and Geography in the Roman Empire*. London.
Alcock, S. E. 1993. *Graecia Capta: The Landscapes of Roman Greece*. Cambridge.
Alcock, S. E., Cherry, J. F., and Elsner, J. (eds) 2001. *Pausanias: Travel and Memory in Roman Greece*. Oxford.
Almagor, E. 2018. 'A literary passage: Polybius and Plutarch's narrator', in Meeus (ed.), 171–209.
Alston, R. 2011. 'Post-politics and the ancient Greek city', in van Nijf and Alston (eds), 307–36.
Amato, E. (ed.) 2005. *Favorinos d'Arles. Oeuvres. Tome 1. Introduction générale; Témoignages; Discours aux Corinthiens; Sur la fortune*. Paris.
2009. *Severus sophista Alexandrinus: Progymnasmata quae exstant omnia*. Berlin.
Amir, Y. 1985. 'Homer und Bibel als Ausdrucksmittel im 3. Sibyllenbuch', in Y. Amir, *Studien zum antiken Judentum*. Frankfurt, 83–100.
Anderson, G. 1989. 'The *pepaideumenos* in action: sophists and their outlook in the early empire', *ANRW* 2.33.1, 79–208.
1993. *The Second Sophistic. A Cultural Phenomenon in the Roman Empire*. London.
Ando, C. 2011. *Law, Language, and Empire in the Roman Tradition*. Philadelphia.
Annas, J. 1995. 'Aristotelian political thought in the Hellenistic period', in Laks and Schofield (eds), 74–94.
Anz, T. 1998. *Literatur und Lust. Glück und Unglück beim Lesen*. Munich.
Appel, W. 2001. 'Grabinschrift für Athenokles (zu IOSPE I^2 687)', *ZPE* 137: 179–82.
Appiah, K. A. 2005. *The Ethics of Identity*. Princeton.

Arendt, H. 1963. 'The crisis in culture', in H. Arendt, *Between Past and Future: Eight Exercises in Political Thought*, introduction by J. Kohn. New York, 2006, 194–222.
Argentieri, L. 2003. *Gli epigrammi degli Antipatri. Le rane 35*. Bari.
  2007. 'Meleager and Philip as epigram collectors', in Bing and Bruss (eds), 147–64.
Armbruster, K. and Wallace, K. R. (eds) 2001. *Beyond Nature Writing: Expanding the Boundaries of Ecocriticism*. Charlottesville, VA.
Armstrong, R. 2009. 'Against nature: some Augustan responses to man-made marvels', in *Paradox and the Marvellous in Augustan Literature and Culture*, ed. P. Hardie. Oxford, 75–94.
Arnaud, P. 1984. 'L'image du globe dans le monde romain: science, iconographie, symbolique', *MEFRA* 96: 53–116.
Arnim, H. von 1896. *Dionis Prusaensis quem vocant Chrysostomum quae exstant omnia, II*. Berlin.
  1898. *Leben und Werke des Dio von Prusa*. Berlin.
Ashcroft, B., Griffiths, G. and Tiffin, H. 2002. *The Empire Writes Back: Theory and Practice in Post-Colonial Literatures*. 2nd ed. London.
Aujac, G. 1992. *Denys d'Halicarnasse. Opuscules Rhétoriques*, v. Paris.
Aujac, G., and Lebel, M. 1981. *Denys d'Halicarnasse. Opuscules rhétoriques*, II: *La composition stylistique*. Paris.
Babut, D. 1969. *Plutarque et le Stoicisme*. Paris.
Bachmann, C. 2015. *Wenn man die Welt als Gemälde betrachtet. Studien zu den Eikones Philostrats des Älteren*. Heidelberg.
Baragwanath, E. 2008. *Motivation and Narrative in Herodotus*. Oxford.
Barclay, J. M. G. 1996. *Jews in the Mediterranean Diaspora: From Alexander to Trajan (323 BCE–117 CE)*. Edinburgh.
Barnes, J. 1997. 'Roman Aristotle', in *Philosophia Togata*, II: *Plato and Aristotle at Rome*, eds J. Barnes and M. Griffin. Oxford, 1–69.
Barrow, R. 1967. *Plutarch and His Times*. London.
Bartlett, J. R. 1985. *Jews in the Hellenistic World*. Cambridge.
Bassino, P. 2013. *Certamen Homeri et Hesiodi: Introduction, Critical Edition and Commentary*. PhD Diss. Durham.
Bate, J. 2000. *The Song of the Earth*. Cambridge, MA.
Battisti, D. G. 1997. *Dionigi di Alicarnasso, Sull'imitazione. Edizione critica, traduzione e commento*. Pisa.
Battistoni, F. 2006. 'The ancient pinakes from Tauromenium: some new readings', *ZPE* 157: 169–80.
Baumann, M. 2011. *Bilder schreiben. Virtuose Ekphrasis in Philostrats Eikones*. Berlin.
  2013. 'Der Betrachter im Bild. Metalepsen in antiken Ekphrasen', in *Über die Grenze. Metalepse in Text- und Bildmedien des Altertums*, eds U. Eisen and P. von Möllendorff. Berlin, 257–91.
  2018. 'Wunderlektüren: Paradoxa und die Aktivität des Lesers in Diodors Bibliotheke', in *Die symphonischen Schwestern. Narrative Konstruktion von*

'Wahrheiten' in der nachklassischen Geschichtsschreibung, eds T. Blank and F. K. Maier. Stuttgart, 227–40.
2020. *Welt erzählen*. *Narration und das Vergnügen des Lesers in der ersten Pentade von Diodors Bibliotheke*. Göttingen.
Baumbach, M. 2017. 'Poets and poetry', in Johnson and Richter (eds), 493–507.
Baumbach, M., and Bär, S. (eds) 2007. *Quintus Smyrnaeus: Transforming Homer in Second Sophistic Epic*. Berlin.
Beagon, M. 2013. 'The burdensome mission of Pliny's *Natural History*', in König and Woolf (eds), 84–107.
Beard, M. 2013. *Confronting the Classics: Traditions, Adventures and Innovations*. London.
Beck, M. (ed.) 2014. *A Companion to Plutarch*. Chichester.
Béranger, J. 1953. *Recherches sur l'aspect idéologique du principat*. Basel.
Bergk, W. T. 1872–94. *Griechische Literaturgeschichte*. Bd. 2, 3 aus dem Nachlass herausgegeben von Gustav Hinrichs; Bd. 4 aus dem Nachlass herausgegeben von Rudolf Peppmüller. Register von Rudolf Peppmüller und Wilhelm Hahn. Berlin.
Berlant, L. 1991. *The Anatomy of National Fantasy*. Chicago.
Berlin, I. 1976. *The Proper Study of Mankind*. New York.
Bernard, S. 2018. *Building Mid-Republican Rome. Labor, Architecture, and the Urban Economy*. Oxford.
Bernard, S., Damon, C. and Grey, C. 2014. 'Rhetorics of land and power in the Polla inscription (CIL I^2 638)', *Mnemosyne* 67: 953–85.
Bernhardy, G. 1836–45. *Grundriß der griechischen Literatur*, 2 vols. Halle.
Bernstein, M. A. 1994. *Foregone Conclusions*. Berkeley.
Besserman, L. (ed.) 1996. *The Challenge of Periodization: Old Paradigms and New Perspectives*. New York.
Bethe, E. 1918. 'Iulius (398) Pollux', *RE* x.1, 773–9.
Bexley, E. M. 2009. 'Replacing Rome: geographic and political centrality in Lucan's *Pharsalia*', *CPh* 104: 459–75.
Bhabha, H. 1990. *Nation and Narration*. London.
1994. *The Location of Culture*. London.
Bichler, R. 1983. '*Hellenismus*'. *Geschichte und Problematik eines Epochenbegriffs*. Darmstadt.
Billault, A. 1995. 'Peut-on appliquer la notion d'asianisme à l'analyse de l'esthétique des romans grecs?', *AAntHung* 36: 107–18.
2004. 'Littérature et rhétorique dans le discours XVIII de Dion Chrysostome *Sur l'entraînement à la parole*', *REG* 117: 504–18.
Bing, P. 2005. 'The politics and poetics of geography in the Milan Posidippus Section One: On stones (AB 1–20)', in *The New Posidippus. A Hellenistic Poetry Book*, ed. K. J. Gutzwiller. Oxford, 119–40 (reprinted in Bing 2009: 253–70).
2008. *The Well-Read Muse. Past and Present in Callimachus and the Hellenistic Poets. With a New Introduction*. 2nd ed. Ann Arbor.
2009. *The Scroll and the Marble: Studies in Reading and Reception in Hellenistic Poetry*. Ann Arbor.

Bing, P., and Bruss, J. S. (eds) 2007. *Brill's Companion to Hellenistic Epigram*. Leiden.
Biraschi, A. M., and Salmeri, G. (eds) 2000. *Strabone e l'Asia Minore*. Perugia.
Blass, F. 1865. *Die griechische Beredsamkeit in dem Zeitraum von Alexander bis auf Augustus. Ein litterarhistorischer Versuch*. Berlin.
  1887. *Die attische Beredsamkeit. 1. Abtheilung: von Gorgias bis zu Lysias*. 2nd ed. Leipzig.
  1893. *Die attische Beredsamkeit. 3. Abtheilung, 1. Abschnitt: Demosthenes*. 2nd ed. Leipzig.
  1901. *Die Rhythmen der attischen Kunstprosa: Isokrates – Demosthenes – Platon*. Leipzig.
  1905. *Die Rhythmen der asianischen und römischen Kunstprosa*. Leipzig.
Bodenhamer, D. J., Corrigan, J., and Harris, T. M. (eds) 2010. *The Spatial Humanities: GIS and the Future of Humanities Scholarship*. Bloomington, IN.
Bommelaer, B. 1989. *Diodore de Sicile, Bibliothèque Historique, Livre III*. Paris.
Bompaire, J. 1958. *Lucien écrivain. Imitation et création*. Paris.
Bonnet, C. 2015. *Les enfants de Cadmos. La paysage religieux de la Phénicie hellénistique*. Paris.
Borg, B. E. (ed.) 2004. *Paideia. The World of the Second Sophistic*. Berlin
  2011. 'Who cared about Greek identity? Athens in the first century BCE', in Schmitz and Wiater (eds), 213–34.
Bosak-Schroeder, C. 2020. *Other Natures: Environmental Encounters with Ancient Greek Ethnography*. Oakland.
Bost-Pouderon, C. 2008. 'Dion Chrysostome et le genre épistolaire: à propos du Περὶ λόγου ἀσκήσεως (Or. XVIII), le seul "discours" de Dion rédigé sous la form épistolaire: un traité ou une lettre?', in *Epistulae Antiquae*, V, eds P. Laurence and F. Guillaumont. Louvain, 37–47.
Boulanger, A. 1923. *Aelius Aristide et la sophistique dans la province d'Asie au IIe siècle de notre ère*. Paris.
Bowersock, G. W. 1965. *Augustus and the Greek World*. Oxford.
  1969. *Greek Sophists in the Roman Empire*. Oxford.
  2004. 'Artemidorus and the Second Sophistic', in Borg (ed.), 53–64.
Bowie, E. L. 1974. 'Greeks and their past in the Second Sophistic', in *Studies in Ancient Society*, ed. M. I. Finley. Rev. ed. London: 166–209.
  1989a. 'Poetry and poets in Asia and Achaia', in *The Greek Renaissance in the Roman Empire*, eds A. Cameron and S. Walker. ICS Bulletin Supplement 55. London, 198–205.
  1989b. 'Greek sophists and Greek poetry in the Second Sophistic', *ANRW* 2.33.1, 209–58.
  1990. 'Greek poetry in the Antonine age', in *Antonine Literature*, ed. D. A. Russell. Oxford, 53–90.
  1994. 'Philostratus: writer of fiction', in *Greek Fiction. The Greek Novel in Context*, eds J. R. Morgan and R. Stoneman. London, 181–99.
  2004. 'The geography of the Second Sophistic: cultural variations', in Borg (ed.), 65–83.

2008. 'Luxury cruisers? Philip's epigrammatists between Greece and Rome', *Aevum(ant)* 8: 223–58 (published 2012).
2011. 'Men from Mytilene', in Schmitz and Wiater (eds), 181–95.
Boym, S. 2001. *The Future of Nostalgia*. New York.
Brancacci, A. 2000. 'Dio, Socrates, and Cynicism', in *Dio Chrysostom. Politics, Letters, and Philosophy*, ed. S. Swain. Oxford, 240–60.
Breckenridge, J. D. 1983. 'Hannibal as Alexander', *AncW* 7: 111–28.
Bremen, R. van 1996. *The Limits of Participation: Women and Civic Life in the Greek East in the Hellenistic and Roman Periods*. Amsterdam.
    2013. '*Neoi* in Hellenistic cities: age class, institution, association?', in Fröhlich and Hamon (eds), 31–58.
Brenk, F. 1977. *In Mist Apparelled*. Leiden.
Bricault, L., and Versluys, J.-M. (eds) 2014. *Power, Politics and the Cult of Isis*. Leiden.
Bridges, E. 2015. *Imagining Xerxes: Ancient Perspectives on a Persian King*. London.
Briquel, D. 2004. 'L'utilisation de la figure d'Héraklès par Hannibal. Remarques sur les fragments de Silénos de Kaléaktè, in *Hispanité et romanité*, ed. J.-M. André. Collección de la casa de Velázquez 88. Madrid, 29–37.
Brock, R. 2013. *Greek Political Imagery from Homer to Aristotle*. London.
Brodersen, K. 2000. *Virtuelle Antike. Wendepunkte der Alten Geschichte*. Darmstadt.
    2003. *Terra Cognita. Studien zur römischen Raumerfassung*. 2nd ed. Hildesheim.
    2014. *Philostratos. Leben der Sophisten*. Wiesbaden.
Brooks, E. (ed.) 1970. *P. Rutilii Lupi De Figuris Sententiarum et Elocutionis*. Leiden.
Brubaker, R., and Cooper, F. 2009. 'Beyond "identity"', *Theory and Society* 29: 1–47.
Brunt, P. A. 1994. 'The bubble of the Second Sophistic', *BICS* 39: 25–52.
Budé, G. de 1948. *Dion Chrysostome, Épitre à un inconnu sur la formation oratoire*. Carouge.
Buell, L. 2001. *Writing for an Endangered World: Literature, Culture, and the Environment in the US and Beyond*. Cambridge, MA.
Bücheler, F. 1883. 'Catalepton', *RhM* 38: 507–25.
    2005. *The Future of Environmental Criticism*. Malden, MA.
Buffière, F. 1956. *Les mythes d'Homère et la penseé grecque*. Paris.
Buitenwerf, R. 2003. *Book III of the Sibylline Oracles and Its Social Setting*. Leiden.
Bulhof, J. 1999. 'What if? Modality and history', *H&Th* 38: 145–68.
Buresch, K. 1892. 'Die sibyllinische Quellgrotte in Erythrae', *Mittheilungen des kaiserlich deutschen archäologischen Instituts, athenische Abtheilung* 17: 16–36.
Burkert, W. 1984. *Die orientalisierende Epoche in der griechischen Religion und Kultur*. Sitzungsberichte der Heidelberger Akademie der Wissenschaften. Philosophisch-historische Klasse. Heidelberg.
Burrus, V. 2018. *Ancient Christian Ecopoetics: Cosmologies, Saints, Things*. Philadelphia.

Burstein, S. M. 1989. *Agatharchides of Cnidus, On the Erythraean Sea*. London.
Burton, A. 1972. *Diodorus Siculus. Book I: A Commentary*. Leiden.
Busse, K. 2006. 'My life is a WIP on my LJ: slashing the slasher and the reality of celebrity and internet performances', in Busse and Hellekson (eds), 207–24.
Busse, K., and Hellekson, K. (eds) 2006. *Fan Fiction and Fan Communities in the Age of the Internet: New Essays*. Jefferson.
Cairns, D. 2016. 'Mind, body, and metaphor in ancient Greek concepts of emotion', *L'atelier du centre de recherche historique* 16, *Histoire intellectuelle des émotions de l'Antiquité à nos jours*, eds D. Boquet and P. Nagy (https://journals.openedition.org/acrh/7416; accessed 26 March 2020).
Cairns, F. 2016. *Hellenistic Epigram. Contexts of Exploration*. Cambridge.
Calabi, F. 2008. *God's Acting, Man's Acting: Tradition and Philosophy in Philo of Alexandria*. Leiden.
Calasso, R. 1993. *The Marriage of Cadmus and Harmony*. New York.
Calboli, G. 1986. 'Nota di aggiornamento', in E. Norden, *La prosa d'arte antica dal VI secolo a.C. all'età della Rinascenza*, tr. and ed. B. Heinemann Campana, 2 vols. Rome, 969–1185.
  1987. 'Asianesimo e atticismo: retorica, letteratura e linguistica', in *Studi di retorica oggi in Italia*, ed. A. Pennacini. Bologna, 31–53.
  1988. 'Asiani (Oratori)', in *Dizionario degli scrittori greci e latini, 1*. Milan, 215–32.
Cameron, A. 1993. *The Greek Anthology from Meleager to Planudes*. Oxford.
  2016. *Wandering Poets and Other Essays on Late Greek Literature and Philosophy*. Oxford.
Canevaro, M., and Gray, B. (eds) 2018. *The Hellenistic Reception of Classical Athenian Democracy and Political Thought*. Oxford.
Caracciolo, M. 2014. 'Experientiality', in *The Living Handbook of Narratology*, eds P. Hühn et al. Hamburg (online edition www.lhn.uni-hamburg.de/article/experientiality; accessed 28 February 2021).
Caragounis, C. 2014. 'Asianism', in *Encyclopedia of Ancient Greek Language and Linguistics, 1: A–F*, ed. G. Giannakis. Leiden and Boston, 178–81.
Carr, E. H. 1986 *What Is History?* Basingstoke.
Casson, L. 1989. *The Periplus Maris Erythraei: Text with Introduction, Translation, and Commentary*. Princeton.
Centrone, B. 2014. 'The pseudo-Pythagorean writings', in *A History of Pythagoreanism*, ed. C. A. Huffman. Cambridge, 315–40.
Champion, C. B. 2004. *Cultural Politics in Polybius' Histories*. Berkeley.
Chaniotis, A. 1987. 'Das Ehrendekret für Diophantos (IOSPE I2 352) und Geschichtsschreibung', in *Acta Centri Historiae Terra Antiqua Balcanica*, II, eds A. Fol, V. Zhivkov and N. Nedjalkov. Sofia, 233–5.
  1997. 'Theatricality beyond the theater: staging public life in the Hellenistic world', in Le Guen (ed.), 219–59.
  2009. 'A few things Hellenistic audiences appreciated in musical performances', in Martinelli (ed.), 75–97.
  2013a. '*Paradoxon, enargeia*, empathy: Hellenistic decrees and Hellenistic oratory', in Kremmydas and Tempest (eds), 201–16.

2013b. 'Emotional language in Hellenistic decrees and Hellenistic histories', in Mari and Thornton (eds), 339–52.
Charlesworth, J. H. 1985. *The Old Testament Pseudepigrapha and the New Testament*. Cambridge.
Cheah, P., and Robbins, B. (eds) 1998. *Cosmopolitics: Thinking and Feeling Beyond the Nation*. Minneapolis.
Christ, W. von, Stählin, O., and Schmid, W. 1920. *Geschichte der griechischen Literatur. Zweiter Teil: die nachklassische Periode der griechischen Literatur*, 2 vols. Munich.
Chuvin, P. 1991. *Mythologie et géographie Dionysiaques: recherches sur l'œuvre de Nonnos de Panopolis*. Clermont-Ferrand.
Cichorius, C. 1922. *Römische Studien. Historisches Epigraphisches Literargeschichtliches aus vier Jahrhunderten Roms*. Leipzig.
Citroni, M. 2006a. 'The concept of the classical and the canons of model authors in Roman literature', in *Classical Pasts: The Classical Traditions of Greece and Rome*, ed. J. I. Porter. Princeton, 204–34.
  2006b. 'Quintilian and the perception of the system of poetic genres in the Flavian age', in *Flavian Poetry*, eds R. R. Nauta, H.-J. van Dam and J. J. L. Smolenaars. Leiden, 1–19.
Civiletti, M. 2002. *Filostrato. Vite dei sofisti. Introduzione, traduzione e note*. Milan.
Clark, T. 2019. *The Value of Ecocriticism*. Cambridge.
Clarke, K. 1997. 'In search of the author of Strabo's Geography', *JRS* 87: 92–110.
  1999. *Between Geography and History: Hellenistic Constructions of the Roman World*. Oxford.
  2008. *Making Time for the Past*. Oxford.
  2018. *Shaping the Geography of Empire: Man and Nature in Herodotus' Histories*. Oxford.
Clauss, J. J., and Cuypers, M. (eds) 2010. *A Companion to Hellenistic Literature*. Malden, MA.
Coates, P. 1998. *Nature: Western Attitudes since Western Times*. Cambridge.
Cogitore, I. 2010. 'Crinagoras et les poètes de la Couronne de Philippe: la cour impériale romaine dans les yeux des Grecs', in *Des rois au prince. Pratiques du pouvoir monarchique dans l'Orient hellénistique et romain (IVe siècle avant J.-C.–IIe siècle après J.-C.)*, eds I. Savalli-Lestrade and M. Amandry. Grenoble, 253–70.
Cohen, A. 2001. 'Art, myth, and travel in the Hellenistic world', in Alcock, Cherry and Elsner eds, 93–126.
Cohen, N. 1995. *Philo Judaeus: His Universe of Discourse*. Frankfurt.
Cohen, S. J. D. 2010. *The Significance of Yavneh and Other Essays in Jewish Hellenism*. Texts and Studies in Ancient Judaism 136. Tübingen.
Cohoon, J. W. 1939. *Dio Chrysostom, Discourses 12–30*. Cambridge, MA.
Cole, T. 1991. *The Origins of Rhetoric in Ancient Greece*. Baltimore.

Coleman, K., and Nelis-Clément, J. (eds) 2012. *L'organisation des spectacles dans le monde romain*. Entretiens Hardt 58. Geneva.
Collins, J. J. 1974. *The Sibylline Oracles of Egyptian Judaism*. Missoula.
  (ed.) 1979. *Apocalypse: The Morphology of a Genre*. Semeia 14. Missoula.
  1986. 'Apocalyptic literature', in *Early Judaism and Its Modern Interpreters*, eds R. A. Kraft and G. W. E. Nickelsburg. Atlanta, 345–70.
  1997. *Seers, Sibyls and Sages in Hellenistic-Roman Judaism*. Leiden.
Colonna, A. (ed.) 1953. 'I Prolegomeni ad Esiodo e la Vita Esiodea di G. Tzetzes', *BPEC* 2: 27–39.
Connolly, J. 2001a. 'Reclaiming the theatrical in the second sophistic', *Helios* 28: 75–96.
  2001b. 'Problems of the past in imperial Greek education', in *Education in Greek and Roman Antiquity*, ed. Y. L. Too. Leiden, 339–73.
  2003. 'Like the labors of Heracles: *andreia* and *paideia* in imperial Greek culture', in *Andreia: Ancient Constructions of Manly Courage*, eds R. Rosen and I. Sluiter. Leiden, 287–317.
  2007. 'Being Greek/being Roman: hellenism and assimilation in the Roman empire', *Millennium Jahrbuch zu Kultur und Geschichte* 101: 93–119.
Conybeare, C., and Goldhill, S. (eds) 2020. *Classical Philology and Theology: Disavowal, Entanglement and the God-Like Scholar*. Cambridge.
Cornell, T. J. (ed.) 2013. *Fragments of the Roman Historians*, 3 vols. Oxford.
Cowley, R. 1999. *What If?* New York.
Cresci Marrone, G. 1993. *Ecumene Augustea. Una politica per il consenso*. Rome.
Cribiore, R. 1996. *Writing, Teachers and Students in Graeco-Roman Egypt*. American Studies in Papyrology 36. Atlanta.
  2001. *Gymnastics of the Mind: Greek Education in Hellenistic and Roman Egypt*. Princeton.
Cronin, S. (ed.) 2008. *Subalterns and Social Protest: History from Below in the Middle East and North Africa*. London.
Curty, O. 2015. *Gymnasiarchika. Recueil et analyse des inscriptions de l'époque hellénistique en l'honneur des gymnasiarques*. Paris.
Cuypers, M. 2010. 'Historiography, rhetoric, and science: rethinking a few assumptions on Hellenistic prose', in Clauss and Cuypers (eds), 317–36.
Danker, F. W. 1982. *Benefactor: Epigraphic Study of a Graeco-Roman and New Testament Semantic Field*. St. Louis.
Davies, P. J. E. 2017. *Architecture and Politics in Republican Rome*. Cambridge.
Dawson, D. 1991. *Allegorical Readers and Cultural Revision in Ancient Alexandria*. Berkeley.
Delcourt, A. 2005. *Lecture des Antiquités romaines de Denys d'Halicarnasse. Un historien entre deux mondes*. Brussels.
della Dora, V. 2011. *Imagining Mount Athos: Visions of a Holy Place from Homer to World War II*. Charlottesville.
Demandt, A. 2001. *Ungeschehene Geschichte*. Göttingen.

De Morais Mota, C. 2010. *The Lessons of Universal History of Diodorus of Sicily's. An Educational Process of Humanity.* Saarbrücken.
Denniston, J. D. 1952. *Greek Prose Style.* Cambridge.
Desideri, P. 1978. *Dione di Prusa. Un intellettuale greco nell'impero romano.* Florence.
Diggle, J. 2005. 'Rhythmical prose in the Euripidean hypotheses', in *Euripide e i papiri*, eds G. Bastianini and A. Casanova. Florence, 27–67.
Dihle, A. 1986. 'Philosophie – Fachwissenschaft – Allgemeinbildung', in *Aspects de la philosophie hellénistique: neuf exposés suivis de discussions*, eds H. Flashar and O. Gigon. Entretiens Hardt 32. Geneva, 185–231.
  2011, 'Greek classicism', in Schmitz and Wiater (eds), 47–60.
Dillon, J. M. 1988. '"Orthodoxy" and "eclecticism": Middle Platonists and Neo-Pythagoreans', in *The Question of 'Eclecticism'. Studies in Later Greek Philosophy*, eds J. M. Dillon and A. A. Long. Berkeley, 103–25.
  1996. *The Middle Platonists. A Study of Platonism 80 BC to AD 220.* 2nd ed. London.
Dörner, F. K. 1996. 'Translation of the *Nomos* inscription', in *Nemrud Daği. The Hierothesion of Antiochus I of Commagene*, 1: *Text*, ed. D. H. Sanders. Winona Lake, 213–17.
Dörrie, H. 1964. *Der Königskult des Antiochus von Kommagene im Lichte neuer Inschriften-Funde.* Göttingen.
Dolar, M. 2006. *A Voice and Nothing More.* Cambridge.
Donadi, F. 2000. 'Il caso Egesia. Sulla possibilità e convenienza di una nuova edizione del *De compositione verborum* di Dionigi d'Alicarnasso', in *Letteratura e riflessione sulla letteratura nella cultura classica*, ed. G. Arrighetti. Pisa, 327–43.
Doulamis, K. 2011. 'Forensic oratory and rhetorical theory in Chariton Book 5', in *Echoing Narratives: Studies of Intertextuality in Greek and Roman Prose Fiction*, ed. K. Doulamis. Groningen, 21–48.
Dover, K. J. 1971. *Theocritus: Select Poems.* London.
Drerup, E. 1901. 'Die Anfänge der rhetorischen Kunstprosa', *Jahrbücher für classische Philologie*, Suppl. 27: 219–351.
Dubuisson, M. 1983. 'Les *Opici*: Osques, occidentaux ou barbares', *Latomus* 42: 522–45.
  1985. *Le latin de Polybe.* Paris.
Dueck, D. 2000. *Strabo of Amasia. A Greek Man of Letters in Augustan Rome.* London.
  (ed.) 2017. *The Routledge Companion to Strabo.* London.
Dueck, D., Lindsay, H., and Pothecary, S. (eds) 2005. *Strabo's Cultural Geography. The Making of a Kolossourgia.* Cambridge.
Duff, T. E. 1999. *Plutarch's Lives. Exploring Virtue and Vice.* Oxford.
  2014. 'The prologues', in Beck (ed.), 333–49.
Eckholdt, J.-F. 2019. *Von göttlicher Vorsehung bis Zufall. Tyche im Werk des Plutarch von Chaironeia.* Berlin.
Eckstein, A. M. 1995. *Moral Vision in the Histories of Polybius.* Berkeley.
Edwards, C. 1993. *The Politics of Immorality in Ancient Rome.* Cambridge.
  2003. 'Incorporating the alien. The art of conquest', in *Rome the Cosmopolis*, eds C. Edwards and G. Woolf. Cambridge, 44–70.

Elliott, J. 2013. *Ennius and the Architecture of the Annales*. Cambridge.
Elsner, J. 1995. *Art and the Roman Viewer. The Transformation of Art from the Pagan World to Christianity*. Cambridge.
  2002. 'Introduction: the genres of ekphrasis', *Ramus* 31: 1–18.
  2014. 'Lithic poetics: Posidippus and his stones', *Ramus* 43: 152–72.
  2017. 'Pfeiffer, Fraenkel and refugee scholarship in Oxford, during and after the Second World War', in *The Ark of Civilization*, eds S. Crawford, K. Ulmschneider and J. Elsner. Oxford, 25–49.
Engelmann, H., and Merkelbach, R. 1973. *Die Inschriften von Erythrai und Klazomenai, II*. Bonn.
Engels, J. 1999. *Augusteische Oikumenegeographie und Universalhistorie im Werk Strabons von Amaseia*. Stuttgart.
  2005. '"Ἄνδρες ἔνδοξοι or "men of high reputation"', in Dueck, Lindsay and Pothecary (eds), 129–43.
  2007. 'Geography and history' in *A Companion to Greek and Roman Historiography*, ed. J. Marincola. Oxford, 541–52.
  2012. 'Artemidoros of Ephesos and Strabo of Amasia', in *Intorno al papiro di Artemidoro, II*, eds B. Kramer and S. Settis. Milan, 139–55.
Errington, R. M. 2002. 'Biographie in hellenistischen Inschriften', in Vössing (ed.), 14–28.
Erskine, A. 1990. *The Hellenistic Stoa: Political Thought and Action*. London.
Evans, R. J. 2014. *Altered Pasts. Counterfactuals in History*. Waltham.
Fabrizi, V. 2015. 'Hannibal's march and Roman imperial space in Livy, *Ab urbe condita*, Book 21', *Philologus* 159: 118–55.
Fairbanks, A. 1931. *Elder Philostratus: Imagines. Younger Philostratus: Imagines. Callistratus: Descriptions*. Cambridge, MA.
Fairweather, J. 1981. *Seneca the Elder*. Cambridge.
Fanon, F. 1963. *The Wretched of the Earth*, tr. R. Philcox, with commentary by J.-P. Sartre and H. K. Bhabha. New York 2004.
Fantuzzi, M., and Hunter, R. 2004. *Tradition and Innovation in Hellenistic Poetry*. Cambridge (original Italian ed. Rome 2002).
Faraone, C. 2019. 'Circe's instructions to Odysseus (*Od.* 10.507–40) as an early Sibylline Oracle', *JHS* 139: 49–66.
Favreau-Linder, A. M. 2004. 'Polémon de Laodicée: l'énigme d'un style', in *L'ultima parola. L'analisi dei testi: teorie e pratiche nell'antichità greca e latina*, eds G. Abbamonte, F. Conti Bizzarro and L. Spina. Naples, 105–21.
Feeney, D. 2001. *The Gods in Epic*. Oxford.
  2005. 'Review: the beginnings of a literature in Latin', *JRS* 95: 226–40.
  2016. *Beyond Greek: The Beginnings of Latin Literature*. Princeton.
Ferguson, N. 1998. *Virtual History. Alternatives and Counterfactuals*. London.
Ferrary, J.-L. 1988. *Philhellénisme et impérialisme. Aspects idéologiques de la conquête romaine du monde hellénistique, de la seconde guerre de Macédoine à la guerre contre Mithridate*. Rome.
Ferrucci, S. 2013. 'L'ambigua virtù: φιλοτιμία nell'Atene degli oratori', in Mari and Thornton (eds), 123–36.

Flatt, T. 2017. 'Desire and limits of lament in Homer', *CJ* 4: 385–404.
Fludernik, M. 1996. *Towards a 'Natural' Narratology*. London.
  2010. 'Experience, experientiality, and historical narrative. A view from narratology', in *Erfahrung und Geschichte. Historische Sinnbildung in Pränarrativen*, eds T. Breyer and D. Creutz. Berlin, 40–72.
Fraenkel, E. 1950. *Aeschylus. Agamemnon*, 3 vols. Oxford.
Forster, F. 2018. *Die Polis im Wandel. Ehrendekrete für eigene Bürger im Kontext der hellenistischen Polisgesellschaft*. Göttingen.
Fox, M. 1993. 'History and rhetoric in Dionysius of Halicarnassus', *JRS* 83: 31–47.
Frede, M. 1999. 'Epilogue', in *The Cambridge History of Hellenistic Philosophy*, eds K. Algra, J. Barnes, J. Mansfeld and M. Schofield. Cambridge: 771–97.
French, R. 1994. *Ancient Natural History. Histories of Nature*. London.
Fröhlich, P. 2005. 'Dépenses publiques et évergétisme des citoyens dans l'exercice des charges publiques à Priène à la basse époque hellénistique', in Fröhlich and Müller (eds), 225–56.
  2013. 'Les groupes du gymnase d'Iasos et les presbyteroi dans les cités à l'époque hellénistique', in Fröhlich and Hamon (eds), 59–112.
Fröhlich, P., and Hamon, P. (eds) 2013. *Groupes et associations dans les cités grecques (IIIe siècle av. J.-C.–IIe siècle ap. J.-C). Actes de la table ronde de Paris, INHA, 19–20 juin 2009*. Geneva.
Fröhlich, P., and Müller, C. (eds) 2005. *Citoyenneté et participation à la basse époque hellénistique. Actes de la table ronde des 22 et 23 mai 2004*. Geneva.
Furtwängler, A. 1884–90. 'Atlas', in *Ausführliches Lexikon der griechischen und römischen Mythologie*, 1, ed. W. H. Roscher. Leipzig, 704–11.
Gabba, E. 1991. *Dionysius and the History of Archaic Rome*. Berkeley.
Gaebel, R. E. 1970. 'The Greek word-lists to Virgil and Cicero', *BRL* 52: 284–325.
Gärtner, U. 2005. *Quintus Smyrnaeus und die 'Aeneis': Zur Nachwirkung Vergils in der griechischen Literatur der Kaiserzeit*. Munich.
Galinsky, K. (ed.) 2005. *The Cambridge Companion to the Age of Augustus*. Cambridge.
Gallagher, C., and Greenblatt, S. 2000. *Practicing New Historicism*. Chicago.
Gandini, C. 2015. *Diplomatico e poeta: Crinagora di Mitilene nella Roma di Augusto*. Reggio Calabria.
Gargola, D. J. 2017. *The Shape of the Roman Order. The Republic and Its Spaces*. Chapel Hill.
Garulli, V. 2012. *Byblos Lainee: Epigrafia, Letteratura, Epitafio*. Bologna.
Garvie, A. F. 1994. *Homer, Odyssey. Books VI–VIII*. Cambridge.
Gasparro, G. S. 1997. *Daimon and Tuche in the Hellenistic Religious Experience*. Aarhus.
Gauthier, P. 1985. *Les cités grecques et leurs bienfaiteurs*. Athens.
Geffcken, J. 1902. *Die Oracula Sibyllina. Die griechischen christlichen Schriftsteller 8*. Leipzig.
Geiger, J. 2014a. *Hellenism in the East: Studies on Greek Intellectuals in Palestine*. Historia Einzelschriften 229. Stuttgart.

2014b. 'The Project of parallel lives. Plutarch's conception of biography', in Beck (ed.), 292–303.
Genette, G. 1972. *Figures III*. Paris.
  2004. *Métalepse: de la figure à la fiction*. Paris.
Geus, K., and Rathmann, M. (eds) 2013. *Vermessung der Oikumene*. Topoi. Berlin Studies of the Ancient World 14. Berlin.
Geus, K., and Thiering, M. (eds) 2014. *Features of Common Sense Geography. Implicit Knowledge Structures in Ancient Geographical Texts*. Antike Kultur und Geschichte 16. Zurich.
Ghosh, A. 2016. *The Great Derangement: Climate Change and the Unthinkable*. Chicago.
Giannakis, G. 2001. 'Light is life, dark is death: an Ancient Greek and Indo-European metaphor', *Philologia* 30: 127–53.
Gibson, B., and Harrison, T. (eds) 2013. *Polybius and His World. Essays in Memory of F. W. Walbank*. Cambridge.
Gill, C. 2003. 'The school in the Roman imperial period', in *The Cambridge Companion to the Stoics*, ed. B. Inwood. Cambridge, 33–58.
Giuliani, L. 2007. 'Die unmöglichen Bilder des Philostrat: Ein antiker Beitrag zur Paragone-Debatte?', in *Übersetzung und Transformation*, eds H. Böhme, C. Rapp and W. Rösler. Berlin, 401–23.
Glacken, C. J. 1969. *Traces on the Rhodian Shore: Nature and Culture in Western Thought from Ancient Times to the End of the Eighteenth Century*. Berkeley.
Gleason, M. 1995. *Making Men: Sophists and Self-Presentation in Ancient Rome*. Princeton.
Goggin, M. G. 1951. 'Rhythm in the prose of Favorinus', *YCS* 12: 149–201.
Goldhill, S. (ed.) 2001. *Being Greek under Rome. Cultural Identity, the Second Sophistic and the Development of Empire*. Cambridge.
  2002. *Who Needs Greek? Contests in the Cultural History of Hellenism*. Cambridge.
  2020. *Preposterous Poetics: the Politics and Aesthetics of Form in Late Antiquity*. Cambridge.
  (forthcoming). 'Latin literature and Greek', in *The Cambridge Critical Guide to Latin Literature*, eds R. Gibson and C. Whitton. Cambridge.
Goldwyn, A. J. 2018. *Byzantine Ecocriticism: Women, Nature, and Power in the Medieval Greek Romance*. Cham.
Gow, A. S. F., and Page, D. 1968. *The Greek Anthology*, II: *The Garland of Philip*. Cambridge.
Grandjean, Y. 1975. *Une nouvelle arétalogie d'Isis à Maronée*. Leiden.
Gray, B. 2013a. 'Philosophy of education and the later Hellenistic polis', in Martzavou and Papazarkadas (eds), 233–53.
  2013b. 'The polis becomes humane? *Philanthropia* as a cardinal civic virtue in later Hellenistic honorific epigraphy and historiography', in Mari and Thornton (eds), 137–62.
  2018. 'A civic alternative to Stoicism: the ethics of Hellenistic honorary decrees', *ClAnt* 37: 187–235.

Gray, J., Sandvoss, C., and Harrington, C. L. (eds) 2007. *Fandom: Identities and Communities in a Mediated World*. New York.
Graziosi, B. 2002. *Inventing Homer: The Early Reception of Epic*. Cambridge.
Greensmith, E. 2018. 'When Homer quotes Callimachus: allusive poetics in the proem of the *Posthomerica*', *CQ* 68: 257–74.
  2020. *The Resurrection of Homer in Imperial Greek Epic: Quintus Smyrnaeus' Posthomerica and the Poetics of Impersonation*. Cambridge.
Grethlein, J. 2013. *Experience and Teleology in Ancient Historiography: 'Futures Past' from Herodotus to Augustine*, Cambridge.
  2020. 'Representation delimited and historicized: metalepsis in ancient literature and vase-painting', in *Metalepsis: Ancient Texts, New Perspectives*, eds S. Matzner and G. Trimble. Oxford, 25–57.
Grethlein, J., and Rengakos, A. (eds) 2017. *Griechische Literaturgeschichtsschreibung. Traditionen, Probleme und Konzepte*. Berlin.
Grieb, V. 2008. *Hellenistische Demokratie. Politische Organisation und Struktur in freien griechischen Poleis nach Alexander dem Großen*. Stuttgart.
Griffin, J. 1993. *Alive in Myth*. New York.
Griffin, M. T. 1997. 'Philosophy, politics, and politicians at Rome', in Griffin and Barnes (eds), 1–37.
Griffin, M., and Barnes, J. (eds) 1997. *Philosophia Togata, 1: Essays on Philosophy and Roman Society*. Rev. paperback ed. (originally published in 1989). Oxford.
Groot, A. W. de 1915. 'Methodological investigations into the rhythm of Greek prose', *CQ* 9: 231–44.
  1919a. *A Handbook of Antique Prose-Rhythm, 1*. Groningen.
  1919b. *De numero oratorio latino*. Groningen.
  1921. *Der antike Prosarhythmus*. Groningen.
  1926. *La prose métrique des anciens*. Paris.
Gruen, E. S. 1992. *Culture and National Identity in Republican Rome*. Ithaca.
  1998a. *Heritage and Hellenism: The Reinvention of Jewish Tradition*. Berkeley.
  1998b. 'Jews, Greeks and Romans in the Third Sibylline Oracle', *in Jews in a Graeco-Roman World*, ed. M. Goodman. Oxford, 15–36.
  2016. *Constructs of Identity in Hellenistic Judaism: Essays on Early Jewish Literature and History*. Deuterocanonical and Cognate Literature Studies 29. Berlin.
Guast, W. 2019. 'Greek declamation beyond Philostratus' Second Sophistic', *JHS* 139: 172–86.
Günther, L.-M (ed.) 2012. *Migration und Bürgerrecht in der hellenistischen Welt*. Wiesbaden.
Güthenke, C. 2020. *Feeling and Classical Philology: Knowing Antiquity in German Scholarship, 1770–1920*. Cambridge.
Guez, J.-P. 2012. 'Magie et sophistique dans la *Vie d'Apollonios de Tyane*', in *Éclats de littérature grecque d'Homère à Pascal Quignard: mélanges offerts à Suzanne Saïd*, eds S. Dubel, S. Gotteland and E. Oudot. Nanterre, 191–231.
Gutzwiller, K. J. 1998. *Poetic Garlands. Hellenistic Epigrams in Context*. Berkeley.
  2007. *A Guide to Hellenistic Literature*. Malden, MA.

Haake, M. 2007. *Der Philosoph in der Stadt: Untersuchungen zur öffentlichen Rede über Philosophen und Philosophie in den hellenistischen Poleis*. Munich.

Habinek, T., and Schiesaro, A. (eds) 1997. *The Roman Cultural Revolution*. Cambridge.

Hadas-Lebel, M. 2003. *Philon d'Alexandrie: un penseur en diaspore*. Paris.

Hadjittofi, F. 2010. 'Nonnus' unclassical epic: imaginary geography in the *Dionysiaca*', in *Unclassical Traditions, II: Perspectives from East and West in Late Antiquity*, eds C. Kelly, R. Flower and M. S. Williams. *Cambridge Classical Journal*, Suppl. 35. Cambridge, 29–42.

Hahm, D. 1990. 'The ethical doxography of Arius Didymus', *ANRW* 2.36.4, 2935–3055.

2007. 'Critolaus and late hellenistic peripatetic philosophy', in *Pyrrhonists, Patricians, Platonizers. Hellenistic Philosophy in the Period 155–86 BC*, eds A.-M. Ioppolo and D. N. Sedley. Naples, 49–101.

Hall, E., and Wyles, R. (eds) 2008. *New Directions in Ancient Pantomime*. Oxford.

Halliwell, S. 2002. *The Aesthetics of Mimesis: Ancient Texts and Modern Problems*. Princeton.

Hallock, T., Kamps, I., Raber, K. L. (eds) 2008. *Early Modern Ecostudies: From the Florentine Codex to Shakespeare*. New York.

Hammer, C. 1898. Rev. von Arnim 1898. *Berliner Philologische Wochenschrift* 18: 836–40.

Hamon, P. 2009. 'Démocraties grecques après Alexandre: à propos de trois ouvrages récents', *Topoi* 16: 347–82.

2012. 'Gleichheit, Ungleichheit und Euergetismus: die *isotes* in den kleinasiatischen Poleis der hellenistischen Zeit', in Mann and Scholz (eds), 56–73.

Haraway, D. 1988. 'Situated knowledges: the science question in feminism and the privilege of partial perspective', *Feminist Studies* 14: 575–99.

Hardwick, L. 2020. 'Aspirations and mantras in classical reception research: can there really be dialogue between ancient and modern?', in *Framing Classical Reception Studies: Different Perspectives on a Developing Field*, eds M. de Pourcq, N. de Haan and D. Rijser. Leiden, 15–32.

Harmon, A. M. 1953. *Lucian, 1*. Cambridge, MA.

Harrison, T. 2005. 'Mastering the landscape', in *Titulus: Essays in Memory of Stanislaw Kalita*, ed. E. Dabrowa. Cracow, 27–33.

Hatzimichali, M. 2013. 'The texts of Plato and Aristotle in the first century BC', in *Plato, Aristotle and Pythagoreanism in the First Century BC. New Directions for Philosophy*, ed. M. Schofield. Cambridge, 1–27.

2017. 'Strabo's philosophy and Stoicism', in Dueck (ed.), 9–21.

Hau, L.I. 2011. 'Tykhē in Polybios: narrative answers to a philosophical question', *Histos* 5: 183–207.

2016. *Moral History from Herodotus to Diodorus Siculus*. Edinburgh.

2018a. 'Diodorus' use of Agatharchides' description of Africa', in *Histoire et géographie chez les auteurs grecs d'époque romaine*, eds M. Coltelloni-Trannoy and S. Morlet. Paris, 27–42.

2018b. 'Narrator and narratorial persona in Diodoros' *Bibliotheke* (and their implications for the tradition of Greek historiography)', in Hau, Meeus and Sheridan (eds), 277–301.

Hau, L., Meeus, A., and Sheridan, B. (eds) 2018. *Diodoros of Sicily: Historiographical Theory and Practice in the Bibliotheke*. Studia Hellenistica 58. Leuven.
Haubold, J. 2013. *Greece and Mesopotamia: Dialogues in Literature*. Cambridge.
Hawthorn, G. 1991. *Plausible Worlds. Possibility and the Understanding in History and the Social Sciences*. Cambridge.
Heath, M. 1989a. 'Dionysius of Halicarnassus "On Imitation"', *Hermes* 117: 370–3.
  1989b. *Unity in Greek Poetics*. Oxford.
Heibges, S. 1911. *De clausulis Charitoneis*. Halle.
Heise, U. K. 2008. *Sense of Place and Sense of Planet*. Oxford.
Heller, A., and Pont, A.-V. (eds) 2012. *Patrie d'origine et patries électives: les citoyennetés multiples dans le monde grec d'époque romaine*. Bordeaux.
Henderson, Jeffrey. 1991. *The Maculate Muse. Obscene Language in Attic Comedy*. 2nd ed. Oxford.
Henderson, John. 2001. 'From Megalopolis to cosmopolis: Polybius, or there and back again', in Goldhill (ed.), 29–49.
Herzog-Hauser, G. 1948. 'Tyche', *RE* VII.A2, 1643–89.
Heßler, J. E. 2014. *Epikur: Brief an Menoikeus*. Basel.
Hidber, T. 1996. *Das klassizistische Manifest des Dionys von Halikarnass: die Praefatio zu 'De oratoribus veteribus'. Einleitung, Übersetzung, Kommentar*. Stuttgart.
  2011. 'Impacts of writing in Rome: Greek authors and their Roman environment in the first century BCE', in Schmitz and Wiater (eds), 115–23.
Hinds, S. 1998. *Allusion and Intertext. Dynamics of Appropriation in Roman Poetry*. Cambridge.
Hinrichs, F. T. 1967. 'Der römische Straßenbau zur Zeit der Gracchen', *Historia* 16: 162–76.
Hinterhöller-Klein, M. 2015. *Varietates topiorum: Perspektive und Raumerfassung in Landschafts- und Panoramabildern der römischen Wandmalerei vom 1. Jh. v. Chr. bis zum Ende der pompejanischen Stile*. Vienna.
Hölkeskamp, K.-J. 1993. 'Conquest, competition and consensus: Roman expansion in Italy and the rise of the *nobilitas*', repr. in Hölkeskamp 2004, 11–48.
  2001. 'Capitol, Comitium und Forum: öffentliche Räume, sakrale Topographie und Erinnerungslandschaften', repr. in Hölkeskamp 2004, 137–65.
  2004. *Senatus Populusque Romanus. Die politische Kultur der Republik - Dimensionen und Deutungen*. Stuttgart.
Hoeschele, R. 2017. 'A lapidary tête-à-tête with Homer: Two epigram cycles from the Villa of Aelian', in *Traditions épiques et poésie épigrammatique. Actes du colloque des 7, 8 et 9 novembre 2012 à Aix-en-Provence*, eds Y. Durbec and F. Trajber. Hellenistica Groningana 22. Leuven, 41–58.
Hoffmann, W. 1907. *Das literarische Porträt Alexanders des Großen*. Leipzig.
Holliday, P. J. 2002. *The Origins of Roman Historical Commemoration in the Visual Arts*. Cambridge.

Hollis, D. L. 2019. 'Mountain gloom and mountain glory: the genealogy of an idea', *Interdisciplinary Studies in Literature and the Environment* 26: 1038–61.

Hollis, D. L., and König, J. (eds) 2021. *Mountain Dialogues from Antiquity to Modernity*. London.

Holmes, B. 2017. 'Foreword: before nature?', in Schliephake 2017a, ix–xiii.

Honigman, S. 2003. *The Septuagint and Homeric Scholarship in Alexandria*. London.

Hoof, L. van 2010. *Plutarch's Practical Ethics: The Social Dynamics of Philosophy*. Oxford.

Horn, F. 2018. 'Dying is hard to describe: metonymies and metaphors of death in the *Iliad*', *CQ* 68: 359–83.

Hornblower, S. 2015. *Lykophron: Alexandra. Greek Text, Translation, Commentary, and Introduction*. Oxford.

Horsley, G. H. R. 1981. *New Documents Illustrating Early Christianity, 1: A Review of the Greek Inscriptions and Papyri Published in 1976*. Sydney.

Hose, M. 1999. 'Post-colonial theory and Greek literature in Rome', *GRBS* 40: 303–26.

Howley, J. A. 2014. '*Heus tu rhetorisce*: Gellius, Cicero, Plutarch, and Roman study abroad', in *Roman Rule in Greek and Latin Writing. Double Vision*, eds J. M. Madsen and R. Rees. Leiden, 163–92.

Hoyos, D. 2006. 'Crossing the Durance with Hannibal and Livy: the route to the pass', *Klio* 88: 408–65.

Hughes, J. D. 2014. *Environmental Problems of the Greeks and Romans: Ecology in the Ancient Mediterranean*. 2nd ed. Baltimore.

Huitink, L., and Rood, T. 2019. *Xenophon, Anabasis Book III*. Cambridge.

Hunter, R. 1983. *A Study of Daphnis and Chloe*. Cambridge.

2009a. 'The *Trojan Oration* of Dio Chrysostom and ancient Homeric criticism', in *Narratology and Interpretation: The Content of Narrative Form in Ancient Literature*, eds J. Grethlein and A. Rengakos. Berlin: 43–62.

2009b. *Critical Moments in Classical Literature*. Cambridge.

Hunter, R., and Jonge, C. C. de (eds) 2019a. *Dionysius of Halicarnassus and Augustan Rome. Rhetoric, Criticism and Historiography*. Cambridge.

2019b. 'Introduction', in Hunter and de Jonge (eds), 1–33.

Huss, W. 2001. *Ägypten in hellenistischer Zeit, 332–30 v. Chr.* Munich.

Hutchinson, G. O. 1995. 'Rhythm, style, and meaning in Cicero's prose', *CQ* 45: 485–99.

2013. *Greek to Latin: Frameworks and Contexts for Intertextuality*. Oxford.

2015. 'Appian the artist: rhythmic prose and its literary implications', *CQ* 65: 788–806.

2018. *Plutarch's Rhythmic Prose*. Oxford.

Hutton, W. 2005. *Describing Greece: Landscape and Literature in the Periegesis of Pausanias*. Cambridge.

Innes, D. C. 2002. 'Longinus and Caecilius: models of the sublime', *Mnemosyne* 55: 259–84.

Inwood, B. 2014. *Ethics after Aristotle*. Cambridge, MA.
Isager, J. (ed.) 2001. *Foundation and Destruction: Nikopolis and Northwestern Greece. The Archaeological Evidence for the City Destructions, the Foundation of Nikopolis and the Synoecisms*. Aarhus.
Isayev, E. 2014. 'Polybius's global moment and human mobility throughout ancient Italy', in *Globalisation and the Roman World: World History, Connectivity and Material Culture*, eds M. Pitts and M. J. Versluys. New York, 123–40.
Jacob, C. 1991. 'Θεὸς Ἑρμῆς ἐπὶ Ἁδριανοῦ: La mise en scène du pouvoir impérial dans la Description de la terre habitée de Denys d'Alexandrie', *CCG* 2: 43–53.
Jameson, F. 1981. *The Political Unconscious*. London.
Janni, P. 1984. *La mappa e il periplo. Cartografia antica e spazio odologico*. Rome.
Jenkins, H. 1992. *Textual Poachers*. London.
  2002. 'Interactive audiences: the "collective intelligence" of media fans', in *The New Media Book*, ed. D. Harries. London, 157–70.
Jocelyn, H. D. 1979. '*Vergilius cacozelus* (Donatus *Vita Vergilii* 44)', *PLLS* 2: 67–142.
Johnson, W., and Richter, D. (eds) 2017. *The Oxford Handbook of the Second Sophistic*. Oxford.
Jolivet, V. 1987. '*Xerxes togatus*: Lucullus en Campanie', *MEFRA* 99: 823–46.
Jones, B. W. 1984. *The Emperor Titus*. London.
Jones, C. P. 1971. *Plutarch and Rome*. Oxford.
  1978 *The Roman World of Dio Chrysostom*. Cambridge, MA.
  2000. 'Nero speaking', *HSCPh* 100: 453–62.
  2004. 'Multiple identities in the age of the Second Sophistic', in Borg (ed.), 13–22.
Jones, H. L. 1917–32. *The Geography of Strabo*, 8 vols. Cambridge, MA.
Jong, I. J. F. de 1987. *Narrators and Focalizers: The Presentation of the Story in the Iliad*. Amsterdam.
  2001. *A Narratological Commentary on the Odyssey*. Cambridge.
Jonge, C. C. de 2008. *Between Grammar and Rhetoric: Dionysius of Halicarnassus on Language, Linguistics and Literature*. Leiden.
  2014. 'The Attic Muse and the Asian harlot: classicizing allegories in Dionysius and Longinus', in *Valuing the Past in the Greco-Roman World*, eds J. Ker and C. Pieper. Leiden, 388–409.
  2017. 'Dionysius on Thucydides', in *The Oxford Handbook of Thucydides*, eds R. Balot, S. Forsdyke and E. Forster. Oxford, 641–58.
  2019. 'Dionysius and Horace: composition in Augustan Rome', in Hunter and de Jonge (eds), 242–66.
  2021. 'Challenging the canon of the ten Attic orators: from kanôn to canon', in *Canonisation as Innovation: Anchoring Cultural Formation in the First Millennium BC*, eds D. Agut-Labordère and M. J. Versluys. Leiden.
Jung, M. 2006. *Marathon und Plataiai. Zwei Perserschlachten als 'lieux de mémoire' im antiken Griechenland*. Hypomnemata 164. Göttingen.

Kah, D. 2012. '*Paroikoi* und Neubürger in Priene', in Günther (ed.), 51–71.
Kah, D., and Scholz, P. (eds) 2004. *Das hellenistische Gymnasion*. Berlin.
Kamen, D. 2013. *Status in Classical Athens*. Princeton.
Kassel, R. 1987. *Die Abgrenzung des Hellenismus in der griechischen Literaturgeschichte*. Berlin.
Keaney, J., and Lamberton, R. (eds) 1996. *Essay on the Life and Poetry of Homer [Plutarch]*. Atlanta.
Keeline, T., and Kirby, T. 2019. '*Auceps syllabarum*: a digital analysis of Latin prose rhythm', *JRS* 109: 161–204.
Kemezis, A. M. 2011. 'Narrative of cultural geography in Philostratus' *Lives of the Sophists*', in *Perceptions of the Second Sophistic and Its Times. Regards sur la Seconde Sophistique et son époque*, eds T. S. Schmidt and P. Fleury. *Phoenix* Suppl. 49. Toronto, 3–22.
Kennedy, G. A. 1972. *The Art of Rhetoric in the Roman World. 300 BC–AD 300*. Princeton.
 1994. *A New History of Classical Rhetoric*. Princeton.
Kennell, N. 2013. 'Who were the *Neoi*?', in Martzavou and Papazarkadas (eds), 228–9.
Kidd, I. G. 1988–99 *Posidonius*, *II.i* and *II.ii: The Commentary; iii: The Translation of the Fragments*. Cambridge.
 1989. 'Posidonius as philosopher-historian', in Griffin and Barnes (eds), 38–50.
Kienast, D. 1982. '*Corpus Imperii*. Überlegungen zum Reichsgedanken der Römer', in *Romanitas – Christianitas. Untersuchungen zur Geschichte und Literatur der römischen Kaiserzeit. Johannes Straub zum 70. Geburtstag am 18. Oktober 1982 gewidmet*, ed. G. Wirth, in collaboration with K.-H. Schwarte and J. Heinrichs. Berlin, 1–17.
Kim, L. 2007. 'The portrait of Homer in Strabo's Geography', *CPh* 102: 363–88.
 2010. *Homer Between History and Fiction in Imperial Greek Literature*. Cambridge.
 2017a. 'Atticism and Asianism', in Richter and Johnson (eds), 41–66.
 2017b. 'Literary history in Imperial Greece: Dionysius' *On Ancient Orators*, Plutarch's *On the Oracles of the Pythia*, Philostratus' *Lives of the Sophists*', in Grethlein and Rengakos (eds), 212–47.
Kindstrand, J. F. 1973. *Homer in der zweiten Sophistik: Studien zu der Homerlektüre und dem Homerbild bei Dion von Prusa, Maximos von Tyros und Ailios Aristeides*. Uppsala.
Knoche, U. 1952. 'Die Augusteische Ausprägung der Dea Roma', repr. in *Römertum. Ausgewählte Aufsätze und Arbeiten aus den Jahren 1921 bis 1961*, ed. H. Oppermann. Darmstadt 1962, 359–99.
Koelb, J. H. 2006. *The Poetics of Description: Imagined Places in European Literature*. New York.
 2009. '"This most beautiful and adorn'd world": Nicolson's *Mountain Gloom and Mountain Glory* reconsidered', *Interdisciplinary Studies in Literature and the Environment* 16: 443–68.
König, A., and Whitton, C. (eds) 2018a. *Roman Literature under Nerva, Trajan and Hadrian: Literary Interactions*. Cambridge.
 2018b. 'Introduction', in König and Whitton (eds), 1–34.

König, A., Langlands, R., and Uden, J. (eds) 2020a. *Literature and Culture in the Roman Empire, 96–235: Cross-Cultural Interactions.* Cambridge.
  2020b. 'Introduction', in König, Langlands and Uden (eds), 1–33.
König, J. 2009. *Greek Literature in the Roman Empire.* London.
  2011. 'Self-promotion and self-effacement in Plutarch's *Table Talk*', in *The Philosopher's Banquet. Plutarch's Table Talk in the Intellectual Culture of the Roman Empire*, eds F. Klotz and K. Oikonomopoulou. Oxford, 179–203.
  2015. 'Greek literature in the Roman world: introducing imperial Greek literature', in *A Companion to Greek Literature*, eds M. Hose and D. Schenker. Chichester, 112–25.
  2016a. 'Strabo's Mountains', in *Landscapes of Value: Natural Environment and Cultural Imagination in Classical Antiquity*, eds J. McInerney and I. Sluiter. Leiden, 46–69.
  2016b. 'Re-reading Pollux: encyclopaedic structure and athletic culture in *Onomasticon* Book 3', *CQ* 66: 298–315.
  2018. 'Representations of intellectual community in Plutarch, Pliny the Younger and Aulus Gellius', *Archimède. Hors série* 1: 54–67.
König, J., and Whitmarsh, T. (eds) 2007a. *Ordering Knowledge in the Roman Empire.* Cambridge.
  2007b. 'Ordering knowledge', in König and Whitmarsh (eds), 3–39.
König, J., and Woolf, G. (eds) 2013a. *Encyclopaedism from Antiquity to the Renaissance.* Cambridge.
  2013b. 'Encyclopaedism in the Roman Empire', in König and Woolf (eds), 23–63.
Kolb, A. 2016. 'The Romans and the world's measure', in *Brill's Companion to Ancient Geography. The Inhabited World in Greek and Roman Tradition*, eds S. Bianchetti, M. R. Cataudella and H.-J. Gehrke. Leiden, 223–38.
Konstan, D., and Saïd, S. (eds) 2006. *The Greeks on Greekness.* PCPS 29. Cambridge.
Korenjak, M. 2000. *Publikum und Redner: ihre Interaktion in der Sophistischen Rhetorik der Kaiserzeit.* Zetemata 14. Munich.
Koumoulides, J. T. A. (ed.) 1987. *Greek Connections: Essays on Culture and Diplomacy.* Notre Dame.
Kraus, M. 1996. 'Exercitatio', in Ueding (ed.), III: Eup-Hör, 71–123.
Kremmydas, C., and Tempest, K. (eds) 2013. *Hellenistic Oratory: Continuity and Change.* Oxford.
Krewet, M. 2017. 'Polybios' Geschichtsbild. Hellenistische Prinzipien seiner Darstellungen menschlichen Handelns', *WS* 130: 89–125.
Kühnert, F., and Vogt, E. 2005. 'Rhetorik', *Lexikon des Hellenismus*, eds H. H. Schmitt and E. Vogt. Wiesbaden, 912–19.
Laks, A., and Schofield, M. (eds) 1995. *Justice and Generosity: Studies in Hellenistic Social and Political Philosophy.* Cambridge.

Lamberton, R. 1986. *Homer the Theologian: Neoplatonist Allegorical Reading and the Growth of the Epic Tradition.* Berkeley.
Lang, M. L. 1989. 'Unreal conditions in Homeric narrative', *GRBS* 30: 5–26.
Laplace, M. 2007. *Le roman d'Achille Tatios: discours panégyrique et imaginaire romanesque.* Bern.
Larmour, D. H. J. 2014. 'The synkrisis', in Beck (ed.), 405–16.
Lateiner, D. 1989. *The Historical Method of Herodotus.* Toronto.
Laurence, R. 1999. *The Roads of Roman Italy. Mobility and Cultural Change.* London.
Laurent, J. 2008. 'Strabon et la philosophie stoïcienne', *Archives de Philosophie* 71: 111–27.
Lausberg, H. 2008. *Handbuch der literarischen Rhetorik. Eine Grundlegung der Literaturwissenschaft.* 4th ed. Stuttgart.
Leach, E. W. 2000. 'Narrative space and the viewer in Philostratus' *Eikones*', *MDAI(R)* 107: 237–51.
Le Guen, B. (ed.) 1997. *De la scène aux gradins: théâtre et représentations dramatiques après Alexandre le Grand.* Toulouse.
Lemarchand, L. 1926. *Dion de Pruse: les oeuvres d'avant l'exil.* Paris.
Levine, A.-J. 1995. 'The Sibylline Oracles', in *Searching the Scriptures*, II: *A Feminist Commentary,* ed. E. Schüssler Fiorenza. New York, 99–108.
Levine, L. I. 2012. *Visual Judaism in Late Antiquity: Historical Contexts of Jewish Art.* New Haven.
Lévy, C. 1998. *Philon d'Alexandrie et le langage de la philosophie.* Turnhout.
Liddel, P. 2018. 'Inscriptions and writing in Diodoros' *Bibliotheke*', in Hau, Meeus and Sheridan (eds), 447–69.
Liddel, P., and Fear, A. (eds) 2010. *Historiae Mundi. Studies in Universal History.* London.
Lightfoot, J. 1999. *Parthenius of Nicaea: The Poetical Fragments and the Erotika Pathemata.* Oxford.
  2007. *The Sibylline Oracles: With Introduction, Translation, and Commentary on the First and Second Books.* Oxford.
  2017. 'Man of many voices and of much knowledge; or, in search of Strabo's Homer', in Dueck (ed.), 251–62.
Lintott, A. 1972. 'Imperial expansion and moral decline in the Roman Republic', *Historia* 21: 626–38.
  1981. 'What was the "Imperium Romanum"', *G&R* 28: 53–67.
Lloyd-Jones, H. 1982. *U. von Wilamowitz-Moellendorff. History of Classical Scholarship.* London.
Long, A. A. 2006. *From Epicurus to Epictetus: Studies in Hellenistic and Roman Philosophy.* Oxford.
Long, A. A., and Sedley, D. N. 1987. *The Hellenistic Philosophers,* 2 vols. Cambridge.
Louden, B. 1993. 'Pivotal contrafactuals in Homeric epic', *CA* 12: 181–93.
Lucarini, C. 2015. 'I due stili asiani (Cic. "Br." 325; "P. Artemid.") e l'origine dell'Atticismo letterario', *ZPE* 193: 11–24.

Lucas, D. W. 1968. *Aristotle, Poetics*. Oxford.
Luzzatto, M. T. 1983. *Tragedia greca e cultura ellenistica. L'or. LII di Dione di Prusa*. Bologna.
Ma, J. 2013. *Statues and Cities: Honorific Portraits and Civic Identity in the Hellenistic World*. Oxford.
Macdonald, E. 2015. *Hannibal. A Hellenistic Life*, repr. as *Hannibal. The Life and Legend*. New Haven.
Maciver, C. 2012. *Quintus Smyrnaeus' Posthomerica: Engaging Homer in Late Antiquity*. Leiden.
Maier, F. K. 2010. '"... zu vertrauten Vorstellungen führen". Die Funktion der Geographie im didaktischen Geschichtskonzept des Polybius', *Geographia Antica* 19: 47–63.
  2012a. 'Learning from history *para doxan*. A new approach to Polybius' manifold view of the past', *Histos* 6: 144–68.
  2012b. *'Überall mit dem Unerwarteten rechnen': die Kontingenz geschichtlicher Prozesse bei Polybios*. Munich.
  2018. 'Past and present as *paradoxon theorema* in Polybius', in *Polybius and His Legacy*, ed. N. Miltsios. Berlin, 55–74.
Maiuri, A. 1925. *Nuova silloge epigrafica di Rodi e Cos*. Florence.
Manfredi, L. I. 1999. 'Carthaginian policy through coins', in *Phoenicians and Carthaginians in the Western Mediterranean*, ed. G. Pisano. Studia Punica 12. Rome, 69–78.
Mann, Chr., and Scholz, P. (eds) 2012. *'Demokratie' im Hellenismus: Von der Herrschaft des Volkes zur Herrschaft der Honoratioren?* Die hellenistische Polis als Lebensform 2. Berlin.
Mansfeld, J., and Runia, D. T. 1996. *Aëtiana. The Method and Intellectual Context of a Doxographer, 1*. Leiden.
Mari, M., and Thornton, J. (eds) 2013. *Parole in movimento. Linguaggio politico e lessico storiografico in età ellenistica*. Studi ellenistici 27. Pisa.
Marías, J. 2015. 'To begin at the beginning. Opening speech 15th international literature festival Berlin, September 9th 2015, House of the Berliner Festspiele' (www.literaturfestival.com/ medien/ texte/ eroeffnungsreden/ opening-of-the-15th-ilb-javier-marias-let2019s-start-at-the-beginning/ view; accessed 22 September 2015).
Markell, P. 2003. *Bound by Recognition*. Princeton.
Martinelli, M. C. (ed.) 2009. *La musa dimenticata. Aspetti dell'esperienza musicale greca in età ellenistica*. Pisa.
Martzavou, P. 2014. '"Isis" et "Athènes": épigraphie, espace et pouvoir à la basse époque hellénistique', in Bricault and Versluys (eds), 163–91.
Martzavou, P., and Papazarkadas, N. (eds) 2013. *Epigraphical Approaches to the Post-Classical Polis, Fourth Century BC to Second Century AD*. Oxford.
Mattingly, D. J. 2013. *Imperialism, Power, and Identity: Experiencing the Roman Empire*. Oxford.
  2014. 'Identities in the Roman world: discrepancy, heterogeneity, hybridity and plurality', in *Roman in the Provinces: Art on the Periphery of Empire*, eds L. R. Brody and G. L. Hoffman. Chestnut Hill, 35–59.

McEwen, I. K. 2003. *Vitruvius: Writing the Body of Architecture*. Cambridge, MA.
Meeus, A. 2018a. 'History's aims and audience in the proem to Diodoros' *Bibliotheke*', in Hau, Meeus and Sheridan (eds), 149–74.
  2018b. 'Introduction: narrative and interpretation in the Hellenistic historians', in Meeus (ed.), 1–22.
  (ed.) 2018c. *Narrative in Hellenistic Historiography*. Histos Suppl. 8. Newcastle.
Meister, J. B. 2012. *Der Körper des Princeps. Zur Problematik eines monarchischen Körpers ohne Monarchie*. Stuttgart.
Meister, K. 1975. *Historische Kritik bei Polybios*. Wiesbaden.
Menn, S. 1997. 'Physics as a virtue', *Boston Area Colloquium in Ancient Philosophy* 11: 1–34.
Mérot, G. 2017. 'Un canon épistolaire? La singularité du discours *Sur l'entraînement à la parole* de Dion de Pruse', in *Sacré canon: autorité et marginalité en littérature*, eds M. Lata and A. C. Baudoin. Paris, 23–39.
Messerschmidt, W. 2003. *Prosopopoiia. Personifikationen politischen Charakters in spätklassischer und hellenistischer Kunst*. Cologne.
Meyer, D. 2005. *Inszeniertes Lesevergnügen. Das inschriftliche Epigramm und seine Rezeption bei Kallimachos*. Stuttgart.
Meyer, D., and Wirbelauer, E. 2007. 'Rom und die Römer in griechischen Epigrammen (2. Jh. v. Chr.–1. Jh. n. Chr.)', in *Visions grecques de Rome. Griechische Blicke auf Rom*, eds M.-L. Freyburger and D. Meyer. Paris, 319–46.
Migliario, E. 2012. 'Intellettuali dei tempi nuovi: retori greci nella Roma augustea', in *Forme della memoria e dinamiche identitarie nell'antichità greco-romana*, eds E. Franchi and G. Proietti. Trento, 111–30.
Millar, F. G. B. 1987. 'Polybius between Greece and Rome', in Koumoulides (ed.), 1–18.
Miltsios, N. 2013. *The Shaping of Narrative in Polybius*. Berlin.
Miltsios, N., and Tamiolaki, M. (eds) 2018. *Polybius and his Legacy*. Berlin.
Minar, E. L., Sandbach, F. H., and Helmbold, W. C. 1961. *Plutarch's Moralia*, XIX. Cambridge, MA.
Moatti, C. 2015. *The Birth of Critical Thinking in Republican Rome*, tr. J. Lloyd (originally published in French 1997). Cambridge.
Möllendorff, P. von 2013. '"Sie hielt ein aufgerolltes Buch in den Händen ..." – Metalepse als mediales Phänomen in der Literatur der Kaiserzeit', in *Über die Grenze. Metalepse in Text- und Bildmedien des Altertums*, eds U. Eisen and P. von Möllendorff. Berlin, 346–86.
Mohm, S. 1977. *Untersuchungen zu den historiographischen Anschauungen des Polybios*. PhD Diss. Saarbrücken.
Moles, J. L. 1978. 'The career and conversion of Dio Chrysostom', *JHS* 98: 79–100.
Molin, M. 2004. *Polybe, Histoires, III: Livre III, texte établi par J. de Foucault, revu et traduit par E. Foulon, commenté par M. Molin*. Paris.
Momigliano, A. 1942. 'Terra Marique', *JRS* 32: 53–64.
Mommsen, T. 1889. 'Zusatz', in *Sitzungsberichte der Königlich Preußischen Akademie zu Berlin*, 973–81.

Morgan, M. G. 1973. 'Pliny, N. H. III 129, the Roman use of stades and the elogium of C. S. Tuditanus', *Philologus* 117: 29–48.
Morgan, T. 1998. *Literate Education in the Hellenistic and Roman Worlds.* Cambridge.
  2011. 'The Miscellany and Plutarch', in *The Philosopher's Banquet: Plutarch's Table Talk in the Intellectual Culture of the Roman Empire*, ed. F. Klotz. Oxford, 49–73.
Morrison, J. V. 1992. 'Alternatives to the epic tradition. Homer's challenges in the *Iliad*', *TAPhA* 122: 61–71.
Morson, G. S. 1994. *Narrative and Freedom: the Shadows of Time.* New Haven.
Morstein Kallet-Marx, R. 1995. *From Hegemony to Empire. The Development of the Roman Imperium in the East from 148 to 62 BC.* Berkeley.
Morton, P. 2018. 'Diodorus Siculus' "Slave War" narratives: writing social commentary in the *Bibliotheke*', *CQ* 68: 534–51.
Most, G. W. 2011. 'Principate and system', in Schmitz and Wiater (eds), 163–79.
Most, G. W., and Laks, A. (eds) 2016. *Early Greek Philosophy*, VIII.1: *Sophists.* Cambridge, MA.
Mülke, M. 2018. *Aristobulos in Alexandria. Jüdische Bibelexegese zwischen Griechen und Ägyptern unter Ptolemaios VI.* Berlin.
Müller, C. 2014. 'La (dé)construction de la politeia. Citoyenneté et octroi de privilèges aux étrangers dans les démocraties hellénistiques', *Annales HSS* 69: 753–75.
Müller, K. 1935. *Die Epigramme des Antiphilos von Byzanz. Einleitende Untersuchungen, Text und Kommentar.* Neue deutsche Forschungen 2. Berlin.
Münscher, K. 1920. *Xenophon in der griechisch-römischen Literatur.* Leipzig.
Muntz, C. E. 2017. *Diodorus Siculus and the World of the Late Roman Republic.* New York.
Murphy, T. 2004. *Pliny the Elder's Natural History: The Empire in the Encyclopedia.* Oxford.
Myers, M. 2011. 'Lucan's poetic geographies: center and periphery in civil war epic', *Brill's Companion to Lucan*, ed. P. Asso. Leiden, 399–416.
Neis, R. 2013. *The Sense of Sight in Rabbinic Culture: Jewish Ways of Seeing in Late Antiquity.* Cambridge.
Nervegna, S. 2013. *Menander in Antiquity: The Contexts of Reception.* Cambridge.
Nesselrath, H.-G. 1992. *Ungeschehenes Geschehen: 'Beinahe-Episoden' im griechischen und römischen Epos von Homer bis zur Spätantike.* Stuttgart.
Nestle, W. 1927. 'Die Fabel des Menenius Agrippa', *Klio* 21: 350–60.
Newby, Z. 2007. 'Reading the allegory of the Archelaos relief', in *Art and Inscriptions in the Ancient World*, eds Z. Newby and R. Leader-Newby. Cambridge, 156–78.
  2009. 'Absorption and erudition in Philostratus' *Imagines*', in *Philostratus*, eds E. Bowie and J. Elsner. Cambridge, 322–42.
  2012. 'The aesthetics of violence: myth and danger in Roman domestic landscapes', *ClAnt* 31: 349–89.

Nicolet, C. 1991. *Space, Geography and Politics in the Early Roman Empire*, tr. H. Leclerc. Ann Arbor.
Nicolson, M. H. 1959. *Mountain Gloom and Mountain Glory: The Development of the Aesthetics of the Infinite*. Ithaca.
Niehoff, M. 2001. *Philo on Jewish Identity and Culture*. Texts and Studies in Ancient Judaism 86. Tübingen.
  2011. *Jewish Exegesis and Homeric Scholarship in Alexandria*. Cambridge.
  2012. *Homer and the Bible in the Eyes of Ancient Interpreters*. Leiden.
  2018. *Philo of Alexandria: An Intellectual Biography*. New Haven.
Nietzsche, F. 1997. *Untimely Meditations*, ed. D. Breazeale, tr. R. Hollingdale. Cambridge.
Nijf, O. van, and Alston, R. (eds) 2011. *Political Culture in the Greek City after the Classical Age*. Leuven.
Nikiprowetzky, V. 1970. *La Troisième Sibylle*. Paris.
Nikolaidis, A. G. 2014. 'Morality, characterization, and individuality', in Beck (ed.), 350–72.
Noël, M.-P. 1999. 'Gorgias et l' "invention" des γοργίεια σχήματα', *REG* 112: 193–211.
Nora, P., and Kritzman, L. D. (eds) 1996–8. *Realms of Memory. Rethinking the French Past*, 3 vols. New York.
Norden, E. 1898. *Die antike Kunstprosa vom VI. Jahrhundert v. Chr. bis in die Zeit der Renaissance*, 1. Leipzig.
  1915. *Die antike Kunstprosa vom VI. Jahrhundert v. Chr. bis in die Zeit der Renaissance*, 1. 3rd ed. Leipzig.
Nünlist, R. 2009. *The Ancient Critic at Work: Terms and Concepts of Literary Criticism in Greek Scholia*. Cambridge.
Nünnerich-Asmus, A. 1993. 'Straßen, Brücken und Bögen als Zeichen römischen Herrschaftsanspruchs', in *Hispania antiqua. Denkmäler der Römerzeit*, eds W. Trillmich et al. Mainz, 121–57.
Östenberg, I. 2009. *Staging the World: Spoils, Captives, and Representations in the Roman Triumphal Procession*. Oxford.
Oldfather, C. H., et al. 1935–67. *Diodorus of Sicily: The Library of History*, 12 vols. Cambridge, MA.
Olson, J. M., Roese, N. J., and Deibert, R. J. 1996. 'Psychological biases in counterfactual thought experiments', in Tetlock and Belkin (eds), 349–52.
Onians, J. 1979. *Art and Thought in the Hellenistic World: The Greek World View 350–50 BC*. London.
Ooms, S. 2019. *How to Compose Great Prose: Cicero, Dionysius of Halicarnassus and Stylistic Theory in Late-Republican and Augustan Rome*. PhD Diss. Leiden.
Osborne, R. 2011. *The History Written on the Classical Body*. Cambridge.
Oudot, E. 2008. 'Aelius Aristides and Thucydides: some remarks about the Panathenaic oration', in *Aelius Aristides: Between Greece, Rome, and the Gods*, eds W. V. Harris and B. Holmes. Boston, 31–49.
Palm, J. 1955. *Über Sprache und Stil des Diodoros von Sizilien*. Lund.

Papanikolaou, D. 2008. *Rhetorical Receptions of Gorgias: Hegesias and the Asianists*. PhD Diss. Cambridge.

2009. 'The aretalogy of Isis from Maroneia and the question of Hellenistic "Asianism"', *ZPE* 168: 59–70.

2012a. '*IG* V.2, 268 (= *SIG³* 783) as a monument of Hellenistic prose', *ZPE* 182: 137–56.

2012b. 'Sophistic oratory and styles in Roman Asia Minor: Hermogenes and the Tlos Sophist (*TAM* II.174)', *C&M* 63: 119–60.

Parke, H. W. 1998. *Sibyls and Sibylline Prophecy in Classical Antiquity*. London.

Parmeggiani, G. 2018. 'Polybius and the legacy of fourth-century historiography', in Miltsios and Tamiolaki (eds), 277–97.

Pasquali, G. 1913. 'Die schriftstellerische Form des Pausanias', *Hermes* 48: 161–233.

Patillon, M. 2002. *Pseudo-Aelius Aristides. Arts Rhétoriques Livre II: Le discours simple*. Paris.

2012. *Corpus Rhetoricum*, IV: *Prolégomènes au De ideis. Hermogène, Les catégories stylistiques du discours (De ideis). Synopses des exposés sur les ideai*. Paris.

Pausch, D. 2011. *Livius und der Leser. Narrative Strukturen in ab urbe condita*. Munich.

Pavlovskis, Z. 1973. *Man in an Artificial Landscape: The Marvels of Civilization in Imperial Roman Literature*. Leiden.

Pearce, S. 2007. 'Translating for Ptolemy: patriotism and politics in the Greek Pentateuch', in *Jewish Perspectives on Hellenistic Rulers*, eds T. Rajak, S. Pearce, J. Aitken and J. Dines. Berkeley, 165–81.

(ed) 2013. *The Image and Its Prohibition in Jewish Antiquity*. Oxford.

Pédech, P. 1964. *La méthode historique de Polybe*. Paris.

Peirano, I. 2012. *The Rhetoric of the Roman Fake: Latin Pseudepigrapha in Context*. Cambridge.

Pelling, C. B. R. 1986. 'Synkrisis in Plutarch's *Lives*', in *Miscellanea Plutarchea*, eds F. E. Brenk and I. Gallo. Ferrara, 83–96.

2002. *Plutarch and History. Eighteen Studies*. London.

Pernot, L. 1993. *La rhétorique de l'éloge dans le monde gréco-romain*, 2 vols. Paris.

2005. *Rhetoric in Antiquity*, tr. W. Higgins. Washington, DC.

2017. 'Greek and Latin rhetorical culture', in Richter and Johnson (eds), 205–16.

Petrain, D. 2014. *Homer in Stone: The Tabulae Iliacae in their Roman Context*. Cambridge.

Pettegrew, D. K. 2016. *The Isthmus of Corinth: Crossroads of the Mediterranean World*. Ann Arbor.

Pfeiffer, R. 1968. *History of Classical Scholarship from the Beginnings to the End of the Hellenistic Age*. Oxford.

1976. *History of Classical Scholarship from 1300–1850*. Oxford.

Pieper, C. 2016. 'Menenius Agrippa als *exemplum* für die frühe römische Beredsamkeit. Eine historische Spurensuche', *RhM* 159: 156–90.

Pier, J. 2016. 'Metalepsis', in *The Living Handbook of Narratology*, eds P. Hühn et al. Hamburg (www.lhn.uni-hamburg.de/node/51.html; accessed 16 March 2021).
Pinkwart, D. 1965. *Das Relief des Archelaos von Priene und die 'Musen des Philiskos'*. Kallmünz.
Pogorzelski, R. 2011. '"Orbis Romanus": Lucan and the limits of the Roman world', *TAPhA* 141: 143–70.
Pollitt, J. J. 1986. *Art in the Hellenistic Age*. Cambridge.
Porter, J. I. 2002. 'Homer: the very idea', *Arion* 10: 57–86.
  2006. 'Feeling classical: classicism and ancient literary criticism', in *Classical Pasts: The Classical Traditions of Greece and Rome*, ed. J. I. Porter. Princeton, 301–52.
  2016. *The Sublime in Antiquity*. Cambridge.
Post Classicisms Collective 2020. *Postclassicisms*. Chicago.
Pothecary, S. 2005. '*Kolossourgia*. "A colossal statue of a work"', in Dueck, Lindsay and Pothecary (eds), 5–26.
Potter, D. 1990. 'Sibyls in the Greek and Roman world', *JRA* 3: 471–83.
Prag, J., and Quinn, J. C. (eds) 2013a. *The Hellenistic West: Rethinking the Ancient Mediterranean*. Cambridge.
  2013b. 'Introduction', in Prag and Quinn (eds), 1–13.
Prandi, L. 2016. 'Hegesias of Magnesia (142)', in Brill's New Jacoby.
Prencipe, V. 2017. 'Impervious nature as a path to virtue: Cato in the ninth book of *Bellum civile*', in Schliephake (ed.), 131–46.
Prendergast, C. 2019. *Counterfactuals. Paths of What Might Have Been*. London.
Pretzler, M. 2005. 'Comparing Strabo with Pausanias: Greece in context vs. Greece in depth', in Dueck, Lindsay and Pothecary (eds), 144–60.
Primavesi, O., and Giuliani, L. 2012. 'Bild und Rede. Zum Proömium der *Eikones* des zweiten Philostrat', *Poetica* 44: 25–79.
Prontera, F. 1984. 'Prima di Strabone. Materiali per uno studio della geografia come genere letterario', in *Strabone. Contributi allo studio della personalità e dell' opera*, ed. I. F. Prontera. Perugia, 187–256.
Purcell, N. 1987. 'Town in country and country in town', in *Ancient Roman Villa Gardens*, ed. E. B. MacDougall. Washington, DC, 187–203.
  1990. 'Maps, lists, money, order and power', review of C. Nicolet, *L'inventaire du monde. Géographie et politique aux origines de l'empire romain*, Paris 1988 (= Nicolet 1991), *JRS* 80: 178–82.
  2002. 'The creation of provincial landscape: the Roman impact on Cisalpine Gaul', in *The Roman Empire in the West*, eds T. Blagg and M. Millett. Oxford, 7–29.
  2005. 'Romans in the Roman World', in Galinsky (ed.), 85–105.
  2012. 'Rivers and the geography of power', *Pallas* 90: 373–87.
Quaß, F. 1993. *Die Honoratiorenschicht in den Städten des griechischen Ostens*. Stuttgart.
Quayson, A. 2000. *Postcolonialism: Theory, Practice or Process?* Cambridge.

Quinn, J. C. 2012. 'Postcolonialism', in *The Encyclopedia of Ancient History*, eds R. S. Bagnall, K. Brodersen, C. B. Champion, A. Erskine and S. R. Huebner. Oxford.
  2013. 'Imagining the imperial Mediterranean', in Gibson and Harrison (eds), 337–52.
Raaflaub, K. A., and Talbert, R. J. A. (eds) 2010. *Geography and Ethnography: Perceptions of the World in Pre-Modern Societies*. Oxford.
Radt, S. 2002–11. *Strabons Geographika. Mit Übersetzung und Kommentar*, 10 vols. Göttingen.
Rajak, T. 2009. *Translation and Survival: the Greek Bible of the Ancient Jewish Diaspora*. Oxford.
Rajewsky, I. 2002. *Intermedialität*. Tübingen.
Rathmann, M. 2016. *Diodor und seine 'Bibliotheke'. Weltgeschichte aus der Provinz*. Klio Beihefte, Neue Folge 27. Berlin.
Rawson, E. 1985. *Intellectual Life in the Late Roman Republic*. London.
  1989 [1997]. 'Roman rulers and the philosophical adviser', in Griffin and Barnes (eds), 233–57.
  1990. 'The antiquarian tradition. Spoils and representations of foreign armour', in *Staat und Staatlichkeit in der frühen römischen Republik*, ed. W. Eder. Stuttgart, 158–73.
Reardon, B. P. 1971. *Courants littéraires grecs des IIe et IIIe siècles après J.-C.* Paris.
Reinhardt, K. 1926. *Kosmos und Sympathie: neue Untersuchungen über Poseidonios*. Munich.
Rengakos, A. 2017. 'The literary histories of the Hellenistic age', in Grethlein and Rengakos (eds), 71–82.
Reydams-Schils, G. 1997. 'Posidonius and the *Timaeus*: off to Rhodes and back to Plato?', *CQ* 47: 455–76.
Ribeiro Ferreira, J., Leão, D., Tröster, M., and Barata Dias, P. (eds) 2009. *Symposion and Philanthropia in Plutarch*. Coimbra.
Richardson, J. S. 1979. 'Polybius' view of the Roman empire', *PBSR* 47: 1–11.
  1991. 'Imperium Romanum: empire and the language of power', *JRS* 81: 1–9.
Richardson, L., Jr. 1992. *A New Topographical Dictionary of Ancient Rome*. Baltimore.
Richter, D. S. 2011. *Cosmopolis: Imagining Community in Late Classical Athens and the Early Roman Empire*. Oxford.
Richter, D. J., and Johnson, W. (eds) 2017. *The Oxford Handbook of the Second Sophistic*. Oxford.
Ridgway, B. 1990. *Hellenistic Sculpture, 1: The Styles of ca. 331–200 BC*. Madison.
Riggsby, A. 2007. 'Guides to the wor(l)d', in König and Whitmarsh (eds), 88–107.
  2019. *Mosaics of Knowledge: Representing Information in the Roman World*. Cambridge.
Robert, L. 1930. 'Pantomimen im griechischen Orient', *Hermes* 65: 106–22.
  1960. *Hellenica 11/12*. Paris.
  1967. 'Sur les inscriptions d'Ephèse', *RPh* ser. 3, no. 4: 7–84.

Robert, L., and Robert, J. 1989. *Claros 1. Décrets hellénistiques*. Paris.
   1954. *La Carie: histoire et géographie historique avec le recueil des inscriptions antiques*, 2 vols. Paris
Robiano, P. 2018. 'D'un tableau l'autre: parcours du discours et parcours de la *poikilia* dans les *Tableaux* de Flavius Philostrate', *REG* 131: 479–520.
Robling, F.-H. 1992. 'Asianismus. II', in Ueding (ed.), 1: A–Bib, 1120–1.
Röllmann, B. 1910. *De numeri oratorii primordiis*. Münster.
Rohde, E. 1886. 'Die asianische Rhetorik und die zweite Sophistik', *RhM* 41: 170–90.
   1876. *Der griechische Roman und seine Vorläufer*. Leipzig.
Roisman, J. 2005. *The Rhetoric of Manhood: Masculinity in the Attic Orators*. Berkeley.
Roller, D. W. 2014. *The Geography of Strabo*. Cambridge.
Romilly, J. de 1975. *Magic and Rhetoric in Ancient Greece*. Cambridge, MA.
Romm, J. S. 1992. *The Edges of the Earth in Ancient Thought: Geography, Exploration, and Fiction*. Princeton.
   2006. 'Herodotus and the natural world', in *The Cambridge Companion to Herodotus*, eds C. Dewald and J. Marincola. Cambridge, 178–91.
Rood, T. 2018. 'Geographical and historical patterning in Diodorus Siculus', in Meeus (ed.), 23–68.
Rosaldo, R. 1989. 'Imperialist nostalgia', *Representations* 26: 107–22.
Rosamilia, E. 2014. 'Biblioteche a Rodi all'epoca di Timachidas', *ASNP, Classe di Lettere e Filosofia* 5: 325–62.
Roseman, C. H. 2005. 'Reflections of philosophy: Strabo and geographical sources', in Dueck, Lindsay and Pothecary (eds), 27–41.
Rosen, K. 1987. 'Ehrendekrete, Biographie und Geschichtsschreibung. Zum Wandel der Polis im frühen Hellenismus', *Chiron* 17: 277–92.
Rosenstein, G. D. 2005. *The World Hitler Never Made. Alternate History and the Memory of Nazism*. Cambridge.
Roskam, G., De Pourcq, M., and van der Stockt, L. (eds) 2012. *The Lash of Ambition. Plutarch, Imperial Greek Literature and the Dynamics of Philotimia*. Leuven.
Roth, P. 1986. *The Counterlife*. New York.
Rothe, S. 1989. *Kommentar zu ausgewählten Sophistenviten des Philostratos: die Lehrstuhlinhaber in Athen und Rom*. Berlin.
Roveri, A. 1982. 'Tyche bei Polybios', in *Polybios*, eds K. Stiewe and N. Holzberg. Wege der Forschung 347. Darmstadt, 297–326.
Rubincam, C. 1987. 'The organisation and composition of Diodorus' *Bibliotheke*', *EMC* 31: 313–28.
   1989. 'Cross-references in the *Bibliotheke Historike* of Diodoros', *Phoenix* 43: 39–61.
   1997. 'The organisation of material in Graeco-Roman world histories', in *Pre-Modern Encyclopaedic Texts: Proceedings of the Second COMERS Congress, Groningen, 1–4 July 1996*, ed. P. Binkley. Leiden, 127–36.
Rudd, G. 2007. *Greenery: Ecocritical Readings of Late Medieval English Literature*. Manchester.

Runia, D. 1990. *Exegesis and Philosophy. Studies on Philo of Alexandria*. Aldershot.
  2012. *Philo of Alexandria: an Annotated Bibliography, 1997–2006*. Leiden.
Russell, D. A. 1981. *Criticism in Antiquity*. London.
  1989. 'Greek criticism of the empire', in *The Cambridge History of Literary Criticism*, 1: *Classical Criticism*, ed. G. A. Kennedy. Cambridge, 297–329.
  1992. *Dio Chrysostom, Orations VII, XII and XXXVI*. Cambridge, MA.
  2001. *Quintilian, The Orator's Education Books 9–10*. Cambridge, MA.
Rutherford, I. 1998 *Canons of Style in the Antonine Age: Idea-Theory in Its Literary Context*. Oxford.
Sacks, K. S. 1990. *Diodorus Siculus and the First Century*. Princeton.
Saïd, S. 2006. 'The rewriting of the Athenian past: from Isocrates to Aelius Aristides', in Konstan and Saïd (eds), 47–60.
Sasse, J. 1979. *Entropie und Wahrscheinlichkeit – Untersuchungen zum Konzept einer elementaren Einführung des Entropiebegriffs auf mikrophysikalischer Basis*. Osnabrück.
Scardigli, B. (ed.) 1995. *Essays on Plutarch's Lives*. Oxford.
Scardino, C. 2018. 'Polybius and fifth-century historiography: continuity and diversity in the presentation of historical deeds', in Miltsios and Tamiolaki (eds), 299–321.
Schippers, A. M. 2019. *Dionysius and Quintilian: Imitation and Emulation in Greek and Latin Literary Criticism*. PhD Diss. Leiden.
Schirren, T. 2009. 'Sophistik und Philologie: Hat das Subversive auch Methode?', in *Was ist eine philologische Frage? Beiträge zur Erkundung einer theoretischen Einstellung*, ed. J. P. Schwindt. Frankfurt am Main, 112–36.
Schlachter, A. 1927. *Der Globus. Seine Entstehung und Verwendung in der Antike nach den literarischen Quellen und den Darstellungen in der Kunst*, herausgegeben von F. Gisinger. Leipzig.
Schlegel, F. 1974 [1802]. *Kritische Ausgabe seiner Werke: Charakteristiken und Kritiken II*, Paderborn.
Schliephake, C. (ed.) 2017a. *Ecocriticism, Ecology, and the Cultures of Antiquity*. Lanham, MD.
  2017b. 'Introduction', in Schliephake (ed.), 1–15.
  2020. *The Environmental Humanities and the Ancient World*. Cambridge.
Schlosser, J. A. 2020 *Herodotus in the Anthropocene*. Chicago.
Schmid, W. 1887–97. *Der Atticismus in seinen Hauptvertretern von Dionysius von Halikarnass bis auf den zweiten Philostratus*, 5 vols. Stuttgart.
Schmidt-Hofner, S. (ed.) 2016. *Raum-Ordnung. Raum und soziopolitische Ordnungen im Altertum*. Heidelberg.
Schmitz, T. A. 1997. *Bildung und Macht. Zur sozialen und politischen Funktion der zweiten Sophistik in der griechischen Welt der Kaiserzeit*. Zetemata 97. Munich.
  2004. 'Alciphron's letters as a sophistic text', in Borg (ed.), 87–104.

2007. 'Die Erfindung des klassischen Athen in der zweiten Sophistik', in *Bilder der Antike*, eds A. Steiner-Weber, T. A. Schmitz and M. Laureys. Super alta perennis 1. Göttingen, 71–88.

2011a. 'The image of Athens in Diodorus Siculus', in Schmitz and Wiater (eds), 235–51.

2011b. 'The Second Sophistic', in *The Oxford Handbook of Social Relations in the Roman World*, ed. M. Peachin. Oxford, 304–16.

2014. 'Plutarch and the Second Sophistic', in Beck (ed.), 32–42.

2017. 'Professionals of *paideia*? The sophists as performers', in Johnson and Richter (eds), 169–80.

Schmitz, T. A., and Wiater, N. (eds) 2011a. *The Struggle for Identity: Greeks and Their Past in the First Century* BCE. Stuttgart.

Schmitz, T. A., and Wiater, N. (eds) 2011b. 'Introduction: approaching Greek identity', in Schmitz and Wiater (eds), 15–45.

Schmitzer, U. 2008. '"Oligostichicus Caesar." Das Bild des Augustus und seines Hauses in der *Anthologia Palatina*', in *Augustus – Der Blick von außen: Die Wahrnehmung des Kaisers in den Provinzen des Reiches und in den Nachbarstaaten*, eds D. Kreikenbom et al. Wiesbaden, 15–28.

Schneider, K. 1935. 'Miliarium', *RE Suppl.* VI, 395–431.

Schofield, M. 1999. *The Stoic Idea of the City*. New ed. with added foreword and epilogue. Chicago.

2012. 'Antiochus on social virtue', in Sedley (ed.), 173–87.

(ed.) 2013. *Aristotle, Plato and Pythagoreanism in the First Century* BC. Cambridge.

Sedley, D. 2003. 'Philodemus and the decentralisation of philosophy', *Cronache Ercolanesi* 33: 31–41.

2009. 'Philosophy in the Artemidorus papyrus', in *Intorno al Papiro di Artemidoro, I: Contesto Culturale, Lingua e Stile*, eds C. Gallazzi, B. Kramer and S. Settis. Milan, 29–53.

(ed.) 2012. *The Philosophy of Antiochus*. Cambridge.

Segre, M. 1935. 'Epigraphica', *RFIC* 63: 214–25.

Seibert, J. 1993. *Forschungen zu Hannibal*. Darmstadt.

Seland, T. (ed.) 2014. *Reading Philo: A Handbook to Philo of Alexandria*. Grand Rapids, MI.

Sessions, G. 1981. 'Shallow and deep ecology: a review of the philosophical literature', in *Ecological Consciousness: Essays from the Earthday X Colloquium, University of Denver, April 21–24, 1980*, eds R. Schultz and J. D. Hughes. Washington, DC, 391–462.

Sharples, R. W. 2010. *Peripatetic Philosophy, 200 BC to AD 200: An Introduction and Collection of Sources in Translation*. Cambridge.

Sheridan, B. 2010. 'Diodorus' reading of Polybius' universalism', in Liddel and Fear (eds), 41–55.

Sherk, R. K. 1963. 'Caesar and Mytilene', in *GRBS* 4: 145–53.

Sherwin-White, A. S. 1980. *The Roman Citizenship*. Oxford.

Shewring, W. H. 1931. 'Prose-rhythm and the comparative method', *CQ* 31: 12–25.

1934. 'Platonic influence in Lucian's "clausulae"', *Berliner Philologische Wochenschrift* 54: 814–16.
Shorrock, R. 2011. *The Myth of Paganism: Nonnus, Dionysus and the World of Late Antiquity.* London.
Shuckburgh, E. S. 1908–9. *The Letters of Cicero.* London.
Sidebottom, H. 1996. 'Dio of Prusa and the Flavian dynasty', *CQ* 46: 447–56.
Sider, D. 1997. *The Epigrams of Philodemos. Introduction, Text, and Commentary.* Oxford.
Siegert, F. 2016. *Einleitung in die hellenistisch-jüdische Literatur. Apokrypha, Pseudepigrapha und Fragmente verlorener Autorenwerke.* Berlin.
Sistakou, E. 2007. 'Glossing Homer: Homeric exegesis in early third century epigram', in Bing and Bruss (eds), 391–408.
Smith, A. C. 2011. *Polis and Personification in Classical Athenian Art.* Leiden.
Smith, R. M. 1995. 'A new look at the canon of the ten Attic orators', *Mnemosyne* 48: 66–79.
Smith, R. R. R. 1991. *Hellenistic Sculpture. A Handbook.* London.
Smith, S. D. 2007. *Greek Identity and the Athenian Past in Chariton: The Romance of Empire.* Groningen.
Somers, M. 1994. 'The narrative constitution of identity: a relational and network approach', *Theory and Society* 23: 605–49.
Sonnabend, H. 2005. 'Zwischen Fortschritt und Zerstörung: Mensch und Umwelt in der Antike', in *Physik/Mechanik*, ed. A. Schürmann. Geschichte der Mathematik und der Naturwissenschaften in der Antike 3. Stuttgart, 118–28.
Spanoudakis, K. (ed) 2014. *Nonnus of Panopolis in Context: Poetry and Cultural Milieu in Late Antiquity with a Section on Nonnus and the Modern World.* Berlin.
Spawforth, A. J. S. 2012. *Greece and the Augustan Cultural Revolution.* Cambridge.
Spencer, D. 2010. *Roman Landscape: Culture and Identity.* Cambridge.
Spina, L. 1989. 'Il racconto di un racconto. Egesia di Magnesia in Dionigi d'Alicarnasso, *de comp. verb.* VI 18.25–27', *Vichiana* 18: 333–40.
Spivak, G. C. 1988. 'Can the subaltern speak?' in *Marxism and the Interpretation of Culture*, eds C. Nelson and L. Grossberg. Chicago, 271–316.
Squire, J. C. 1999. *Wenn Napoleon bei Waterloo gewonnen hätte – und andere abwegige Geschichten.* Munich.
Squire, M. 2009. *Image and Text in Graeco-Roman Antiquity.* Cambridge.
  2011. *The Iliad in a Nutshell: Visualizing Epic on the Tabulae Iliacae.* Oxford.
  2013a. 'Apparitions apparent: ekphrasis and the parameters of vision in the Elder Philostratus's *Imagines*', *Helios* 40: 97–140.
  2013b. 'Embodied ambiguities on the Prima Porta Augustus', *Art History* 36: 242–79.
  2015. '*Corpus imperii*: verbal and visual figurations of the Roman "body politic"', *Word & Image* 31: 305–30.
Staab, G. 2004. 'Athenfreunde unter Verdacht: der erste Asianist Hegesias aus Magnesia zwischen Rhetorik und Geschichtsschreibung', *ZPE* 148: 127–50.
Stefec, R. S. 2016. *Flavii Philostrati Vitae Sophistarum.* Oxford.

Steinmetz, P. 1964. 'Gattungen und Epochen der griechischen Literatur in der Sicht Quintilians', *Hermes* 92: 454–66.
Stella, L. A. 1949. *Cinque poeti dell' Antologia Palatina*. Bologna.
Stevens, K. 2019. *Between Greece and Babylonia: Hellenistic Intellectual History in Cross-Cultural Perspective*. Cambridge.
Stewart, A. 1990. *Greek Sculpture: An Exploration*. New Haven.
Stewart, O. 2017. '"I will speak ... with my whole person in ecstasy": instrumentality and independence in the *Sibylline Oracles*', in *Sibyls, Scriptures, and Scrolls: John Collins at Seventy*, II, eds J. Baden, H. Najman and E. Tigchelaar. Leiden, 1232–46.
Stockt, L. van der 2014. 'Compositional methods in the *Lives*', in Beck (ed.), 321–32.
Stray, C. 2015. 'A teutonic monster in Oxford: the making of Fraenkel's *Agamemnon*', in *Classical Commentaries*, eds C. Krauss and C. Stray. Oxford, 39–57.
Struck, P. 2004. *Birth of the Symbol: Ancient Readers at the Limits of Their Texts*. Princeton.
Sulimani, I. 2011. *Diodorus' Mythistory and the Pagan Mission: Historiography and Culture-heroes in the First Pentad of the Bibliotheke*. Leiden.
Susemihl, F. 1891–2. *Geschichte der griechischen Litteratur in der Alexandrinerzeit*, 2 vols. Leipzig.
Swain, S. 1989. 'Plutarch: chance, providence and history', *AJP* 110: 272–302.
  1996. *Hellenism and Empire: Language, Classicism, and Power in the Greek World AD 50–250*. Oxford.
  (ed.) 2000. *Dio Chrysostom. Politics, Letters, and Philosophy*. Oxford.
  2004. 'Bilingualism and biculturalism in Antonine Rome. Apuleius, Fronto, and Gellius', in *The Worlds of Aulus Gellius*, eds L. Holford-Strevens and A. Vardi. Oxford, 3–40.
Tacoma, L. E., and Tybout, R. A. 2016. 'Moving epigrams: migration and mobility in the Greek east', in *Migration and Mobility in the Early Roman Empire*, eds L. de Ligt and L. E. Tacoma. Studies in Global Social History 23. Leiden, 345–89.
Tait, J. G., and Preaux, C. (eds) 1955. *Greek Ostraca in the Bodleian Library at Oxford*, II: *Ostraca of the Roman and Byzantine Periods*. London.
Tatum, W. J. 2010. 'Another look at Tyche in Plutarch's Aemilius Paullus-Timoleon', *Historia* 59: 448–61.
Tavernini, N. 1953. *Dal libro decimo dell'Institutio Oratoria alle fonti tecnico-metodologiche di Quintiliano*. Turin.
Tellenbach, G. 1994. 'Ungeschehene Geschichte und ihre heuristische Funktion', *HZ* 258: 297–316.
Tetlock, P. E., and Belkin, A. (eds) 1996. *Counterfactual Thought Experiments in World Politics. Logical, Methodological, and Psychological Perspectives*. Princeton.
Thomas, R. 2019. *Polis Histories, Collective Memories and the Greek World*. Cambridge.

Thommen, L. 2012. *An Environmental History of Ancient Greece and Rome*, tr. P. Hill. Cambridge.
Titchener, F. B. 2014. 'Fate and Fortune', in Beck (ed.), 479–87.
Too, Y. L. (ed.) 2001. *Education in Greek and Roman Antiquity*. Leiden.
Touloumakos, J. 1971. *Zum Geschichtsbewußtsein der Griechen in der Zeit der römischen Herrschaft*. Göttingen.
Trapp, M. B. 1997. 'Philosophical sermons: the *Dialexeis* of Maximus of Tyre', *ANRW* 2.34.3, 1945–76.
  2007. *Philosophy in the Roman Empire: Ethics, Politics and Society*. Aldershot.
Trevisan, R. 2010. 'Un' eterogenea descrizione del mondo: i libri I–V della Biblioteca Storica di Diodoro Siculo', in *Linguaggi del Potere, Poteri del Linguaggio*, eds E. Bona and M. Curnis. Alessandria, 265–88.
Tsouni, G. 2019. *Antiochus and Peripatetic Ethics*. Cambridge.
Tueller, M. A. 2010. 'The passer-by in archaic and classical epigram', in *Archaic and Classical Epigram*, eds M. Baumbach, A. Petrovic and I. Petrovic. Cambridge, 42–60.
Ueding, G. (ed.) 1992–2015. *Historisches Wörterbuch der Rhetorik*, 12 vols. Tübingen.
Usener, H. 1889. *Dionysii Halicarnassensis librorum de imitatione reliquiae epistulaeque criticae duae*. Bonn.
Usher, M. D. 2020. *Plato's Pigs and Other Ruminations: Ancient Guides to Living with Nature*. Cambridge.
Usher, S. 1974. *Dionysius of Halicarnassus, The Critical Essays*, I. Cambridge, MA.
  1985. *Dionysius of Halicarnassus, The Critical Essays*, II. Cambridge, MA.
Valgimigli, M. 1912. *La critica letteraria di Dione Crisostomo*. Bologna.
Vanacker, W., and Zuiderhoek, A. (eds) 2017. *Imperial Identities in the Roman World*. London.
VanderKam, J. 2018. *Jubilees*, 2 vols. Minneapolis.
Vatri, A. 2020. 'The nature and perception of Attic prose rhythm', *CPh* 115: 467–85.
Versluys, M. J. 2017. *Visual Style and Constructing Identity in the Hellenistic World: Nemrud Dağ and Commagene under Antiochos I*. Cambridge.
Veyne, P. 1976. *Le pain et le cirque: sociologie historique d'un pluralisme politique*. Paris.
Vössing, K. (ed.) 2002. *Biographie und Prosopographie. Internationales Kolloquium zum 65. Geburtstag von A. R. Birley*. Düsseldorf.
Vogt, J. 1929. '*Orbis Romanus*, ein Beitrag zum Sprachgebrauch und zur Vorstellung des römischen Imperialismus', repr. in *Orbis. Ausgewählte Schriften zur Geschichte des Altertums*, eds F. Taeger and K. Christ. Freiburg 1960, 151–71.
Vogt, K. M. 2008. *Law, Reason, and the Cosmic City. Political Philosophy in the Early Stoa*. Oxford.
Vogt-Spira, G. 1992. *Dramaturgie des Zufalls. Tyche und Handeln in der Komödie Menanders*. Munich.
Volkmann, R. 1853. *De Oraculis Sibyllinis dissertatio: supplementum editionis a Friedliebio exhibitae*. PhD Diss. Leipzig.

Vretska, K. 1976. *C. Sallustius Crispus, De Catilinae coniuratione*, 2 vols. Heidelberg.
Walbank, F. W. 1948. 'The geography of Polybius', repr. in Walbank 2002, 31–52.
  1957. *A Historical Commentary on Polybius*, I. Oxford.
  1972. 'Some structural problems: time and place', in *Polybius*. Sather Classical Lectures 42. Berkeley, 97–129.
  1975. 'Symploke. Its role in Polybius' Histories', *YClS* 24: 197–212.
  1993. 'Η ΤΩΝ ΟΛΩΝ ΕΛΠΙΣ and the Antigonids', repr. in Walbank 2002, 127–36.
  2002. *Polybius, Rome and the Hellenistic World. Essays and Reflections*. Cambridge.
  2007. 'Fortune (tychē) in Polybius', in *A Companion to Greek and Roman Historiography*, II, ed. J. Marincola. London, 349–55.
Waldis, J. 1920. *Sprache und Stil der großen griechischen Inschrift vom Nemrud-Dagh in Kommagene (Nordsyrien)*. Heidelberg.
Waldmann, H. 1973. *Die kommagenischen Kultreformen unter König Mithradates I. Kallinikos und seinem Sohne Antiochus I*. Leiden.
Walker, S., and Cameron, A. (eds) 1989. *The Greek Renaissance in the Roman Empire*. London.
Wallace-Hadrill, A. 1998a. '*Mutatio morum*: the idea of a cultural revolution', in *The Roman Cultural Revolution*, eds T. Habinek and A. Schiesaro. Cambridge, 3–21.
  1998b. 'To be Roman, go Greek: thoughts on Hellenization at Rome', *BICS* 71: 79–91.
  2008. *Rome's Cultural Revolution*. Cambridge.
Walsh, J. J. 1996. 'Flamininus and the propaganda of liberation', *Historia* 45: 345–63.
Walter, J. 2017. 'Poseidon's wrath and the end of Helike: notions about the anthropogenic character of disasters in antiquity', in Schliephake (ed.), 31–43.
Walter, U. 2004. *Memoria und res publica. Zur Geschichtskultur im republikanischen Rom*. Frankfurt.
Walters, B. 2020. *The Deaths of the Republic: Imagery of the Body Politic in Ciceronian Rome*. Oxford.
Warf, B., and Arias, S. (eds) 2009. *The Spatial Turn. Interdisciplinary Perspectives*. Routledge Studies in Human Geography 26. London.
Warren, J. 2007. 'Diogenes Laertius, biographer of philosophy', in König and Whitmarsh (eds), 133–49.
Weaire, G. 2002. 'The relationship between Dionysius of Halicarnassus' *De imitatione* and *Epistula ad Pompeium*', *CPh* 97: 351–9.
Webb, R. 2006. 'The *Imagines* as a fictional text, *ekphrasis, apatê* and illusion', in *Le défi de l'art. Philostrate, Callistrate et l'image sophistique*, eds M. Costantini, F. Graziani and S. Rolet. Rennes: 113–36.
  2009. *Ekphrasis, Imagination and Persuasion in Ancient Rhetorical Theory and Practice*. Farnham.

2012. 'The nature and representation of competition in pantomime and mime', in Coleman and Nelis-Clément (eds), 221–60.
Webster, J., and Cooper, N. (eds) 1996. *Roman Imperialism: Post-Colonial Perspectives*. Leicester.
Weißenberger, M. 2002. 'Das Imperium Romanum in den Proömien dreier griechischer Historiker: Polybios, Dionysios von Halikarnassos und Appian', *RhM* N.F. 145: 262–81.
2012. Review of Wiater 2011, *Gnomon* 84: 588–91.
Welch, K. E. 2006. '*Domi militaeque*: Roman domestic aesthetics and war booty in the republic', in *Representations of War in Ancient Rome*, eds S. Dillon and K. E. Welch. Cambridge, 91–161.
West, M. L. 1997. *The East Face of Helicon: West Asiatic Elements in Greek Poetry and Myth*. Oxford.
1999. 'The invention of Homer', *CQ* 49: 364–82.
2010. *The Making of the Iliad: Disquisition and Analytical Commentary*. Oxford.
White, L., Jr. 1967. 'The historical roots of our ecologic crisis', *Science* 155: 1203–7.
Whitmarsh, T. 2001a. *Greek Literature and the Roman Empire: The Politics of Imitation*. Oxford.
2001b. '"Greece is the world": exile and identity in the Second Sophistic', in Goldhill (ed.), 269–305.
2005. *The Second Sophistic*. Oxford.
2008. *The Cambridge Companion to the Greek and Roman Novel*. Cambridge.
(ed.) 2010a. *Local Knowledge and Microidentities in the Imperial Greek World*. Cambridge.
2010b. 'Thinking Local', in Whitmarsh (ed.), 11–16.
2011. 'Greek poets and Roman patrons in the late Republic and early empire', in Schmitz and Wiater (eds), 197–212.
2013a. *Beyond the Second Sophistic: Adventures in Greek Postclassicism*. Berkeley.
2013b. 'The "invention of fiction"', in Whitmarsh 2013a, 11–34.
2013c. 'Politics and identity in Ezekiel's *Exagoge*', in Whitmarsh 2013a, 211–27.
2013d, 'Adventures of the Solymoi', in Whitmarsh 2013a, 228–47.
2017, 'Greece: Hellenistic and early imperial continuities', in Johnson and Richter (eds), 11–24.
2020. *Achilles Tatius. Leucippe and Clitophon. Books I–II*. Cambridge.
Whitmarsh, T., and Thomson, S. 2013. *The Romance between Greece and the East*. Cambridge.
Wiater, N. 2006a. 'Geschichte als imaginäres Museum. Zum Geschichtsmodell in Diodors *Bibliotheke*', *WJA* 30: 59–85.
2006b. 'Geschichtsschreibung und Kompilation. Diodors historiographische Arbeitsmethode und seine Vorstellungen von zeitgemäßer Geschichtsschreibung', *RhM* 149: 248–71.
2011. *The Ideology of Classicism: Language, History, and Identity in Dionysius of Halicarnassus*. Berlin.

2014a. 'Hellenistische Rhetorik', in Zimmermann and Rengakos (eds), 860–86.
2014b. *Dionysius von Halikarnass. Römische Frühgeschichte, I: Bücher 1 bis 3. Eingeleitet, übersetzt und kommentiert*. BGL 75. Stuttgart.
2016. 'Shifting endings, ambiguity and deferred closure in Polybius' *Histories*', in *Knowing Future Time in and through Historiography*, ed. A. Lianeri. Berlin, 243–65.
2017. 'The aesthetics of truth. Narrative and historical understanding in Polybius' *Histories*', in *Truth and History in the Ancient World. Pluralising the Past*, eds I. Ruffell and L. I. Hau. London, 202–25.
2018a. *Dionysius von Halikarnass. Römische Frühgeschichte, II: Bücher 4 bis 6. Eingeleitet, übersetzt und kommentiert*. BGL 85. Stuttgart.
2018b. 'Documents and narrative: reading the Roman-Carthaginian treaties in Polybius' *Histories*', in Miltsios and Tamiolaki (eds), 131–65.
2018c. 'Getting over Athens: re-writing Hellenicity in the *Early Roman History* of Dionysius of Halicarnassus', in Canevaro and Gray (eds), 209–35.
2019. 'Experiencing the past: language, time, and historical consciousness in Dionysian criticism', in Hunter and de Jonge (eds), 56–82.
Wiemer, H.-U. 2016. 'Römische Aristokraten oder griechische Honoratioren? Kontext und Adressaten der Verhaltenslehre des Stoikers Panaitios', *Chiron* 46: 1–45.
Wilamowitz-Möllendorff, U. 1900a. 'Asianismus und Atticismus', *Hermes* 35: 1–52.
1900b. 'Lesefrüchte LX', *Hermes* 35: 536–42.
1902. *Griechisches Lesebuch*. Berlin.
1922. *Pindaros*. Berlin.
Williams, R. 1977. *Marxism and Literature*. Oxford.
Winston, D. 1990. 'Judaism and hellenism: hidden tensions in Philo's thought', *StudPhilon* 2: 1–19.
Winterbottom, M. 1982. 'Cicero and the Silver Age', in *Éloquence et rhétorique chez Cicéron*, eds W. Stroh and W. Ludwig. Geneva, 237–74.
1983. 'Declamation, Greek and Latin', in *Ars Rhetorica antica e nuova*. Genoa, 57–76.
1988. 'Introduction', in *Sopatros the Rhetor. Studies in the Text of the Διαίρεσις Ζητημάτων*, eds D. Innes and M. Winterbottom. London, 1–20.
2011. 'On ancient prose rhythm: the story of the Dichoreus', in *Culture in Pieces. Essays on Ancient Texts in Honour of Peter Parsons*, eds D. Obbink and R. Rutherford. Oxford, 262–76.
Woelk, D. 1966. *Agatharchides von Knidos, Über das Rote Meer. Übersetzung und Kommentar*. Bamberg.
Wörrle, M. 1995. 'Vom tugendsamen Jüngling zum "gestreßten" Euergeten. Überlegungen zum Bürgerbild hellenistischer Ehrendekrete', in Wörrle and Zanker (eds), 241–50.
Wörrle, M., and Zanker, P. (eds) 1995. *Stadtbild und Bürgerbild im Hellenismus*. Munich.
Woerther, F. 2015. *Caecilius de Calè-Actè. Fragments et témoignages*. Paris.
Wolf, W. 2005. 'Metalepsis as a transgeneric and transmedial phenomenon. A case study of the possibilities of "exporting" narratological concepts', in

Narratology beyond Literary Criticism. Mediality, Disciplinarity, eds J. C. Meister, T. Kindt and W. Schernus. Berlin, 83–107.

Woolf, G. 2000 *Becoming Roman: The Origins of Provincial Civilization in Gaul*. Cambridge.

2006. 'Playing games with Greeks: one Roman on Greekness', in Konstan and Saïd (eds), 162–92.

Wooten, C. 1975. 'Le développement du style asiatique pendant l'époque hellénistique', *REG* 88: 94–104.

1987. *Hermogenes' On Types of Style*. Chapel Hill.

Worthington, I. 1994. 'The canon of the ten Attic orators', in *Persuasion: Greek Rhetoric in Action*, ed. I. Worthington. London, 244–63.

1999. *Dinarchus, Hyperides, edited and translated*. Greek Orators 2. Warminster.

Wright, W. C. 1921. *Philostratus, Lives of the Sophists; Eunapius, Lives of the Philosophers and Sophists*. Cambridge, MA.

Wyss, B., Hirsch-Luipold, R., and Hirschi, S.-J. (eds) 2017. *Sophisten in Hellenismus und Kaiserzeit*. Tübingen.

Yarrow, L. M. 2006. *Historiography at the End of the Republic. Provincial Perspectives on Roman Rule*. Oxford.

Young, R. J. C. 1990. *White Mythologies*. London.

1995. *Colonial Desire: Hybridity Theory, Culture and Race*. London.

2001. *Postcolonialism: An Historical Introduction*. Chichester.

Ypsilanti, M. 2010. 'Deserted Delos: a motif of the *Anthology* and its poetic and historical background', *GRBS* 50: 63–85.

2018. *The Epigrams of Crinagoras of Mytilene: Introduction, Text, Commentary*. Oxford.

Yunis, H. 2011. *Plato, Phaedrus*. Cambridge.

Zangara, A. 2007. *Voir l'histoire: théories anciennes du récit historique, IIe siècle avant J.-C.–IIe siècle après J.-C.* Paris.

Zarmakoupi, M. 2014. *Designing for Luxury on the Bay of Naples: Villas and Landscapes (c. 100 BCE–79 CE)*. Oxford.

Zeitlin, F. 2001. 'Visions and revisions of Homer', in Goldhill (ed.), 195–268.

Ziegler, K. 1952. 'Polybios', *RE* XXI, 1440–578.

Zimmermann, B., and Rengakos, A. (eds) 2011. *Handbuch der griechischen Literatur der Antike*, I: *Die Literatur der archaischen und klassischen Zeit*. HdA VII.1. Munich.

2014. *Handbuch der griechischen Literatur der Antike*, II: *Die Literatur der klassischen und hellenistischen Zeit*. HdA VII.2. Munich.

Zinserling, G. 1959–60. 'Studien zu den Historiendarstellungen der römischen Republik', *Wissenschaftliche Zeitschrift der Friedrich-Schiller-Universität Jena, Gesellschafts- und sprachwissenschaftliche Reihe* 9: 403–48.

Ziolkowski, A. 1992. *The Temples of Mid-Republican Rome and their Historical and Topographical Context*. Rome.

Zucker, F. 1956. 'Der Stil des Gorgias nach seiner inneren Form', *Sitzungsberichte der Deutschen Akademie der Wissenschaften zu Berlin* 1: 3–19.

Index Locorum

Aelian
  Varia Historia 13.22, 183
Aelius Aristides
  On Rome
    36, 220
    60, 220
    100–1, 130
  Panathenaicus 13.98 Jebb, 220
Aëtius
  I, Pr. 2 = II 35 SVF, 244
  I 27.5 = I 176 SVF, 246
Agatharchides
  On the Red Sea
    GGM I, 120, ll. 4–5, 292
    GGM I, 120, ll. 12–14, 292
    GGM I, 120, ll. 35–42, 295
    GGM I, 121, ll. 4–5, 292
Alpheus
  Anth. Pal. 9.101, 74
Anthologia Palatina
  1.22, 200
  4.2.5–6, 70
  5.132.7–8, 78
  6.161, 80
  7.17, 84
  7.376.3–6, 81
  7.741, 82
  9.58, 89
  9.101, 74
  9.122.1–2, 86
  9.178, 78
  9.216, 85
  9.250, 74
  9.283, 91
  9.284, 71
  9.288, 87
  9.419, 90
  9.423, 74
  9.550, 74
  9.553, 88
  9.559, 76
  9.561.1–6, 90
Antipater
  Anth. Pal. 9.58, 89
Antiphilus
  Anth. Pal. 9.178, 79
Apollonius of Athens
  ap. Philostr. *VS* 2.58.2–3 = II.20, 601–2, 283
Appian
  1.pr.1, 47
Aristophanes
  Knights 31, 187
Aristotle
  De anima 474a14, 55
  Nicomachean Ethics 1152b1–3, 168
  Poetics 1459a17–18, 43
  Politics 1280b31–40, 168
Artemidorus of Ephesus
  Geographoumena Col. 1, 13–15, 239
Aulus Gellius
  2.21.4, 78
Bianor
  Anth. Pal. 9.423, 74
Cassius Dio
  21.2, 49
  37.21.2, 48
  43.14.6, 49
  62.16, 131
  62.18.3, 188
Cicero
  Brutus
    51, 221
    314–16, 221
    325–7, 221
    226, 310
  De domo sua 124, 45
  De finibus
    5.1, 226
    5.1.1, 213
    5.1.2, 214
    5.1.3, 214–15
    5.2.4, 216

Cicero (cont.)
  5.2.5, 216
  5.3, 226
  De lege agraria
    1.26, 45
    3.4, 45
  De natura deorum 2.133, 248
  De officiis 1.85, 38
  Epistulae ad Atticum 8.1.1, 38
  Epistulae ad familiares 5.12.4–5, 109
  Epistulae ad Quintum fratrem 2.15.4, 110
  In Catilinam 1.31, 45
  Orationes Philippicae 8.15–16, 38
  Orator
    25, 221
    27, 221
    28, 222
    212, 221
    230–1, 221
  Pro Archia
    23, 228
    30, 228
  Pro lege Manilia 17, 45
  Tusculanae disputationes 1.79, 232
Crinagoras
  Anth. Pal.
    6.161, 80
    7.376.3–6, 81
    7.741, 82
    9.283, 91
    9.284, 71
    9.419, 90
    9.559, 76
Dio Chrysostom
  18.1, 327, 330
  18.5, 327
  18.6, 330, 333
  18.6–8, 332
  18.7, 334
  18.10, 338, 340
  18.11, 346
  18.12, 347–8
  18.13, 348
  18.13–17, 339, 344
  18.14, 341, 343
  18.15, 342
  18.16, 329, 342
  18.17, 329
  18.18, 350
Diodorus Siculus
  1.1.1, 158
  1.1.1–2, 111
  1.1.3, 157, 164
  1.1.4–5, 162
  1.2.1–3, 239

  1.4.4, 238
  1.51.5, 142
  1.51.5–6, 126
  1.51.7, 137
  1.56.2, 137
  1.57.1–3, 137
  2.13.5, 143
  2.7.2, 138
  2.9, 138
  3.38.4–6, 95
  3.38–48, 94–5, 101, 117
  3.39.1, 96
  3.39.4–6, 97, 104
  3.39.5, 98
  3.40.2–3, 98, 106
  3.40.4–8, 107
  3.44.4–5, 107, 112
  3.44.7–8, 99
  4.19.3, 143
  4.66, 201
  11.2.4, 141
  11.3.6, 141
  11.5.1, 141
  13.47.4, 143
  14.49.3, 143
  14.51.1, 144
  17.40.5, 144
  17.41.1, 144
  17.41.2, 144
  17.41.5–6, 144
  17.42.6, 145
Diogenes Laertius
  1.1, 244
  7.155, 248
Dionysius of Halicarnassus
  De compositione verborum
    4.11, 296
    4.16–20, 233
    18.26, 296
  Letter to Ammaeus 1.6, 233
  Letter to Pompeius
    3.1, 323
    3.2–15, 339
    3.2–6.11, 338
    3.16–21, 339
    4.1–3, 339–40
    4.3, 341
    4.4, 340–1
    5, 340
    6, 340
  On Demosthenes
    6, 233
    8.4, 346
  On Imitation 6, 233
    1.2–3, 323

1.4, 324
2.1, 332
2.10, 325, 332
2.11–13, 333
2.2, 325
3.1–12, 338
3.2, 325
3.3, 325
4.1–3, 344
4.2, 344
5.1–7, 345
5.2, 325
5.4, 346
fr. 1, 325
fr. 7, 338
On the Ancient Orators
   1, 221
   1.1–7, 347
   1.2, 25
   1–2, 237
   2.2, 25
   4.5, 345
On Thucydides 1.1, 323, 325
Roman Antiquities
   1.1.1, 238
   1.2.1, 238
   1.3.3, 238
   1.5.1, 212, 238–9
   1.8.4, 238
   1.89.2, 217, 219
Duris of Samos
   FGrH 76 F 14, 50
Euenus
   Anth. Pal. 9.122.1–2, 86
Eusebius
   Praeparatio evangelica 13.12.13, 205
Galen
   The Best Doctor Is Also a Philosopher (*Med.Phil.*)
     1, 53 K, 240
     1, 59–60 K, 240
     1, 60–1 K, 240
Geminus
   Anth. Pal. 9.288, 87
Gorgias of Leontini
   Encomium to Helen (82 B 11 D-K = 32 D 24 Most-Laks)
     4, 292
     7, 279
   Funeral Oration
     82 B 6 D-K = 32 D 28 Most-Laks, 281, 293
Hadrian of Tyre
   ap. Philostr. *VS* 2.43.1 = II.10, 590, 316
Hegesias of Magnesia (FGrH 142)
   F 5, 296

F 6, 292
F 7, 292
F 12, 295
F 14, 292
F 24, 294
Herodes Atticus
   ap. Philostr. *VS* 2.18.3 = II.1, 564, 316
Herodotus
   1.82, 82
   1.174, 125
   3.60, 125
   3.117, 125
   4.33, 75
   6.44, 126
   7.22, 126
   7.23, 127
   7.24, 126
   7.35, 127
   7.37, 127
   7.130, 127
   7.131, 127
   7.143.1, 265
Hesiod
   Theogony
     22–8, 209
     517–19, 37
   Works and Days 650–1, 73
Homer
   Iliad
     2.484–92, 209
     6.357–8, 198
     8.19–26, 37
   Homeric Hymn to Apollo (3)
     166–72, 190
   Homeric Hymn to Artemis (9)
     1–4, 200
Honestus
   Anth. Pal.
     9.216, 85
     9.250, 74
Horace
   Epistles 2.1, 156–7, 358
   Odes
     4.15.14–15, 37
     4.15.21–4, 37
Inscriptions
   FD III 4.77, ll. 24–6, 159
   I.Iasos 98, 162
   I.Mylasa 109, ll. 4–10, 169
   I.Priene[2]
     68, ll. 13–14, 165
     68, ll. 73–6, 166
     69, ll. 55–6, 171
     69, ll. 63–7, 172
   I.Sestos 1, ll. 1–10, 160

Inscriptions (cont.)
  IG II² 1011, ll. 42–3, 159
  IG v.2.268, 277
  IG v.2.268 ll. 32–42, 308–9
  IG VII.4148, ll. 5–6, 159
  IGRom. IV, 1540, 189
  ILLRP 454, 65
  IOSPE I² 39 (Olbia), ll. 36–9, 164
  OGIS 383, 277, 309–11
  Robert and Robert 1954, 11
    no. 167, ll. 28–30, 159
  SEG 26.821, 277, 305–7
Isaeus of Assyria
  ap. Philostr. *VS* 1.50.5 = 1.20, 514, 278
Isocrates
  Panegyricus 34.7 , 220
Josephus
  Jewish Antiquities 12.11–118, 363
Lactantius
  Divine Institutes 1.6.9, 189
Laurea
  Anth. Pal. 7.17, 84
Livy
  21.21.9, 61
  41.28.8–10, 52
Lucian
  De mercede conductis 42, 117
  Imagines 9, 117
  Verae historiae
    2.20, 184
    2.24, 202
    2.25, 197
Manilius
  Astronomica 3.19–21, 128
Marcus Aurelius
  Meditations 12.14, 249
Menander fr. 191 K-A, 270
Nonnus
  Dionysiaca
    40.319–22, 356
    42.181, 209
Onomarchus of Andros
  ap. Philostr. *VS*
    2.54.1 = 11.18, 598, 286
    2.54.2–4 = 11.18, 599, 286
Ovid
  Fasti 2.684, 37
  Tristia
    2.211–12, 36
    2.215–18, 36
    2.219–34, 36
Pausanias
  8.33.2, 74
  10.12.2, 188
  10.12.3, 188

  10.12.6, 188
  10.12.7, 188
Philip of Thessalonica
  Anth. Pal.
    4.2.5–6, 70
    9.561.1–6, 90
Philo
  Life of Moses
    2.37, 362
    2.41, 362
  On Dreams 2.117–19, 128
Philodemus
  Anth. Pal. 5.132.7–8, 78
Philostratus of Athens
  Lives of the Sophists
    1.pr., 480–1, 23
    1 pr., 481, 115
    1.45.1 = 1.19, 511, 24–5, 316
    1.50.2, 278
    1.50.5 = 1.20, 514, 278
    1.55.5 = 1.21, 518, 316
    2.18.3 = 11.1, 564, 316
    2.43.1 = 11.10, 590, 316
    2.47.4 = 11.12, 593, 280
    2.47.5–6 = 11.12, 593, 284
    2.54.1 = 11.18, 598, 286
    2.54.2–4 = 11.18, 599, 286
    2.58.2–3 = 11.20, 601–2, 283
    2.61.3 = 11.21, 604, 316
Philostratus the Elder
  Imagines
    pr. 4–5, 101
    2.17, 94
    2.17.1, 101
    2.17.4, 103
    2.17.5, 104, 106, 112
    2.17.12, 103, 113
Plato
  Hippias Minor 365b, 201
  Phaedrus
    244b, 187
    264c2–5, 42
  Republic 353e7–354a9, 169
Pliny the Elder
  Natural History
    6.44–5, 61
    6.61–3, 61
Plutarch
  De cohibenda ira 455e, 130
  De defectu oraculorum 410 a, 93
  De facie in orbe lunae 927 a–b, 248
  De fortuna Alexandri
    336d, 269
    339a, 269

Index Locorum 407

340–5, 269
341e–f, 270
De Pythiae oraculis 397a, 187
Life of Alexander
  20.1, 259
  20.2–3, 259
  45.5, 257
  49.2–4, 258
  62.1–9, 262
Life of Antony 33.2–3, 260
Life of Caesar
  37.5–8, 262
  63, 257
  66, 257
Life of Coriolanus 1.2, 261
Life of Fabius
  2.4–7, 263
Life of Pericles
  18.1, 263
  22.1, 263
Life of Pompey 1.1–2, 261
Life of Sulla 13.1, 218
Quaestiones convivales
  1.1, 613b, 246
  7.8, 712b, 337
  8.2, 718b–c, 116
Pollux of Naucratis
  ap. Philostr. *VS*
  2.47.4= II.12, 593, 280
  2.47.5–6 = II.12, 593, 284
Polybius
  1.1.5, 44
  1.1.6, 41
  1.2.1–7, 44
  1.3.1–2, 55
  1.3.4, 42, 44, 55
  1.4.1, 41
  1.4.2–3, 41
  1.4.6, 41
  1.4.7, 41, 44
  1.4.8, 44
  1.69.4–5, 265
  2.56, 271
  3.9.8, 267
  3.35.7–8, 56
  3.36.1–5, 56
  3.37.6, 56, 63
  3.37.7, 56
  3.37.9, 56, 63
  3.37.10, 63
  3.37.11, 57, 62
  3.38.2, 57, 63
  3.38.7–8, 58
  3.39.2–5, 57
  3.39.4, 58, 60

3.39.8, 63
3.39.9, 57–8
3.39.10, 57–8
3.39.11, 57–8
3.39.12, 58
3.40.1, 58
3.42.1, 58
3.58.2, 63
3.59.3–4, 63
4.40.2, 75
5.35–7, 265
5.101.10, 62
8.11.3–6, 5
9.9.9–10, 269
9.12.1, 270
16.28.2, 270
36.12, 238
Posidonius
  Fr. 18 Edelstein-Kidd, 245
  Fr. 90 Edelstein-Kidd, 245
  Fr. 103 Edelstein-Kidd, 248
Proclus of Naucratis
  ap. Philostr. *VS* 2.61.3 = II.21, 604, 316
Pseudo-Alcaeus
  Anth. Pal. 1.22, 200
Quintilian
  10.1.19, 334
  10.1.46–84, 331
  10.1.54, 321
  10.1.67–8, 336
  10.1.69, 336
  10.1.73–5, 338
  10.1.76, 346
  10.1.76–80, 345
  10.1.77, 346
  10.1.81–4, 344
  10.1.82, 338, 342
  10.3.19–21, 350
Scopelian of Clazomenae
  ap. Philostr. *VS* 1.55.5 = 1.21, 518, 316
Sextus Empiricus
  Adversus mathematicos 11.170, 245
  Outlines of Pyrrhonism 3.239–41, 245
Sibylline Oracles
  3.350–80, 195
  3.388–400, 195
  3.401–10, 195
  3.410, 196
  3.410–18, 196
  3.412, 196
  3.414, 197
  3.419, 198–9
  3.419–32, 179, 198
  3.420, 199

Sibylline Oracles (cont.)
  3.421–2, 202
  3.423, 199, 202
  3.423–4, 200
  3.424–5, 201
  3.426–30, 202
  3.429, 203
  3.432, 204
  3.545–50, 203
  3.774, 198
  3.809–29, 206
  3.813, 207
  3.823–8, 208
Statius
  Silvae 2.2.54–9, 130
Stobaeus
  Eclogues 2.7.5^{b10}, 245
Strabo
  1.1.1, 238, 240–2
  1.1.2–10, 241
  1.1.4, 243
  1.1.12–15, 242, 245
  1.1.15, 242
  1.1.16, 242
  1.1.17, 242
  1.1.18, 167–8
  1.1.21, 243
  1.2.3, 173, 244
  1.2.34, 244
  1.4.3, 241
  2.3.5, 242
  2.3.8, 244
  2.4.7, 56
  2.5.2, 245
  2.5.8, 241–2
  2.5.34, 243
  3.2.8–11, 134
  3.9.6, 93
  4.4.4, 243
  5.3.8, 247, 249
  6.4.1, 76
  7.F15a, 134
  8.6.23, 72
  9.1.16, 294
  12.3.16, 233
  13.1.54, 218, 233, 236
  14.1.41, 291
  14.1.48, 235
  14.5.4, 233, 235
  14.5.12–15, 169
  14.5.13, 236
  14.5.14, 235
  14.5.15, 237
  14.6.5, 134
  15.1.59, 243
  15.1.70, 243
  16.1.6, 243
  16.1.9–11, 134
  16.1.11, 134
  16.2.24, 233
  16.4.27, 244
  17.1.3, 243
  17.1.36, 248–9
  17.1.46, 243
SVF
  I 176, 246
  II 35, 244
Theocritus
  Idyll 15, 355
Thucydides
  1.22.4, 340
  2.37.1, 220
Virgil
  Aeneid 6.854–92, 79
Vitruvius
  On Architecture
    1.1.3, 239
    1.1.7–10, 239
Xenophon
  Anabasis 3.1.4, 259, 265

General Index

Achilles, 178, 184, 201, 203
Achilles Tatius, 276, 317, 356
Actium, 7, 19, 88
Aelian, 183, 317
Aelius Aristides, 130, 220, 289, 358, *See also* Pseudo-Aelius Aristides
Aeschines, 23, 219, 319, 322–4, 345–8, 350
Aeschylus, 82–4, 322, 325, 332–8, 342, 349–50, 353
  Agamemnon, 351
  Persians, 128
Agatharchides, 4, 95, 292, 295
Alcaeus, 200, 325, 332, *See also* Pseudo-Alcaeus
Alexander the Great, 51, 61–4, 66, 68–9, 74, 89, 132, 134–5, 144–5, 183, 195, 257–9, 262–3, 269–70, 295–7
  in historiography, 27
  in periodisation, 7–8, 347
Alexandria, 98, 178, 181–3, 192, 231, 357, 362–3
  as cultural centre, 20, 150, 156, 169, 234–7
Alexandrian Jews, 17–18, 194, 204, 357, 361, 365
Alexandrian literature, 2–3, 6–8, 14, 31, 184, 209, 321, 353
Alps, 32, 57–8, 90–1, 139, 143
Anacreon, 84
Anaximander, 240
Andocides, 345
Androcottus, 262
Antimachus, 332
Antiochus I, 309
Antiochus III, 264
Antipater, 74–5, 89
Antiphilus, 79
Antiphon, 345
antithesis, 280, 282, 284, 288, 292–7, 307, 311–12, 314–15
Antony, 88, 170, 227, 260, 266
Apellicon of Teos, 218, 233
Apollonius of Athens, 277, 282–4

Apollonius of Rhodes, 332, 353
Appian, 47–8
Aratus, 332
Archelaos relief, 181–3, 186, 199, 201–2, 210
  representation of *Oikoumene*, 50
  representation of Poetry, 185
Archilochus, 332
architecture, Roman, 51–3
Argos, 183
Aristarchus, 321
Aristobulus, 204–5, 210
Aristophanes, 9, 84, 187, 207, 319, 332
Aristophanes of Byzantium, 321
Aristotle, 7, 55, 153, 167–8, 218, 231–3, 236, 344
  Aporemata Homerica, 194
  Poetics, 42–4, 46
Arsinoe III, 51, 62
Artapanus, 18
Artemidorus of Ephesus, 239
Asia Minor, 125, 133, 160, 165, 169, 188–9, 192, 231, 233–4, 236–7, 250, 320, 328, 359
Asianism, 24–6, 33, 222, 277, 289, 291, 313–18
  definitions of, 273–7, 289–90
  imperial, 303–5
  late Hellenistic, 301–3, 305–13
Athens, 2, 17, 22–3, 26–7, 86, 168–9, 231–2, 234–6, 278, 316, 353
  as geographical epithet, 84
  cultural representations of, 45, 155, 211–12, 294–6, 357–8
  sack of Athens, 150, 213, 231
Athos, Mt, 126–7, 130, 134–5, 140–2
Atilius Calatinus, 52
Atlas, 37
Atticism, 25–6, 33, 211–12, 215–17, 219–22, 227, 229, 273, 275, 345–8
Atticus. *See* Pomponius Atticus, Titus
Augustan literature, 1–2, 22, 119, 319, 323, 332, 338

409

Augustus, 2, 7, 32, 36–8, 47–9, 72–3, 79, 88, 90–1, 132–3, 146, 187, 226–7, 229, 235, 260
    Res Gestae, 48
Aulus Gellius, 78

Babylon, 138, 183, 195, 284
Baetis, 296
Baiae, 130
Batrachomyomachia, 182, 185
beauty, 246
    aesthetic pleasure of unity, 42–5
    of language, 323–6, 340, 342, 346, 349
benefaction, 119, 132, 134, 137–44, 146, 151–2, 158–65, 170–1, 174–5
Bergk, Theodor, 8
Berlin, Isaiah, 253
Bernhardy, Gottfried, 8
Bible, 194, 205
biography, 27–9, 352
blindness, 178, 190, 199
body metaphor, 36–47, 54–5, 66–8, 89
Buitenwerf, Rieuwerd, 193, 197, 207
burial, 81, 189

Caecilius of Caleacte, 345
Caesar, 8, 49–51, 72–3, 110, 132, 138–9, 170, 217, 256, 260, 262–3, 269
Caligula, 88, 130, 361, 364
Callimachus, 332, 364
    Pinakes, 84
Campania, 78, 129
canals, 126–7, 134–5, 137, 142, 355
canon formation, 26–7, 33, 84, 212, 219–25, 228–9, 325, 345, 360
Capua, 64–5
Carneades, 216
Carthage, 100, 265
    expansion of power, 57–8, 61, 66, 68
    war with Rome, 52, 55, 267
Cassius Dio, 48, 130–1, 188
cataracts, 134–5
Catullus, 78
    Poem 65, 224
centre and periphery, 33, 37, 65, 69, 89–93, 150, 156, 231, 236
Chaeronea, 87–8
Chariton, 303, 313
Charmuthas, 99–100
Chios, 178, 183, 190, 199–200
Christian literature, 10, 210, 357, 363
Christianity, early, 122, 180
Cicero, 23, 109–10, 212, 220, 223
    and Asianism, 310, 313
    and Atticism, 17, 221–2, 357–8

body metaphor, 38–9, 44–6
De finibus, 156, 212–18, 225–7, 229–30
De officiis, 153
    on prose style, 290–1, 301–3, 344
    Pro Archia, 227–9
    Tusculan Disputations, 224–5
Circe, 206, 208
citizenship, 154, 165, 170
    cultural citizenship, 212, 227–9
cityscape, Roman, 32, 52–4, 68
civic rhetoric, 152–3, 155, 164, 175
clarity (of language), 325
Clark, Timothy, 123
classicism, 22–3, 26, 28, 33–4, 219, 221, 231–4, 276–8, 289, 316–17, 320, 348–9
Clement of Alexandria, 353
Cleombrotus of Sparta, 93
Clitarchus, 338
closure, 251–3
Cnidos, 125
Coates, Peter, 122
Columns of Heracles, 56–7, 60
comedy, 333–5, 338, 353
    personification of, 181
Conon, 347
continuity between late Hellenistic and imperial texts, 14, 19, 23, 26–9, 256, 263, 272, 313, 316–17, 320
Corcyra, 76–7
Corinth, 71–3, 83
Coriolanus, 261, 269
corpus imperii, 32, 36–8, 44–7
corpus rei publicae, 38, 44, 46
cosmopolitanism, 28, 149–77, 356
counterfactuals, 61, 197, 261, 266–8
Cratinus, 332
Crinagoras, 71–3, 76–7, 79–82, 89–92
cross-cultural interaction, 17, 30, 195, 228, 231, 236, 357–8, 361–5
Curia Hostilia, 214
Cyclades, 76–7, 234
Cynics, 156, 172
Cyprus, 134

danger, 81, 97–8, 101, 106–9, 111–14
Darius, 61, 259, 266
death, 98, 108, 110
declamation, 183, 272, 278, 281–4, 317
decrees, honorific, 4, 151, 154–5, 158–66, 169–72, 174–6
Delos, 74–5, 83, 188
Delphi, 89, 93, 125, 159, 188, 201, 285
Demetrius of Phalerum, 60, 345
Demetrius Poliorcetes, 62

General Index

Demosthenes, 216–17, 219, 278, 284, 289, 298–300, 316, 319, 322, 325, 345–8
determinism, 252–7, 260–3, 267–9, 271
dialogue, 116, 354, 363–4
   between late Hellenistic and imperial texts, 19–20, 27–9, 73, 94, 117–18, 180–1, 263
   between late Hellenistic Greek literature and Latin literature, 13–14, 38–9, 359
   between late Hellenistic texts, 12–14, 119, 149, 212
   definitions of, 14–17
Dinarchus, 38, 45
Dio Chrysostom, 1, 21, 26, 29–30, 183, 276–8, 289, 316–17, 319–23
   On Training for Public Speaking, 326–50
   Trojan Oration, 184, 197
Diodorus Siculus, 12, 15, 18, 21, 28, 31–4, 201, 225–6, 238–9, 242–3, 247, 314, 355–6, 358
   and classicism, 22, 220
   cosmopolitanism, 150–1, 155, 157–66, 168, 171, 176–7
   experientiality of literature, 106–7, 111–13, 117
   generic inventiveness, 94–101
   representations of landscape alteration, 119, 124, 131–3, 135–47
Dionysius of Halicarnassus, 4, 12, 15, 153, 173, 232–3, 237–8
   and classicism, 219, 225–8, 289, 319–20
   and Rome, 9, 22, 34, 218
   civic virtues, 154
   On Imitation, 320–7, 330–50
   on prose style, 30, 291, 296
   On the Ancient Orators, 24–7, 221, 237
   Panegyricus, 219
   providence, 247, 249
   Roman Antiquities, 212, 217
Dionysius of Syracuse, 143–4
Dionysius Periegetes, 69
distances, 57–68, 73–4, 81–2, 96
diversity of Hellenistic literary production, 1–7
divine will, 124–5, 131, 144, 203
Domitian, 320
Dover, Kenneth, 8
Droysen, Johann Gustav, 7–10
Duilius, 52
Duris of Samos, 50, 347

ecocriticism, 120–1, 123, 130, 146–7
ecphrasis, 94, 102–3, 113–15, 117, 355–6, 361
education. *See paideia*
Egypt, 93, 97, 137, 139, 183, 192, 237, 247, 249
emotion, 78, 86–7, 93, 107, 113, 166, 175, 218, 221, 224, 332–3, 339, 356

encomium
   Mantineia inscription, 151, 301–3, 308–11
   of Isis, 301–3, 305–11
encyclopaedism, 136, 146
energeia, 39–40, 42–5, 51, 54–5, 67–8
engineering, 124, 129–30, 133–6, 140, 142–4
environmental humanities, 32–3, 120–3
environmental justice, 123, 125
Ephesus, 172
Ephorus, 5, 338
epic, 29, 43, 185, 332
Epicureans, 4
Epicurus, 215–16, 318
epigrams, 30, 32–4, 70–92, 189, 198, 200, 355
Eratosthenes, 134, 173, 240–1
Erythrae, 188, 207
Ethiopia, 94
Euenus, 85
Euphorion, 332
Eupolemus, 18, 193
Eupolis, 332
Euripides, 8, 26, 116, 197, 219, 319, 322, 328–9, 332–8, 342, 349–50, 353
expansion of Roman power, 39, 47, 51
experientiality, 109–14, 117, 214, 218, 221, 266, 353, 360
Ezekiel (poet), 18, 193

Fabius Maximus, 263
Fabius Pictor, 5
fandom, 212, 223–5, 228–30
fate, 85, 246, 248–9, 260,
   See also determinism, *tyche*
Favorinus, 276, 317
Flavian literature, 320, 323, 332, 338, 350
fortune, 110, 260, 269–70
Fraenkel, Eduard, 351
freedom, 157, 348
   loss of, 88
Frontinus, 343

Galen, 240, 246
Geminus (poet), 87–8
genre
   categorisation, 31, 34
   inventiveness, 6, 23, 27, 101
geography, 30, 34, 94, 101, 104, 150
   representation in epigram, 70–92
global level. *See* local and global perspectives
globalisation, 8, 69, *See also* local and global perspectives
Gorgianic figures, 280, 282, 288, 290–8, 300, 305, 307–18

Gorgias of Leontini, 23–4, 272–3, 278, 289, 305, 313, 318, 342
  Encomium to Helen, 197, 277, 279–80
  Funeral Oration, 277, 281–2
Gracchus, Tiberius Sempronius, 52–3
grandeur (of language), 325, 332–3, 336, 339–40, 344, 349, 356
Greek language, 362
Gutzwiller, Kathryn, 3

Hadrian of Tyre, 313, 316–17
Hamilcar, 267
Hannibal, 32, 39–40, 55–64, 66–8, 263
harbours, 96, 99–100, 108, 355–6
Hebrew, 205, 362
Hebrew Bible, 203
Hecataeus, 240
Hector, 184, 203
Hegesias of Magnesia, 277, 289–317
Helen, 184, 188, 197–9, 203, 324
Hellenismus, 8
Hellenistic literature, late, 1–2
  definitions of, 6–7, 10–11
  periodisation, 7–12
  prose, 3–4, 149–50, 153, 181–6, 273, 359–61
  verse, 2–3, 12, 29, 185, 363
Hellespont, 127–8, 130–1, 141, 145
Heracles, 37, 62, 138
  Temple of Heracles, 62
  via Heraclea, 61, 139, 143
Heraclitus, 187–8, 192
Hermogenes of Tarsus, 289
  On Types of Style, 321, 343
Herodes Atticus, 316–17
Herodotus, 75, 82, 124–8, 132, 141, 143, 197, 219, 238, 265–7, 319, 321, 325, 338–42, 349–50
Hesiod, 73, 205, 325, 332
  Theogony, 209
hexameter, 170, 178, 180, 182, 188, 193, 209, 300, 363
hindsight (narrative), 252–4
historiography, 4–5, 27, 42, 101, 109–12, 118, 156, 158, 252, 256, 266–7, 271, 322, 332, 339
Homer, 26, 178, 209, 243, 265, 322, 328, 332, 334–5, 337–8, 357, 363
  biographical tradition, 198, 200, 204
  birthplace, 179, 199
  Iliad, 37, 181, 184–5, 190, 197, 202
  mortality, 199, 205
  Odyssey, 77, 181, 184–5, 190, 197, 202
  on geography, 240–1
  reception of, 29, 179–86, 190–9
Honestus, 85
Horace, 37, 229, 358, 364

Hughes, J. Donald, 122
hybris, 32, 119, 124, 128, 133, 141, 144–6
Hyperboreans, 74–5
Hyperides, 38, 45, 324, 345–6

identification, 212, 218, 222, 226–30
imagination, 92, 108–10, 114, 218, 223, 230
imitation, 43, 173, 224, 232, 295, 319, 324
India, 209, 243, 262
inscriptions, 4–5, 17, 31–2, 34, 39–40, 51–3, 65, 67, 151–3, 155–6, 170, 173, 176–7, 277, 318, 356–7
'Asianist', 301–3, 305–13
intermediality, 31, 102, 106, *See also* mediality
intertextuality, 15, *See also* dialogue
intratextuality, 30, 119, 121, 146
Ionia, 183
Isaeus of Assyria, 278–9
Isocrates, 128, 219–20, 227, 284, 298–300, 324, 345–6
Isthmus of Corinth, 131
Italy, 38, 42, 55–8, 60–4, 68, 75–7, 79–80, 93, 129, 133
Ithaca, 80
itineraries, 65–7

Jerome, 363
Jerusalem, 361–2
Jewish literature, 10, 17–19, 179–81, 186, 189–91, 204–5, 208–10, 357, 361–5
John of Gaza, 356
Josephus, 10, 131, 303, 363

Kim, Lawrence, 184, 201, 334
kleos, 91, 197–8
König, Jason, 116

labour force, 140, 143–4, 146
Lactantius, 188
landscape, 73, 86–9, 247
landscape alteration, 29, 32–3, 40, 89, 119, 121, 123–48
  continuity of narrative, 122, 141
Laqueur, Richard, 8
Laurea, 83–4
Lesbos, 81, 102–3
Letter of Aristeas, 17, 194, 361, 363
libraries, 218, 236
lieux de mémoire, 32, 86–9
Lightfoot, Jane, 180
Livy, 62, 223
local and global perspectives, 30–3, 40–1, 46, 59, 61–2, 64, 68, 70, 123–4, 132, 147, 149, 220, 229, 238, *See also* centre and periphery
Longinus, 343–4, 348

General Index

Longus, 276, 313, 317
Lucian, 28–9, 183, 186, 276, 289, 316, 331, 355, 364
   De mercede conductis, 116–17
   Imagines, 117
   On the Hall, 317
   Pro imaginibus, 117
   True Histories, 184, 197, 199–204, 210
Lucius Verus, 189
Lucullus, 129
Lycurgus, 324, 345–6
lying, 178, 201, 206, 209
lyric, 84, 325, 332
Lysias, 128, 278, 298, 316, 324–5, 345–7

Magnesia, 172
Malinowski, Bronisław, 352
Manilius, 128
Mantineia. *See* encomium, Mantineia inscription
Marcellus, Marcus Claudius, 79–80, 235
Marcus Aurelius, 232, 249
Marías, Javier, 253
Mark Antony. *See* Antony
Maximus of Tyre, 184, 276, 313, 317
mediality, 94, 100, 103, 112, 115, 118, *See also* intermediality
medicine, 239–40, 358
Mediterranean, 5, 11, 32, 44, 56–7, 62, 73, 77, 89, 104, 120, 122, 132, 138, 146, 149, 154, 156–7, 166, 176, 183, 211, 220
Melanion (ephebarch), 160–2
Meleager, 70
Menander, 26, 270–1, 319, 322, 332–8, 342, 349–50
Menelaus, 197, 269
Menippus of Pergamum, 270–1
mental maps, 30, 32–3, 52–3, 73, 354–5
metalepsis, 103, 106, 115–17
metapoetics, 198
migration, 236
milestones, 32, 40, 60, 63–8, 89
Miletus, 172
mimesis. *See* imitation
mining, 133–4
miscellanism. *See* encyclopaedism
Mithridatic Wars, 20, 195, 213
monotheism, 204, 208
Morson, Gary Saul, 252–6
Moses, 204–5
mountains, 75, 96–7, 99, 104–5, 108, 119, 125, 127, 129–30, 133, 137, 139, 142, 145, 259, *See also* Alps, Athos, Mt, Pyrenees
Muses, 208–9, 347
Mycenae, 74

myth, 75, 79, 84–6, 93, 105–6, 138–43, 146, 189, 196–7
Mytilene, 84–5

narrator, overt, 98, 101–2
Neleus, 218
Nemrud Dağ, 277, 302–4, 309–12, 315–17
Nero, 24, 79
Nerva, 320, 327–9
Nicander, 332
Nicetes of Smyrna, 23, 316, 348
Nicolaus of Damascus, 11, 220, 347
Nicopolis, 88
Nietzsche, Friedrich, 354
Niketes of Smyrna. *See* Nicetes of Smyrna
Noah, 208–9
Nonnus
   Dionysiaca, 209–10, 356
Nora, Pierre. *See* lieux de mémoire
Norden, Eduard, 273–7, 291, 294, 309, 312, 316, 318

Octavian. *See* Augustus
Odysseus, 77, 184, 201
Oedipus, 85, 214–15, 217
oikoumene, 22, 30, 32, 39–42, 44–8, 54–63, 66–8, 100, 150, 158, 219, 242, 249
   and movement, 55, 60–1
   female personification of, 38, 49–51
Onomarchus of Andros, 277, 286–9, 293, 317
oracles, 125, 179–81, 186–9, 192–3, 201, 203–5, 207–10, 285, *See also* Sibyl, *Sibylline Oracles 3*
   relationship with poetry, 188, 194, 203
orality, 29, 94, 103, 106, 114–16
oratory, 219, *See also* Asianism, Atticism
   decline and revival, 23–6
   Hellenistic, 24, 289, 317
   performance, 1, 23–4, 115
orbis terrarum, 37, 47, 49, 227
Orpheus
   Testament of Orpheus, 204, *See also* prophecy, *pseudographos*
Ovid, 15, 92, 364
   Metamorphoses, 193
   Tristia, 36–9, 47–8, 67

paideia, 17, 34, 83, 115, 159, 164, 179, 181, 185, 215, 220–1, 224–5, 236, 241, 323, 331
Panaetius, 232
   On Duty, 153
Panyasis, 332
paromoeosis, 278–82, 288, 292, 296, 307, 312, 315

Parthenius, 12
patronage, 20–1, 34, 77–9, 132, 235–7
Pausanias, 33, 69, 74, 86, 115
performance, 114, 232, 355
Periander, 131
Pericles, 216, 219–20, 263, 342
periodisation, 2, 20, 185, *See also* Hellenistic literature, late, periodisation
Peripatetics, 4, 152–5, 233
periplus, 31, 41, 61, 68, 94–114, 117
Pernot, Laurent, 275–6
Persia. *See also* Aeschylus, *Persians*
Persians, 126, 134–5, 142, 259
Pharos, 361–2
Philetas, 332
Philip of Thessalonica
   Garland, 70–1, 73, 77–9, 85, 88, 90–3
Philip V, 62
Philistus, 321, 338–40
Philo, 10, 313, 353, 361–5
   On Dreams, 128–9
Philodemus, 21, 77–8
philosophy, 27–8, 344–5
Philostratus of Athens, 1, 20, 28, 34–5, 183, 201, 210, 272, 280
   Heroicus, 184
   Lives of the Sophists, 23–6, 277–8, 282, 286, 289, 292, 297, 304–5, 313–18, 347–8
Philostratus the Elder
   Imagines, 94, 100–7, 112–18, 356
Phylarchus of Athens, 5, 347
Pindar, 319, 325, 332, 351–2
Plato, 27, 38–9, 43, 46, 116, 153, 173, 201, 205, 214, 217, 219, 231–3, 289, 316, 344
   Phaedrus, 42–3, 173, 187
   Republic, 167–9, 174
Platonism, 248–9, 324, 361
Pliny, 61
   Natural History, 129, 134
Plutarch, 1, 6, 21, 71–93, 187–8, 214, 218, 220, 246, 248–9, 330–1, 358–9
   De Pythiae oraculis, 187
   On the Control of Anger, 130
   Parallel Lives, 27–8, 256–71
   Sympotic Questions, 116
   Table-Talk, 337
Plution, 347
Polemo, 213–14, 274–6, 313, 317
Pollux of Naucratis, 277, 280–1, 284–6, 315, 317
Polybius, 3–6, 8–12, 15, 19–20, 27, 34–5, 54–68, 75, 111, 132, 173, 238, 241–2, 256, 354, 358, *See also* body metaphor
   and biography, 27–9
   and contingency, 31, 263–71

   as starting point, 11–12, 360, 363
   geographical 'digression', 39–41, 56, 58–9, 66–8
   prose style, 314, 347
   representations of *oikoumene*, 30–2, 41–7, 50–1, 150, 156–7
polymatheia, 241–4, 250
Pompey, 48–51, 73, 129, 132, 235, 256, 260–2
Pomponius Atticus, Titus, 212–17, 226
Pomponius Mela, 69
Popillius Laenas, Publius, 65
portents, 144, 187
Porus, 262
Posidonius, 4, 28, 134, 150, 232, 240–2, 245, 248–9
Priene, 50, 155–6, 160, 165–6, 171–5, 181, 356
Proclus of Naucratis, 316
Procopius, 356
pronoia. *See* providence
prophecy, 188, 192, 196–200, 202–4, 207, 210, *See also* oracles
prose rhythm, 151, 298–305, 313–14
prose style, 273, 279, 301, 310, 319–50, 365
providence, 158, 246–50
provinces, 47, 49, 54, 224, 229
Pseudo-Aelius Aristides, 343–4
Pseudo-Alcaeus, 200
pseudographos, 178, 199–200, 204
pseudopatris, 199
psychagogia, 173–4
Ptolemy II, 62, 356
Ptolemy IV, 51, 62, 264
Pyrenees, 56–60, 90–1
Pyrrhus, 62
Pythagoras, 205, 216, 232
Pythagoreans, 153
Pytheas of Massilia, 241–2
Python of Byzantium, 278

Quintilian, 26, 220, 321–3, 329, 331–9, 342–6, 349–50
Quintus Curtius, 144

reader response, 94, 107–14, 116–17
reading lists, 33, 319–27, 331–50
Red Sea, 31, 94–7, 99, 101–3, 106–7, 110–12, 117, 292
Rengakos, Antonios, 9
revisionism, 18, 34, 197, 201, 210
Rhegium, 64–5
rhetoric, 2, 4, 25, 109, 272, 319–50
Rhodes, 23, 79, 172, 231
road building, Roman, 32, 64–6, 68, 247
Rohde, Erwin, 273–5

General Index

Roman empire, 2, 21, 30, 38, 54, 69, 80, 89, 136, 155, 230, 249, 355
  expansion of, 13–14
  geography of, 44, 49, 355
  Greek attitudes to, 72–3, 92–3, 365
  visualisation of power, 37–8
Rome, 9, 11, 31–2, 37–8, 44–54, 73, 129, 146, 153, 179, 196, 205
  cultural revolution, 13, 21–2
Roth, Philip, 251–2, 255

Samos, 125, 172
Sappho, 78, 84–5, 319
Sardinia, 52
Sardis, 74
Sceptics, 4
Scheria. *See* Corcyra
Schlegel, Friedrich, 253–4, 271
Schmid, Wilhelm, 9, 273–5
Schmitz, Thomas A., 22, 225
Scopelian of Clazomenae, 316
Scythia, 90
Second Sophistic, 1, 21, 24–5, 115, 132, 180–1
  treatments of Homer, 184–6, 194
seers, 260, 266, *See also* oracles, prophecy, Sibyl
self-referentiality, 91, 98, 100, 102
Semiramis, 138, 140, 143, 146
Seneca the Elder, 24
Seneca the Younger, 131
senses, 97, 106, 109
Septuagint, 205, 353, 360–3
Sesoösis, 137, 140, 143, 146
Sextus Empiricus, 245
shipwrecks, 107, 109, 112, 126
Sibyl, 178–210, 358
  birthplace, 207
  Erythraean Sibyl, 188–9, 201, 206–7
  mortality, 190, 205
  portrayal as an old woman, 186
Sibylline Oracles 3, 17, 34, 179–81, 186–210, 357, 361, 363
Sicily, 76, 105, 238, 291
sideshadowing, 6, 254–9, 263, 267–8, 271
Simonides, 214, 332
simplicity (of language), 343–4, 346
Smyrna, 183, 190, 199–200
snakes, 97–8, 104
Socrates, 168–9, 173, 204, 219
Socratic writers, 338–9, 344–5
sophists, 23, 113–14, 280, 286, 304, 314–15, *See also* Asianism, oratory
  imperial style, 277–92, 301, 305, 307, 312, 318
Sophocles, 8, 84, 214–15, 217, 219, 319

space, knowledge and representation of, 10, 30–4, 40, 47, 49, 53, 58–70, 83, 86, 94, 115, 191, 354–5
Spain, 55, 58–9, 61, 90, 134
Sparta, 82, 85, 188, 197
spatial turn, 32, 69
Spendius, 265
Speusippus, 213–14
Stählin, Otto, 9
Statius
  Silvae, 130, 355
Stesichorus, 325, 332
Stoicism, 4, 31, 40, 149–50, 153–6, 167, 170–2, 176, 220, 231–2, 241, 244–50, 344
Strabo, 4, 6, 9, 12, 15, 21, 28–34, 56, 69, 72, 76, 93, 124, 131–5, 218–19, 261, 291, 294
  and cosmopolitanism, 155, 166–77
  and philosophy, 31, 33, 150
  as end point, 11, 360, 363
  Geography, 11, 119, 231–50
  representations of landscape alteration, 137–8, 143, 145–7, 355
  structures of feeling, 212–19
style. *See* prose style
sublimity, 325, 333, 335–6, 340, 349
Suetonius, 131, 328
symploke, 5, 39, 44, 47, 55, 59, 62, 67–8

Tabulae Iliacae, 183, 185
Tacitus, 343
Tarsus, 93, 169–72, 175, 235–7
Temple of Apollo at Rome, 187
Temple of Fortuna, 52
Temple of Janus, 52
Temple of Mater Matuta at Rome, 52
Temple of Spes, 52
Tenos, 74–5
terra marique, 48, 63
Thebes, 74, 85, 172, 292–6
Theocritus, 8, 332, 353, 355, 364
Theodorus of Gadara, 347
Theopompus, 4–6, 27–8, 319, 321, 338, 340–1
Thessaly, 23, 127
Thrace, 277, 305
Thrasymachus, 168–9
Thucydides, 219–20, 266, 298–300, 325, 338–9
Tiberius, 11, 89, 188, 207, 347
Timaeus of Tauromenium, 291
Timagenes, 338
Titus, 320, 328
Tolstoy, Leo, 254–5
tragedy, 18, 43, 197, 219, 224, 333, 335
  personification of, 181
Trajan, 320

Tralles, 172
translation, 17, 205, 361–3
triumphs, 48–9, 51–3
Trojan War, 92, 179, 184, 195–8, 201
Troy, 203, 205
tyche, 42, 256, 263, 268–71,
 See also fate
tyranny, 125–7, 132, 142–3
Tyre, 356
 siege of Tyre, 143–4
Tyrtaeus, 332

Valerius Maximus, 214
Varro, 188, 207, 225–6
Vespasian, 320
villas, Roman, 129
Virgil, 359, 364
 Aeneid, 79
virtual history, 266–8
Vitruvius, 239, 243, 246

Weston, Jessie, 352
Wiater, Nicolas, 22, 111, 218, 225, 324
Wilamowitz-Möllendorff, Ulrich von, 7–8, 272–7, 318, 354
 Pindaros, 351–2
Wolf, Friedrich August, 7–8
wonders, 89, 97, 101, 112, 124, 129, 137, 140

Xenocrates, 213–14
Xenophon, 4, 289, 319, 321–2, 328–9, 338–45, 349–50
 Anabasis, 259–60, 265–6, 329, 343–4
Xerxes, 61, 87, 126–31, 134–5, 137, 140–3, 145

Zeitlin, Froma, 181, 183–4
Zeno, 244
Zeuxis of Croton, 324–5
Zimmermann, Bernhard, 9
Zosimus, Aulus Aemilius, 155, 160, 165–6, 171–6, 356–7, 365

For EU product safety concerns, contact us at Calle de José Abascal, 56–1°,
28003 Madrid, Spain or eugpsr@cambridge.org.

www.ingramcontent.com/pod-product-compliance
Lightning Source LLC
LaVergne TN
LVHW011754060526
838200LV00053B/3599